CHAIRING THE ACADEMIC DEPARTMENT

CHAIRING THE ACADEMIC DEPARTMENT

Leadership among Peers

Third Edition

Allan Tucker

AMERICAN COUNCIL ON EDUCATION
Series on Higher Education
ORYX PRESS
1993

Published by The Oryx Press
4041 North Central at Indian School Road
Phoenix, AZ 85012-3397

Printed in the United States of America

Library of Congress Cataloging in Publication Data
Tucker, Allan, 1921–
    Chairing the academic department : leadership among peers / Allan Tucker.
    p. cm. — (American Council on Education/Oryx series on higher education)
    Originally published: 3rd ed. New York : American Council on Education, c1992.
    Includes bibliographical references and index.
    ISBN 0-89774-826-3 Case; ISBN 1-57356-254-8 Paper
    1. Departmental chairmen (Universities)—United States.
2. Universities and colleges—United States—Administration.
I. Title. II. Series: American Council on Education/Oryx series on higher education.
[LB2341.T78 1993]   93-4915
378.1'11—dc20   CIP

Contents

Preface   *vi*

Acknowledgments   *viii*

Part I   THE ACADEMIC DEPARTMENT   *1*

   1. Vital Signs of a Healthy Department   *3*

   2. History and Development of Academic
Departments   *14*

Part II   THE DEPARTMENT CHAIR   *25*

   3. Roles, Functions, and Characteristics of
Department Chairs   *27*

   4. Power and Authority of a Chair   *44*

   5. Leadership and Decision Making   *56*

   6. The Chair's Role in Bringing About Change   *73*

   7. Delegation and Department Committees   *89*

Part III   FACULTY, STAFF, AND STUDENTS   *101*

   8. Full-Time Faculty   *103*

   9. Part-Time Faculty and Graduate Teaching
Assistants   *118*

  10. Support Staff in the Department   *131*

  11. Students   *141*

Part IV RECRUITING, AFFIRMATIVE ACTION, AND RETENTION ... *155*

12. Procedures and Practices for Recruiting, Employing, and Retaining Faculty ... *157*
13. Affirmative Action: Finding, Hiring, and Retaining Women and Minority Faculty ... *183*

Part V WORKLOAD ASSIGNMENTS, FACULTY EVALUATION, AND PERFORMANCE COUNSELING ... *193*

14. Workload Assignments and Reporting Faculty Activities ... *195*
15. Faculty Evaluation ... *216*
16. Performance Counseling and Dealing with Unsatisfactory Performance ... *246*

Part VI PROFESSIONAL GROWTH, FACULTY DEVELOPMENT, AND IMPROVING THE QUALITY OF COLLEGE TEACHING ... *261*

17. Professional Growth and Faculty Development ... *263*
18. Improving the Quality of College Teaching ... *283*

Part VII WRITING GOALS AND DEVELOPING PLANS ... *295*

19. Writing Departmental Missions, Goals, and Objectives ... *297*
20. Departmental Planning ... *311*

Part VIII RESOURCES ... *329*

21. Generating University and College Budgets ... *331*
22. Funding the Department ... *353*

Part IX   CURRICULUM MANAGEMENT,
TEACHING ASSIGNMENTS, AND
EFFECTIVE USE OF FACULTY TIME   *369*

   23.   Curriculum Management   *371*
   24.   Teaching Assignments and Effective Use of
       Faculty Time   *383*

Part X   CONFLICT   *395*

   25.   Managing Conflict   *397*
   26.   Grievances and Faculty Unions   *417*
   27.   Legal Implications of Being a Chair   *446*

Part XI   DEALING WITH DEANS, UNIVERSITY
ADMINISTRATIVE OFFICES, AND
EXTERNAL AGENCIES   *481*

   28.   Dealing with Deans and University
       Administrative Offices   *483*
   29.   Dealing with External Agencies   *494*

Part XII   ASSESSMENT   *507*

   30.   Evaluating the Department   *509*
   31.   Evaluating the Chair   *530*

Part XIII   PERSONAL AND PROFESSIONAL
WELFARE OF THE CHAIR   *541*

   32.   Getting the Position, Finding Satisfactions,
       Coping with Stress, and Moving to the Next
       Job   *543*

Index   *560*

Preface

A key position in college and university administration is that of department chairperson. It is the chairperson who must provide leadership to the faculty and at the same time supervise the translation of institutional goals and policies into academic practice. Yet most chairpersons are drawn from faculty ranks, and assume the position having had little administrative experience. Moreover, few opportunities for orientation and training are available to them.

This paradox became more and more apparent to me during the eleven years I served as academic vice-chancellor of the State University System of Florida. Subsequently, after joining the faculty of Florida State University as professor of higher education, I submitted to the W. K. Kellogg Foundation a proposal requesting funds to design and test a model for enhancing the planning, management, and leadership competencies of department chairpersons. The Kellogg Foundation awarded a major grant for developing, testing, and implementing such programs both in Florida and throughout the country.

To help define the primary issues confronting departments, chairpersons in the nine state universities of the Florida university system were questioned about their own experiences. In addition, information was gathered from their counterparts in many institutions of higher learning outside Florida. Materials were developed to address the topics suggested by the initial inquiry. These materials were presented and tested in a series of seminars and workshops for chairpersons in Florida's state universities, and subsequently for chairpersons in many colleges and universities throughout the United States. The workshop materials were eventually published in book form in 1981. The second edition, published in 1984, was an expansion and update of the first edition. This third edition is in response to the many comments and suggestions made by chairpersons who read the first and second editions and/or participated in one or more department leadership workshops wherein the book was used as both text and basis for discussion. Concerns expressed by community college chairpersons were also taken into account and incorporated in some of the chapters, thus making the contents of the book applicable to community colleges as well as to baccalaureate granting institutions.

The third edition consists of thirty-two chapters, as compared to seventeen contained in the second edition. Eight of the thirty-two are completely new chapters. Five are expanded discussions of five topics which in the second edition were discussed briefly as parts of other chapters. The remaining chapters are reorganizations, rearrangement, expansions, and revisions of materials contained in the second edition.

The eight completely new chapters are:

Chapter 1. Vital Signs of a Healthy Department
Chapter 13. Affirmative Action: Finding, Hiring, and Retaining Women and Minority Faculty
Chapter 18. Improving the Quality of College Teaching
Chapter 28. Dealing with Deans and University Administrative Offices
Chapter 29. Dealing with External Agencies
Chapter 30. Evaluating the Department
Chapter 31. Evaluating the Chair
Chapter 32. Getting the Position, Finding Satisfactions, Coping with Stress, and Moving to the Next Job

The five chapters consisting of expanded discussions of topics that were discussed briefly in the second edition are:

Chapter 8. Full-Time Faculty
Chapter 9. Part-Time Faculty and Graduate Teaching Assistants
Chapter 10. Support Staff in the Department
Chapter 11. Students
Chapter 20. Departmental Planning

Besides the revisions and additions mentioned above, the lists of references for each chapter have been updated and the number of questions at the end of the chapter has been expanded. These questions are especially designed to help the reader relate the contents of the chapter to his or her own institution and situation. The questions can also be used as a basis for discussion in department leadership seminars and workshops.

Departments vary considerably in size, age, and level of maturity. Modes of department governance also vary greatly, as do chairpersons' personalities and leadership styles. To develop a set of absolute prescriptions that would provide every chairperson with solutions to every problem would be an almost impossible task; no such attempt has been made here. The book does, however, present examples of common department problems, and shows how some of these were solved. It suggests ways to recognize and approach these problems, but it is not intended to be a definitive document that must be slavishly followed if a department is to be effective. Rather, the book will, I hope, spur chairpersons to analyze their own departments and to compare them with those described here. The cases discussed may or may not be directly applicable to each department, but the process of comparison may help generate solutions to similar problems.

Acknowledgments

I am deeply indebted to the Kellogg Foundation for its financial assistance in the development and implementation of our project designed to enhance the leadership, management, and planning competencies of department chairpersons in universities and colleges in the United States. Dr. E. T. York, former chancellor of the State University System of Florida, Dr. Bernard Sliger, former president of Florida State University, and Dr. Jerry Miller, former vice president of the American Council on Education provided vital encouragement and moral support during the design and testing of various formats for conducting workshops for department chairpersons. Many other persons, including deans and chairpersons at institutions both in and outside Florida where we conducted department leadership workshops, also provided assistance in the form of suggestions and critiques.

I want to express appreciation to many of my colleagues for their patience and tolerance in allowing me to share with them my ideas regarding the contents of the workshop materials, and for their willingness to read and criticize my manuscripts and make suggestions for improvement. I particularly want to thank the following individuals from Florida State University who, over the years, participated in the writing and/or editing of several segments of the workshop materials from which the first, second, and third editions of this book evolved: Joseph C. Beckham, attorney and professor of higher education; Neil Betten, professor of history; David W. Leslie, professor of higher education; Emanuel I. Shargel, associate professor of educational foundations and policy studies; Ilona Turrisi, former director of budget and analysis; and John S. Waggaman, associate professor of higher education.

I also wish to acknowledge the assistance of Mrs. Barbara Allen, whose patience was beyond the call of duty as she typed and retyped the many drafts of the manuscripts as they were being written, revised, and rerevised.

Part *I*

THE ACADEMIC DEPARTMENT

Chapter 1.   Vital Signs of a Healthy Department

Chapter 2.   History and Development of Academic Departments

Chapter *1*

Vital Signs of a Healthy Department

A healthy department is one whose faculty and staff are motivated, productive, appreciated, secure in their jobs, work well together as a group, and able to reach consensus on issues concerning the governance and welfare of the department. A healthy department has well-defined operational and visionary goals that are attainable and contribute not only to the mission of the department but to that of the university as a whole. They are understood and accepted by the faculty, and provide direction for both collective and individual decisions.

Goals

Realism characterizes goals in healthy departments. Even the visionary aspects of goals are within reach. A healthy department, for example, may aspire to increase its research output or to enhance its reputation for excellent teaching. It will not, however, thoughtlessly aspire to "be number one" in the country in its field if such an aspiration is clearly not within reach. It may, on the other hand, aspire to increase external research funding (and even set a particular dollar target) or to be represented on the program of certain national scholarly meetings every year.

In a healthy department, conflict is minimal even in departments that have multiple goals. Healthy departments recognize that trying to accomplish different goals simultaneously almost invariably will lead to conflict. Goals in these departments are modulated to avoid serious disagreements over priorities. As mentioned in the preceding paragraph, a healthy department might focus on incremental and measurable increases in research output as one of its goals, and at the same time select as a second goal the improvement of its undergraduate curriculum. Although faculty members in this department take signals from both goals, they will receive reasonably clear targets toward which they can direct proportional effort. Faculty in healthy settings at major universities are not stressed by trying to develop a national reputation for their department and by working intensively on curriculum change at the same time. But they also know that *some* effort needs to be aimed at maintaining and enhancing their teaching skills. Goals in healthy departments do not typically divide people and cause them to be uncertain about what they are supposed to be doing. Instead, goals provide a guide to what *is* important, and serve to focus efforts to achieve those things. They help people pull together, especially when a department is trying to accomplish an agenda that has many different themes.

In a healthy department, faculty work cooperatively in communal efforts. Although individuals play unique and special roles in an effective academic unit, they also must contribute to a purposeful social enterprise. Goals provide them with guidance and rationales for committing themselves to achieving cooperatively those things a department cannot do as a mere collection of individual entrepreneurs.

Faculty in healthy departments share an *explicit* awareness of goals. They have a sense of ownership in their goals, and indeed have internalized them. Goals that are shared in this way become effective guides to action. Faculty will also have an *implicit* understanding of what kinds of activity support the department's goals, and what kinds of activity detract from them. They not only can be self-directing, but can shape others' behavior as well. Healthy departments in this way do not need a great deal of direction and hierarchical control. People know what they are supposed to do, and they do it with a minimum of supervision.

Strategies

Healthy departments have strategies that are expressed as plausible scenarios for accomplishing their most important goals, rather than as rigid militaristic plans. Widely shared and understood, they use imagery and simple scripts that help people to visualize the future in concrete ways. A strategy is a map that people use to figure out their own role in achieving the department's goals. Healthy departments also think a few years ahead, and so know in advance what they need to accomplish. While having a sense of their own role within the university, they also become skilled at scanning the environment to spot which factors might help or handicap the department's fortunes.

Healthy departments pursue realistic opportunities, conserving their energies and resources by concentrating on things they know they can achieve. All departments face a changing environment, new social pressures, and shifting trends in the bases of knowledge and practice—but healthy departments view change positively. They develop a wide array of information sources about what is likely to happen, and they sort this information out to search for opportunities. Healthy departments are selective in what they choose to do; they do not jump randomly at every target of opportunity. Strategic thinking is done collaboratively, so that faculty and staff can contribute information and ideas, and so that all members of the department feel informed and aware.

Resources

A healthy department has resources adequate to do its job and accomplish its goals, whether its resources are based on student enrollments, contracts and grants, or funding from other sources. Although many departments accomplish a great deal without truly sufficient resources, no one can live for an indefinite period in a state of perceived deprivation. Morale declines, real problems cannot be solved, and adaptation is impossible because everyone is working close to the outer limits of their energies.

In a healthy department the resource base is stable and secure enough to permit the department to perform its mission in a predictable way. Some departments go through "boom and bust" cycles. They may have large grants for a short period, or they may benefit from a surge in student interest in their field. It is easy to fall into a trap in such periods. One might allow the base budget of the department to erode in times of good fortune, only to find that when "normalcy" returns it is not possible to restore faculty lines, expense funds, and other resources that were available only temporarily because external factors made them available. Likewise, resources that are withdrawn during times of stringency are hard to replace when the institution finds itself more fortunate. Healthy departments are cognizant of these ebbs and flows, and attempt to preserve a base budget that will serve them well when other factors are *not* equal.

The most effective way to sustain a healthy resource base is to find and fill a "niche," either in the internal economy of the college or university, or in the flow of funding for research and development. The idea of niches comes from the world of marketing. One looks at the market to determine needs, and develops products to fill gaps. Establishing a niche for oneself means finding a gap that badly needs to be filled with a certain kind of filling, and concentrating on filling it. Healthy departments know their "products," and they know what the market for those products is. The resource base of a healthy department is carefully built and cultivated through good marketing—which means nothing more than identifying and filling important needs. Not all departments have found niches in all areas, or even in the same areas. Some departments are predominantly research departments that bring in large amounts of external funds to the university's budget. Others may engage in some research, but their main niche lies in providing service courses to large numbers of undergraduate students. Still other departments have as their main contribution service to state government and business. Even though departments may have broad ambitions and goals which encompass several areas of activity, faculty members know which of their contributions provide the major source of their funding. They understand that if their research productivity is not of sufficient quality, quantity, or relevance to generate research funds from either the university or external sources, a significant contribution in one or more areas other than research will help sustain the department.

In a healthy department, faculty members not only strive to maintain and capitalize on the reputation they have earned for the niche they have found for themselves, but are not deterred from being involved in some aspect of research even though research funds may not be forthcoming for their particular project or discipline. To stay healthy, a department needs at least one dependable and stable source of funding. A really robust department has several different niches, meaning that it does not have to rely on only one source but has several.

Administration

In a healthy department there exists just the right amount of administration, neither too much nor too little. Sufficient organization is present both to accomplish routine work and to provide the support that faculty need to fulfill their assigned responsibilities. It is focused on its essential contributions to the university and to the broader community, discipline, or profession. It is effective (and is recognized as being so) because it achieves what it is supposed to achieve. In the process it does not consume resources inefficiently or excessively. What it has, it uses to good effect. A healthy department is a net *contributor* to the university's long-term well-being because it draws money, students, status, a reputation for excellence, and other important resources to the institution.

Healthy departments also respect the democratic culture of the academic world. Departmental governance is fair, open, equitable, and humane. Policies are developed in a thoughtful, participatory, and cooperative way. Healthy departments develop a sense of involvement and commitment among the faculty and staff. People feel they have sufficient opportunity to take initiatives, to air their opinions, and to make needed changes. Factions and political maneuvering are minimized by the open sharing of information and by an ethic of collaborative decision making.

When conflicts or disputes arise in a healthy department (and they inevitably arise in all human enterprises), they are handled with fairness, patience, objectivity, and a regard for individual rights. People at all levels in the department have a sense of security, a sense that their work is appreciated and that they are making a contribution. They feel that rewards are commensurate with their efforts, that extra effort will bring an appropriate measure of additional appreciation, and that those who are not pulling their fair share of the load will be encouraged to perform at a higher level. A healthy department will administer reasonable sanctions for undesirable behavior when necessary, but the bounds of acceptable behavior are clearly established and understood from the outset. Sanctions are used only when alternatives have been exhausted and after appropriate due process has been afforded.

Administration in a healthy department is neither heavy-handed, nor so low-key as to be invisible. Faculty and staff expect that a tone and climate will be established that focuses on work that the department must do to be effective. Although they want to be appreciated and recognized, they also know that everyone must accept a certain measure of discipline and harnessing to the collective tasks of the unit. Faculty, of course, often are energetic, autonomous, high achievers who thrive on self-direction. Yet they still require recognition and security, and the department needs them to work collaboratively for the common good. In a healthy department, faculty sense and respect a reasonable balance between their personal ambitions and the more general needs of the unit.

Program

Academic programs are the fundamental reason why departments are in business. Healthy departments work consciously to run excellent programs, and the faculty and staff collaborate to maintain a high standard for their "product." Feedback on program quality is sought and welcomed. Information is used to design and implement change. It is understood that all members of the department have a stake in the quality and reputation of the program.

A healthy department has relevant curricula in place and makes revisions that are consistent with trends in the field, with the demands of the marketplace, and with the needs and interests of its students. It embraces new knowledge, new specializations, and new standards of professional practice, and is receptive to change in the organization of its programs. It actively gathers intelligence about new developments, and it openly discusses and debates the intellectual and pedagogical premises of its programs.

This kind of department has a reputation for good teaching in all of its courses, not just those for its own majors. It pays attention to the nuts and bolts of sound pedagogy, and provides a supportive environment for faculty who want to devote effort to improving their teaching skills. In a healthy department, good teaching is respected and rewarded. It is accepted that good teaching helps attract good students to the program, and it is accepted that good teaching is essential to effective learning. Faculty feel free to share their ideas about teaching and their experiences in the classroom. They promote each other's efforts to master the art of excellent pedagogical practice. Perhaps most importantly, faculty in a healthy department feel free to share feedback on teaching performance. Like actors in a theater company, they will work offstage to critique and strengthen each other's techniques and methods of approaching subject matter. They will also explore and adopt new technology when it is likely to improve efficiency of instruction, or to enhance important learning outcomes.

Healthy departments meet both enrollment demand and professional accrediting standards. At the same time, they provide challenging, but not unrealistic, standards for their students to meet. The department achieves a balance between marketplace pressure for access to its programs, and the constraints that accrediting bodies put on them in the name of quality.

A healthy department channels its students' energies in a variety of ways so they may learn and apply the knowledge of the field. It recognizes that many students need to use ideas and principles, to test their understanding through experience, and to act on knowledge before they internalize it. The department will provide at least a modest extracurricular program to foster students' identification with the field, and to promote opportunities for active application of knowledge.

A healthy department balances faculty assignments so it can assure that research productivity is acceptable, if research is part of the department's mission. Many institutions accept a broad definition of research, often including creative activity, or general scholarship, within its scope. A healthy department accommodates the broadest definition of research commensurate with its acknowledged role within the institution. Faculty are encouraged to do as much creative, scholarly and intellectual work as it is reasonable to expect. For some, such activity will pay off principally in more relevant and challenging learning experiences for students. For other faculty members, it will result in grants, publications, and international recognition. Healthy departments are able to accept the varied kinds of intellectual activity its faculty are best equipped to do, and they acknowledge this work with appropriate recognition and reward.

A healthy department gives its faculty time to be of meaningful service to the university and to the broader community. Not only is it ethically and morally important for them to make a contribution to the communal welfare, but faculty often serve as effective ambassadors for a department and its programs when they are visible in the external world. Service activities help project a human image on a department, and broaden its base of friends and supporters. A healthy department will actively develop programs of interest to both the community and the university, and selectively encourage its faculty to do promotional work in ways that capitalize on their own interests and abilities.

People

A healthy department has the right mix of people. Faculty and staff form the core, but often there are others contributing as well. In a healthy department the mix of people who do the essential work is balanced to avoid inequities, the right skills are matched to the right jobs, and roles are well-understood. People share, and are committed to, the general values of the department.

The mix of faculty in a healthy department provides places for youth and maturity alike. It is important on the one hand to have faculty with relatively recent training, so that newer ideas and methodological developments in the field continue to refresh and renew the department's programs. On the other hand, a core group of senior faculty usually acts to provide a leavening influence, tempering intellectual enthusiasms with long experience and wisdom. A healthy department's vitality is fresher when this kind of generational interplay takes place in a positive and constructive way.

Perhaps more importantly, however, a healthy department appreciates the limitations of the career span and intentionally appoints faculty across the generational spectrum. A general plan, perhaps informal but a plan nevertheless, exists that plots inevitable retirements against the department's long-term needs. New faculty are hired to fill acknowledged and understood roles, sometimes before a retirement occurs. A healthy department understands the importance of continuity and of overlapping the generations so that newer members learn and appreciate the traditions and values of those who have built a successful enterprise.

Although stability and continuity are important, faculty must also have skills that are kept current and appropriate to the responsibilities they are asked to assume. Healthy departments support faculty who make efforts to expand their own interests and skills. A healthy department also brings gentle pressures to bear on faculty whose teaching and research may no longer be keeping pace. Through judicious use of rewards and sanctions, it encourages faculty to take advantage of opportunities to learn, grow, and integrate new experiences and ideas into their work.

Faculty members and staff alike are clear about their roles as well as the expectations that others have of them. Each member of a department contributes a special blend of qualities, both personal and professional. In a healthy department, not all faculty are expected to be world-class researchers. Some clearly play a valuable role in mentoring and advising undergraduate students. Others are particularly valued for their skills in developing curricula, courses, or field experiences. Healthy departments openly honor the variety of roles played by faculty and staff alike. People come to enjoy and thrive on playing their own distinctive roles, and feel rewarded for doing so.

Healthy departments allow for differences in the roles people play, and do not insist that everyone's contribution be measured against a single scale. One mark of an immature department is its insistence that everyone measure up to some arbitrary standard, such as number of publications or dollar value of grants received. In a healthy department, people are neither underworked, nor overworked; fresh challenges and opportunities to suggest and try new ideas are encouraged. It is recognized that a range of talents, abilities, and interests is necessary to keep the department alive and vital.

The department has cohesion and morale is good. An informal social life exists, and people share in the personal triumphs and tragedies of the department as a community. In a healthy department, people care about each other as human beings and treat each other with fairness, respect, courtesy, and warmth. Divisions on real gut issues are not allowed to divide the department. Among other things, people are paid at rates commensurate with what is expected of them; equity prevails. In short, faculty and staff feel appreciated.

Communication

Healthy departments support an open and collegial atmosphere. People communicate freely with one another, and information is shared in appropriate ways. Faculty and staff alike are kept informed about new developments, emerging issues, problems, opportunities, and news of the department and the institution.

Appropriate formal channels of communication are established and maintained. Newsletters, memoranda, reports, and other "media" are professionally composed and circulated. On the other hand, communication in a healthy department is not excessively formal. Good informal networks exist, and people know how and when to talk with each other about subjects that do not "fit" in the formal channels. Humor and "play" are accepted as part of the department's culture, and are valued for how they stimulate creativity and people's feeling of belonging and participation.

A healthy department keeps a balance between formal and informal communication. Meetings are held with appropriate frequency and for substantive reasons. They are treated as formal and important occasions and are not held when the agenda would be trivial. On the other hand, social occasions are held sufficiently often to maintain the human connections that are psychologically important, and to foster bonds among faculty, staff, and students. Special occasions are invented to celebrate achievements and recognize accomplishments.

Culture

A healthy department shares a set of values and actively uses the idea of corporate culture to maintain and promote those values. For example, in a healthy department, traditions are established and maintained. People and rites of passage are recognized with ceremony and ritual. Stories and legends are told to illustrate what the department "stands for."

In order to have a culture that binds members of the department together, new "members" must be oriented and initiated into the department's value system and folklore. A healthy department intentionally arranges occasions to welcome new faculty, staff, and students and to initiate them with celebrations of the department's history and mythology. The department is proud of its special way of doing business, and takes particular pains to assure that everyone associated with it learns the culture.

The culture of a healthy department goes well beyond ways of doing the routine work of the unit. People share a commitment to values beyond the instrumental. They come to appreciate that it is important to do more than just meet their classes and go home. They know that the department stands for something more, and they know what that "something" is. There is no single set of values or symbols that fits all departments. Some prize human relationships above all else. Others honor creativity and independence. Some are bound to certain ideas or points of view, and others to a more general atmosphere of inquiry that emphasizes process rather than substance. Occasionally a department reveres a great or talented professor or a particularly noteworthy accomplishment by one or more department members. Although history adds and subtracts specific details over the years, healthy departments consciously build on core values and consciously work to inculcate those values in new initiates.

Although healthy departments build and maintain a culture, they also honor academic freedom and tolerate diversity and idiosyncrasy. They do not enforce cultlike conformity, and they do not punish those who choose to differ. The larger norms of the academic community take hold and require wide latitude for alternative perspectives and points of view. A healthy department culture is strong enough to give people a reason to commit their energies and talents to a collaborative enterprise, but not so strong that they suppress their individuality and creativity.

Summary

A healthy academic department is a businesslike social enterprise with a strong sense of its place in the larger college or university enterprise. Its work is optimized by its clear sense of how to put the right people to work on the most important tasks, how to motivate and reward them in fair and equitable ways, and how to bind people to the organization through shared vision and shared values. Although no department meets all the criteria of health outlined in this chapter, it is important to keep them in focus as targets one might hope to hit in a reasonable amount of time. Healthy departments are most readily recognized as those that achieve results commensurate with their role and the resources available to them. But healthy departments also enjoy an internal coherence and a sense of bonding among their members that makes cooperation and coordination of their jobs stimulating and rewarding.

Questions

Review in your mind the department and/or programs under your supervision and contemplate answers to the questions below:

1. What problems or circumstances prevent your department from achieving the ideal state of health described in chapter 1? For example, how would you complete the following thoughts?

   a. Not enough budget to do _____

   _____

   b. Not enough personnel to do _____

   _____

   c. Enough personnel, but none qualified to do _____

   _____

d. Lack of equipment to do _____

_____

e. Inability to satisfy faculty needs or wants, which are _____

_____

f. Poor relationship with the dean or academic vice-president in areas such as _____

_____

g. Not enough good students, thus affecting the department in ways such as _____

_____

h. Some faculty members don't get along with each other, resulting in consequences such as _____

_____

2. List other problems that prevent your department from achieving the ideal state of health.
3. What steps can be taken to improve some of the situations?
4. What situations can never be improved?

References

ANDERSON, G. LESTER. "Organizational Diversity." In *New Directions for Institutional Research: Examining Departmental Management,* no. 10, edited by John C. Smart and James R. Montgomery. San Francisco: Jossey–Bass, 1976.

ATWELL, ROBERT H., and GREEN, MADELINE, F. *Academic Leaders as Managers.* San Francisco: Jossey–Bass, 1981.

BENNETT, JOHN B., and FIGULI, DAVID J. (Eds.) *Enhancing Departmental Leadership: The Roles of the Chairperson.* New York: Macmillan, 1990.

BIRNBAUM, ROBERT. *Individual Preferences and Organizational Goals: Consistency and Diversity in the Futures Desired by Campus Leaders.* ASHE Annual Meeting Paper, Baltimore, Maryland, 1987. (ERIC Document Reproduction Service No. ED 292 384)

BOK, DEREK. *Higher Learning.* Cambridge: Harvard University Press, 1986.

CLARK, BURTON R. *The Academic Life. Small Worlds. Different Worlds.* A Carnegie Foundation Special Report. Princeton: The Carnegie Foundation, 1987.

COHEN, ARTHUR M., and BRAWER, FLORENCE B. *The American Community College.* 2nd ed. San Francisco: Jossey–Bass, 1988.

EHRLE, ELWOOD B. "Selection and Evaluation of Department Chairmen." *Educational Record,* 56(1), 1975, pp. 29–38.

GIES, JOSEPH. *The Liberal Arts College: The Next Twenty-five Years.* 1984. (ERIC Document Reproduction Service No. ED 261 604)

HERR, KAY U. *Chairperson's Handbook.* 1989. (ERIC Document Reproduction Service No. ED 311 838)

KAIKAI, SEPTIMUS M., and KAIKAI, REGINA E. *Chairpersons as Promoters of Community Service.* Catonsville, MD: Catonsville Community College, 1990. (ERIC Document Reproduction Service No. ED 321 801)

KERSSEN, JEFF. *Accuracy in Academia? "Professor" as a Problematic Cultural Term.* 1987. Paper presented at the Annual Meeting of the Western Speech Communication Association, Salt Lake City, 1987. (ERIC Document Reproduction Service No. ED 281 257)

KONRAD, ABRAM G., and MCNEAL, JOANNE. "Goals in Canadian Universities." *Canadian Journal of Higher Education,* 14, 1984, pp. 31–40.

LARSON, JON (et al.) "Higher Education Planning Perspectives: an Historical Overview, the Administrators' Perspectives, and the View from Two-year Colleges." *CUPA Journal,* 39, 1988, pp. 1–14.

MALM, LINDA. *Leadership Practice: How I Raised $100,000 This Year With No Fund Raising Experience.* 1990. (ERIC Document Reproduction Service No. ED 319 423)

MITCHELL, MARY B., and WHEELER, DANIEL W. *A Grounded Theory of Chairperson Management Strategy.* ASHE 1987 Annual Meeting Paper, San Diego, 1987. (ERIC Document Reproduction Service No. ED 281 465)

REYES, PEDRO, and MCCARTY, DONALD J. *The Power of Lower Participants in Educational Organizations.* ASHE Annual Meeting Paper, San Antonio, 1986. (ERIC Document Reproduction Service No. ED 268 868)

SCHAFFER, ROBIN. "Role Conflict in Academic Chairpersons." *Occupational Therapy Journal of Research,* 7, 1987, pp. 301–313.

SEAGREN, ALAN T. *Perception of Chairpersons and Faculty Concerning Roles, Descriptors, and Activities Considered Important for Faculty Development and Departmental Vitality.* 1986. (ERIC Document Reproduction Service No. ED 276 387)

SEMLACK, WILLIAM D. *Corporate Culture in a University Setting: An Analysis of Theory "X," Theory "Y," and Theory "Z" Cultures Within University Academic Departments.* 1986. Paper presented at the Annual Meeting of the Central States Speech Association, Cincinnati. (ERIC Document Reproduction Service No. ED 269 822)

SERGIOVANNI, THOMAS J., and CORBALLY, JOHN E. *Leadership and Organizational Culture.* Chicago: University of Illinois Press, 1988.

SPICER, CHRISTOPHER H., and STATON-SPICER, ANN Q. "Communication in the Socialization of the Academic Department Chairperson." *Bulletin of the Association for Business Communication,* 65, 1988, pp. 46–54.

STATON-SPICER, ANN Q., and SPICER, CHRISTOPHER H. "Socialization of the Academic Chairperson: A Typology of Communication Dimensions." *Educational Administration Quarterly,* 23, 1987, pp. 41–64.

WINANS, GLEN T. *Determinants of Budget Allocations to Academic Departments: A Case Study.* 1987. ASHE 1987 Annual Meeting Paper, San Diego. (ERIC Document Reproduction Service No. ED 281 464)

Chapter 2

History and Development of Academic Departments

Universities have not always been organized into discipline departments. In fact, if one looks back over the some six hundred years that universities have existed, departmentalization is a relatively recent idea. While scholars point to an exception here and there, equivalents of academic departments do not show up until the second half of the 1700s; even then such a pattern was an exception. Prior to and shortly after the Civil War, American colleges were administered by presidents who personally served as scholar, leader, teacher, chief disciplinarian, librarian, admissions officer, keeper of student records, business manager, secretary of the faculty, and secretary of the board of governors.

As enrollments began to grow, presidents found it necessary to appoint individuals with special expertise to assume some of these presidential functions. The first appointment was that of librarian and the second was that of registrar. The need to establish a registrar's office became apparent in the 1880s, according to some historians, when elective curricula began to appear at some of the colleges and the task of keeping academic records became more complicated. As enrollments and curricula continued to expand, increased numbers of disciplinary and academic problems could not be solved with routine answers. In the 1890s the first deans were appointed to whom curricular and disciplinary authority was gradually delegated. Academic deans became chief personnel officers for the faculties, and deans of men and deans of women assumed responsibilities for student services. The addition of new administrative positions such as director of admissions, business manager, and public relations officer continued well into the twentieth century.

The office of vice-president was first established in the late 1800s in a few of the larger universities. By the middle of the twentieth century, however, this office was in place at most institutions of higher learning in the United States. In the beginning, librarians, registrars, deans, and other appointed officials considered their administrative responsibilities as part-time jobs and continued to serve in faculty capacities as scholars, teachers, and student advisers. As the number of students increased, it was necessary for presidents to employ full-time tutors and professors. In the middle 1800s faculty members at both Harvard and the University of Virginia began to group themselves into separate departments of instruction.

The rise of departments grew out of a need to improve the organization and management of the academic process as knowledge expanded at an ever accelerating pace. The day of the "tired clergyman" teaching everything from rhetoric to natural philosophy was over. The influence of the German universities and their search for scientific truth led to the era of disciplinary specialization. Kerr[1] and others point to this influence, especially at the graduate level, as the driving force behind undergraduate departmentalization of American colleges and universities. In retrospect, it appears inevitable that the increase in specialization and departmentalization would change the perspective of the faculty. Critics charged, and still charge, that publishing, research, and concern for tenure have pushed teaching into a subordinate position. Allegiance to the discipline has become more important than loyalty to, and concern for, the college or university. Can students learn interdisciplinary approaches to living in a complex, sophisticated world at universities divided into departments?

In the 1950s some of the larger American universities began to establish institutes, centers, and bureaus for specialized teaching and research. These new units frequently cut across departments and were intended to encourage interdisciplinary studies and activities. Although there are many such units in institutions of higher learning throughout the country, the discipline department remains the mainspring in the organization of academic work at our colleges and universities.

Organization of Academic Departments and Divisions

Departments often are designated as either pure or mixed. A pure discipline department is one in which all its faculty members are trained, have common backgrounds, and teach in the same discipline. "Pure" departments such as history, chemistry, English, and mathematics are more apt to occur in large colleges and universities. In smaller colleges, where a discipline has too few faculty members to justify departmental status, several discipline programs may be housed in one department for administrative and economic efficiency; for example, a department of sociology and anthropology, or a department of history, philosophy, and religion. Such are called "mixed" departments.

---

1. Clark Kerr, "Administration in an Era of Change and Conflict," *Educational Record,* Winter 1973, p. 41.

At some institutions, mostly small ones, an administrative unit containing several different academic or vocational disciplines is not called a mixed department. Instead it is called a division, and has a division director or division chairperson who reports to a dean or a vice-president, depending on the size of the division and the institution. At other institutions the disciplines within a division may be departmentalized, with each department having a chairperson responsible to the division director or chairperson. It is sometimes the case that at the same institution some divisions are departmentalized and some are not. Divisional structure is found at some small-to-medium-sized baccalaureate granting colleges, but mostly it is found in community colleges, with each division responsible for several academic disciplines or vocational programs. In large community colleges, divisions are sometimes subdivided into departments according to discipline, depending on the size of the program offered in that discipline.

Size and Maturity of Departments

For the sake of analysis, departments may be divided into four categories: small, large, immature, and mature. Overlappings among these categories do occur, of course, but the categories can serve as benchmarks for our discussion of departments. We shall define a "small" department as one that has up to nine full-time faculty members, including the chairperson. Departments with four or fewer members are not really departments but programs that have achieved department status because of their excellence or because of tradition, sentiment, nostalgia, or tolerance on the part of the central administration. We shall define a "medium-sized" department as one that has between ten and nineteen full-time faculty members, and a "large" department as one that has twenty or more full-time faculty members.

Hersey and Blanchard define *maturity* as "the capacity to set high but attainable goals . . . , willingness and ability to take responsibility, and education and/or experience of an individual or group. *These variables of maturity should be considered only in relation to a specific task to be performed.*"[2] According to this definition, a mature academic department is one in which the faculty members have the experience and capacity *as a group* to work together, set high but attainable goals, reach group decisions, and readily accept responsibility for their decisions and assignments. Not only are some departments more mature than others, but a department may display more maturity in one situation than another, depending on the problem or task with which it is dealing. An immature department is one that has great difficulty in reaching consensus or in developing and implementing a plan of action; its members are either unable or unwilling to work together effectively. Generally, mature departments are those

2. Paul Hersey and Kenneth H. Blanchard, *Management of Organizational Behavior: Utilizing Human Resources,* 3rd ed. (Englewood Cliffs: Prentice–Hall, 1977), p. 161.

that have been in existence for a long time, say fifteen years or more. Of course, age does not guarantee maturity; in fact, a mature department can regress to immaturity. Generally, however, a young department, whether small or large, is an immature department, according to our definition, simply because the process of learning to work cooperatively takes time and effort.

IMMATURE SMALL DEPARTMENTS

The members of an immature small department are usually highly self-conscious and defensive about its existence in the college or the institution. Repeatedly, the department is called on to justify its own existence, to defend its intellectual premises and its place in the great chain of academic being, and to resist budget raids by older, more powerful departments. In the formation and development of its curriculum, such a department often tends toward polarization; it may become faddish or wildly eclectic in its course offerings and degree programs, or it may hunker down behind a stodgy, traditional program in an attempt to gain instant respectability and acceptance from the rest of the institution. Its value system for promotion and tenure is undeveloped, although guided by institutional policy. Often it either rebels against such policy by claiming the virtues of innovation and uniqueness, or it interprets institutional policy as rigidly and conservatively as possible in an attempt, once again, to gain acceptance and credibility within the institution.

These polarities of behavior tend to follow disciplinary lines. The new, small science department—particularly the chemistry department—is likely to be more traditional and conventional than its mature counterparts in other institutions. The new social science department—especially the sociology department, which is itself a newcomer to the pantheon of academic disciplines—is likely to be innovative, eclectic, and chaotic as it struggles to establish itself.

The extreme behavioral patterns exhibited by immature small departments often lead the dean or central administration to appoint as chairperson a faculty member with a dominant personality who will try to run the department like a platoon. This response is only a natural one and usually quite necessary.

Leaders of immature small departments must continually remind themselves and their faculty members that they are going through a necessary stage of development and that life will not always be so difficult. The curriculum established now will have an effect on the department's future, as will promotions, tenure awards, and resource allocations. This phase of a department's existence is the stormiest, and all department members should try to remember that since things will inevitably change, they should not commit themselves to decisions that will make change more difficult to realize.

MATURE SMALL DEPARTMENTS

In the mature small department, conditions are entirely different. This type of department has long since lived through the development stage and often takes on the relaxed air of a country club as it goes about its business. Since all its members know each other, they usually share a unity of purpose and a sense of group cooperation seldom found in any other kind of department. Of course, there may be personality clashes or grave philosophical differences among the members, but the strife is genteel, as it is in a country club. Seldom is the chairperson of such a department a hard-driving platoon leader. Usually he or she comes from the faculty ranks. Often the position in such a department becomes, intentionally or not, a rotating position, institutional policies to the contrary notwithstanding.

Yet beneath this serene surface, danger abounds. The department's very strength, its close-knit unity, and its lack of strife may be its undoing. Decisions tend to be made in town-hall fashion; the whole department may decide, with the chairperson as presiding officer, on resource allocations, curriculum development and reform, course assignments and teaching loads, and, if institutional policy permits, promotion and tenure.

The problem with this kind of democratic activity is that it makes establishing and implementing priority systems extremely difficult, although not impossible. Everyone defers to everyone else, and even the chairperson may follow the path of least resistance—spreading the resources evenly, giving each faculty member's courses and programs equal billing in the catalog and in the schedule of courses, promoting everyone's friend, tenuring all newcomers as soon as possible, and trying to give everyone the same salary (prorated, of course). In five years—at the most—such a department will be in serious trouble with its faculty members, the dean, and the central administration.

Chairpersons of mature small departments must be perhaps more strong-willed than those of other kinds of departments. Not only must they be strong-willed; they must also be the most graceful and patient diplomats of them all. The chairperson's position in the mature small department may offer a severe test, and anyone who takes the job should not be deceived by the surface calm, for he or she will have to work continually to keep the department from sliding into senility.

The preceding examples represent the extremes of maturity ranges of small departments. Real departments may lie anywhere between these extremes.

IMMATURE LARGE DEPARTMENTS

Immature large departments tend to have the same sorts of problems as their smaller counterparts. If anything, such departments more compellingly invite the implementation of the department-as-platoon concept than do smaller departments. To state it simply, a strong will and steel nerves are necessary requisites for leading an immature large department. Again, in every decision made with colleagues, the chairperson's best course of action is to remind them continually that present decisions affect the department's future. An immature large department should be almost wholly concerned with the future, not with the present. An immature large department is often the result of a merger of several more mature, smaller ones. The new organization makes it imperative that the members learn to work with their new colleagues to overcome the tribulations of immaturity.

Mature large departments have a tendency to organize themselves either into feudal territories or into assembly lines. In the last thirty years department organization has tended toward internal atomization or fragmentation. This tendency is a natural one, for as knowledge increases and becomes ever more specialized, units within academic disciplines begin growing apart from the parent discipline.

The classic example of this kind of fragmentation is found in the psychology department, typically a mature large department. It often has so many subunits that it can be considered a school. In psychology, the experimentalists are a breed apart, as are the clinical psychologists. Indeed, there appears to be a trend in some institutions to set up the clinical psychology subunit as a separate department. Add to these subunits such groups as the social psychologists, the school psychologists, and the consumer behavior psychologists—to name a few—and the problems of a psychology department chairperson are easy to understand. Chemistry departments also tend to become atomized. The larger and more mature the chemistry department, the greater the differences among the organic, inorganic, theoretical or quantum, and analytical groups. In such departments, the chairperson's major challenge lies, of course, in resource allocation. Each territorial group, powerful in itself, presents its case to the chairperson, and consensus-based decisions are extremely difficult to achieve.

In the mature large department, promotion and tenure issues are generally easier to resolve than resource allocation problems, for the competing units develop a sense of pride and *esprit de corps* and seldom recommend weak cases to the entire department. The best course of action for the chairperson is to encourage, not discourage, competition among subunits. Fostering open competition is better than stiffling initiative and innovation or attempting to administer these warring units according to the principle of sharing the wealth. But competition means that in the resource allocation process there will be some winners and some losers, and departments that adopt this mode of operation should be prepared to make and accept decisions that recognize firmly established priorities.

In addition to the tendency towards fragmentation, mature large departments also exhibit a tendency to adopt the assembly-line concept of operation. This approach is almost inevitable. Large numbers of freshmen must be run through the introductory courses in such departments as chemistry, English, mathematics, economics, and speech. At the same time, there are large numbers of graduate students who must be taught, whose theses and dissertations must be approved, and whose teaching assistantships must be supervised. Under these circumstances the chairperson and the faculty have a difficult time maintaining the necessary collegial mode of operation, and the family ambience of a small or medium-sized department begins to dissolve under these pressures. The administrative hierarchy begins to grow under the pressures of numbers: the chairperson has to appoint an associate or vice-chairperson, a director of freshman English, a director of the undergraduate chemistry labs, and a director of introductory speech courses. With its increasing variety of assistant and associate chairpersons, the department's internal structure begins to resemble the hierarchy of the institution's central administration.

These developments may be inevitable, but they tend to isolate the chairperson. To resist this isolation, the chairperson must continually seek ways to improve communication with faculty members; he or she must continually "get out among 'em" and not succumb, for example, to the tempting argument that because the department is so large, department faculty meetings are useless.

Department meetings in mature large departments are almost always stressful for the chairperson, and it is only natural to wish to avoid stress. Such meetings must be held regularly with agenda posted in advance. The chairperson must spend time with heads of department divisions and, above all else, communicate to each division head the needs and goals of the other divisions. Only in this way can a spirit of teamwork and department unity be maintained. This approach is time-consuming and requires hard work, but if the chairperson of a mature large department is to avoid becoming just another academic bureaucrat, he or she must bend every effort to the goal of personal communication and interaction with faculty members.

A Theory of Departmental Development

Robert K. Murray, in his article "On Departmental Development: A Theory," describes a model tracing five stages of growth and evolution in a typical department. A department in the first stage of growth—especially a department in a small, undistinguished institution—has only a few members and is ruled autocratically and arbitrarily. The second stage, frequently coinciding with an increase in department size, is characterized by turmoil and power struggles, during which faculty members fight for a greater voice in decision making. This infighting often leads to the chairperson's resignation; faculty morale is low, and the department atmosphere is antagonistic. The third stage of a department's evolution is marked by "rampant democracy." A department in this stage spends an inordinate amount of time making democratic decisions and having committee meetings. Such a department is characterized by a rotating chairmanship and a sense of drift; the chairperson simply rubber-stamps the decisions of the faculty. The fourth stage is characterized by the department's large size and a split between nontenured junior professors and tenured senior professors, who make the important governance and policy decisions. The chairperson has a good deal of power but knows that his or her authority comes from the peer group of senior professors. The fifth stage, occurring in some very large distinguished departments and in a few small ones, leaves ordinary governance matters to competent secretaries and specially selected academic bureaucrats. A department in this stage of development is at the peak of prestige and influence but is beginning to collapse because of lack of organization.

A department need not evolve consecutively through all five stages. In a given institution at any given time, departments may be in different stages, and the progression from stage to stage is not necessarily smooth nor inevitable. Murray's theory does, however, provide an interesting conceptual scheme that can be used to explain the organizational problems of some departments.

Determining the Maturity Level of Your Department

In determining the maturity level of your department, it may be helpful to review briefly what constitutes maturity in group behavior. As has already been stated in this chapter, a mature department is defined as one in which faculty members as a group have the experience, capacity, and willingness to (1) work together effectively; (2) set high but attainable goals; (3) reach group decisions; and (4) accept responsibility for their decisions and assignments.

A corollary to this definition is that a department is neither mature nor immature all the time. The maturity of a department can be assessed separately for each issue or activity being dealt with. A department may deal maturely with one issue and immaturely with another. The frequency with which issues are resolved in a mature way is the basis for judging the overall maturity of a department. In the case of each issue or activity there are four categories of behavior:

1. A group which is neither willing nor able to take responsibility
2. A group which is not willing but able
3. A group which is willing but not able
4. A group which is willing and able

Category 1 represents groups with the least maturity. Category 4 represents groups with the most maturity. Moderate maturity would be represented by categories 2 and 3.

Chairpersons of departments containing more than one program (mixed departments) must decide whether they wish to assess the maturity level of the department as a whole or the maturity level of each subgroup within the department. Chairs of departments with only one program (pure departments) will not have to make this decision.

The chairperson should recall how many significant issues required departmental action within the last twelve months. Consider each issue separately. How did the faculty as a group deal with the issue? Were they willing and able to deal with it? Were they able to reach a consensus without too much prodding from the chairperson? If so, the group dealt with the issue in a mature way. Consider-

TABLE *2.1*   Relationship Between Frequency of Mature Behavior and
Overall Maturity of Departments

FREQUENCY OF MATURITY	LEVEL OF MATURITY	
About 25% of the time	Low	1
About 50% of the time	Low to Medium	2
About 75% of the time	Medium to High	3
Most of the time	High	4
What maturity level is your group?		

ing all of the issues, determine what percentage of them were dealt with in a mature way. Refer to Table 2.1, which indicates the relationship between frequency of mature behavior and the overall maturity level of the department. For example, if a department dealt with twenty significant issues during the past twelve months and acted maturely in dealing with fifteen of them (75 percent), then, according to Table 2.1, the maturity level of the department would be medium to high, or level 3.

The above procedure has not been tested or validated. It is intended to help chairpersons obtain an approximate measure of their department's maturity level, which in turn may provide guidance in the kind of department leadership that is needed.

Questions

1. Does your department or division contain only one discipline program or does it contain more than one? If only one, indicate how many full-time and part-time faculty.
2. If more than one, please name the number of different discipline programs contained in your department or division and indicate how many full-time and part-time faculty members there are in each program.
3. How many years has your department or division been in existence in its present form? Was it originally established this way or has it undergone one or more changes in organization to reach its present administrative arrangement?
4. The following review of "group maturity" is provided as a basis for responding to questions about the maturity of your department or division.

   Maturity is defined by Hersey and Blanchard in their Situational Leadership Theory as the capacity of a group of individuals to set high but attainable goals, the willingness and ability to take responsibility, and the education and/or experience of the group to accomplish those

goals. A group is neither mature nor immature about everything. The variable of maturity should be considered only in relationship to specific tasks or activities. In considering maturity we can divide groups into four main categories:
- Those who are neither willing nor able to take responsibility
- Those who are willing but not able to take responsibility
- Those who are able but not willing to take responsibility
- Those who are willing and able to take responsibility

The lowest level of maturity is the first category listed; the highest level is fourth.

a. On the basis of the preceding definition, how would you rate the maturity of your whole department or division on the majority of those issues requiring a department or division consensus—low, moderate, or high?

b. How would you rate the maturity of the group of faculty members in each program in your department or division on the majority of issues requiring a program consensus—low, moderate, or high?

References

Adams, Hazard. *The Academic Tribes.* 2nd ed. Champaign, IL: University of Illinois Press, 1988. (ERIC Document Reproduction Service No. ED 297 632)

American Association Of Community And Junior Colleges. *Community, Junior and Technical College Directory.* Washington, DC, 1990.

Anderson, G. Lester. "Organizational Diversity." In *New Directions for Institutional Research: Examining Departmental Management,* 10, edited by John C. Smart and James R. Montgomery. San Francisco: Jossey–Bass, 1976.

Barzun, Jacques. *The American University: How It Runs, Where It Is Going.* New York: Harper & Row, 1968.

Bobbitt, H. Randolph, and Behling, Orlando C. "Organizational Behavior: A Review of the Literature." *Journal of Higher Education,* January–February 1981, pp. 29–44.

Bowker, Lee H., and Lynch, David M. *Chairing a Small Department.* Paper presented at the National Conference for Department Chairs, Orlando, 1985. (ERIC Document Reproduction Service No. ED 256 222)

Brubacher, John S., and Rudy, Willis. *Higher Education in Transition.* 3rd ed. New York: Harper & Row, 1976.

Cohen, Arthur M. and Brawer, Florence B. *The American Community College.* 2nd ed. San Francisco: Jossey–Bass, 1988.

Corson, John J. *The Governance of Colleges and Universities.* New York: McGraw–Hill, 1960.

Cummings, L. L., and Dunham, Randall B. *Introduction to Organizational Behavior: Text and Reading.* Homewood, IL: Richard D. Irwin, 1980.

Durnin, Richard G. "The Role of the Presidents in the American Colleges of the Colonial Period." *History of Education Quarterly,* 1, June 1961, pp. 23–30.

GIES, JOSEPH. *The Liberal Arts College: The Next Twenty-five Years.* 1984. (ERIC Document Reproduction Service No. ED 261 604)

HERSEY, PAUL, and BLANCHARD, KENNETH H. *Management of Organizational Behavior: Utilizing Human Resources.* 3rd ed. Englewood Cliffs: Prentice–Hall, 1977.

JOHNSONI, F. CRAIG. "Data Requirements for Academic Departments." In *New Directions for Institutional Research: Examining Departmental Leadership,* 10, edited by John C. Smart and James R. Montgomery. San Francisco: Jossey–Bass, 1976.

KERR, CLARK. "Administration in an Era of Change and Conflict." *Educational Record,* Winter 1973, pp. 38–46.

KOPECK, R. I., and CLARKE, R. G. "One Dimension of Organizational Structures of Middle-Size Community Colleges." *Community College Review,* 10, 1982, pp. 33–40.

MAACK, MARY. "Women in Library Education: Down the Up Staircase." *Library Trends,* 34, 1986, pp. 401–432.

MARCH, JAMES G. *How We Talk and How We Act: Administrative Theory and Administrative Life.* Urbana: University of Illinois Press, 1980.

MILLETT, JOHN D. *New Structures of Campus Power: Success and Failures of Emerging Forms of Institutional Governance.* San Francisco: Jossey–Bass, 1978.

———. *Management, Governance and Leadership: A Guide for College and University Administrators.* New York: American Management Association, 1980.

MURRAY, ROBERT K. "On Departmental Development: A Theory." *The Journal of General Education,* October 1964, pp. 227–236.

RYAN, DORIS W. "The Internal Organization of Academic Departments." *Journal of Higher Education,* June 1972, pp. 464–482.

SAMUELS, KEITH T. *A Study of Community College Division Chairpersons with Comparisons to University Department Chairpersons in Florida's System of Higher Education.* Unpublished Doctoral Dissertation, Florida State University, 1983.

SEAGREN, ALAN T., and CRESWELL, JOHN W. *A Comparison of Perceptions of Administrative Tasks and Professional Development Needs of Chairpersons/Heads of Departments in Australia and the U.S.* 1985. (ERIC Document Reproduction Service No. ED 257 328)

SMART, JOHN C., and ELTON, CHARLES F. "Administrative Roles of Department Chairmen." In *New Directions for Institutional Research: Examining Departmental Management,* 10, edited by John C. Smart and James R. Montgomery. San Francisco: Jossey–Bass, 1976.

STEWART, W. G. *Selected Management Functions in the Role of Division Chairpersons in Multi-Campus Community Colleges.* Doctoral Dissertation, North Texas State University, 1981. (Dissertation Abstracts International, 1982, 42, 3034-A University Microfilms No. 812898)

Part II

THE DEPARTMENT CHAIR

Chapter 3.   Roles, Functions, and Characteristics of Department Chairs

Chapter 4.   Power and Authority of a Chair

Chapter 5.   Leadership and Decision Making

Chapter 6.   The Chair's Role in Bringing About Change

Chapter 7.   Delegation and Department Committees

Roles, Functions, and Characteristics of Department Chairs

The present economic crisis in higher education raises a fundamental question concerning the ability of colleges and universities to fulfill their traditional functions. Specifically, can institutions of higher learning maintain flexibility and viability, preserve quality, remain accountable, and respond effectively to the changing needs of society within the context of continuing inflation and steady-state or even declining resources? Academic departments are the organizational units within an institution that are most severely affected by steady-state or declining resources, and those who chair these departments can have considerable influence in resolving this problem.

Paradoxically, most department chairpersons are drawn from faculty ranks and have had, at best, very little administrative experience. Recent surveys found over two-thirds of them had no prior administrative experience, the turnover rate was 15 to 20 percent per year, and the chairpersons' term of service was usually six years.

Some chairpersons are appointed by the dean and serve at the dean's pleasure; others are appointed by the dean from a list of candidates recommended by a faculty search committee; and still others are elected by their colleagues to serve for one or more terms. In some departments, the position of chairperson rotates among its members. In many cases, chairpersons receive extra compensation and other perquisites, such as full-time summer appointments and more luxurious office space. The material and psychological rewards of the position are intended to compensate for frustrations encountered in the job, such as abrasive incidents with both deans and faculty members, longer hours, and reduced time for teaching and research. Occasionally the frustrations cause chairpersons to resign, especially when the dissatisfactions outweigh the benefits. The department whose chairperson serves a fixed term, usually two or three years, gives the chairperson an option to exit gracefully after a full cycle or two of experience.

While specially designed national and regional workshops are conducted for new presidents, vice presidents, and deans to help prepare them for their new responsibilities, few such opportunities are available to department chairpersons, who outnumber all other types of university administrators combined. The increasing complexities of operating institutions of higher education, along with shrunken budgets, have led deans and other university administrators to delegate more and more tasks to department chairpersons. Thus, it is in the best interests of colleges and universities to ensure that department chairpersons become as knowledgeable as possible about planning, management, and leadership techniques. The following list shows, by category, the astonishing variety of responsibilities and duties that face the department chairperson:

Responsibilities of Chairpersons

Department governance
> Conduct department meetings
> Establish department committees.
> Use committees effectively.
> Develop long-range department programs, plans, and goals.
> Determine what services the department should provide to the university, community, and state.
> Implement long-range department programs, plans, goals, and policies.
> Prepare the department for accreditation and evaluation.
> Serve as an advocate for the department.
> Monitor library acquisitions.
> Delegate some department administrative responsibilities to individuals and committees.
> Encourage faculty members to communicate ideas for improving the department.

Instruction
> Schedule classes.
> Supervise off-campus programs.
> Monitor dissertations, prospectuses, and programs of study for graduate students.
> Supervise, schedule, monitor, and grade department examinations.
> Update department curriculum, courses, and programs.

Faculty affairs
> Recruit and select faculty members.
> Assign faculty responsibilities, such as teaching, research, committee work, and so forth.

Monitor faculty service contributions.

Evaluate faculty performance.

Initiate promotion and tenure recommendations.

Participate in grievance hearings.

Make merit recommendations.

Deal with unsatisfactory faculty and staff performance.

Initiate termination of a faculty member.

Keep faculty members informed of department, college, and institutional plans, activities, and expectations.

Maintain morale.

Reduce, resolve, and prevent conflict among faculty members.

Encourage faculty participation.

Student affairs

Recruit and select students.

Advise and counsel students.

Work with student government.

External communication

Communicate department needs to the dean and interact with upper-level administrators.

Improve and maintain the department's image and reputation.

Coordinate activities with outside groups.

Process department correspondence and requests for information.

Complete forms and surveys.

Initiate and maintain liaison with external agencies and institutions.

Budget and resources

Encourage faculty members to submit proposals for contracts and grants to government agencies and private foundations.

Prepare and propose department budgets.

Seek outside funding.

Administer the department budget.

Set priorities for use of travel funds.

Prepare annual reports.

Office management

Manage department facilities and equipment, including maintenance and control of inventory.

Monitor building security and maintenance.

Supervise and evaluate the clerical and technical staff in the department.

Maintain essential department records, including student records.

Professional development

Foster the development of each faculty member's special talents and interests.

Foster good teaching in the department.

Stimulate faculty research and publications.

Promote affirmative action.

Encourage faculty members to participate in regional and national professional meetings.

Represent the department at meetings of learned and professional societies.

Responsibilities· of Chairpersons in Community Colleges

Some community colleges have only division chairpersons and some have both division and department chairpersons. The nomenclature varies from one college to another even though the functions of the chairpersons may be similar. In any case, the number of division and department chairpersons per community college ranges from seven to seventy-five with an average of about twenty-one per institution. The total number for all community colleges is approximately 27,000.

Although most institutions, regardless of type, will have similar lists of responsibilities for chairpersons, the real or perceived importance of any particular responsibility on the list may vary from one chairperson to another depending on the missions, goals, and functions of the institution. The discipline oriented research function obviously separates community colleges from universities but not from all four-year colleges. Some of their course offerings and types of curricula, especially in vocational areas, also set them apart from other types of institutions, resulting in a difference in the rank ordering of responsibilities according to importance.

Comparing the roles of chairpersons from different types of institutions is made more difficult because of the differences in personalities, goals, and abilities of the chairpersons themselves. Provided with a menu of possible tasks and activities, chairpersons tend both to select those items which better match their strengths and to shun, or at least put off, those items that fall into areas in which they are less comfortable. Such avoidance behavior may have a significant impact on shaping the role of an individual chairperson and the importance he or she attaches to specific responsibilities. Conversely, a dean may recognize certain abilities in a chairperson and by way of special assignments contribute a shift in the individual's actual role.

An interesting pattern emerges when comparing community college chairpersons with university chairpersons in terms of how they rate the importance of each of the responsibilities listed earlier in this chapter. They were asked to select the ten responsibilities they considered most important. Both groups of chairpersons included the following five in their top ten although not necessarily in the same rank order.

- Fostering of good teaching
- Maintenance of faculty morale
- Recruitment and selection of faculty

- Communicating needs to the dean and interaction with upper-level administration
- Updating curriculum courses and programs

Three additional responsibilities included in the community college chairpersons' top ten were ranked considerably lower in importance by university chairpersons. These were:

- Providing for the flow of information to the faculty to inform them of plans, activities, and expectations at various organizational levels
- Dealing with unsatisfactory performance
- Preparation and presentation of proposed departmental budgets

Three additional responsibilities included in the university chairpersons' top ten were ranked considerably lower in importance by community college chairpersons. These were:

- Recognition and rewarding of faculty in accordance with their contribution to academic programs
- Evaluation of faculty for tenure, raises, and promotions
- Encouragement of faculty to participate actively in professional meetings

The data obtained from this survey showed that overall, university and community college chairpersons are fairly close in how they rank-ordered the importance of most of the responsibilities. Both groups agree on the top importance of five of the responsibilities. There was marked disagreement, however, in their rankings of six of the responsibilities, which may be a reflection of the differences between the two groups in how they perceived their roles as chairpersons. As can be seen from the data, community college chairpersons ranked the importance of administrative and bureaucratic tasks much higher than did their university colleagues. University chairpersons, on the other hand, placed greater importance on activities that are faculty related.[1]

With the exception of references to graduate instruction and research, most of the topics discussed in the remainder of this book will have as many implications for community college chairpersons as for chairpersons of other types of institutions. Community college chairpersons will find that from an administrative and leadership point of view, their institutions may have more in common with four-year institutions than they realized.

---

1. Keith T. Samuels, "A Study of Community College Division Chairpersons With Comparisons To University Department Chairpersons in Florida's System of Public Higher Education." Unpublished doctoral dissertation, Florida State University, 1983, p. 130.

Roles of Chairpersons

As part of their responsibilities, chairpersons find it necessary to deal with various categories of people, within and outside the institution. Within the institution, chairpersons deal with presidents, vice-presidents, deans, registrars, personnel officers, maintenance personnel, faculty committees, students, other department chairpersons, department associates, staff personnel, and others. Individuals and agencies outside of the institution with whom chairpersons must relate include alumni, legislators, civic organizations, regional and national professional organizations, high school and junior college students, high school and junior college counselors, townspeople, and professional colleagues.

In dealing with various kinds of persons, the chairperson assumes those roles most appropriate to accomplish his or her objectives. The role indicates how or in what capacity the chairperson relates to an individual or a group in performing an activity. Following is a list of twenty-eight possible roles that chairpersons assume to some degree at one time or another:

teacher	representer	decision maker
mentor	communicator	problem solver
researcher	evaluator	recommender
leader	motivator	implementor
planner	supervisor	facilitator
manager	coordinator	entrepreneur
advisor–counselor	anticipator	recruiter
mediator–negotiator	innovator	peer–colleague
delegator	peacemaker	
advocator	organizer	

The chairperson's job, obviously, is difficult and complex. A brilliant university or college administration with inept chairpersons cannot survive; an inept administration, with the help of a group of brilliant chairpersons, usually can. The position of department chairperson, then, is an important one. The discussion that follows is an attempt to describe and, to some degree, define the role of the chairperson.

The Paradoxical Nature of the Role

One distinctive characteristic of the chairperson's role is its paradoxical nature. The chairperson is a leader, yet is seldom given the scepter of undisputed authority. He or she is first among equals, but any strong coalition of those equals can severely restrict the chairperson's ability to lead. Deans and vice-presidents look to chairpersons as those primarily responsible for shaping the department's future, yet faculty members regard themselves as the primary agents of change in department policies and procedures. The chairperson, then, is both a manager and a faculty colleague, an advisor and an advisee, a soldier and a captain, a drudge and a boss.

Chairpersons are the only academic managers who must live with their decisions every day. The dean and the vice-president make many important administrative decisions, such as which colleges or departments will get the lion's share of the year's operating budget. The dean and the vice-president, however, do not have to say good morning—every morning—to their colleagues in the department; they do not have to teach several times a week alongside their colleagues; they do not have to maintain a family relationship with their faculty members. The department chairperson, on the other hand, does. He or she must be acutely aware of the vital statistics of each family member—births, deaths, marriages, divorces, illnesses, and even private financial woes.

This intimate relationship is not duplicated anywhere else in the college or university because no other academic unit takes on the ambience of a family, with its personal interaction, its daily sharing of common goals and interests (with frequent contention over how those goals are to be pursued), and its concern for each member. No matter how large the department, no matter how deeply divided over pedagogical and philosophical issues it may be, its members are bound together in many ways: they have all had the same general preparation in graduate school; their fortunes generally rise or fall with the fortunes of the discipline to which they all belong; and they share the same general value system of their profession. Working alongside the members of this "family" is the chairperson, a manager who is sometimes managed, a leader who is sometimes led, a parent who continually strives to keep peace for the sake of mutual benefit and progress.

These conditions are not the only ones that make the department chairperson's role paradoxical. He or she must deal with the expectations and desires of the students in the department, the personal and professional hopes and fears of the department faculty members, the goals and priorities of the college dean, the often perplexing and—from the department's perspective—sometimes shadowy priorities of the central administration, the sometimes naïve and sometimes jaundiced views of the alumni, and the bureaucratic procedures of accrediting agencies. Few administrators can, by themselves, face these conflicting constituencies and find solutions to all problems. Yet the chairperson must induce these constituencies to work together to help solve the problems they themselves generate.

A department chairperson's constituencies, in addition to department faculty members, include students and alumni. Students often seem to want less work and more entertainment. Undergraduates generally want the department to reduce the number of required courses for the major or to abolish certain degree requirements, such as specific courses in foreign languages, statistics, mathematics, humanities, or laboratory science. Graduate students generally want the scope of the qualifying examinations reduced and the language requirement modified or abolished; graduate assistants often want their teaching and research duties reduced. Students, until they become alumni, want "interesting" lecturers who give "fair" tests and don't require much outside reading or problem solving. Alumni want almost the opposite. Faculty members often want to increase the requirements for the department major to equal the number of credits necessary for the baccalaureate degree; they also are inclined to double the duties of the teaching and research assistants.

An astute chairperson will strive to establish a creative tension among these three constituencies—students, alumni, and faculty members—to reach a rational compromise on these particular issues. The compromise should not revolutionize higher education, fragment the already delicately balanced undergraduate curriculum, or increase the cost of the graduate program to the point that it drives the department into bankruptcy.

College deans, the central administration, and professional accrediting agencies pose other problems. The first two groups are seldom at odds with each other over department priorities, and only a powerful and supremely confident department chairperson should attempt to generate creative tension between them. The professional accrediting agencies, with their seemingly narrow interests and excessive demands, are seldom concerned with the institution's general academic welfare. Occasionally the chairperson can persuade the college dean and the central administration to join with the department against the accrediting agency. He or she could also enlist the aid of the agency and the dean to educate the idealists in the central administration about the hard realities of life in the department trenches. Or, in a daring maneuver, the chairperson could, in a pincer movement, catch the college dean between the central administration and the accrediting agency and, for example, make the dean surrender more resources to the department. Whatever the alignment of forces and whatever the issues at hand, the department chairperson almost always becomes the fulcrum in the balancing act of allocating institutional resources.

A conflict which occurs frequently within a chairperson is whether he or she is primarily a faculty person with some administrative responsibilities or an administrator with some faculty responsibilities. In baccalaureate granting institutions, department chairpersons perceive themselves primarily as faculty members with some administrative responsibilities. In community or junior colleges, division chairpersons generally perceive themselves as administrators with some faculty and teaching responsibilities. Even in instances when the amount of effort devoted to administration is the same in both cases, the difference in self-perception of these chairpersons still persists.

Since university departments are more likely to be pure in the sense that most faculty members have similar training and teach in the same discipline, faculty members of these departments are usually able to reach a consensus in matters of curriculum and department policy without too much difficulty. This may explain in part why department chairpersons who emerge from this type of faculty tend to think of themselves primarily as faculty members rather than as administrators. Community college divisions, on the other hand, usually contain several different and perhaps unrelated programs taught by faculty members with diverse backgrounds. Because of their diversity, division faculty members are likely to have more difficulty in reaching consensus on some issues than members of a pure university department. Community college chairpersons therefore may tend to conduct their division business in a somewhat less collegial fashion and to work more closely with central administrators than do chairpersons of departments in four-year institutions. The former seem to have greater opportunity to be involved in college-wide decisions and are expected to serve more as extensions of the administration than as advocates of the faculty. Many of them have been employed in a community college for several years prior to obtaining a doctorate and hence may be less discipline oriented than their university counterparts. Their loyalty therefore is generally stronger to their institution than to their discipline, and because of the nature of their responsibilities they perceive themselves more as administrators than as faculty members. A chairperson is really both an administrator and a faculty person. From a contractual point of view, however, a chairperson is faculty if it is so stated in his or her contract, or administrator if so stated. On the other hand, if it is not stated one way or the other, chairpersons are free to call themselves whatever they want. From a functional point, however, they are a lot of things, but only one thing at a time, depending on which duty they are performing at that time.

Special Roles and Responsibilities of Chairpersons

Many of the chairperson's standard functions automatically make him or her the department's chief planner. This role is an almost imperceptible one, because seldom does any of these standard functions appear to be solely a planning function. The sum of these standard functions, pursued almost on a daily basis, makes the chairperson the chief architect of the department's future.

Consider once again how the chairperson's actions affect the department's future. The appointment of the curriculum committee members helps shape the department's enrollment patterns, its degree programs, its standing in the institution and in the profession. The appointment or selection of promotion and tenure committee members helps shape the character of the department, as well as its programmatic strengths and weaknesses and its standing in the institution and the profession. The allocation of department resources down to the smallest detail—who gets the new line item for a secretary, for example—has obvious implications for the department's future. Assigning courses and teaching loads profoundly affects the lives of the faculty members. The way in which the chairperson conducts the annual faculty evaluations and renders these judgments also affects the lives of individual faculty members. And, finally, recommending or setting salaries will stimulate a series of behavior patterns that, for better or worse, will deeply affect the department's future.

In any organization with the ambience of a family, someone must be the magister, the trainer of tyros; and in the academic department, this duty generally falls to the chairperson. The chairperson—initially, at least—is perceived by the new faculty members as the leader, for he or she knows about the local folkways, the institutional pitfalls, and the way in which a faculty member may succeed professionally. If graduate advisors had done their job properly, their students, upon becoming faculty members, would not need so much coaching from a department chairperson, and the chairperson's chore would be considerably lightened.

The majority of the nation's graduate schools successfully educate and train their candidates in the mastery of a subject, but few new Ph.D.s are well versed in how to conduct themselves as teachers and as department members. The chairperson must remember that although many new faculty members have had experience as teaching assistants, that experience may have been poorly monitored and generally unstructured. Often graduate teaching assistants, through the neglect of their superiors, have picked up bad teaching habits and have brought them along to their first full-time faculty job. One of the worst habits new teachers can bring to the classroom is an attitude that implies that students somehow hinder the faculty's serious work. Although this attitude is seldom ingrained, many new faculty members have assimilated it while working on their dissertation or preparing for doctoral qualifying examinations. Under those circumstances, they come to the mistaken opinion that teaching is only of secondary importance.

The chairperson, then, must see to it that the new faculty members learn how to conduct themselves in a classroom. The attitude that students are hindrances is easy to overcome, for it is not a natural attitude; otherwise faculty members would not be faculty members but would be pursuing other goals in industry or government. But someone must tell newcomers about the department's traditions, its goals, and its place in the college and in the institution. Someone has to tell them about the feuds within the department, the idiosyncrasies of its members, the whole rhythm and flow of department life. In short, someone has to socialize the new members, else they are likely to have a bruising first year or two. In some quarters, this bruising experience may be viewed as a necessary rite of passage, but it is nonetheless an inefficient use of time and resources and can be of seriously damaging experience. The chairperson or a trusted faculty member must conscientiously train new members. The chairperson cannot ignore these matters; for the general welfare of the department, he or she must take a personal interest in new faculty members.

Earlier, the paradoxical nature of the chairperson's job was noted and the role of advocate briefly discussed. That role should be examined more closely, because it is no simple matter. Clearly, the chairperson must be an advocate for the department. He or she must be an advocate in budget negotiations with the college dean and the central administration. Success in these negotiations depends on how carefully data are prepared to support the needs of the department, how clearly and honestly the data are presented, and how relevant the data are to regional and national priorities of the profession or discipline represented by the department. For example, the chairperson of the English department should never march into the dean's office and invidiously compare the budget of the English department with that of the chemistry department. A dean who knows something about cost analysis and who has the priority system of the institution's departments firmly in mind can easily ignore internal comparisons. Most deans, provosts, and vice-presidents hate to be told that one department gets better budget treatment than another, and these administrators are generally well armed with elaborate defenses built around cost analyses and priority systems. In a budget fight, for example, the best way to be a successful advocate for the department is to shame the dean into concessions by comparing the department's budget and its professional standing with other departments of the same discipline in competitive institutions in the state, region, or nation. This tactic, however, can be successful only if the department has a good record of performance and, in the uncomfortable language of budgeteering, has been "productive."

The chairperson must at times be an advocate for one or more faculty members. These kinds of situations generally arise from salary allocations and promotion and tenure cases. Again, rhetoric seldom wins the day in salary allocation disputes. The presentation of simple, compelling, honest data is the chairperson's best instrument as advocate. Sometimes the dean, the institutional review board, or even the president will not agree with a department recommendation on tenure or promotion. Immediately, all concerned are treading on dangerous ground. If the department has insisted on sending forward a promotion or tenure recommendation with which the department chairperson disagrees, if the institution's policies and procedures allow the recommendation to go to the next highest level, and if, at that and subsequently higher levels, the recommendation is turned down, the chairperson should not fight the case. The chairperson, however, must tell the department at the outset what his or her recommendation is going to be and inform the department that he or she will not fight. In this difficult situation, to state one's intention is a more honest way to conduct oneself than to yield to the temptation to be a hero and "fight for the department."

Although fighting for the department has great possibilities for high drama—or comedy—it is not good for one's self-esteem or intellectual integrity. If the chairperson and the department are fully united in a promotion or tenure case, however, then they should fight for it all the way. If they lose, the loss is an honorable one, and at least they gain markers that can be called in at the next confrontation with the higher administration, whether it be over budget, curriculum, space, or personnel.

But turnabout, as college deans are fond of saying, is fair play, and sometimes the chairperson must be the advocate of the dean or the central administration. Just as departments must have priorities, so too must colleges and institutions. Not every department can always be designated a high-priority department. Indeed, some, because of the character of the institution, can never attain prominent status. (One such example might be a humanities department in a technological university.) When resources are allocated for each year's operating budget, the chairperson must report as fully and as honestly as possible not only on the resources allocated to the department, but also on the reasons for those allocations. When decisions that adversely affect the department are handed down, the chairperson must be able to share the institution's perspective and try to implement even an unfavorable decision with some grace and style. If the chairperson is strongly opposed to a decision and, consequently, his or her relationship with the faculty and the dean deteriorates, he or she should consider resigning. The matter is as simple and as cold as that. The chairperson who cannot accept the decisions of the higher administration in resource allocation or other institutional matters does no one a service by staying on; all that results is the embitterment of everyone concerned. The chairperson can always devote his or her energies to changing those institutional or collegiate priorities—and even have fun mounting such a challenge—but once the decisions are made for the year, the only thing to do is to put those decisions to work for the good of the institution and wait until next year.

Perhaps the most important of the chairperson's special responsibilities is that of faculty evaluator. Here he or she becomes the judge on the bench, the dispassionate, if possible, evaluator of each faculty member's performance. In an increasing number of institutions around the country, the process of evaluation has been formalized as a legal requirement that must be fulfilled each year. But even in those institutions in which the evaluation process is not formalized, chairpersons cannot escape the role of evaluator. Wittingly or unwittingly, they enact this role in all their functions: appointing committees, assigning courses, allocating resources, recommending promotion and tenure, and setting or recommending annual salaries. Hence, the annual evaluation meeting between chairperson and faculty member, even if not required, is a good way of fulfilling the evaluation responsibility. The meeting should have a specific agendum, or an external frame of reference, to give each participant a sense of purpose; otherwise, the meeting is likely to become a social visit or the discussion is apt to turn to more agreeable business than the awkward matter of how one has performed one's job during the past year.

The agendum should be related to department priorities, resource allocation, or the department's plans for itself. It is easier for the chairperson and the faculty member to discuss job performance if the department has established certain goals for itself and its members. How did the faculty member help fulfill the department's objectives during the past year? If there were problems, what were they and what caused them? Not all faculty members are team players, nor should they be. Some persons cannot be judged by what they contribute toward achieving the department's stated goals for the year or the next five years. Too much emphasis on team playing can inhibit or even stifle a faculty member's creativity.

If certain members of the department have not overtly contributed to the department's goals and are not likely to, then it becomes necessary for the chairperson to establish, year by year, a set of individual goals for these persons. The goals should not be too specific, or else both the chairperson and the faculty member may find themselves trapped by undue specificity. For example, to suggest that the faculty member should, in the next year, publish three articles in learned journals is probably too bureaucratic, but both chairperson and faculty member can comfortably agree that a reasonable goal for next year would be the publication of some research in a reputable journal. Sometimes, however, the chairperson must be specific, both for the good of the faculty and the reputation of the department. The associate professor who has spent three years writing a book may have to be told that for only one more year will he receive special resources (clerical help, graduate assistants, and so forth) to help bring the book to completion. Or the bright young assistant professor may have to be told that she has conducted enough experiments to validate a hypothesis; next year she must send off a research grant proposal to a funding agency and free up some department resources so that others in the department can begin to write research proposals. All these matters are relative and depend on the chairperson's good judgment and personal knowledge of each faculty member's capabilities.

The important point is that evaluation must be viewed as a constructive, not a destructive, act. For it to be constructive, the chairperson must establish goals against which yearly job performance can be measured. If no goals have been set, then the evaluation inevitably becomes either too personalized or so vague as to be worthless or insulting. The chairperson must realize that most faculty members *want* to be evaluated; they want their performance judged and, of course, praised. But no faculty member can walk into an annual evaluation conference expecting to be praised if he or she knows that the goals agreed upon last year have not been met. And even if they have not been met, the faculty member will usually welcome the opportunity to explain why not.

The annual evaluation conference, then, should not be viewed by the chairperson or the faculty as a painful or awkward ordeal. It can and should be a chance for colleagues to examine together what the year's work has produced, what went right, what went wrong, and why it went wrong. But this useful and constructive experience is possible only if chairpersons set goals for colleagues—with, of course, their help—and address those goals each year, no matter how painful it may be at times to keep the evaluation process focused on those goals.

As we have seen, the department chairperson assumes many roles, and some of these roles may, at times, conflict with others. The dean may have certain expectations about the chairperson's role, the faculty may have others, and the chairperson may have yet others that do not correspond to those of the dean or the faculty. Such a dilemma may have no easy or satisfactory solution. The chairperson must become accustomed to being in an atmosphere beset by contradiction.

Characteristics and Skills of an Effective Chairperson

The roles of the department chairperson, as we have noted, may vary considerably. Not the least important role is that which the chairperson develops for himself or herself. A chairperson who is both an effective leader and an efficient facilitator often possesses many of the following characteristics:

- Good interpersonal skills; ability to work well with faculty members, staff, students, deans, and other chairpersons
- Ability to identify problems and resolve them in a manner acceptable to faculty members
- Ability to adapt leadership styles to fit different situations
- Ability to set department goals and to make satisfactory progress in moving their departments toward those goals
- Ability to search for and discover the optimum power available to them as chairpersons; ability to maximize that power in motivating faculty members to achieve department goals and objectives
- Active participation in their professions; respect of their professional colleagues

The job of chairperson varies so much from department to department that a detailed standard job description is difficult to compose. Each chairperson, to a large degree, creates the role according to his or her own talents and skills within a framework that is consistent with institutional, department, and personal goals, both academic and administrative.

Chairpersons must determine what goals they can realistically set for themselves and for their departments during the period of their leadership. They must ultimately decide what roles they must and want to play, and how best to play them. Chairpersons must decide whether they want to provide leadership to their faculty members or act in the capacity of executive secretary, whose prime responsibility is to implement the faculty's wishes. Chairpersons must be sufficiently perceptive to judge the extent to which their faculty members and deans will permit them to be the kind of leaders they want to be, and they must be able to satisfy these expectations, as well as follow their own goals. Their effectiveness as chairpersons will depend on their being able to judge which roles to fulfill under any given set of circumstances and then to fulfill them.

A job description will not relieve chairpersons of the necessity or the responsibility for making such judgments; they themselves must decide the nature of the position. The elements that make the chairperson's job ambiguous and frustrating are the same elements that also make it challenging and interesting. When the position becomes only frustrating and loses its interest and challenge, it is time for the chairperson to consider seriously whether he or she can continue as an effective leader.

Questions

1. Review the functions and responsibilities of department chairpersons as listed at the beginning of this chapter. Which ones do not apply to the chairperson of your department? List other functions that your chairperson performs that are not included in the list.

2. Review the roles of department chairpersons as listed at the beginning of this chapter. Which ones do not apply to the chairperson of your department? List other roles that your chairperson plays that are not included in the list.

3. What roles do you think your faculty expects you to assume as chairperson?

4. What roles do you think your dean expects you to assume as chairperson?

5. What roles would you like to assume most as chairperson?

6. Which of these roles seem to conflict? Why and how do they conflict? What problems do conflicting roles pose for the chairperson? How may chairpersons resolve these problems?

7. What are your personal visions or goals toward which you would like to move your department during your time as chairperson?

8. Some chairpersons are elected to the position by faculty members; others are appointed by the dean with or without faculty consultation. What are the similarities and differences between these two kinds of chairpersons in terms of (1) tasks for which the chairperson is responsible; (2) how the chairperson relates to his or her faculty and dean; and (3) strategies used in getting the job done? What are the reasons for these similarities or differences?

References

ADAMS, HAZARD. *The Academic Tribes.* 2nd ed. Champaign, IL: University of Illinois Press, 1988. (ERIC Document Reproduction Service No. ED 297 632)

AVI-ITZAK, TAMAR E. "On 'First-timers' Vis-à-vis 'Experienced' Department Chairpersons' Perceptions of Role Fulfillment: The Case of Fluid Participation in Organization." *Higher Education in Europe,* 10, 1985, pp. 31–36.

BARE, ALAN C. "Managerial Behavior of College Chairpersons and Administrators." *Research in Higher Education,* 24, 1986, pp. 128–138.

BENNETT, JOHN B., and FIGULI, DAVID J. (Eds.) *Enhancing Departmental Leadership: The Roles of the Chairperson.* New York: Macmillan, 1990.

BOGUE, E. GRADY. "Administrative Malpractice: The Limits of Common Sense." *Educational Record,* Winter 1978, pp. 77–86.

BOOTH, DAVID B. "Institutional and Disciplinary Ideas for Development." *Educational Record,* Winter 1977, pp. 85–90.

BRANN, JAMES, and EMMET, THOMAS A. (Eds.) *The Academic Department or Division Chairman: A Complex Role.* Detroit: Balamp, 1972.

CHACKO, HARSHA E. *Administrators' Method of Upward Influence and Perceptions of Their Supervisors' Leadership Styles.* Paper presented at the Annual Meeting of the AERA, New Orleans, 1988. (ERIC Document Reproduction Service No. ED 296 476)

COHEN, ARTHUR M., and BRAWER, FLORENCE B. *The American Community College.* 2nd ed. San Francisco: Jossey–Bass, 1988.

DAUWALDER, DAVID P. "A Ranking of Major Challenges Facing Business Education by Department Chairpersons in NABTE-Member Institutions." *Delta Pi Epsilon Journal,* 27, 1985, pp. 19–35.

DRESSEL, PAUL L.; JOHNSON, F. CRAIG; and MARCUS, PHILIP M. *The Confidence Crisis.* San Francisco: Jossey–Bass, 1971.

FARH, JING LIH (et al.) "An Empirical Investigation of Self-Appraisal-Based Performance Evaluation." *Personnel–Psychology,* 41, 1988, pp. 141–156.

FINK, L. DEE. "The Lecture: Analyzing and Improving its Effectiveness." In *New Directions for Teaching and Learning: The Department Chairperson's Role in Enhancing College Teaching,* 37, Spring 1989, pp. 17–30.

FREDERICK, PETER J. "Involving Students More Actively in the Classroom." In *New Directions for Teaching and Learning: The Department Chairperson's Role in Enhancing College Teaching,* 37, Spring 1989, pp. 31–40.

GREEN, MADELEINE (Ed.) *Leaders for a New Era: Strategies for Higher Education.* New York: ACE/Macmillan, 1988.

HAYWARD, PATRICIA C. "A Discriminant Analytic Test of Biglan's Theoretical Distinction Between Biology and English Department Chairpersons." *Research in Higher Education,* 25, 1986, pp. 136–146.

HEIMLER, CHARLES H. "The College Departmental Chairman." *Educational Record,* Spring 1967, pp. 158–163.

KNIGHT, W. HAL, and HOLEN, MICHAEL C. "Leadership and the Perceived Effectiveness of Department Chairpersons." *Journal of Higher Education,* 56, 1985, pp. 677–690.

KREMER-HAYON, LYA, and AVI-ITZAK, TAMAR E. "Roles of Academic Department Chairpersons at the University Level." *Higher Education,* 15, 1986, pp. 105–112.

LESLIE, DAVID W. "The Status of the Department Chairmanship in University Organization." *AUP Bulletin,* 59, 1973, pp. 419–426.

———. "NLRB Rulings on the Department Chairmanship." *Educational Record,* 53, 1972, pp. 313–320.

LYNCH, DAVID M. (et al.) "Chief Liberal Arts Academic Officers: The Limits of Power and Authority." *Studies in Higher Education,* 12, 1987, pp. 39–50.

MARCH, JAMES G. *How We Talk and How We Act: Administrative Theory and Administrative Life.* Urbana: University of Illinois Press, 1980.

McCARTY, DONALD J., and REYES, PEDRO. "Organizational Models of Governance: Academic Deans' Decision-making Styles." *Journal of Teacher Education,* 38, 1987, pp. 2–8.

McKEACHIE, WILBERT J. "Memo to New Department Chairmen." *Educational Record,* Spring 1968, pp. 221–227.

MITCHELL, MARY B. "The Process of Department Leadership." *Review of Higher Education,* 11, 1987, pp. 161–176.

RASCH, CARLA. "Sources of Stress Among Administrators at Research Universities." *Review of Higher Education,* 9, 1986, pp. 419–434.

ROACH, JAMES H. L. "The Academic Department Chairperson: Functions and Responsibilities." *Educational Record,* Winter 1976, pp. 13–23.

SCHAFFER, ROBIN. "Role Conflict in Academic Chairpersons." *Occupational Therapy Journal of Research,* 7, 1987, pp. 301–313.

SCHULTZ, MAX F. "Management of the Multi-Department." *ADE Bulletin,* May 1978, pp. 34–39.

SHREEVE, WILLIAM. *University Department Chairs: Who Are We?* Washington, DC, 1987. (ERIC Document Reproduction Service No. ED 285 464)

SINGLETON, BRENDA S. "Sources and Consequences of Role Conflict and Role Ambiguity Among Department Chairs." *Capstone Journal of Education,* 7, 1987, pp. 39–50.

SMART, JOHN C., and ELTON, CHARLES F. "Administrative Roles of Department Chairmen." In *New Directions for Institutional Research: Examining Departmental Management,* 10, edited by John C. Smart and James R. Montgomery. San Francisco: Jossey–Bass, 1976.

STATON-SPICER, ANN Q., and SPICER, CHRISTOPHER H. "Socialization of the Academic Chairperson: A Typology of Communication Dimensions." *Educational Administration Quarterly,* 23, 1987, pp. 41–64.

TRASK, KERRY A. "The Chairperson and Teaching." In *New Directions for Teaching and Learning: The Department Chairperson's Role in Enhancing College Teaching,* 37, Spring 1989, pp. 99–107.

WATSON, ROY E. "The Role of the Department Chair: A Replication and Extension." *Canadian Journal of Higher Education,* 16, 1986, pp. 13–23.

WINNER, CORNELIA W. *The Role of the Department Chairperson at Delaware Technical and Community College.* Dover, DE: University of Delaware, 1989. (ERIC Document Reproduction Service No. ED 308 898)

Chapter 4

Power and Authority of a Chair

To be an effective chairperson, one must start with some power and authority. Yet, many chairpersons believe they are not given sufficient power or authority to carry out the responsibilities of the position. Although the term "power" is acceptable in government, military, and business organizations, it is an intimidating word in the academic community. The discussion that follows is based primarily on the dictionary definition which states that power is the ability of an individual to effect a change in someone's behavior—a change that might not otherwise occur.

In many cases, power is acquired by having access to or actually possessing certain resources that others desire. These resources may be physical, personal, economic, or psychological. In a college or university setting, the ability to persuade or influence may be the most effective power available to individuals in positions of leadership. Generally speaking, the power of administrators, managers, and leaders can be categorized into three types, depending on how and from where it is acquired—namely, power from authority, position power, and personal power.

POWER FROM FORMAL AUTHORITY

Authority granted officially from a higher level in the bureaucracy of the institution is called "formal authority." It gives an individual the right to command resources or to enforce policies or regulations. The ultimate power from this source exists when a person to whom the authority is granted is able to make final decisions and firm commitments for his or her department without requiring additional signatures of approval. In the case of a state college or university system, the board of regents or board of trustees is empowered by the state legislature to operate and control the system. The board, in turn, delegates authority and responsibility to the college or university presidents for the operation of the individual institutions. The presidents delegate authority to vice-presidents and deans. Any official authority chairpersons may have has been delegated to them by their deans; deans cannot delegate more authority than has been delegated to them by their vice-presidents. Faculty members will permit their behavior to be influenced or affected by the chairperson if they believe that he or she has formal authority or is close to someone who has it. Generally speaking, chairpersons and deans are perceived by their faculties to have more formal authority than they really have. In any case, the ability to influence or effect a change in some people's behavior will depend to some extent on the amount of formal authority that a chairperson is perceived to have.

POSITION POWER

Power that comes from having an appropriate title or being in an important position is called "position power." Recommendations made by people with certain types of "position power" are generally given more serious consideration than recommendations made by individuals who do not have it. Department chairpersons by virtue of holding the title may have influence, not only with faculty members of their own respective departments but with people in and outside of the college over whom they have no authority or jurisdiction. Those who have such influence are perceived by some as having power. Chairpersons not only have the authority and responsibility to recommend salary raises, promotion, tenure, and teaching assignments, but they can often provide certain types of assistance to faculty members that faculty members need but cannot provide for themselves, such as helping them develop professional acquaintances, recommending them for membership in select professional associations, nominating them for executive positions in these associations, helping them obtain sabbaticals or funds for travel to professional meetings, and helping them make contacts leading to paid consulting jobs. Moreover, chairpersons frequently are asked by their faculty members to write letters of reference to other institutions in support of applications for new positions, or to banks or mortgage companies in support of applications for loans.

Many of the preceding prerogatives of chairpersons are possible because of the misconception that the title "chairperson" carries with it considerable formal authority. Chairpersons who use the influence of their position or title are often able to obtain opportunities for individual faculty members or for the department as a whole. Position power, however, may not be enough. What may be needed to complement it is "personal power."

PERSONAL POWER

In providing leadership to their faculty members, chairpersons also use whatever personal power they may have. The definition of "power" used in this chapter is the ability of an individual to effect a change in someone's behavior. Faculty members will permit themselves to be influenced or affected in some way by the chairperson if they respect the particular individual holding the position. Personal power derives from peers' respect for and commitment to the chairperson. It is informally granted to the chairperson by the faculty members and depends on how they perceive him or her as an individual and as a professional. A chairperson with a great amount of personal power is usually perceived by the faculty as possessing some of the following characteristics: fairness and evenhandedness in dealing with people; good interpersonal skills; national or international reputation in the discipline; expertise in some area of knowledge; influence with the dean; respect in the academic community; ability and willingness to help faculty members develop professionally; ability to obtain resources for the department; highly regarded by upper-level administration; knowledgeable about how the college operates; privy to the aspirations, plans, and hidden agendas of the institution's decision makers; and ability to manage the department efficiently.

Personal power is not a power that can be delegated: it is a power that a chairperson must earn—and not just from faculty members. The same characteristics which earn the respect of the faculty members can earn the respect of the dean and vice-president. A chairperson who has developed credibility with the dean and is respected for being knowledgeable, fair, and reasonable will influence the dean more frequently than will a chairperson who lacks these characteristics. Chairpersons who are successful in influencing the deans are perceived by their faculty members to have power.

Special Roles and Powers

Leadership, especially in the collegial environment, has seldom been simply a function of personal charisma. Charisma can help one amass power and authority, but charisma alone will not get the job done. The department chairperson begins with a good deal of power and authority, most of which is not readily discernible to the casual observer. It is best for all concerned if he or she uses the levers of power and authority unobtrusively. In this way, he or she can become an invisible leader, which, most will agree, is the best kind, especially in an institution of higher education.

In most colleges and universities the chairperson's power is manifested by the exercise of certain roles. Following are examples of roles that can provide the chairperson with power and authority: the bearer of news—good and bad—to department faculty members; the defender of the department; the primary contact for the department faculty members with regard to external professional assignments and consulting; the appointer of committees and committee members; the sometime initiator and constant arbitrator of curriculum development and reform; the allocator of department resources; the maker, even if by proxy, of the schedule of course offerings; the final arbiter for assigning courses and teaching loads to individual faculty members; one of the most influential voices in tenure and promotion cases; in most institutions, the official evaluator of faculty members; and the person who usually sets or recommends salaries for the department faculty members.

Even some of the most onerous tasks that a department chairperson must undertake can bestow a power and authority that, if used consciously and carefully, help enhance his or her leadership role. Consider three relatively minor aspects of the chairperson's professional administrative life: bearing good and bad news; defending the department; and being the primary contact for outside organizations seeking to enlist department members for various professional activities and consulting.

We all know that knowledge is power, and the chairperson generally is the first department faculty member to know what the institution's budget for the next year will be or what programmatic priorities the board of trustees, the board of regents, the central administration, or the college dean have decreed for the future. It is the chairperson who must make this news, good or bad, known to the faculty members. If, in sharing bad news, the chairperson is quick to blame the dean, the central administration, the institution's control agency, or specific individuals among those groups, he or she is probably unhappy or insecure in the job. Sometimes, of course, specific persons are to be blamed for bad news, but within the complex social structure of a college or university, there is seldom one villain responsible for the setbacks suffered by a department faculty. The same can be said for good news: rarely is one person in an institution responsible for a department's good fortune. In imparting information, however, the chairperson can shape the faculty members' opinion about that news and, in the process, establish an ambience—a set of attitudes, a good psychology—that can last for a year or perhaps longer. It is important, then, that chairpersons learn how to share information with colleagues.

The first lesson for chairpersons is that knowledge must be shared. A department that is kept in relative ignorance about budget, programs, and personnel development is a department mismanaged and unable to defend itself against decisions made about its destiny by those outside it.

The chairperson generally is the first line of defense for the department and the spokesman for the department in budget fights with the dean's office and the central administration offices. The faculty members expect their leader to be a vigorous advocate of the department's programmatic and philosophical positions, and the proper exercise of this role confers a degree of authority. A wise chairperson, of course, makes sure that his or her own advocacy of a certain issue reflects the department faculty's consensus or at least has the support of the senior faculty members, who are often responsible for the chairperson's appointment. If the chairperson's aspirations for the department are continuously inconsistent with the faculty's, one of two things can be safely assumed: the department will soon have a new leader, or the department has been in such serious trouble that the dean or the central administration has appointed the chairperson to act as a troubleshooter and to implement drastic change.

The chairperson is also responsible for the department's external communications. Outsiders flood the department chairperson's desk with requests for help and advice. An alumnus wants a speaker for a luncheon or a dinner; a high school principal wants a commencement speaker; a professional organization wants a consultant; a newspaper feature writer wants to write a story on what is going on in the department. Other requests come from the dean's office or the central administration. The president wants expert advice on an issue he or she is writing about; the vice-president is establishing yet another university-wide committee, council, or task force and wants "some good people who will make constructive contributions"; a new visiting trustee or regent must be entertained or educated.

That the chairperson must respond to these requests is in itself a sign of authority and power. But more important, these requests generally represent golden opportunities for advancing the cause of the department and its members. These requests, in their innocent form, are also acid tests of the chairperson's judgment, for the wrong responses can turn the opportunities from gold to brass, damage the department's reputation, and ensure a brief term of office for the chairperson.

Yet another seemingly innocent duty, that of appointing committees and committee members, turns out, on close examination, to be a source of power and authority, especially in medium-sized and large departments. An academic department can be led—but not run—by one person. It is too familial in character to be organized along the lines of a military hierarchy. Authority must be dispersed so that the collegial nature of this important academic unit can flourish; hence, the necessity for committees.

The department chairperson has the power to establish new committees and, although not always without a fight, dispense with old ones. Through this influence on committee structure, the chairperson's strength of purpose is tested. At least three important functions are assigned to committees: tenure and promotion recommendations, salary matters, and curriculum development. In small departments the entire faculty may serve as the committee that deals with each of these tasks. In larger departments separate committees are formed for each function. Sometimes the department faculty elects committee members, sometimes not.

Generally, institutional policy limits membership on the tenure and promotion committee to senior faculty, although some institutions make a point of including junior faculty. The policy of including junior faculty seems democratic and laudable, but the junior members of tenure and promotion committees almost always suffer from the conflicts within these committees. If the members of the promotion and tenure committee are elected, the chairperson must act as a precinct captain and get out the vote—the right vote—or risk losing a large measure of control over the department's future. The salary committee is usually shunned by the wiser faculty members, for much unhappiness results from its deliberations. But a department should have such a committee, even though it, like all other committees, is advisory. With the advice and, indeed, the protection of such a committee, the chairperson is able to face the faculty each fall when classes begin. Prudent appointments to the curriculum committee can help maintain a delicate balance of firebrands and wary old conservatives. A department must avoid the extremes of a silly, faddish curriculum that earns the derision of faculty members outside the department and of an obsolescent curriculum that arouses the contempt of funding agencies, the profession itself, and the students.

A department may have other committees, including a search committee, a library committee, an equipment committee, and a social committee. The only one that possesses any real leverage is the faculty appointments or search committee, which recommends the hiring of new faculty members. This committee, like the tenure and promotion committee, makes recommendations to the chairperson (and sometimes to the department faculty) about scholars who may eventually become part of the family. It is of utmost importance, therefore, that the members of this committee be of one mind with the chairperson. The chairperson, moreover, must see to it that the committee conducts its business in a manner that ensures the future health of the department.

Although administrators may be the least likely agents of curriculum development and reform, the chairperson can—and should—have a strong influence on such activities within the department. Most faculties are exceedingly conservative about curriculum development and reform unless faced with such harsh realities as dramatically declining enrollments. The advent of such realities usually causes an unnatural burst of creativity among the faculty; new courses, programs, and proposals for reduced prerequisites bloom like flowers in May. In such cases it is the chairperson's responsibility to protect the discipline and the profession that the department represents and to see that the department's curriculum and degree programs maintain their integrity.

At the same time, the chairperson must be the conscience of the faculty members. He or she must continually prompt them on many matters: the dangers of a rigid curriculum; new developments in the profession; the dire consequences of sliding into obsolescence; new teaching techniques; the services available to them through the institution's office of instructional resources (or other similar agency); the condition of the department's library holdings, its laboratories, and its research and teaching equipment. This concern, visibly and continually expressed, automatically confers the power that goes with conscientious leadership. The performance of these duties, as routine as many of them may seem, gives the chairperson what he or she most needs—the trust and respect of the faculty.

In most departments, a key role of the chairperson is the allocation of resources within the department. Resources are always limited; there are never enough for everyone. And someone must be the final arbiter in the allocation of these resources. Rarely can a group of single-minded, aggressive individuals reach a rational compromise on the distribution of limited resources. Such things may happen in utopian novels but seldom in the real world. Hence the chairperson must preside over this important task. The authority to allocate resources is the most visible of the chairperson's levers of power; consequently, it must be used with great tact and courage. Decisions about resource allocation will never be enthusiastically received by all concerned, but such decisions must be made. Furthermore, the rationale for these decisions should be logical and openly stated.

One great temptation that any chairperson faces is the urge to spread the department resources as evenly as possible. Such a procedure gives everyone a little piece of the action and avoids arguments over the *bête noir* of all academic administrators—enforcing program or personnel priorities. The problem with spreading resources evenly is that this practice inevitably pleases no one and irritates everyone. Departments, like colleges and universities, must have priorities and must follow them. If a college or university has no priorities, department chairpersons are usually the first to argue that the institution lacks leadership, that it is rudderless, and that no one knows where it is going. The same observations apply to departments in which certain programs and certain faculty members get more resources than others.

One way to get the department faculty to agree on a priority system for resource allocation is to reach a consensus that strength must be built on strength. Nearly every department has its strengths, and the faculty is well aware of these strengths. For example, the senior professors in organic chemistry may be the best teachers and researchers and have the best laboratory in the department; the three young associate professors in European history may be the best teachers and researchers and may have the best library holdings; the microelectronics group may have the greatest national visibility and the most contract and grant work. Certain programs and faculty members are the obvious choices for receiving the biggest share of the department resources, and few in the department (and virtually no one outside the department) will long contest a decision to allocate these programs and professors a goodly share of the budgeted operating resources for the year.

The rub comes when the department chairperson must, with the support of at least part of the faculty, decide whether to let a weak program die, whether to keep a weak program alive at the expense of stronger programs, or whether to start a program that, because of new developments in the field, will aid in attracting students and federal or private financial assistance. Sometimes department members cannot be persuaded to let a weak program die with dignity; sometimes such a program has a life of its own, usually because those involved in it are incapable of working on another program or because of tradition, sentiment, or nostalgia or any combination of these factors. Clearly, the chairperson has the duty to assess the program's weakness and then act on the assessment and cut the program's resources. If the chairperson keeps alive a weak program, he or she has a further duty to point out to department colleagues that the program survives at the expense of resources that could go to stronger programs.

Establishing and implementing a new program is almost always a risky business, and leadership plays a crucial role. Almost any chairperson, regardless of leadership style or personal authority, can impede and usually stifle the establishment and growth of a new program. Department faculty members generally recognize this fact; consequently, the chairperson is apt to be heavily lobbied in these affairs. There is no sure formula for success in such an undertaking, but certain caveats are relevant.

- Woe to the chairperson who tries to establish a new program without the support of an influential segment of the department faculty.
- Woe also to the chairperson who, at the behest of a starry-eyed dean or a zealot in the central administration, tries to start a program without the consent or advice of the department's best faculty members.
- Woe to the chairperson who starts a program, for whatever reason, without consulting others in the discipline outside the university, outside the state, and outside the region.
- Woe to the chairperson who does not inform the faculty that the financial consequences of starting a new program will affect the entire department.

Another somewhat obscure but real source of the chairperson's power is his or her jurisdiction over assigning courses and teaching loads to faculty members. Clearly this task is not as visible, glamorous, or influential an activity as resource allocation, but it affects the emotional and intellectual life of every faculty member.

The heart's and mind's desire of most faculty members is to teach the subject that is, to them, the most important thing in their life. A person does not become a professor to make money or to acquire power, although these latent yet thoroughly natural motivations can burst into bloom in a sometimes alarming manner after a few years of teaching and research. Most professors can lead a happy and useful life if they are allowed to teach courses they *want* to teach to those students who will profit most from that teaching. Nothing—except salary—so concerns a professor as much as what he or she is scheduled to teach. (Younger faculty members who are building a knowledge of their subjects and the platform for their professional careers are especially concerned with course assignments.) Nothing—again, except a low salary—so dispirits a faculty member as to be relegated to teach three sections of a Western civilization survey, three sections of trigonometry and algebra, or four sections of the principles of physics. Most faculty members live to teach their subject specialty to superior students. This happy state is the edenic vision, the academic Shangri-la, that lurks in every professor's mind and is often the prime motivation for his or her work. Consequently, the chairperson, by means of authority to assign courses, can shape the careers and professional destinies of most of the department members and, in essence, make the majority of them basically happy or unhappy.

The responsibility for assigning courses plays such a crucial role in the life of the department that its power is generally shared by department committees that recommend who should teach what courses and when they should be taught. The task is delegated to a committee not because it is drudgery, but because the function itself is so important to all faculty members. Yet, as in resource allocation, there must be a final arbiter, and that arbiter is the department chairperson. Hence, like it or not, the authority to assign courses and teaching loads becomes a source of power that may be used to reward deserving faculty members.

Obviously, the department chairperson plays an extraordinarily influential role in matters of promotion and tenure. At many universities and colleges the chairperson can override the vote of the faculty in promotion and tenure decisions; at others, the vote of the faculty must be sent to the dean, whether or not the chairperson agrees with that vote. But at virtually all institutions, the chairperson must make his or her recommendation to the dean regarding every tenure and promotion case. This recommendation is almost always heavily weighed by the dean, the central administration, and whatever institution-wide review board or committee may exist. Last but not least, the institution's president or chancellor takes seriously the recommendation of the department chairperson; consequently, his or her views on a particular candidate for tenure or promotion are critical.

As in the case of resource allocation, the decisions on promotion and tenure are not going to please everyone. It is impossible for the chairperson to avoid facing at least one difficult promotion or tenure decision every two or three years. Those who try to avoid making a difficult decision are apt to find themselves in the same predicament that results when available resources are spread evenly across all programs. Such nonactions—which, in fact, *are* actions—please no one and irritate everyone. Chairpersons who stand before the department faculty or the dean and wash their hands of the matter fool no one; furthermore, they lose the respect of the faculty, the dean, and the central administration. Chairpersons who ask a higher level of review to make a hard tenure or promotion decision that they failed to make are evading responsibility. They may succeed in escaping the pain once—or maybe even twice in a very tolerant administration—but a third attempt usually leads to a request from the dean for a change in department leadership. The chairperson's role in promotion and tenure decisions, as in resource allocation decisions, is an important and highly visible one. Here again, power must be used with tact and prudence.

The act of evaluation—at most universities an annual occurrence—is clearly linked to promotion and tenure, and at almost all institutions the responsibilities for this spring ritual falls to the chairperson. But woe to those who regard it *only* as a ritual, because each evaluation will become a plank in the platform upon which rests other crucial decisions of the chairperson's highly visible levers of power, and a merely ritualistic observance of the evaluation process might erode its effectiveness. This particular function is very important and will be discussed later at greater length.

The final and most visible of all the chairperson's powers is the responsibility to set or recommend annual salaries for each faculty member in the department. At some institutions the chairperson has sole authority for setting salaries (within his or her budget, of course); at other institutions he or she merely makes recommendations about salaries to the college dean. Whatever the institution's procedure, the chairperson, through this power, establishes the value system by which the department lives and operates. As noted earlier, a faculty salary committee usually assists the chairperson in this responsibility. The chairperson's interaction with this committee is probably unique, for, having done the annual evaluation of all the faculty members, the chairperson can better judge the relative value of each of them. Of course, the committee members are in the awkward position of having to consult with the chairperson, at least in an indirect way, about their own salaries. Setting salaries and recommending the setting of salaries is a job no one wants, and the committee is usually less than zealous in its recommendations. Inevitably, the basic decisions turn out to be the chairperson's, and with this painful task comes the final and most important source of his or her power.

The various kinds of power that chairpersons exercise daily have been discussed. Few of these powers are based on formally delegated authority. Instead, these powers may depend, to a large degree, on precisely how they are perceived by the chairperson as well as by the faculty members. Chairpersons who perceive that they have no power usually have none; chairpersons who perceive that they have power usually do. In any event, the exercise of this power must be tempered with sound judgment.

Questions

1. Generally speaking, will a dean delegate more formal authority to one chairperson than to another with regard to the fulfillment of similar departmental responsibilities? Give reasons for your answer.

2. Is it conceivable that the dean may delegate more informal authority to one chairperson than to another? What factors determine the amount of informal authority that deans delegate to their chairpersons?

3. Many department chairpersons say they do not have enough formal authority to do all of the things they have to do—or, if they had more authority, they could be a more effective chairperson. What authority or power does the dean currently have that you as a chairperson would be interested in acquiring through delegation? (Remember, the dean cannot delegate authority that he or she does not have.)

4. To what extent do you believe that most chairpersons use all the power available to them in carrying out their responsibilities?

5. What kind of power or influence does a chairperson use in getting faculty members promoted or tenured? Is it power from formal authority, position power, personal power, or a combination of two or more? With whom is the power used?

6. What kind of power or influence does a chairperson use (formal authority, position power, personal power), and with whom is it used, in helping faculty members obtain opportunities to:
   a. Travel to professional conferences.

    b. Be members of important committees in the institution.

    c. Be members of important committees in professional and scholarly societies.

    d. Engage in consulting activities.

7. Some chairpersons believe that each institution should have a written statement spelling out in detail the duties, responsibilities, and formal authority of its chairpersons. Other chairpersons strongly oppose the idea. To what extent, if any, might such a written statement be helpful to the chairperson? To what extent might it be a hindrance? If it were decided at an institution that such a statement should be developed, what sorts of things should be included—what might best be excluded? Why?

8. How might a chairperson deal with a situation in which the dean and the faculty members are on the opposite side of an issue? Give examples of such situations.

9. Suppose a chairperson came to you for advice. He claimed that at least half of his recommendations to the dean were turned down. He knows for a fact, however, that two of his fellow chairpersons had most of their recommendations accepted by the same dean. He wants to know why the dean seems to be more favorably disposed to his colleagues than to him, and what can he do to improve his standing with the dean. What additional information do you need before you can make any suggestions? What possible kinds of suggestions could you make?

10. Other than being able to recommend dismissal, no promotion, or no merit increases, what powers are available to a chairperson for penalizing faculty members who continue to perform in an unsatisfactory manner?

11. Compare formal authority with personal power as they relate to the chairperson's effectiveness.

References

BUCKLEY, WILLIAM F. *God and Man at Yale: The Superstitions of "Academic Freedom."* Chicago: Regnery Books, 1986.

CHACKO, HARSHA E. *Administrators' Method of Upward Influence and Perceptions of Their Supervisors' Leadership Styles.* Paper presented at the Annual Meeting of the AERA, New Orleans, 1988. (ERIC Document Reproduction Service No. ED 296 476)

DOUGLAS, JOEL M. *Power Relationships on the Unionized Campus.* 1989. (ERIC Document Reproduction Service No. ED 318 354)

HAYWARD, PATRICIA C. "A Discriminant Analytic Test of Biglan's Theoretical Distinction Between Biology and English Department Chairpersons." *Research in Higher Education,* 25, 1986, pp. 136–146.

HERR, KAY. *Chairperson's Handbook.* 1989. (ERIC Document Reproduction Service No. ED 311 838)

HILL, WINSTON W., and FRENCH, WENDELL L. "Perceptions of the Power of Department Chairpersons by Professors." *Administrative Science Quarterly,* March 1967, pp. 548–574.

LITTLE, DORIC. *Addressing the Issue of Appropriate Professional Ethics on Community College Campuses.* 1989. (ERIC Document Reproduction Services ED 306 999)

LYNCH, DAVID M. (et al.) "Chief Liberal Arts Academic Officers: The Limits of Power and Authority." *Studies in Higher Education,* 12, 1987, pp. 39–50.

MILLETT, JOHN D. *New Structures of Campus Power: Success and Failures of Emerging Forms of Institutional Governance.* San Francisco: Jossey–Bass, 1978.

MITCHELL, MARY B., and WHEELER, DANIEL W. *A Grounded Theory of Chairperson Management Strategy.* ASHE 1987 Annual Meeting Paper, San Diego, 1987. (ERIC Document Reproduction Service No. ED 319 423)

NEUMANN, YORAM. "The Perception of Power in University Departments: A Comparison Between Chairpersons and Faculty Members." *Research in Higher Eduction,* 11(4), 1979, pp. 283–293.

RAU, WILLIAM, and BAKER, PAUL J. "The Organized Contradictions of Academe: Barriers Facing the Next Academic Revolution." *Teaching Sociology,* 17, 1989, pp. 161–183.

REYES, PEDRO, and McCARTHY, DONALD J. *The Power of Lower Participants in Educational Organizations.* ASHE Annual Meeting Paper, San Antonio, 1986. (ERIC Document Reproduction Service No. ED 268 868)

RICHMAN, BARRY M., and FARMER, RICHARD N. *Leadership, Goals, and Power in Higher Education: A Contingency and Open-Systems Approach to Effective Management.* San Francisco: Jossey–Bass, 1974.

WHITE, AUSTON. *Organizational Structure and Design in Higher Education: A Literature Review of Organizational Structures in Higher Education with a Focus on the Co-Existence of Academic and Non-Academic Structures.* 1990. (ERIC Document Reproduction Services No. ED 319 354)

Chapter 5

Leadership and Decision Making

Leadership may be defined as the ability to influence or motivate an individual or a group of individuals to work willingly toward a given goal or objective under a specific set of circumstances. The term "leadership" implies that where there is a leader, there must be one or more followers and a goal or objective toward which the followers are being led. This definition applies to any situation in which one person influences the behavior of another. An individual does not necessarily have to be in a position of authority to be a leader. The leader–follower relationship can occur between friends, colleagues, associates, students, relatives, and so on.

Just as there are many kinds of departments, so there are many kinds of department chairpersons: their variety is as infinite as the variety of human nature. It is possible, however, to generalize about human nature and to categorize the types of leadership styles. Several models will be described in this chapter. Some chairpersons will be able to identify completely or partly with one or more of the styles described below. Others may find no leadership style described here to which they can relate and may wish to search the literature or describe their own. In either case, what follows is found to be the situation to some degree in many academic departments.

The Directive–Supportive Behavior Model

Leadership styles may be categorized as directive or supportive. Some leaders are very directive. "Directive" behavior at its extreme consists primarily of one-way communication from the chairperson to faculty members in which he or she explains what is to be done, when, where, and how. In addition to providing detailed guidance, the leader carefully monitors the department's performance. Chairpersons who practice this type of leadership evidently believe that the task or assignment will not be accomplished properly without detailed direction and monitoring. In some cases, this chairperson may be correct in his or her belief. Conversely, there are chairpersons who are nondirective in their approach. After explaining what needs to be done, they give very little direction or guidance and provide practically no monitoring during the course of the activity. The expectation is that the faculty members are capable and willing to do what is necessary without much direction. Most chairpersons are neither 100 percent directive nor nondirective but fall somewhere between the two extremes.

Some leaders are very supportive. "Supportive" behavior consists of two-way communication between the chairperson and the faculty members. Here the chairperson provides personal or psychological support, including encouragement, praise, and general concern for the personal and professional welfare of each faculty member. On the other hand, there are chairpersons who are nonsupportive. They communicate very little with their faculty members and do not encourage faculty members to communicate with them. Here again, most chairpersons are neither 100 percent supportive nor nonsupportive but fall somewhere in between the two extremes. Some chairpersons are capable of moving from one extreme to another in terms of how supportive they are and try to provide the amount of support that faculty seem to need. The extent to which a chairperson is supportive may also be related to his or her ability to communicate and encourage communication in return.

A chairperson's behavior is neither exclusively directive nor supportive; leadership style consists of a mix of both. Leadership behavior varies, however, according to the particular mix of these behavior patterns. The proportion of directive behavior to supportive behavior indicates the chairperson's leadership style. We can visualize four different mixes of behavior patterns by plotting directive behavior on a horizontal axis and supportive behavior on an intersecting vertical axis. The result is a graph with four quadrants, with each quadrant representing a different mix of directive and supportive behavior (see Fig. 5.1).

Quadrant 1—High directive and low supportive (a great deal of direction to the faculty members, not much personal and psychological support)

Quadrant 2—High directive and high supportive (a great deal of direction to the faculty members, a great deal of personal and psychological support)

Quadrant 3—Low directive and high supportive (not much direction to the faculty members, a great deal of personal and psychological support)

Quadrant 4—Low directive and low supportive (not much direction to the faculty members, some—but not much—personal or psychological support)

Each quadrant in Fig. 5.1 represents a different leadership style in terms of directive and supportive behavior. The most effective leadership style, according

FIGURE *5.1* Leadership style graph

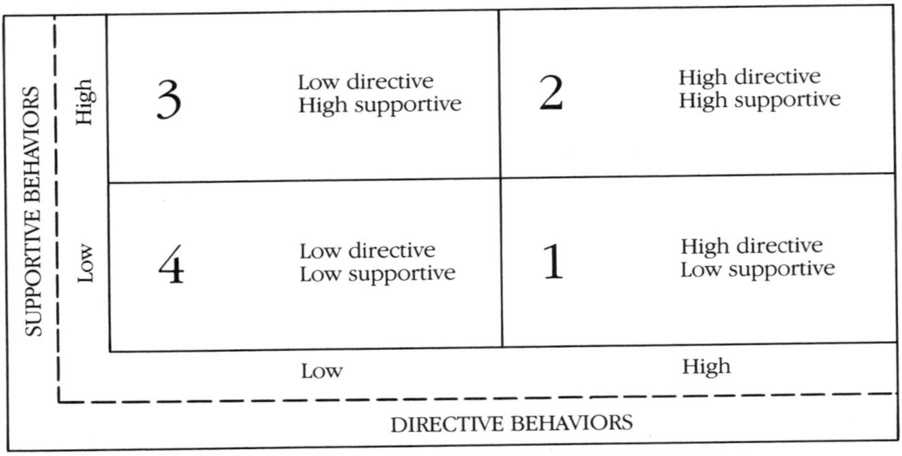

according to some authors, is one that takes into account the maturity level of the group and provides the appropriate amount of direction and support needed to achieve a specific goal or objective. Academic departments, like other groups, vary in their levels of maturity. As described in chapter 2, a mature academic department is one in which the faculty members have the experience, capacity, and willingness to work effectively as a group, to set high but attainable goals, and to reach group decisions, and they readily accept responsibility for their decisions and assignments. The maturity of a group should not be confused with the maturity of the individual members who comprise the group. Each member of the department may be mature on an individual basis, but the members may not be able to work together effectively as a group. Since a group may perform maturely in achieving one objective and immaturely in trying to achieve another, it is neither mature nor immature all the time.

Immature groups or departments generally need more direction than mature groups. The need for direction decreases as a department becomes more mature and its members learn to work together effectively. Mature departments need very little direction most of the time and often resent receiving too much. Although most faculty members enjoy receiving personal and psychological support from their chairpersons, mature departments, as a whole, do not need as much psychological support as do less mature departments. The notion of the directive supportive behavior model assumes that an effective chairperson will be able to adjust his or her leadership style to meet different situations. If the department is immature, the chairperson spends a lot of time being directive, assigning tasks, and monitoring them. As the department matures, the chairperson gives proportionately less direction but becomes more supportive. A department's progression toward maturity can be viewed as a continuum, and the chairperson must be able to estimate the level of maturity with which he or she is dealing at any given time. When the department approaches the highest level of maturity, the chairperson according to this model must be able to change styles to one of nondirection.

Each of the four quadrants in the figure represents not only an identifiable leadership style but also a stage in a continuum of changing leadership styles, which can accommodate the appropriate maturity level in the continuum of changing maturity levels of a group. It can be argued that Quadrant 1 exemplifies the best approach for dealing with an immature department, while Quadrants 2, 3, and 4, in that order, exemplify styles appropriate to a department as it progresses to a higher degree of maturity.

When a department begins to display less maturity than it has in the past, the department chairperson may need to make what is called a regressive intervention and provide more direction. In a regressive intervention, the department chairperson applies a leadership style appropriate for the present lower level of maturity rather than employing the style that was effective when the department was at a higher level of maturity with regard to the task under discussion. Once the department is again able to cope with the task, the department chairperson may return to the former leadership style.

Keep in mind that, according to this conceptualization, there is no one most appropriate leadership style. The best leadership style varies for different departmental situations. Some academic departments may be best served by one kind of leadership style at any particular time; other departments or even the same departments under different circumstances may be better served by another style.

The Autocratic–Democratic Model

The style of a chairperson may range from autocratic to democratic across a broad spectrum or continuum. As departments evolve, mature, grow, and perhaps even decline, one can see that the style of the chairperson must change to suit the changing needs of the department. While one's style may be a matter of personal choice or preference, an autocratic chairperson may be most appropriate for a young and relatively immature department. At such a time an autocratic chairperson can set a course for the department and give it direction. For example, a prominent department in a large college began its existence with an extremely autocratic and authoritarian chairperson who personally molded the fledgling department. The first chairperson was succeeded by a less autocratic, more democratic type who continued with the plan of the original chairperson, but who allowed the faculty a much greater degree of participation in policy-making decisions. The department now has a national reputation, elects its chairpersons on a rotating basis, and arrives at crucial decisions in a democratic manner. If the evolutionary history of a department follows the expected pattern, an autocrat may be desirable in its formative years. This may conceivably be true even when the individual members are mature scholars and the department itself is new, or is strife-torn and divided. As the department matures, however, its individual members may expect to become more involved in the governing process. The chairperson may then decide to adopt a less autocratic and more participatory style of leadership. Unfortunately, some chairpersons choose an autocratic style because it suits their personalities rather than because it is the style best suited to the needs of the department. Such individuals are frequently too rigid to allow the faculty to become involved in policy decisions. When a chairperson cannot become less authoritarian as the department matures, he or she may need to be replaced. The average six-year period during which an individual serves as chairperson may be related to the cycle of change in the evolution of a department.

The Gamesman Model

Michael Maccoby, in *The Gamesman,* describes four types of leadership styles of corporation executives: the spectator, the technician, the jungle fighter, and the gamesman. Maccoby assigns to each type characteristics which, while especially appropriate in the context of corporate affairs, are not exactly applicable to academic affairs. We use Maccoby's terminology because it is interesting and provocative, but we have altered his definitions to fit realities in the academic department. Chairpersons may be interested in seeing how closely these types resemble their colleagues or themselves. The terminology should not be taken too seriously or too literally, but rather in a lighthearted though inquiring spirit.

The spectator chairperson is a passive and acquiescent manager who flourishes in mature departments, either small or large. In the small department, the chairperson leaves the faculty alone; in the large department, the administrative hierarchy is so well developed that the faculty is generally unaware of the chairperson's presence. The spectator does very little except make sure that the department's business is conducted on time; seldom does he or she become an advocate for anything except a trouble-free life for the department. All power and authority are turned over to department committees, and generally compromises are sought on such troubling matters as curriculum reform, resource allocation, and promotion and tenure cases.

This role closely approaches the ideal of a chairperson, who serves as clerk of the court. It is often a useful role, for departments, like nations, have their cyclical movements of reform and orthodoxy, of strife and peace. The spectator chairperson functions best in a department that has just experienced a stormy period of reforms, leaving an exhausted faculty that needs serenity in order once again to focus its attention on the cardinal functions of teaching, research, and service. The spectator should not, however, be left in place too long, lest the department slide into stagnation, and decline. A chairperson who assumes this role in an immature department, whether small or large, may be ineffective unless he or she has been picked deliberately by the dean or the central administration to preside over the dissolution of a unit that should never have been made a department.

The technician chairperson is a superb bureaucrat. He or she always submits staff reports on time, follows to the letter the directions given by the college, knows all the rules and regulations of the institution, the state, and the federal government, and knows how to follow those regulations to keep everyone out of trouble. The technician chairperson has read all the literature on management techniques and assiduously follows the best advice given there; even so, he or she often appears to lack vision, imagination, and courage. Such a chairperson can function well in any kind of department and has the great virtue of being able to bring order out of chaos. By virtue of knowing the rules and regulations, the technician chairperson can inhibit the zealots and pilgrims among the faculty; by the same token, he or she can use that knowledge to prod a sluggish, lazy department.

The technician chairperson is seldom the head of a high-priority department, which requires relentless pursuit of excellence. He or she is content to ensure that the department functions well in accordance with commonly accepted procedures and policies. Being able to maintain the status quo is no mean virtue, however, and many departments in transition from immaturity or from nonpriority status to priority status are often well served by the technician. Unlike the spectator, the technician does not turn over all power and authority to committees—he or she knows the rules and regulations too well to do that—but generally conducts affairs in a democratic fashion. The style of the technician is one step further removed from the Platonic ideal of the chairperson.

The jungle fighter chairperson has taken the position for two reasons: to make the department better and perhaps someday to become dean. He or she is unabashedly ambitious and understands that a strong, successful department is the best self-advertisement. Such a chairperson is sometimes brilliant, possibly dangerous, and during his or her term department life is never dull. Next to personal success, the jungle fighter chairperson wants nothing more than the department's complete victory in all major issues; he or she becomes its forceful advocate for all its positions. If this ambition were only for the department, the college dean or the central administration would find it extremely difficult to negotiate with the jungle fighter. The either-you-give-me-what-I-want-or-I'll-resign attitude in confrontation with the upper-level administration, however, seldom results in the chairperson's resignation; this approach is likely to be a brinksmanship approach, with the jungle fighter usually pulling back before superior forces.

The jungle fighter flourishes in large departments, both immature and mature, and is most successful in large, mature, high-priority departments. Such a person is capable of making truly significant—even brilliant—contributions to the department, but his or her value to the rest of the university or college depends on what priority level the department has been assigned. Although not a team player, the jungle fighter is probably the best agent of change among all types of chairpersons. He or she tends to be less democratic than the technician and plays a heavy hand in the affairs of department committees, consequently relinquishing little power or authority. Indeed, such a chairperson pretends to speak and act for the faculty at times when he or she is speaking or acting only for personal aims or for the goals of a few department members. But jungle fighters get their way more often than not. They can make a weak department strong and lay the foundation for a great department. This role is yet one step further removed from the Platonic ideal.

The gamesman chairperson is one who takes the job in order to improve the department, the college, and the institution. While not above ambition for higher office, the gamesman is not necessarily devoted to a future in academic administration. The gamesman plays life like a game and is interested in both strategy and tactics. Such a chairperson is cool and dedicated. He or she likes to win, as much for the pleasure of winning as for any other reason, but remains a sportsman and knows how to accept defeat.

The gamesman's leadership style embodies all the paradoxes inherent in the chairperson's difficult and perplexing job. He or she is strong but flexible, a manager who is sometimes managed, a leader who is sometimes led, a Janus-like advocate who can defend, at different times, the interests of the department faculty as well as the interests of the whole institution. He or she tries to reduce the number of occasions when the department's goals are perceived to be at odds with the institution's goals by convincing others that everyone's interests are best served by keeping the department strong. The gamesman is intelligent and courageous and probably has a highly developed sense of humor.

Although the terms *spectator, technician, jungle fighter,* and *gamesman* refer to an overall leadership style, a chairperson may combine in varying proportions characteristics of two or more of these types. A gamesman may become so carried away with the game that he or she becomes a jungle fighter. A spectator, confronted with a dilemma, may be forced to learn to use rules and regulations as a technician does. A jungle fighter who has been bruised in combat or who has mellowed with age may decide to forsake ambition and try being a gamesman. A real chairperson generally does not exhibit only one type of behavior; rather, his or her personality more likely reflects a melding of all these types.

Determining Your Leadership Style Following the Directive–Supportive Model

Following is a list of questions to evaluate yourself in terms of how directive and supportive you perceive yourself to be in providing leadership to your faculty members. By answering the questions and following the instructions, you will be able to place yourself in one of the quadrants on the leadership style graph. This questionnaire has not been validated, nor is there any intention to try to validate it. The results, therefore, should not be taken too seriously. However, working through the exercise will help clarify the concept of leadership style and give you a general idea of your style. Those who chair departments or divisions composed of two or more distinct academic or vocational programs may prefer to determine their leadership style as applied to the group of faculty members in one of the programs rather than to the department as a whole.

How directive are you? (In each question, circle the number preceding the response that best describes your situation.)

1. How often do you review the department's goals and missions with at least one-third of your faculty members?
   0 Hardly ever
   1 Occasionally but not too often (1 or 2 times a year)
   2 Fairly often (3 to 5 times a year)
   3 Quite often (more than 5 times a year)

2. When you give an assignment to a faculty member or a committee, how much detail do you give the individual or committee on how to carry out the assignment?
   0 Hardly any detail
   1 Some but not much detail
   2 A fair amount of detail
   3 Lots of detail

3. During the period that the faculty member or committee is carrying out the assignment, how much monitoring do you do of the progress being made?
   0 Hardly any monitoring
   1 Occasional but not much monitoring
   2 A fair amount of monitoring
   3 Lots of monitoring

4. In meeting with individual faculty members to discuss their assignments, how specifically do you discuss the assignments?
   0 Not specifically at all
   1 Not too specifically
   2 Somewhat specifically
   3 Very specifically

Add the four numbers you circled above. On the leadership style graph, Fig. 5.2, place an "X" above the number on the horizontal axis that corresponds to the sum of your four circled numbers. This number represents, on a scale of 1 to 12, the extent to which you are directive. Draw a straight vertical line from the "X" upward.

How supportive are you? (In each question, circle the number preceding the response that best describes your situation.)

1. How many of your faculty members have come to you to relate personal accomplishments or problems during the past year?
   0 Hardly any
   1 Less than 25 percent
   2 Between 25 and 50 percent
   3 More than 50 percent

2. With how many of your faculty members have you made a point of meeting socially during the past year?
   0 Hardly any
   1 Less than 25 percent
   2 Between 25 and 50 percent
   3 More than 50 percent

FIGURE *5.2*   Leadership style graph—style determination

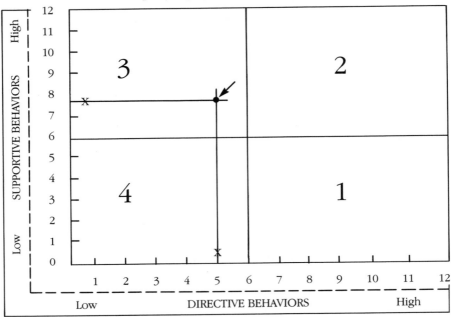

3. To how many of your faculty members have you made a point of giving personal encouragement during the past year?

0 Hardly any   2 Between 25 and 50 percent
1 Less than 25 percent   3 More than 50 percent

4. To how many of your deserving faculty members have you written unsolicited informal or formal notes commending them for special achievement during the past year?

0 Hardly any   2 Between 25 and 50 percent
1 Less than 25 percent   3 More than 50 percent

Add the four circled numbers. On the leadership style graph, place an "X" to the right of the number on the vertical axis that corresponds to the sum of your four circled numbers. This number represents, on a scale of 1 to 12, the extent to which you are supportive. Draw a straight horizontal line from the "X" to the right.

The vertical line and horizontal line which you have drawn will intersect in one of the four quadrants of the graph. For example: suppose your "directive" sum was 5 and your "supportive" sum was 8. The vertical and horizontal lines which you have drawn will intersect in Quadrant 3 (see Fig. 5.2). Your leadership style, according to this simple and nonvalidated test, is low directive and high supportive (see Table 5.1).

TABLE 5.1 Appropriate Leadership Styles for Different Levels of Maturity

LEVELS OF MATURITY	QUADRANT	LEADERSHIP STYLE APPROPRIATE FOR MATURITY LEVEL
Low	1	High directive Low supportive
Moderate	2	High directive High supportive
Moderately high	3	Low directive High supportive
High	4	Low directive Low supportive

*Paul Hersey and Kenneth H. Banchard, *Managment of Organizational Behavior: Utilizing Human Resources,* 3rd ed. (Englewood Cliffs: Prentice–Hall, 1977), p. 165

Case Study

Following is a case study that illustrates two different types of departments and the leadership style most appropriate for each.

Gemini University, a small to middle-size institution, had four language departments: French, German, Spanish, and Russian. These departments had existed separately for more than thirty years and each had between three to seven faculty members including the chairperson. The board of trustees, after some study and upon recommendation of the president, combined these four departments and their faculties into a single eighteen-member Department of Modern Languages with one chairperson to be appointed. The faculty members of the original four separate language departments were not happy about becoming part of a single large department and resisted the idea to the very end. Although they participated in the search for a new chairperson, they were unable to reach consensus about any of the candidates. The dean, in desperation, finally offered the job to Dr. Sidney King, chairperson of the Department of Modern Languages at Apollo University for the past five years. The Modern Languages Department at Apollo University was established as a single unit about twenty five years ago when the university first opened its doors and now consisted of fifteen faculty members. Students in this department could major in French, Spanish, German, Italian, or Russian. Dr. King was offered the position of chairperson of the new Modern Languages Department at Gemini University because of his reputation as an effective chairperson of a smoothly operating department. Dr. King's interest in the new position was his desire for a change and the added incentive of a potential salary much larger than what he was now receiving.

From the information contained in the case study one may conclude:

1. At Gemini University the faculty members of the Modern Languages Department that was recently formed by merging four separate language departments are unable to reach consensus or work cooperatively. By definition, therefore, the department can be classified as a group with low maturity level. The leadership style most appropriate for a group with low maturity level falls into Quadrant 1—high direction with increasing amount of support.

2. The Modern Languages Department at Apollo University had been a single department for twenty-five years. It actually started out as a single department. Since it operates smoothly, one can assume that it is a mature department. The leadership style most appropriate for a group with high maturity level falls into Quadrant 4—not much direction, and some but not lots of support. Dr. King, chairperson of that department, probably used that leadership style.

3. At this particular time in the development of the Modern Languages Department at Gemini University, a chairperson is needed who can use a leadership style appropriate for an immature department. If Dr. King of Apollo University accepts the position of chairperson of the Modern Languages Department at Gemini University, he must be able to modify his leadership style from being nondirective to being directive, at least during the initial period of his appointment. If he uses the same nondirective leadership style at Gemini University as he used with the Modern Languages Department at Apollo University, the Gemini Modern Languages Department will continue to flounder. If, on the other hand, he is able to modify the style he used for his Modern Languages Department at Apollo to fit the immature department at Gemini, then he has a good chance of succeeding.

4. The main point is that just because Dr. King is an effective chairperson at Apollo University it does not necessarily follow that he will be effective at Gemini University unless he is able to change his leadership style to fit the new situation.

Department Decision Making

Every department, at some time or another, has to make decisions. The matters to be decided vary considerably, ranging from issues of great import to more transient ones. Departments must make decisions about larger issues—such as priorities, goals, and the allocation of department resources—as well as smaller issues, including the extent to which the department should become active in off-campus programs, the allocation of travel funds, and the teaching load of department faculty members.

The examples list above are familiar ones. The list could be expanded to include decisions about personnel problems, budgetary problems, interpersonal problems, organizational problems, and so on. A study of the decision-making process reveals that most decisions are based on the use of a simple problem-solving model. Ordinarily when a person becomes aware that a problem exists, the first step is to identify and clarify the nature of the problem. Then a list of possible solutions can be formulated. (The possibility of doing nothing is frequently the first item on the list.) Thinking about solutions generally leads to a consideration of the possible consequences of each alternative. A person decides which solution seems most likely to produce the desired results and then proceeds to carry it out.

In the academic department, there are times when several decisions must be made simultaneously and other times when only a single, though difficult, decision must be made. Within this context, some chairpersons come to think of themselves as firemen, rushing about trying to extinguish small fires before they become conflagrations. Others fail to see the first signs of impending difficulties and react only after a crisis has occurred. Although the chairperson's personality greatly influences his or her approach to decision making, he or she can consciously adopt methods that seem best suited to the problem.

The chairperson must take the lead in deciding if things are to change or stay the same in the face of the exigencies of academic life. The questions of how to decide and who is to be involved in the decision-making process are difficult and perplexing. Most administrators recognize the desirability of involving faculty members and students in the problem-solving and decision-making processes. Nevertheless, many problems do not permit a great deal of faculty or student participation, simply because they must be dealt with swiftly. In any event, the question of the degree of faculty and student involvement in department decision making is one that most chairpersons must address.

The degree of faculty and student involvement in department decision making is often related to the chairperson's attitude and style. (A chairperson's mode of operation is probably also related to personality variables that need not be discussed here.) The chairperson's style of department leadership can range across a broad continuum, from extremely authoritarian or autocratic to extremely democratic.

The variety of styles within these extremes has been described by Robert Tannenbaum and Warren H. Schmidt in their article "How to Choose a Leadership Pattern." Summarized below is their list of leadership styles. Notice that the styles become more democratic and less autocratic, more relationship-oriented and less task- or directive-oriented, as we proceed down the list.

1. *The chairperson makes the decision and announces it.* The chairperson identifies the problem, evaluates alternative solutions, chooses one of them, and announces to the faculty which solution will be implemented. Little faculty participation is encouraged.

2. *The chairperson makes the decision and tries to sell it.* The chairperson recognizes that his or her decision may not be accepted outright by all concerned. He or she seeks to reduce any resistance by indicating what the faculty will gain.

3. *The chairperson makes the decision and invites questions.* The chairperson seeks acceptance of his or her decision by helping the faculty understand it by means of a question-and-answer session.

4. *The chairperson presents a tentative decision subject to change.* This style permits the faculty to exert some influence on the decision.

5. *The chairperson presents the problem, gets suggestions, and makes the decision.* The chairperson comes to the faculty with a problem that he or she has identified and analyzed but has not solved. He or she asks the faculty for suggestions; however, all understand that the final decision is the chairperson's.

6. *The chairperson defines the limits and asks the faculty to make the decision within these limits.* The chairperson delegates to the faculty (including himself or herself) the freedom to make the final decision. Before doing so, however, the chairperson states the problem as he or she sees it and sets the boundaries, or areas of freedom, within which the decision can be made.

7. *The chairperson permits the faculty to make the decision within broadly defined limits.* This situation occurs when problems are vague and require a high degree of freedom of exploration if creative solutions are to be found. Only broad limits are imposed and the chairperson, if he or she participates at all, participates as an equal.

Criteria for Degree of Faculty Involvement in Decision Making

The continuum of leadership styles suggests that chairpersons can perform their functions in a variety of ways. Although many believe, as a matter of principle, that faculty and student involvement in decision making should be maximized, the truth of the matter is that not all faculty members and students can be, should be, or should even wish to be involved in every decision a chairperson makes. Do any guidelines or rules exist that suggest when faculty members and students should be asked to participate in the decision-making process?

When problems confront a department and decisions must be made, the chairperson might ask himself or herself several basic questions that can help determine the degree to which the faculty should be involved. These questions are based on three relevant criteria:

- *Expertise*—Who knows how to solve the problem? The chairperson alone? A particular faculty member or group within the department? The whole department?
- *Acceptance*—Is faculty acceptance of the decision crucial for effective implementation? Will implementation fail if the faculty refuses to go along with the decision?
- *Time*—Is there enough time to get the faculty involved in the process of decision making? Is the issue so crucial that an immediate decision is necessary?

While these criteria are logically independent of one another, they should all be considered when an important problem or issue arises. It would be possible to construct a matrix of hypothetical issues, with different values for each criterion, but instead we will discuss each criterion separately.

EXPERTISE.   Some decisions require expertise in specific areas. If the chairperson possesses such expertise, he or she is perfectly capable of making a decision alone. Lacking that expertise, the chairperson may seek it from faculty members in the department and should not hesitate to call on those who have experience and interests in areas connected with the problems to be addressed. Frequently the expertise needed for rational decision making may be found outside the department, within the institution, and is available for the asking. Sometimes simple pride or fear of asking for help can prevent a chairperson from using staff resources wisely and advantageously.

ACCEPTANCE.   Some decisions, important or not, require that the department faculty accept them if they are to be carried out. Important decisions that affect the well-being or survival of the department will require the faculty's acceptance if they are to be implemented. Some decisions that are seen as unimportant are readily accepted by the faculty, who is grateful not to have been bothered with them. In such instances, the chairperson can make the decision alone or delegate the matter to a staff member. On the other hand, some seemingly unimportant decisions may require faculty involvement in order to gain acceptance. The chairperson must rely on his or her judgment to evaluate the faculty members' mood.

People willingly participate in an activity when they can see the benefits that accrue from a common endeavor, when they see the department's success as synonymous with their own. On the other hand, the most benign and rational decision can be resisted, subverted, or diverted by a group if it feels that it had no share in making the decision. What better way is there to encourage faculty members to accept and implement decisions than to have them participate in the process of making decisions?

TIME.   Occasionally problems arise and decisions must be made with great speed. In the context of modern bureaucratic organizations, opportunities arise that must be seized without hesitation or they will be lost. The chairperson must judge whether an immediate decision is better than no decision at all.

The three criteria we have been discussing—expertise, acceptance, and time—vary in importance according to circumstance. Considering these criteria when the question of faculty involvement arises will help a chairperson decide whether, in those particular circumstances, the faculty ought to be involved. A related problem is *how* faculty members can be encouraged to participate in the decision-making process. Some are ready and eager to be involved in department problem solving, while others show little interest in sharing in the hard work that is a part of intelligent decision making. No single method of involving faculty members in the decision-making process is best. Departments vary considerably in size, tradition, role and mission, and the personalities and skills of their members. Each chairperson's decisions about the methods and techniques of faculty involvement must take into account the special, often idiosyncratic, characteristics of the department. Nevertheless, each chairperson must determine whether a matter should be brought to a meeting of the full faculty, referred to a committee, discussed informally with faculty members, or acted upon according to his or her own best judgment. These determinations depend partly on how the chairperson views his or her role and partly on his or her experience in working with each option.

Most department chairpersons, on the basis of their past experience, choose to share the decision-making process with their faculty members for the following reasons. First, faculty members will have to implement almost any decision the chairperson makes and are therefore more likely to be cooperative if they are involved in making the decision. Second, as mentioned earlier, individual faculty members often have expertise or experience to contribute to the decision-making process. Third, when conflicts do occur, resolving them in the context of open discussion is less disruptive than neglecting them altogether and possibly causing them to multiply unnecessarily. Finally, department decisions take place within the broader contexts of academe and a democratic society. The university, as an institution, has a long tradition of collegiality; the idea of a community of scholars is compatible with processes of shared decision making by equals.

Questions

1. In chapter 2, you were asked to estimate the maturity level of your department or division. Using the directive–supportive model, what style of leadership would appear to be most effective for that level of maturity?

2. What is your leadership style, as determined by the instrument in this chapter? How does it compare with the style that would appear to be most effective for your department, given your estimation of its level of maturity?

3. What are some fairly important types of decisions that you as chairperson could make for your department without involving the faculty members in the decision-making process and that they would accept without serious complaint?

4. What are some fairly unimportant types of decisions that you could make without involving the faculty members in the decision-making process and that they would not accept?

5. What types of department decisions would your faculty members prefer that you make without bothering them?

References

ABRELL, RONALD L. "Educational Leadership Without Carrot and Club." *The Clearing House,* February 1979, pp. 280–285.

ARGYRIS, CHRIS; CYERT, RICHARD M.; RAILEY, STEPHEN K.; and MAEROFF, GENE I. *Leadership in the 1980s.* Cambridge, MA: Institute for Educational Management, Harvard University, 1980.

ARGYRIS, CHRIS. "Interpersonal Barriers to Decision-making." *Harvard Business Review,* February 1966, pp. 84–97.

ARGYRIS, CHRIS, and SCHON, DONALD A. *Theory in Practice: Increasing Professional Effectiveness.* San Francisco: Jossey–Bass, 1974.

ASTIN, ALEXANDER W., and SCHERRI, RITA A. *Maximizing Leadership Effectiveness: Impact of Administrative Style on Faculty and Students.* San Francisco: Jossey–Bass, 1980.

ATWELL, ROBERT H., and GREEN, MADELINE F. *Academic Leaders as Managers.* San Francisco: Jossey–Bass, 1981.

BALDRIDGE, J. VICTOR (et al.) *Policy Making and Effective Leadership: A National Study of Academic Management.* San Francisco: Jossey–Bass, 1978.

BLAKE, ROBERT R., and MOUTON, JANE S. *The Management Grid.* Houston: Gulf, 1964.

BROWN, DAVID G. *Leadership Vitality: A Workup for Academic Administrators.* Washington, DC: American Council on Education, 1980.

BURNS, TOM, and STALKER, G. M. *Management of Innovation.* New York: Methuen, 1961.

CHACKO, HARSHA E. *Administrators' Method of Upward Influence and Perceptions of Their Supervisors' Leadership Styles.* Paper presented at the Annual Meeting of the AERA, New Orleans, 1988. (ERIC Document Reproduction Service No. ED 296 476)

CHILDERS, MARIE E. "What Is Political About Bureaucratic–Collegial Decision-Making?" *The Review of Higher Education,* 5(1), Fall 1981.

CLEARY, ROBERT. "University Decision Making." *Educational Forum,* November 1978, pp. 89–98.

COHEN, MICHAEL D., and MARCH, JAMES G. (Eds.) *Leadership and Ambiguity: The American College President.* Carnegie Commission on Higher Education, New York: McGraw–Hill, 1974.

CORSON, JOHN J. *The Governance of Colleges and Universities.* New York: McGraw–Hill, 1960.

GUEST, ROBERT H.; HERSEY, PAUL; and BLANCHARD, KENNETH H. *Organizational Change Through Effective Leadership.* Englewood Cliffs: Prentice–Hall, 1977.

HAYWARD, PATRICIA C. "A Discriminant Analytic Test of Biglan's Theoretical Distinction Between Biology and English Department Chairperson." *Research in Higher Education,* 25, 1986, pp. 136–146.

HERSEY, PAUL, and BLANCHARD, KENNETH H. *Management of Organizational Behavior: Utilizing Human Resources.* 3rd ed. Englewood Cliffs, NJ: Prentice–Hall, 1977.

HOBBS, WALTER G., and ANDERSON, G. LESTER. "The Operation of Academic Departments." *Management Science,* December 1971, pp. 134–144.

KOWITZ, ALBERT C., and KNUTSON, THOMAS J. *Decision Making in Small Groups: The Search for Alternatives.* Boston: Allyn & Bacon, 1960.

LYNCH, DAVID M. (et al.) "Chief Liberal Arts Academic Officers: The Limits of Power and Authority." *Studies in Higher Education,* 12, 1987, pp. 39–50.

MACCOBY, MICHAEL. *The Gamesman.* New York: Simon & Schuster, 1977.

MARCH, JAMES G. *How We Talk and How We Act: Administrative Theory and Administrative Life.* Urbana: University of Illinois Press, 1980.

McCARTY, DONALD, and REYES, PEDRO. "Organizational Models of Governance: Academic Deans' Decision-Making Styles." *Journal of Teacher Education,* 38, 1987, pp. 2–8.

MEETH, L. RICHARD. "Administration and Leadership." *Power and Authority.* San Francisco: Jossey–Bass, 1971.

MIDDLEHURST, ROBIN. "Evaluation and Development of a Leadership Course for Heads of Academic Departments in the United Kingdom." *Higher Education Management,* 1, 1989, pp. 170–182.

NEUMANN, YORAM. "The Perception of Power in University Departments: A Comparison Between Chairpersons and Faculty Members." *Research in Higher Education,* 11 (4), 1979, pp. 283–293.

NEWMAN, FRANK. *Taking the Helm in the Third Century: Twenty-six Prominent Americans Speculate on the Educational Future.* New Rochelle, NY: Change Magazine Press, 1976.

PALMER, RUPERT E., JR. "The Chairman as Servant: Or, How to Lead a Department from a Position of Weakness." *ADE Bulletin,* May 1979, pp. 38–40.

RICHMAN, BARRY M., and FARMER, RICHARD N. *Leadership, Goals, and Power in Higher Education: A Contingency and Open-Systems Approach to Effective Management.* San Francisco: Jossey–Bass, 1974.

SERGIOVANNI, THOMAS J., and CORBALLY, JOHN E. *Leadership and Organizational Culture.* Chicago: University of Illinois Press, 1988.

SPRUNGER, BENJAMIN E., and BERGQUIST, WILLIAM H. *Handbook for College Administration.* Washington, DC: Council for the Advancement of Small Colleges, 1980.

TANNENBAUM, ROBERT, and SCHMIDT, WARREN H. "How to Choose a Leadership Pattern." *Harvard Educational Review,* March–April 1957, pp. 95–101.

WHETTEN, DAVID A. "Effective Administrators: Good Management on the College Campus." *Change,* November/December 1984.

Chapter 6

The Chair's Role in Bringing About Change

In most social groups a creative tension exists between forces that operate to bring about change and forces that operate to resist change. Although the American education system in general and institutions of higher education in particular are conservative and resistive of change, the continuous pressures of political and social events demand responses, and these responses result in a good deal of change. During the turbulent sixties, it seemed as if the pressures for a thorough democratization of educational curriculum and governance would revolutionize the structure of higher education. The seventies showed a great decline in student unrest, and many predictions of the preceding decade failed to materialize. Nevertheless, there is now a good deal more student participation in academic affairs than occurred in the fifties and sixties—for example, students now sit on boards of regents and on many academic committees.

Economic uncertainties and changing enrollments have combined to threaten the optimistic predictions of unlimited growth in the power, size, and influence of academic institutions. In fact, in many instances, programs and institutions are themselves threatened. The demands of minorities, particularly blacks and women, have led to numerous changes in school policy and procedure. The rise of teacher militancy at the elementary and secondary level has been followed by increasing unionization in many colleges and university systems. Changes in technology have led to changes in instructional techniques; educational television and computer-assisted instruction are becoming more common. These are but a few of the many pressures toward change that come from within and outside the college. Therefore, to ask what changes will be required is more realistic than to ask whether change will be required.

Departments have been and are subjected to many pressures for change from within and without the institution. The discussion of decision making is related to the kinds of change departments will be required to make. The chairperson's role in bringing about needed change can be central in determining whether change is indeed desirable, in planning for change, and in providing leadership in the process of implementing change.

While the question of change and the problems of implementing it can be easily discussed and the need for change readily acknowledged, the actual processes of bringing about change are quite perplexing. The results of some social science research suggests that many methods used to effect changes in human behavior are quite inefficient.

Amitai Etzioni, who has investigated problems of change, argues that attempts to effect behavioral change in humans through educational and advertising methods may not be successful unless there are accompanying changes in the environment. In his article "Human Beings Are Not Very Easy to Change, After All," he cites failures in antismoking campaigns, alcohol and drug abuse programs, and traffic safety programs that depended primarily on advertising and propagandizing. He then contrasts these failures with efforts that succeeded in altering behavior when persons were removed from situations or environments that contributed to the problem in the first place. In discussing the dismal failures of the intensive educational campaigns to help disadvantaged children, Etzioni concludes that educational programs will continue to fail as long as the children's total environments are unchanged. Change has been implemented successfully when persons *willingly* enter a new social community. Etzioni suggests that the total change approach, exemplified by people who join a kibbutz or an organization like Alcoholics Anonymous, is often successful. While total change appeals to a radical perspective, it obviously works only with volunteers, and many persons will simply not volunteer for a radical revision of their social environment.

Although Etzioni's research is not primarily concerned with change in academic organizations, some of his findings are applicable to this discussion. For example, a department chairperson, the sole representative of her institution, participates in a regional or national workshop for academic administrators. She returns with enthusiasm and many ideas for implementing change, only to encounter a resistive and unyielding environment. In this case, motivating the department chairperson to desire change was in itself not sufficient to bring it about.

Etzioni's research also suggests that finding new persons to implement decisions for change may be easier than obtaining cooperation from those whose ways are set. Unless positions are available for new faculty members, chairpersons of some departments must wait for recalcitrants to retire before attempting any change. In those instances when the chairperson is the obstruction to changes necessary for the department's survival, the dean must seek ways of changing the chairperson's behavior or perhaps of changing the chairperson.

In his article "Hauling Academic Trunks," J. B. Lon Hefferlin notes that few institutions change spontaneously and suggests that the most important factor influencing change is the market conditions under which educational institutions operate. Colleges and universities and their departments must attract resources or fail in their mission. Departments compete, within and without the institution, for scarce resources. If they fail to compete, they are liable to wither away. A department's curricular offerings must attract students, and the working conditions must attract faculty members, or mediocrity and stagnation will result. Many, if not most, departments closely watch what departments at other institutions are doing and try to do the same sorts of things—i.e., they sail with the wind rather than trying to go against it.

The second most powerful factor influencing academic change, according to Hefferlin, is the institution's ethos toward change. Each college or university and its departments have their own historic orientation toward change. This orientation, whatever it is, tends to be self-perpetuating, since those in power usually choose persons like themselves to succeed them. Yet choosing innovative successors often results in meaningful change. It is easier to replace persons than to change their attitudes, and frequently curricular or structural changes in universities or colleges must take place at the time when old professors retire or leave and new ones replace them. Dwight Ladd's study *Change in Educational Policy* indicates that changes in colleges and universities do not take place unless the faculty is convinced of the desirability of change.

A third factor that influences change in higher education is the institutional structure, which can be an aid or a barrier to change. The same is true of department structure as well. The department's decision-making process may be facilitated by clear procedures, by the nature of committees within the department, and by the rules that govern curricular issues and personnel policies. Some departments have written bylaws that outline the structure, while others have a structure based on higher authority. Departments that have no formal rules or procedures often have informal rules based on precedent or tradition. A problem in most large institutions is the rigidity of the bureaucracy. Strict, bureaucratic rules and procedures certainly operate against policies that are flexible, adaptive, and responsive.

In certain areas within departments, the need for change seems to crop up with some regularity. The first is the area of department goals and objectives. The goals of colleges and universities change with societal needs and conditions, and department goals may have to be altered to remain consistent with the institution's larger goals. To avoid mere rhetoric, goals and objectives should be stated realistically within the institutional and societal framework.

A second area of change is the department curriculum. The curriculum should be consistent with the department's goals and responsive to the needs of students, the discipline or profession, the community, and the institution. While the curriculum necessarily reflects the capabilities of the faculty, it can become ossified if not monitored.

A third area of change is the department's research and service activities. Here, too, there is the question of whether the research activities of faculty members within the department are consistent with department goals. Another serious question concerns the relationship between the department's research and service activities and its curricular and instructional activities; some research and service activities might conceivably weaken the department's course offerings. Finally, departments can address the question of the quality and worth of the research carried out in the department. This question most commonly arises during considerations of promotion and tenure for faculty members, but it might be addressed more profitably in the context of a general department evaluation.

Hefferlin, in the article cited earlier, lists five techniques for implementing academic change: the administrator must determine the obstacles, provide reassurance, build on existing concerns, avoid rejection, and respect the past. Although Hefferlin is speaking of change at the institutional level, his techniques may be applied when implementing change within a department. If changes are contemplated, the chairperson should anticipate possible obstacles to implementing these changes. These obstacles may be internal or external. They may be due to apathy, indifference, or lack of information.

Change is sometimes threatening, and the threats can be real or imagined. The chairperson should think of ways to assuage fears and consider techniques of conciliation, co-optation, and confrontation in the attempt to implement changes. When discussing change, try to avoid distorting and misrepresenting ideas. The chairperson can avoid opposition by clarifying the ideas and activities being considered. The more information the faculty members receive, the more likely they are to feel reassured. Change that builds on the existing concerns of the department is more likely to gain acceptance than change that does not. Changes should address problems that the faculty sees as urgent. The task force approach to change, which allows interested faculty members to participate, is recommended as a way of channeling the concerns of faculty members.

One way to avoid rejection is to propose change for a specific experimental period. If such a proposal is rejected, an optional, parallel program can be suggested. Then, if the proposed change works well, the rest of the faculty is more likely to accept it. Optional, parallel programs work well in the area of curriculum.

Finally, change in academia may be garbed in tradition. Hefferlin cites President Lowell of Harvard, who in 1938 said of the college president:

> If he desires to innovate he will be greatly helped by having the reputation of being conservative, because the radicals who want a change are little offended by the fact of change, while the conservatives will be likely to follow him because they look on him as sharing their temperament and point of view.[1]

This sage political advice can be applied to the governance of a department as well. Tradition should be respected while change is fostered.

In his article "Organizational Reform Is Not Enough," H. Bradley Sagen lists conditions that affect the adoption of academic innovation. His ideas, presented in terms of institutional changes, will be discussed here in terms of department

---

1. J. B. Lon Hefferlin. "Hauling Academic Trunks," *Elements Involved in Academic Change* (Washington, DC: Association of American Colleges, 1972), p. 10.

changes. He favors incentives and institutional support for innovations. In fact, one common criticism voiced about department change is the lack of rewards for those who attempt to innovate. Sagen suggests that faculty members might be encouraged to develop new ideas, goals, and programs through such small incentives as secretarial assistance, student assistantships, and released time.

Proposed changes are also easier to implement if they do not conflict with the values held by the department faculty members. If proposed changes are compatible with the faculty members' values and beliefs, the changes should not meet with resistance. A chairperson interested in innovations should be aware of the faculty members' academic and personal values and should be able to show that proposed changes are compatible, or at least not too incompatible, with those values. Sagen also stresses the importance of "participative involvement" in bringing about change. Compatibility of values is a necessary part of participative involvement.

Another desirable prerequisite to change is the clarification of the present situation. To know where you are going requires not only a clear idea of how you are going to get there, but also a clear idea of where you are. Sagen also recommends identifying and using faculty leaders to facilitate change. Some faculty members are admired and respected by their colleagues for their intelligence, honesty, and integrity; their opinions and attitudes carry a good deal of weight with their peers. A chairperson who can mobilize department leaders to support desired changes may find the path to change smoother than the chairperson who ignores department leaders.

Dealing with Change and Resistance to Change

Clark Kerr, a former president of the University of California, once said that changing a university curriculum is like trying to move a cemetery. His statement aptly characterizes faculty resistance to change. Though colleges and universities are characterized by massive inertia, in the long run they must yield to the pressure of changes. Because faculty members perceive change as threatening and manipulative, chairpersons tend to shy away from talking about it directly in order to avoid provoking anxiety and resistance. Faculty members feel less anxious, however, when discussing such subjects as self-renewal, organizational development, or faculty and staff development, all of which are actually efforts for planned change. For chairpersons to act as leaders or facilitators in these efforts, they should know and understand the process of change.

When faculty members resist change, what are they really resisting? Will a plan be automatically accepted if it is logical and educationally well conceived? Not necessarily. As we noted earlier, plans for change that rely exclusively on rationality are typically not successful. A faculty member's first reaction to a proposed change is to ask how it will affect him or her personally in terms of opportunity for professional development, promotion, salary increases, and work assignments. Faculty members will also be concerned about how the change will affect their future relationships with coworkers, students, administrators, colleagues, and so forth. To ensure the greatest likelihood of acceptance, therefore, a proposed plan for change should not only be logical and well conceived but should take into consideration the personal concerns of those involved. The chairperson should seek out those who feel that they will lose status if the change occurs. If their fears are unfounded they should be given the necessary assurances. If indeed the change may cause them to lose status, the chairperson should think about what, if anything, could be done to make up for this loss or to improve their present status. When the chairperson shows proper concern and interest, resistance may be converted to support.

Proper and frequent communication with faculty members before, during, and after a change will help alleviate many of their personal concerns. Those who will be affected by a proposed change should be provided with as much information as possible about the situation. Lack of knowledge about what is going on causes insecurity, and insecurity increases resistance, regardless of the merits of the proposed change. Information that presents the rationale for suggested changes may be sufficiently persuasive to reduce resistance or gain support for a proposed plan. Changing a person's knowledge base is frequently a prerequisite for changing attitude and behavior.

Another impediment to change often results from the requirement that plans for proposed changes must be reviewed and approved by many persons and groups in the institution's governance hierarchy. Any faculty committee or administrator may veto an idea as it travels the hierarchy from department to dean's office to president's office. Whenever a new idea for change is presented to a faculty committee for the first time, the reaction is generally negative, and after the initial rejection, committee support for the idea is difficult to obtain. In some instances, it is better to discuss the idea individually with several members of the committee before making the presentation to the committee as a whole. If individual members are persuaded that the idea has merit, they will help obtain support from the rest of the committee. Proper and frequent communication with committee members and administrators during the development of the plan can reduce resistance.

Change involves considerable risk because it will not necessarily solve a problem. Not every new approach will prove effective, and when a change fails, the innovator may be criticized or even terminated. A wrong change could stir up conflict, upset sensitive balances and relations, and waste faculty members' energy. Therefore, before the chairperson decides to implement a plan for a change, he or she could collect data that will help determine the probability of the plan succeeding without demoralizing the faculty. If the probability of success is low, the plan should not be implemented. Keep in mind also that the smaller the change, the less resistance it will generate. If a change is necessary, select one that will solve the problem in the simplest and least noticeable way. Do not amputate a leg to cure a toe infection. Remember also that if faculty members have not been involved in the planning, they will resist even the smallest change that might affect them.

What motivates faculty members to change? First, many are motivated by the desire for competence and the need to achieve. These persons are primarily interested in job mastery and professional growth and are constantly thinking of better ways of doing things. They are willing to participate in planning and implementing change for the sake of their own professional improvement and the department's improvement. Second, some faculty members are motivated to change only if they can anticipate a more tangible reward that they can share with their families. Third, some faculty members are motivated to change only when they consider the consequences of not changing—if, for example, they thought that unwillingness to change could cause them to lose privileges or face possible termination. A department with decreasing enrollments might be motivated to modify its recruitment policies, its curriculum, and its goals and activities if decreasing enrollment could lead to a reduced department budget and perhaps a reduced number of faculty positions. Faculty members' response to the need for change is generally based on a combination of all three factors, each of which may be weighted differently for different persons. But there are some faculty members who just won't change under any circumstances. The question of what to do with them is one of the challenges facing the department chairperson.

When considering the feasibility of implementing a plan for change, the chairperson should try to anticipate who will support the plan and who will resist it. The chairperson should make a list of potential supporters and the reasons for their support and another list of those who are expected to resist the plan and the reasons for their resistance. The supporting faculty members and their rationale can be thought of as "driving forces," the resisters and their rationale as "restraining forces."

Because the faculty members on each list will vary in the degree to which they support or resist the plan, the chairperson should rate the strength of each person's support or resistance on a scale of 1 to 5. When all the driving and restraining forces have been listed and the strength of each force has been rated, totals of the driving forces and the restraining forces can be calculated and then compared.

In his book *Field Theory in Social Science,* Kurt Lewin, a well-known social psychologist, has developed what is called the force field analysis theory, which says that change takes place when an imbalance occurs between the sum of the driving forces and the sum of the restraining forces. The greater the imbalance, the more acceptable the change will be. When the two sets of forces are balanced, the status quo continues. To bring about change, the driving forces must become strong enough to overcome the restraining forces, or the restraining forces must be sufficiently reduced or weakened to be overcome by the existing driving forces.

Applying Lewin's theory to the chairperson's role, we see that the chairperson should determine what kind of and how much influence is needed to attain the optimum pressure of driving forces necessary to bring about the desired change. He or she must then calculate whether there is enough support—or enough influence to obtain support—for the change. At this point the chairperson can decide whether the efforts for change are likely to be successful. If the decision is made to go ahead with the plan, a decision must also be made about the strategy to be used.

Strategies for bringing about change include the participative model and the power model. The participative, or involvement, model is used most often in organizations. In this model, new knowledge is made available to the group with the hope that the group will accept the data and develop a commitment to the desired change. The group is involved in reviewing the data and helping select or develop new methods for choosing the desired goal. In the power model, the chairperson imposes the plan for change on the faculty members in the hope that when they see how well it works, they will support it. In a university setting, the participative model is the most appropriate most of the time. The power model, however, can be more efficient and effective when the faculty's acceptance is not crucial to the implementation of the plan.

In evaluating the need for the change, the department chairperson must learn how to ask the right questions. He or she should talk to faculty members, the dean, other chairpersons, students, and recent alumni. The questions should include these: What is good about the department? What is not so good? What might happen in the future if the status quo remains unchanged? What would faculty members like to see happen in the future?

These questions will elicit mounds of useful information. Moreover, the process will generally please those who are asked to comment and will thereby earn the chairperson a measure of positive support. These interviews will result in a tentative list of proposed changes that should be considered.

In selecting and implementing plans for change, then, the following points should be kept in mind:

- Select changes that are most timely and appropriate for the department's current situation.
- Select plans for change that have a reasonable chance of success—e.g., sufficient faculty support, sufficient resources, and so forth.
- Select plans that require the least drastic change to solve a problem.
- Develop plans for responding to the personal needs of those who will be affected by the changes.
- Develop strategies for communicating appropriately with those who will be affected by the change as well as those who must approve it.
- Develop strategies for obtaining faculty members' commitment to supporting and participating in the implementation of the plan.
- Be sensitive to values held by members of the department.

In bringing about needed change, the department chairperson should have the ability to perform the following functions:

- Provide guidance to the faculty in developing and updating department goals and objectives.

- Assess local, regional, and national needs for education services provided by the department.
- Develop action plans for the needed changes.
- Implement action plans for the needed changes.

Examples of specific skills helpful to department chairpersons in dealing with change include these:

- ability to design and implement strategy for bringing about needed curriculum and program change
- ability to develop long-range plans and strategies—for example, strategies for timely appointment, promotion, tenure, and retirement of faculty members—that will enable a department to remain responsive to new and changing needs
- ability to identify and develop programs to meet the professional development needs of faculty members in times of retrenchment

Intervention Plans

For our purposes, an *intervention* is defined as a person's action or series of actions that causes a change in the behavior of another person or group. Literally, it is an interruption in the direction in which a person or group is moving. A department chairperson can devise an intervention plan that will move a department in the desired direction and at the same time improve faculty motivation and morale. A well planned intervention may further the goals of collegiality and shared governance. In its simplest form, such a plan would consist of a statement of the intervention and its expected outcome. Evidence for these expectations should be specified so that a follow-up can determine whether the intervention was effective.

Some interventions seem especially appropriate to the university setting, with its horizontal structure and its traditional framework of collegiality. Nine particularly appropriate kinds of interventions are described below, with examples of how such interventions might be useful.

The first kind of intervention calls attention to a contradiction in action or attitudes. Recently a chemistry department had the opportunity to fill a vacant position at the associate professor level. In establishing the criteria for the application, the faculty members stipulated at least five years' teaching experience, significant publications in major journals, national visibility, demonstrated service in the profession, and the ability to direct graduate students. Some months later an assistant professor in the department with four years of teaching experience, two publications, a good service record to the university, and a pleasant personality applied for a promotion to the rank of associate professor. Since he was well liked and seemed to show promise as a researcher, the department members were anxious for him to be promoted. The chairperson called their attention to the discrepancy between their criteria for someone coming from outside the institution and their criteria for someone within the institution. After some discussion, they decided to ask the faculty member to wait another year and work toward coming closer to department standards. In this case, the department chairperson's intervention modified the way in which the department developed and used its human resources.

The second kind of intervention relies on the use of research findings or conceptual understandings to help faculty members broaden their perspective on a particular problem. A communications department chairperson was faced with the problem of having too many sections of an extremely popular speech course and too few instructors. The faculty's desire to maintain the twenty-to-one student–faculty ratio in the classroom was opposed by the dean, who said that he simply could not find the additional faculty positions to support so low a student–faculty ratio in a lower-division course. The chairperson looked into the research on students evaluating their peer's performance, which showed that students' evaluation of their fellow students was reliable and permitted a larger class size by reducing the amount of time the instructor spent on grading. She shared the information with the faculty members, who were convinced by the evidence. The appeal to research findings was persuasive and allowed the department chairperson both to double her class size and to maintain the faculty member's morale.

The third kind of intervention reexamines the existing methods for solving problems within the department. A new economics department chairperson wished to involve junior faculty members in the department's decision-making process. When he met resistance from the existing oligarchy, he used the occasion of a university self-study to appoint a committee composed of junior and senior faculty members to review the department's decision-making process. The committee concentrated on the methods used to make decisions and, with the input from the junior faculty members, recommended a revision of the department's decision-making processes. The committee workload was distributed more evenly and the senior faculty members' time used to better advantage.

The fourth kind of intervention focuses on lowering situational conflict within the group by improving group relationships. The faculty members of an English department were unable to modify their selection of requirements for their undergraduate general education courses. The modernist faction felt that the traditionalists were being stubborn in their devotion to the past, while the traditionalist faction felt that many of the modernists' innovations were too avant garde and that faculty members who espoused curricular revisions were merely trying to promote their own ends. Tensions had increased when the department chairperson organized a weekend retreat for the faculty members at the university convention center some twenty-five miles from campus. During the retreat, as the faculty members walked together on the beaches or sat in front of the fire, many of the superficial emotional elements of the conflict were reduced. On the last day of the retreat, the faculty members were able to resolve the problem to everyone's satisfaction.

The fifth kind of intervention allows for the adoption of two or more options rather than a single forced choice. This approach is particularly appealing to science departments and other departments that are quantitatively oriented. Although the procedures for comparing courses of action are not scientifically exact, they do add an element of logic to the decision-making process. A graduate psychology department wished to modify its comprehensive examination procedures by substituting a research project assignment for the written examination. The faculty members disagreed about the appropriateness of this course of action, so the department chairperson allowed one group of doctoral students to select either the examination or the project for one academic year. After the year's experience with both options, the faculty decided to adopt the research project as an option for students.

The sixth kind of intervention identifies significant alternatives and examines the consequences that might follow the adoption of each alternative. The chairperson of a history department found that she was unable to provide adequate office space for a growing number of faculty members and graduate students. A morale problem developed. The dean told the chairperson that she could have all the office space she wanted in a vacant house on the edge of campus. The chairperson met with the faculty members to explore the advantages of being housed in spacious quarters but away from the center of campus life and the advantages of being housed in cramped quarters but close to the center of campus life. After much discussion, they decided in favor of more cramped quarters closer to classrooms and other students. The intervention resulted in increased understanding, thus reducing the morale problem.

The seventh kind of intervention objectively applies a historical perspective to the present situation. A geology department chairperson wished to encourage faculty members to solicit research proposals from outside agencies. To this end he conducted a review of outside funding received by the department over the preceding ten years and compared it with research activities and funding both of other science departments within the university and of other geology departments within the university system. The evidence indicated that the department was missing out on some research opportunities. Faculty members began to write proposals and to receive outside funding.

The eighth kind of intervention identifies the source of the problem as something related to an institutional policy or constraint. A humanities department chairperson was challenged by a group of her faculty members for her failure to secure enough travel money for them to attend the national convention. The department chairperson met with the group and reviewed the board of regents' budgetary procedures, the university's restrictions on travel, and appropriations of travel funds throughout the university. She was able to demonstrate that while the absolute amount of travel money was ridiculously low, the department had received more than its fair share, given the institutional constraints. She also indicated that those departments that had more travel money usually obtained it from outside sources. By showing the faculty members the structure of the system, she was able to spur their requests for funds from outside agencies.

The final kind of intervention relies on one of the strongest arguments of all—tradition. Faculty members, it has been said, never like to do anything for the first time; appeals to tradition can, therefore, be particularly persuasive. An education administration department chairperson wished to encourage the faculty members to be more active in ordering books for the library. Ordering books was consuming a great deal of his time, but he knew from experience that a general request for more book orders would generate little response. He began his strategy by assigning students in his own classes to read books that he considered basic to areas in his field but that were unavailable in the library. When students reported that the library did not possess the books that were assigned, the chairperson relayed those reports to a meeting of the faculty. At the meeting, the chairperson spoke of the great libraries at the universities at which many of the faculty members had earned their doctorates. He stated that funds were available to the department for the purchase of books in their respective fields; thus a library could be built that would at least equal those they had used as students. With the expertise of the faculty mobilized, a first-class collection representing the highest tradition of university scholarship could be amassed. As a result of the discussion, the book-ordering function was taken over by a faculty committee.

The nine intervention techniques that seem especially appropriate for use in universities may be summarized as follows:

1. Call attention to a contradiction in action or in attitudes.
2. Rely on the use of research findings or conceptual understandings.
3. Reexamine the existing methods for solving problems.
4. Focus attention on lowering intergroup conflict by improving group relationships.
5. Test the adoption of two or more options, as opposed to a single forced choice.
6. Identify significant alternatives and examine the consequences of adopting each alternative.
7. Apply a historical perspective to the present situation.
8. Identify the source of the problem as related to an institutional policy or constraint.
9. Argue from tradition.

In this chapter we have discussed the need for chairpersons to obtain information from faculty members when contemplating department changes. Faculty members who have not had the opportunity to become involved in the decision-making process sometimes resist, actively or passively, the implementation of the resulting decision, regardless of its potential benefit to the department. Too much involvement, however, can be just as detrimental as too little. We have described various ways of determining the extent to which faculty members should be involved, how to involve them, and how to help them overcome some of their feelings of resistance to a proposed change. Some attitudes of resistance, if unchecked, can develop into difficult conflict situations. Dealing with potential and active conflict is described in some detail in chapter 25.

Questions

1. Following are three factors which influence change. How would you evaluate your department on each of these factors?
   a. The market conditions—does the curriculum of your department attract students? Does the department attract good faculty?
   b. What attitude do faculty members have toward change—why would they be for or against change?
   c. Is the institutional or departmental structure an aid or barrier to change—how would it be an aid? How would it be a barrier?

2. Areas of change which surface most often in many departments are:
   a. Goals of the department
   b. Curriculum
   c. The relationship between research, service, and teaching.
   Which of these areas have been considered for change during the past five years? Have changes been implemented during the past five years?

3. Following is a case study concerning a "high failure mathematics department." Please answer questions at the end of the case study. If more details are needed in order to answer the questions, please fill in the missing aspects of the case with hypothetical information based on your own experience. To the extent possible, apply the suggested methods in the chapter as well as your own ideas in attempting to reduce the resistance to the change.

   The department of mathematics in a middle-size university has an unusually high failure rate in freshman-level mathematics courses. In a meeting called to discuss the problem, the dean of arts and sciences points out that he has received numerous complaints from the dean of engineering because too many students were failing the mathematics courses required to enter full-time study in the college of engineering.

   The mathematics faculty feels that the high level failure rate simply reflects inadequate preparation on the part of entering students. The director of institutional research counters this suggestion by revealing that many students who ranked in the top quartile of the College Board Examination were included in the large number of failing students. The dean of engineering is threatening to develop mathematics courses within the college of engineering if the situation persists any longer. The mathematics chairperson wants the faculty to see that a problem exists. He recognizes that they must develop a plan for changing the grading policy or the structure of the freshman mathematics courses, otherwise engineering students might be required to take their mathematics courses in the college of engineering.

   a. How can the chairperson get the department to recognize that the present situation cannot continue?
   b. What type of faculty members would support change? What type would resist change?
   c. What might be the concerns of those who oppose change?
   d. What can be done to alleviate their concerns?
   e. How might the chairperson involve faculty in developing a plan for solving the problem?
   f. Review the nine interventions described in this chapter. Is one or more of them appropriate in this case? Which one(s)? If none is appropriate, design another intervention strategy that might work.
   g. How might the chairperson handle faculty members who adamantly refuse to consider changing the grading policy of the course structure?

4. Do you currently have a specific problem in your department, the solution to which requires a change that will be resisted by some faculty members?

   a. Knowing your faculty members as you do, can you identify in your mind:
      i. Those who would immediately support your idea (?)
      ii. Those who would have an open mind and therefore could be persuaded (?)
      iii. Those who follow the opinion of the majority when a consensus has been reached (?)
      iv. Those who would adamantly oppose the idea (?)
   b. What interventions would seem to have the most positive effects on faculty members in your department? (See interventions listed in this chapter.)
   c. What procedures and strategies would you use to win over those faculty members who might create opposition?

References

CHAMBERLAIN, PHILLIP C. "Resistance to Change in Curriculum Planning." In *The Academic Department or Division Chairman: A Complex Role,* edited by James Brann and Thomas A. Emmet. Detroit: Balamp, 1972, pp. 250–262.

CARTWRIGHT, DORWIN. "Achieving Change in People: Some Applications of Group Dynamics Theory." *Human Relations,* November 1951, pp. 381–392.

CARTWRIGHT, DORWIN, and ZANDER, ALVIN (Eds.) *Group Dynamics: Research and Theory.* 3rd ed. New York: Harper & Row, 1968.

COCH, LESTER, and FRENCH, JOHN R. P., JR. "Overcoming Resistance to Change." *Human Relations,* August 1948, pp. 512–32.

CONRAD, CLIFTON F. "A Grounded Theory of Academic Change." *Sociology of Education,* April 1978, pp. 101–112.

CORSON, JOHN J. *The Governance of Colleges and Universities.* New York: McGraw–Hill, 1960.

ETZIONI, AMITAI. "Human Beings Are Not Very Easy to Change After All." *Saturday Review,* 3 June 1972, pp. 45–47.

GUEST, ROBERT H.; HERSEY, PAUL; and BLANCHARD, KENNETH H. *Organizational Change Through Effective Leadership.* Englewood Cliffs: Prentice–Hall, 1977.

HAYWARD, PATRICIA C. "A Discriminant Analytic Test of Biglan's Theoretical Distinction Between Biology and English Department Chairpersons." *Research in Higher Education,* 25, 1986, pp. 136–146.

HEFFERLIN, J. B. LON. *Dynamics of Academic Reform.* San Francisco: Jossey–Bass, 1969.

———. "Hauling Academic Trunks." In *Elements Involved in Academic Change,* edited by Charles U. Walker, pp. 1–10. Washington, DC: Association of American Colleges, 1972.

LAWRENCE, PAUL R. "How to Deal with Resistance to Change." *Harvard Business Review,* May–June 1954, pp. 49–57.

LEVINE, ARTHUR. *Why Innovation Fails: The Institutionalization and Termination of Innovation in Higher Education.* Albany: State University of New York Press, 1981.

LEWIN, KURT. *Field Theory in Social Science,* edited by Dorwin Cartwright. Westport, CT: Greenwood, 1975.

LINDQUIST, JACK. *Strategies for Change: Academic Innovation and Adaptive Development.* Washington, DC: Council for the Advancement of Small Colleges 1980.

LIONBERGER, HERBERT F. *Adoption of New Ideas and Practices.* Ames, IA: Iowa State University Press, 1960.

LIPPETT, RONALD (et al.) *Dynamics of Planned Change: A Comparative Study of Principles and Techniques.* New York: Harcourt Brace, 1958.

LYNCH, DAVID M. (et al.) "Chief Liberal Arts Academic Officers: The Limits of Power and Authority." *Studies in Higher Education,* 12, 1987, pp. 39–50.

MARROW, ALFRED J.; BOWERS, DAVID G.; and SEASHORE, STANLEY E. (Eds.) *Strategies of Organizational Change.* New York: Harper & Row, 1967.

MILGRAM, STANLEY. "Group Pressure and Action Against a Person." *Journal of Abnormal and Social Psychology,* August 1964, pp. 137–143.

RONKEN, HARRIET O., and LAWRENCE, PAUL R. *Administering Changes: A Case Study of Human Relations in a Factory.* Boston: Harvard University Press, 1952.

SAGEN, H. BRADLEY. "Organizational Reform Is Not Enough." In *Elements Involved in Academic Change,* edited by Charles U. Walker, pp. 20–29. Washington, DC: Association of American Colleges, 1972.

SCHUSTER, JACK H. "The Faculty Dilemma: A Short Course." Phi Delta Kappan, 68, 1986, pp. 275–282.

————. *Governing Tomorrow's Campus, Perspectives and Agendas.* Washington, DC: American Council on Education, 1989.

SERGIOVANNI, THOMAS J., and CORBALLY, JOHN E. *Leadership and Organizational Culture.* Chicago: University of Illinois Press, 1988.

TRASK, KERRY A. "The Chairperson and Teaching." In *New Directions for Teaching and Learning: The Department Chairperson's Role in Enhancing College Teaching,* 37, Spring 1989, pp. 99–107.

TRINKHAUS, JOHN W., and BOOKE, ALVIN L. "The Curriculum Change Process: Participants, Strategies, and Tactics." *Research in Higher Education,* 13, 1980, pp. 307–319.

VON HADEN, HERBERT I., and KING, JEAN MARIE. *Educational Innovator's Guide.* Worthington, OH: Charles A. Jones, 1974.

Chapter 7

Delegation and Department Committees

One of the first questions that a newly appointed department chairperson asks is, "How can I effectively fulfill all my responsibilities as chairperson and at the same time not reduce my teaching, research, and service activities?" Chairpersons who singlehandedly try to carry out all their administrative tasks and simultaneously maintain their previous levels of professional activity are bound to find that the workload is impossible to manage. At some point they must decide to what extent they wish to retain their commitment to teaching, research, and professional activities. Some chairpersons give up most or all of their teaching and research in order to fulfill their administrative and leadership tasks. Others, by carefully delegating many administrative tasks to faculty members and department committees, manage to schedule sufficient time for some teaching and research. Then there are those chairpersons who continue to carry out all their customary teaching, research, and service activities, paying attention to administrative tasks only when absolutely necessary. Chairpersons usually choose the model most suited to their talents, abilities, and professional objectives.

Academic vice-presidents and deans are not seriously concerned with the extent to which the chairperson personally carries out the department's administrative activities—so long as the tasks are carried out. Nor do deans and academic vice-presidents apply pressure on department chairpersons to conduct research. Faculty members, however, often expect chairpersons to continue their research and scholarly activities even while administering the department. Some chairpersons who are no longer actively engaged in research complain openly about the difficulties and frustrations of the chairperson's job and indicate repeatedly to their colleagues that they can hardly wait to return to the classroom or laboratory. The sincerity with which these statements are made cannot be overlooked. In a recent survey of department chairpersons, however, 90 percent responded that they would serve an additional term in the position if invited to do so.[1] For those who envision a career in the area of university

---

1. Survey conducted in 1987 by Allan Tucker, unpublished.

administration, the relinquishing of research activity may simply mark the beginning of a new career interest. On the other hand, many chairpersons try to maintain their earlier activities simply for love of their discipline or in anticipation of returning to their former roles when their time as chairperson is over.

Clearly the role of chairperson involves many tasks that are quite time-consuming. In their study of chairpersons at one state university, Gerald W. McLaughlin, James R. Montgomery, and L. F. Malpass found that chairpersons considered the following tasks most demanding: providing informal leadership for faculty members; representing the department to the central administration; allocating financial resources; maintaining faculty morale; encouraging organizational improvement; managing academic programs; planning for the long term; advising students; and encouraging faculty members' professional development.

Even though these tasks were considered most demanding, they provided some satisfaction. Still other tasks were perceived as providing no satisfaction at all. These included maintaining student records, serving on college and university committees, managing facilities, and preparing and presenting budgets. Especially onerous were tasks governed by federal, state, and university laws and administrative rules and requiring much detail work.

Incidentally, chairpersons in the study cited above reported that they worked an average of fifty-five hours per week. They spent an average of twenty-six hours on department leadership and administrative tasks, ten hours on teaching and student counseling, nine hours on research and professional development, and four hours on college and university activities. Several of the chairpersons polled had been in office for five years, and their schedules indicated the extent to which they had adapted their professional lives to their administrative role.

A national survey of chairpersons of medium-sized to large university departments, conducted by John C. Smart and Charles F. Elton and reported in their article "Administrative Roles of Department Chairmen," revealed that the types of roles that the chairperson assumed were related to the department's academic discipline. For example, chairpersons in the basic disciplines, whether the sciences or the humanities, spent more time in the "faculty role" than did those in applied sciences departments. They spent relatively more time recruiting, selecting, and evaluating department faculty members; encouraging their professional development and research and publication efforts; maintaining a healthy department climate by reducing conflicts among the faculty members; and providing informal leadership for the faculty members.

Chairpersons of social science departments—such as anthropology, political science, psychology, and sociology—spent more time in the "instructional role." They spent more time than others teaching and advising students; managing clerical and technical personnel in the department; and maintaining accurate student and department records.

Chairpersons of departments of pure and applied science—such as biology and agriculture departments—spent more time in the "research role" than did chairpersons of the nonscience departments, such as English, history, and communications. They spent relatively more time obtaining and managing grants, gifts, and contracts; recruiting, selecting, and supervising graduate students; and managing department finances, equipment, and grants. Chairpersons in this group also showed low commitment to the instructional role.

The "coordinator role" was not predominant among chairpersons of any particular discipline but was most often associated with chairpersons of education departments. Those in the coordinator role spent more time than their colleagues soliciting ideas to improve the department, planning and reviewing the curriculum, and assigning teaching, research, and other duties to faculty members. They also spent more time coordinating department activities with external groups, representing the department at professional meetings, participating in college and university committee work, and interacting with university administrators on behalf of the department. Education chairpersons also spent less time in the faculty role. Perhaps this emphasis on coordinating is related to the fact that education professors spend a great deal of time supervising practice teaching and working with public school personnel; this coordinator role may be carried over when the professor becomes a chairperson.

Whatever the reasons for favoring one of the roles described above, the chairperson must still attend to those tasks that are part of other roles. These tasks may be secondary, but they cannot be totally neglected. To chairpersons who complain of having insufficient time for filling all their roles, university administrators often respond by suggesting that they learn better time management skills. In fact, administrators often suggest that the busiest faculty member be chosen chairperson because busy people manage their time successfully. Many books offer valuable techniques for organizing and managing one's time, and these are helpful for those who are not skillful at getting tasks scheduled and accomplished. Effective time management, however, will not significantly reduce a chairperson's work; such a reduction is possible only if the chairperson learns to delegate tasks. The extent to which chairpersons learn to delegate tasks will determine the amount of time they will have available for teaching, research, and other activities of their choice.

Some chairpersons, as we have noted, continue to carry out all their customary teaching, research, and service activities, but they do this at the expense of administrative tasks; in effect, the administrative tasks are assumed only when absolutely necessary. The attitude that characterizes this kind of administration is that nothing deserves attention until a crisis erupts. The chairperson sees the job as a chore and never bothers to learn about either the intricacies of leadership or the techniques of organization and delegation.

The crisis-fighting approach to department administration leads to an accumulation of unopened mail, unsubmitted reports, missed deadlines, and unattended faculty concerns. The result is a department with low morale and an unfavorable work environment. Often, in the face of faculty disapproval or even rebellion, the chairperson assigns more and more responsibility to the clerical staff. The staff, then, may take on airs of administrative authority, thus further antagonizing faculty members. In such a case, the department chairperson is not really fulfilling his or her responsibility. If a chairperson wants to have time for teaching and research and still effectively lead the department, he or she must learn to practice the art of delegation.

How, then, does a chairperson become an organizer and coordinator of tasks and activities? By delegating tasks and responsibilities to staff members, to faculty members, or to committees. The ability to delegate functions, tasks, and responsibilities requires a trust and confidence in peers and staff members, a trust that occurs when there is consensus within the department about goals, objectives, policies, programs, and priorities. Delegation also requires a willingness to accept the results of the delegated effort, even if these results are not as extraordinary as those the chairperson might have achieved working alone. A chairperson who is compelled to oversee every detail and to operate with "zero defect" standards is often unable to tolerate the work of those who seem less competent.

The chairperson's responsibilities for the completion of a certain task do not end once the task had been delegated. The work of others must be evaluated, checked, and occasionally endorsed. To evaluate something, however, usually takes less time than to do it. The chairperson, by careful delegation, can save between 60 to 90 percent of the time he or she might devote to a single task, especially if the instructions are clear and precise and if those delegated are in tune with the chairperson's style and thinking. Although not every task can be assigned to any person, many detailed but routine tasks can be easily relegated to secretaries, graduate student assistants, and staff associates.

Often, the chairperson can find faculty members who will willingly perform some administrative chores. Department tasks that provide growth and development opportunities are useful governance training for junior faculty members, and they should be given credit for service to the department. For example, these tasks could be made a part of the assigned workload, or the faculty members could be rewarded with some perquisite or a special title. A chairperson must be careful not to overload the unpromoted, untenured junior faculty member to the point that his or her career is threatened.

Senior faculty members who are having difficulty adjusting to the department's changing teaching or research goals or who are in an unproductive phase of their career might also welcome the opportunity to contribute to the department by assuming some delegated responsibility. In delegating tasks to senior faculty members, the chairperson must be sure that these persons are both willing to accept and competent to perform the assignment. Great tact and delicacy may be required in enlisting the efforts of senior faculty members.

Committee Structure

Department committees are useful to the chairperson because he or she can delegate certain tasks to them. They also help provide a logical order to the department decision-making process. Moreover, the faculty is more likely to accept decisions that are made or recommended by a committee, especially if the process for selecting committee members has been approved by the faculty. Much of a department's work is accomplished through committees, and the chairperson should understand how they work and the various ways in which they can be organized.

In a survey of fifteen selected academic departments at Ohio State University, reported in her article "The Internal Organization of Academic Departments," Doris Ryan found that the number of committees per department ranged from sixteen to none, with an average of seven.[1] The larger the department, the more committees it had; small departments often operated, in their entirety, as a single committee.

The size of a committee is clearly related to the tasks that it is assigned, as well as to the department structure. Large committees frequently occur in large departments that have formal subgroups, especially when each subgroup desires representation on those committees. For example, in a large psychology department, the clinical psychologists, who were not represented on the admissions committee, argued that the experimental psychologists, who dominated the selection process, were rejecting many good applicants. Generally, committees consisting of three to nine members seem to be more productive than larger committees. An odd number of members eliminates ties when voting.

There are two general types of committees—standing and ad hoc. A standing committee operates on a permanent basis. Although its membership may change, it continues to operate from year to year unless some administrative decree terminates its activities. Two examples of standing committees that operate on a permanent basis are admissions committees and faculty evaluation committees. Ad hoc committees, on the other hand, are formed for specific tasks and cease operation when their tasks are completed. Ad hoc committees may include search committees and others that respond to immediate needs. The frequency with which committees meet depends on the tasks assigned to them; some meet on a regular schedule, others on call.

Committee functions may logically be divided into three categories: developing policies, performing administrative activities, and providing technical advice. The policy-making function consists of developing rules, regulations, and criteria for governing certain department activities, such as evaluating faculty performance, admitting students, determining equitable workloads for faculty, assigning space, and so forth. The administrative function consists of making decisions on specific issues or recommending positions to the department chairperson. These administrative functions, all based on predetermined policies and criteria, include reviewing the applications of persons seeking admission to a program and making a decision as to whether they should be admitted; evaluating the performance of faculty members; recommending equitable workloads for specific faculty members; and assigning space to faculty members.

---

1. Doris W. Ryan, "The Internal Organization of Academic Departments," *Journal of Higher Education,* June 1972, p. 467.

A committee may be established for the sole purpose of developing policies and criteria to govern a single activity, and a second committee may be appointed to implement those policies. In some instances, a single committee is charged not only with developing such policies, procedures, and criteria, but also with implementing them. For example, a faculty evaluation committee may be required not only to develop department policies and criteria for evaluating the faculty but also to evaluate individual faculty members. Similarly, an admissions committee may be required not only to develop policies, procedures, and criteria for admitting students, but also to act on applications for admission.

Committees that provide technical advice are usually composed of faculty members with special expertise for addressing particular problems. These committees are usually ad hoc and are given assignments such as designing and planning new facilities, deciding what types of equipment should be purchased, developing core and specialized curricula for specified programs, and so forth.

Members of these committees may be appointed by the department chairperson, elected by the department, or chosen by a combination of both methods. Similarly, the committee chairperson may be appointed by the department chairperson, elected by the committee members, or elected by the department. In some cases, the department chairperson may also be the committee chairperson, a voting member of the committee, or an ex officio member, or he or she may not be a member at all. How these matters are handled depends on the department's nature and size and the tasks that must be accomplished.

The department chairperson must provide sufficient guidance and direction for the committee. The committee's charge should be clear and precise, and the committee should be apprised of its responsibilities, including what criteria must be followed, under what constraints it must operate, what its members can and cannot do, and what deadlines must be met. Most committees operate in an advisory capacity to the chairperson or to the department. Some advisory committees, however, are perceived as having a decision-making responsibility. One example is the admissions committee, whose task is so important that wise chairpersons rarely overrule its recommendations. In any event, an advisory committee should know that it operates in an advisory function. For committee members to work hard on some problem and then have their work ignored or rejected is disheartening, especially if they think that they are part of a decision-making rather than an advisory committee.

Sometimes chairpersons do not give clear guidance to committees. When a committee is not given a specific charge, criteria to follow, or deadlines to be met, it often accomplishes little or nothing at all. Possibly this result is just what the chairperson desired. Occasionally, a chairperson is pressured to do something that he or she is reluctant to do. Leaving the matter to a committee without giving it guidance, direction, or deadlines—especially if the committee members are at odds with each other—will give the chairperson time to let things simmer.

Some department administrative tasks can easily be delegated to committees, especially when the chairperson is willing to accept a decision that is arrived at fairly. Sometimes, however, the chairperson wants the department to take a certain course of action, which, if he or she proposed it, would arouse some opposition. In such a case, a chairperson could form a committee to recommend to the department that particular course of action.

Can there be any degree of certainty that a committee's conclusions will coincide with the chairperson's ideas? Some administrators use the following strategy. First, they discuss their ideas informally with individual faculty members to identify those who are or who might be sympathetic to the plan. These chairpersons do not use hard-sell tactics and are careful not to show undue eagerness to implement the action. Second, they select a committee of faculty members who are sympathetic to the plan and who also enjoy the respect of their colleagues. An appointed committee of this kind, properly instructed and charged, will usually come up with conclusions and recommendations that are consistent with the chairperson's original plan. If committee members or other faculty members suspect the Machiavellian nature of the chairperson's procedures, they may firmly resist adopting the intended action, regardless of its merits. Many faculty members consider machinations of this sort questionable; nevertheless, many chairpersons have been known to use such tactics. Our description of these tactics, however, is not intended to be an endorsement of them.

An elected committee may not be as predictable in terms of the recommendations it will make. If the chairperson wants an elected committee to recommend a certain course of action, he or she should talk to the committee members individually to gauge their feelings and attempt to persuade them to his or her way of thinking. If the chairperson cannot obtain the support of the committee, he or she might temporarily abandon the issue. Some chairpersons have been known to appoint two committees to work independently on the same problem in order to have a choice of recommendations. Faculty committees and departments as a whole almost always react negatively to a fresh proposal when it is introduced at a formal meeting, especially if the chairperson introduces it without having done any groundwork or having issued previous warning. And a negative reaction is not easily changed. A wise chairperson, therefore, will informally prepare committee members or department members before presenting a new concept at a formal meeting.

The work of department committees may be summarized as follows:

- Committees may function in policy-making, administrative, or technical roles.
- Committee members may be appointed, elected, or both.
- Committees may function in an advisory or decision-making capacity.
- Committees may meet regularly or on call.
- Committees may be permanent or ad hoc.
- The department chairperson may be the committee chairperson, a voting member of the committee, or an ex officio member, or not serve on the committee at all.

- The optimum number of members should be an odd number between three and nine.
- The charge to the committee should be clear and precise.

A department should, on occasion, examine the number and functions of its committees. Their value has been emphasized, but to overburden the faculty with a plethora of committees is counterproductive; only those committees that are necessary should be formed. Some large departments even have a committee to control the tendency of committees to multiply needlessly.

Following is a representative, though far from inclusive, list of department committees and a brief summary of the main functions of each. Few departments have all these committees, and some may not have any.

- *Admissions committee*—usually reviews applications of students for admission to the department and makes recommendation to admit or to deny admission
- *Graduate policy and programs committee*—determines admission and graduation requirements and standards; monitors quality of graduate programs
- *Student recruitment committee*—develops and implements methods of publicizing to prospective students the department's program and professional opportunities within the field
- *Seminars and symposia committee*—arranges and publicizes lectures, seminars, and symposia for faculty members and students within and outside the department
- *Governance committee*—at request of chairperson, considers the structure and functions of department committees; makes recommendations or advises chairperson concerning a broad range of department business
- *Field liaison committee*—establishes and maintains relationships with outside agencies and organizations; coordinates service activities of department faculty
- *Curriculum committee*—develops and monitors curriculum, including core and required courses
- *Promotion and tenure committee*—reviews the records of faculty members eligible for promotion or tenure and recommends appropriate action; in some departments, establishes the standards and criteria for these decisions
- *Faculty evaluation committee*—reviews records of faculty members for purposes of annual evaluation and merit increases; in some cases, establishes criteria for these reviews
- *Faculty development committee*—develops, implements, and monitors procedures that contribute to the professional advancement of faculty members

- *International students committee*—develops and implements procedures for meeting special needs of foreign students
- *Faculty assignment committee*—schedules classes; develops and implements procedures for ensuring that the department's work is equitably divided
- *Student advisory committee*—a student-directed and student-run committee, concerned with student welfare; nominates student members to certain faculty committees
- *Search committee*—develops and implements procedures for recruiting new faculty members and recommends appropriate appointments
- *Examination and grading committee*—sets standards for and reviews the grading system; administers qualifying and comprehensive examinations for graduate students
- *Off-campus program committee*—recommends and supervises courses and programs offered off campus
- *Placement committee*—develops and implements procedures for placing graduates of the program
- *Planning committee*—assesses the department's future needs and develops short- and long-range plans for consideration by the chairperson and the department; sometimes plans new buildings and facilities

Well-organized departments sometimes develop rules and guidelines for the operation of their committees; other committees operate on the basis of unwritten rules. More energy is sometimes spent in developing bylaws for committees than in dealing with the issues. Following is an example of committee guidelines that were adopted by a large department in a large university. This example is not offered as a model but only as an illustration for chairpersons interested in formalizing their department's committee structure. Note that the guidelines stipulate the committee's purposes and duties, describe how members are selected, outline operating procedures, and provide for a periodic evaluation of the committee's activities.

Appropriate guidelines could be drawn up for each committee within the department. The guidelines need not be lengthy or complex, but the charge should be clear.

GUIDELINES FOR THE FACULTY EVALUATION COMMITTEE

Purposes and Duties
1. To design faculty evaluation criteria and procedures for use within the department.
2. To communicate the evaluation criteria procedures to the faculty in a timely fashion.
3. To implement the evaluation procedures for department promotion and tenure, annual evaluation, and merit, and for master's and doctoral directive status
4. To advocate review and monitor procedures that contribute to professional

advancement of untenured and junior members (e.g., to establish conditions suitable for research, writing, and publishing)

Committee Memberships

1. Each of the three degree programs in the department will elect three faculty members as representatives on the committee to serve for a one-year term.
2. The committee chairperson will be named by the department chairperson from among those elected.

Committee Procedures

1. The committee will meet as frequently as may be required to do its work.
2. All candidates for promotion, tenure, and merit, as well as candidates for master's and doctoral directive status within the department shall be reviewed by the committee.
3. The committee will make a brief report of its work to the faculty at the end of the winter quarter.
4. The department chairperson will explain and discuss with the committee the reasons for any action that is contrary to the committee's recommendations. The committee members will inform the faculty of such instances.

Review

The committee will be responsible for conducting a yearly review of its procedures. If necessary, the committee will propose recommended changes to the governance committee.

The many tasks that confront department chairpersons can be extremely time-consuming. To avoid being totally consumed by these tasks and to find sufficient time for desired scholarly activities, chairpersons must learn to delegate some of their tasks. Some chairpersons cannot bear the thought of sharing their responsibilities with colleagues; they fear that other persons are unable to do the job as well as they themselves. Delegation, however, is the only solution to the chairperson's problem of finding time to do all that he or she must do or wants to do. Chairpersons who recognize this fact are continually looking for the right person or committee to whom some department tasks can be entrusted.

Questions

List the ten most time-consuming activities that you personally performed during the past year in your capacity as department chairperson (refer to the chairperson's tasks and responsibilities listed at the beginning of chapter 3). Beside each activity that you list, indicate which of these tasks must be performed only by you; which could be delegated to a person in the department, such as a student assistant, secretary, or faculty member; and which could be delegated to a committee. If you think the task could be delegated, write the title of the person or the name of the committee to whom it could be delegated.

1. How many time-consuming tasks did you list?
   a. How many of these tasks could you delegate to a person or to a committee?

    b. How many could you not delegate to a person or a committee? Explain why not.

2. How many committees does your department have?

3. Which ones help you most with your administrative responsibilities?

4. Do you believe that your department has the right number of committees? Too many? Too few?

5. Which committees would you add, eliminate, or change? Give reasons.

References

ADAMS, HAZARD. "Humanitas and Academic Politics." *ADE Bulletin,* 90, 1988, pp. 18–26.

AMERICAN SOCIETY OF ASSOCIATION EXECUTIVES. *So You're on a Committee.* Washington, DC: ASAE, 1976.

ANDERSON, G. LESTER. "Organizational Diversity." in *New Directions for Institutional Research: Examining Departmental Management,* 10, edited by John C. Smart and James R. Montgomery. San Francisco: Jossey–Bass, 1976.

BOWKER, LEE H., and LYNCH, DAVID M. *Chairing a Small Department.* Paper presented at the National Conference for Department Chairs, Orlando, 1985 (ERIC Document Reproduction Service No. ED 256 222)

BROESAMLE, JOHN J. *Academic Turbulence and the Crisis of Professional Satisfaction.* 1984. (ERIC Document Reproduction Service No. ED 253 155)

CORSON, JOHN J. *The Governance of Colleges and Universities.* New York: McGraw–Hill, 1960.

CUMMINGS, L. L., and DUNHAM, RANDALL B. *Introduction to Organizational Behavior: Text and Reading.* Homewood, IL: Richard D. Irwin, 1980.

McLAUGHLIN, GERALD W.; MONTGOMERY, JAMES R.; and MALPASS, L. F. "An Investigation of Department Heads at a State University." Paper presented at the American Educational Research Association Conference, New Orleans, 1973.

RABINOWITZ, SAMUEL, and STUMPF, STEPHEN A. "Facets of Role Conflict, Role-Specific Performance, and Organizational Level Within the Academic Career." *Journal of Vocational Behavior,* 30, 1987, pp. 72–83.

RAU, WILLIAM, and BAKER, PAUL J. "The Organized Contradictions of Academe: Barriers Facing the Next Academic Revolution." *Teaching Sociology,* 17, 1989, pp. 161–183.

RYAN, DORIS W. "The Internal Organization of Academic Departments." *Journal of Higher Education,* June 1972, pp. 464–482.

SCHUSTER, JACK H. *Governing Tomorrow's Campus, Perspectives and Agendas.* Washington, DC: American Council on Education, 1989.

SMART, JOHN C., and ELTON, CHARLES F. "Administrative Roles of Department Chairmen." In *New Directions for Institutional Research: Examining Departmental Management,* 10, edited by John C. Smart and James R. Montgomery. San Francisco: Jossey-Bass, 1976.

requested under separate cover by the person responsible for monitoring affirmative action procedures. The data thus gathered may not be linked to the individuals' applications.

Closing Dates

The closing date contained in the advertisement is the date after which no further applications are accepted. The practices surrounding this general rule may vary from institution to institution. In some cases, all the information requested must be postmarked by the announced closing date. In other cases, only the letter of application needs to be received by the closing date, while the supporting materials may be accepted up to the time the committee meets to evaluate the applications. Either way, the committee must decide on the policy it will follow and should so inform the applicants. Some position vacancies are announced with an application deadline listed as "open." If a desirable candidate applies for the position, great care be taken until another advertisement is published. In any case, with a closing date, the closing date should not be sooner than one week after the publication of the advertisement.

Part *III*

FACULTY, STAFF, AND STUDENTS

Chapter 8. Full-Time Faculty

Chapter 9. Part-Time Faculty and Graduate Teaching Assistants

Chapter 10. Support Staff in the Department

Chapter 11. Students

Chapter 8

Full-Time Faculty

In colonial times, faculty at the few colleges then existing were largely populated with young men who served as tutors. They had no special qualifications as academics, and certainly did not hold advanced degrees. Their principal responsibilities lay as much in student discipline as in serious intellectual pursuits. It was not until the period of the late 1700s to the early 1800s that tutors gradually were expected to specialize in a subject. Indeed, "professors" were comparatively scarce until the early decades of the twentieth century—few Americans held the Ph.D., and scholarship was as often conducted outside the academy as inside it.

Several important developments have led to the organization and character of "faculties" as they now appear in the contemporary college and university. Most importantly, each of these developments has increased both the *independence* and the *autonomy* of faculty from the corporate university.

First, in the late 1800s, universities increasingly were able to appoint newly minted Ph.D. holders to their faculties. Having been trained to do research, they began to organize their work into disciplines, and to create within the university subunits called "departments." Departments encouraged specialization in a comparatively narrow area of intellectual inquiry. Faculty across the country began to identify with colleagues at other universities whose intellectual interests were similar. Their correspondence eventually was shared through the journals of learned societies, few of which existed prior to 1900. Publication of research increasingly became the standard by which faculty were judged.

Second, faculty organized politically to promote academic freedom—an idea imported from German universities where the earliest American Ph.D.s were obtained. In 1915 the American Association of University Professors was formed to advance the academic freedom interests of the profession. Protracted discussions with the American Council on Education resulted in wide adoption in 1940 of the joint statement *Academic Freedom and Tenure*. With that statement, protection of faculty independence through the institution of tenure became, if not universal, certainly the norm at institutions of stature. In subsequent years, "shared authority" for decisions on many key issues, including faculty appointments and promotions, became the model by which faculty and their employing institutions customarily operated.

The third significant element supporting faculty independence was access to external funding. As the federal government undertook massive support of research in the post–World War II era, faculty in many fields, but especially in the physical, biological, engineering, and medical sciences, built very substantial research centers and became managers of their own semiautonomous enterprises. Universities acquiesced because research funding meant the power to compete for still more illustrious faculty and doctoral students. It also meant enhanced prestige.

Each of these trends has reinforced the others, until faculty have established— at the major research universities—a powerful culture of autonomy. Individual faculty members operate very much as independent entrepreneurs, each negotiating his or her own terms with the university with such leverage as can be brought to bear.

The fundamental theme of relations with the full-time faculty, then, centers on autonomy. The corporate university needs to exercise some measure of control, and is expected by its various sponsors to do so. Faculty, on the other hand, have erected some powerful countermeasures, and expect to be left alone to pursue their independent scholarly (and sometimes personal) interests. The department often becomes a field of play on which skirmishes over autonomy are held and tests of wills are conducted.

The Ideal Professor

The ideal department would be populated by faculty all of whom are ideal professors. The ideal professor is a composite of all the best traits and talents a department chair might wish for. Some will be present in every department in some measure, but not everywhere and not always. Recognizing and capitalizing on the good qualities that are present is one of the principal arts a chair will bring to the job.

The ideal professor, of course, would be a superior teacher. His or her courses would be current and stimulating. He or she would organize and present material in ways that respected principles of human learning. Students would engage in class activities that bring broad principles to life. They would learn to think analytically, to ask serious questions, to reason, and to engage in penetrating critiques. The ideal professor would be popular and draw students from many departments, some of whom would even be recruited as new majors. Lectures, demonstrations, labs, and assignments would be thoroughly planned, exquisitely organized, and presented with flair and drama—without trivializing the subject. Assignments would be progressively calibrated to challenge and interest students, being neither "Mickey Mouse" nor beyond their abilities. Grades would be assigned in a completely objective and neutral fashion. Standards would be clear, and a respectable distribution of grades would be similar to the college's norms, neither too easy nor too strict. The ideal professor would be an understanding counselor, a wise mentor, an inspiring coach, and a stellar role model. He or she would be accessible to undergraduate students, patient and understanding with graduate students, and utterly humane in his or her work with all students.

The ideal professor would conduct research commensurate with the university's expectations. Faculty at a community college, for example, might conduct research that could be used in the classroom or laboratory. Faculty at a major university might be seeking more than one major grant at any given time, and would have a staff at work on various projects. Some would publish regularly if that were expected; others would occasionally report their work to civic clubs and local government agencies. The ideal professor would fit his or her research agenda to the expectations of the institution and would neither underachieve nor overreach.

The ideal professor would be an energetic, wise, and respected participant in the civic dialogues of both the community and the university. His or her talents would be brought to bear on the pressing business of the department with dedication and loyalty to the common good. He or she would be a clever and witty social companion, and would respect Aristotle's admonition to be moderate in all things.

The ideal professor is of course a dream in the minds of department chairs! In the normal world, faculty are as enormously varied a population as any other. From some of the world's great scientists and humanists to garden-variety pedants and ideologues, from heroically moral and altruistic human beings to petty tyrants and bullies, from profoundly creative minds to rigid and schizoid charlatans, college and university faculty bring their flawed humanity to the classroom—and into the intimate community that is the department.

Characteristics of Full-Time Faculty[1]

The average age of faculty in American colleges is about forty-seven years, with about 60 percent over age forty-five. Faculty in business and the health sciences tend to be younger; faculty in education and the humanities tend to be older. (Some fields will experience rather significant retirements in the mid- to late 1990s, but this will not affect all fields equally.) Affirmative action notwithstanding, faculty are still overwhelmingly white (90 percent), and predominantly male (73 percent). In all classes of institutions but the community college, faculty hold the Ph.D. or first professional degree. Over 90 percent of those at research universities hold these degrees; about two-thirds of those at comprehensive and liberal arts colleges do so; and about one-fifth of community college faculty have terminal degrees.

---

1. *Faculty in Higher Education Institutions, 1988: 1988 National Survey of Postsecondary Faculty* (Washington, DC: U.S. Department of Education, 1990).

Sixty percent of faculty at four-year institutions and about 36 percent of those at community colleges have tenure. Average salary for faculty at four-year institutions is just over $41,000, while at community colleges it is just over $32,000. Faculty at research universities average about $50,000 in salary. Some faculty also earn substantial outside income. On the average, faculty at private research universities, for example, earn over $22,000 from sources other than their basic salary. Increasing signs of inequity among fields is evident. Health sciences faculty average over $56,000 a year in salary; those in business average just over $39,000; and the average in fine arts is $33,500. Faculty report that they work fifty-one hours per week at public research universities, and forty hours per week at community colleges. Faculty at other types average between these two extremes.

Faculty average 56 percent of their time on instruction, 16 percent on research, and 13 percent on administration. Research assignments average 29 percent in research universities; teaching assignments average 71 percent in community colleges. Women typically report a heavier teaching assignment (61 percent vs. 54 percent for men). Men typically report a heavier research assignment (18 percent vs. 12 percent for women).

The wants and needs of faculty are very much like those of other "employees"—their professional station and prestige notwithstanding. Faculty need to be paid at a level commensurate with their value to the university and in the marketplace. They need status and security, and will work toward both as long as the effort required is reasonable. They need freedom from bureaucratic control and intellectual constraints, and have quick triggers if they feel they are being coerced. Perhaps above all, faculty need to feel that they can maximize satisfaction of these wants and needs, and that the institution will commensurately recognize and reward their effort. Recent surveys show that, on the whole college and university faculty are satisfied with their choice of profession, with their jobs, and with the conditions that go with both.

Faculty Cultures

Even though their wants and needs are much like those of other employees, faculty are not *like* other employees. They are an intellectual and cultural elite. They endured an extensive period of personal sacrifice to achieve advanced degrees, and have been through an intense socialization experience that has resulted in a set of very strong values—values shared by faculty across disciplines and generations alike. They are commonly said to form the core of a distinct faculty "culture."

Faculty culture is shaped by an overriding commitment to the advancement of knowledge. Though they feel called to pursue truth independent of conventional wisdom and free from institutional constraints, faculty nevertheless have a towering regard for method, logic, and process. They have learned to examine the means by which conclusions are reached as the principal test of truth. They are not impressed with persuasiveness, slickness, emotional appeals, or rhetorical gamesmanship. Faculty inhabit a world in which peer judgment is the single standard by which truth is certified, and they almost always opt for collegial modes of decision making as an extension of this ethic.

Characteristically, faculty will demand that all decisions be made in a collective mode—by committee, by consultation, by consensus, by democratic process. Unilateral, executive-style decision making violates a deeply held sense of how to behave in doing the department's business. Although they will insist on a collegial style of deciding, they will also, and simultaneously, struggle to impose high standards of logic, rationality, and consistency on policies, rules, and decisions. They will want to "see the data," to haggle over interpretation, and to construct elaborate and comprehensive rules to govern all foreseeable anomalies and problems. This is directly analogous to their interest and skill in the construction and elaboration of theory, but it is also exasperatingly pure for conditions that are changeable, chaotic, and lacking in hard information. Irony #1, then, is that faculty try to apply standards of pure rationality to a decision arena that is often better suited to pragmatism and compromise.

Irony #2 is that faculty who favor collegiality, consensus, and democracy also thrive on autonomy and competition. They prefer to work independently. They consider committee meetings and faculty meetings to be intrusions on their time, and openly resent the time they spend on such duties. They also thrive on competition, especially when competing brings grants, publications, and national recognition. There is a very thin veneer covering this intense competitive streak in many faculty. Collegial occasions sometimes result in ritualistic displays of competitive behavior, complete with verbal sparring and intellectual one-upmanship. Therefore, although faculty will insist that decisions be made collegially and rationally, they sometimes behave in ways that make it impossible to do so.

A third irony is built into the faculty culture. Faculty show a high regard for peer review processes, and the critical rites of passage in an academic career are governed by peer review. Faculty sit in judgment of each other's work whenever a promotion or tenure decision is made, and they would not have such decisions made in any other way. Nevertheless, promotion and tenure decisions, instead of being perceived as purely rational decisions, often are seen as carrying the taint of politics associated with departmental or disciplinary schisms. A tenure decision that carries such a taint—no matter that it is perceived rather than real—can divide faculty for years, and create conflict that carries over into many areas of department life.

Academic Freedom: Serious Business

Faculty culture is more than just an informal set of values. It is based on strong traditions codified by the American Association of University Professors

(AAUP), and enjoying some measure of protection under the first amendment to the federal Constitution.

The 1940 Statement on Academic Freedom and Tenure has been widely adopted by both professional associations and those representing virtually every kind of college or university in the U.S. The Statement essentially sets forth common understandings shared in the academic community about privileges and rights to speak freely and to be protected from undue institutional pressure via tenure. An extensive series of clarifying and supplementary statements have been issued since 1940, and provide a complex set of specified protections for faculty rights. The AAUP interprets these various standards, and occasionally is called on to investigate infractions thereof by colleges or universities. In a few cases each year the Association may consider sanctions, the worst of which amounts to public censure.

Academic freedom became a serious issue during the McCarthy era and during the student upheavals of the 1960s and 1970s. In the former case, faculty who were suspected of Communist sympathies attempted to shield themselves from firings (and worse) by relying on the protection of academic freedom and its enforcement by the AAUP. In the latter, faculty sometimes sided with students radicals and became embroiled in disputes that ultimately tested the first amendment's protections of academic freedom.

Without going into technical detail, it is sufficient to say that faculty independence and autonomy are considerably buttressed by the standards of academic freedom and tenure, and by certain protections afforded under the first amendment. The precise extent of protected freedoms has never been (and probably will never be) carved in stone. But it should be assumed that faculty have the right to express themselves freely in public; to exercise broad judgment about the quality of academic work; to determine the curriculum and standards for appointment, promotion, and tenure; and to pursue lines of research with only essential regulation to protect public safety and the rights of human (and animal) subjects.

Academic freedom, while affording broad protections, and while taken with a life-or-death seriousness by many faculty, is nevertheless *not* license to neglect one's duties, to disrupt orderly departmental work, to abuse students or research subjects, to be insubordinate, or to impose purely personal and/or political will on colleagues. Although it is often the most obstreperous and uncooperative faculty members who wave the flag of academic freedom, the department and its chair may legitimately assert their own rights to pursue their collective business without chaos and disorder.

Governance

Faculty, although they disavow any personal interest in conducting the university's corporate business, nevertheless will insist that governance be participatory, consultative, and democratic. By long-standing custom, and often also by statutes and rules governing university organization, all important academic matters (and others, too) are the province of senates, councils, commitees, and other consultative bodies.

On many campuses, faculty governance will become the province of a semiprofessional "elite." The same individuals will occupy committee chairs, senate offices, and other positions of nominal power, year after year. They are either elected by their peers or appointed by those who are elected. In any event, it is usually easy to identify faculty who are continuously associated with the academic power structure. They accumulate considerable expertise in procedure, and build information bases that are sources of considerable power. They also have strong networks of colleagues and associates that enable them to get things done as others cannot. It is not uncommon to find faculty politicians who remain officially anonymous while wielding considerable influence over much of the core business of the campus.

Senates and committees, not unlike their counterparts in civilian government, often are conservative, unreceptive to reform initiatives. They exercise enormous veto power and can exact a price for their approval of a proposal. When they function as forums for faculty views, senates (in particular) may become arenas for ideological attacks on almost any administration position. Seasoned veterans of faculty politics know and understand that such posturing and display help release tension, and actually may galvanize cooler heads into making responsible and progressive decisions.

Most departments operate with a standing committee structure with variations on at least three major committee types: an executive committee that works closely with the chair on overall department management; a curriculum committee; and a committee to handle the major faculty personnel decisions— appointment, promotion, tenure, and salary. A chair may find that these committees exercise considerable discretion over many policy matters and that they effectively make most of the key decisions controlling the department's future. A chair may be put in the position of serving as executive secretary to the department's standing committees, and the faculty may well expect the chair to play just such a limited role.

It pays to learn about the culture of faculty governance at an institution or in a particular department because either by rule or by entrenched custom faculty may have collective authority over a great deal of the agenda. Chairs may be more or less effective at such institutions, depending on how adept they are at working through the system.

Faculty Leaders

Faculty expect to be involved, to be consulted, and to exercise veto power (or the power to consent). Some departments are fortunate enough to have faculty who are willing to take some of the burdens of leadership. Recognizing faculty leaders and encouraging them to assume some of the responsibility for department affairs helps build an effective and legitimate decision-making structure.

There are different kinds of faculty leaders. Some may be characterized as "politicians," others as "statesmen." The difference is not trivial. Politicians are sophisticated, manipulative, self-interested, and persistent. They often care very much about mastering and controlling the levers and gears of policy making. In some cases they exercise very effective and entrenched control over a wide array of department affairs. Statesmen, on the other hand, engage in leadership out of a sense of *noblesse oblige*. They may be willing to take on particular responsibilities, and to work at leadership and governance, but only for a certain period of time. Their leadership tends to be substantive and disinterested (in the sense that they work toward the "best" or "optimal" solutions to problems—as distinguished from the politician's self-interestedness).

Departments that enjoy faculty leadership of either kind will generally realize a higher level of information, awareness, and understanding of problems and issues. The faculty not only will be involved, but will be unable to hide from participating in important decisions. Responsibility is more readily shared, and decisions may be more readily perceived as reasonable, legitimate, and correct. Departments with faculty leadership may also be quicker to change and adapt when conditions require, because more people are informed and can perceive the need for change.

Some departments may have faculty in leadership roles who provide *no* leadership. Occasionally, the decision-making structure itself is sclerotic. Through accident, historical precedent, and inattention the least productive and least effective faculty may hold titular chairs and committee memberships. But these are place holders, not leaders. No meaningful work is done, and the department fails to face both issues and the need for change.

Other departments may have very active systems of faculty governance dominated by faculty who exercise a negative and conservative kind of leadership. Sometimes retrograde and negative leadership can be traced to fear. Faculty, very much like other humans, may find their status and security threatened by more energetic and productive younger people. Or they may find themselves falling behind on the intellectual curve in their fields. Whatever the reason, they become mobilized and activated to preserve their interests and the status quo alike via political involvement in department affairs. It is one arena in which they can feel effective and competent, prevent unwelcomed change, and at the same time enjoy the legitimation of faculty cultural expectations. This kind of leadership is often associated with the "politician" pattern.

Statesmen, too, may exercise conservative leadership. Perhaps they are not so well informed, or are diffident about creating too much upset or conflict. But often they are the more able to play the roles of moderates and progressives in departmental leadership. Most likely to be drawn from the ranks of researchers, often they enjoy high status within the institution or nationally. With a broader frame of reference, a secure reputation, and no vested interest in the status quo, statesmen faculty can more freely consider alternatives and explore avenues for change.

All things considered, a department that enjoys some measure of faculty leadership is probably a more vital department than one in which faculty have become disengaged and disaffected. Even the more conservative and "political" kind of leadership will help to assure that faculty are to some extent involved and informed. Many departments will be more fortunate in having statesmanlike leadership on which to draw. The chair benefits from the exercise of faculty leadership when responsiblity for decisions is spread and when such leadership promotes readiness for change.

Faculty Careers

Although it is often assumed that faculty are preoccupied with research, the vast majority carry substantial teaching loads and, in fact, prefer teaching over research. Mythology aside, then, for most faculty, teaching is the essence of their careers. Comparatively little is known about the evolution and sociology of teaching careers. However, as greater and greater attention is paid to the quality of undergraduate education, more institutions are recognizing the importance of rewarding excellent teaching.

In the past, teaching has been a mostly solitary art, but increasingly, faculty who teach can call on technological aids, instructional design and support staff, evaluation and assessment specialists, and colleagues who willingly share ideas, tips, and experiences. As the culture of teaching becomes more open at some institutions (particularly the liberal arts and community colleges), and as faculty appreciate the strength they can draw on in working cooperatively with colleagues, teaching as not only an art but also a source of pride and accomplishment may be revived.

A second career path is pursued by faculty who devote the largest share of their energies to scholarship and research. Faculty with research interests dominate most departments at research universities. Many have developed large, well-funded, heavily staffed enterprises that require virtually full-time administrative attention. They may have extensive relations with federal government agencies, and with the corporate world as well. In some disciplines, research involves travel in the field—marine biology, geology, and anthropology are examples. In others, it may necessitate extended periods of such work as that with rare documents in remote countries. The term "scholarship" applies for the most part to different kinds of activities. For example, writing plays, novels, or poems would be considered scholarly activity in the humanities.

Faculty who pursue scholarly careers may be distracted from the mundane work of the department (teaching and governance) for extended periods. They are often consumed by grantsmanship and by the actual research activity itself. They "teach" in ways that are frequently not appreciated. Graduate and some outstanding undergraduate students may be apprenticed to faculty research teams. The experiences gained in these activities have strong educative value for the students and frequently result in dissertations, honors theses, and publications.

Research-oriented faculty bring both money and prestige to the institution, and are often valued highly for this. The respect they are accorded, however, is not always reciprocated. They often work in a tense and difficult relationship with their institutions. They often feel constrained by the demands on their time and energy, even when those demands are legitimate. They will negotiate for the lightest teaching loads the institution can tolerate; they will resist orderly commitments to office hours and advisement of undergraduates; they will complain about rampant bureaucracy in the administration of grants and contracts; and they will resent openly the university's insistence on receiving overhead, or indirect cost funds as a portion of each research grant. Their loyalties will often seem directed outside the university—to colleagues and organizations in the discipline, to funding agencies, and to various boards and committees on which they may be serving. They become progressively more specialized over the course of their careers, and seem less interested in the civilized discourse of the liberal arts, and therefore less intellectually accessible to their departmental colleagues and students. It has often been pointed out that research faculty do more to *fragment* the university than to *unify* it.

For all of that, research-oriented faculty bring vitality, excitement, challenge, and real intellectual adventure to a department. They are a main source of support for graduate students, and frequently provide the same for important departmental activities that would otherwise be unfunded by institutional sources. It is trite to speak of a "margin of excellence," but research faculty, with their grants and extensive travel, their writing, speaking, and publishing, often are in a position to add greatly to the depth and breadth of what a department is able to offer its students.

Some faculty in almost every department, however, eschew serious, competitive scholarship. They settle into a pedestrian teaching career. Their serious commitments are to the institution and its various rituals. They attend every commencement, perhaps serving as marshals or on committees to select speakers. They master the means and routines of institutional governance, becoming experts in parliamentary procedure or in certain arenas of policy. They entertain students and colleagues in their homes, take on heavy advisement loads, and aspire no further than to represent the traditional values of the institution. The common term for these loyalists is "locals" (as opposed to "cosmopolitans," the jet-setters of the academic world).

Locals make their careers in one institution, become fixtures in the community, frequently speak to civic groups, write columns in local newspapers, and may even be active in local politics. Although often treated with thinly disguised contempt by research faculty, they may in fact do more for the public image of the institution than anyone else. As keepers of traditions and as avuncular mentors to students, they carry on the legends and the spirit of the institution. They *are* the university to the undergraduates, and present the accessible, human face of the university to the community.

Perhaps the least visible and least tractable of faculty are those who pursue quasi-independent careers as entrepreneurs and consultants. Although sometimes confused with researchers, they do not really have substantial agendas in that arena. Often lonewolves, the consultant class of faculty spend sometimes unconscionable amounts of time away from the campus. They contract with business, government, publishers—any and all who will pay the going rates for their services. Sometimes, consultant–faculty even incorporate themselves and conduct a business (or two or three) out of their faculty offices or homes. With highly developed skills and a sense of the market, some even manage to double or triple their salaries with outside income.

This group of faculty often provides a legitimate service, and may be highly valued, particularly if their consulting work provides a financial return to the department or university. (Faculty in some departments organize themselves into an informal consulting firm, and for both altruistic and tax purposes run their income through the department to help provide student financial aid, a pool of travel funds, and small research grants for their own and colleagues' work.) Consulting may also serve as a training ground for graduate students, and may provide good data for research projects. Consulting with government agencies and business may also lay the foundation for future research contracts.

But consultant–faculty can also be abusive of their association with the university and its students. They may slough off their teaching assignments by using graduate students to substitute for them. They may fail to prepare, or to stay current. They are notoriously unavailable to students for counseling and advisement. Too, they decline committee assignments. Consultant faculty may be absent from the campus for extended periods of time—periods when they are nominally employed by the university and legitimately expected to perform on-campus assignments. They also openly use university facilities and resources to conduct their private business dealings, charging telephone calls to department budgets, demanding work on consulting reports by secretarial staff, using computing facilities to analyze data, and clearing substantial income without reimbursing the university. These abuses may, of course, in essence be borderline criminal activity, and so must be monitored and controlled.

A healthy department will encourage development of a mixture of talents and interests among its faculty. Each type of faculty member is valuable to a department, and ought to be put to work in a way that maximizes his or her contribution. Teachers carry the most important freight, the lifeblood of the department's funding: the student credit hour. Excellent teachers who draw students to the department should be encouraged, supported, and rewarded to a far greater extent than has been so in recent decades. Researchers establish a climate of intellectual adventure, external funding, and visibility and prestige that may be turned into new resources. Locals maintain the department and university, performing the daily routines and chores that at least some part of every human grouping must perform to keep functioning. They are honest citizens, and their work is too often underappreciated. Consultant–faculty are the renegades, the freewheelers. They may contribute in a positive way, but as often as not are the deviants who must be disciplined and reformed. When they are at their best, they provide much the same kind of benefit to the department that researchers do.

Balancing these roles and blending the talents and interests of a diverse faculty constitute the art of the chair. Knowing that a committee chaired by a consultant will probably meet only sporadically when its leader can afford to be on campus, for example, means knowing which kind of issue could safely be entrusted to that kind of committee. Assigning a local to a committee charged with a major innovation in curriculum would be placing a conservative in a spot that might require someone more adventuresome. Asking a researcher to take on a speaking engagement at a local civic club might result in a minor disaster, particularly if the researcher "goes technical" in his or her talk. The department chair who can recognize faculty types will be in a position to play on their strengths, and to engage their interests and energies in ways that help the department.

Maintaining a diversity among the types of faculty in a department is important. A department that strives to appoint only researchers is asking for trouble. Rivalries and competition will intensify; resentments over time spent on routine departmental chores and on teaching will bubble to the surface; and territorial problems with laboratories, facilities, graduate students, and faculties will erupt. On the other hand, departments composed entirely of locals will be widely viewed as stagnant, conservative, and in decline. Comfortable as a group of unambitious faculty may be with one another, they cannot compete for students and status if they are not represented in the broader world by their publications, by some stellar teaching, and by some visible signs of ambition. Success for a department depends on finding a mix and on giving people due reward for playing each of the valuable and legitimate roles that every department must see played if it is to get its work done.

Questions

1. How many full-time faculty members are in your department?

2. What characteristics do your faculty have in common with the characteristics of those described in the chapter?

3. Using this chapter's discussion of faculty culture as a basis for your response, describe the faculty in your department in terms of their attitudes, loyalties, culture, career objectives, and so on.

4. Has your faculty ever discussed at scheduled department meetings such subjects as academic freedom, ethics, roles of faculty, etc.? Would faculty in your department be willing to spend time on these subjects?

5. What is the dominant faculty culture at your institution? Where does your department fit into this culture?

6. Does your department have a written policy on academic freedom? Written faculty bylaws? Would you consider your department to be a group of independent entrepreneurs? How do these factors affect your leadership style?

7. As chair, what can you do to encourage development of "ideal professors" in your department?

8. Is there a faculty senate at your institution? List several ways the senate (or if there is no senate, use union or collective bargaining agreement) activities impact upon faculty members within your department.

9. Who are the faculty leaders in your department? How would you characterize their leadership style: Politicians? Statesmen? Is it compatible or conflicting with your personal leadership style?

10. List several activities currently underway in your department that contribute to the development of faculty careers. What possibilities can you think of to provide more opportunities for faculty development?

11. If you had an unlimited budget, what three faculty development activities would you incorporate in your department's faculty development program?

12. If you had *no new funds* available, what three activities could you incorporate into your department's faculty development program?

References

ADAMS, HAZARD. "Humanitas and Academic Politics." *ADE Bulletin, 90, 1988, pp. 18–26.*

BALDWIN, ROGER G. "Faculty Career Stages and Implications for Professional Development." In Jack H. Schuster (et al., *Enhancing Faculty Careers.* San Francisco: Jossey–Bass, 1990.

BOK, DEREK. *Beyond the Ivory Tower: Social Responsibility of the Modern University.* Cambridge: Harvard University Press, 1982.

BOWEN, HOWARD R., and SCHUSTER, JACK H. "Faculty Tasks and Talents." *The American Professors: A National Resource Imperiled.* New York: Oxford University Press, 1986.

BOWKER, LEE H., and LYNCH, DAVID M. *Chairing a Small Department.* Paper presented at the National Conference for Department Chairs, Orlando, 1985. (ERIC Document Reproduction Service No. ED 256 222)

CLARK, BURTON R. *The Academic Life. Small Worlds. Different Worlds.* A Carnegie Foundation Special Report. Princeton: The Carnegie Foundation, 1987.

———. "The Imperatives of Academic Work." *The Academic Life.* Princeton: The Carnegie Foundation, 1987.

CORSON, JOHN J. *The Governance of Colleges and Universities.* New York: McGraw–Hill, 1960.

DILL, DAVID D. "The Management of Academic Culture: Notes on the Management of Meaning and Social Integration." *Higher Education, 11,* May 1982.

DOUGLAS, JOEL M. (Ed.) *Salary and Compensation Methodology in Academic Collective Bargaining.* New York: National Center for the Study of Collective Bargaining in Higher Education and the Professions, 1983. (ERIC Document Reproduction Service No. ED 230 140)

———. "Faculty in Higher Education Institutions, 1988: 1988 National Survey of Postsecondary Faculty." Washington, DC: U.S. Department of Education, 1990.

FENCHEL, ALLAN H. *The Academic Corporation: Justice, Freedom, and the University.* New York: Black Rose Books, 1987.

GMELCH, WALTER H. "Dimensions of Stress Among University Faculty: Factor-analytic Results from a National Study." *Research in Higher Education,* 24, 1986, pp. 266–286.

KEYNES, MILTON. *Academic Freedom and Responsibility. Society for Research into Higher Education.* Philadelphia: Open University Press, 1988.

LESLIE, DAVID W. "NLRB Rulings on the Department Chairmanship." *Educational Record,* 53, 1972, pp. 313–320.

———. "The Status of the Department Chairmanship in University Organization." *AAUP Bulletin,* 59, 1973, pp. 419–426.

LEWIS, LIONEL S. "Publish or Perish: Reality or Myth." *Scaling the Ivory Tower, Merit and Its Limits in Academic Careers.* Baltimore: Johns Hopkins Press, 1975.

MANDEL, RICHARD D. "A Little Bit of History." *The Professor Game.* Garden City: Doubleday, 1977.

McCARTY, DONALD J., and REYES, PEDRO. "Organizational Models of Governance: Academic Deans' Decision-making Styles." *Journal of Teacher Education,* 38, 1987, pp. 2–8.

McCONNELL, T. R., and MORTIMER, KENNETH P. *The Faculty in University Governance.* Berkeley: Center for Research and Development in Higher Education, University of California, 1971.

McDOWELL, EARL E., and MROZLA, BRIDGET A. *An Explanatory Study of the Academic Résumé and Employment Interview Practices.* Paper presented at the Annual Meeting of the Speech Communication Association, Boston, 1987. (ERIC Document Reproduction Service No. ED 290 187)

NEAR, JANET P., and SORCINELLI, MARY DEANE. "Work and Life Away from Work: Predictors of Faculty Satisfaction." *Research in Higher Education,* 25, 1986, pp. 377–394.

O'TOOLE, JAMES; VAN ALSTYNE, WILLIAM; and CHAIT, RICHARD. "A Conscientious Objection." *Three Views of Tenure.* New Rochelle, NY: Change Magazine Press, 1979.

PAGE, JANE A., and PAGE, FRED M. *Collegiate Instruction: Some Differences Among Faculty Members Based on Rank, Years of Experience, and School Affiliation.* Paper presented at the Annual Meeting of the Mid-South Educational Research Association, Mobile, AL, 1987. (ERIC Document Reproduction Service No. ED 289 445)

REYES, PEDRO, and SMITH, GREGORY. *Faculty and Academic Staff Participation in Academic Governance: The Social Contract Model.* ASHE 1987 Annual Meeting Paper, San Diego, 1987. (ERIC Document Reproduction Service No. ED 281 446)

REYES, PEDRO, and TWOMBLY, SUSAN B. "Perceptions of Contemporary Governance in Community Colleges: An Empirical Study." *Community College Review,* 14, 1987, pp. 4–12.

RUSSELL, SUSAN H. *Faculty in Higher Education Institutions, 1988, Contractor Report.* Washington, D.C.: National Center for Higher Education Statistics, 1990. (ERIC Document Reproduction Service No. ED 321 628)

SEAGREN, ALAN T. *Perception of Chairpersons and Faculty Concerning Roles, Descriptors, and Activities Considered Important for Faculty Development and Departmental Vitality.* 1986. (ERIC Document Reproduction Service No. ED 276 387)

SORCINELLI, MARY DEANE, and NEAR, JANET P. "Relations Between Work and Life Away from Work Among University Faculty." *Journal of Higher Education,* 60, 1989, pp. 59–81.

VAN DOREN, MARK. "The Educated Person." *Liberal Education.* New York: Holt, 1943.

Chapter 9

Part-Time Faculty and Graduate Teaching Assistants

Many colleges and universities employ part-time faculty and graduate teaching assistants to provide instruction in courses for undergraduate students, particularly at the freshman and sophomore levels. They are less expensive to hire than full-time faculty, and at those institutions where enrollments are increasing but allocated budgets are not, administrators are tempted to utilize part-time instructors and graduate teaching assistants in lieu of some full-time faculty. Discussions and debates continue as to whether the overall quality of instruction provided by part-time faculty and graduate teaching assistants compares favorably with that provided by full-time faculty, and whether savings in costs realized by using part-timers is derived at the expense of quality instruction. This chapter deals with the advantages and disadvantages to institutions who employ part-time instructors and graduate teaching assistants. It also addresses the problems involved for department chairs in determining what roles and functions should be expected of part-time instructors in other departmental activities such as governance, student advising and to what extent they should be reimbursed for their involvement in these other activities.

Part-Time Faculty

Part-time faculty are not a new phenomenon in higher education, but their numbers are now quite large. In the fall of 1980, for example, Florida's twenty-eight community colleges employed almost 9,000 part-time faculty as compared to half that number of full-time faculty. The growth of part-timers in American community colleges began in the 1960s with an 80 percent increase during the

1970s. This contrasted dramatically with only an 11 percent gain in full-time faculty. Even the four-year institutions in this period had a 38 percent increase in part-time faculty, with only a 9 percent increase in full-time staff. In general, full-time faculty continue to outnumber part-time persons because four-year institutions employ mostly full-time staff and do not count graduate teaching assistants as part-timers. Clearly, part-time instructors are here in large and probably increasing numbers. For purposes of the following discussion, the terms part-time faculty and instructors are used interchangeably.

Some institutions find that part-time faculty members provide flexibility, since they can be hired as needed to meet changing student course and program enrollments and because their salaries are generally lower than those of their full-time counterparts. Also they may bring vitality and new ideas to programs suffering from static faculties and declining enrollments. Part-time faculty members are often used to staff new and experimental programs to test the student market before an institution makes any firm commitments. Part-timers have proven so useful that some institutions are converting certain of their full-time positions into a greater number of part-time positions.

A 1980 study of part-time faculty by a select committee of Florida community college presidents identified the following eight key advantages in the employment of this group:

1. The cost is less.
2. The commitments of the college are fewer.
3. They generally have a positive attitude.
4. They are usually up-to-date in their fields.
5. They are an excellent source of recruitment for full-time positions when openings occur.
6. They may understand the part-time students and their problems better than their full-time counterparts.
7. They are rarely unionized.
8. They provide a vital link with the local community from which they are drawn.

There are also problems associated with employing part-time faculty. Those most often mentioned include:

1. Part-time faculty members often feel exploited with respect to salary.
2. There is a lack of program continuity when a large share of the faculty is part-time.
3. They are often not available for student advising or counseling during regular office hours or before class which in some cases also imposes heavier than normal counseling responsibilities on full-time faculty.

4. They are suspected of devoting insufficient time and effort to their course preparations.

5. They do not contribute to the out-of-class tasks of the faculty, such as committee work, curriculum development, et cetera.

6. Full-time faculty members, when outnumbered by the part-time group, often fear that departmental program governance could be taken over by the part-timers.

7. The cleavages and frictions between full and part-time faculty members may be more disruptive to the program than the existence of a completely full-time though obsolescent faculty.

The successful utilization of part-time faculty members requires a substantial understanding of their characteristics and special needs. A large survey of part-time instructors undertaken by the Tuckmans[1] in 1980 reveals some interesting facts about the makeup of this group. Following is a slightly modified and expanded version of the classification and description of the seven categories of part-timers contained in the Tuckman report.

1. *Full-mooners* are persons who, in addition to their part-time jobs, hold full-time positions elsewhere of at least thirty-five hours per week for eighteen weeks of the year. This group, comprising 27.6 percent of the sample, includes many full-time faculty members at nearby universities and community colleges, as well as local business and professional persons. A good example of a full-mooner is a certified public accountant who is recruited to teach introductory accounting courses.

2. *Students* are persons employed in departments other than those in which they are seeking degrees. These part-timers, 21.2 percent of the sample, are often graduate students from near or distant colleges or universities. Some are still doing course work while others are writing their dissertations. It should be noted that graduate teaching assistants within their own departments are usually not reported as part-time instructors by the universities for whom they work. If they were counted, the numbers reported would be quite different.

3. *Hopeful full-timers* are persons holding part-time positions because they are unable to find full-time employment and comprise 16.6 percent of the sample. These fully qualified persons are becoming a national concern because they represent a generation of scholars who are unemployed due to the lack of academic jobs. They hope that their part-time positions will develop into full-time employment.

4. *Part-mooners* are persons who simultaneously hold two or more part-time jobs of less than thirty-five hours per week for more than one week. They comprise 13.6 percent of the sample and like the hopeful full-timers often seek full-time employment. Members of groups 3 and 4 are the so-called itinerant or gypsy scholars of the 1980s.

---

1. Howard P. Tuckman and Barbara H. Tuckman, "Who Are the Part-timers and What Are Colleges Doing for Them?" In *Current Issues in Higher Education,* 4, 1981, pp. 4 and 5.

5. *Homeworkers* are persons who do not want full-time employment because they are taking care of a relative or child at home and comprise 6.4 percent of the sample. These individuals are often unemployed spouses who possess a variety of graduate credentials and experiences. Along with the full-mooners they provide a stable cadre of part-time instructors.

6. *Semiretired* are persons who seek activities to fill time made available by retirement and make up only 2.8 percent of the sample. These individuals who often possess considerable talent and ability may also contribute to the stable core of part-timers. They may need the extra income to compensate for inflation and rising taxes which have reduced their fixed retirement income. In rural areas, the homeworkers and semiretired can be the main sources of part-timers.

7. *Part-unknowners* comprise the remaining 11.8 percent of the sample. They give a variety of reasons for becoming part-time which do not fall into any of the other categories.

Traditionally, part-time faculty members have been used to meet unexpected needs for additional instructional staff when full-time instructors become ill, are given sabbaticals, or receive unexpected leaves of absence. They have been the typical source for teaching courses offered at night, weekends, and in the summer, and for courses taught offcampus through extension and continuing education programs. Part-time faculty most often teach one or more courses with no other responsibilities assigned. They are usually paid less than the salary rate of full-time faculty members because they have not been required to advise students, participate in the governance system, and so on. Most writers point out that to require such participation will lead to increased costs.

The enrollment of the typical younger student is decreasing in many colleges and universities. These diminished numbers are being partially compensated for by increased enrollments of older students in evening, weekend, and off-campus programs. Since these programs are often taught by part-time instructors, it is clearly in an institution's best interests to insure that part-time faculty members are of a quality sufficient to meet the instructional goals of the institution. If part-time instructors are either unhappy with their conditions of employment or inadequately skilled to do a satisfactory job of teaching, the resulting student dissatisfaction could affect enrollments. At the same time, questions about the rights and privileges of part-time faculty have been raised in collective bargaining negotiations and in lawsuits in state and federal courts. Consequently, some institutions have begun to think seriously about establishing separate personnel policies for part-time faculty members.

Institutions that have concerns about the present or future use of part-time faculty need to develop clear policies about the expected duties and responsibilities of these individuals. Does the department wish part-time faculty members to be involved in departmental affairs beyond the single task of teaching courses? Should they participate in curriculum development, departmental governance, committee work, and student advisement? What provisions will be made to ensure that part-time faculty are providing quality instruction to their students?

Few part-time instructors are willing to assume additional responsibilities without expecting additional compensation. Moreover, the involvement of part-timers in issues of governance and curriculum could alter the direction and character of the department. It therefore behooves a department to consider carefully the extent to which it wishes to employ part-time faculty for the many different types of services which they may be capable of providing. These questions are not intended to either encourage or discourage the use of part-time faculty for noninstructional tasks but rather to illuminate the implications and possible concerns that may arise when extensive use is made of part-timers. Whatever is decided and agreed upon should be included in a written policy statement which clarifies what the institution expects of them and what they can expect from the institution in terms of length of appointment, remuneration, and assigned duties. It is also important that the part-timer not be given any false expectations concerning the probability of future employment, either part- or full-time. Some of the topics and issues which have arisen in selecting and utilizing part-time faculty are discussed in the following paragraphs.

RECRUITMENT AND SELECTION. Part-timers currently available to an institution are often able to recommend acquaintances who may be qualified and interested in a particular part-time teaching assignment. Department chairpersons can telephone or write their counterparts in nearby institutions. Community college division chairpersons can make contacts at the better high schools in order to identify the most experienced teacher, including outstanding teachers. Affirmative action officers and professional women's network coordinators can also be contacted. If need be, a classified advertisement can be placed in nearby city and college newspapers.

To aid in selection of candidates, a job description could be written listing, for example, all of the desired qualifications and expected duties, as well as the pay range and whatever benefits might be available. If the posiiton is not tenure earning or not renewable, the written description should so indicate. If feasible, the chairperson should involve full-time faculty in the selection decision. In an emergency, the chairperson may not have the opportunity to check credentials until after a selection decision is made, but such emergency hiring without checking credentials should be kept at an absolute minimum. Since at present there exists a large supply of unemployed persons with graduate degrees, there is no reason why a part-time person should not be as qualified as a full-time instructor in the same department.

SALARY. There are several bases for determining the salary to be paid a part-timer. The most common is to pay a flat rate for a course. Sometimes a part-timer is paid at the same rate that a new full-timer receives for teaching the same course. Occasionally, hourly rates are used. At some institutions the rate of pay will depend on the size of the class, with more pay for enrollments above a minimum number, such as thirty-five. The purpose is to provide a modest incentive to the instructor to teach the "oversize" class. Another factor often considered in salary determination is the formal educational and professional experience of a part-timer. One with more formal educational or recognized professional experience, such as a certified public accountant, might command more than the minimum amount per course.

Perhaps the most important factor to be considered here is the relation between the typical amount per course paid to part-timers and the overload payments available to regular faculty. Whereas the difference between computed hourly rates for part- and full-time faculty members can be justified on the basis of responsibilities that full-time faculty have in addition to teaching, the argument does not hold for differences between the pay which part-timers receive and the overload pay which a full-time faculty member receives for teaching the same course. At institutions where financial difficulties preclude annual salary increases, an offer of overload pay at the part-timers' rate may be used as an economic incentive to regular faculty. Incidentally, once these pay differences are determined, it could be the institution's policy that full-timers be given the option of overload pay before the part-timers are sought and hired. A byproduct of such a policy could be a rise in faculty morale.

A number of other pay issues raise concerns about basic fairness to part-timers. Part-timers new to an institution may be required to attend orientation sessions. Whether they should be remunerated for this attendance depends upon local policy, but if the services of a particular person are valued, a modest payment can be a good incentive. Other issues focus on the matter of compensation for time spent in course preparation. What if a course does not fill with the minimum number of students? If the institutional policy is firm that the course should be terminated after the first meeting when a minimum is not met, then it seems only fair to compensate the part-timer for some course preparation effort and for the time spent meeting the first class. A policy of this kind shifts the responsibility for marketing and forecasting anticipated revenues to the administration and away from the part-timer. Of course, if a college or university does not want to guarantee a minimum compensation in the event that the class is canceled for lack of enough students, then the minimum enrollment for earning compensation must be stated forthrightly in the employment offer and contract which the part-timer receives.

FRINGE BENEFITS.   The area of fringe benefits is important for the part-time faculty because about 70 percent of them are not employed elsewhere in places where they qualify for such benefits. A 1980 study published by the American Association of University Professors indicates that as many as 60 percent of the part-time faculty with Ph.D.s who work more than half- but not full-time receive a wide variety of fringe benefits. Fewer of those Ph.D.s working less than half-time receive the same benefits. Health insurance, often perceived as the most important benefit, is extended to about 85 percent of part-timers who work more than half-time, and to about 60 percent of those employed for less than half-time. Health insurance as part of the total compensation package is also the benefit for which part-timers have the greatest need because so few of them have another job. Many group insurance carriers are willing to discuss special programs for part-timers.

EXPECTATIONS.   As mentioned earlier, the formal expectations of the part-timer's duties should be stated clearly in a written document. A genuine meeting of the minds is desirable before a formal contact is drafted. One of the ways to begin the effort of clearly stating expectations is to include them in a formal memorandum to the part-timer who is being offered employment. The prospective part-timer then can respond by asking for desired clarifications or modifications. This somewhat formal procedure can help ensure clear and complete communications before the new term is at hand.

The items to be included in the memorandum should cover the title of the course and related details, the position title, pay and benefits offered, the course cancellation policy, the extent of duties beyond teaching the course and whether pay will be provided for other than nonteaching duties. In addition, the memorandum should include information about required texts or tests, and the rights and restrictions relating to tenure, renewal, and the consideration for full-time employment. It is important that office hours, if any, be stated explicitly, and that office space be assigned for this activity. Details about other rules and regulations that may apply to the part-timer in addition to those appearing in the memorandum and contract should be stated. If a part-time person is covered under a collective bargaining agreement, this should be explained. The prospective part-timer should be invited to examine the college catalog, bargaining contract, faculty constitution, and so on.

VESTED INTERESTS.   One of the more difficult issues concerning the employment of part-time faculty members is whether they may acquire a vested or property interest in their part-time jobs. This is, of course, a legal question, but at the present time it is without clear definition. Some community college administrators are sufficiently concerned that they do not permit the same person to be employed part-time for more than two years continuously. This very cautious and conservative attitude could prevent retention of very able part-time instructors. The other end of the spectrum is to treat part-timers the same as full-time faculty, but on a prorated basis. To date hardly any institutions follow the latter pattern. Currently a number of statements have been drafted for inclusion in contracts which explain the limits of an institution's responsibilities to a part-timer. For example, some contracts clearly state that successful teaching does not guarantee that the part-timer will necessarily be considered again for another part-time job. Similarly, if it is institutional policy that part-timers are ineligible for tenure, this is stated explicitly in the contract. In some states a part-time person who works more than half-time for several years and is paid at a prorated full-time faculty salary may qualify for tenure.

These issues also have impact on policy decisions providing for increases in compensation or addition in benefits after a part-timer has worked successfully two or three years. The concern here is that these rewards may be perceived as resulting from seniority rights, and imply an entitlement to continuing employment in the part-time position. If these rewards were based only on the results of systematic evaluations and specific evidence of meritorious performance, perhaps a disclaimer could be inserted stating that length of time in continuous service on a part-time job is not sufficient to qualify a part-timer for those rewards.

In sum, the employment contract should state both what is intended and not intended when a person is hired as a part-timer. Furthermore, part-timers who work more than 50 percent on a regular basis may acquire a vested interest in their jobs that may require the institution to treat them like full-time faculty. Obviously, legal counsel should be sought before a firm policy is set. Clearly, a department chairperson would benefit from advance planning if part-timers are to be used.

MANAGEMENT OF PART-TIME FACULTY. It is very difficult to supervise part-time faculty members in the same ways as full-time faculty members. Institutions may have to provide "night" deans, secretaries, and support personnel to help part-timers perform their assigned responsibilities effectively. The remoteness of part-timers from mainstream activities makes it necessary that they too be evaluated, counseled about their performance during the term, and given suggestions for improvement. These activities allow the institution to exercise a degree of quality control over their part-time teachers. Below are some frequently made recommendations for improving the performance and morale of part-timers.

SUPPORT SERVICES. Part-timers who work in the week day during regular hours can usually obtain support services with proper advance notice to typists, librarians, media specialists, etcetera. But those who work in the evenings and on weekends have greater difficulty. One solution is to have some secretaries and librarians work flexible hours, and provide the part-time faculty and their students with the adjusted schedules. Most clerical support services need to be available only through the first half hour or hour after a class begins in the evening. Arrangements for support services on weekends require a specific cost-benefit or feasibility analysis to ensure that the institution does not commit unavailable resources.

INSTITUTIONAL INFORMATION FOR PART-TIMERS. One of the best ways to confront the many concerns which can divide full- and part-time faculty is to involve a committee of full-time faculty, working with department heads and deans in drafting a handbook of policy information for part-timers. Policies for part-timers should be based on principles of equity. Where full- and part-timers face similar tasks and are equipped with similar qualifications, they should be governed by the same policies; where full- and part-timers have different tasks and responsibilities they should be treated differently.

The institution's community can be informed about the part-time faculty in a variety of ways. The part-timers can be listed in the annual catalog, or a separate publication containing information about full-and part-time faculty could be distributed. Frequently, a yearbook format is used, with photographs and biographical sketches including degrees earned and special expertise. If the full- and part-timers are listed together under their department, division, or discipline, then both day and night students would be informed about their entire faculty.

PERFORMANCE EVALUATION AND PROFESSIONAL DEVELOPMENT.   Given the direction of the courts in expanding the due process rights of part-time faculty, it would be wise for department heads and deans to arrange for a performance evaluation of each part-timer at least once a year. Evaluation is also desirable as a quality assurance policy, and should be implemented whenever a significant number of part-time persons is employed in an academic year. Such a number might be five persons or 50 percent of the number of full-time faculty, whichever is larger.

Part-time faculty may not resist performance evaluation as much as full-time faculty. The evaluation of part-timers will usually be based primarily on their teaching effectiveness, and the same techniques used for evaluating teaching performance of full-time faculty may apply unless they are specifically assigned and compensated for additional duties. Many, if not most, part-timers have had no teaching experience, nor have they been instructed in testing and measurement procedures. The results of performance evaluation can be used to determine which areas of subject matter or technique need improvement. Then, opportunities should be provided so that the part-timers who desire to be reemployed can learn ways to improve their teaching. Some opportunities might include seminars on instructional methods and grading procedures.

DEALING WITH PART-TIMERS' CONCERNS.   Part-timers are often isolated from ongoing discussions and explanations of institutional policies and procedures, especially when they teach nights or on weekends. Therefore, they stand a good chance of misperceiving, misunderstanding, or simply not being aware of new or changed directives and requirements about which other faculty members have been informed. Some of these changes may appear arbitrary or capricious to an uninformed part-timer. A way to avoid conflict may be the periodic scheduling, perhaps once a semester, of a conference to explain institutional policy and procedure. Part-timers have expressed concerns about a number of issues in which they feel the need for more involvement, information, or equitable treatment. Following is a list of some of these concerns:

1. The right to participate in selecting textbooks, making up exams, and structuring courses
2. Criteria for evaluation of performance
3. Criteria for continued employment in the part-time position
4. Information on who represents their interests in the department, college, or university when working conditions are being discussed.

5. Information about their rights to negotiate, grieve about, or appeal salary offerings, especially when their salaries for subsequent terms reflect no increase for inflation or no relationship to the increments of full-time faculty

6. Information on how to receive consideration when full-time openings occur

7. Assurances that exercise of rights to academic freedom will not result in nonrenewal.

Whether part-timers are entitled to use the grievance procedures which may have been established for full-time faculty depends on institutional policy. Providing access to existing grievance procedures may provide the isolated part-timers with confidence in their institution, and assurance that a reliable means is available for processing their concerns.

ENHANCING PRESTIGE. It is useful to enhance the prestige of part-time faculty. This may be accomplished in many ways, including holding an official orientation especially for them, displaying pictures of both full- and part-time faculty in the same brochures and welcoming their attendance at fall and spring faculty meetings. Also, they might be sent personal invitations to attend receptions or social affairs hosted by the president, dean, or board of trustees. A chairperson can do much good by shepherding and introducing part-time faculty at annual or term presidential receptions. If the chairperson can recruit full-time faculty to assist in the shepherding and introducing, then so much the better. The good feelings and benefits from social activities often provide the beginning of trust which, when honored on all sides, provides the absolutely best means by which to solve problems and build a viable institution.

Graduate Teaching Assistants

Universities that have graduate degree programs employ many of their graduate students to assist in the instruction of undergraduate students. Teaching assistants with master's degrees who are working towards a doctorate often are assigned as primary instructors for classes, studios, or laboratories and are given responsibility for most of the following activities: prepare tests, grade examinations, hold office hours, lecture, develop and write course syllabi, lead discussions, provide advice and counsel to undergraduate students. They receive minimum supervision from faculty members. In major research universities, about half of all graduate teaching assistants are in this category and between 30 and 50 percent of all freshmen and sophomore courses are taught by them. Graduate teaching assistants who are baccalaureates working towards the masters degree generally do not lecture, lead discussions, or prepare syllabi. They may help with grading papers and tests, but they work under the supervision of a faculty member. Although the number of junior- and senior-level courses taught by graduate teaching assistants is relatively small, in the past few years the number has been increasing.

As graduate teaching assistants, graduate students acquire some college-level teaching experience and receive stipends which help pay for part of their educational expenses. Unfortunately, the stipends are usually low for the amount and kind of work they represent. Often the long hours required to carry out the duties of the graduate teaching assistantship result in an unreasonable extension of time to complete the degree. At some universities, the low stipends and the exploitative nature of their assignments have led the graduate teaching assistants to organize unions which negotiate on their behalf with university administrators.

In spite of the fact that graduate teaching assistants teach large numbers of undergraduate courses, most graduate teaching assistants start out ill-prepared for the task. Most universities don't require or even encourage graduate students to take teaching-methods courses or supervised teaching.

The best way to ensure improved teaching from graduate teaching assistants and future professors is to require them to take a course in how to teach, how to design courses, and how to mount effective presentations.

Much depends on the number of undergraduate classes offered by the department that are taught by the graduate teaching assistants. Departments like English and mathematics, with large numbers of undergraduate service courses, will usually have someone in charge of orienting graduate teaching assistants to their teaching responsibilities. Departments with fewer numbers of undergraduate courses and fewer graduate teaching assistants will probably have to depend on centrally administered programs, in which case the chairperson should make his or her dean and/or provost aware of the need for a central program. A system for training teaching assistants which has proven to be effective at some universities is one that includes a generic program administered centrally, and a departmental program which deals with the unique aspects of teaching a specific discipline.

Questions

1. Does your department utilize the services of part-time faculty? If so, how many?

2. Does your department have procedures for evaluating part-time faculty? How do the procedures compare to those used for full-time faculty?

3. Are part-time faculty invited or expected to attend department meetings? Are they permitted to vote? If so, in what areas?

4. Are they provided with adequate orientation to the ways of the department? How are they oriented?

5. Does your institution and/or department have a written set of policies regarding part-timers? When was it last revised? Is there an institutional or departmental committee to address these issues?

6. Does your department assign primary responsibility for teaching any classes to graduate teaching assistants? If so, what training or orientation is provided by the institution and/or department to graduate teaching assistants in the area of teaching? Is it adequate?

References

ABBOTT, ROBERT D. "Review of Research on TA Training." In *New Directions for Teaching and Learning: Teaching Assistant Training in the 1990s,* Fall 1989.

ALLEN, R. R., and RUETER, THEODORE. *Teaching Assistant Strategies: An Introduction to College Teaching.* Dubuque: Kendall/Hunt, 1990.

BOWKER, LEE H., and LYNCH, DAVID M. *Chairing a Small Department.* Paper presented at the National Conference for Department Chairs, Orlando, 1985. (ERIC Document Reproduction Service No. ED 256 222)

BUERKEL-ROTHFUSS, NANCY L., and GRAY, PAMELA. *Graduate Teaching Assistant (GTA) Training: The View from the Top,* 1989. (ERIC Document Reproduction Service No. ED 318 351)

BURKE, DELORES L. "The Academic Marketplace in the 1980s: Appointment and Termination of Assistant Professors." *Review of Higher Education,* 10, 1987, pp. 199–214.

COHEN, ARTHUR M., and BRAWER, FLORENCE B. *The American Community College.* 2nd ed. San Francisco: Jossey–Bass, 1988.

COMEAUX, PATRICIA, and AAITKEN, JOAN E. *Assuring Quality and Standard Evaluation in the Basic Course: Training and Supervising Graduate Students,* 1989. (ERIC Document Reproduction Service No. ED 315 801)

FRYER, THOMAS W., JR. "Designing New Personnel Policies: The Permanent Part-Time Faculty Member." *College and University Personnel Association,* Spring 1977, pp. 14–21.

GREENLAW, PAUL S., and BIGGS, WILLIAM D. *Modern Personnel Management.* New York: Holt, 1980.

LOUIS, KAREN S. (et al.) *University Policies and Ethical Issues in Graduate Research and Education.* Results of a Survey of Graduate School Deans. ASHE 1988 Annual Meeting Paper, 1988. (ERIC Document Reproduction Service No. ED 303 100)

McDOWELL, EARL E., and MROZLA, BRIDGET A. *An Explanatory Study of the Academic Resume and Employment Interview Practices.* Paper presented at the Annual Meeting of the Speech Communication Association, Boston, 1987. (ERIC Document Reproduction Service No. ED 290 187)

MOHANTY, DANELL Q. "Faculty Salary Analyses by Region, Rank, and Discipline from 1977–78 to 1983–84." *Research in Higher Education,* 24, 1985, pp. 304–317.

RIGGS, MATT. "Using Discriminant Analysis to Predict Faculty Rank." *Research in Higher Education,* 25, 1986, pp. 365–376.

RODDY, MARY ELLEN. *Qualifications and Productivity of Nontenure-track Faculty.* Paper presented at the Annual Meeting of the American Educational Research Association, Washington, DC, 1987. (ERIC Document Reproduction Service No. ED 284 488)

SEAGREN, ALAN T. *Perception of Chairpersons and Faculty Concerning Roles, Descriptors, and Activities Considered Important for Faculty Development and Departmental Vitality.* 1986. (ERIC Document Reproduction Service No. ED 276 387)

STANLEY, BARBARA. *Teaching Research Ethics: Methods and Practice.* Paper presented at the Annual Meeting of the APA, Toronto, 1984. (ERIC Document Reproduction Service No. ED 251 019)

TRANK, DOUGLAS M., and SHEPARD, GREGORY A. *Textbook Selection Criteria for a Multisection Basic Course Taught Exclusively by Graduate Teaching Assistants.* 1987. (ERIC Document Reproduction Service No. ED 287 183)

TUCKMAN, HOWARD P., and BARBARA H. "Who are the Part-timers and What are Colleges Doing for Them?" *Current Issues in Higher Education, 4,* 1981.

TUCKMAN, HOWARD P., and VOGLER, WILLIAM D. "The Part in Part-Time Wages." *AAUP Bulletin,* May 1978, pp. 70–77.

WRIGHT, DELIVEE L. "TA Training Resources." In *New Directions for Teaching and Learning: Teaching Assistant Training in the 1990s.* Fall 1989.

Chapter 10

Support Staff
in the Department

Departments are complicated organizations, and depend heavily on many different people to accomplish their work. Although the chair often thinks of faculty as the most important people in the department, others may play equally important but less visible roles. A large department may have a number of key staff people who do important jobs. In fact, the staff are often the ones who represent the department to students and the public. In some departments, staff with considerable seniority may effectively run things, and constitute the department's de facto management. Chairs come and go, faculty come and go, but some staff assistants stay on for decades.

It is important, therefore, that department chairs observe and assess their staff situations on a continual basis. In this chapter, some of the issues that affect staff and their work are discussed. Staff are viewed as essential to a department's effectiveness, but only insofar as the chair elects to manage and supervise their work in ways that assure accomplishment of important goals and objectives.

Staff Characteristics

The system used in staffing departments of state-supported colleges and universities is in many ways similar to that used in staffing branches of the state civil service. Staff in all but the very highest positions (persons with college degrees and some management training or experience) will be drawn from the local labor market, and will reflect the skills and quality of people in that market. Some institutions are able to select from a broad pool of very well qualified people. They enjoy the luxury of a seller's market. Other institutions, particularly those in rural areas, may have to recruit intensively and extensively in order to meet the minimum needs of the institution. Inevitably, some institutions will find the supply is less than adequate to meet their needs.

Depending on what the labor market has to offer, and on which level of position departments may be able to fill, staffing may be highly variable from one institution to another. Consequently, a department chair may have to supervise inexperienced staff with serious deficiencies in their qualifications, or may enjoy the support of a highly skilled and experienced staff. Since the local labor market defines the level of skill and availability, and since the selection and screening is usually done by some sort of civil service mechanism, a department is likely, on the average, to have no better or worse staff than the institution as a whole.

On the low end of the spectrum is a staff who have no more than basic skills, and who may have completed vocational courses or programs but have never attended college. They have never been involved in the academic culture in even the most rudimentary ways. Many of them view the university from the perspective of a real outsider. It is a place to work; it offers the entertainment of major sporting events, concerts, and so on; but it is not really perceived to be substantially different from any other corporate place of employment. Adjusting to this type of staff support is difficult for any chairperson but is especially difficult for new chairs. However, with patience from the chairperson and faculty members, careful supervision, opportunities to attend short training programs, mentoring by experienced staff members from other departments, a large dose of stroking and encouragement, and a little bit of luck, such staff can be effective in providing the support that the department needs.

The range of staff in a given department depends on its size and general importance to the university. Some smaller departments are lucky if they do not have to share a clerk–typist of the lowest classification with two or three other departments. Others may be able to hire (in effect) a professional manager. This person may have a business degree and substantial experience, and can, with a minimum of guidance and supervision, effectively manage the entire scope of the department's routine business. Other staff may include professional-level people who advise students and assist in the academic administration of the department.

The Work of Department Staff

The most important work of staff is, for the most part, the day-to-day routines. They receive visitors and prospective students, manage telephone traffic and messages, process words, maintain files, keep faculty calendars (when faculty consent to have their calendars kept!), purchase and store supplies, maintain equipment, schedule and sometimes proctor examinations, keep the department's financial records, process faculty personnel and pay forms, handle travel reservations and reimbursements, record and transcribe minutes of faculty meetings, update rule books and manuals, and manage grant and contract records.

All of these duties fall within the formal job descriptions of staff. They also assist in a variety of other less-recognized roles: They keep the coffee pot going, help students solve personal problems, give new faculty advice about the community, prepare for and clean up after department social events, and provide the chair with the latest rumors and intelligence from the halls and back-channels.

Working Conditions

Working conditions in an academic department often are somewhat different from those that most traditional training may lead prospective workers to expect. Trained for roles in a standard bureaucracy, many staff have trouble adapting to the apparently chaotic and eccentric behavior they encounter in the university.

The most seemingly bizarre behavior is that of faculty. They come and go apparently at will, keeping no predictable hours. They occasionally miss classes without forewarning. They fail to return telephone messages—when they choose to receive them at all. They demand instant turnaround on work that is lengthy, impenetrable to the civilian, and in need of a great deal of technical production work on tables, graphs, and bibliographies. Staff may come to resent particularly certain faculty who are both demanding and pathologically unresponsive. (A faculty member who drops off a manuscript with a tight deadline and promptly vanishes from all known means of contact may wonder why he wasn't called to clear up a misunderstanding about format for the references, and may complain bitterly about the errors and "quality" of the word-processing person.)

Staff people find it difficult to comprehend why faculty members in their department are apparently able to misbehave with impunity while they themselves are held to strict working hours, limited and perhaps inadequate benefits, and a dress code, and may find promotion hard to secure even for exemplary performance. Supervision for staff people may range from nonexistent to harsh and authoritarian, but is all too often less than exemplary.

It is a credit to many staff people that they perform their work with integrity and pride in the face of what they honestly consider provocative and contemptuous behavior from some of the most privileged members of the academic community. Many quietly cover for inadequate and incompetent behavior of faculty and chairs—and, in this regard, they are neither more nor less heroic than staff people in all other major organizations in our society. But they are seldom enough recognized, rewarded, or thanked for what they do.

Terms and Conditions of Employment

Although staff members work in and are supervised by the department, they are usually recruited, classified, hired, paid, evaluated, transferred, and promoted by a personnel unit. They may be members of a collective bargaining unit, or they may be covered by state laws and rules. If they have com-

plaints or grievances, these are processed by specialists in the personnel department who ordinarily have little reason to be involved in the department's
business.

A department chair may have very little to say about many aspects of staff
employment because staff members are covered so completely by separate rules
and regulations. Authority over staff may reside in a remote bureaucracy, and it is
sometimes difficult to figure out who is really in charge when a crisis breaks. If
the crisis can be managed informally and within the department, so much the
better. (The most likely candidate for this kind of treatment is the staff person
who has an illness or family problem and may need to arrange more flexible
hours for a limited period of time.) On the other hand, some staff problems arise
because rules are misunderstood, inconsistently enforced, or actually violated.
Many such disputes, if not handled in the right way by the right people, can
result in legal exposure for the university. It is important to call on professional
personnel administrators for advice, counsel, and mediation when such conflicts
appear headed out of control.

Managing the Staff

Although department chairs may expect to manage the staff, ironically, staff
often "manage" department chairs. Staff with long experience are often the most
knowledgeable people in the university. They have control of files and information. They know who really decides things. They can anticipate the cycle of
events. They know the quirks and idiosyncrasies of the system. They have seen it
all before, and they know that every new administrator is bound to make very
avoidable mistakes. It is a wise department chair who takes advantage of his
staff's knowledge and lets himself be managed by the staff when such will
prevent major errors or embarrassment.

But staff can only legitimately function within the formal boundaries of
their jobs. Department policies are essentially the province of the faculty, and
staff need to be directed in the implementation of those policies. The chair is the
link between the faculty and the staff, and between policy and implementation.
Unless they get a clear explanation and clear direction, staff will not be in a
position to either understand or implement department policies.

The chair is usually the only person with the necessary authority to provide
direction and guidance to staff. He or she must assume responsibility for seeing
that the staff receives appropriate training and feedback. When new policies or
rules are adopted, staff need to be counseled and advised about how to implement them. When new technology is adopted, staff will need opportunities to
attend training sessions, and they will need to adapt their familiar work patterns
to the new equipment. When job responsibilities are ambiguous or conflict with
others' responsibilities, staff need the opportunity to seek an authoritative resolution. The chair may feel it is inappropriate to act decisively and authoritatively,
having absorbed the consultative norms of the faculty culture, but staff usually

expect and need the chair to exercise direction and control. It is the only way they get clear signals about what they are supposed to be doing.

Evaluating the Staff

New staff usually are hired with a probationary period of some specified length. During this period, the department chair may have a good opportunity to work closely with an employee who is motivated and receptive to suggestions. Although it sometimes takes a considerable investment of time and energy to orient and train a new employee, that investment may pay important dividends. Expectations are made clear, lines of authority and communication are established, performance standards are set, and the new employee learns enough to be able to perform his or her functions independently. The personal contact one invests in a new employee can also result in a healthy bonding of that person to the department. Competence and loyalty are two of the products of such a healthy induction process.

Occasionally a new employee may not be able to meet expectations. When either side determines (or both do) that the person is not working out well, this must be communicated in some appropriate way. Perhaps personnel training specialists can be brought in to suggest ways of salvaging the situation. But if the cost is more than either side is willing (or both are) to bear, the relationship ought to be terminated. That is the purpose of the probationary period, and no one would fault the department chair for making a reasonable judgment that a staff person is not going to meet standards.

Routine evaluation of staff job performance usually is carefully orchestrated according to the institution's rules and/or whatever collective bargaining agreement may be in place. Annual evaluations often are a matter of life-and-death importance to staff. Their salaries, benefits, promotional opportunities, and long-term futures depend on achieving satisfactory evaluations. They are usually far less mobile than faculty, and cannot afford to see their work opportunities affected by marginal or poor evaluations. Strong feelings will be provoked whenever a staff member receives a less-than-glowing annual evaluation.

Nevertheless, not all staff perform at glowing levels all the time, and many need performance counseling. Marginal or unacceptable performance should be dealt with whenever it seems necessary. Staff will respond to feedback if it is legitimate, fair, and humane. Informal conferences focused on problem solving, and conducted with a careful regard for the staff person's dignity, may be a highly productive way to achieve improvements and behavior change. They must be conducted very close to the time of the incident or the display of the poor behavior in order to have maximum impact. This kind of daily observation and feedback may be more intense than many department chairs feel comfortable with, but it is the only effective way to get change. Waiting until the end of the year and dropping a detailed bill of particulars on a staff member with an unsatisfactory evaluation will almost surely create conflict and hostility, thus exacerbating the extent of the problem rather than moving it toward solution.

Conflict with Faculty

Staff and faculty may be expected to engage in a modest amount of skirmishing over a variety of issues. Faculty usually want more service and productivity than staff can reasonably be expected to provide. Demands multiply at very predictable times of the year—usually shortly before a semester begins or ends. Faculty can be peremptory and rude with staff when they feel under pressure, and often issue direct orders regardless of their own authority to do so. In most situations there is a good deal of ambiguity over who can order whom around and who is responsible for what. For much of the time, relations between faculty and departmental staff are informal and unstructured. This pattern breeds familiarity, and it is a congenial state of affairs until a crunch hits. Then the comfortable ambiguity breeds conflict and misunderstanding.

The chair will inevitably hear complaints from either or both sides, and will sometimes have to intervene in a direct clash of wills between a faculty member and a staff person. The perceptive chair will anticipate this kind of conflict, and will develop a sense of when and over which issues it is likely to occur.

Staff are good judges of the course of events in the department, and can help the chair estimate when and how conflict may develop. Staff often know more than the chair about the flow of work, and the chair sometimes knows about faculty projects that might come due when the staff is likely to be unprepared for additional work. Holding periodic planning sessions with staff could serve two purposes: to anticipate cycles in the flow of work, and to develop cooperatively a plan of action for the peak periods. When the chair takes time to help staff in this way they usually are grateful, and the impact on their morale is very positive. Pooling good information, and planning ahead, collectively are obviously the most intelligent way to avoid crises.

The chair, however, must be careful to play a neutral and objective role in preventing or resolving faculty/staff conflicts. The main goal—getting the work done—must be the chair's focus. Even when careful planning has been done, even when everyone is prepared to do his or her part, unexpected crisis will occur. The chair will inevitably field complaints from either one side or both sides. Usually a crisis means that someone is upset over a deadline, so time is almost always of the essence. Although the chair may wish to resolve disputes through careful fact-finding, adjudication is not going to do more than find the fault. Finding fault should be avoided in these tense situations because it wastes valuable time and creates a "winner" and a "loser." The chair's interest is better served by helping the combatants turn their energies to cooperation and to productive solutions. The chair might get a conversation under way in which both sides air their needs and their priorities, and in which the chair's role is to seek a middle ground, and a practical solution that leaves everyone reasonably content.

Conflict between faculty and staff can substantially weaken the chair's authority and effectiveness if it gets out of control. Staff, if they perceive that they lack the chair's backing and support, can bring the work of the department to a halt. They can also tie the chair's time up by going into a "passive aggressive" mode: They simply stop taking responsibility and initiative, requiring the chair to direct and coordinate their every task.

Faculty, on the other hand, will see management of the staff as one measure of the chair's effectiveness. If they sense that the staff has become unresponsive or unproductive, they will be quick to blame the chair, and they will also consume more of the chair's time with complaints. When they cannot see results, they will naturally question the chair's ability to do the job.

The chair's best strategy is usually to develop a good teamwork climate for the staff, to engage in regular planning and feedback sessions with them, and to signal that they have his or her support and commitment as long as they continue to perform in good faith. If they sense that the chair is approachable and that they can discuss problems and solutions openly, they will respond. They can almost always appreciate the need to accommodate faculty and to adapt and change when unusual conditions arise. But they cannot (and should not be expected to) sacrifice their pride and their interests in a onesided relationship in which the chair simply fails to consider or support them.

Staff and Students

Students may consume a great deal of the chair's time and attention. In some departments the chair may gratefully delegate a large amount of routine student contact to staff. It is fairly common for a staff person to become, either formally or informally, the ultimate departmental authority to most students. This becomes widely known, and the staff person achieves the status of a department legend. Students seek advice on academic, personal, and professional problems, and turn to the staff person much more readily than they would turn to either the chair or a faculty advisor.

The chair should consider this situation a mixed blessing. On the one hand, it may be considered effective management to delegate away a distracting assignment. It may also be wise to have a warm and helpful person dealing with students' problems—especially if the chair is not particularly interested in or attracted to this kind of work. (Some chairs simply cannot afford to spend the time involved, much as they may be interested in young people.) If the department is large enough, it is probably a good idea to hire someone with training in counseling or student development to fill this role.

Student-related issues are nevertheless part of the chair's responsibility, and total abdication is unwise. No matter how legendary or how effective a staff person may be in dealing with students, there are important limits to be observed. The faculty and the chair are charged to manage the academic program, to introduce students to the performance standards and expectations of the various professions, and to exercise judgment about the quality of student work. They cannot delegate these things away to a nonfaculty person, and they deprive students of an education if they do not exercise these responsibilities. This often means substantial out-of-class contact and counseling. Staff can assist by scheduling group advisement, by providing emotional and other support to students who may be under stress, and by providing the chair with feedback from the student grapevine. But staff should never be given responsibility for students' academic or professional development.

It is particularly important that the chair monitor staff to be sure they are not assuming more authority than they should. Some staff, by reason of long experience and personal qualities, may be quick to assume a mentor relationship with students, guiding them through the program, providing extensive counsel, steering them to certain faculty advisors, and suggesting courses to take. Their impact on students can be considerable, and everyone can become comfortable with a kind of tacit arrangement that allows staff a great deal of latitude. The chair, however, must keep in mind that staff are neither trained nor authorized to educate students. Education is both the province and the responsibility of faculty, and the chair must assure that staff neither usurp this job, nor assume it by default.

Staff Development

Staff have aspirations and ambitions, and (like other people) hope to improve their salaries and status through advancement. They can be expected to seek promotional opportunities and, from time to time, to test their marketability for better jobs. This seems to be especially true for younger, more junior staff people. They view the university, and not just the department, as their employer, and they will want to take full advantage of training, education, and developmental opportunities offered as benefits.

It is good personnel policy to help staff realize their ambitions, even when it may mean that the department has to deal with periodic turnover. Employees who feel that they are developing new skills, advancing their own knowledge, and improving their careers are likely to be more loyal, responsible, and ambitious. The department itself can do a lot to help its younger staff people develop. It can undertake informal training and provide counsel and support within the normal course of business. It can also provide released-time or flexible working hours for staff to attend special training sessions or to take courses.

Helping staff advance themselves may at first seem counter to the department's interest, and it may, in fact, result in turnover on a fairly regular basis. But investing in people by helping them realize their needs and ambitions is simply good employee relations. Ultimately it helps the university to compete for good people in the local job market. It means that entry-level employees will be of a better quality over the longer term, and it means that the university is able to attract a work force that has the energy and talent to advance to higher-level jobs. The last thing an employer wants is to have to accept the low end of the labor pool—those who have neither the talents nor the ambition to do more than hold a minimally demanding job. Staff development should therefore be seen as a long-term investment in the university's ability to attract and hold a high-quality work force.

Questions

1. What functions do your support staff (administrative assistants, secretaries, etc.) perform for the department?
2. How many support staff are there in your department, and how many faculty do they serve?
3. Do they, or are they expected to, assist or counsel students?
4. Are they involved in any kind of decision making?
5. Are support staff in your department given adequate facilities and equipment to perform effectively? List priorities for improvements. Think of ways to incorporate support staff in the decisions.
6. What is the attitude of support staff regarding periodic evaluations? Does the process need to be improved? Could you enlist the advice of the support staff, faculty, and/or personnel officer in making the improvements?
7. Does your department have a sufficiently developed policy for addressing staff complaints and grievances?
8. Are staff aware of professional development opportunities available to them?

References

BERRYMAN-FINK, CYNTHIA. *The Manager's Desk Reference*. New York: American Management Association, 1989.

BOWKER, LEE H., and LYNCH, DAVID M. *Chairing a Small Department*. Paper presented at the National Conference for Department Chairs, Orlando, 1985. (ERIC Document Reproduction Service No. ED 256 222)

BYARS, LLOYD L., and RUE, LESLIE W. *Personnel Management: Concepts and Applications*. New York: Holt, 1980.

DESATINICK, ROBERT L. *The Business of Human Resource Management: A Guide for the Results-Oriented Executive*. New York: Wiley, 1983.

GREENLAW, PAUL S., and BIGGS, WILLIAM D. *Modern Personnel Management*. New York: Holt, 1980.

HALLORAN, JACK. *Applied Human Resources: An Organizational Approach*. Englewood Cliffs: Prentice–Hall, 1987.

KOSSEK, ELLEN ERNST. *The Acceptance of Human Resource Innovation.* London: Greenwood, 1989.

LEVESQUE, JOSEPH D. *Manual of Personnel Policies Procedures, Operations.* Englewood Cliffs: Prentice–Hall, 1986.

RAELIN, JOSEPH A. *The Clash of Cultures: Managers and Professionals.* Boston: Harvard Business School Press, 1986.

REYES, PEDRO, and McCARTY, DONALD J. *The Power of Lower Participants in Educational Organizations.* ASHE Annual Meeting Paper, San Antonio, 1986. (ERIC Document Reproduction Service No. ED 268 868)

SPENCER, LYLE M. *Calculating Human Resource Costs and Benefits: Cutting Costs and Increasing Productivity.* New York: Wiley, 1986.

WEISS, W. H. *Supervisor's Standard Reference Handbook.* Englewood Cliffs: Prentice–Hall, 1988.

WILLIAMS, ALLAN P. O. *Changing Culture: New Organizational Approaches.* Washington, DC: Institute of Personnel Management, 1989.

YOE, MARY RUTH. "MBTI in the Workplace." *Alumni Magazine Consortium,* 1984.

Chapter 11

Students

Students are the department's lifeblood. Ironically, they are both customers and "products." The department has fiduciary responsibilities to educate them, but it also has to satisfy them, or they will—practically speaking—take their business elsewhere. If the department fails to educate, it will be held accountable; if it fails to satisfy, it will lose student credit hours. Therein lies the chair's eternal dilemma in dealing with students. And students come in all imaginable varieties: Although many are from the traditional white, middle-class, college-going population between the ages of eighteen and twenty-one, it is increasingly common for students to be older, to be from minority groups, to have had significant life experiences, to be parents, to be retooling for a new career, and/or to be recent immigrants.

Traditional Students

The traditional student is between the aforementioned typical ages of eighteen and twenty-one, and comes from a white, middle-class background. These students and their parents believe college will prepare them for success (part of the popular mythology), and they invest heavily in the college experience. Although most have adequate academic skills, in fact a substantial number are only marginally prepared. Many will have benefited from (and perhaps even enjoyed) some measure of independence and responsibility, but others will have led sheltered and unexamined lives. Most are stable, healthy, growing young people, but some will have serious emotional or developmental problems. Most are goal-oriented and achievement-driven, whereas others simply drift along, hoping for the best. The admissions office admits all who meet admission standards, and then assumes that they will sort themselves out with the wise and mature counsel of the faculty.

The traditional student and his or her parents trust the college or university to educate. They expect goals to be stated, courses to be taught by professors, skills and knowledge to be learned, and some kind of payoff for their large investment of time, effort, and money. Although a sophisticated educator understands that students must learn through their own initiative and effort—reading, studying, questioning, discussion, doing research, applying their knowledge— most students come to college feeling that they are going to *receive* knowledge by the same relatively passive and unchallenging methods they mastered in high school. Many go through a period of shock and dismay when they discover that their professors answer questions by presenting both sides of a debate; that they are expected to take positions on issues without much preparation; that they are open to attack for their ideas; that they have to take responsibility for laboratory experiments; and that they have to do independent research without a syllabus or guidelines. For many traditional students the college experience creates more anxiety and frustration than it does growth. Faculty and the chair sometimes have to consider how far these students may be pushed before the challenge becomes too inhibiting.

Adult Students

Adult students form an increasing proportion of many departments' "new" student body. Many of these nontraditional students have substantial experience. They have, in some cases, already completed degrees, worked, retired from military careers, raised families, traveled, read widely, served as civic leaders, and/or otherwise functioned as competent citizens. They will often have a specific reason for attending college, and may take a very active role in deciding which courses to take. As adult learners they will behave quite differently in the classroom from the traditional college-age student. They will show considerable initiative, bring perspectives and experience to bear in class discussions, and more frequently challenge instructors' premises or points of view. Inevitably at least some will pose a challenge to faculty, and often to the department chair as well. (Chairs are as likely as anyone else to hear from adult students.) Major adjustments in standard programs of study, in scheduling of courses, in teaching styles, and in the overall philosophy of education may be necessary in order to deal successfully with this category of student.

Chairs may find it useful to have a consultative committee of students and faculty to recommend and discuss ideas for making courses and programs more appealing and accessible to nontraditional groups. As we shall now see, this may be especially needed if there is any significant number of "reentry" women.

Returning Women

In recent years, women have increasingly turned to higher education for a variety of reasons. Some wish to prepare themselves for independence in ways that generations in previous eras could not always manage. Others desire career advancement, or are changing careers. Some are reentering professions after time out for childbearing. Whatever the case, the motives and needs of returning women students usually are different from those of most traditional students. Some may, for example, already have a bachelor's degree in one field, and plan to acquire one in another. Some may not want to follow the traditional four-year program, and will seek ways to waive general education requirements as well as other introductory courses. Some may be combining childrearing and a job with their return to school; they in particular may need more time to finish, and probably face chronic scheduling problems.

Sometimes the standard ways of doing academic business create artificial barriers to the aspirations of this group, and a little effort to adapt can make a major difference in their chances to succeed. Chairs will find themselves being called upon more frequently to make adjustments in the department's customary practices and requirements if there are very many such students in the department.

Transfer Students from Community Colleges

Another group that is becoming increasingly common on many campuses is the population of transfer students from community colleges. Although they register as advanced undergraduates, they are still new to the institution. It often takes them a full semester to adjust to new faculty, new performance expectations, and new living arrangements. Some must adjust to independence and freedom for the first time as well. As this population expands, more universities will develop "articulation agreements" with two-year colleges in the states or regions from which transfer students come in large numbers. Within the parameters of the articulation agreements, or on their own, departmental chairs can arrange for their faculty to compare course syllabi and talk about expectations with the faculty of the same academic disciplines in the two-year colleges. Arrangements can be made for the early orientation for potential transfer students, including the setting up of departmental committees of faculty and students to serve as hosts and mentors to new transfer students—thus providing a support system for those who may need help in making the adjustment to a new institution.

Multicultural Students

As more new groups seek higher education, student populations are becoming increasingly multicultural. The experiences, backgrounds, languages, and cultural viewpoints of these groups are more and more often centered in the Caribbean Basin, the Far East, and the lesser-developed world in general. They come from backgrounds in which the traditional values of higher education, reflected in the classics of Western culture, in the tradition of logical positivism, and in the dominance of free-market economics, often seem alien and biased. Institutions are increasingly adopting multicultural curricula to accommodate these new points of view and value systems. Traditional students can also benefit from a multicultural perspective, and are required in some institutions to take courses in non-Western culture. The chair may need to consider whether his or her department has adequately adopted a broad perspective, and whether the department is hospitable—intellectually as well as socially—to students from other cultures. In many fields it may be desirable to add courses or experiences designed to explore non-Western thought. In all departments it would be very desirable to honor cultural diversity with, at the very least, informal events that involve foreign students and their families, giving them opportunities to express their heritage and traditions.

Graduate Students

Graduate students present the chair with a different set of concerns. Although they are often treated as adults and as junior colleagues in the department, they still are students. Since much of the university's attention is focused on undergraduates, comparatively few resources are devoted to the support of graduate student needs.

Graduate students make enormous sacrifices to earn advanced degrees. They often have families to support. Lots of them leave jobs and homes to live for a period of years in students ghettos. They find low-paying jobs as teaching assistants, but many also have to support themselves with other work at the low end of the local economy—clerical work, night-clerking in hotels, delivery jobs, and odd-job yard work probably sustain more graduate students than anyone imagines. They may have to literally live from week to week without benefit of self-owned transportation and with only marginal nutrition. Indeed, graduate students sometimes invest everything, psychologically as well as materially, in the pursuit of advanced training. And often they make these sacrifices without being able to expect a substantial return in the form of a secure, prestigious, high-paying job.

For many graduate students, particularly foreigners who must adapt to a new culture and a new language, the stress level is very high, especially during the latter stages when they are doing dissertation research. Some of this stress may be due to a personality conflict between a graduate student and a major professor. The student may find that after a long and intense period of research on that candidate's part, the major professor's criticism becomes grating, perhaps intolerable. Sometimes genuine intellectual disputes arise and neither side is willing to compromise. For the student, the stakes are often perceived to be very high. The chair may be asked to intervene at some point to resolve the conflict if possible, perhaps by suggesting that the student change major professors (without prejudice to either the student or the professor). If a change is to take place it must be done very diplomatically in order to minimize possible trauma on both sides.

Graduate students often are taken for granted. They seldom complain, and usually suppress their own personal problems. But they undergo great upheavals nevertheless. Marriages become strained; some break down. Self-concepts are tested and reformed. Physical health is hard to maintain. Alienation from family and culture—while still in only a marginal role in the university or profession—leaves them feeling isolated.

Many graduate students are required to teach as part of their training. But they get little guidance or support in the art of teaching, and so may be judged harshly by students and faculty alike. Others work as junior members of a research team, taking on the most difficult, tedious, and unrewarding jobs as part of the initiation process. In short, the life of a graduate student can be grim and stressful. Seldom is account taken of their needs and problems. Most departments could not function without a cadre of such dedicated teaching and research assistants—but they are quick to exploit the dependency of these worthy young people.

The *chair,* however, *is* in a position to provide support and recognition to graduate students who perform valuable services for the department. The chair is *also* in a position to help locate jobs and other kinds of support for graduate students. Although it is easy to let graduate students fend for themselves, they deeply appreciate even small gestures—a kind word, an invitation to lunch or dinner, the opportunity to talk about personal or career matters, encouragement and support for preparation of a paper or article, funds to travel to a professional meeting once in a while.

Dealing with Students Who Have Problems

Most students do not need to see the chair on an individual basis. Much of the chair's contact with individual students will be to conduct routine business. Granting required approvals, signing forms, handling drop-add and late registration matters, providing routine academic advisement, and dealing with exceptions and waivers to rules are likely to be the usual reasons students see the chair. But much of this business can be, and often is, handled by a staff assistant or by an assistant chairperson.

STUDENTS WHO COMPLAIN ABOUT INSTRUCTION

There are several common situations in which students will wish to see the chair for decidedly nonroutine reasons. Students and faculty may have misunderstandings or disagreements, and fail to reach a satisfactory resolution after several attempts to communicate. When this happens, the "breakage" often winds up in the chair's office, with the student seeking solace, counsel, justice, or revenge.

Some students will come to the chair with complaints about a professor's teaching style, coverage of the material, assignments, or expectations. Younger students, for example, may feel threatened by the degree of independence they are expected to assume. More mature students may complain about a professor's patronizing attitude. Sometimes, two students will lodge conflicting complaints— say, that assignments are too hard *and* that they are too easy.

The chair's role is a delicate one. The first responsibility is to be sure that faculty are doing reasonable things. Their courses should have reasonably clear goals, their instructional methods should be responsible and valid, and their demands on students should be fair and connected to the proposed outcomes of the course. Occasionally, students have a bona fide complaint, and the chair will have to answer twice: once for why he or she didn't know there was likely to be a problem, and the second time for not fixing what has gone wrong. Obviously it pays to stay in touch with what faculty are doing in their courses, and to keep them from committing pedagogical stunt-flying. (On the other hand, a faculty preoccupied with safe, conventional, and dull methods may be guilty of failing to educate in equal proportion.)

On occasion, students may have been challenged beyond their expectations or their ability to cope. They may express considerable anger and emotion, and may even shed tears. Sometimes a parent or guardian will become involved. On very rare occasion the student poses a danger to the self or others. The chair may well be unprepared for this latter kind of confrontation because the student may not have attempted resolution by talking directly with the faculty member.

The chair has several objectives in mind when a student challenges either a professor or the institution. The first is to defuse anger and hostility. The second is to focus on and discover the facts. The third is to educate—helping student and/or faculty member to understand the broader goals of the institution and the department, and how the issue at hand seems to relate. The final objective is to assist and participate in finding a resolution. (The wise chair does not *impose* solutions, except as a last resort.) Although it is almost always tempting to come to the defense of a faculty member or the institution as the first line of defense, such a closed and presumptuous response will almost surely alienate the student and preclude a chance to educate, teach, and perhaps send the student away with insight into him- or herself.

All of the possible outcomes can be reduced to *two* choices: Either the student adjusts to the institution's way of doing things, or the institution admits to an error and adjusts its own procedures. But there is never any need for the chair to meet with a student and promise something on the spot. Rather, the chair will want to assess the student's feelings and be sure time is allowed for learning and perspective to take root. The chair will also want to buy time to assess the facts of the situation.

The chair's essential posture is that of an educator. The most desirable outcome is that the students learn and grow. Sometimes getting the university to admit a mistake and to change is an enormously productive learning experience, and the chair needs to be prepared for that outcome.

One common mistake chairs can make in dealing with student issues is to take on the burdens of mediation. The student will register a complaint, and the chair will agree to mediate on the theory that the student needs protection and support. The chair then goes to the faculty member or members to present the student's complaint and seek resolution. Faculty correctly resent such an approach and treat it as a breach of professional courtesy by both the student and the chair. Students need to learn that they bear responsibility for solving their own problems, and should deal directly with the faculty member. The faculty member will not appreciate being put on the defensive by the chair, and will feel accused of something, no matter how trivial.

STUDENTS WHO COMPLAIN ABOUT GRADES

Although such is not as frequent as one might expect, students do register complaints about grades they receive on individual assignments or at the end of courses. The chair must handle these complaints with great care, and perhaps with more conservatism than may seem humane.

Some students fail. They do not live up to expectations, they do not go to class, they do not complete assignments, they do not prepare for examinations, they write poorly, they hate being in school. They may just be unable to handle independence, but they may also be unable to do the work. All institutions have (and are expected to have) standards for performance. They should only apologize if they do not have standards. Students who do not or will not meet standards of performance must be and should be penalized, perhaps by exclusion from the institution.

The chair may expect to deal with the consequences of failure whenever it occurs. Students and parents can get highly emotional about it, and sometimes are litigious. The chair should remember that the faculty are the final arbiters of performance in the classroom, on graduate theses and dissertations, and on clinical performance in whatever setting. The chair's authority may be over procedural matters, such as grade appeals, but no more. Issues having to do with failure, probation, dismissal, or any imposition of penalties are almost always governed by the institution's formal rules, and there may be substantial legal risk in dealing with these matters informally or ad hoc.

Chairs must exercise considerable self-discipline and care in dealing with a student who has failed. Instinctively, a humane chair will wish to forgive and salvage—perhaps even to exercise the well-honed desire to educate. Certainly, many students who fail can present themselves as deserving exceptions. (Virtually every one will have a tale of considerable woe and injustice to tell, some valid and some not even exaggerated.) It is a truly heartless chair who cannot muster some sympathy and caring for a student who throws him- or herself on the mercy of the university.

In these cases long experience, as well as sometimes unhappy legal encounters, have led to the development of sound and useful procedures. Students must be counseled as to their rights and concerning the available recourse. They may pour their hearts out to the chair, but they must be firmly reminded that the chair may not be in a position either to ascertain facts or to offer solutions. Such may only be done in the proper channels at the proper time.

Occasionally a student will be sufficiently upset to engage legal counsel. The chair should never respond directly to someone representing (or purporting to represent) a student. Privacy regulations almost certainly prevent a chair from discussing someone's status with a third party. Furthermore, everything a chair says to legal counsel can and will be used against the institution in any formal proceeding. Legal counsel should therefore be referred—without exception—to the university's attorney. Some students will not reveal that they have attorneys. They may, however, be acting on counsel's guidance and instructions. For this reason it is sometimes wise to refuse to see a student if it is clear that the chair has no authority to deal with a complaint or cannot effect any resolution of the situation. Instead, one must insist that the student follow written procedures and direct his or her concerns to the person with authority in this matter. Under conditions where the chair feels a meeting is unavoiable, it might be wise to ask a neutral third party to be present as a witness. That third party may well be the university's legal counsel.

The chair would almost always like to avoid the hard decisions and formal procedure that go along with enforcing academic standards. But such decisions, and their consequences for all involved, are inevitable in the course of doing the university's business—one part of which is certifying to the outside world that its graduates have met high expectations. If employers, graduate schools, and accrediting bodies lose confidence in a university's willingness to enforce and maintain high standards, the damage will be far worse than that from sitting through a nuisance lawsuit.

STUDENTS WHO SEEK PERSONAL COUNSELING

Students may wish to visit with the chair for guidance and advice. Some will simply be seeking emotional support, but career guidance, surrogate parenting, personal friendship, and intellectual exchange may all be reasons why students visit with the chair. Chairs have to decide how much time they wish to spend visiting with students. A warm, engaging personality and an open door may attract students to the point where the chair is distracted from a normal work routine.

It is probably wise to sort out the kind of student contact one can handle effectively. Keeping regular office hours should limit the informal walk-ins. Much student counseling can be referred elsewhere. Students who seem to be looking for career advice, for example, can be steered toward the career development center or to faculty who may be especially knowledgeable. Students who apparently display a need for emotional support (and who may cling tenaciously to whoever offers it) should be encouraged to seek help from the counseling center. Students looking for intellectual companionship can be gently steered to faculty members whose interests might prove stimulating.

In very rare cases, students develop dangerous psychological or behavioral disorders. They can be threatening to themselves or others, and may actually carry out acts that are damaging to persons or property. Chairs should never hesitate to contact security personnel when they have a concern about safety. Assaults and worse have taken place on campuses, sometimes over minor academic disputes. It is only prudent to take protective steps when the situation seems to warrant action.

None of this is to suggest that the chair avoid students or refuse to see them. It is, however, to suggest that the chair direct students to people from whom they might receive the most gratifying advice and counsel appropriate to their apparent or expressed needs. It is also to strongly urge that the chair exercise prudence in protecting his or her own time and psychic energy.

Creating New Learning Environments for Students

Most undergraduate students are bright, energetic, hopeful young people. They come to college expecting to change, grow, and meet challenges. Often they find their most stimulating opportunities to learn and develop useful skills in extracurricular activities. There is some concern in the academic world, however, that faculty have withdrawn from opportunities to educate, and that much more could be done to enhance the college experience.

Some institutions are experimenting with new approaches to undergraduate education in which students are involved in some kind of intensive experience by means of which they can apply what they are learning in the classroom, and can sharpen their civic and ethical values. They are required to deepen their understanding by engaging in problem-solving activities. These activities often are conducted in cooperative, team-oriented projects in real-world settings, for example, an internship with an appropriate legislative committee or a role in some community service. Adopting these experimental methods requires important changes in how faculty and students approach the business of learning.

Since few academics, especially in research-oriented institutions, readily show an interest in innovative undergraduate education, the chair may have to do some very clever "internal marketing" to help sell ideas that work. The chair may, in fact, have to lead by example. Students themselves may prove to be strong allies, since they often enjoy planning and designing their own experiences, and since they can usually draw other faculty into activities more readily than the chair can either order or bribe faculty to show an interest. A few bright, civic-minded seniors, especially those with some interest in teaching, could form the nucleus of a very effective conspiracy to "reinvent" the undergraduate experience.

Accommodating to Changing and Diverse Learning Styles of Students

As the student population diversifies, institutions of higher education are finding that the preferred learning styles of incoming students are changing dramatically. While colleges could once expect students to be comfortable learning and expressing themselves via the written word, this is no longer true for many students.

The diversity of students attending colleges and universities is likely to increase in the foreseeable future, and there will almost certainly be *more* need to provide alternative learning options. There will be more students from other cultures, more with language deficiencies, and more whose principal media for learning are television, audio tape, and computers. The chair would be wise to invest some time exploring the power and potential of these new learning tools. Students will someday expect to use them as a standard alternative to lectures and books.

Many institutions now have highly effective learning centers in which students may try alternative methods of learning, such as listening to tapes or doing lessons on computers. These learning centers sometimes provide diagnostic and remedial services. A department that finds itself dealing with a significant number of nontraditional students may want to develop close working relations with such a campus learning center in order to ensure that its students have alternatives, as well as opportunities to seek whatever help they may need with treatable learning deficiencies.

The chair may have to provide a significant level of leadership within the department to help faculty focus on the learning needs of the new student population. The chair can bring the issue into the open, stimulate discussions about what to do, invite learning specialists in to serve as resource people, and give faculty released time to experiment with nontraditional learning methods. Faculty may have to be encouraged to develop or provide alternative learning options for some of their courses and lessons. They need to be introduced to the concept, and to develop a familiarity with, and confidence in, the personnel of the learning center.

Students in Governance

Prior to the 1960s, a role for students in governance was unthinkable. Since the "revolution" it has become equally unthinkable to exclude students from department committees and meetings. The impact of student involvement has been mixed. On balance it has not resulted in major change, but it has added an important voice to departmental discussions.

Since student involvement is now a permanent part of the academic culture, it is wise to focus on what it adds and how it can strengthen the decisions a department must make. For the most part, students bring energy and interest to the positions they fill on various committees. They are not, as a rule, deeply knowledgeable when they start out, but students often work hard, prepare thoroughly, and offer sincere opinions. Most importantly, they bring their interests as consumers, and they have a high ethical awareness.

Students almost always serve as members of student committees that are advisory to the department or the college. Student advisory committees tend to reflect cycles of student interest. An apathetic student body today may well be mobilized over a new issue at any time. The chair will find student advisory committees particularly useful as consultative bodies that can help explore options and can survey students to establish opinions on important issues. Although such committees may pursue a principally social agenda, or lapse altogether for periods of time, the chair should support them. Their advice and ability to represent the student view is very important.

Students also serve as representatives on faculty committees—for example, on the department's elected executive or steering committee or on the curriculum committee. They may also serve on search committees, but they do not often serve on promotion and tenure committees. Student members of faculty committees expect to see a body of rational professionals discussing important matters. Although few faculty meetings would measure up to civilian expectations, the presence of students in the room almost certainly has a moderating effect. Faculty will be more likely to try rational behavior if they are being observed, and so, if for this reason alone, a chair should welcome student participation.

Students who do their homework and prepare for meetings are sometimes the best-informed people in the room. Certainly they can add perspective to discussions, and they often ask the kind of simple question that a faculty member would avoid asking. They force issues to be discussed with more clarity, and press for solutions to problems to be more carefully explored, particulary when they can add views on how students may be affected. When decisions are reached, students will have had a say in the outcome, and are more likely to accept the result. Student involvement results in better decisions, made in a more rational way, and understood and accepted by more of those who will be affected. For all of these reasons, the chair will see student involvement in governance as a positive factor.

It has been argued that students serving on committees and voting bodies automatically bring with them conflicts of interests. They presumably would vote on issues directly affecting them, thereby voting in their self-interest instead of rationally. This argument seems not to have survived in the face of experience. Students have a very strong interest in receiving a quality education—theoretically the same interest pursued by faculty. A rational student will vote to protect the value of his or her investment in a degree, and may, in fact, actively oppose changes that appear to weaken the quality of that degree.

Finally, students may attend faculty meetings either as representatives of an advisory committee or as observers. Laws governing open meetings may, in fact, require that students have notice of such meetings, and may provide them with the right to be present. They may or may not have the privilege of the floor, and there may or may not be provision for them to be represented in any votes taken. Chairs may have to rule on such procedural matters, and should be thoroughly knowledgeable about both bylaws and department customs.

There are few, if any, arguments against involving students as described.

For the most part they have proved serious and responsible about their governance activities. Participation in representative democracy has a strong educative value. Students who participate are learning civic skills, and forming values that well may carry over into life after college. Chairs should defend student participation for this effect alone, but they have many other practical reasons to welcome student involvement in departmental affairs. Doing so is, in brief, good management, good politics, and good education.

A chair may wish to invite all the students in the department to meet with him or her once or twice a year. Some chairs will feel uncomfortable doing so, and may actively avoid such meetings. But at least three important purposes are served by such meetings. First, the chair may learn a great deal from talking with students in an informal setting. (If the chair lays out ground rules that allow open conversation, but do not oblige him or her to take any immediate action on complaints, little is risked, and students may feel that they can share important concerns.) Second, students may feel gratified to consider that they have an open channel for the expression of their interests and problems. (By meeting with them periodically the chair gives them a chance to talk about their concerns, and to relieve the kind of tension that often builds up when students feel they cannot find a way to express themselves and solve problems.) Third, this kind of open communication runs both ways: The chair may be able to educate the students about issues to which they may have been blind. (Problems that have begun to irritate the faculty or the chair may be discussed, and students may be put in the position of taking some responsibility for change.) For these reasons and more, meeting with students can be productive, and the chair *should* consider doing so once or twice a year—or even more frequently if that seems appropriate and potentially fruitful.

Questions

1. Describe the dominant student cultures in your department. What are the approximate percentages of traditional, adult, returning women, transfer, multi-cultural, graduate students? List several implications for your department associated with each student group.

2. Review departmental policies for dealing with frequently encountered student problems. Are clearly written guidelines available to students to explain grievance procedures?

3. What campus referrals are available for students with personal problems that might impact their academic success? Does your department give faculty advisers current information on campus resources?

4. Are there student members on departmental committees? If so, which committees? Are students utilized in departmental decision making? If so, how?

References

ALTBACH, PHILIP G. "American Student Activism: The Post Sixties Transformation." *Journal of Higher Education,* January/February 1990.

ASTIN, ALEXANDER W. "The Educational Pipeline for Minorities." *Minorities in American Higher Education.* San Francisco: Jossey–Bass, 1988.

ASTIN, ALEXANDER W., and GREEN, KENNETH C. "The American Freshman: An Overview of the Data." *The American Freshman: Twenty-Year Trends, 1966–1985.* Los Angeles: Cooperative Institutional Research Program of the American Council on Education and UCLA, 1987, pp. 7–17.

ATTINASI, LOUIS C., JR. "Getting In: 'Mexican Americans' Perceptions of University Attendance and the Implications for Freshman Year Persistence." *Journal of Higher Education,* 60, May/June 1989.

BARBER, ELINOR G., and MORGAN, ROBERT P. *Boon or Bane: Foreign Graduate Students in U.S. Engineering Programs.* New York: Institute for International Education, 1988.

BECKER, HOWARD S.; GEER, BLANCE; and HUGHES, EVERETT C. "Studying College Students: The Nature of Our Problem." *Making the Grade: The Academic Side of College Life.* New York: Wiley, 1968.

BOWEN, HOWARD M. "Is Higher Education Worth the Cost?" *Investment in Learning: The Individual and Social Value of American Higher Education.* San Francisco: Jossey–Bass, 1977.

BOYER, ERNEST W. *College: The Undergraduate Experience in America.* New York: Carnegie Foundation for the Advancement of Teaching, 1987.

BRUBACHER, JOHN S. "Higher Education for Whom?" *On the Philosophy of Higher Education.* San Francisco: Jossey–Bass, 1977.

CHICKERING, ARTHUR W. "Adult Development: A Workable Vision for Higher Education." *Current Issues in Higher Education.* Washington, DC: American Associate for Higher Education, 1980.

FELDMAN, KENNETH A., and NEWCOMB, THEODORE M. *The Impact of College on Students.* 2 vols. San Francisco: Jossey–Bass, 1969.

HOROWITZ, HELEN LEFKOWITZ. "The Changing Student Culture: A Retrospective. *Educational Record,* 70, Summer/Fall 1989.

KINGSTON, NEAL M. *The Graduate Record Examinations Validity Study Service: Yesterday and Tomorrow.* Princeton: Educational Testing Service, 1986. (ERIC Document Reproduction Service No. ED 300 452)

LOUIS, KAREN S. (et al.) *University Policies and Ethical Issues in Graduate Research and Education.* Results of a Survey of Graduate School Deans. ASHE 1988 Annual Meeting Paper, 1988. (ERIC Document Reproduction Service No. ED 303 100)

MALANEY, GARY D. "Differentiation in Graduate Education." *Research in Higher Education,* 25, 1986, pp. 82–96.

PEARSON, J.; SHAVLIK, D.; and TOUCHTON, J. *Educating the Majority.* New York: ACE/Macmillan, 1989.

Ronkowski, Shirley. *Changing in Teaching Assistants Concerns Over Time.* (ERIC Document Reproduction Service No. ED 315 012)

Schlossberg, Nancy K.; Lynch, Ann Q., and Chickering, Arthur W. *Improving Higher Education Environments for Adults: Responsive Programs and Services from Entry to Departure.* San Francisco: Jossey–Bass, 1989.

Sedlacek, William E. "Black Students on White Campuses: Twenty Years of Research." *Journal of Student Personnel,* 28(6), 1987, pp. 484–495.

Stanley, Barbara. *Teaching Research Ethics: Methods and Practice.* Paper presented at the Annual Meeting of the APA, Toronto, 1984. (ERIC Document Reproduction Service No. ED 251 019)

Staton, Ann Q., and Darling, Ann L. "Socialization of Teaching Assistants." In *New Directions for Teaching and Learning: Teaching Assistant Training in the 1990s.* Fall 1989.

Tinto, Vincent G. *Leaving College: Rethinking the Causes and Cures of Student Attrition.* San Francisco: Jossey–Bass, 1987.

Warren, Jonathan. "The Changing Characteristics of Community College Students." In *ASHE Reader on College Students,* Needham Heights, MA: Ginn Press, 1989.

Wigington, Henry. "Students' Ratings of Instructors Revisited: Interactions Among Class Instructor Variables." *Research in Higher Education,* 30, 1989, pp. 331–344.

Willer, Barry. "Survey of U.S. and Canadian Medical Schools on Admissions and Psychiatrically At-risk Students." *Journal of Medical Education,* 59, 1984, pp. 928--936.

Part IV

RECRUITING, AFFIRMATIVE ACTION, AND RETENTION

Chapter 12. Procedures and Practices for Recruiting, Employing, and Retaining Faculty

Chapter 13. Affirmative Action: Finding, Hiring, and Retaining Women and Minority Faculty

Procedures and Practices for Recruiting, Employing, and Retaining Faculty

In the past, during times of expanding enrollments, increasing budgets, and no affirmative action regulations, the recruitment and selection process was much less complex than it is today. An expanded enrollment would automatically create an increased number of faculty positions, and in certain fields the number of available positions would often exceed the number of qualified faculty members to fill them. When minorities and women were hired, it was primarily due to personal values held by enlightened presidents, deans, and department chairpersons. If after one or two years, newly employed faculty members did not perform as well as expected, they would be advised to seek employment elsewhere. This was called "counseling them out." These "counseled out" individuals offered little resistance because they knew that they would have no difficulty finding employment at another institution. Turnover among faculty members in those days was quite high, as was faculty mobility, and the process for screening and selecting new faculty members was quite informal.

There were times when a position needed to be filled rather quickly and the faculty member's area of specialization within the discipline was not a key factor in his or her selection. This resulted in continual modification of department goals to fit faculty members' areas of specialization and interest rather than the overall mission of the institution. Departmental goals were changed every time one or two new faculty members were hired.

Today the situation is different.[1] Even though at some institutions enrollments are expanding, budgets are not increasing proportionately, and the number of available faculty positions is decreasing. There is very little voluntary turnover, and mobility has slowed down to a snail's pace. Faculty members are no longer willing to be counseled out because they have few places to go. Moreover, it is becoming increasingly difficult to terminate faculty members whose performance is barely marginal. Some department vacancies are reclaimed by the central administration of the institution and never returned to the department. Therefore, when a department does have a vacancy which it is permitted to fill, every care should be taken to insure that the person selected to fill it is the best person for the job in terms of the department's future as well as its present. It is well to remember that whoever is selected for the position, bad or good, may be with the department for a long time.

Recruitment Within the Context of Departmental Planning

Recruitment of faculty members should not be an ad hoc affair carried out in isolation but rather an integral part of a long-range departmental plan which includes a clearly defined set of departmental goals. After a department's goals have been reviewed and updated, they can be used to assess the current extent to which the existing faculty members possess the skills and interests required to meet the needs stated in the goals. Where there are some unmet needs, the chairperson and the appropriate faculty committee can begin to consider the kind of person who might be sought in the recruitment process.

A department should develop and keep current an inventory of existing faculty specializations and competencies including skills in teaching, research, service, student advising, and mentoring of graduate students. This human resource inventory can serve the chairperson as a planning tool and, when measured against the department's goals, can provide guidance in determining which skills or competencies need to be added and which are no longer necessary and should be phased out. An important part of the inventory is a job description for each faculty member. Job descriptions should include data about average assignment, subjects taught, whether applied or basic research is conducted, and the range of services and other activities that are carried out or expected.

The department should also keep a list of those specialties and commitments which clientele groups such as students, private industry, and government agencies have grown to expect from the department. The combined use of the human resource inventory, the list of clientele expectations, and the goal statements of the department allows the chairperson to see which areas of specialization are presently over- or understaffed, which current areas are not addressed,

---

1. Some elements of this chapter are drawn from a research project prepared in 1982 for the Institute for Departmental Leadership, Florida State University, by John S. Waggaman.

and which areas may need to be addressed in the future. The strength or weakness of each department specialty is linked to the quality of performance of each individual faculty member. An analysis of faculty evaluation data can help the chairperson determine whether there are areas of weakness. Depending on the goals and resources of the department, a decision can then be made to strengthen, retain as is, or phase out certain areas of weakness.

The department should attempt to anticipate the occurrence of any position vacancies and include this information in its inventory. Vacant faculty positions emerge for many reasons, such as retirement, recruitment by another institution, noncontinuation of contract, illness, or death. A sensitive department chairperson will often have many clues that members of the faculty are in various stages of career development which may lead them to leave their current position. Personal health and life-styles of individuals sometimes provide early warning signals of future disabilities. Making reliable estimates when vacancies are likely to occur requires that the chairperson thoroughly understand a great variety of circumstances that precede the departure of faculty members.

Having a variety of information available allows the chairperson to anticipate the course of events prior to the occurrence of a vacancy, and to avoid hasty, ill-conceived measures that might jeopardize the attainment of departmental goals. The numerical decline of the traditional college-age group, poor economic conditions which limit parental support, and the reduction of federal aid to students all augur little or no expansion in enrollment, and indeed a real possibility for decline, at many institutions. There will probably be few vacancies in the 1990s. It is therefore especially important that recruitment efforts be consonant with departmental goals and that the recruitment process be well organized and conducted fairly within equal employment guidelines so that the best qualified candidate may be selected. If the recruitment process becomes an integral part of a long-range departmental plan and dates of vacancies are anticipated, the occurrence of a vacancy will not be the occasion for departmental crises, confusion, or despair over missed opportunities.

Obtaining Clearance Before the Recruiting Effort

The chairperson cannot assume that just because a vacancy has occurred in the department he or she will automatically receive permission to fill it. The central administration at most institutions has the power to sweep the unfilled position from the department and reallocate it to a more favored department— one which is deemed to have greater need. This practice is becoming more common where enrollments decline and few if any new positions are created. It is also possible that the administration may feel the need to use the salary money allocated to the vacated position for other exigencies, such as a demand from the state or governing board to turn back a percentage of the allocated budget. In such a case, the departmental faculty may have to assume heavier teaching loads or cancel courses. A chairperson who desires to fill a sudden vacancy, or for that matter any vacancy, must be prepared to justify the need for the position. In any event, before beginning a formal recruiting effort, clearance for the recruitment must be obtained from the dean of the school or college.

Restructuring the Position

The occurrence of a vacancy presents a good opportunity to restructure the position and to bring it in line with the department's long-range goals. What area of specialty is desirable from the department's point of view? Should it be the same as or different from that of the preceding occupant? The department may recognize a need for a different set of disciplinary skills in some new academic specialty or research area. Should interdepartmental responsibilities be built into the position? What are the salary constraints? Is it better to replace a senior professor with another of equal rank or stature, or for the same money to hire one or possibly two promising junior scholars whose potential is as yet unproven? If the salary constraints are severe, would a part-time or temporary appointment meet the needs? If a change in enrollment or faculty workload is imminent, would it be more prudent to recruit a person for a fixed contract period with no assurance of an additional appointment? A department with large aspirations and a need for new positions may find its opportunities severely restricted by financial constraints. This problem needs to be identified as early as possible so that the chairperson can present the administration with the best arguments for new positions.

When a vacancy occurs and the requirements of the new position are in the process of being developed, the chairperson should circulate copies of the tentative job description to the departmental faculty so that they will be able to react to it. Perhaps a faculty member already in place has a mind to develop the very same specialty which is being sought. If it is learned that one of the current faculty members is interested in developing the desired specialty area, the chairperson should discuss the possibility with that individual *before* the job description is completed and the recruitment process is begun. The same advice holds if the chairperson learns that a faculty member wishes to teach the courses formerly taught by the person who vacated the position. This may be an opportunity to rekindle professional interest and energy within tired or bored faculty members by rotating them through different teaching assignments; assuming, of course, that they are qualified and other faculty members have no serious objections.

Affirmative Action Procedures

While the position description is being developed, and before any advertising or other active recruiting is undertaken, a copy of the latest affirmative action guidelines should be obtained from the office responsible for monitoring affirmative action in the institution. These guidelines often contain everything a chairperson needs to know about affirmative action procedures. It may be a requirement of the college or university that the department maintain a file of the recruitment activities in order to demonstrate that the process has been carried out fairly. Such a file should be started at the very beginning of the search and at a minimum should contain the following information which becomes a part of the department's affirmative action documentation.

1. The name and title of the person who will appoint a search and screening committee if one is to be constituted; if no committee is to be appointed, an exact description of the recruitment process should be included

2. The size and composition of the committee

3. The manner in which the committee chairperson is selected

4. In the absence of a screening committee, the name of the person responsible for seeing that the search is carried out properly and in a timely manner

5. The name and title of the staff person who maintains the documents and files of applicants

6. Instructions to the file keeper concerning the removal of photographs and any other inappropriate information from the files

7. Arrangements for obtaining and recording information about the race and sex of nominees and candidates to demonstrate that recruitment took place from a nondiscriminatory pool of applicants

If the information suggested above is kept on file, the department will be able to document its response to any questions that may arise.

The Search and Screening Committee

It is a commonly accepted practice to constitute a search and screening committee whose task is to find applicants for a vacant position. The functions of the committee include: (1) seeking and finding qualified individuals who are interested in applying for the position; (2) receiving, reviewing, and evaluating the applications of the candidates; (3) interviewing qualified candidates; and (4) recommending the top candidates to the chairperson and dean. In searching for qualified individuals the committee is charged with the responsibility for actively seeking out and recruiting blacks, women, and other minority members. The committee also must use objective screening procedures, which insure fair and equitable treatment of all applicants, thus providing a basis for a legal defense against charges of discrimination, arbitrary, capricious, and unreasonable behaviors, or constitutionally impermissible activities. The size of the search committee is dependent on several factors but is usually made up of from three to seven individuals. When the duties of the vacant position cross departmental lines or involve close interaction with other departments or areas, the committee needs representation from those other departments or areas. If there are no black, female, or other minority members within the department who can be appointed to the committee, the appointer must seek such individuals elsewhere. If the vacancy is for a senior faculty member it may be desirable that the committee include senior faculty members from other areas. Often the search committee includes a student who is majoring in the specialty or area in which the candidate will teach. The committee needs a chairperson, one who ordinarily is a member of the department in which the vacancy exists. Sometimes the committee elects its chairperson, but usually he or she is appointed by the department chairperson or the dean.

The function of the search-and-screening committee, like most departmental committees, is advisory. One of its first tasks is to review the job description for currency and completeness. The deparment chairperson should lead this review and revision, thus insuring that the committee members will be fully aware of the department's expectations for the next holder of the position. Having completed the review and made the necessary revisions, the committee can then prepare the vacancy announcements.

Position Vacancy Announcement

Two kinds of announcements need to be prepared. The first is a short statement used to advertise the position. The second is a longer detailed description which can be sent to all those who respond to the advertisements and to individuals who are thought to be possible candidates. In addition, copies may be sent to departments in other institutions and to members of professional associations.

The short statement, used as an advertisement, might include the following ingredients:

1. The name of the department and institution
2. The academic rank or ranks of the open position
3. Minimum degree and experiential requirements for the applicant
4. Description of special characteristics or expertise desired
5. Brief description of teaching, research, and service responsibilities
6. Whether the position is tenure-earning or for a fixed period of time
7. Employment period—academic or calendar year
8. Salary range or statement that salary is competitive
9. Name, title, and address of person to whom inquiry should be made
10. Closing date for application

The longer detailed position description should repeat all the information contained in the advertisement, together with clear instructions on how to make application and submit credentials, and should be expanded to include all relevant information which the applicants need to know. The degrees offered by the department should be listed and if the department's name is ambiguous, the disciplines taught should be spelled out. If the position is nontenure-earning but the contract is renewable, it should be so stated, and the availability of any possible supplementary salary such as summer employment or overload work should be mentioned. If the location of the institution is not well known, a geographic description might be in order. General information about the institution need not be included in the short or long announcements; however, descriptive brochures, if available, might be sent to those who request them. If interviews will be held at a professional conference such as the Modern Language Association or the American Educational Research Association, specific dates and places need to be mentioned. Equal opportunity employers should state that fact in their advertisements. Generally, institutions that receive federal assistance or whose students receive federal aid fall into this category. A church-sponsored college that restricts its hiring to members of its faith should so indicate.

Instructions on applying and submitting credentials should be clear and precise. Applicants are usually asked to submit a letter of application, three or more letters of reference, and a current résumé or vita. In some cases the committee may wish to ask for a copy of the applicant's placement file from the institution that granted his or her advanced degree. Other materials or documents such as publications may be required as well.

It may be desirable to ask the candidate to include a written statement expressing his or her special qualifications in the letter of application. In some cases the applicant may be asked to state the earliest date employment could begin. When the salary is open, it may be appropriate to ask the candidate what expectations he or she holds and whether special conditions must be met before the applicant will accept the position.

The applicants need to be informed as to how many and what sorts of letters of reference are required. General letters of reference from a placement file are sometimes submitted by the applicant but are really not as useful as those expressly written for the purpose. Letters of reference should be current and are most valuable when they address the candidate's suitability for a particular position. Full mailing addresses and telephone numbers of the referees should be requested when references are to be checked.

If information not appearing on a standard résumé or vita is desired, it should be asked for. If there is interest in evaluating the quality as well as the quantity of publications, copies of recent published materials should be requested. If the position is in the field of music or the arts, specific instructions should be given concerning the shipment of tape recordings, photographs, slides, or artworks.

In their application materials, candidates should not be requested to submit information concerning their race, national origin, sex, age, possible handicap, family plans, maiden name, or any other items precluded under the affirmative action guidelines. However, for statistical purposes such information may be requested under separate cover by the person responsible for monitoring affirmative action procedures. The data thus gathered may not be linked to the individuals' applications.

Closing Dates

The closing date contained in the advertisement is the date after which no further applications are accepted. The practices surrounding this general rule may vary from institution to institution. In some cases, all the information requested must be postmarked by the announced closing date. In other cases, only the letter of application needs to be received by the closing date, while the supporting materials may be accepted up to the time the committee meets to evaluate the applications. Either way, the committee must decide on the policy it will follow and should so inform the applicants. Some position vacancies are announced with an application deadline listed as "open." If a desirable candidate applies for the position, it cannot be filled until another advertisement is published which announces a closing date. The closing date should not be sooner than one week after the publication of the announcement.

If no attractive candidates apply for the position by the time of the closing date, or a superior candidate appears after the closing date, the position must be readvertised with a new deadline before the latecomer or any other applicant may be considered. If the rank, salary, or other important aspect of the position is changed after advertising has begun or is completed, the changed position should be readvertised for at least two more weeks. Furthermore, no position should be filled, nor should a firm commitment be made to any candidate, before the application deadline date.

Where to Announce the Vacancy

In order to meet affirmative action guidelines and to conduct a meaningful search for possible candidates, search and screening committees must often go to great lengths in locating a variety of potential sources. Many institutions are regional in character and draw their faculty largely from residents of their own geographical area or from graduates of nearby universities. The composition of the faculty, then, frequently reflects the manpower situation of that region, which may not include many qualified minority or women candidates. In such cases, the committee must look beyond the traditional area in its effort to attract a wider variety of applicants. Even quite cosmopolitan departments may need to increase the numbers and kinds of institutions from which they have traditionally recruited faculty. An accurate record of these search efforts should be kept for accountability purposes.

Job registries are published by various agencies such as state departments of education, state postsecondary or higher education coordinating councils, and statewide equal employment job agencies. Such registries may have wide circulation, and departmental position vacancies should be listed with them. Departments in private institutions should check to see if their statewide or regional association of private universities and colleges maintains such a job registry and should announce their openings in it. Many disciplines and professions have active state and regional associations which publish position openings in their newsletters and journals, and search committees should take advantage of these opportunities. In addition, it may be possible to obtain membership lists or even purchase mailing labels from these associations in order to send announcements to the members. Of course, announcements should always be mailed to departments in the discipline that have graduate programs of quality.

Large, comprehensive institutions generally advertise in publications of national professional associations such as The American Psychological Association and The American Association for the Advancement of Science. In the last several years, *The Chronicle of Higher Education* has been used extensively to advertise position vacancies. The more specialized the desired competency, the greater is the need to consult the appropriate national discipline association. Here, too, one might be able to obtain a set of mailing labels to be used to contact a targeted set of potential candidates. Recognized leaders in the field are often able to suggest names of qualified individuals who may be ready for a change.

Most professional associations are committed to the principles of affirmative action and many maintain, as a service to colleges and universities, a list of qualified women and minority members who might be willing to consider a position vacancy. Professional associations, therefore, are a source of information that should not be overlooked. Announcements should also be sent to colleges and universities that predominantly serve blacks or women. The committee chairperson should work with the departmental staff to build a mailing list of institutions, departments, associations and key individuals who can be helpful in identifying a broad range of potential candidates.

Position Changes Which Need Not be Advertised

In general, all instructional and research positions of a continuing nature which are half time or more need to be advertised following affirmative action guidelines. However, some positions do not need to be advertised, even in institutions with stringent guidelines. Following are examples, drawn from a list developed by the State University System of Florida, of positions "not required to be advertised."

1. Promotion from assistant to associate professor
2. Selection of chairperson or assistant chairperson, when the existing faculty serve on a rotating basis; however, external recruiting for a chairperson should be advertised

3. A principal investigator or recipient of a contract or grant

4. An existing position whose funding source has changed but whose duties remain the same, for example, a shift from a grant or contract to a regularly funded general budget; should the duties be redefined, the position needs to be advertised

5. Visiting scholars or exchange professorships

6. Positions less than half time during a term

7. "Adjunct" or visiting or other temporary faculty who are not appointed for more than a year

---

Record Keeping

Throughout our discussion we have mentioned the importance of keeping records of the search and screening process. Here is some additional information, along with a summary of what has been stated earlier. The records should be kept in a specific location, known to the departmental secretary, the department chairperson, and the search committee chairperson. A record of all mailings announcing the position should be maintained. When written inquiries about the position are received, they should be dated and stamped. When responding to these inquiries, a statement should be included explaining that persons found eligible to be considered for the position will be sent a survey form asking for information about their race and sex along with other data, which will be aggregated to document the affirmative action efforts of the committee.

When each application is received it should be dated and placed in an individual folder. Each applicant's folder should contain a checklist which can be used to determine quickly whether the file is complete. The application folders should be grouped alphabetically by last name. On the day after the application period closes, the head secretary should compile a master list of all persons who have made inquiry about the position vacancy. In preparation for the first meeting of the search committee following the closing date, someone should be assigned the task of inspecting the files and placing a mark beside the names of all persons whose files are incomplete. At this first meeting, the search committee should confirm that those files are indeed incomplete and retire them from further consideration for the time being. No photographs of candidates should be included in the files. They should be removed by the secretary opening the mail, labeled or tagged, and kept together in a separate file. If too much extraneous material is submitted by an applicant it should be pulled by the search committee chairperson and filed by the secretary along with the pictures. It is advisable that all records be kept for at least three years for each recruitment effort. The committee chairperson should contact the individual designated as the institutional affirmative action officer at the planning stage of the recruitment effort and stay in constant touch with this person to assure compliance with national and state policy as well as institutional regulations. It is also important that the affirmative action officer be sent copies of the advertisement and the long position vacancy announcement. In some instances this person must approve the advertising copy before it is sent out; the same approval may be required for the long announcement. Some institutions have developed a handbook containing a checklist of all the procedures that must be followed in the recruiting process. One or two copies of such a handbook, if available, should be obtained for members of the search committee early in the process.

Separating Ineligible from Eligible Applicants—The First Screening

The search committee now has the difficult task of reviewing and evaluating applicants on the basis of written information contained in each applicant's file. The committee may decide in advance to declare ineligible for consideration those applicants whose files are still incomplete by a certain date. On the other hand, the committee may decide that in the case of incomplete files, missing documents will be requested if the information thus far received suggests that the applicant has strong qualifications. Fairness would dictate, however, that if such a request were made, it should be made of every applicant with an incomplete file. The lack of a terminal degree such as a doctorate may also be sufficient reason for not considering an application. This requirement is sometimes waived for individuals who are otherwise well qualified and can certify that their degrees will be received by a certain date.

Other reasons for finding candidates ineligible may be related to the inability of applicants to meet state and institutional regulations. For example, many institutions have a nepotism rule which forbids hiring relatives or dependents of the department chairperson or dean. Often, this rule applies only to those who would be under direct supervision of a relative already employed. Some institutions follow a strict policy of not hiring their own graduates because they fear the consequences of academic inbreeding. Other objections to hiring one's own products are based on the well-known tendency of senior professors to continue to direct their former students' activities rather than accept them as equals. Conversely, there are institutions that deliberately employ selected alumni who have made names for themselves elsewhere. Such alumni, it is claimed, identify with and understand the traditions of their alma mater better than outsiders. Many institutions which forbid the hiring of their own graduates allow exceptions to be made in special circumstances, such as a need for a temporary faculty member to fill a sudden vacancy or the lack of resources to recruit an outside candidate.

Mention should be made of a class of applicants who are particularly annoying. There are individuals who state in a letter "If you are seriously interested in me I will send . . ." (an updated vita, letters of reference, or whatever to complete their applications). These persons are game-players who are trying to place themselves in an advantaged position before the competition gets under-way. If the committee chairperson responds with an indication of interest, it may create false expectations on the part of the applicant and raise questions of fairness to other applicants with incomplete files.

During the first screening, the files of candidates may be separated into three categories. Some candidates are clearly "ineligible" in terms of qualifications or institutional or departmental policies; others are "eligible" and still others are "marginal" in that their files may not be complete or they do not quite meet all of the criteria for eligibility. The files of those who have been declared ineligible should be set aside and a note containing the reason for the ineligibility should be inserted in each file. It is not yet appropriate to send letters of rejection to the ineligible applicants.

Evaluating the Qualifications of Eligible and Marginal Candidates—The Second Screening

Now the committee members read the files carefully and prepare for the second cut. During this review, the committee decides how well each applicant meets the criteria and the desired job qualifications listed in the position announcement. Search committees frequently develop a checklist that members can use when reviewing the application materials. Some committee members find it easier to arrive at an overall rating of individual applicants if separate ratings can be given to each of a number of items on a well-developed list. Such a list contains items concerning past experience, letters of recommendation, and every agreed upon criterion contained in the long position vacancy announcement. Several copies of the checklist, at least one for every committee member, are placed in each applicant's folder.

At present, given the condition of the academic market place, there is likely to be a veritable flood of applicants for each advertised position. A large number of these applicants may submit all the required credentials and documents but do not provide evidence that they meet the specified required characteristics. Many who do not meet the formal requirements believe they may be qualified by virtue of their special experiences in previous positions. Others want to move from where they are just to get away, and still others want a first-time, full-time job in academe. Those who do not meet the expected criteria should be declared ineligible and have the reasons for their ineligibility noted in their files. Examples of reasons are "inappropriate specialization," "wrong degree," "insufficient experience," "no teaching experience," and "too little research." It may be the case that most of the applicants are ill qualified and that the list of eligible candidates is disappointing.

The search committee may then decide to consider the "marginal" candidates, those who do not quite meet all of the criteria but nevertheless appear to have better-than-average qualifications. Marginals who are retained will be considered again in the third screening along with all other eligible candidates who are still in contention. In reviewing application materials, the committee members should keep in mind the affirmative action policies of the institution. As many women and minority candidates as possible should be retained in the "eligible" or "marginal" category for consideration in the third screening. If a committee is unable to identify a sufficient number of well-qualified candidates from the pool of "eligible" or "marginal" applicants, the committee may consider modifying the eligibility criteria. Affirmative action policies may then dictate that the position needs to be readvertised.

Formal agreement by the committee to use the advertised position characteristics as criteria needs to be taken seriously by the members and adhered to religiously unless unusual circumstances intervene. The search committee may need to decide in advance how it will proceed when it feels that equity and fairness would be served if it altered its own policies. Only rarely does a set of procedures cover all contingencies, even when expert guidance is used in their development. A search committee might agree that any of its procedures may be temporarily changed by a unanimous, or nearly unanimous, vote and submission of a written resolution explaining the perceived need. A policy of this kind might enable the committee to consider a good potential applicant who might otherwise be excluded on procedural grounds.

The chairperson of the search committee with the help of committee members should once again screen the files of all applicants who have survived the second screening to ensure that they are sufficiently worthy to be included in the third screening. If any additional unqualified applicants are found, their files should be reviewed by the entire committee and differing interpretations should be worked out. A secret ballot may be needed to resolve a genuinely sticky case. Some of these cases might be handled by designating them as "marginals," which would automatically move them to the third stage of consideration. Those applicants who do not survive the second screening, for whatever reasons, should be noted on the master list of applicants and their files pulled from further consideration. The remaining applicants have now been judged to meet the minimum set of requirements for the position and will become the official pool of "nominees" from which the best qualified will be selected.

Selection of the Finalists—The Third Screening

Each search committee member working individually now will need to read each nominee's file and select the top six to ten candidates. The chairperson should collect a copy of each committee member's list and compile them into an aggregate table of choices. The resulting table becomes the focus of the next meeting of the committee, at which each committee member explains his or her choices and discusses their strengths and weaknesses. The chairperson next should attempt to develop a consensus about the rank order position for each nominee. The object of this meeting is to select the top three nominees, any of whom would be clearly acceptable to the faculty. The chairperson of the search committee should then draft a memorandum to the department chairperson listing the names of those nominees being recommended along with their strengths and weaknesses. If only one or two are clearly consensus nominees, then only those names should be submitted.

Checking the References

Upon receiving the search committee's memorandum and the accompanying files, the department chairperson is ready to start checking each of the recommended nominee's references. This is usually done by telephone. The number of references to be checked will depend on the kinds of responses obtained from the referees. At least three should be contacted. What should one search for in these telephone checks? Initially, level of competence, promise of career growth, ability to work with colleagues and students, outstanding achievement, other strengths, and such weaknesses as missing classes, not completing work on time, student complaints, et cetera.

If conversations with three referees do not provide clear answers to these questions, then additional ones should be called until clear answers are obtained. If comments from some referees cause other questions to be raised, or if the nominee is described as nearly perfect, then it is appropriate to "network" a larger set of referees by asking the original ones for the names and telephone numbes of two other persons who would know the nominee, and if still more information is needed, asking this second group for a third list. The department chairperson may ask members of the search committee to make some of the telephone calls.

One of the more common difficulties facing a chairperson is how to check references of nominees who don't want their current employers to know that they are contemplating a move. In such cases, recommended nominees must be informed that they are being considered and be given the opportunity to drop the names of certain referees temporarily. It may be that a nominee's colleagues, except for the department chairperson and dean, could be called at this time. Similarly, if a nominee's letters of reference were written more than two years previously, he or she should be asked to provide more current ones. Some referees have nothing positive to say about anyone, whereas others will make only laudatory comments about everyone. To obtain information that will be helpful in evaluating the candidates, it is important to be able to identify the response style of the referee and to ask questions that will elicit useful answers. A member of the search committee or the department chairperson should prepare a written summary of what has been learned in these telephone reference checks.

One of the nagging fears of a search committee, department chairperson, college dean, and the dean of faculties is that a genuinely undesirable person will be hired. The kinds of personal conduct that cause the most problems and should be listened for in these interviews are: pernicious irascibility, mental health problems, alcoholism, criminal behavior, dismissal from a college or university in the last five years, and disciplinary action in the last two or three years. Persons found to be described with any of these problems need some evidence of being fully qualified and rehabilitated to be seriously considered for appointment.

Conceivably a nominee may have to be dropped from consideration as a result of the reference checks. Minor discrepancies in important characteristics can be pursued directly with the nominee over the phone or personally if he or she is invited to visit the campus.

Before Inviting the Candidate to the Campus

Toward the end of the final screening, the credentials of those candidates likely to be invited to the campus for an interview should be verified. Institutions from which they obtained degrees can easily be contacted to verify that the degrees have been conferred. Similarly, previous titles and ranks of nominees can be checked by contacting institutions where they were formerly employed. If there is a period of time unaccounted for in the employment record of the individual or if there is a long period between degrees, it is appropriate to ask the candidate to explain these time gaps. In most instances credentials provided by the candidates will be genuine. However, when such is not the case, the situation can be traumatic and embarrassing to the department and indeed the entire university, especially if the discrepancies are not discovered until one or more years after an appointment has been made.

Once again the departmental expectations should be compared with the candidate's qualifications and career objectives. A primarily research oriented person will not be happy in a position which requires that most of his or her time be spent teaching, and conversely a primarily teaching oriented person would be unhappy in a position which requires a major research output. To mismatch people in this way would be a disservice to the candidate and to the department. Yet mismatches sometimes occur.

As soon as the final group of nominees has been checked, the support staff should send a package of materials to them *before* they are invited to the campus for a visit. The materials should include such items as a faculty handbook, an institutional catalog, a copy of the collective bargaining agreement if one exists, a minimal description of the governance of the institution, any separate statements about a continuing contract or tenure status, opportunities for career advancement, academic freedom, grievance procedures, nature of the annual contract, budgetary facts, personnel policies, fringe benefits, and patent and copyright policies. Many of the latter items are contained in faculty handbooks, faculty constitutions, or bargaining agreements.

Before extending invitations to recommended nominees, the department chairperson should confer with the dean to make sure that the original approval to initiate the recruitment is still valid. Sometimes institutions undergo financial difficulty or policy changes after the initial approval was given. In such cases, the dean may try to persuade the department to fill the position temporarily with a part-time person, or postpone filling it for one year—which is less than what was first promised. Also, under certain circumstances the dean might suggest that the search committee review the pool of applicants once again to see if a woman or minority person can be recommended—or perhaps a qualified younger person with whom students can identify more closely. A department chairperson who regularly keeps the dean up to date on the progress of the recruiting effort is likely to learn of any funding problems or policy changes that might have occurred in the interim. Moreover, a dean who is kept informed of the results of the various screenings is more likely to accept the recommendations of the search committee. In any event it is usually the dean who must authorize travel expenses for candidates who are invited to the campus for an interview. With the dean's approval reaffirmed, the department chairperson can start inviting them to visit the campus.

The invitation is usually extended in a telephone conversation and a follow-up letter of confirmation. The telephone conversation provides the department chairperson with an opportunity to find out if the candidate is still interested in the position. The chairperson also has the opportunity to ask questions that have been raised by the search committee and to make sure that the candidate understands the pay range, rank, and other vital data about the position. Some departments expect each candidate to make a formal presentation to the faculty members during the visit regarding his or her areas of expertise and interest. If such is the case, the format of the presentation can be discussed in the telephone conversation. And finally, a mutually acceptable date for the visit can be scheduled.

The Campus Visit and the Interview

If more than one candidate is to be invited to the campus, schedules should be developed so that there is at least a day's interval between visits. Each candidate should be interviewed by the department head, members of the search committee individually or as a group, faculty members with whom he or she will be working, student representatives, the dean, and perhaps a member of the central administration. It is important that candidates be made to feel welcome and at ease, and that common courtesies be extended. If possible, candidates should be met at the airport and escorted to their appointments. Otherwise, they may conclude that there is a lack of serious interest in them or that the institution is a cold and unfriendly place. If time permits, they should be taken on a tour of the city and shown appropriate residential areas and other interesting and attractive features of the community. A candidate who, for salary or other reasons, has not yet decided whether to accept the offer, may choose to do so because of the warmth and friendliness communicated by the faculty and administrators.

When conducting interviews, a recommended technique is the use of open-ended questions. Such questions elicit detailed responses from candidates rather than "yes" or "no" answers, which are neither revealing nor constructive. For example, if candidates are asked whether they enjoyed their last job, a simple yes or no is not helpful. If on the other hand, they are asked "What did you enjoy about your last job?" their responses may provide insight into their character. Other examples of closed- and open-ended questions are:

CLOSED-ENDED QUESTIONS	OPEN-ENDED QUESTIONS
Did you apply for this position because of the research opportunities?	What was it that led you to apply for this position?
Do you feel that you are qualified for this position?	Describe your feelings on how well qualified you are for this position.
Have you ever had personality clashes with your colleagues?	All in all, how do you feel about the people you work with in your present (or previous) position?
Have you been required to demonstrate leadership?	In what ways have you been required to demonstrate leadership in the past?

An arrangement that can make the interview more effective is to have the chairperson or a member of the search committee sit through each of the scheduled sessions or meetings. This person can make the proper introductions and summarize the candidate's qualifications and interests for the benefit of those who have not had access to the application folder.

During the interview, it is important to avoid asking certain questions that violate fair employment practices. Such unlawful questions include direct inquiries about national origin, and whether one is naturalized or native born. Questions about nationality, race, or religious affiliations, or the religious affiliation of schools attended, are also unlawful. It is improper to inquire about family planning, size of family, ages of children, child care plans, and spouse's employment or salary. One may not inquire about military service in countries other than the United States or request military service records. One should not inquire about ancestry, the birthplace of applicants' parents, grandparents, or spouses, about clubs and organizations to which applicants belong, about medical history of pregnancies, and other health matters. The overall criterion is to avoid asking nonjob-related questions, the answers to which would provide information that could be used as a basis for unlawful discrimination.

It is permissible to inquire into the place and length of current and previous addresses, to ask if an individual is or intends to become a U.S. citizen, and if the spouse is a citizen. The candidates may be asked whether they have any criminal convictions which may have a bearing on job performance, but they may not be asked about arrests. Instead of asking about family size or family responsibilities, it is proper to inquire about freedom to travel if required by the job, and ability to meet work schedules. If any candidate is asked lawful questions about convictions, ability to travel, anticipated absences, or disabilities that may affect performance, *all* candidates must be asked those questions.

Many excellent guides for effective interviewing are available. For those who prefer a handy checklist, here in paraphrased form is one taken from the *Handbook for Search and Screening Committees at Florida State University.*

1. Avoid interruptions. Do not take telephone calls during the interview.

2. Treat each candidate as a unique individual.

3. Provide a good first impression of the department, college and university. Be prompt, adhere to the schedule, and provide an attractive location for the interview.

4. Listen carefully to what the candidate has to say; do not dominate the conversation.

5. Avoid unlawful questions and those not job-related.

6. Avoid entering into arguments with candidates.

7. Do not make promises that cannot be kept.

8. Conduct the interview in private and assure the candidates of the confidentiality of the information they provide.

9. Allow sufficient time for the interview, for movement between meetings, and for refreshment and restroom stops.

10. Ask questions about the candidates' ideas, philosophies, or achievements in lieu of direct questions about their attitudes.

11. Avoid lengthy notetaking during the interview. If necessary, expand notes and complete rating forms promptly after the interview.

12. Try not to turn the interview into an interrogation. Rather than launch a barrage of questions, make interesting and appropriate comments which stimulate the candidate to respond.

13. Try to avoid making hasty judgments about the candidate based solely on appearance or mannerisms—ask the candidates questions, answers to which may help dispel negative impressions.

14. Do not show impatience when the candidate does not seem to be responding in the manner expected. Ask open-ended questions which may help the candidate to come around to the point of information being sought.

The search committee chairperson may desire to prepare and distribute a simple evaluation form to each of the interviewers. The form might list those characteristics to be evaluated and provide space for written comments. Interviewers should be reminded to observe and be prepared to comment on the behavior and mannerisms of the candidates.

- Does the candidate look better on paper than in person? If so, what personal characteristics contributed to a negative impression?
- How did the candidate's energy level appear? Active? Normal? Lethargic?
- Did the candidate's body stance give the impression that he or she was nervous, relaxed, unsure, confused, defensive, or rigid?
- What was seen in the candidate's facial expressions? Openness? Arrogance? Puzzlement? Pleasantness? Boredom? Alertness?
- Were the expected weaknesses of the candidate confirmed by the interview? Were other weaknesses apparent?
- Were strengths confirmed? Were new strengths revealed? Did the candidate show genuine promise?
- Did the interview reveal any unexpected problems?

The chairperson of the search committee should promptly collect the written evaluations of the interview so that the committee can use them in its deliberations.

The Dean's Choice

The department chairperson sends the dean a memorandum containing the list of recommended candidates. A complete file with credentials and references for each person should accompany the memorandum. Generally, a dean will prefer to receive the list in alphabetical rather than rank order. There are subtle ways in which the department chairperson can let the dean know what the search committee really felt about each candidate. The most obvious is to describe the impressions that were made during the interviews. The dean, of course, will want to know whether any of the candidates is a woman or a member of a minority group. After discussing the matter with the chairperson and upon due deliberation, the dean will rank order those persons who are recommended and give the chairperson permission to make a job offer to the leading one.

The Job Offer

The chairperson usually makes the job offer by telephone. During the phone call the chairperson reiterates the proposed salary, the rank, and the date of appointment. Often, the candidate may ask for some time to make a final decision; and a week or two should be sufficient for this purpose. It is not uncommon for candidates to seek counteroffers from their current institutions, or from other institutions with whom they may be negotiating. If the chairperson at the offering institution knows or suspects that this is the case, he or she must decide whether the candidate is so valuable that additional inducements should be offered. These inducements could take the form of higher salary, moving expenses, or released time for scholarly activities. It is possible that there are no additional inducements available, and the candidate must be persuaded on the basis of intangibles such as the quality of life in the university or the community. In any event, the chairperson should insist on a decision by a fixed date.

There is always the possibility that a candidate will not accept an offer. In fact, it is possible that the top three candidates may, one after another, reject it. A desired counteroffer at the home university, a perceived better opportunity at another institution, or other conditions may lead all of them to turn the offer down. It would be unfortunate if the turndowns occur because the department is making the mistake of trying to recruit out of its league or creating negative impressions about itself.

For the candidate who does accept, several things need to be made clear. First, a letter will be sent making the formal job offer, to which the candidate should respond promptly and affirmatively. Second, a contract may be forthcoming, but only after a board of trustees or regents approves the proposed contract. If a letter of intent to employ is signed by a dean or other college official, the candidate may begin to make plans to move to the new institution. However, until the *official contract* is received and signed by the candidate, he or she is not legally bound to the new position nor can the candidate be absolutely certain of being employed at the new institution; and the candidate should be so informed. Obviously, the department chairperson or secretary should follow the progress of the appointment papers, the payroll forms, and the contract as they move through the institutional bureaucracy. A candidate who is relatively assured of being appointed needs to find housing, arrange for childen's schooling, et cetera. The department should arrange for one or two faculty members or their spouses to help the candidate identify a desirable residential area. The new faculty member should be encouraged to move to the area two weeks or a month before the term begins, if possible. This will give the new person time to adjust to the community as well as to the new institution and department.

Terminating the Search

After a search has been completed, letters need to be sent to the original applicants. It is important to indicate only that a person was found who best met the needs of the department. Written comments about the rejected person's capabilities could result in misinterpretation, arguments, and lawsuits and therefore should not be included in the notification. The chairperson should be thoroughly conversant with the requirements for compiling, submitting, and storing the records or each recruitment effort. Some institutions will not process appointment papers for the selected candidate until the affirmative action file of the search is complete. Generally, a three-year holding period is sufficient for records of a search, and a specific place may be designated for final disposition of these records.

In the event the search was unsuccessful it is still necessary to compile a complete set of records. These can be helpful later if the search is reopened. At present it seems necessary to notify each of the former applicants when a search is reopened and ask them whether they wish to be considered again. It is apparent from actual experience that such a communication tends to raise the hopes of many persons who were previously judged unqualified or unsuitable. Many applicants evidently are not sophisticated enough to realize that if they were not called or invited to campus during the first search they stand little chance the second time around. On the other hand, if the second search specifies lower criteria for the position, some of the previous applicants may qualify as candidates or nominees. Also, it may be the case that other former applicants who in the meantime have had articles and books published may have upgraded their qualifications. If the initial search is unsuccessful, it is important not to send out letters of rejection until a decision has been made to terminate the search. If the search is to be reopened, all former applicants must be notified and the search process must begin again at its first phase.

In summary, recruitment should be an integral part of a long-range departmental plan which includes a clearly defined set of goals. As part of the planning process, departments should keep an inventory of current faculty specializations and competencies as well as a list of other areas which need to be developed, including projected time frames for their development. A central part of any recruiting effort is the commitment to principles of equal opportunity and affirmative action. Clearly written affirmative action procedures need to be developed and followed and careful records of the process need to be kept. Departments should make special efforts to expand the traditional pool of qualified applicants so that more women and minority members are considered.

A search committee must be established according to set criteria and should conduct its business in an orderly and planned manner. Part of its responsibility is to advertise a vacant position properly and screen all applicants. The task of the committee is less onerous if it is directed by a specified set of policies and procedures for evaluating all application materials, screening applicants, and designating those deemed best qualified. During the search process and subsequent candidate interviews, it is as important for the institution to make a good impression on potential faculty members as it is for these faculty members to demonstrate their best attributes. Choosing the right person is more important now than ever before in light of increasing economic problems, changing curricula, fluctuating enrollments, and the great difficulties encountered when attempting to discharge unsatisfactory and nonproductive colleagues. There is a strong likelihood that the person selected today may be a member of the department for a very long time to come.

Retention of Faculty

Completing a proper search and filling the position with a carefully selected candidate is no guarantee that the candidate will succeed, especially if it is his or her first academic position. Effort must be made on both sides to assure that a sound and productive relationship is built. From the department's perspective, this means following a few fairly simple principles of good human-resource development.

New faculty, just like other new employees, need to feel that they are a part of the unit. They need to be included in the social and professional events that are important to veteran members. Small but visible rituals of initation symbolize a new person's entry and acceptance. Each department will have its own way of welcoming and initiating a junior faculty member, but it often takes a conscious effort to make sure this happens. The welcome should be an unforced occasion, a natural event in the course of departmental life. A brief welcoming speech at the first faculty meeting of the Fall term might be an appropriate occasion in one department; something more informal, like an invitation to play or sing in a musical ensemble, would be more natural in another. There is no magic formula—whatever seems appropriate as a symbolic welcoming gesture will probably meet the needs of the department and the new person alike.

Although a new faculty member may *feel* welcomed, he or she must still master the rules of behavior and the expectations that the department and the institution will ultimately enforce. A period of orientation, socialization, and induction is important, even if sometimes uncomfortable for everyone involved. A new Ph.D. from a major research university, for example, may be surprised or shocked to discover that a heavy undergraduate teaching load—with a good number of marginally prepared students—is the norm at Cornfed U. Having graduated from a department in which senior professors taught a single graduate seminar every semester and otherwise only occasionally conducted an undergraduate honors course, the new person will have to go through a major reorientation of expectations. Not only will expectations have to be revised, but an array of new skills will have to be learned, often quickly and without warning. Having imagined a career in which one could spend large chunks of time doing research and writing papers, one suddenly realizes that twelve contact hours a week with up to fifty students in each class is draining work. This is particularly true if one or more of the preparations happens to be in an area well outside one's training and interests.

An effective department chair will empathize with the crisis that such a transition to "the real world" may precipitate and will see to it that new faculty members are helped to visualize the actual assignments they will undertake. Assistance and support in getting started will be offered. Opportunities for feedback and counseling will be readily available. Rewards for mastering new tasks will be quickly extended. Forgiveness for errors and blunders will initially be generous, and will be accompanied with good-natured but clear and firm advice. The margin for error, however, will be progressively reduced. A new faculty member is not different from a new employee in any other situation. He or she must learn the new role, accommodate to the realities of the job, adjust his or her ideals and ambitions, and perceive a compensating measure of support and appreciation for the sacrifices one ordinarily makes when one agrees to work for an organization.

Although the first step in building a healthy relationship is to assure that the induction and initiation phase goes well, the long-term prospects depend on how well the parties understand and accommodate the basic needs and interests of the other. Retaining faculty will require attention, not only to the basic needs of the department, but to the basic needs of the faculty members, too.

Among the fundamental needs that all ambitious people try to satisfy are those for money, security (both physical and psychological), achievement, and esteem or status. Faculty, who certainly as a group are as ambitious as any other, need these things in no less signficient ways than any other. Unless their departmental home can offer them what they need, they will become demoralized and look for exits.

Salary and benefits, although hardly ever perceived by faculty as ample compensation for either their work or their fundamental value to society, must nevertheless be perceived as both adequate and equitable. Large salary differentials in a department have perhaps the most explosive potential of any source of conflict. Although differentials based on rank, length of service, or bona fide merit can be accepted in most settings, differentials that are perceived to be based on favoritism or other subjective biases may have a profound impact on morale. Further, a department that consistently fails to achieve merit or other salary increases for its faculty (commensurate with those achieved elsewhere on campus) will face serious morale problems when faculty perceive that they have fallen too far behind their colleagues in other fields.

Faculty expect to achieve tenure and to hold it in the face of all disasters of whatever magnitude. This is the bedrock institution of security for faculty, and it is viewed by all with the utmost seriousness. New faculty, particularly, need to learn how tenure may best be achieved. Mentoring them so they can get over the tenure hurdle may mean the difference between a successful career and a failed one. The chair may not be the best person to provide such mentoring, especially if he or she will eventually have to make a binding recommendation on tenure. But mentoring should be available, and the chair must take pains to assure that the new faculty member understands clearly what the standards and expectations are. If an institution is serious about publication as the principal criterion for tenure, that ought to be made perfectly clear.

Because the motivation for security is profoundly important to most people, and because tenure is one of the sacred aspects of faculty culture, an institution must consider whether it is in a position to award tenure to faculty it hires. Although many faculty are explicitly hired for nontenure-track positions, they often have expectations, realistic or not, that they may be able to earn tenure if their efforts prove them worthy. Similarly, individuals who are hired on tenure-track positions have every reason to believe that the institution is acting in good faith and that they will almost certainly achieve tenure with their obvious talents and value to the institution. Needless to say, the grounds for fundamental and catastrophic misunderstandings are built into these relationships.

Closely related is the ability of faculty to achieve. Not only is this a basic need, but achievement is the basis on which rewards are distributed. Shaping one's achievements to the expectations of the institution means the difference between succeeding and failing. Providing opportunities to succeed is the essential ingredient in retaining faculty. A department that assigns a heavy teaching load to a new faculty member who will be expected to publish to earn tenure is not only assuring a very public failure, but is acting unethically. Basic fairness requires that a new faculty member understand the grounds on which tenure will be awarded or denied, that he or she have a reasonable opportunity to live up to the expected standards, and that the judgment ultimately be made on objective grounds. No reasonable person expects to achieve security without producing, but reasonable people do expect to be rewarded in proportion to their efforts. When fundamental needs like that for security are at stake, people will work hard when they have a fair opportunity.

Even the most jaded and secure senior professor has basic needs for status and esteem. People need to feel appreciated. If they are un- or underappreciated for too long, their morale will plummet. Although not everyone can win Nobel Prizes, or even get work published more often than once in five years, he or she still needs to hear praise and other words of appreciation. For new faculty, who may go as long as seven years before earning tenure, and for older faculty who may feel that others are anxiously awaiting their retirement, this need to feel appreciated may be especially strong. No one expects or needs rewards or praises that are out of proportion to their accomplishment, and they may be embarrassed by any such display. But a word of thanks for a job well done, a quiet compliment, or a note of praise for an article or paper may have psychological importance of a degree far beyond the effort it may take to offer it.

Although these largely commonsense ideas are critical to the department's ability to keep morale high and to retain new and more senior faculty alike, they often are ignored by faculty and department chairs alike. Somehow, it is assumed that faculty are different, that they are not "regular employees." That assumption carries with it a corollary: that faculty are not human, either. To the contrary, faculty are unusually perceptive and sensitive human beings. Although seemingly immune to the normal rules and rituals of organizational life, they are nevertheless extremely perceptive and attentive to the small symbolic cues in their environment. Keeping them attuned to their jobs and rewarding them for doing things they are supposed to be doing is nothing more or less than an investment in their long-term value to the department.

Questions

1. Does your institution or department have written policies governing recruitment of new faculty? What are the similarities and differences between the procedures of your institution and those described in this chapter?

2. How many new faculty have been hired in your department during the past five years? What procedures were followed in recruitment and selection?

3. a. List the discipline specialties represented by the current members of your department.

   b. Are there specialties among them for which there no longer seems to be a need (for whatever reason)?

   c. Do you expect any retirements or resignations during the next five to ten years that will leave the department without some of its needed specialties?

   d. What additional specialties does your department need to achieve its goals over the next five to ten years?

4. Let us assume that two of the faculty members in your department are planning to retire two years from now. You are told by the dean that you will be able to fill the two vacant positions and that the two new faculty members need not have the same specialties as their predecessors.

   a. What procedures does your institution have regarding recruiting and searching for replacements?

   b. Would you look for new people with the same specialties as those of the retirees? How would you go about deciding which specialties you would be looking for?

5. How does your department deal with faculty whom you want to retain but who have, or look for, opportunities to move elsewhere?

References

BOWEN, HOWARD R., and SCHUSTER, JACK H. *The American Professoriate: A National Resource Imperiled.* New York: Carnegie Corporation, 1986.

BOWKER, LEE H., and LYNCH, DAVID M. *Chairing a Small Department.* Paper presented at the National Conference for Department Chairs, Orlando, 1985. (ERIC Document Reproduction Service No. ED 256 222)

BRENEMAN, DAVID W., and YOUN, TED I. K. (Eds.) *Academic Labor Markets and Careers.* Philadelphia: The Falmer Press, Taylor & Francis, Inc., 1988.

CAPLOW, THEODORE, and McGEE, REECE J. *The Academic Marketplace.* Garden City NY: Doubleday, 1958.

CARNEGIE COUNCIL ON POLICY STUDIES IN HIGHER EDUCATION. *Making Affirmative Action Work in Higher Education: An Analysis of Institutional and Federal Policies with Recommendations.* San Francisco: Jossey–Bass, 1975.

DOUGLAS, JOEL M. (Ed.) *Salary and Compensation Methodology in Academic Collective Bargaining.* New York: National Center for the Study of Collective Bargaining in Higher Education and the Professions, 1983. (ERIC Document Reproduction Service No. ED 230 140)

ELMORE, GARLAND C. "A Second National Survey of Faculty Salaries in Radio and Television." *ACA Bulletin,* 56, 1986, pp. 36–42.

FELD, SHELIA. "The Academic Marketplace in Social Work." *Journal of Social Work Education,* 24, 1988, pp. 201–210.

FLORIDA STATE UNIVERSITY. *Handbook for Search and Screening Committees.* Tallahassee: Human Affairs Office, Florida State University, 1980.

GADDY, DALE. *Faulty Recruitment.* Washington, DC: American Association of Junior Colleges, 1969.

HOWE, RICHARD D., and URQUHART, MARYON. *Salary Trend Study of Faculty in Social Sciences for the Years 1984–85 and 1987–88.* Boone, NC: Appalachian State University, 1988. (ERIC Document Reproduction Service No. ED 302 165)

MANN, MARY PAT. *An Analysis of Faculty Goals: Personal, Disciplinary, and Career Development Decisions.* Paper presented at the Annual Meeting of the AERA, San Francisco, March 1989. (ERIC Document Reproduction Service No. ED 305 874)

MCDOWELL, EARL E., and MROZLA, BRIDGET A. *An Exploratory Study of the Academic Résumé and Employment Interview Practices.* Paper presented at the Annual Meeting of the Speech Communication Association, Boston, 1987. (ERIC Document Reproduction Service No. ED 290 187)

MCINTOSH, THOMAS H., and KOEVERING, THOMAS E. "Six-year Case Study of Faculty Peer Reviews, Merit Ratings, and Pay Awards in a Multidisciplinary Department." *Journal of the College and University Personnel Association,* 37, 1986, pp. 5–14.

NOE, NICHOLAS N. *Measures of Salary Inequality.* AIR Annual Forum Paper, Orlando, 1986. (ERIC Document Reproduction Service No. ED 280 423)

PINGREE, SUZANNE (et al.) "Anti-Nepotism's Ghost: Attitudes of Administrators Towards Hiring Professional Couples." *Psychology of Women Quarterly,* 3 Fall 1978, pp. 23–29.

SAGARIA, MARY ANN. "Administrative Mobility and Gender: Patterns and Processes in Higher Education." *Journal of Higher Education,* 59, 1988, pp. 306–326.

STECKLEIN, JOHN E., and LATHROP, ROBERT L. *Faculty Attraction and Retention.* Minneapolis: Bureau of Institutional Research, University of Minnesota, 1960.

STEELE, CLAUDE M., and GREEN, STEPHEN G. "Affirmative Action and Academic Hiring: A Case Study of a Value Conflict." *Journal of Higher Education,* July 1976, pp. 413–435.

THOMAS, TRUDELLE. "Demystifying the Job Search: A Guide for Candidates." *College Composition and Communication,* 40, 1989, pp. 312–327.

WAGGAMAN, JOHN S. *Faculty, Recruitment, Retention, and Fair Employment: Obligations and Opportunites.* ASHE–ERIC/Higher Education Research Report No. 2. Washington, DC: Association for the Study of Higher Education, 1983.

WEAVER, FREDERICK STIRTON. "Scholarship for the Teaching Faculty." *College Teaching,* 34, 1986, pp. 51–58.

Chapter 13

Affirmative Action: Finding, Hiring, and Retaining Women and Minority Faculty

Since the department is the locus of the recruitment process and the heart of the equal-employment effort, it should assume responsibility for making a serious effort to locate women and minority candidates. In those discipline areas where women and minority faculty members are in short supply, departments should do what they can to expand the pool of qualified candidates. Departments also have a moral obligation to eliminate all departmental policies and practices that could result in discrimination, and to ensure that affirmative action and equal-opportunity policies are followed.

Current Status of Women and Minorities in Faculty Positions

As recently as 1988, when the National Center for Education Statistics surveyed faculty characteristics, 73 percent of all full-time faculty were male.[1] Men are more concentrated in the research and graduate institutions (about 80 percent of full-time faculty at these institutions were male), and in certain fields (97 percent of the full-time faculty in engineerng were male). Women were more likely to be serving in part-time faculty positions, and to be working in community colleges. Fewer women faculty than men had received the doctorate.

Just over 10 percent of all full-time faculty in 1988 were drawn from

1. *Faculty in Higher Education Institutions, 1988: 1988 National Survey of Postsecondary Faculty* (Washington, DC: U.S. Department of Education, 1990).

minority groups. Asians made up the largest minority group, accounting for 4.4 percent of all faculty. Blacks were seriously underrepresented in proportion to their numbers in the general population; they accounted for only 3.3 percent of all faculty. Hispanics accounted for 2 percent of all faculty, also a comparatively small number. Private universities and liberal arts colleges were reported to have greater proportions of minorities on their faculties than public institutions. Asian faculty appear to be most prominently represented in business, engineering, and the health sciences. Black faculty are more heavily represented in education and the social sciences. Hispanics are most heavily represented in the humanities and fine arts. Individual fields seem to have particular difficulty finding minority faculty from certain ethnic groups. There are very few black engineering faculty, for example. (The national sample surveyed by NCES contained *one* black engineering professor.) Although great strides have been made, women and minorities are still substantially underrepresented in many fields, and the pipeline is not producing enough Ph.D.s to go around.

Current Hiring Practices and Discrimination

In spite of the fact that there is a shared moral objection to discrimination, the simple continuation of traditional hiring practices within the university tends to perpetuate the underrepresentation of women, minorities, and others in academe. The federal government and the federal courts have established guidelines and given instructions on how discrimination in higher education may be avoided. These guidelines address the problems of inadvertent as well as intentional discrimination. Affirmative action may be defined as the process whereby qualified individuals with minority status are actively sought to fill vacancies, and when found are given preference over equally qualified nonminority persons. Some departments in state universities stipulate the percentage of women and minorities to be attained over a specific period of time. To reach these goals, some officials feel so pressured that they may, after advertising a vacancy, defer filling the available position until a women or minority candidate is found who can be successfully recruited and employed. Such a practice is itself a violation of fair-employment criteria since, once a position is announced and an open search is conducted, the best available person should be selected for the job, regardless of sex, age, race, religion, et cetera.

Many institutions have made extraordinary efforts to remove vestiges of discriminatory practice. Nevertheless, allegations of discrimination continue to be made in courts, in grievances, and in published reports. Department chairpersons should be aware that each new appointment of a white male to the faculty may be seen over time as evidence of discrimination. That is, the effect of existing practices has been seen to lead to discriminatory outcomes. In contrast to this point of view, some courts have ruled that a clear intent to discriminate must be found before any special change in recruitment is required. Affirmative action does not mean that institutions are required to hire less-qualified minority members over better-qualified nonminority individuals.

Many grievances concerning discrimination have found their way into state and federal courts. Court cases generally concern alleged discrimination against women and minority members in matters of hiring practice and salary allocation. The outcome of many of these court cases has led universities to establish their own formal guidelines, which must be followed in all cases of hiring. Guidelines vary from institution to institution, and chairpersons should be familiar with affirmative action procedures in their respective institutions. Good records of recruiting efforts should be kept in anticipation of possible litigation.

Increasing the Pool of Qualified Women and Minority Faculty Members

If institutions are serious about meeting their ethical obligations, they have to do more than fulfill the letter of the law in conducting searches. Although they cannot expect to solve a major social problem on their own, they can *help* by working with others. The pools are small, and there are not enough women and minorities to fill all of the positions in the fields that especially need more of both. Institutions of higher education *must* help increase the pool of women and minorities qualified to fill faculty positions.

STARTING WITH GRADE SCHOOL STUDENTS

One way of increasing the pool is going to the root of the problem, which can be as early as the elementary school level. Most current analyses suggest that certain important choices are made by children at relatively young ages. For example, many girls and minorities show evidence of disinterest in mathematics and science by the time they reach middle school. It may be the way the subjects are taught (unimaginatively, emphasizing rote drills), or it may be that teachers of these subjects are predominantly white males. But middle school is a time when students should be starting to take courses that will lead to preparation for college. Many colleges are now beginning to form partnerships with individual schools and school districts in order to help students in this age group to make good choices. If this is the time when the pipeline begins shutting off for women and minorities, it is precisely the time when strong recruitment efforts should begin.

Colleges and universities can help schools to identify talented young people from nontraditional backgrounds, and assist in developing experiences that will interest those young people in careers to which they have traditionally not aspired. The students could be invited to college laboratories, to go on field expeditions, to attend summer camps in certain subject areas, to work with an undergraduate mentor who may be planning a teaching career in the field, to enter contests or competitions, and to participate in a variety of other entertaining and motivating activities. It is, of course, important that they have contact in these experiences with role models—women and minority students or faculty who have enthusiasm and demonstrable interest in what they are doing as nontraditional people in their particular fields.

Although motivation is important, it is no less important than real opportunities to study and prepare academically. Once again, faculty from a college or university can play a supportive role. Teachers and school districts often need and welcome assistance in developing curricula in specialized subject areas. In fields like mathematics, science, and foreign languages, teachers, particularly at the elementary level, may feel unprepared to provide more than routine drill-and-practice lessons. It is hard for them to convey the excitement and power of real science, or the exotic aspects of another culture, if they have had limited preparation and immersion in these fields in their own careers. College and university faculty, although they may feel uncomfortable in an elementary or middle school classroom, could work effectively with a teacher (or a team of teachers) to develop new lessons and curricula that would help young children to understand and pursue topics in some of the important specialized subject areas that, for whatever reason, youngsters seem to avoid. It is critically important that the "pipeline" issue be addressed at the early and middle school grade level. Department chairs can help by supporting and encouraging faculty who are willing to get involved.

ATTRACTING MORE WOMEN AND MINORITY HIGH SCHOOL GRADUATES TO PURSUE COLLEGE DEGREES

Ultimately, each department must also take responsibility for attracting more women and minorities to study and to major in its own subject areas. It may lay the groundwork for recruitment by engaging in early recruitment and cooperation with the lower schools. A department that has involved itself with younger students will have several advantages. It may have expanded the pool of interest in the field, and it may have stimulated an interest in its institution among the students who have had contact with faculty and facilities. Perhaps more subtly, it may have learned how better to approach and engage the interests of women and minority students, and may therefore become far more adept at working with these students.

The expansion of opportunity requires this kind of willingness to learn and adapt. It does not require "watering down" or changing basic subject-matter content, but it may require new ways of teaching, and new efforts to engage and motivate younger students to see the exciting and challenging possibilities of studying in fields that at first may not be attractive to them.

Finding Women and Minority Faculty

Going through the motions and completing a valid affirmative action search is one thing. Actually locating, recruiting, and hiring a new person from one of the "protected" groups is another. Depending on the depth of the particular pool, the search may have to be particularly aggressive. Some institutions collaborate in the establishment of national "vita banks" to assist in pooling names of minority candidates for faculty positions. Professional associations may also have networks or subgroups dedicated to finding and promoting women and minorities for faculty positions. Some universities have been particularly successful in producing women and minority Ph.D.s, and may be good recruiting grounds.

Special Burdens Carried by Women and Minority Faculty Members and How Department Chairs Can Help

Women and minorities who accept faculty positions sometimes bear special burdens. They may often be "the only one" in the department, and find their position awkward for a variety of reasons. Although the department may take great care to treat everyone equally, to foster a sense of openness and fairness, and to provide encouragement and support to faculty who may be pathbreakers among their gender or race, it may also unwittingly contribute to the burdens they already feel.

Women and minority faculty often assume (or are assigned) heavier-than-average teaching loads. Whether this is because they prefer to teach, whether it is because someone feels that they are needed in the classroom, or whether it is because of subtle discrimination, is something only the department will be able to answer. It may be important to provide female and minority students with good role models, and it may be that women and minority faculty are better able to do this than anyone else. But it is also an inequity to ask women and minority faculty members to take on more teaching assignments than others have to, and it is a handicap if a person's tenure will depend on having time to do research.

Committee service is another burden that women and minority faculty sometimes carry in greater proportion than others do. Naturally, a sensitive department chair will wish to balance the characteristics of search committees and other groups doing important work. But if there is one women or one black on the department's faculty, he or she is more than likely to be appointed to almost *every* committee. Further, that person will sometimes be expected to carry the burden of representing a particular set of values or point of view. More subtly, that person may also be expected to validate the overall fairness of committee procedures and decisions ("We had a black/Hispanic/ woman on the committee, and I'm sure they would have spoken up if anything looked discriminatory. . . .").

But it doesn't always work that way. Having one woman or minority person (of whichever sex) on the committee does not always guarantee outcomes that are free from bias or prejudice. A lone woman or minority member is often reluctant to speak in opposition to an action favored by the majority of a committee composed of nonminority members, even when the action may be patently wrong. This is especially true if the woman or minority member is a junior faculty person and doesn't feel secure in his or her role. He or she doesn't want to play the martyr by being the only one speaking against the action. Neither does he or she want to be typed as an advocate for something "wrong"—for example, an action extending special privileges to certan categories of people, or breaking rules for others. This person is aware that by not speaking against the proposed action it might look as if he or she has personally benefited from special breaks in the rules, when in fact not only has this person played by the normal rules, but has had to overcome barriers along the way.

Here is the quintessential no-win situation: You are damned if you do and damned if you don't. Far from seeing committee service as a privilege or a duty, women and minority faculty may see it as a time-consuming burden, and as a trap in which they can do themselves as much damage as they can do the department or the university good. Chairpersons must do their best to protect women and minority faculty from falling into these types of situations.

"Tokenism" is another affliction that may hurt the morale and the career prospects of women and minority faculty. A person hired solely because of his or her race or gender—and not because he or she is especially well qualified to fill the position—is almost sure to fail. Not only will it become clear that the person really cannot handle the demands of the job, but this may reinforce sexist or racist attitudes among faculty and students who consciously or unconsciously anticipated failure. The damage is magnified because the department has not gotten important work done, and because attitudes have regressed. Most seriously, an individual has wasted important years of a career, and may be injured in ways that cannot ever be compensated.

The most subtle problem facing women and minority faculty is usually social. They often feel isolated and uncomfortable because there are no natural peers among the department faculty. They cannot share common experiences, interests, ideas, and personal matters with people who might not be understanding and supportive. The morale of women and minority faculty members may be seriously affected if others in the department have strong personal relationships and openly pursue social and friendship bonds among themselves without including the women and/or minority faculty members.

Raiding

When recruiting women or minority faculty, a department may be tempted to raid established people at other universities. This is the easy, but ultimately unproductive, solution to a short-term need. Raiding does not help increase the pool of qualified people. Instead, it just rotates the problem from institution to institution. The positions left by women and minorities at one institution may be just as significant as those they are filling at the recruiting institution. No new minority faculty have been added to the work force, and the net result is that just as many openings exist as existed before.

Sensitivity to Women and Minority Faculty Issues

Bringing women and minority faculty into departments that have been predominantly male and white opens new issues that must be discussed with the faculty in a candid fashion. It is the chair's responsibility to open and lead such discussions. One agenda item is to simply encourage accepting and helpful attitudes towards new colleagues.

Other issues may be more sensitive, and so more difficult to handle with candor. For example, it may be necessary to add salary or benefit premiums to attract *outstanding* women or minority candidates in certain fields. Faculty must understand that this is a common educational problem which does not reflect on their own competence or worth. It may not seem fair, but it needs to be done if women and minorities are to be added to the faculty.

The chair must also focus sensitivity on the problems that women and minorities have over and above the problems of nonminorities. They must persuade nonminority faculty that these problems are real and that they deserve attention, and perhaps some kind of compensating forgiveness. At the same time, the chair who successfully attracts a nontraditional faculty member should counsel the new person about the concerns and worries of the current faculty. Both sides may have to work at being understanding, sensitive, and accepting if the relationship is going to work.

Some women or minority faculty will bring additional concerns that majority faculty will find hard to identify with. For example, minorities may have great concerns about where they can live comfortably, especially those with young children. How they will be accepted in various neighborhoods, what kind of social lives they can lead in the community, where their children can go to school and feel safe, secure, and accepted, all may consume a great deal of energy. Department chairs cannot of course solve all of these problems. They can, however, offer advice, provide contacts in the community, and handle the concerns with sensitivity and understanding.

Although department chairs should develop sensitivity, it is also important not to overreact. No faculty member, whether majority or minority, wishes for extraneous attention or unwarranted solicitude. They want to do their jobs well, and to enjoy the rewards that come with making a serious contribution to the department. They want to be judged by the same standards that apply to everyone else, and to be accpted for who they are as human beings—not because they belong to someone's arbitrary category. They certainly do not want to carry added burdens, though, and they do expect that they will be treated fairly, objectively, and equitably. The chair often must tread a fine line between achieving more opportunity for groups who have been traditionally excluded, and patronizing those who become the vanguard and the pioneers.

Questions

1. Are there programs in the university community or campus community to mentor women and minority high school students who are entering higher education and who might benefit from presentations by one or more of your faculty members?
2. List several pools from which you might recruit to bring qualified women and minority candidates to your department. Do you have sufficient resources to bring candidates from these pools to the campus for interviews?
3. Are there professional journals, magazines, creative conference recruitment activities, and so on, that can be added to your departmental recruitment efforts? If yes, what are they?
4. Does your department make a special effort to orient new faculty to their professional and personal surroundings? Is so, what kind of efforts?

References

ATKINSON, DONALD R. "Ethnic Minority Representation in Counselor Education." *Counselor Education and Supervision, 23*, 1983, pp. 7–19.

BOGENSCHUTZ, MARGARET M., and SAGARIA, MARY ANN. *Aspirations and Career Growth of Mid-Level Administrators in Higher Education.* Paper presented at the Annual Meeting of the American Educational Research Association, New Orleans, 1988. (ERIC Document Reproduction Service No. ED 296 652)

BRAITHWAITE, RONALD L., and BEATTY, LULA. "Minority Male Participation in Educational Research and Development: A Recruitment Selection Dilemma." *Journal of Negro Education, 50*, Fall 1981, pp. 389–400.

DOUGLAS, JOEL M. (Ed.) *Salary and Compensation Methodology in Academic Collective Bargaining.* New York: National Center for the Study of Collective Bargaining in Higher Education and the Professions, 1983. (ERIC Document Reproduction Service No. ED 230 140)

Faculty in Higher Education Institutions, 1988: 1988 National Survey of Postsecondary Faculty. Washington, DC: U.S. Department of Education, 1990.

FELD, SHEILA. "The Academic Marketplace in Social Work." *Journal of Social Work Education, 24*, 1988, pp. 201–210.

FLEMING, JOHN E.; GILL, GERALD R.,; and SWINTON, DAVID H. *The Case for Affirmative Action.* Washington, DC: Howard University Press, 1978.

KLUGER, ELIZABETH. "Sex Discrimination in the Tenure System at American Colleges and Universities: The Judicial Response." *Journal of Law and Education, 15*, 1986, pp. 319–339.

LIE STIVER, SUZANNE, and O'LEARY, VIRGINIA E. *Storming the Tower: Women in the Academic World.* East Brunswick, NJ: Nichols Publishing, 1991.

LINNELL, ROBERT H. "Age, Sex and Ethnic Trade-offs in Faculty Employment: You Can't Have Your Cake and Eat It Too." *Current Issues in Higher Education,* 4, 1979, pp. 3–9.

MAACK, MARY. "Women in Library Education: Down the Up Staircase." *Library Trends,* 34, 1986, pp. 401–432.

MINGLE, JAMES R., and RODRIGUEZ, ESTER M. *Building Coalitions for Minority Success: A Report of the SHEEO Project on Minority Achievement in Higher Education.* Denver: State Higher Education Executive Officers, 1991.

MITCHELL, JOYCE M., and STARR, RACHEL R. "A Regional Approach for Analyzing the Recruitment of Academic Women." *American Behavioral Scientists,* 15, Nov.–Dec. 1971, pp. 183–205.

MOORE, KATHRYN M., and JOHNSON, MICHAEL P. "The Status of Women and Minorities in the Professoriate: The Role of Affirmative Action and Equity." In *New Directions for Institutional Research,* no. 63 (Managing Faculty Resources), 16, 1989, pp. 45–63.

MOORE, KATHRYN M. *Women and Minorities. Leaders in Transition: A National Study of Higher Education Administrators.* Washington, DC: American Council on Education, 1982. (ERIC Document Reproduction Service No. ED 225 459)

MOORE, WILLIAM, JR., and WAGSTAFF, LONNIE H. *Black Educators in Elite Colleges.* San Francisco: Jossey–Bass, 1989.

NOE, NICHOLAS N. *Measures of Salary Inequality.* AIR Annual Forum Paper, Orlando, 1986. (ERIC Document Reproduction Service No. ED 280 423)

PEARSON, CAROL S.; SHAVLIK, DONNA L., AND TOUCHTON, JUDITH G. *Educating the Majority: Women Challenge Tradition in Higher Education.* New York: Macmillan, 1989.

SAGARIA, MARY ANN. "Administrative Mobility and Gender: Patterns and Processes in Higher Education." *Journal of Higher Education,* 59, 1988, pp. 306–326.

SAGARIA, MARY ANN, and KROTSENG, MARSHA V. "Deans' Managerial Skills: What They Need and What They Bring to a Job." *Journal of the College and University Personnel Association,* 37, 1986, pp. 1–7.

SAGARIA, MARY ANN, and JOHNSRUD, LINDA K. *Administrative Intrainstitutional Mobility: The Structuring of Opportunity.* ASHE Annual Meeting Paper, San Francisco, February 1987. (ERIC Document Reproduction Service No. ED 281 445)

Salaries, Tenure, and Fringe Benefits of Full-time Instructional Faculty. Washington, DC: Center for Education Statistics. HEGIS Data available from Office of Educational Research and Improvement, Washington, DC 20208, 1986.

SIMEONE, ANGELA. *Academic Women Working Toward Equality.* South Hadley, MA: Bergen & Garvey, 1987.

SIMPSON, WILLIAM A., and SPERBER, WILLIAM E. "Salary Comparisons: New Methods for Correcting Old Fallacies." *Research in Higher Education,* 28, 1988, pp. 49–56.

WATTENBARGER, JAMES L., and NICKEL, DONNA A. "An Investment in Quality: An Example of the Impact of a Title III Project upon a Community College." *Community College Review,* 15, 1987, pp. 22–27.

Part *V*

WORKLOAD ASSIGNMENTS, FACULTY EVALUATION, AND PERFORMANCE COUNSELING

Chapter 14.   Workload Assignments and Reporting Faculty Activities

Chapter 15.   Faculty Evaluation

Chapter 16.   Performance Counseling and Dealing with Unsatisfactory Performance

Workload Assignments and Reporting Faculty Activities

Department chairpersons differ greatly in the way they perceive their roles and responsibilities in assigning activities to faculty members. Some believe that the professional nature of university teaching and research forbids the formal assignment of faculty duties. Others hold that a chairperson is a manager of resources, especially human resources, and that he or she is responsible for the department's success or failure in helping achieve the university's mission and goals. The latter view clearly requires that the chairperson take an active role in assigning faculty duties. In recent years, legislative demands for accountability and union demands for explicitness in faculty–administration relationships have strengthened the view that the chairperson must play a role in assigning faculty activities.

The trend is for chairpersons to assume *more* rather than less authority and responsibility in faculty assignment. The State University System of Florida, for example, has for several years required a formal assignment of faculty activities; it even requires a periodic audit of such assignments. Further, the collective bargaining agreement between the United Faculty of Florida and the Florida Board of Regents specifically requires faculty assignments. Many other public and private colleges and universities have similar kinds of requirements.

Finally, college and university budget models may be based on minimum or average workload data of this kind; some multicampus university systems also have such standards. In some states the legislatures have passed laws establishing minimum workloads for faculty, such as twelve student contact hours per term for university faculty and fifteen for junior college faculty. Some departments wrongly implement this policy by treating the established minimum workload as if it were a maximum workload. A chairperson may not believe in the worthiness of such laws, but where they exist, legislators expect faculty activities to reflect the laws' intent. Compliance with the law, however, does not mean that the university should use the twelve-hour law as the framework within which all assignments are made. Assignments should be based on the department's goals, objectives, priorities, and policies, including the needs of the faculty and students. In implementing these goals and policies, every effort must be made not to violate the twelve-hour law, should one exist.

Benefits and Purposes of Explicit Assignments

The chairperson has extensive responsibilities for assigning faculty duties, and this task is directly related to faculty evaluation. Most college and university administrators now understand that evaluations should be based on the performance of specifically assigned activities. They realize that individual faculty members and the groups who represent them wish to ensure that faculty members are not denied promotion, tenure, or salary adjustments because of failure to perform tasks they were never explicitly assigned in the first place.

Explicit assignments serve other important purposes in addition to evaluation. The development of equitable workloads among the department faculty almost demands a record of the particular assignments made to each faculty member. Systems for equalizing workloads are sometimes included in department policies. On the other hand, some faculty members believe that workload equity is a matter that they themselves must determine, rather than some absolute institutional standard of equivalency that they must follow. Such policy statements as those passed by the American Association of University Professors recommending numbers of teaching credit hours on the basis of the number of new and old preparations have been helpful guidelines in this matter. By making formal, explicit assignments, however, the chairperson is able to adhere to the department's policy, implement its goals and objectives, and maintain data to explain his or her good judgment in managing human resources.

Similarly, as students' needs are assessed and changes required, the chairperson can modify faculty assignments, thereby shifting faculty effort to cover these needs. If some subject areas are not covered or developed, the department can undertake some long-range planning so that it can do more than just fill the gap at the last minute. An analysis of the extent to which explicit assignments are completed may show the need for new faculty resources or professional career and development counseling.

Policies governing formal assignment of faculty duties generally include statements such as the following:

> Faculty members should be assigned duties and activities in writing. These assignments must be clearly stated, and those receiving them should acknowledge them as understood.

The department chairperson, by virtue of his or her responsibility for attaining department goals and objectives, is the person who should make faculty assignments.

Effective faculty assignments require clear statements of department goals, objectives, and workload policies. The proper functioning of the department depends on the chairperson's maintaining adequate records and consulting extensively with faculty members before and after the assignments are completed.

Preparation of Assignments

What are the essential requirements of an assignment of duties? How detailed must the assignment be? How often should an assignment be made?

The department chairperson who tries to understand the many conflicting requirements for faculty assignments can reach several conclusions. A chairperson may conclude that the best procedure is to make assignments as brief and as general as possible. In this way maximum flexibility may be preserved, thereby ensuring that all bases are covered, no matter what needs may come up during the year. Unfortunately, assignments that are brief and general are usually vague and subject to broad interpretation by the faculty member as well as the chairperson. Vagueness can make it impossible to determine whether the assignment has been completed successfully. In the event of a faculty grievance over tenure or promotion, the chairperson may be hard-pressed to substantiate any judgments made if he or she can present no clear evidence of duty assignment and performance criteria.

A chairperson who has faced only one grievance resulting from an assignment that is too vague or general is usually convinced that highly detailed assignments are necessary and justified. Even so, endless arguments may ensue, depending on how the assignment is worded, about the degree to which the various assignments were completed. In some cases, faculty members may demand tenure, promotion, or salary increases, claiming they have completed all the detailed assignments given them and then submitting evidence to support their claims. A problem may also surface if a faculty member refuses to complete a task that needs to be done but that was not listed as part of the agreed-upon detailed assignment made earlier in the year.

The two problems described above might have been avoided if the assignments had been precise. An assignment must be general enough to provide some flexibility for both the chairperson and faculty member, and it must be detailed enough so that both understand what performance is expected and what will serve as a basis for evaluation.

Chairpersons should be particularly alert to the information about assignments contained in the various documents that must be acknowledged by each faculty member. Some institutions notify faculty members of their next period of employment by means of a salary letter; it may contain general language indicating, for example, that for the fiscal year the person will be paid a specific sum for teaching, research, service, and other such functions as assigned. A person may be appointed for only part of a year or as a part-time employee during a school year; the assignment for a part-time faculty member may be more specific than for the full-time faculty member, e.g., the teaching assignment may consist of one specific course.

As the formal employment relationship between faculty members and the institution evolves, however, the salary letter often becomes merely a notification of salary award, whereas the contract document becomes the actual instrument of notification of employment and salary level. The contract document may contain a variety of other information, including a detailed statement of requirements in legal terminology. The assignment in the contract still may be given in functional terms (i.e., teaching, research, and service), but it may also list specific tasks (e.g., teaching one graduate course off-campus). In preparing a contract, the dean's office may solicit information from the chairperson about any special assignment terms to be entered in faculty contracts. At the same time, a chairperson should check with the dean's office to make sure that a faculty member is not assigned activities that are not likely to be required or performed—for example, a faculty member who has been assigned teaching as a full-time workload should not be assigned any research or service activities.

A chairperson might be required to solicit from each faculty member a projected work plan for an entire academic year. This plan might be the basis for the annual contract and the assignment of workloads each term. Note that institutions operating on the quarter calendar sometimes attempt to spread the annual department workload as evenly as possible over the four quarters. In such instances, full-time faculty members may have an opportunity to work during the summer quarter in lieu of another quarter. This type of arrangement, if approved by the chairperson, would be indicated in the work plan. Because plans of this kind are developed in early spring for the subsequent academic year, they are subject to change. Regular consultation with each faculty member should enable the chairperson to anticipate any changes and to make the necessary adjustments to the plan.

The chairperson usually is not required to agree to faculty members' requests concerning workloads; nevertheless, the assignment of a faculty member's workload or schedule should not be arbitrary or capricious. Consultation is a standard of collegiality; to impose a work assignment on academic professionals may be a denial of their expertise. In emergencies, of course, faculty members must be assigned certain tasks to ensure coverage.

In some universities, the annual projected work plan for each faculty member may be converted to an official document, and as such it will often include the details for each term of the contract year. The plan is not always implemented as originally prepared, however. The chairperson may change an assignment before it is fulfilled; the faculty member may undertake one or more activities not included in the assignment; or the faculty member may not perform an assigned activity. The alert chairperson will discover the existing discrepancies during periodic consultation each term and take appropriate corrective action. A consultation before a term begins, specifically to confirm and adjust the assignment as needed, should reveal the changes a faculty member is planning or anticipating. Such preterm conferences also inform the faculty member of possible changes that the chairperson may request to meet changing conditions in the department.

The chairperson should adjust the assignment planning or workload projection records to reflect the activities actually performed. Similarly, he or she should obtain explanations from faculty members as to why certain assigned activities have not been performed, especially when nonperformance represents a breach of agreement or a failure to support important goals, objectives, and priorities of the department. It is equally important that faculty members be commended, in writing, for tasks well done, new activities successfully undertaken, and so on. The chairperson should communicate to the dean and other appropriate university officials any extraordinary achievements by faculty members.

Equitable Assignments

A chairperson must be concerned not only with each faculty member but also with the department's total functioning and how its workload can be distributed equitably among all the faculty. He or she must not only keep in mind the needs of individual faculty members but must also assess the effect that a person's assignment may have on the other faculty members in the department. If, for example, a faculty member is assigned to teach a course for the first time and is given some released time from other teaching responsibilities for course development, who will assume the other teaching responsibilities of that faculty member?

When assignments are shifted among the faculty members to distribute the workload equitably, the chairperson may have a difficult time trying to find the proper combination of activities for each person. The chairperson will have to assess each faculty member's skills and competencies to make sure the workload is spread equally among those who can best perform it. In some departments, the faculty may decide to assign priority factors for various activities. Some activities have higher priority than others, depending on the effort required and the comparative importance of the activity as perceived by the department. The priority factors expressed as points are used in calculations that result in the assignment of equitable workloads to the faculty.

Very few departments find a priority system either necessary or desirable, but some have used it successfully. Table 14.1 shows a system used by one large, research-oriented social science department in a major university in allocating points for specific activities.

The department that used this system listed all its activities, regardless of who carried them out, and allocated to each activity the number of points

TABLE *14.1* **Point System in Which Points Are Assigned for Specific Tasks Included in Faculty Assignments**

ACTIVITY	POINTS
Teaching	
COURSE TEACHING	
One lecture course	8 points
One seminar course	5 points
One lab course	3 points for first 25 students; 1 point for each additional 25 students
ONE-ON-ONE SUPERVISION*	
Director of master's thesis	4 points
Member of master's committee	1 point
Director of doctoral dissertation	6 points
Member of doctoral committee	2 points
Directed individual study, supervised research, or supervised internship	1 point per student; maximum 4 points per term
Research†	
Sponsored research project:	
Under $10,000	4 points
Over $10,000	10 points
Other activities	
Member of department or university committees	The number of points allowed for each activity is determined by the chairperson based on the time and effort involved and the importance of the work to the department.
Chairperson of department or university committee	
Administrative assignments within the department	

*The maximum number of points allowed for all one-on-one supervision during any academic year is 30. Points for the first four classifications listed in this section are given on completion of the graduate degree.
†The maximum number of points allowed for sponsored research during any academic year is 40.

designated. The sum of all the points was divided by the number of department faculty members to determine the average point load. The workload for this particular department amounted to 1056 points. Since the department contained sixteen faculty members, the average, or equitable, load was sixty-six points per academic year. Table 14.2 shows three examples of faculty workloads and point allocations.

This point system was not used for evaluation purposes but only to help equalize the assignments given to individual faculty members. Any point system is cumbersome, and the result may not be much different from the result obtained by means of another system. Faculty members with heavy teaching loads continue to be assigned heavy teaching loads, and productive researchers are

TABLE *14.2*   Sample of Workloads and
Point Allocations

	POINTS
Faculty Member A	
Six lecture courses (8 points each)	48
One-on-one supervision	19
No grants	0
No committees	0
Total	67
Faculty Member B	
Three lecture courses (8 points each)	24
One lab (3 points each)	3
One-on-one supervision	22
Two grants (10 points each)	20
Total	69
Faculty Member C	
Four lecture courses (8 points each)	32
One lab (3 points each)	3
One graduate seminar	5
One-on-one supervision	13
Committee assignment	5
One grant	10
Total	68

allowed reduced teaching loads. Some faculty members, however, feel more secure with a point system of this nature. Quite often, a faculty member will challenge the point values that the chairperson has allocated to certain activities.

Equitable faculty workloads can be accomplished in two ways: (1) by assigning workloads that are equitable term by term; or (2) by assigning workloads that are equitable when averaged over the academic or fiscal year. Averaging workloads over an academic year allows the chairperson to assign heavier teaching loads during terms when enrollment is unusually high and lighter teaching loads during terms when enrollment is usually lower. Moreover, faculty members may be willing to undertake an extra heavy load one term in order to have a light load the following term, during which they will have more time to concentrate on their own professional interests.

The first step in preparing teaching schedule assignments for a given term is to review the teaching schedules of previous years for the same term. This information—together with information from the faculty and an awareness of personnel changes, curriculum changes, changing student interests, and so forth—can serve as the basis for developing teaching schedules for the current term.

In assigning teaching activities, the chairperson should ask the following questions about each faculty member's assignment:

- Has this faculty member taught this particular course before? Does he or she have more than one new course to teach?
- How many new preparations does this faculty member have? Will special assistance be needed for labs, computer usage, and so forth?
- Do these courses require any special activities, e.g., field trips, demonstrations, and so forth?
- How much evaluation of student work will be required?
- What is the mix of level of courses? The size of the estimated enrollment?
- How many thesis and dissertation projects is each faculty member directing? On how many committees is each serving? How many students is each counseling?
- How many undergraduates are being advised by each faculty member? What other undergraduate activities is each supervising or sponsoring?

Clearly, the chairperson must be flexible in assigning percèntages of effort for each faculty activity. He or she should move away from rigid formulas and toward individual judgments about the workloads assigned to each faculty member. The examples given in Table 14.3 indicate that a wide range of assignments may be equivalent and, hence, equitable. Note that two faculty assignments can appear quite disparate and yet be considered functionally equivalent. The explanation following each example presents the factors used by an academic vice-president of a major university to determine that the percentages assigned each category of activities were in agreement.

The number of credit hours of teaching, generally, is not a good measure of workload. For example, a sixteen-credit-hour load that consists of teaching the same course to four different undergraduate classes of twenty students each might be a light load for an experienced faculty member who has taught that course many times before. In contrast, an eight-credit-hour load that consists of teaching two entirely different courses to two different classes of forty students each might be a heavy load for a new, inexperienced faculty member who has never taught either course before, especially if the two courses required more themes and reports from the students than did the first faculty member's course. The chairperson should not hesitate to assign the same courses to two faculty members, giving one a 50 percent teaching assignment and the other an 80 percent assignment if the faculty members' relative experience and qualifications warrant the difference in assignment and would result in a similar "real" workload for each faculty member. To be more consistent, the chairperson may wish to assign the faculty member with less experience to 80 percent of full time for teaching a course that includes time for course development. Clearly, department needs and course workloads—not some requirement for a report—should determine the most efficient and effective use of faculty resources.

TABLE *14.3*   **Sample of Equitable Faculty Assignments**

		FACULTY MEMBER A	FACULTY MEMBER B
Example 1			
Teaching	67%	2 classes (8 hours)	4 classes (16 hours)
Research	20%	Research Grant	Research grant
Service	13%	1 committee	3 committees
	100%		
EXPLANATION OF EXAMPLE 1			
Teaching		*Graduate classes; 2 in-depth preparations*	*Same course; no additional preparation*
Research		*Self-explanatory*	*Self-explanatory*
Service		*University committee*	*Routine department committees*
Example 2			
Teaching	75%	3 classes (12 hours)	3 classes (9 hours)
Research	20%	No funded research grant	Research grant
Service	5%	2 committees	1 committee
	100%		
EXPLANATION OF EXAMPLE 2			
Teaching		*2 sections of same class*	*3 different classes*
Research		*In process of preparing a grant for funding*	*Funded grant*
Service		*Routine department committee*	*College committee*
Example 3			
Teaching	67%	5 classes (20 hours)	3 classes (15 hours)
Research	18%	No research project	No research project
Service	10%	No definite service activity	1 committee
Advisement	5%	Advisement	Advisement
	100%		
EXPLANATION OF EXAMPLE 3			
Teaching		*Undergraduate sections of same class; 4 activity classes; 1 lecture class*	*3 large classes (different course taught each term requiring preparation and work outside of class)*
Research		*Needs to develop some research and creativity pursuits*	*Needs to develop some research and creativity pursuits*
Service		*Chairperson will make a definite curriculum assignment prior to the beginning of the term*	*Department work*
Advisement		*Assigned students*	*Assigned students*

The equitable assignment of faculty duties systematically allows the chairperson to formulate and implement plans for attaining department goals while assisting faculty members in reaching some of their personal goals. This harmonizing, after all, is one of the purposes of assigning activities. The chairperson's success in this activity may well determine his or her effectiveness as an academic administrator and leader, since personnel assignment activities and decisions constitute a major function of the chairperson's role. Chairpersons who are inadequate personnel managers could become liabilities to their departments. Some chairpersons find personnel decisions so disturbing and distasteful that they resign. On the other hand, chairpersons who are interested in these kinds of problems and learn to cope with them may find rewarding careers in university administration.

Performance Criteria for Functional Assignments

For the busy chairperson, the task of assigning faculty activities commonly becomes a chore that must be done hurriedly. All too often the task is performed by making a simple list of the things the faculty member will probably be doing in the next few months. An even more unfortunate situation occurs when the faculty member is allowed to complete the assignment form without consulting the chairperson. In neither case has a real assignment been made, and the chairperson is forfeiting an opportunity to manage valuable human resources for the improvement of the department. Yet making periodic term assignments can sometimes be a distasteful waste of time. Assignment schedules that consist of a simple listing of the same set of duties each term are basically useless.

How can assignments be transformed into useful aids to the chairperson's already difficult task of resource management? A few suggestions about activities for each performance area should provide an indication of the essentials of a good assignment and should stimulate further thinking about the subject. The key is to think of each assignment in terms of how a chairperson should evaluate success in completing the assignment, i.e., what criteria should govern each assignment in each area?

TEACHING ASSIGNMENTS

The assumption that teaching assignments should consist only of a list of courses to be taught is invalid. About the only thing that can be evaluated with such an assignment is whether or not the courses have been taught! More important, the performance of such an assignment must certainly be evaluated as "average." What could be the basis for an above- or below-average performance when everyone completes the assigned courses?

At the very least, a teaching assignment should rest on a clear understanding that the *quality* of the teaching will be evaluated. Further, a clear statement, preferably in writing, should be provided as to the types of evidence, such as student evaluations or peer review, that will be used in making the evaluation. It is the chairperson's responsibility to ensure that clearly stated criteria for evaluation are established by the department and are understood by all the department members.

Teaching assignments can be made with a degree of sophistication. The success of a teaching assignment should probably be measured in terms of what students learn, either in absolute terms or in relative terms (such as student growth). But have you, as the chairperson or as a department member, defined what is expected of a student who completes a given course? If so, and if the learning outcomes are stated in measurable terms, successful course instruction will be measurable in terms of student learning. Of course, many faculty members will object to this method of measuring teaching success, citing inaccuracy of tests, differences in student ability or motivation, and a variety of other arguments. Admittedly, precise measurement of effective outcomes, such as attitude changes, does lag behind precise measurement of cognitive outcomes. Nevertheless, student learning is the primary goal of teaching and can be taken as one measure of successful teaching.

Other activities that might be included in the teaching assignment are developing courses; revising syllabi; updating laboratory experiments; converting courses to computer-assisted instruction; training, monitoring, and evaluating graduate teaching assistants; and other related activities. To avoid misunderstandings, the department faculty should agree that these teaching assignments are appropriate.

RESEARCH AND CREATIVE ACTIVITY ASSIGNMENTS

Research and creative activities seem to play an increasing role in the assignment process and, in many departments, are necessary conditions for promotion and tenure. Again, the necessity of specific assignments and the insistence on clearly stated criteria for evaluation are essential. Probably everyone can think of faculty members who have been talking research for years but have yet to produce a successful grant proposal, research report, publishable paper, or anything else that might be considered a significant contribution. These "wheel spinners" could write books of excuses and reasons for their failure to finish various projects—if only they had a little more time!

If research or creative activity is to be included as part of a faculty assignment and if it is to be evaluated at a specific time, the faculty member should be able to provide a documented plan of action with some sort of time schedule for completing various parts of the research activity. The action plan might include such information as the title of the project; whether a library review of the literature is required; when the project will be completed; whether a proposal for outside funding is planned and when it will be completed; whether laboratory equipment must be acquired and assembled and how much of the laboratory effort can be completed this term; and what efforts at data collection and processing are required. If the faculty member is writing an article for publication, he or she should note whether a rough draft can be completed this term. If a graduate student is scheduled to complete a thesis, note what must be done to assure that he or she will be able to complete the research.

If the faculty member cannot provide a detailed action plan, perhaps the research should *not* be assigned! If the plan can be stated clearly, the assignment should indicate that the research effort will be formally evaluated in the future. Failure to accomplish set goals means that the assignment has not been completed, and this failure should be reflected in an evaluation. Of course, the faculty member may have good reasons for failing to complete an assignment. The chairperson has the responsibility for ascertaining and assessing the validity of these reasons, converting this information to appropriate evaluation judgments, and adjusting the assignments for the next term accordingly.

The term *failure* may be considered unduly harsh when assignments are being evaluated; perhaps *noncompletion* would be less grating. Regardless of the term used to describe this unfortunate situation, the chairperson must make sure that failure is not rewarded or allowed to slip by without appropriate reaction.

SERVICE ASSIGNMENTS

Service is an assignment activity that may include a range of activities, such as attending local service club meetings or serving as a member of campus or interinstitutional committees. For example, a faculty member may be assigned to develop and deliver off-campus presentations designed to alert the public to services offered by the university, gain support for an on-campus program, or attract students to the campus.

Again, the chairperson should think seriously about the real purpose of making such assignments and how their success can be evaluated. If a faculty member is assigned to a university committee, is regular attendance at meetings expected? Is regular attendance considered "outstanding" or just "average" performance of this assignment? Should the department chairperson ask the head of this committee to provide an evaluation of the faculty member's performance? If the faculty member was assigned to contact local high schools and explain new department programs, is the mere making of the contacts sufficient for successful completion of the assignment? Or does success require that a larger percentage of students in the schools contacted attend the university? Just why is this assignment being made? Will it really benefit the department, college, or institution?

Another kind of service assignment is holding office in a state or national professional society. Most chairpersons will insist that such activities bring "honor" to the home university. No doubt they do, but the effect is difficult, if not impossible, to measure. Fortunately, a chairperson is seldom called on to explain such benefits to taxpayers or legislators. Although service assignments can be made considerably more specific than most currently are, it is difficult to assign these types of activities in a way that makes objective evaluation possible. On the other hand, membership in professional societies has traditionally been considered a part of the academic life, and holding office in those societies has traditionally been deemed worthwhile. Some public institutions now require a written report from faculty members about the benefits—academic and other—of attending regional and national conferences.

Reporting of Faculty Activities

The discussion so far has focused essentially on the distribution of the department workload. The formalization of these assignments has come about because of such developments as collective bargaining, increased disagreement with tenure and promotion decisions, and, in some cases, state statutes.

The reporting of faculty activities, however, is a result of the quest for increased accountability. Specifically, any university that accepts federal or state contract and grant funds must be able to provide proof that the contracted amount of effort has indeed been expended on the contracted activity. Payroll certifications that would satisfy accountability requirements are often deemed too cumbersome; therefore, a quarterly or semester report on activity is generally substituted. Universities that have recently been audited by federal agencies have been told that the effort of the support personnel, as well as the effort of the faculty, must be certified. In the absence of clear federal guidelines, universities have developed their own reporting systems. Many of these systems not only satisfy federal agencies but also provide chairpersons and deans with pertinent information and allow cost studies to estimate costs more closely. Thus, many colleges and universities have developed detailed categories of activities, coupled with standard definitions, in order accurately to record data about faculty workload. The amount of detail reported on these activity forms seems to be increasing; the forms all focus on standardized reporting techniques and rely on computer processing for handling the increasing volume of data.

Recommendations for the data elements and counting procedures, as well as for the activities to be reported, can be found in relevant technical reports of the National Center for Higher Education Management Systems and in circulars. Following is a list of broad categories adopted by one state:

A. General academic instruction
  1. Lower-division instruction
  2. Upper-division instruction
  3. Graduate instruction
  4. Thesis supervision
  5. Dissertation supervision
  6. Department research
  7. Academic advisement
  8. Other instructional activities
B. Community education
C. Preparatory and adult basic education
D. Institutes and research centers
E. Individual or project research
F. Patient services

G. Community services
H. Cooperative extension services
I. Academic administration—management
J. Academic administration—governance
K. Curriculum development
L. Academic personnel development

The data recorded for each category are the percentages of effort a faculty member has spent on each activity. When compiled, the data are circulated through the organizational hierarchy to state budget, legislative and federal officers. Academicians almost always view these reports negatively, seeing them as yet more bureaucratic encroachments on their lives.

The requirements for reporting faculty activities can have a significant effect on a department, however, and the chairperson should be sure that the reports accurately reflect not only the assignment but also the actual work accomplished. Accurate and complete reporting is essential for a number of reasons. First, the reported activities must not violate previous contractual agreements with a federal agency. For example, a faculty member who, for a given term, has contracted to spend 100 percent of full time on a research project funded by a federal agency cannot teach a course or otherwise share in the department workload during that term. If he or she does teach a course and therefore does not provide 100 percent of full time to the research project, the university may be required to repay a portion of the funds secured. Thus the chairperson must be familiar with faculty commitments when making assignments and reviewing reports of actual activities.

Second, many universities, under state legislative directive, annually conduct a cost study across all disciplines. These cost studies use information about faculty workload data as primary data. Cost-study reports, now being published across the nation, show instructional costs and cost per credit hour by discipline for each university. Since information about faculty workload may be the primary data for these calculations, the assignments made by the department chairperson can significanly affect the cost results in his or her discipline. The cost study could become the basis for legislative funding in future years and thus takes on major significance.

Third, faculty activity reports are used internally by institutions for various studies of costs and faculty workloads, and, sometimes, for collective bargaining purposes. Again, the accuracy of these data may have some effect on the department in terms of the allocation of financial resources and faculty positions and in possible grievance actions.

Reporting Assignments in Terms of FTE (full-time equivalents)

Faculty activity assignments are generally reported as fractions of a full-time equivalent (FTE) faculty position. The chairperson usually specifies the fraction of a full-time workload (1.00) for each assigned set of activities for each faculty member. For reporting purposes, each assignment is specified in terms of a decimal fraction of an FTE position, e.g., 0.50, or as a percentage (50 percent) of an FTE workload; the total of the fractional assignments must not exceed 1.00 FTE.

Many chairpersons, however, have difficulty accepting this concept because *full-time* cannot easily be defined in terms of hours per week. Some chairpersons insist that their faculty members work sixty hours per week and should, therefore, be assigned more FTE, perhaps 1.50 FTE. An exception to the 1.00 limit may occur when a faculty member is assigned a full load, whatever that happens to be, and then is also assigned some overload activities, such as teaching in a division of continuing education. On the other hand, part-time faculty members are always assigned some fraction of an FTE, e.g., 0.50 FTE. Thus, what constitutes an overload, or a workload greater than 1.00 FTE, is determined by circumstances and by policies of institutional offices and divisons other than the department.

Although some chairpersons would argue to the contrary, a full-load assignment cannot exceed 1.00 FTE for full-time faculty members, regardless of the number of credit hours taught, the total hours worked per week, or the "extra" activities that the faculty member may plan to do during the term. Previous examples (Table 14.3) have shown that functionally equivalent percentages of an FTE for two faculty members may not necessarily reveal the great differences in their patterns of activities. Furthermore, the same activity for two persons, each teaching a section of the same course, may result in significantly different FTE percentages. Accurate assignment of FTE fractions for each faculty member's activities depends greatly on the chairperson's understanding and experience in reviewing assignment reports and in questioning faculty members about their actual efforts with different assignments. Consulting with an experienced chairperson and with the technical staff processing these data can also be helpful.

In colleges or universities where minimum workload standards are important policy matters, chairpersons must be extra cautious not to use the minimum standard as the definition of a 1.00 FTE or as a basis for assigning fractions of FTEs to faculty activities. As repeatedly stated, the standard is a minimum, not a maximum, and usually refers only to the minimum number of class contact hours expected of a faculty member. This minimum number of class contact hours, be it twelve or fifteen, may constitute whatever percentage of an FTE workload is deemed appropriate by the chairperson and the department. A faculty member complies with the law or policy by satisfying the minimum contact hour requirement, but the law or policy does not tie the required minimum number of contact hours to any particular percentage of FTE workload assignment.

Chairpersons who misinterpret the minimum workload policy and make assignments on the basis that twelve class contact hours is a maximum load and thus represent 1.00 FTE often complain that no time is left for teaching, research, or service. This misunderstanding creates problems at those universities where every faculty member has been instructed by contract to perform some research and service in addition to teaching. Moreover, a faculty member who is teaching more than twelve contact hours may or may not be overloaded. As indicated in the section dealing with equitable assignments, a twenty-contact-hour load may not be heavy at all, while an eight-hour load for a new faculty member may be a weighty fifty-hour-a-week job. In sum, the workload standards should not be a basis for making assignments per se but should be implemented by ensuring that the faculty members perform their assigned activities and that the total department effort complies with the workload policy.

Sometimes workload policies may be satisfied by the compliance of a complete academic unit, such as a department or college, rather than by the compliance of each person in the unit. In such cases, workloads are averaged for each unit; that is, all instruction hours are totaled for a given unit and divided by the aggregate FTE faculty. A related problem concerns the interpretation of the differences between workload standards expressed as contact hours and as credit hours. For example, three contact hours in a lecture class per week per term are considered three hours of credit, but three hours of laboratory class per week per term may be considered only one hour of credit. Lecturing for one hour supposedly requires more effort on the instructor's part than supervising a laboratory class for one hour. The concept of the contact hour is also used to measure counseling and advising time with students. In any event, the chairperson should know precisely what is required for each particular FTE reporting category.

Faculty activity is generally reported in terms of percentage of effort. For example, a faculty member might report 75 percent of his or her effort in instruction and 25 percent in research, regardless of whether the total effort constitutes a 1.00 FTE salaried appointment or any fraction thereof. To reiterate, assigning a specific portion of a 100 percent effort to each of the categories of teaching, research, and service is a distributive measure of effort not necessarily related to the source or fraction of an FTE salary assigned to each category. Federal authorities no longer recognize the concept of "donated time." A faculty member cannot, within a given term, expend 100 percent of his or her effort within a research project and also "donate" the time required to teach a course.

In addition, the concept of "loans and borrows" is no longer accepted by federal authorities. Thus, a faculty member paid 100 percent from a contract during a given term cannot teach a course that term and be released from teaching during a following term to work on the contracted activity. If federal auditors observe this type of arrangement, they will recommend that the university repay the federal agency for the portion of time the faculty member did not expend on contracted activities during the term of the contract and will ignore the effort of the following term.

"Donated time" and "loans and borrows" are just two concepts that chairpersons must fully understand. A knowledge of external commitments is extremely important in making assignments and reviewing activity reports.

A General Assignment Strategy for Chairpersons

Clearly the chairperson's task of making faculty assignments is complex. It requires an understanding of many rules and regulations; it depends on a clear understanding of department goals and objectives; and it requires a significant number of judgmental decisions. A convenient and useful strategy by which to establish term assignments is outlined below. This strategy assumes that the chairperson already has department goals, objectives, and priorities clearly in mind; that the faculty have consented to these; and that the chairperson is fully aware of the department members' interests, strengths, and experiences. The strategy comprises eight major steps.

1. Establish the instructional, research, and service workload that the department as a whole can be expected to accomplish during the term. Questions to be answered include these: What total FTE can be assigned? (That is, how many full-time equivalent faculty members, including graduate assistants and faculty adjuncts, are available to accomplish the department's work?) What relative effort among the categories of instruction, research, and service would best serve department interests and contribute to department goals?

2. Identify the courses to be taught during the term and the courses that are optional. Consult with faculty members, students, and other department chairpersons to assess the needs and demands here.

3. Determine the special requirements that have been imposed on faculty members for the term. Ask the faculty for this and other pertinent data. Which faculty members will have released time on research grants? What institution, college, or department committee assignments have already been committed for the term? (Note: If you as chairperson find these "external" commitments heavy, remember that *you* have control over most of them! If you do not, it is time to get your data together and have a long talk with the dean!)

4. List, for each faculty member, adjunct, and graduate assistant available to your department, the activities to which you tentatively expect each person to be assigned, without reference to time or fraction of FTE for each activity. Your choices of assignment should reflect both the department's needs and each faculty member's professional development (tenure, promotion, research, and so forth). The total listing for all faculty members should include each area and activity identified in items 2 and 3 above.

5. Determine how much effort, preferably in terms of fractions of FTE, you expect the faculty member to devote to each activity listed; double-check this with the faculty members as needed. If you use fractions of FTE, remember that the total FTE must equal exactly 1.00. If you use hours, the total hours assigned are not too important since, for reporting purposes, hourly assignments for each activity will ultimately be converted to the appropriate fraction of the total hours assigned (i.e., to a fraction of a 1.00 FTE). However, be aware that a twenty-hour teaching load, if otherwise equivalent, may be 0.50 FTE for the

forty-hour-a-week person but only 0.36 FTE for the fifty-five-hour-a-week person. If hours are to be taken seriously, some standard hourly effort rates may have to be developed to ensure that persons doing equivalent work share the same workload report fractions. For these and other reasons, the standard fractional FTE for particular activities may be the best understood and simplified measure of assigned (and reported) effort.

The crucial issue is whether or not the final assignment is realistic in terms of what a faculty member can be expected to accomplish and perform well. In making the FTE assignment, the chairperson's judgment on such matters as faculty experience and department needs in teaching, research, and service activities is extremely important.

6. Assess the reasonableness of each faculty assignment both in terms of the activities assigned and the time or fractional FTE allowed for the activity. If inequities exist, adjustments among the faculty or in the total effort assigned may be necessary, but note that some equity adjustments may be moved to another term.

7. Identify evaluative criteria that you will use to assess each assignment being made; these activities typically are faculty activities but may include expected outcomes. Be as quantitative as possible. Both you and the faculty member must share an understanding of how the level of success in completing the assignment will be determined.

8. Discuss each assignment with the appropriate faculty member. Consultation may be required by a collective bargaining agreement or state laws. A consultation may reveal new information or become a negotiation session, making futher assignment changes necessary. The final assignment decisions, however, should remain in the hands of the chairperson.

These steps provide a reasonable and sound strategy for assigning faculty duties. The chairperson will want to involve the faculty in as many of the steps as possible but particularly in steps 1 and 2, where the department's goals, objectives, and priorities are established and form the basis for the planned term activities. In addition, the chairperson should consult with each faculty member after the start of a term to make sure all is going as planned.

Questions

1. What ways are there to define "work load" other than one of the following:
   a. Total hours per week (including all activities)(?)
   b. Total (100%) professional effort (including all activities)(?)
   c. Total credits of courses taught (?)
2. Discuss the pros and cons of each way listed in question 1.
3. How can institutional expectations of faculty be incorporated into a departmental definition of a work load?

4. Should a department definition of faculty workload be considered a minimum or maximum expectation for evaluation purposes? Give reasons for your answer.

5. a. What are the advantages of keeping on file a written list of institutional assignments or expectations for each faculty member?

   b. What are the disadvantages of too much detail in the written list?

6. a. In determining a proper workload for an individual faculty member, should more time for class preparation be allowed to a faculty person who is teaching a course for the first time than to a faculty member who has taught the course before? Give reasons for *not* allowing it.

   b. Should time for research be included in a faculty member's contracted workload? Give reasons and circumstances for a "yes" answer. Give reasons and circumstances for a "no" answer.

7. In your department, what is considered a maximum teaching load? Is it a certain number of courses or course credits taught per term, a certain number of contact hours per week, or something else?

8. If a person is assigned a maximum teaching load in your department, does this teaching constitute a full-time workload? If it constitutes less than a full-time workload, what other assignments do you give to make a full-time workload?

9. Is the teaching load of your department divided equitably among the faculty members, or do some members have larger teaching loads than others? Do faculty members who have the same size teaching loads receive the same percentage of FTE for teaching? In your department, what constitutes the workload of one FTE faculty member?

10. Have you ever reduced a faculty member's teaching load in order to assign him or her to other activities? Please explain.

11. In making assignments, do you follow any special procedures to ensure that the assignments are equitable? For example, do you assign a faculty member a specific number of points for each activity, and is he or she considered to have a full workload when the sum of all the earned points reaches a predetermined number? Or do you have some other method for ensuring equitable assignments among your faculty? Please explain.

12. Have any of the teaching, research, or service assignments to your faculty members ever been tailored to help them develop a special competency or overcome a weakness?

References

BOWEN, HOWARD R., and SCHUSTER, JACK H. *The American Professoriate: A National Resource Imperiled.* New York: Carnegie Corporation, 1986.

BROWN, STEPHANIE. "Approaching Faculty Productivity as a Mechanism for Retrenchment." *New Directions for Institutional Research,* Winter 1979, pp. 45–54.

BURKE, DELORES L. "The Academic Marketplace in the 1980s: Appointment and Termination of Assistant Professors." *Review of Higher Education, 10,* 1987, pp. 199–214.

CRESWELL, JOHN W. "Faculty Acceptance of a Workload Survey in One Major University." *Research in Higher Education,* May 1978, pp. 205–226.

DYER, JAMES S., and MULVEY, JOHN M. "Computerized Scheduling and Planning." *New Directions for Institutional Research,* Spring 1977, pp. 67–86.

EASTMAN, JULIA A. "The Different Organizational Requirements of Scholarship and Service." *Review of Higher Education,* 12(3), Spring 1989.

EHRLE, ELWOOD B. "Selection and Evaluation of Department Chairmen." *Educational Record,* 56(1), 1975, pp. 29–38.

Faculty Activity Analysis Overview and Major Issues. TR 24, Boulder, CO: NCHEMS, 1974.

Faculty Activity Analysis Procedures Manual. TR 44, Boulder, CO: NCHEMS, 1973.

FRYER, THOMAS W., JR. "Designing New Personnel Policies: The Permanent Part-Time Faculty Member." *College and University Personnel Association,* Spring 1977, pp. 14–21.

HAY, ELLEN. "The Variable of Teaching Effectiveness in Tenure and Promotion Decisions." *ACA Bulletin,* 68, 1989, pp. 52–59.

HARPER, RONALD L. "Faculty Activity Analysis." *New Directions for Institutional Research,* Spring 1978, pp. 73–81.

HOBBS, WALTER G., and ANDERSON, G. LESTER. "The Operation of Academic Departments." *Management Science,* December 1971, pp. 134–144.

JOHNSON, F. CRAIG. "Data Requirements for Academic Departments." In *New Directions for Institutional Research: Examining Departmental Leadership,* no. 10, edited by John C. Smart and James R. Montgomery. San Francisco: Jossey–Bass, 1976.

KAIKAI, SEPTIMUS M., and KAIKAI, REGINA E. *Chairpersons as Promoters of Community Service.* Catonsville, MD: Catonsville Community College, 1990. (ERIC Document Reproduction Service No. ED 321 801)

LEWIS, LIONEL S. "Publish or Perish: Reality or Myth." *Scaling the Ivory Tower, Merit and Its Limits in Academic Careers.* Baltimore: The Johns Hopkins Press, 1975.

MARCH, HERBERT W., and DILLON, KRISTINE E. "Academic Productivity and Supplemental Income." *Journal of Higher Education,* 51, 1980, pp. 546–555.

MARCH, JAMES G. *How We Talk and How We Act: Administrative Theory and Administrative Life.* Urbana: University of Illinois Press, 1980.

McGEE, GAIL W., and FORD, ROBERT C. "Faculty Research Productivity and Intention to Change Positions." *Review of Higher Education,* 11, 1987, pp. 1–16.

NATIONAL SCIENCE FOUNDATION. *Systems for Measuring and Reporting the Resources and Activities of Colleges and Universities.* NSF 67–15. Washington, DC.: National Science Foundation, June 1967.

NEAR, JANET P., and SORCINELLI, MARY DEANE. "Work and Life Away from Work: Predictors of Faculty Satisfaction." *Research in Higher Education,* 25, 1986, pp. 377–394.

PAGE, JANE A., and PAGE, FRED M. *Collegiate Instruction: Some Differences Among Faculty Members Based on Rank, Years of Experience, and School Affiliation.* Paper presented at the Annual Meeting of the Mid-South Educational Research Association, Mobile, AL, 1987. (ERIC Document Reproduction Service No. ED 289 445)

PORTER, JOHN D. *Classroom Utilization: Pacing Departments on a Scheduling Diet.* AIR, 1986. (ERIC Document Reproduction Service No. ED 280 390)

RIGGS, MATT. "Using Discriminant Analysis to Predict Faculty Rank." *Research in Higher Education,* 25, 1986, pp. 365–376.

RODDY, MARY ELLEN. *Qualifications and Productivity of Nontenure-track Faculty.* Paper presented at the Annual Meeting of the American Educational Research Association, Washington, DC, 1987. (ERIC Document Reproduction Service No. ED 284 488)

RUSSELL, SUSAN H. *Faculty in Higher Education Institutions, 1988, Contractor Report.* Washington, DC: National Center for Higher Education Statistics, 1990. (ERIC Document Reproduction Service No. ED 321 628)

SCHULTZ, JERELYN B., and CHUNG, YONSUK L. "Research Productivity and Job Satisfaction of University Faculty." *Journal of Vocational Education Research,* 13, 1988, pp. 33–48.

SEAGREN, ALAN T. *Perception of Chairpersons and Faculty Concerning Roles, Descriptors, and Activities Considered Important for Faculty Development and Departmental Vitality.* 1986. (ERIC Document Reproduction Service No. ED 276 387)

SOMMERS, ALEXIS N. "University Productivity." *Educational Record,* Winter 1977, pp. 251–256.

SORCINELLI, MARY DEANE, and NEAR, JANET P. "Relations Between Work and Life Away from Work Among University Faculty." *Journal of Higher Education,* 60, 1989, pp. 59–81.

SPRUNGER, BENJAMIN E., and BERGQUIST, WILLIAM H. *Handbook for College Administration.* Washington, DC: Council for the Advancement of Small Colleges, 1980.

STIER, WILLIAM F., JR. *Physical Education Workload Policies, Practices and Procedures on the Junior/Community College Level—A National Inquiry.* Paper presented at the National Convention of the American Alliance for Health, Physical Education, Recreation and Dance, Cincinnati, 1986. (ERIC Document Reproduction Service No. ED 273 586).

TUCKMAN, HOWARD P., and TUCKMAN, BARBARA H. "Who Are the Part-timers and What Are Colleges Doing for Them?" *Current Issues in Higher Education,* 4, 1981.

WINANS, GLEN T. *Implementing Microcomputers in Academic Departments: Changing the Face of Academic and Administrative Life at the University of California, Santa Barbara.* 1986. (ERIC Document Reproduction Service No. ED 265 767)

WRIGHT, TED. *Who Uses Institutional Research and Why?* Research Report No. 85–22. Miami: Miami–Dade Community College, 1985.

Chapter 15

Faculty Evaluation

Evaluation of faculty performance is one of the chairperson's most difficult and important responsibilities. Probably no other activity has more potential for strengthening or weakening the department over a period of years. One of the most important components of faculty evaluation is communication with each faculty member regarding what is expected and what will be evaluated. This communication can be in the form of a contract, a written memorandum of understanding, or an official assignment statement. A verbal understanding not in writing may not be enough. Handled properly, evaluation can improve faculty morale and result in a strong, effective department. Handled improperly, evaluation can destroy morale, decrease the chances for the department's success in meeting objectives, and place the chairperson on the receiving end of a long succession of grievances. Most colleges and universities have or should have official documents that provide specific information about the evaluation process, such as how often evaluations will be conducted, who will do the evaluating, in what form the evaluations will be submitted, who may use them, how they will be used, and what may be placed in the faculty member's personnel file.

A necessary condition for effective evaluation is clear, specific criteria. In addition, there must be a reasonable, definitive assignment of activities and an ongoing system of performance counseling. If faculty members' assignments are sufficiently clear and if discussion between chairperson and faculty members regarding performance becomes a regular activity, evaluation will no longer be seen as a dreaded annual exercise. In effect, the process could become no more than a report of a faculty member's performance—a report that would hold no surprises for either the faculty member or the chairperson.

This chapter will focus on four questions: Why is evaluation necessary? What should be evaluated? Who should do the evaluating and what should be the process? How should performance be evaluated? Examples of different procedures used to evaluate faculty performance are presented. No single procedure is advocated as being better than another. It should be noted, however, that each of the procedures described in the following pages is used by at least one department at some institution.

Why Is Evaluation Necessary?

Every department chairperson who has held the position for at least a year has been faced with the need to evaluate staff and faculty members. Evaluation is required by the dean, the collective bargaining contract (if the institution has one), the vice-president, the president, the board of trustees, and even the faculty. In times of limited resources, competition becomes intense and decisions are sometimes challenged. State legislators, parents, and citizens are requiring more accountability with regard to the quality of teaching, benefits from research, and time away from campus for service.

Faculty members themselves are no longer satisfied with an arbitrary and paternalistic evaluation by a department chairperson. They insist on a more formal evaluation based on specific criteria, and this desire seems to increase as the discretionary funds available for merit raises decrease. Faculty members also want the option to appeal in the event that they disagree with the evaluation. Leaders in education, therefore, need to find ways to perform evaluations that are reliable and acceptable to students, to the faculty, to faculty unions, to university administrators, and to state legislators and other groups responsible for providing financial support.

Performance evaluation of faculty has several purposes. One has always been to provide faculty with some measure of how well they are performing in their professional roles so that they can improve their performance. Other purposes are related to personnel decisions that must be made each academic year, such as (1) continuation of contract, (2) recommendation for merit pay, (3) promotion decisions, and (4) tenure decisions. Evaluation of nontenured faculty members to determine whether their contract should be continued is done annually and is usually based on what the individual has achieved over the past year. Evaluation of faculty for merit raise purposes is also based on what the candidate has done during that time. Evaluation for promotion is based on what the candidate has accomplished while serving in the present rank. Evaluation for tenure is based on a comprehensive assessment of past performance and a projection of future contributions to the university.

Because evaluation for tenure is more than a perfunctory assessment of a candidate's recent performance, it must be more than an assessment of that person's ability to meet minimum expectations on his or her present assignment. Not unlike the award of partnership in a professional firm, the award of tenure is essentially a grant of a permanent interest in the university's future. Evaluating a candidate for tenure requires a serious effort to project whether the party will perform at a high level throughout his or her career. Since evaluation for tenure may result in a long-term commitment *by* the institution, it is important that it obtain an assessment of the candidate's potential long-term commitment *to* the institution. The candidate is judged as a colleague, an institutional citizen, a teacher, a researcher, and a general partner in the educational enterprise. This kind of judgment is necessarily subjective, and so necessarily requires a searching and thorough consideration of *all* aspects of the candidate's professional behavior. Although a candidate for tenure may be quite strong on as many as two dimensions, that does not mean he or she is equal to the university's expectations for someone to whom it stands to make a lifetime commitment, even if one of those dimensions is research performance.

A few universities, and most community colleges, do not give merit raises. Salary increases are based on schedules which automatically provide set increments each year for all faculty members. At these institutions the results of performance evaluation has very little impact on salary increases. Some of the same institutions do not have a tenure system, either. Instead, all faculty whose contracts are continued for two or more years are automatically considered to be permanently employed. Many community colleges do not provide academic rank or promotion in rank for their faculty; all are titled instructors. At institutions which do not have merit, promotion, *or* tenure systems, the result of performance evaluation would be used primarily for self-improvement of faculty and for contract continuation purposes.

What Should Be Evaluated?

The central academic functions of most universities and baccalaureate granting colleges include teaching, research, and service. The amount of effort allotted to each of these functions varies from institution to institution. The main functions of community colleges are teaching and service. Community college faculty members are not expected to conduct research as part of their workload and hence research is not evaluated. Some of their professional efforts, however, are devoted to special projects and could fall into a general category called "special assignments." Community college department chairpersons and division directors may wish to ignore those sections in this chapter dealing with research and include instead a category of "special assignments" as a performance area to be evaluated along with teaching and service. A department committee or the department as a whole will have little difficulty in developing a list of activities to be evaluated under each of the broad areas of performance as determined by the institution. Questions about the minimal level of performance quality and the kinds of evidence that will be accepted for the evaluation, however, are considerably more difficult.

One point that has emerged in the last several years, especially at those institutions that have faculty unions, is the importance of evaluating only what has been formally assigned. Penalizing faculty members for failing to complete unassigned duties or for failing to accomplish more than what has been assigned has created legal problems in some instances when faculty members were not subsequently promoted or awarded tenure. It behooves chairpersons, therefore, to anticipate what activities within each major category will be evaluated and to include them in the formal assignments.

Receiving an assignment does not necessarily mean that a faculty member is called into the chairperson's office and told "This is what you are assigned to do this year." The most common practice is for the faculty member to tell what courses he or she plans to teach, and what other activities are planned. The chairperson may make suggestions, and when a plan is agreed upon by the faculty member and the chairperson, the plan is written up as the faculty member's assignment. The word "assignment" seems to have a negative connotation in the minds of some academics because of its perceived authoritarian implication. Nevertheless, it is a term commonly used in official faculty contracts. Such contracts often stipulate that faculty may be evaluated only on activities contained in the formal assignment. Regardless of semantics, however, a faculty member needs to know what is expected of him or her and upon what basis an evaluation will be made. At some institutions the "official" assignment and the expectations may not be the same. For example, the "official" assignment may contain only the amount of teaching that is expected. Although faculty members at these institutions are expected to engage in other activities such as research, these expectations are not included in the formal assignment but are called "add ons" and are often interpreted by newly appointed faculty members as voluntary. Yet, the awarding of promotion or tenure at some of these institutions is often based on the performance evaluation received for the "add-on" activities. Faculty members who are denied promotion or tenure because they performed poorly or not at all in an "add-on" activity sometimes file grievances. They claim that they were not explicitly informed that a recommendation for their promotion and tenure would depend on a satisfactory performance in that activity.

PERFORMANCE AREAS TO BE EVALUATED

Performance areas to be evaluated are generally listed in various official documents, such as the university constitution, the state system personnel policy manual, or a union contract. The list may vary in detail from one university to another, from one department to another within the same university, or from one faculty member to another. Most lists, however, will include the following performance areas, compiled from a variety of official documents. Note the mixture of activities, outcomes, and the quantitative and qualitative characteristics included.

TEACHING. Teaching involves the presentation of knowledge, information, and ideas by methods that include lecturing, discussion, assignment and recitation, demonstration, laboratory exercise, practical experience, direct consultation with students, and so forth. In an evaluation, the use and effectiveness of each method should be considered. The evaluation of teaching effectiveness should also be related to the written objectives of each course, which should have been given to each class at the beginning of the term. Evaluation of teaching should include consideration of:

- Correlation of imparted knowledge and skills to course objectives
- Stimulation of the students' critical thinking and creative ability in light of the course objectives
- The faculty member's adherence to accepted standards of professional behavior in meeting his or her responsibilities to students

In an informal sample taken in 1987, chairpersons in two major state universities in Florida listed the following as their preferred sources of evidence for evaluating teaching: (1) systematic rating by students; (2) chairperson's evaluation; (3) colleagues' opinions; (4) committee evaluation; (5) content of course syllabi and examinations; (6) informal rating by students; (7) colleagues' ratings based on classroom visits; (8) long-term follow-up of students' performance; (9) faculty member's interest in teaching improvement activities (workshops and so forth); (10) faculty member's self-evaluation or report; (11) students' examination performance; (12) popularity of elective courses (e.g., enrollment); and (13) opinions of alumni.[1]

RESEARCH, SCHOLARSHIP, AND OTHER CREATIVE ACTIVITIES. Contribution to and discovery of new knowledge, new educational techniques, and other forms of scholarly and creative activity should be considered for evaluation. Evidence of research and other creative activity should include, but not be limited to, published books; articles and papers in professional journals; paintings and sculpture; works for performance (musical compositions, dances, plays, and so forth); papers presented at meetings of professional societies; and current research and creative activity that has not yet resulted in publication, display, or performance. Evaluation of research and other creative activities should include consideration of:

- quality and quantity of productivity of both short-term and long-term research and other creative programs and contributions
- Recognition by the academic or professional community of work accomplished (for judgments pertaining to the decision to award tenure, evaluation should be sought from qualified scholars in pertinent disciplines both within and outside the university)

SPECIAL ASSIGNMENTS. Community colleges may use this category in lieu of research. Each institution must determine for itself what projects or activities should be included under this category and what criteria and evidence will be used in evaluating the activities.

SERVICE. Service should include, but not be limited to, involvement in department, college, and university committees, councils, and senates; service in

---

1. Informal survey conducted by Allan Tucker, unpublished.

appropriate professional organizations; involvement in organizing and expediting meetings, symposia, conferences, and workshops; participation in radio and television; and service on local, state, and national governmental boards, commissions, and other agencies. Only those activities that are related to a person's field of expertise or to the university's mission should be evaluated. Evaluation of service should include consideration of:

- Contribution to the orderly and effective functioning of the academic administrative unit (program, department, school, college) and the whole institution
- Contribution to the university community
- Contribution to local, state, regional, and national communities, including scholarly and professional associations

OTHER DUTIES.   Reasonable duties other than those usually classified as teaching, research or other creative activity, or service are occasionally assigned to faculty members. The performance of these duties—which might include academic administration, academic advising, career counseling, or the supervision of interns—should also be evaluated. A dean or director may be the best person to conduct the evaluation of these activities, so the chairperson should consult them about correct procedures.

EVALUATION BASED ON ASSIGNMENTS

If evaluations are to be based on assignments, then the assignments must specify what constitutes successful and acceptable completion. Such specification requires an understanding of the difference between activities and outcomes, for both may be evaluated. Typically, faculty members are paid for participating in an acceptable set of professional activities, such as conducting classes, preparing syllabi and other materials for classes, advising and counseling students, serving on department and institutional governing committees, reviewing manuscripts, collecting and analyzing data, conducting research, and so on. Simply assigning activities without some idea of what is expected or what constitutes satisfactory completion of the assignment, however, makes it difficult to differentiate the performance of faculty members, especially when they are given similar activity assignments—the same number of courses to teach, the same percentage of time to conduct research, and so forth.

Outcomes are the results of activities. Whereas activities emphasize process, outcomes focus on achievements and end products. Examples of simple outcome assignments made by department chairpersons include preparing and duplicating for students a research bibliography on subject X for course Y; completing the first draft of the third chapter of a book manuscript on topic Z; and reviewing the professional literature on subject R for inclusion in a consulting paper for government agency A. All these outcomes are clearly observable.

Examples of complex outcome assignments would be completing manuscript M and finding a publisher for it; submitting a completed proposal for funding and having it accepted in principle; and completing a consulting project by a specific deadline date and arranging for publication of the final report. These outcome assignments are "complex" because they include more than one condition that must be met. Two other complex outcome assignments, drawn from the literature of educational performance objectives, are teaching introductory course S so well that at least 75 percent of the students believed it was worthwhile and teaching course R so well that 85 percent attain a grade of C or higher on the final exam. Some controversy surrounds the idea that outcomes can be clearly specified, particularly when an arbitrary figure—such as 85 percent—appears in the statement. Such figures should be specified only after careful thought about what constitutes a satisfactory outcome; they should not be included merely to give an appearance of precision. Note that faculty members can meet these kinds of performance objectives by lowering standards.

Outcome assignments, if properly made, lend themselves more easily to an objective evaluation of performance quality than do activity assignments, which usually focus on quantity rather than quality of performance. Chairpersons who try to evaluate faculty performance on the basis of outcomes usually consult in advance with their faculty members to determine what each person plans to accomplish during the year and to stipulate the intended outcomes. The chairperson and the faculty member together develop the annual assignment, incorporating as far as possible the faculty member's plan. Some chairpersons and faculty members claim that faculty members generally resist a request to provide an advance list of the individual activities, projects, and outcomes that they plan for the coming year. They do not object, however, to submitting a detailed list of their accomplishments and their performance outcomes during the past year in order to prepare for an annual performance evaluation.

An interesting exercise for chairpersons would be to review some lists prepared by faculty members of their accomplishments of the past year, changing the tense of the verbs from past to future. By doing so, chairpersons can see what the anticipated outcome of assignments made at the beginning of the year might have been. Would these faculty members have been able to anticipate their accomplishments one year in advance? Would it have been helpful to them and to the department if they had been required to think in terms of intended accomplishments? Each person has his or her own opinion on these issues, and the arguments on both sides would provoke an interesting discussion.

Chairpersons who wish to specify desired outcomes in faculty members' annual assignments should obtain the following information about each person's activities. As far as teaching is concerned, the chairperson should know what level of effectiveness the faculty member plans to attain in helping students reach stated course objectives; what innovations are anticipated; how much effort will be expended in preparing for class; and what level of satisfaction will be expected from the students. If research or creative activity is part of the faculty member's assignment, the chairperson should know what progress can be expected by the end of the year and what kind of evidence (short of a published article or book) is acceptable to demonstrate that progress has been made; whether a grant proposal will be written by the end of the term; whether a rough draft of an article for publication will be completed; whether a special seminar or recital will be given; whether a specified amount of progress can be expected on a research project; and whether a library literature search will be completed by the end of the year. If a service assignment is made, the chairperson should know what outcome is expected; whether attendance at committee meetings is all that is expected; whether, if the assignment is on an ad hoc department committee, a report is due and who has responsibility for writing the report; whether contacts with potential students are part of a service assignment; and, if so, how many contacts are expected. These are the kinds of questions that department chairpersons should consider in making faculty assignments on which evaluations are based.

Obvious and specific procedures are necessary for interpreting whatever evidence is deemed appropriate for a faculty evaluation. For example, there must be procedures for reading and interpreting student ratings of teachers and some basis for assigning an overall quality rating, i.e., for stating whether the faculty member's teaching is "outstanding," "very good," "satisfactory," "weak," or "unsatisfactory." Similarly, standard procedures for interpreting all other evidence are also needed, so that a chairperson can demonstrate the extent to which the final evaluation is based on objectively assessed evidence.

Who Should Do the Evaluating and What Should Be the Process?

Evaluation of a faculty member's performance is usually derived from some or all of the following sources: the faculty member's chairperson or other administrator; the faculty member's self-evaluation; the faculty member's peers; professional colleagues at other universities (in matters of promotion and tenure); students; and other university officials.

The department chairperson is usually the person responsible for collecting evaluations about each faculty member from these sources. Even though a faculty committee may have assisted the chairperson in the evaluation, most universities hold the department chairperson responsible for the official evaluation. Each faculty member should be told who will perform the official evaluation, the nature of the process, the performance criteria to be used, and so on. Similarly, all persons involved in submitting evidence or making judgments should be informed of their particular roles. One point cannot be overemphasized: the chairperson's official evaluation rests on his or her informed judgment of all the appropriate evidence. The evaluation process gains substantial legitimacy in the eyes of the faculty members if they have been able to participate in the development of department goals and objectives.

Another way to involve faculty members in their own evaluation is to have each of them prepare a "brag sheet" describing his or her activities and accomplishments. Faculty members should be afforded the opportunity to describe in detail what they consider their important contributions to the department, the institution, the profession or discipline, and the community. Sometimes they cannot easily enumerate their outstanding accomplishments on a standardized form. Therefore, the self-evaluation could be written in narrative form, which would allow them the freedom to describe their achievements in their own words. Faculty members feel more confident that their actions are appreciated and valued if they have the opportunity to describe them adequately. On the other hand, the chairperson, when reading the brag sheets, should be able to distinguish between rhetoric and reality.

Students are often invited to participate in the institutional evaluation of faculty members. At some institutions they also conduct their own evaluation of teaching faculty members and publish the results for the benefit of fellow students. The results of these evaluations are quite interesting, to say the least.

How Should Performance Be Evaluated?

The questions of what should be evaluated and who should do the evaluating are relatively simple to answer compared with the question of how performance should be evaluated. The art of evaluating the performance of faculty members is not that well developed. Experts who are invited to make presentations on how to evaluate such performance will adequately explain why evaluation is important, what should be evaluated, who should do the evaluating, and what procedures should be followed to obtain maximum involvement of appropriate faculty members, students, and administrators in the evaluation process. Usually, however, these experts are unable to provide a magic formula that will make the evaluation process more simple or less painful.

At most universities faculty performance is evaluated in at least three areas, namely: teaching, research, and service. No matter which of the three is being evaluated, the evaluation process requires an understanding of the following elements: criteria, standards, and evidence. *Criteria* are the activities, behaviors, and outcomes that are to be examined under each of the areas to be evaluated. Examples of criteria often used in evaluating teaching performance are: enthusiasm, preparation of the syllabus, organization of the course, method of presenting information, attempt to be innovative, and method of grading. Similarly, criteria can be specified under the research and the service areas.

Institutions and/or departments must also decide what type of rating scale will be used in evaluating each of the criteria. Some institutions rate criteria under only two categories (satisfactory of unsatisfactory), others use five (outstanding, very good, satisfactory, weak, and unsatisfactory), and still others use a numerical scale (1 through 5).

When it has been determined which areas of performance will be evaluated, the criteria to be rated under each of the areas and the rating scale to be used, methods need to be developed for rating the quality and/or quantity of the performance for each of the criteria. The performance ratings for all the criteria in the area being evaluated can then be treated mathematically to arrive at a single measurement or rating for the overall performance in that area.

Standards need to be established for each of the criteria in each area to be evaluated. A *standard* is the minimum quality or quantity rating that is acceptable for each of the categories in the rating scale. For example, what standard (minimum ratings) will be used for awarding evaluations of "satisfactory" or "very good" or "outstanding"? Also important is the need for the institution or department (or both) to decide what *evidence* will be accepted to justify the ratings.

Reaching a consensus on what should be included in a list of criteria for each area of performance is not a difficult task for a group of experienced faculty members. The group can be fairly objective in compiling the list. However, developing and agreeing on ways to measure or rate performance is very difficult, especially in the area of teaching. The ratings on many of the criteria will, of necessity, be subjective—but subjectivity may be acceptable if the ratings are done by acknowledged experts in the field. The setting of standards will also be difficult, especially since they will be based on measurements that may be subjective. But, here again, the perceived expertise of the evaluators will have a lot to do with the acceptability of the evaluation results.

The evaluation system that a department uses will depend on a variety of factors: the institution's requirements, the school or college's procedures, and the kinds of personnel decisions that need to be made. In some cases different personnel decisions may use the same evaluation data, but at most institutions these decisions are distinct in terms of legal requirements. Moreover, each personnel decision should be based on evaluation data that represent more than the subjective and arbitrary response of a chairperson or a committee of peers. Therefore, as these decisions become more complex, the chairperson should seek to implement or improve quantitative evaluations, rather than to avoid them.

Not every faculty member in a department is outstanding, but the difficult task for the chairperson is to differentiate among the members, most of whom perform their assigned duties at least satisfactorily. The department faculty members should help determine the specific criteria to be used for personnel decisions, whether these decisions are related to promotion, tenure, annual assessment, or merit recommendations. The chairperson must work with the faculty to delineate the particular evaluation criteria used in each part of the evaluation. The chairperson should also state how the criteria will be applied to the evidence in each person's evaluation folder.

In thinking about devising a system for evaluation, the chairperson and the faculty members together must confront several questions: First, what constitutes 100 percent of a full-time workload for a given term or year? Does a 100 percent assignment demand all of a faculty member's professional time and effort, regardless of the number of hours worked? Or does it consist of a specified number of hours, say forty hours per week? Is a formal definition of what constitutes 100 percent of a full-time workload even necessary? Will a faculty member's teaching duties alone make up 100 percent of his or her assigned full-time workload, with research and service activities considered as "add-ons"? If so, will such additional activities be required or voluntary? Will the performance of these additional activities, even though they are not part of a formal assignment, be evaluated for promotion and tenure purposes? Will a subjective evaluation be made of each faculty member's overall worth to the department without separate evaluations of the performance in each activity and regardless of whether the activity was formally assigned?

After the chairperson and the faculty members have thought through these questions and arrived at answers that are acceptable to them as a department, they must consider further questions. If each faculty member is expected to engage in some teaching, research, and service activities, will this expectation be stated formally in an assignment contract? If activities in these three areas are formally or informally assigned, will each faculty member receive a separate performance rating for each area? Will a faculty member's overall performance evaluation be determined by simply averaging the three ratings? Or will the ratings also take into consideration the amount of time and effort expended in each area? Is good teaching just as important to the department as good research? If a faculty member receives an "outstanding" rating for research and a "poor" rating for teaching, will the "poor" rating for teaching pull down his or her overall evaluation?

Some evaluation procedures are more complex and quantitative than others. The more quantitative the system, the more objective it is perceived to be. For some reason, the use of numbers is supposed to dilute the subjectivity of human judgment. In reality, this is not necessarily the case, especially in evaluating the quality of performance. Much to the surprise of some chairpersons, however, there are faculty members in some departments who insist on the use of detailed quantification. Quantification involves the use of arabic numbers rather than descriptive words to express human judgment. Numbers can be added, averaged, and otherwise subjected to statistical treatment. Descriptive words cannot. But human judgment is still the only basis upon which many qualitative evaluations can be made. When evaluations are based on human judgment, the evaluator in effect becomes the evaluation instrument. The number and range of experiences in a given field, together with common sense and good judgment, contribute to the degree of precision of the human evaluation instrument.

Examples of Evaluation Processes and Performance Ratings

SIMPLE SUBJECTIVE EVALUATION OF OVERALL CONTRIBUTION TO THE MISSION OF THE DEPARTMENT

In this type of evaluation the chairperson bases his or her evaluation on the faculty member's performance of department activities without necessarily listing the activities and without prescribing what percentage of time or effort of full-time workload is to be spent on each activity and without a separate detailed scrutiny of each activity performed. The chairperson reviews each faculty member's performance over the past year, including the self-evaluation report, and then asks the question, "How valuable, in my opinion, is this faculty member to the department?" This process is repeated for all the faculty members, and then they are ranked according to how much the chairperson values their contributions to the department. In the process of ranking, the chairperson assigns a number to each subjective evaluation and by so doing gives a quantitative measure to each faculty member's performance. This simple type of evaluation, as well as the types described later, may be done by the chairperson alone, with or without the help of consultants; by a department committee headed by the chairperson; by a department committee without the chairperson's participation; or by the entire department.

At this point, the matter of rating faculty members as "above average" should be mentioned. Every department chairperson must face the fact, difficult as it may be to acknowledge, that all the members of his or her department are not necessarily "above average." If the evaluations of all faculty members in a single department are averaged, the evaluation of some faculty members will be below that average. To evaluate faculty members as "above average" or "below average" does not make sense unless the group with which they are being compared can be clearly specified. Is the reference group another department in the same school or college, another department in the institution, or a similar department in another university? To give ratings higher than faculty members deserve simply because everyone else is doing so is not good policy.

Performance ratings can range from simple to complex. A chairperson might simply rate the faculty members as "O.K." or "not O.K.," "merit" or "no merit," or "acceptable" or "not acceptable." Faculty members can also be rated on a three-point scale, such as "high merit," "low merit," and "no merit." The difference between a rating of 73 percent and 75 percent, however, may be insignificant in determining whether the performance of one faculty member should be rated higher then another's.

An evaluation procedure based on a four-point scale is also suggested for use.[2] This approach is helpful because the scale is familiar to anyone who has graded academic performance. Simply translate the value terms "outstanding," "very good," "satisfactory," "weak," and "unsatisfactory" to the numbers 4.0, 3.0, 2.0, 1.0, and 0 (see Table 15.1 for performance rating key). For example, if the performance of a teaching activity is evaluated as "very good," the faculty member would receive a performance rating of 3.0. This scale will be used in subsequent discussions of more complex systems of evaluation, but it should be remembered that other schema can be used with equal effectiveness.

Before a number system is adopted to designate levels of performance as "outstanding," "very good," "satisfactory," and so forth, the chairperson and the de-

---

2. Developed by Allan Tucker.

TABLE *15.1* Performance
Rating Key

LEVEL OF PERFORMANCE	PERFORMANCE RATING
Outstanding	4
Very Good	3
Satisfactory	2
Weak	1
Unsatisfactory	0

partment should have some idea of what those ratings imply. In terms of performance, what is the difference between being "outstanding" and just "satisfactory"?

SEPARATE EVALUATION OF EACH OF SEVERAL COMPONENTS OF A FACULTY MEMBER'S ACTIVITIES

The question of value at the next level of complexity takes into account the faculty member's contributions in each of the three major performance areas—teaching, research, and service. In this system, the faculty member's performance in each area is rated separately on a four-point scale, and his or her ratings are averaged. Table 15.2 shows the performance ratings, by area and based on the four-point scale, of three faculty members.

In our example, Jones comes out with an average rating of 3.33, which can be interpreted as somewhere between "very good" and "outstanding." Smith's average rating is "very good," and Brown's is "satisfactory." If this type of evaluation were being done by a committee rather than the chairperson, each committee member could give each department member a separate rating for each area of performance. These ratings could then be averaged to produce a committee rating for each performance area.

TABLE *15.2* Rating of Faculty Members, By Area of Performance, Using Four-Point Scale

	FACULTY MEMBERS		
Area of Performance	*Jones*	*Smith*	*Brown*
Teaching	4.0	2.0	2.0
Research*	3.0	4.0	1.0
Service	3.0	3.0	3.0
Total of Ratings	10.0	9.0	6.0
Average Rating	3.33	3.0	2.0

*Community colleges may wish to use "special assignments" as an area of performance instead of "research."

The system described above is used in departments that are not particularly concerned with the percentage of full-time workload that is assigned to any given activity. These same departments probably consider teaching, research, and service equally important in achieving department goals and do not rate outstanding researchers higher than outstanding teachers.

WEIGHTING THE EVALUATION OF EACH COMPONENT ACTIVITY
PROPORTIONATELY TO EFFORT EXPENDED

Faculty members in some departments are not satisfied with a laissez-faire system of assignment. They want evaluations to take into account the percentage of full-time workload that is assigned to each of the three major performance areas; in addition, they want the evaluations to count activities that fall under a fourth category called "other." The fourth category generally includes assignments such as administrative duties, career counseling, supervision of interns, and so forth. Such calculations are not difficult.

Subsequent discussion will make use of the following terminology:

- *Performance ratings* (PR)—These ratings are based on a four-point scale and are used to differentiate "outstanding, "very good," "satisfactory," "weak," and "unsatisfactory" performance (see Tables 15.1 and 15.2).
- *Rating points* (RP)—Rating points are calculated for a given area or activity by multiplying the performance rating for that activity by the percentage of full-time workload assigned to that activity. For example, if 60 percent of a faculty member's full-time workload is assigned to teaching and if her rating for that assignment is "outstanding," she would receive 240 rating points (4×60).
- *Rating point average* (RPA)—The rating point average is calculated by totaling the rating points obtained for the areas of performance being evaluated and dividing that total by the sum of the percentages of the full-time workload assigned to the several areas or activities being rated. (See Tables 15.3, 15.4, and 15.5).

For example, Faculty Member A is rated 4.0 for his teaching assignment, which constitutes 60 percent of his full-time workload. He therefore would receive 240 rating points (4×60) for the area of teaching. He is rated 3.0 for his research assignment, which constitutes 30 percent of his full-time workload. For the areas of research, therefore, he would receive 90 rating points (3×30). His assigned percentage of full-time workload for service was 5 percent; his assigned percentage of full-time workload for "other," which consisted of supervising interns, was also 5 percent. For each of the latter two areas he was rated 3.0 and thus received 15 rating point (3×5) for each. The total number of rating points for the four areas—teaching, research, service, and "other"—therefore was 360 ($240 + 90 + 15 + 15$). The sum of assigned percentages of full-time workload for the four areas was 100 percent ($60 + 30 + 5 + 5$). The rating point average (RPA) for this faculty member was 3.6 ($360 \div 100$).

TABLE *15.3* Rating of Faculty Member A's Performance, By Area of Performance and By Percentage of Full-Time Workload Assigned to Each Area

AREA OF PERFORMANCE	I PERFORMANCE RATING	II ASSIGNED % OF FULL-TIME WORKLOAD	RATING POINTS (RP) (I × II)
Teaching	4.0	60	240
Research*	3.0	30	90
Service	3.0	5	15
Other	3.0	5	15
Total	13.0	100	360

$$\text{Rating Point Average (RPA)} = \frac{\text{Total of Rating Points}}{\text{Total of Assigned Percentages}} = \frac{360}{100} = 3.6$$

*Community colleges may wish to use "special assignments" as an area of performance instead of "research."

(The calculations used to derive the RPA for Faculty Member A appear in Table 15.3). Since "full time" constitutes 100 percent of a faculty member's workload, the sum of the percentages assigned to the several areas cannot exceed 100 percent, and since 4.0 is the highest performance rating that can be given to any area, a rating point average can never be greater than 4.0.

Following are examples of assignments and ratings given to two other faculty members in the same department, Faculty Member B and Faculty Member C. Forty percent of Faculty Member B's full-time workload was assigned to teaching, for which she was rated 2.0; 40 percent was assigned to research, for which she was rated 4.0; 10 percent was assigned to service, for which she was rated 3.0; and 10 percent was assigned to "other" (in this case, administrative duties), for which she was rated 2.0. Sixty-five percent of Faculty Member C's full-time workload was assigned to teaching, for which he was rated 1.0; 20 percent was assigned to research, for which he was rated 1.0; 10 percent was assigned to service, for which he was rated 4.0; and 5 percent was assigned to "other" (in this case career counseling), for which he was rated 3.0. Tables 15.3, 15.4, and 15.5 show how the rating point averages (RPAs) can be calculated for each faculty member.

Had Faculty Member A's ratings been averaged without regard for the percentage of full-time workload assigned to each area, he would have received a rating of 3.25 (13 ÷ 4). Taking the percentage of full-time workload assigned to each area into account, his rating point average is 3.60. Faculty Member B, who would have received an average rating of 2.75 (11 ÷ 4), receives a rating point average of 2.90 when consideration is given to the percentage of full time workload assigned to each area. Faculty Member C, who would have received an

TABLE 15.4 Rating of Faculty Member B's Performance, By Area of Performance and By Percentage of Full-Time Workload Assigned to Each Area

AREA OF PERFORMANCE	I PERFORMANCE RATING	II ASSIGNED % OF FULL-TIME WORKLOAD	RATING POINTS (RP) (I × II)
Teaching	2.0	40	80
Research*	4.0	40	160
Service	3.0	10	30
Other	2.0	10	20
Total	11.0	100	290

$$\text{Rating Point Average (RPA)} = \frac{\text{Total of Rating Points}}{\text{Total of Assigned Percentages}} = \frac{290}{100} = 2.9$$

*Community colleges may wish to use "special assignments" as an area of performance instead of "research."

average rating of 2.25 (9 ÷ 4), now receives a rating point average of 1.40 when percentage of full-time workload assigned to each area is considered.

Keeping in mind that human judgment is a factor to be reckoned with in the assessment of faculty members' performance, the chairperson must address the question of the quantity of work completed in the amount of time assigned to the effort. For example, if a faculty member receives an "outstanding" rating

TABLE 15.5 Rating of Faculty Member C's Performance, By Area of Performance and By Percentage of Full-Time Workload Assigned to Each Area

AREA OF PERFORMANCE	I PERFORMANCE RATING	II ASSIGNED % OF FULL-TIME WORKLOAD	RATING POINTS (RP) (I × II)
Teaching	1.0	65	65
Research*	1.0	20	20
Service	4.0	10	40
Other	3.0	5	15
Total	9.0	100	140

$$\text{Rating Point Average (RPA)} = \frac{\text{Total of Rating Points}}{\text{Total of Assigned Percentages}} = \frac{140}{100} = 1.4$$

*Community colleges may wish to use "special assignments" as an area of performance instead of "research."

for assigned research that constitutes 10 percent of a full-time workload, should that person receive an "outstanding" rating for the same effort and end product if research constitutes 30 percent of a full-time workload?

WEIGHTING THE EVALUATION OF EACH COMPONENT ACTIVITY PROPORTIONATELY TO ITS IMPORTANCE TO MISSION OF THE DEPARTMENT

So far we have discussed two types of evaluation: (1) a simple type based only on performance rating without regard for percentage of full-time workload assigned to each area; and (2) a more complex type that takes into account separate performance ratings for each area and the percentage of full-time workload assigned to each of the areas rated. We have not yet considered the question of priority of performance areas.

Some departments prize research more highly than other performance areas and wish to reward good research more highly than good teaching or good service. On the other hand, some departments with enormous undergraduate teaching loads are primarily concerned with encouraging and rewarding their outstanding teachers. Such departments not only evaluate faculty members in terms of their assigned duties, as already illustrated, but also assign priority factors to the various areas according to the priority given to each. If a department wishes to encourage its members to do more research, for example, it could reward its more productive members by assigning larger percentages of their full-time workload to research, or it could assign a higher priority factor to the research portion of the assignment.

Tables 15.3, 15.4 and 15.5 describe a department that assigns a priority factor of 1 to each performance area; in this way the department indicates that it believes all areas to be of equal importance and that "outstanding" performance should be rewarded equally, regardless of area. A department that wishes to give more priority to research than to other assigned areas can do so in several ways within the four-point system. A chairperson, after consulting with department members, could arbitrarily decide that research is 1.5 times as important as any other area and accordingly multiply each faculty member's assigned percentage of full-time workload devoted to research by a priority factor of 1.5.

Consider Faculty Member B, who in Table 15.4 was assigned 40 percent of her full-time workload to research and received a rating of 4.0 for research. If Faculty Member B's assigned percentage of full-time workload for research is multiplied by a priority factor of 1.5, her adjusted assigned percentage of full-time workload for research becomes 60 percent (40 percent × 1.5). Table 15.6 shows these calculations. When Faculty Member B's percentage of full-time workload assigned to research (40) is multiplied by the area priority factor for research (1.5), her rating point average rises from 2.90 to 3.08.

If a priority factor is applied to the percentage of full-time workload assigned to a given performance area for one faculty member, then the same priority factor has to be applied to that performance area for all faculty members. The adjustment described in Table 15.6 would result in a lower rating point

TABLE *15.6* Rating of Faculty Member B's Performance, By Area of Performance and By Percentage of Full-Time Workload Assigned to Each Area, Taking into Account the Area Priority Factor

AREA OF PERFORMANCE	I PERFORMANCE RATING	II ASSIGNED % OF FULL-TIME WORKLOAD	III AREA PRIORITY FACTOR	IV ADJUSTED ASSIGNED % OF FULL-TIME WORKLOAD (II × III)	V ADJUSTED RATING POINTS (I × IV)
Teaching	2.0	40	1.0	40	80
Research*	4.0	40	1.5	60	240
Service	3.0	10	1.0	10	30
Other	2.0	10	1.0	10	20
Total	11.0	100	N/A	120	370

$$\text{Adjusted Rating Point Average (RPA)} = \frac{\text{Total Adjusted Rating Points}}{\text{Total Adjusted Assigned \%s}} = \frac{370}{120} = 3.08$$

*Community colleges may wish to use "special assignments" as an area of performance instead of "research."

average for Faculty Members A and C. Faculty Member A's would drop from 3.60 to 3.50, and Faculty Member C's would drop from 1.40 to 1.35. These differences might affect the distribution of merit money. Note that the higher the priority factor in any activity, the greater will be the change in the rating point averages.

A chairperson who does not want to assign a priority factor that could be considered arbitrary might conduct a survey of the faculty members, asking each to indicate on a ten-point scale the value that should be given to each assigned area. For example, on a form similar to Table 15.7, each faculty member would circle the number that, in his or her opinion, reflects the priority of the performance area to the department's mission.

The average of the faculty members' responses for each performance area would be the priority factor for that area. In Table 15.7, therefore, the department has given a priority factor of 8 to teaching, 10 to research, 5 to service, and 5 to "other." In Table 15.8, Faculty Member B's assigned percentages of full-time

TABLE *15.7* Faculty Rating of the Priority of Performance Areas to the Department's Mission

Teaching	1	2	3	4	5	6	7	(8)	9	10
Research*	1	2	3	4	5	6	7	8	9	(10)
Service	1	2	3	4	(5)	6	7	8	9	10
Other	1	2	3	4	(5)	6	7	8	9	10

*Community colleges may wish to use "special assignments" as an area of performance instead of "research."

TABLE 15.8 Rating of Faculty Member B's Performance, By Area of Performance and By Percentage of Full-Time Workload Assigned to Each Area, Taking into Account the Area Priority Factor

Area of Performance	I Performance Rating	II Assigned % of Full-Time Workload	III Area Priority Factor	IV Adjusted Assigned % of Full-Time Workload (II × III)	V Adjusted Rating Points (I × IV)
Teaching	2.0	40	8.0	320	640
Research*	4.0	40	10.0	400	1600
Service	3.0	10	5.0	50	150
Other	2.0	10	5.0	50	100
Total	11.0	100	N/A	820	2490

$$\text{Adjusted Rating Point Average (RPA)} = \frac{\text{Total Adjusted Rating Points}}{\text{Total Adjusted Assigned \%s}} = \frac{2490}{820} = 3.09$$

*Community colleges may wish to use "special assignments" as an area of performance instead of "research."

workload have been adjusted by multiplying the assigned percentages by the department priority factor for each area.

By the same method of calculation, Faculty Member A's rating point average would become 3.58 and Faculty Member C's 1.25. Note that the effect of applying priority factors, while not great, has increased the rating point average (RPA) of the department's best researcher, Faculty Member B, from 2.90 to 3.10, thus raising her evaluation on the four-point scale from "satisfactory" to "very good." This adjustment, however, has not greatly reduced the other faculty member's rating point averages.

In the calculations thus far, performance ratings have been used for the major categories of teaching, research, service, and "other." Each of these major categories may be broken down into several components. For example, the area of teaching can be divided into these components: amount of teaching; fulfillment and educational objectives; use of innovative techniques; and student evaluations. Each component could then be rated individually on the four-point scale, and from these individual ratings a composite rating for the area of teaching could be calculated. The areas of research and service can also be broken down into component activities and rated accordingly.

EVALUATION USING THE POINT SYSTEM

Some departments have developed a point system to help in the evaluations. They have a comprehensive list of all activities in each area, and a specific number of points is awarded for the completion of each activity. For example, some departments award a certain number of points for publications in refereed journals and fewer points for those in nonrefereed journals. In some fields there exists a well-known and generally accepted hierarchy of journals. Publications in the most prestigious journals are awarded more points than publications in less prestigious journals. A small number of points might be given for submitted publications and a larger number of points for accepted publications. A certain number of points may be given for papers presented at national meetings and a smaller number for papers presented at regional or local meetings of professional societies. The number of points given for the publication of a book might differ according to the publisher's prestige.

In the area of service, questions about allocation of points may be complex and difficult. Consideration might be given to the number and importance of committees on which the faculty member serves. A department might award more points for chairing a committee than for serving on it and might vary the number of points for service on national, regional, and state committees. The number of points earned by each faculty member for each activity is then totaled. The department must then determine how to translate these totals into performance ratings. This system is mentioned as a matter of information but is not necessarily advocated for use.

Following is an example of a point system for evaluation developed by a small, primarily research-oriented department. The system specifies the number of points to be awarded for each activity included in the areas of teaching, research, and service.

SAMPLE OF POINT SYSTEM FOR FACULTY EVALUATION

A. Teaching
  1. Teaching load
     a. Graduate courses—each 0.50 points × number of credit hours
     b. Undergraduate courses—each 0.30 points × number of credit hours
     c. Directed individual study, supervised research, or supervised teaching—each 0.10 points
  2. Students' evaluation of faculty member; evaluation of peer or supervisor may also be conducted according to this form
     a. 90th percentile ranking—20 points
     b. 75th–89th percentile ranking—16 points
     c. 60th–74th percentile ranking—12 points
     d. 50th–59th percentile ranking—8 points
  3. Supervisory committees or positions
     a. Director of doctoral committee—5 points for each Ph.D. granted during faculty member's evaluation period; 3 points for each ongoing doctoral committee
     b. Member of doctoral committee—2 points
     c. Director of master's committee—3 points for each master's degree granted during faculty member's evaluation period; 2 points for each continuing student

      d. Member of master's committee—1 point

      e. Graduate student advisor—1 point for every three students

      f. Laboratory director—10 points

B. Research and scholarly activity

   1. Publications

      a. Writing

         1) Article for refereed national journal—5 points

         2) Article for nonrefereed national journal—3 points

         3) Article for state journal—2 points

         4) Book with major publishing company—15 points

         5) Revised book—7 points

         6) Section of book with major publisher—5 points

         7) Book with local publisher—5 points

         8) Section of book with local publisher—2 points

      b. Editorial activities

         1) Editor of book—7 points

         2) Editor of national professional journal—15 points

         3) Editor of state professional journal—10 points

         4) Associate editor or reviewer for national journal—10 points

         5) Associate editor or reviewer for state journal—5 points

         6) Manuscript reviewer for major publisher—2 points each manuscript

         7) Reviewer for federal agency—5 points

   2. Research projects

      a. Author of R&D project funded by outside agency—15 points

      b. Author of R&D project funded by university—10 points

      c. Author of R&D project submitted to outside agency but not funded—5 points

      d. Author of R&D project submitted to university but not funded—3 points

   3. Papers and speeches

      a. Presented at national or international meeting, by invitation—10 points

      b. Submitted to national or international meeting—5 points

      c. Presented to regional or state meeting, by invitation—5 points

      d. Submitted to regional or state meeting—3 points

      e. Presented at another institution, by invitation—5 points

      f. Presented at local meeting—1 point

C. Service

   1. Committee activities

      a. Chairperson of university committee—10 points

      b. Member of university committee—5 points

      c. Chairperson of school or college committee—5 points

      d. Member of school or college committee—3 points

      e. Chairperson of area or program committee—3 points

      f. Member of area or program committee—1 point

      g. Member of faculty senate—7 points

      h. Chairperson of search committee—5 points

      i. Member of search committee—3 points

   2. Professional activities

      a. Chairperson of national committee—5 points

      b. Member of national committee—3 points

   c. Chairperson of regional or state committee—3 points
   d. Member of regional or state committee—1 point
   e. Officer at regional or national level—10 points
   f. Officer at state level—7 points
   g. Leader for in-service training—3 points
   h. Organizer for workshop—5 points
   i. Member of professional association—1 point
   j. Attendance at professional meeting—1 point each
3. Consulting (each visit—2 points)

This point system was used until the department was merged with several others that were less research oriented. The resulting larger department felt that this system was too rigid and too specific and abandoned it.

This system is highly quantitative in that it assigns a number of points for each activity. It is also qualitative, however, in that it allocates more points to good teaching performance than to average teaching performance, more points for papers published in prestigious journals than for papers published in lesser journals, and more points for membership on important committees than for membership on less important committees.

Another system of point allocation used by some departments rates faculty members' teaching performance on a ten-point scale, with "outstanding" performance receiving a full ten points and "poor" performance receiving no points at all. The average score for faculty members in the department is fixed beforehand at five points. Thus a department with ten members will have a total of fifty points to be divided among all the faculty members for teaching performance. This system is sometimes called the "constant sum" method. If a rater gives three faculty members ten points each for teaching performance, there would be only twenty points left to be divided among the other seven members. The same method is used for evaluating research and service.

This rating system, by limiting the total number of points that can be allocated, keeps a department from giving high ratings to all its members. In practice, if a small committee does the rating, the result will be sharp differentiations between faculty members, with some receiving high scores and others recieving low scores. When a large number of persons does the rating, the result will be a regression towards the mean, and the system loses much of its discriminating force.

The Evaluation Folder

The rules and regulations governing faculty members usually require that an official evaluation folder be established for each member. The folder is to be accessible only to the faculty member and to administrators who must make evaluative decisions. It may contain any information that will be used in the evaluation process, including summaries of performance counseling actions as well as annual formal evaluations prepared by the department chairperson.

In this age of due process, a faculty member may challenge any item placed in the evaluation folder and, by mutual agreement, the item may be removed from the folder. Also note that anonymous material, except systematic student evaluations and committee summaries, may not be placed in the folder. Some state laws may give even greater protection to personnel files.

Linking Merit Increases to Rating Point Averages

The following example will focus only on the allocation of moneys for merit increases. Assume that cost-of-living increases and other types of salary adjustments, if any, have already been made. The four-point system can link merit increases with performance evaluations in several ways. In this example, merit is divided into several levels—"high merit," "medium merit," "low merit," and "no merit." The department has seven members. They have been evaluated using the four-point system, and their rating point averages are as follows: Faculty Member A—3.8; Faculty Member B—3.4; Faculty Member C—3.2; Faculty Member D—2.8; Faculty Member E—2.6; Faculty Member F—2.5; and Faculty Member G—1.9.

The first question the department must address is, "Where should the lines be drawn to differentiate the levels of merit?" In this example, the lines will be drawn as follows: "high merit"—3.5–4.0 RPA; "medium merit"—3.0–3.4 RPA; "low merit"—2.5–2.9 RPA; and "no merit"—0–2.4 RPA. This merit level key is shown in Table 15.9.

Three units of money are allocated for "high merit," two units for "medium merit," and one unit for "low merit." The number of faculty members in each merit category and the number of merit units are illustrated in Table 15.10.

Assume that $3,900 has been made available to the department for merit increases. The total number of merit units in the example is 10, and each unit is therefore worth $390 ($3900÷10). The amount of merit raise that each faculty member in the department will receive is shown in Table 15.11. If the department had decided to draw the lines differently, the money would have been allocated differently. The fewer the merit units, the greater would be the dollar value per unit. The fewer the faculty members earning merit raises, the greater would be the amount of money per faculty member deemed meritorious. In some departments, less than 50 percent of the faculty receive merit money.

TABLE *15.9* **Merit Level Key**

	RPA
High merit	3.5–4.0
Medium merit	3.0–3.4
Low merit	2.5–2.9
No merit	0–2.4

TABLE *15.10* Calculation of Number of Merit Units Available for Distribution

	RATING POINT AVERAGE	NUMBER OF FACULTY MEMBERS		MERIT UNITS PER FACULTY MEMBER		TOTAL MERIT UNITS
High merit	3.5–4.0	1	×	3	=	3
Medium merit	3.0–3.4	2	×	2	=	4
Low merit	2.5–2.9	3	×	1	=	3
No merit	0–2.4	1	×	0	=	0
				Total	=	10

Determining policy in the allocation of merit money is a vexing matter and the subject of some controversy.

At institutions that have faculty salary schedules, merit moneys are often allocated not in dollars, but in units. The central administration takes upon itself the responsibility of determining the dollar value of each unit and specifying the number of units each department will receive. At such institutions, the chairperson has the responsibility for determining only the number of units to be awarded to each faculty member. The process used could be the same as described above.

In this chapter we have described a wide variety of procedures for evaluating faculty performance. The art of evaluating the quality of performance has been a perplexing problem ever since there have been faculty members. In most cases, quality is still best measured in terms of the opinions, values, and perceptions held by students, peers, alumni, and other persons who have actually observed or been the beneficiaries of the performance. Quality of performance is best described with words and phrases, but words and phrases cannot be added, multiplied, or averaged. To overcome this difficulty, numbers are often assigned to various words and phrases that describe quality of performance. Numbers can be processed mathematically for the purpose of yielding a final number that supposedly represents a faculty member's overall evaluation. This

TABLE *15.11* Calculation of Merit Raises

FACULTY MEMBER	NUMBER OF MERIT UNITS		VALUE OF MERIT UNIT		MERIT RAISE
Faculty Member A	3	×	$390	=	$1,170
Faculty Member B	2	×	$390	=	$ 780
Faculty Member C	2	×	$390	=	$ 780
Faculty Member D	1	×	$390	=	$ 390
Faculty Member E	1	×	$390	=	$ 390
Faculty Member F	1	×	$390	=	$ 390
Faculty Member G	0	×	$390	=	$ 0

final number can then be transposed into words or phrases that describe the quality of the overall performance. The number, regardless of how sophisticated the mathematical process that yielded it, still represents a collection of human judgments. Attempting to quantify the quality of faculty performance, nevertheless, does force the evaluator to examine more carefully all facets of the faculty member's professional life. Quantification makes it easier to compare faculty members in terms of their performance and contribution to the department.

Questions

1. Evaluating Teaching Performance
   a. Which of the following items can be evaluated objectively and which can only be evaluated subjectively?
   - Is the teacher enthusiastic in presenting material?
   - Does the teacher show concern with whether students learned the material?
   - Does the teacher encourage students to express opinions?
   - Does the teacher encourage class discussion?
   - Does the teacher present material at the right speed?
   - Does the teacher organize the course well?
   - Are students told what is expected of them?
   - Is the teacher a good lecturer?
   - Does the teacher have any bad speaking habits?
   - Has the teacher prepared a syllabus?
   - Are the material and the syllabus up to date?
   - Does the teacher keep punctual office hours?
   - Do examinations reflect course objectives?
   - Is the grading done fairly?
   - How well do students learn in the class?
   - How attentive are the students in the class?
   - How well does the teacher make use of audio visual aids?
   - Does the teacher try to be innovative?
   - In the case of laboratory classes, how well organized are the classes?
   b. If you were responsible for obtaining evaluations about the quality of teaching performance, whose evaluation or judgment would you seek? Would you be willing to settle for just one person's judgment or would you want judgments from more than one person? How many? Why?
   c. Should individuals whose evaluation judgments are sought have special qualifications? What should be the qualifications?
   d. When evaluations are based on the evaluator's subjectivity, the evaluator in effect becomes the evaluation instrument. What can or should be done to sharpen or hone the instrument? Can individuals be trained to be good evaluators?

e. How important is it for those whose teaching performance is to be evaluated to agree on who should evaluate their teaching? Give reasons for your answer.

f. Identify the faculty member whom you consider the most valuable to your department. Also identify the faculty member whom you would consider the least valuable. Using the four-point scale and the format described in this chapter, calculate the rating point average (RPA) of each of the two faculty members. Assume that all activities—teaching, research, service and so forth—are of equal importance to the department's mission, and that for each faculty member you have either formally assigned percentage of full-time workload to each activity or you know the percentage of effort devoted to each activity.

2. Evaluating Research Productivity

a. List some characteristics of good research that could be considered in evaluating the quality of the published research paper.

b. In the case of a faculty member who is conducting research but has not yet published a paper on it, what interim accomplishments or milestones toward the completion of the project could be considered in evaluating the faculty member's research efforts?

c. In an annual faculty evaluation, should a faculty member receive credit toward a merit increase or promotion for an above satisfactory research effort even though a paper has not yet been published? Give reasons for your answer.

d. In the case of the performing or visual arts, what criteria can be used to evaluate interim or final accomplishments?

e. What should be the qualifications of individuals selected to evaluate the quality of research?

f. If more than one qualified individual evaluates the quality of the research paper, can it be assumed that all will give the paper the same rating? Give reasons for your answer.

g. Who should decide who is or is not qualified to evaluate research?

h. How important is it for those whose research is to be evaluated to agree on who should evaluate their research? Give reasons for your answer.

3. General Questions

Which of the following would be most desirable? Please give reasons for your answer.

a. The department receives exact instructions from some office in the institution on how to carry out faculty evaluations including the instrument, criteria, and procedures. The department is expected to follow the instructions without deviation.

b. The department is given general criteria and a framework within which it must develop its own instrument and procedures for carrying out faculty evaluations.

    c. The department is instructed to develop its own criteria, instrument, and procedures for carrying out faculty evaluation. It receives no guidance whatsoever from the office of the dean or academic vice-president.

4. Case Study

    The following abridged case study on "A Discrepancy in Rating Between Two Evaluation Procedures" is presented as a basis for thought. Please answer the questions at the end of the case study.

> The chairperson of a certain department has rated Professor Smith as being more productive than Professor Jones for each of the past four years. His method of evaluation was based primarily on his overall impression of these two faculty members. This year, however, on the advice of his faculty, he decided to follow a more complex evaluation system which required that each of the three primary activities—teaching, research, and service—be broken down into its component activities, that each component activity be rated separately using numbers rather than descriptive words, and that the numbers be treated statistically so that an overall numerical rating could be determined for each faculty member. The chairperson was surprised to find that Professor Jones came out with a higher overall rating than Professor Smith. But in his heart, the chairperson felt that Smith was the more productive professor.

    a. Give reasons that might account for the discrepancy.
    b. What must the chairperson do to resolve his inner conflict?

References

ARGYRIS, CHRIS, and SCHON, DONALD A. *Theory in Practice: Increasing Professional Effectiveness.* San Francisco: Jossey-Bass, 1974.

ASTIN, ALEXANDER W., and LES, CALVIN B. T. "Current Practices in the Evaluation and Training of College Teachers." *Educational Record,* Summer 1976, pp. 361–375.

BRASKAMP, LARRY A.; ORY, JOHN C.; and PIEPER, DAVID M. "Student Written Comments." *Journal of Educational Psychology,* 73(1), 1981, pp. 65–70.

BRENEMAN, DAVID W., and YOUN, TED I. K. (Eds.) *Academic Labor Markets and Careers.* Philadelphia: The Falmer Press, Taylor and Francis, Inc., 1988.

CARTWRIGHT, DORWIN. "Achieving Change in People: Some Applications of Group Dynamics Theory." *Human Relations,* November 1951, pp. 381–392.

COCH, LESTER, and FRENCH, JOHN R. P., JR. "Overcoming Resistance to Change." *Human Relations,* August 1948, pp. 512–532.

COHEN, ARTHUR M., and BRAWER, FLORENCE B. *The American Community College.* 2nd ed. San Francisco: Jossey–Bass, 1988.

CONRAD, CLIFTON F. "A Grounded Theory of Academic Change." *Sociology of Education,* April 1978, pp. 101–112.

COOK, MARVIN J., and NEVILLE, RICHARD F. *The Faculty as Teachers: A Perspective on Evaluation.* ERIC Clearinghouse on Higher Education, Report no. 13, Washington, DC: George Washington University, 1971. (ERIC Document Reproduction Service No. ED 054 392).

DENT, PRESTON L., and NICHOLAS, THOMAS. "A Study of Faculty and Student Opinions on Teaching Effectiveness Ratings." *Peabody Journal of Education,* January 1980, pp. 135–143.

EBLE, KENNETH E. *Professors as Teachers.* San Francisco: Jossey–Bass, 1972.

ECKARD, PAMELA J. "Faculty Evaluation: The Basis for Rewards in Higher Education." *Peabody Journal of Education,* January 1980, pp. 94–100.

EHRLE, ELWOOD B. "Selection and Evaluation of Department Chairmen." *Educational Record,* 56(1), 1975, pp. 29–38.

ETZIONI, AMITAI. "Human Beings Are Not Very Easy to Change After All." *Saturday Review,* 3 June 1972, pp. 45–47.

FARH, JIING LIH (et al.) "An Empirical Investigation of Self-Appraisal-Based Performance Evaluation." *Personnel–Psychology,* 41, 1988, pp. 141–156.

GRAY, CHARLES E. "The Teaching Model and Evaluation of Teaching Performance." *Journal of Higher Education,* November 1969, pp. 636–642.

GREENLAW, PAUL S., and BIGGS, WILLIAM D. *Modern Personnel Management.* New York: Holt, 1980.

HAY, ELLEN. "The Variable of Teaching Effectiveness in Tenure and Promotion Decisions." *ACA Bulletin,* 68, 1989, pp. 52–59.

HEFFERLIN, J. B. LON. *Dynamics of Academic Reform.* San Francisco: Jossey–Bass, 1969.

———. "Hauling Academic Trunks." In *Elements Involved in Academic Change,* edited by Charles U. Walker, pp. 1–10. Washington, DC: Association of American Colleges, 1972.

HILDEBRAND, MILTON. "How to Recommend Promotion for a Mediocre Teacher Without Actually Lying." *Journal of Higher Education,* January 1972, pp. 44–62.

HIND, ROBERT R.; DORNBUSH, SANFORD M.; and SCOTT, W. RICHARD. "A Theory of Evaluation Applied to a University Faculty." *Sociology of Education,* Winter 1974, pp. 114–128.

HOLCOMB, BRIAVEL. "The Tenure Review Process." *Journal of Geography in Higher Education,* 11, 1987, pp. 85–98.

LAWRENCE, PAUL R. "How to Deal with Resistance to Change." *Harvard Business Review,* May–June 1954, pp. 49–57.

LEVINE, ARTHUR. *Why Innovation Fails: The Institutionalization and Termination of Innovation in Higher Education.* Albany: State University of New York Press, 1981.

LEWIN, KURT. *Field Theory in Social Science,* edited by Dorwin Cartwright. Westport, CT: Greenwood, 1975.

LINDQUIST, JACK. *Strategies for Change: Academic Innovation and Adaptive Development.* Washington, DC: Council for the Advancement of Small Colleges, 1980.

LIONBERGER, HERBERT F. *Adoption of New Ideas and Practices.* Ames, IA: Iowa State University Press, 1960.

LIPPETT, RONALD (et al.) *Dynamics of Planned Change: A Comparative Study of Principles and Techniques.* New York: Harcourt Brace, 1958.

Mann, Mary Pat. *An Analysis of Faculty Goals: Personal, Disciplinary, and Career Development Decisions.* Paper presented at the Annual Meeting of the AERA, San Francisco, March 1989. (ERIC Document Reproduction Service No. ED 305 874)

Marrow, Alfred J.; Bowers, David G.; and Seashore, Stanley E. (Eds.) *Strategies of Organizational Change.* New York: Harper & Row, 1967.

Marsh, Herbert W.; Overall, J. U.; and Kasler, Steven P. "Validity of Student Evaluations of Instructional Effectiveness: A Comparison of Faculty Self-Evaluations and Evaluations by their Students." *Journal of Educational Psychology,* April 1979, pp. 149–160.

McIntosh, Thomas H., and Koevering, Thomas E. "Six-year Case Study of Faculty Peer Reviews, Merit Ratings, and Pay Awards in a Multidisciplinary Department." *Journal of the College and University Personnel Association,* 37, 1986, pp. 5–14.

McKeachie, Wilbery J. "Student Ratings of Faculty: A Reprise." *Academe: Bulletin of the AAUP,* October 1979, pp. 384–397.

Miller, Richard I. *Evaluating Faculty Performance.* San Francisco: Jossey–Bass, 1972.

Morgan, Henry H., and Cogger, John W. *The Interviewer's Manual: Fair and Effective Interviewing.* 2nd ed. New York: Drake–Beam & Associates, 1980.

Nelson, T. M. "Rating of Scholarly Journals by Chairpersons in the Social Sciences." *Research in Higher Education,* 19, 1983, pp. 469–497.

Russell, Susan H. *Faculty in Higher Education Institutions, 1988, Contractor Report.* Washington, DC: National Center for Higher Education Statistics, 1990. (ERIC Document Reproduction Service No. ED 321 628).

Seagren, Alan T. *Perception of Chairpersons and Faculty Concerning Roles, Descriptors, and Activities Considered Important for Faculty Development and Departmental Vitality.* 1986. (ERIC Document Reproduction Service No. ED 276 387)

Schuster, Jack H. "The Faculty Dilemma: A Short Course." *Phi Delta Kappan,* 68, 1986, pp. 275–282.

Scott, W. Richard; Dornbusch, Sanford M.; Busching, Bruce C.; and Laing, James D. "Organizational Evaluation and Authority." *Administrative Science Quarterly,* June 1967, pp. 93–117.

Seldin, Peter. *Successful Faculty Evaluation Programs: A Practical Guide to Improve Faculty Performance and Promotion/Tenure Decisions.* New York: Coventry Press, 1980.

————. *Evaluating and Developing Administrative Performance: A Practical Guide for Academic Leaders.* San Francisco: Jossey–Bass, 1988.

Smith, Albert B. *Faculty Development and Evaluation in Higher Education.* ERIC/Higher Education Research Report no. 8, Washington, DC: American Association for Higher Education, 1976.

Smith, Richard, and Fiedler, Fred E. "The Measurement of Scholarly Work: A Critical Review of the Literature." *Educational Record,* Summer 1971, pp. 225–232.

Trask, Kerry A. "The Chairperson and Teaching." In *New Directions for Teaching and Learning: The Department Chairperson's Role in Enhancing College Teaching,* 37, Spring 1989, pp. 99–107.

Von Haden, Herbert I., and King, Jean Marie. *Educational Innovator's Guide.* Worthington, OH: Charles A. Jones, 1974.

WALBERG, HERBERT J. (Ed.) *Evaluating Educational Performance: A Sourcebook of Methods, Instruments, and Examples.* Berkeley: McCutchan, 1974.

WEAVER, FREDERICK STIRTON. "Scholarship for the Teaching Faculty." *College Teaching,* 34, 1986, pp. 51–58.

WIGINGTON, HENRY. "Students' Ratings of Instructors Revisited: Interactions Among Class Instructor Variables." *Research in Higher Education,* 30, 1989, pp. 331–344.

WHITMORE, JON. *Handbook for Theatre Department Chairs.* Association for Communication Administration, Annondale, VA: Council of Theatre Chairs and Deans, 1988. (ERIC Document Reproduction Service No. ED 305 855)

Chapter 16

Performance Counseling and Dealing with Unsatisfactory Performance

The Importance and Purpose of Performance Counseling

Performance counseling offers the chairperson a valuable communications tool that, properly used, can significantly enhance relations with faculty members and improve the department's chances for attaining its goals. *Performance counseling* is here defined as a regular although not necessarily formal contact between the chairperson and individual faculty members for the purpose of discussing successes and failures in completing assignments and duties. It is a two-way communications device that affords chairpersons and faculty members an opportunity to express their concerns and needs. Failure to provide this opportunity can become a grievance issue in the case of faculty members whose performance has been labeled deficient at evaluation time. At many institutions, performance counseling is required by state law, institutional policy, or collective bargaining agreement.

Some department chairpersons shirk the responsibility of providing performance counseling because they view this activity as nonprofessional or even degrading. They regard faculty members as professional peers and feel that infringing on or criticizing a fellow faculty member's professional activities is unjustifiable. This attitude is particularly prevalent in institutions in which department chairpersons serve on a rotating basis; it also exists in departments in which the chairperson's academic rank happens to be lower than that of his or her peers. Both chairpersons and faculty members will find performance counseling more acceptable, however, when they see that it can pave the way for more palatable decisions about promotion, tenure, and salary increases.

Chairpersons are also reluctant to provide performance counseling because it demands a complete understanding of department goals and objectives, the ability to make specific assignments for faculty members, and experience in assessing what constitutes acceptable performance standards. Meeting these requirements is no small matter and requires a great deal of thought and maturity. Further, the skills involved cannot easily be taught, because they require an intuitive judgment that not all chairpersons possess equally.

Perhaps the most important advice that can be given to performance counselors is, "Avoid distorting the record." Chairpersons often tend to look for strong points that can offset weak points or to gloss over problems, especially those considered minor. Another distortion results when justifiable criticisms are turned into compliments. For example, a faculty member who gives unreasonably difficult examinations and fails an excessive number of students may be described by the chairperson as a teacher who "demands a high standard of excellence from students"! Such distortions merely avoid the issues and undermine the counseling approach, if not the entire evaluation procedure.

Dealing with Unsatisfactory Performance

One of a chairperson's most difficult and unpleasant duties is to inform faculty members that their performance has been unsatisfactory. Nevertheless, unsatisfactory performance must be dealt with, since bad situations often deteriorate even more if left unattended. Because chairpersons are colleagues of the faculty members whose performance is deemed inadequate, the problem of how to confront those colleagues is often perplexing. Some basic principles, practices, and techniques can be useful when attempting to remedy certain situations.

Unsatisfactory performance is handled most effectively if it is identified early. Early detection of an unhealthy situation allows time for diagnosis and remediation. How, then, does a chairperson recognize a developing problem that requires attention? First, the faculty member's performance must be compared with predetermined standards of satisfactory performance (see chapter 15 on faculty evaluation). In this discussion we will assume that the department has developed criteria that are used to determine whether or not a faculty member's performance is acceptable in the areas of teaching, research, service, and other assigned duties.

Some unsatisfactory behaviors, such as unethical or illegal conduct, must simply be stopped to prevent irreparable harm. Other problems that occur because of rule or policy infractions generally are easily handled *provided* the chairperson adopts a strong managerial position. Institutional policy statements, faculty constitutions, or collective bargaining agreements may give the chair-person significant authority in such matters. For example, most institutions re-quire that faculty members who accept outside employment report such employ-ment before beginning the work. Such activity may well affect performance, especially if the faculty member is off campus one or more days per week. A faculty member's failure to follow this rule should be dealt with directly and firmly if the violation appears to be intentional.

Another example of unacceptable behavior is a faculty member's failure to hold office hours as required by university regulations or to meet scheduled classes. Repeated behavior of this type simply cannot be tolerated. The chair-person's job is *not* to be a policeman but to correct actions that are not in the best interests of students and the department. The effective chairperson may initially make light of the problem, but direct action, through informal as well as formal means, is appropriate if the situation does not improve.

Unsatisfactory performance, like most behavior, usually has a discernible cause or cluster of causes. The chairperson must learn to search for possible causes before attempting to discuss unsatisfactory behavior with a faculty mem-ber. Most instances of unsatisfactory performance on the part of faculty members can be linked to the presence or absence of elements in one or more of the following groups of factors.

1. Knowledge of subject matter and skills in teaching and conducting research
2. Psychological and physical characteristics
3. Personal or family situations
4. Working conditions

KNOWLEDGE OF SUBJECT MATTER AND SKILLS IN TEACHING AND CONDUCTING RESEARCH

A faculty member may perform poorly in teaching a certain course because he or she was trained in another area and does not possess the requisite knowl-edge to teach the assigned course. Other persons may have the knowledge but lack pedagogic skills or are unable to organize course content, manage field experiences, and so on. Poor performance in research productivity may be due to a faculty member's inability to conduct independent research. The research completed for his doctoral dissertation may have been suggested by his adviser and carried out under continuing direction and supervision which is now not available to him.

PSYCHOLOGICAL AND PHYSICAL CHARACTERISTICS

APTITUDE. Certain faculty members may not only demonstrate incompe-tence but also lack the aptitude to improve their skills or acquire new ones. For example, a biology professor whose training was in taxonomy lacked the detailed knowledge of biochemistry and physiology necessary for teaching courses in modern biology. No matter how hard he tried, he was unable to master the new material.

Physical Stamina.   Occasionally there is a faculty member who has a low energy level or perhaps a minor heart ailment and may not have the stamina required to conduct long seminars or travel long distances to teach off-campus courses. The chairperson may not be aware of this situation.

Social Skills.   There are faculty members who lack the social skills necessary to maintain good relations with colleagues, students, and staff. Quality of performance can suffer if proper relationships are not maintained.

Maturity.   Some faculty members have difficulty in adjusting to new situations. When a change is needed in a department program to accommodate the new needs of students or society, certain faculty members are not sufficiently flexible to modify their work habits. Some faculty members are unable or unwilling to carry out assignments that may not be their first choice and thus do not perform at their best.

Judgment.   At most colleges and universities, each faculty member faces more activities than he or she can possibly do in the time available. Some faculty members lack the necessary judgment for deciding which activities should receive high priority in terms of what is best for the department and for their own professional development. These faculty members may spend more time on activities that are only tangentially related to their formal assignments and that are considered of little importance to the mission or goals of the department.

Attitude.   Some faculty members do not have the appropriate attitude to carry out certain assignments. For example, some extremely competent scholars seem temperamentally incapable of teaching undergraduate general education courses. Although very successful with graduate courses in their specific fields, they lack patience and understanding with students whose major interests may lie elsewhere. Other faculty members are resentful of duties that they consider demeaning. Such duties may include undergraduate counseling, off-campus teaching, service on certain committees, attendance at official functions, and so forth. These negative attitudes often lead to poor performance.

Reliability and Dependability.   There are faculty members who find difficulty in meeting commitments they have made. This lack of dependability may range from never being on time or not coming to scheduled meetings or classes, to not keeping promised office hours, not turning in grades on time, or not turning in required reports.

PERSONAL AND FAMILY SITUATIONS

There are many problems faced by faculty members that are unrelated to their work except when stress from these problems affects performance. Examples are physical and mental problems, marital problems, problems with illness in the family, problems with difficult children, financial problems, and so forth.

WORKING CONDITIONS

LACK OF INCENTIVES. Some faculty members are not motivated to perform well because of insufficient incentives. These incentives may include adequate financial rewards, public recognition for achievements, and perquisites such as travel expenses for professional meetings or even parking space.

LACK OF APPROPRIATE FACILITIES AND A PLEASING ENVIRONMENT. A faculty member's performance may suffer because of inadequate physical facilities and resources such as laboratory equipment, office space, libraries, and classroom environments. Dissatisfaction with the social and physical climate of the community at large may also affect the quality of his or her performance.

INSUFFICIENT ORIENTATION IN TERMS OF WHAT IS EXPECTED. A faculty member may never be explicitly told by the chairperson or any other designated faculty member what her duties are and how she will be evaluated. For example, a faculty member who felt that teaching was her main responsibility received a poor evaluation because of her lack of research activity. She was told that all members of her department were expected to conduct research. Another faculty member thought that teaching off-campus courses fulfilled his service responsibilities. He was never told that membership in committees was expected and therefore refused to serve on them. As a result, his overall evaluation in the area of service was unsatisfactory.

CONFLICT WITH THE CHAIRPERSON. In some instances a faculty member's poor performance may be directly related to counterproductive interaction with the department chairperson. The faculty member may receive insufficient encouragement, praise, direction, or supervision. As a result, he or she may perceive a lack of concern on the chairperson's part. Other chairpersons may supervise too closely, thereby causing undue anxiety and tension.

In attempting to deal with a faculty member whose performance is considered unsatisfactory, the chairperson should first learn as much as possible about the personal and environmental matters that may be affecting the faculty member's behavior. Some of these circumstances may be known to the chairperson from personal observation, some from observations of other faculty members. In most instances it is advisable for the chairperson to meet with the faculty member in question to discuss the matter. The chairperson should prepare for the encounter by giving thought to the following suggestions.

First, it is difficult to tell someone that his or her performance has been unsatisfactory without provoking a defensive reaction. Even the chairperson may become defensive when confronting a faculty member whose performance is unsatisfactory. But being defensive is counterproductive and should be minimized whenever possible. If the discussion regarding the faculty member's performance is seen as a counseling session rather than as an interview for formal evaluation, any potential conflict may be diffused. The discussion should be just that—a discussion, not a lecture. The chairperson should try to involve the faculty member, rather than reprimand him or her. As mentioned earlier, the chairperson should start a dialogue with a faculty member at the first hint of difficulty and continue the dialogue at regular intervals. In this way, discussion of instances of poor performance will arise within a context of openness and will not provoke an immediate negative reaction. The chairperson should avoid lumping all of a faculty member's shortcomings into one bundle and dumping it on the unsuspecting person without warning.

The chairperson may perceive unsatisfactory faculty performance as a personal insult or as a poor reflection of his or her leadership abilities. He or she may also feel guilty about a faculty member's shortcomings. These reactions should not be allowed to become anger or hostility toward the faculty member. The chairperson should be as self-controlled and as calm as possible, since emotional responses may get out of hand. Yet the chairperson needs to recognize his or her feelings and anxieties and not try to repress them completely. At times, however, poor performance may be caused by the chairperson's behavior. In such cases, the chairperson should admit to this possibility and not try to project an image of omniscience and infallibility.

The faculty member should be made to feel that the chairperson is genuinely interested in bringing about positive changes and is willing to spend as much time and effort as is necessary to do so. The facutly member should also be made to feel that his or her poor performance need not be shouldered alone, that it is a problem for the whole department and can be solved cooperatively for the good of the department. What must be determined, therefore, is how best to solve the problem, not who should be blamed. Problem solving requires the chairperson's empathetic understanding of the faculty member and the ability to see the other person's point of view. To relieve the faculty member's anxiety, the chairperson must point out that others have had similar problems that have been successfully resolved.

When the chairperson has achieved the proper frame of mind for performance counseling, he or she should again review the possible reasons discussed earlier to see if anything can be done to change the situation. The faculty member should be encouraged to participate in the dialogue and make suggestions for change. If the dialogue goes well, some of these suggestions may correspond to those the chairperson has thought of. At the same time, the chairperson should be flexible enough to change his or her mind when new insights emerge as the result of dialogue. Some measures within the realm of the departments' authority or control include providing opportunities for retraining faculty members who lack certain competencies; providing opportunities for reassignment for those who lack the ability to gain competence or whose health requires less demanding tasks; providing more preparation time for those who are overloaded or overworked; and changing or upgrading facilities for a better research atmosphere. Faculty members who are experiencing a personal crisis may benefit from a new assignment, for the change may give them a renewed sense of importance and productivity.

Sometimes unsatisfactory performance cannot be remedied. Although an attempt should be made to resolve the problem, the chairperson must be able to recognize and accept the fact that some faculty members' performance cannot be improved.

INITIATING AND CONDUCTING A DIALOGUE ABOUT UNSATISFACTORY PERFORMANCE

The importance of dialogue in solving problems of poor performance has been emphasized. Following are some concrete suggestions to the chairperson about how to initiate and conduct a discussion with a faculty member. Some of the suggestions are contained in standard college textbooks on counseling, interviewing, and personnel management. Others were obtained from experienced administrators who participated in department leadership workshops.

- Do not send a memorandum to the faculty member listing his or her areas of unsatisfactory performance and asking that an appointment be made with you to discuss them. It is better to make a personal contact, during which you can invite the faculty member to meet with you to talk about his or her progress toward reaching performance expectations.
- Try to allay the faculty member's anxiety by being calm and cool. Let the faculty member know that he or she is respected as a person and that his or her abilities are appreciated, but that specific changes in performance are necessary.
- Be open-minded, tolerant, and cooperative, and encourage the faculty member to express his or her point of view. Be considerate. Listen attentively to what is being said without interrupting, and keep sufficient control over the discussion so that it does not develop into a shouting match or an abusive argument.
- Be as empathetic as possible and give credit where credit is due, but try to focus on those areas that need improvement and on the possible solutions to the problem. Personal feelings toward the individual whether positive or negative should not be allowed to stand in the way of challenging unsatisfactory performance.
- When pinpointing poor performance, be specific and descriptive, rather than ascribe a blanket negative value to the performance. Be ready to offer concrete suggestions about what needs to be done, especially when

the faculty member seems unable to develop his or her own plan. At the same time, keep the plan flexible. (See chapter 14 on Workload Assignments and Reporting Faculty Activities.)

The meeting should result in the development of a course of action that is agreed upon by both chairperson and faculty member and that includes specific objectives and a schedule for achieving them. The chairperson should arrange additional meetings, if necessary, and keep a written record of the dialogue and its conclusions. The faculty member deserves to have a copy of the record of the meeting. A note of caution: The chairperson should not try to give psychological counseling to the faculty member or even suggest that it is needed. Experience has shown that giving this kind of advice, even when it is solicited, sometimes results in legal action against the chairperson or the university or both.

Encouraging Good Performance

A department recently hired a temporary faculty member to teach two classes. During the term, she spent an inordinate amount of time on the assigned courses and developed some innovative activities that were adopted for continued use in the class. An evaluative questionnaire completed by the students rated both the classes and her teaching "excellent." At the end of the term, the chairperson's only comment to her was, "You may be interested to know that I didn't receive any negative comments on your work this term." Needless to say, the faculty member did not feel that her efforts were sufficiently appreciated!

In facing the day-to-day problems of running a department, the chairperson can easily overlook the importance of encouraging acceptable performance. Most faculty and staff members feel encouraged when their chairperson makes the effort to identify good performance and offers a sincere comment on the work. Chairpersons must find time to compliment special efforts by faculty members. Obvious performance—such as unusually high student ratings, a published paper, a successful grant proposal, or an outstanding presentation to a group of local businessmen—is easy to identify and deserves favorable comment. The recognition of less obvious accomplishments—such as completing an assignment ahead of schedule, spending extra time with a group of students, or being available to help with an unexpected problem—can be an even greater boost for a faculty member's morale.

The chairperson should also take every opportunity to encourage actions by faculty members that will lead to successful promotions and tenure decisions and to ensure that good performance is properly documented. The chairperson's task is *not* to build the case for the faculty member but to have as much supporting evidence as possible when making a case for promotion or tenure.

Maintaining a Record of Performance Counseling

The chairperson's responsibility for maintaining a record of performance counseling, including comments on successful and outstanding accomplishments as well as problem areas, is increasingly important. This record need not be extensive or detailed, and it should not be kept secret from the faculty member involved. It can be as valuable to the faculty member as it is to the chairperson, since the faculty member soon gains a clearer picture of the performance standards expected by the chairperson. The performance counseling record is a valuable document when decisons about promotion, tenure, and salary adjustments are made. When promotion, tenure, or salary adjustments must be denied, the chairperson must be able to document that a reasonable effort has been made to assist the faculty member to improve poor performance. Summaries of performance counseling actions should go in the faculty member's evaluation folder.

The department chairperson, then, should establish a regular pattern of performance counseling with department faculty members. This effort may be formal or informal, but the real purpose of the counseling is to establish a close working relationship with faculty members and to encourage actions that the chairperson feels will benefit both the faculty member and the department. Counseling must be based on clear, definite assignments and on reasonable standards of performance in each major academic area—teaching, research, and service. The chairperson must document performance counseling activities as accurately and as quantitatively as possible without overreacting with either positive or negative comments.

The improvement in faculty members' performance as a result of performance counseling can play a significant role in promotion, tenure, and salary adjustment decisions. Performance counseling may also prove to be important to the chairperson as a way of establishing and maintaining meaningful communication with faculty members.

Questions

1. Identify one or two faculty members in your department or in another department who have performed unsatisfactorily in teaching, research, service, or some other area that is important to the department.

2. For each faculty member so identified, ask yourself the following questions:
   a. In what way was the performance in each case unsatisfactory? Against what criteria was each performance compared?
   b. Are you familiar with any personal factors that may have contributed to the poor performance of the faculty member concerned, such as

lack of competence, lack of mental or physical ability to carry out assigned data, lack of understanding of what is expected, or lack or proper attitude? Give examples.

c. Are you familiar with any environmental factors that may have contributed to the poor performance of the faculty member concerned, such as lack of acceptance by colleagues, lack of incentives, lack of appropriate facilities, or lack of adequate leadership. Give examples.

d. To your knowledge, did the faculty members in question receive any kind of performance counseling? What kind, if any?

e. Assuming that you have decided to provide these faculty members with performance counseling, how would you go about it? Prepare a mental script that you would use with each faculty member. Under what circumstances would you meet with each of them? Anticipate their response. What kind of assistance would you offer them? How would you motivate them?

3. Following is a list of situations that call for some performance counseling. Expand each situation into a scenario based on your experience and/or imagination. Assume that you are the chairperson who will deal with the faculty members in question. What would you say to them? Under what circumstances would you meet with each of them? Anticipate their response. What kind of help could you offer them?

a. Dealing with the faculty member whose teaching performance is unsatisfactory. Assume that the faculty member in this instance has never been counseled before regarding this problem.

b. Dealing with the faculty member whose research output is inadequate. Assume that the faculty member in this instance has been counseled once before regarding this same problem.

c. Informing a nontenured assistant professor who has been in the department for three years that his contract will not be renewed the following year. Assume that the assistant professor has received no performance counseling prior to this meeting.

d. Dealing with a productive faculty member whose morale is low because his application for promotion was denied.

e. Dealing with the faculty member who is productive in areas not related to the department's mission. His efforts need to be redirected.

f. Counseling with the faculty member who casually visits your office to talk about an apparent simple problem while underneath is a considerably more fundamental problem.

g. Counseling with the faculty member who has been the subject of gossip about improper behavior but there is no hard evidence.

h. Rewarding the high performer who may not receive promotion and who sees others performing at a barely acceptable level.

4. Perhaps you could persuade one or two of your colleagues to role-play with you. One of you could be the chairperson, another the faculty

member who is being counseled, and a third person could be the observer and critic of the role-playing.

5. The following case study of "An Unsuccess Story" is presented for thought. Please answer the questions at the end of the case study.

This case is based on an actual incident that occurred after a chairperson attended a department leadership seminar sponsored by the Institute for Academic Leadership, Florida State University.

When Harry Casper, a social science department chairperson, returned home from a workshop on collegial administration, he decided to test his new knowledge. The first problem he wanted to approach was the issue of inequitable workloads among the faculty members. This problem was uppermost in his mind because it was time to work out the class schedule for the next term. After several days of effort he developed an assignment plan using several ideas that were discussed at the workshop. He designed a basic system of points for various activities and a form for recording the planned assignments. To make sure the plan was understandable and that the point weights reflected the priorities agreed upon by the faculty members, he sought out some of his colleagues to get their reactions and made a few important changes based on their suggestions.

While creating and obtaining acceptance of the plan, Casper contemplated ways of making assignments that would be equitable and at the same time allow for faculty development that could be recognized and rewarded. As he reviewed the latest student evaluations of faculty members' performance and considered those persons who were most strongly criticized, his thoughts turned especially to one faculty member, Anne Stone.

Stone, an associate professor, was the first woman social scientist recruited by the department search committee. She had been an outstanding undergraduate social science major, graduating cum laude from this very institution. She completed her doctorate at Indiana University six years previously and had continually done good research. She published regularly and had a book manuscript in process. Her otherwise good record was marred by continuous complaints about her teaching. Students reported that she was uninteresting, disorganized, unfriendly, and rarely available to those seeking advice. In fact, of the department's nineteen full-time faculty members, she always had the lowest rating for teaching.

Stone's record seemed to be getting worse, and Casper wanted to make some special assignments that would enable her to improve her performance. He began work on an assignment that would provide released time for consultation with some instructional design professionals in the university; he also would propose that she teach a few small sections of the introductory courses, as well as a reduced graduate teaching load. In all, he spent almost two weeks working out the details for her faculty development program and for each term of the next academic year's assignment. He felt a genuine sense of accomplishment, tinged with altruism, and felt that Stone would be pleased with his plan for improving her teaching and advising capabilities.

A meeting with Stone was scheduled for the Wednesday morning preceding Thanksgiving holidays. She came into his office, seeming a bit fidgety; her manner was friendly, but she showed some anxiety. Casper explained the new assignment system first, then elaborated on the special assignments that could be worked out for her growth and development as a faculty member. As he began to unfold the details of the plan, her face changed from a look of mild curiosity to one of growing anger. Her first response was to ask why Casper did not like her teaching, and he answered that his plan was based on complaints about her teaching. She responded forcefully that she was one of the best teachers in the department and that he was judging her on the basis of incomplete, unreliable, and bad evidence. Casper tried to reason with her, offering to change the plan in any way that she thought would help improve her teaching. At the end of the third exchange about the plan, Stone jumped from her chair and without another word walked out and slammed the door. Casper made some minor changes in her assignment and then prepared for the consultation with the next faculty member.

Just before the term ended at Christmas, Casper received a call from the president that surprised, saddened, and angered him. Stone had filed an official faculty grievance against him. She claimed that he was harassing her and embarrassing her by requiring that she seek help in improving her teaching from professionals who were not faculty members when she already was an accomplished and experienced teacher. An informal conference with the president's faculty grievance representative could not resolve the issues, so they were to be heard formally by a university grievance committee at the end of January.

a. Assuming that the chairperson was well-intentioned in his attempt to help Stone improve her performance, why were his efforts rebuffed?

b. What could or should the chairperson have done to have aroused a less negative response from Stone?

c. Was Casper wrong in trying to design an annual assignment for Stone that included a program to help her improve her teaching?

    d. Should Casper have involved other faculty members of the department in designing an improvement program for Stone? If so, how should they have been involved?

    e. How would you have handled the situation?

References

BASKIN, OTIS W., and ARONOFF, CRAIG E. *Interpersonal Communication in Organization.* Santa Monica: Goodyear, 1980.

BLAKE, ROBERT R., and MOUTON, JANE S. *The Management Grid.* Houston: Gulf, 1964.

BOLTON, ROBERT H. *People Skills: How to Assert Yourself, Listen to Others, and Resolve Conflicts.* Englewoood Cliffs: Prentice–Hall, 1979.

BRAMMER, LAWRENCE M. *The Helping Relationship.* 2nd ed. Englewood Cliffs: Prentice–Hall, 1979.

COCH, LESTER, and FRENCH, JOHN R. P., JR. "Overcoming Resistance to Change." *Human Relations,* August 1948, pp. 512–532.

CONRAD, CLIFTON F. "A Grounded Theory of Academic Change." *Sociology of Education,* April 1978, pp. 101–112.

CUNNINGHAM, PATRICK J. "Disciplinary Counseling: The First Step Toward Due Process." *The Journal of the College and University Personnel Association,* Summer 1980, pp. 1–6.

EGAN, GERARD, and COWAN, MICHAEL A. *People in Systems: An Integrative Approach to Human Development.* Monterey: Brooks–Cole, 1979.

FOURNIES, FERDINAND F. *Coaching for Improved Work Performance.* New York: Van Nostrand Reinhold, 1978.

GMELCH, WALTER H. "Dimensions of Stress Among University Faculty: Factor-analytic Results from a National Study." *Research in Higher Education,* 24, 1986, pp. 266–286.

HASENFELD, YEHESKEL, and ENGLISH, RICHARD A. *Human Service Organizations: A Book of Readings.* Ann Arbor: The University of Michigan Press, 1974.

HAY, ELLEN. "The Variable of Teaching Effectiveness in Tenure and Promotion Decisions." *ACA Bulletin,* vol. 68, 1989, pp. 2–59.

HEFERLIN, J. B. LON. *Dynamics of Academic Reform.* San Francisco: Jossey–Bass, 1969.

———. "Hauling Academic Trunks." In *Elements Involved in Academic Change,* edited by Charles U. Walker, pp. 1–10. Washington, DC: Association of American Colleges, 1972.

LAWRENCE, PAUL R. "How to Deal with Resistance to Change." *Harvard Business Review,* May–June 1954, pp. 49–57.

LEAVITT, HAROLD J., and PONDY, LOUIS R. (Eds.) *Readings in Managerial Psychology.* 2nd ed. Chicago: University of Chicago Press, 1974.

LEVINE, ARTHUR. *Why Innovation Fails: The Institutionalization and Termination of Innovation in Higher Education.* Albany: State University of New York Press, 1981.

LEWIN, KURT. *Field Theory in Social Science,* edited by Dorwin Cartwright. Westport, CT: Greenwood, 1975.

LINDQUIST, JACK. *Strategies for Change: Academic Innovation and Adaptive Development.* Washington, DC: Council for the Advancement of Small Colleges, 1980.

LIONBERGER, HERBERT F. *Adoption of New Ideas and Practices.* Ames, IA: Iowa State University Press, 1960.

LIPPETT, RONALD (et al.) *Dynamics of Planned Change: A Comparative Study of Principles and Techniques.* New York: Harcourt Brace, 1958.

MARROW, ALFRED J.; BOWERS, DAVID G.; and SEASHORE, STANLEY E., (Eds). *Strategies of Organizational Change.* New York: Harper and Row, 1967.

MILGRAM, STANLEY. "Group Pressure and Action Against a Person." *Journal of Abnormal and Social Psychology,* August 1964, pp. 137–143.

NEAR, JANET P., and SORCINELLI, MARY DEANE. "Work and Life Away from Work: Predictors of Faculty Satisfaction." *Research in Higher Education,* 25, 1986, pp. 377–394.

PAGE, JANE A., and PAGE, FRED M. *Collegiate Instruction: Some Differences Among Faculty Members Based on Rank, Years of Experience, and School Affiliation.* Paper presented at the Annual Meeting of the Mid-South Educational Research Association, Mobile, AL, 1987. (ERIC Document Reproduction Service No. ED 289 445)

ROMAN, PAUL M. "Employee Alcoholism and Assistance Programs: Adapting an Innovation for College and University Faculty." *Journal of Higher Education,* March–April 1980, pp. 135–149.

SCHUSTER, JACK H. "The Faculty Dilemma: A Short Course." *Phi Delta Kappan,* 68, 1986, pp. 275–282.

SHERTZER, BRUCE E., and STONE, SHELLEY C. *Fundamentals of Counseling.* 3rd ed. Boston: Houghton–Mifflin, 1980.

SIMEONE, ANGELA. *Academic Women Working Toward Equality.* South Hadley, MA: Bergen & Garvey, 1987.

STEINMETZ, LAWRENCE L. *Managing the Marginal and Unsatisfactory Performer.* Reading, MA: Addison–Wesley, 1969.

Part VI

PROFESSIONAL GROWTH, FACULTY DEVELOPMENT, AND IMPROVING THE QUALITY OF COLLEGE TEACHING

Chapter 17.   Professional Growth and Faculty Development

Chapter 18.   Improving the Quality of College Teaching

Chapter 17

Professional Growth and Faculty Development

The case can be made that the department chairperson's most important function is to foster the growth and development of faculty and staff members within the department. Experts in staff and personnel development contend that an organization's effectiveness depends heavily on an ongoing, self-renewing program of human resources development. In the same way, an academic department's effectiveness depends largely on *faculty development,* a term coined to denote self-renewing activities for faculty members. In this regard, one vital question emerges: To what extent should the department chairperson help faculty members acquire the requisite knowledge, skills, and attitudes for maintaining their effectiveness, improving their approach to fulfilling responsibilities, and making satisfactory adjustments to the changes in their environments?

Although the need for staff or personal development has been recognized in the past, such development has been mainly a "background" activity. Sometimes it was relegated to the chairperson, for whom it was probably a minor concern. Occasionally, sabbaticals were granted to those who could afford to survive on a reduced income for a limited time. More recently, centers for the improvement of instruction have been established to help faculty members improve the quality of their instruction. By and large, however, faculty development has been allowed to happen naturally through ongoing professional activity, such as attending or participating in conferences or consulting with old friends and colleagues.

In times of expanding resources and faculties, the need for a deliberate faculty development effort was perhaps not as acute or obvious as it is now. New ideas were imported with the everflowing stream of new faculty members. With the influx of new and energetic talents, it was easy to cover up or overlook maturing but nonproductive faculty members. But circumstances have changed. Colleges and universities are now faced with budgetary problems, a population of maturing faculty members who hold tenure and have little chance of obtaining more rewarding positions at other institutions, and the mixed opportunities of unionization. In addition, a growing number of nontraditional students demand that their rights and expectations be upheld.

How then should institutions of higher education respond to these powerful forces that demand change? Before addressing this question, colleges and universities must first identify the nature of such forces and formulate a reasonable guess as to how these forces may affect university systems, institutions, departments, and ultimately the faculty, which actually delivers the services. Then the question may be raised: What is the department chairperson's responsibility in enhancing faculty members' continuing development to meet emerging institutional needs, their own needs, and the needs of students?

A Case for a Deliberate Development Effort

The following trends that have begun to emerge may well compel college faculty members, as individuals and as department members, to reexamine their professional careers:

- An increase in numbers of older students
- A decline in the level of public support, resulting in an economic crunch for universities
- An emerging awareness of new skills and understandings that will be required for effective functioning in a changing society
- A high percentage of tenured faculty members, most of whom are in their forties and fifties
- A buyer's market for students with regard to educational opportunities
- An increasing number of students who are not awed by a teacher's authority and who are willing to bring legal action if they don't get what they pay for
- An increased demand for accountability by parents, members of governing boards, legislators, and the general public

Three trends from this list deserve special consideration in light of their effect on faculty members—namely, an increase in numbers of older students; the decline in public support for higher education; and the demand for new knowledge, skills, and attitudes in a changing society.

INCREASE IN NUMBERS OF OLDER STUDENTS

This "new clientele" for higher education is composed of different kinds of learners, with wide ranges of abilities, interests and life experiences. They may have more experience than the instructor and be as knowledgeable in some subjects. They often challenge time-tested and traditional ways of perceiving how knowledge is organized and may not want credit or degrees for their efforts. Adult learners may also desire learning that is relevant to current issues and problems, since most are not in training for a position or job. Finally, they may wish to be involved in educational decision-making processes, such as needs assessment, goal setting, selection of content and method, and evaluation.

The major question facing higher education today may well be, "To what extent can faculty members learn to relate effectively to the learning needs, styles, and personal attributes of adult students, a potential clientele larger than the total number of persons now enrolled in the education system, from kindergarten through graduate school?" To address such changes, a faculty development effort may include activities that familiarize faculty members with research about learning characteristics of adults.

DECLINE IN PUBLIC SUPPORT FOR HIGHER EDUCATION

Unfortunately, public confidence in higher education is declining at the same time that financial support is eroding. The public is telling higher education to do more with less. This adaptation will be difficult because of the relative affluence of the past decade. With the curtailment of institutional funds to support many valued activities, faculty members may be required to develop skills in obtaining funds from external sources to support these activities. For example, one strategy would be to initiate a deliberate effort to help faculty members acquire skills in grantsmanship to support their research interests.

DEMAND FOR NEW KNOWLEDGE, SKILLS, AND ATTITUDES

Perhaps the most compelling reason for planned renewal efforts can be derived from analyses and forecasts made by futurists, such as Alvin Toffler, Herman Kahn, and Daniel Bell. For example, Toffler forecasts negative psychological and sociological consequences brought about by accelerating social change and details these negative consequences under the now familiar concept of "future shock." Toffler is highly critical of current education and refers to it as "a hopeless anachronism" because of its orientation toward the past rather than the future. He argues that education appropriate for an industrial age is no longer adequate for the postindustrial age. As he puts it, "For education the lesson is clear: its prime objective must be to increase the individual's 'copeability'—the speed and economy with which he can adapt to continual change. And the faster the rate of change, the more attention must be devoted to discerning the pattern of future events."[1] In Toffler's view, a curriculum is required that effectively helps students learn how to learn, how to relate to others, and how to clarify their values so that they can effectively choose among competing alternatives.

---

1. Alvin Toffler, *Future Shock* (New York: Random House, 1970), p. 357.

From the Perspective of the Futurists

Approaching the problem from another perspective, the futurists Kahn and Bruce-Briggs envision a traumatic future for the human race. In *Things to Come: Thinking About the Seventies and Eighties,* they point out the irony that technology—the means of production that has raised our standard of living so dramatically—may also be responsible for a series of environmental and economic disasters. They predicted a world-wide crisis around 1985 brought on by thoughtless use of technology. Did their prediction come true? Perhaps Toffler is correct in advocating values clarification and the opportunity to choose among competing alternatives as appropriate curricular goals. Values based on consumption and growth may have to be changed to values based on conservation and more humanistic concerns if these predicted disasters are to be averted.

Daniel Bell, in his book *The Coming of Post-Industrial Society,* describes several changes that create strain as society moves from an industrial to a post-industrial age. The sources of strain include the inclusion of disadvantaged groups into society; the growth of global economic interdependence and the creation of international societies; the increasing substitution of political decision making for market decision making; the creation of fully urbanized societies and the erosion of an agricultural population; and the introduction of a multitude of technological products. According to Bell, the "elite" approach to higher education must change to accommodate the ever-increasing number of students from lower- and working-class backgrounds. Bell sees the university as becoming society's primary institution for the dissemination of required survival skills. Many of these skills can be deduced from his analysis: the ability to codify, store, and retrieve theoretical knowledge for the purpose of solving human problems; ability to coordinate human behavior in complex systems; ability to engage in participatory decision making; ability to play; ability to regulate individual and group behavior; and ability to resolve conflict. Bell posits that decision-making processes will be political in nature in the postindustrial society. As a result, tension and conflict will probably increase, and conflict resolution will become a necessary skill.

Analyses by these futurists provide much food for thought. Observation of recent trends and events lends credibility to many of their forecasts. We need only examine the advent of legislative mandates for minimum contact hours, collective bargaining by public employees, land use legislation, affirmative action programs, energy control legislation, and pollution control legislation to find evidence of the new kinds of decision-making processes and interest groups described by Bell. Clearly, each of these trends has critical significance for the role of faculty members in higher education.

In response to such dramatic changes in society, renewal activities for faculty members may include an introduction to the concepts of global interdependence, to techniques in values clarification, and to principles of attitude development and change. Nevertheless, perhaps the most compelling rationale for a deliberate faculty development effort is the severe curtailment and ineffectiveness, due to these trends, of the informal and spontaneous forces that have fostered faculty growth, development, and change in the past. Faculty members must now accept greater responsibility for conducting and managing their own change and renewal processes. Without these processes, stagnation and irrelevance in both teaching and research may well increase.

State of the Art

Given a case for a deliberate faculty development effort, what are some of the ways in which such efforts have been conducted? One salutary effect of the student unrest of the mid- and late 1960s was that it drew attention to the quality of college teaching. Not surprisingly, the American Council on Education chose as the theme for its 1966 Annual Meeting the topic of improving college teaching. Papers and commentaries on "teaching the teachers" were presented there; proceedings of the conference were published the following year. Interestingly enough, Calvin Lee, who edited the paper (*Improving College Teaching: Aids and Impediments*) noted that only two paragraphs were devoted to the teaching of older teachers, but at least the matter was raised.

Several relevant monographs on the topic have appeared since then, however. *Career Development of the Effective College Teacher,* by Kenneth E. Eble, appeared in 1971 through the sponsorship of the American Association of Colleges and the American Association of University Professors. Jossey–Bass, in its New Directions for Higher Education series, featured a collection of essays by Mervin Freedman entitled *Facilitating Faculty Development.* Perhaps the most cogent and provocative statements regarding the teaching of older teachers can be found in the book *Faculty Development in a Time of Retrenchment,* by the Group for Human Development in Higher Education. The work that resulted in this latter monograph was supported at various times by the Carnegie Corporation, Lilly Endowment, and the Hazen Foundation. As a matter of fact, the Lilly Endowment has committed funds to several liberal arts schools for the purpose of establishing faculty development programs. The question no longer seems to be whether or not, but when and how.

When we examine the existing literature on faculty development, we find that nearly all of it focuses on only one of the faculty members' roles—teaching. Yet in most institutions faculty members serve as researchers, curriculum developers, information analysts, disseminators of knowledge through the mass media, theory builders, providers of service, problem solvers, consultants, advisors, and counselors. Some also serve as administrators, managers, and members of government committees. Thus, faculty roles and responsibilities span far more than the teaching function itself. The term *faculty development,* as used in this chapter, therefore, refers to establishing activities and procedures that assist faculty members in acquiring knowledge, skills, and attitudes that enable them to become more effective in performing all functions related to professional academic life.

What, then, are some activities that could aid a department faculty development effort? The following list includes only a few of the many possible activities, some of which may already be available at some institutions. Two criteria govern the selection of the activities listed here: faculty members can engage in such activities without great cost to the university and without the assistance of elaborate service facilities or massive bureaucratic effort; and little effort beyond individual initiative is required in order to participate. The list was adapted from a list compiled by David G. Brown and William S. Hanger.[2]

SUGGESTED SELF-DEVELOPMENT ACTIVITIES FOR FACULTY MEMBERS

A. New experiences
    1. Exchanges and sabbaticals
        a. Exchanges within your college or university
        b. Exchanges between colleges and universities regionally, nationally, and internationally
        c. Short visits to neighboring colleges or universities
        d. Exchanges with government, industry, or foundations
        e. Joint appointments
        f. Assignments in other universities or institutions
        g. New, unusual, or unfamiliar committee assignments
    2. Special assignments in administrative posts
        a. Work in dean's office
        b. Work in contracts and grants office
        c. Prepare a grant proposal for a faculty development project sponsored by your institution
B. Development of expertise
    1. Research practices
        a. Submit articles, monographs, books, book reviews, or poetry for publication
        b. Attend research colloquia within and outside the department
        c. Team with a colleague from outside the department to write a grant proposal or article
        d. Join a research center or institute
        e. Participate in local, regional, or national conferences
        f. Participate in consortia activities
        g. Read literature in your field
    2. Developments in peripheral areas
        a. Audit courses given in your field or a related field
        b. Enroll in a new degree program
        c. Take a continuing education course
        d. Enroll in an undergraduate short course
        e. Attend a dissertation defense in another discipline

2. David G. Brown and William S. Hanger, "Pragmatics of Faculty Self-Development," *Educational Record,* Summer 1975, pp. 202–206.

  f. Read literature about higher education (e.g., *Chronicle of Higher Education, Journal of Higher Education, Educational Record, Change, Higher Education and National Affairs,* and so forth)

C. Instructional development

  1. New techniques and materials

    a. Organize or participate in instructional improvement seminars or luncheons

    b. Visit classes conducted by colleagues

    c. Sponsor a session at a professional conference or convention on teaching techniques within your discipline

    d. Develop and use audio-visual aids

    e. Experiment with one of the new teaching technologies—computer-assisted instruction (CAI), individually guided instruction (IGI), instruction television (ITV), simulation and gaming

    f. Talk with book salesmen or equipment dealers

    g. Write and distribute to students clear objectives for the courses you teach

    h. Vary teaching techniques—for example, if you teach primarily by lecturing, introduce some discussion techniques

    i. Try the case-study method

  2. New skills and knowledge about the teaching and learning processes

    a. Take a psychology course or education course in language development or cognitive development

    b. Seek out colleagues familiar with objective test design, criterion-referenced assessment, evaluation strategies, performance testing

    c. Make an item analysis of your tests

  3. Curriculum development

    a. Develop a new specialty area

    b. Attempt to assess and evaluate the effectiveness of a series of courses or a program

    c. Learn about competency-based education

  4. New teaching experiences

    a. Prepare to teach a new course in your discipline or in a related discipline

    b. Teach a continuing education course

    c. Teach an in-service workshop for practicing professionals

    d. Take over a colleague's class in another discipline when he or she is away

    e. Teach an intensive short course

    f. Teach a high school class or a graduate seminar for a few days

    g. Team teach with a colleague or student

  5. Evaluation

    a. Have students evaluate your teaching effectiveness

    b. Form a student feedback committee to advise you on teaching effectiveness

    c. Invite a teaching specialist to sit in on your classes and offer constructive criticism

    d. Xerox your lecture notes and have peers react to them

    e. Videotape your lectures and have colleagues critique them

    f. Develop a peer evaluation system with your colleagues

D. Service
1. Advisement
   a. Solicit current information about employment possibilities for students majoring in your discipline
   b. Study counseling techniques and human development theories
   c. Advise a campus student group (fraternity or sorority, political group, campus newspaper, service club, and so forth)
   d. Keep up with rules and regulations regarding curriculum options outside your discipline
   e. Help with registration advisement or drop-add advisement
   f. Learn to recognize abnormal behavior patterns persons use when coping with stress or anxiety
   g. Find out about community mental health services and how to make referrals
   h. Learn about campus services available to students
2. Interaction with students
   a. Entertain students in your home
   b. Live in a residence hall for two days
   c. Host a foreign student
   d. Attend an intercollegiate athletic event
   e. Lead a group of students to Europe, Mexico, Asia
   f. Participate on a faculty intramural team
3. Community involvement
   a. Run for local office
   b. Serve on local or state government committees and councils
   c. Do volunteer work with a hospital board or local charity
   d. Consult
   e. Participate in academic fairs, workshops, or other activities with elementary and secondary teachers or counselors
4. Work for the college or university
   a. Assist the admissions office in recruiting students
   b. Prepare attractive materials or publications for recruiting students to your field
   c. Call on prospective donors of gifts and bequests asking for time, money, equipment, artifacts
   d. Serve on an admissions committee
E. Personal development
1. Personal knowledge
   a. Enroll in a skill development course such as typing, bookkeeping, auto repairs
   b. Enroll in a continuing education course
   c. Enroll in a leisure education course
   d. Join a group to watch a public television course
   e. Participate in an "outward bound" program
   f. Try to attend a dozen special lectures on campus next year
   g. Analyze how you spend your free time
   h. Attend a personal growth group (assertiveness training, stress management, interpersonal communication, and so forth)
   i. Join a book club

2. Cultural experiences
   a. Attend an artist series on campus
   b. Travel to a foreign country
   c. Learn a new foreign language or sign language
3. Career development
   a. Schedule brown-bag sessions to discuss life and careers of important or interesting persons
   b. Organize a panel on nonacademic career opportunities related to your discipline
   c. Develop a contract with your department chairperson that allows you to pursue a special area of interest in the year ahead
   d. Work at another profession or develop new sources of income that complement but do not detract from academic responsibilities
4. Physical development
   a. Jog with a group of colleagues
   b. Form a faculty intramural team
   c. Learn a new sport

The Question of the Chairperson's Role

In all likelihood, when aspiring faculty members assumed their roles as chairpersons, no clause was included in their contracts or job descriptions that alluded to responsibilities regarding faculty development. The question naturally follows, "How much responsibility should a chairperson have in ensuring that faculty members continue to upgrade their knowledge and skills as researchers and instructors?" Below are three short scenarios describing possible role models for the ways in which chairpersons might respond to this issue.

THE CARETAKER

Chairperson Smith, fifty-five years old, has been a department chairperson for four years. The faculty members in his department are all tenured; half are associate professors, and the other half are full professors. Most are between the ages of thirty-five and fifty-five, and they are generally satisfied with their lot professionally. Smith has noticed lately, however, that many of them are beginning to invest more of their effort in nonprofessional activities—such as camping, jogging, and community affairs— and that department productivity in research and student credit hours is beginning to fall off.

Smith recognizes the need for faculty development in general but feels that each person should assume complete responsibility for finding activities that foster his or her own growth and development. He does, however, have a good reputation for helping faculty members who come to him for advice, and he encourages them to pursue their own initiatives, particularly in research. Merit pay is awarded primarily on the single criterion of research productivity. Smith sees his role as chairperson mainly as that of a caretaker who manages routine administrative duties. He plans to resume eventually the role of full-time faculty member.

THE BROKER

Chairperson Jones, fifty years old, has been department chairperson for three years. Approximately 20 percent of the department faculty members are untenured. Ten percent are assistant professors; 30 percent are associate professors; and 60 percent are full professors. Their ages range from thirty to sixty; forty-five is the median age. Jones has stated that the primary criterion for determining merit pay should be effective teaching, but the department's tenure and promotion committee clearly rewards those who demonstrate productivity in research. The department enrollment has held steady over the past several years and probably will continue to do so since the department's admissions standards are now somewhat selective. Should applications decline, the department would simply decrease admissions standards to compensate. The faculty morale is good, but none of the faculty members are exerting unusual efforts—such as serving on editorial boards or establishing clearly focused research programs—to distinguish themselves nationally.

Jones's view of her role regarding faculty development is that of facilitator and broker. She is familiar with services available to faculty members within the institution and in the community. During the annual evaluation conferences, she reviews with the faculty members their career objectives, suggests resources to help them, and often makes referrals to the contracts and grants office, the instructional design center, and, for personal and career problems, the campus or community counseling centers. But she definitely sees her role as helping faculty members realize their personal and professional goals by encouraging them to seek help from specialized services outside the department. To this end, she maintains a complete file of brochures pertaining to faculty development services and opportunities for growth, such as sabbaticals and exchange programs. Jones has stated publicly that she does not seek a higher administrative office, but she has indicated to close associates that if she were nominated for the position of dean, she would accept the nomination.

THE DEVELOPER

Chairperson Adams, forty-five years old, has been chairperson for three years. The department faculty members are all tenured; 65 percent are associate professors, and 35 percent are full professors. The median age is forty. The faculty members are highly competitive and ambitious. Adams, who entertains the goal of some day assuming greater administrative responsibility as a dean, seeks to help his department gain a strong regional and perhaps even a national reputation. The department's goals are to increase the number and quality of students enrolled in the program, to have each faculty member in the department establish a focused research program, and to have each member demonstrate service to the profession and the community in ways that will enhance the first two goals.

As a result, Adams has established and organized a rather sophisticated faculty development effort. He has established a committee on research that coordinates and encourages grant-writing efforts and publication. A seminar on grantsmanship is held once a year, and a colloquium in which faculty members report their research efforts is held once a month. A curriculum committee is also active; it coordinates matters concerning the content of the curricuium and encourages new delivery mechanisms as well. To expand enrollments, the curriculum committee plans an outreach effort to offer, through the continuing education office, special interest courses to the community. Through this effort the department hopes to enroll many students in full-credit courses or degree programs. The chairperson realizes that the faculty members have had little experience in conducting programs like that planned by the curriculum committee and feels that a series of seminars is necessary to help them acquire the requisite skills for the new program.

Thus Adams views his role regarding faculty development as that of developer. He actively helps faculty members acquire skills and knowledge to implement department goals. The faculty members realize that by contributing toward department goals, they, in turn, will be more able to attain individual professional goals. Adams has also established a reward system that recognizes achievement in these areas and requires that faculty members demonstrate how they have helped the department achieve its goals.

Whether a department chairperson acts as a caretaker, broker, or developer or wishes to assume some other role depends on several factors, such as his or her career goals, self-image, or leadership skills. These factors then interact with the collective will of the department faculty. Does the department want to be led by the caretaker, broker, or developer? A department's capability to survive and grow in an era of declining resources may well depend on the chairperson's ability to lead within the constraints of the faculty's expectations and aspirations.

If the idea of a faculty development program seems attractive, the chairperson and each department faculty member should ponder the following questions: What important trends will affect the department in the next five to ten years? What should be the department's response to these trends? Where does each faculty member want to be, with respect to his or her own life and career, five or ten years from now? Tentative answers to these questions can provide the foundation on which to build a faculty development program and a serious commitment to professional development.

Planning a Development Program

Once the faculty has decided to explore the possibility of establishing a deliberate faculty development effort, a first step in planning is to analyze how local, regional, and national trends might affect the department. One planning technique that is helpful in analyzing how trends may affect a department is the matrix method. One dimension of the matrix lists important trends, while the other identifies components of a program, such as curriculum, faculty members, students, and research (see Table 17.1). Intercepts in the matrix show how the trends will affect particular program components. Using a five-year planning horizon might be helpful—i.e., project how the trend will affect the program component five years from now. Information organized in this way can provide a basis for establishing priority goals and activities in the area of faculty development. Table 17.1 presents hypothetical data on how certain local and national trends may affect a department in a school of education.

Anyone using the matrix technique must be able to identify those trends that would exert the strongest influence. Otherwise, one may plan to scratch where no itch develops. Assuming, though, that the predictions resulting from this analysis are correct—or at least defensible—gaps between the existing state of affairs and the desired state of affairs become readily apparent.

Initiating a Development Program: Six Caveats

After analyzing important trends and ways in which it could effectively respond, the department should consider strategies for change. Certain caveats should be kept in mind when initiating faculty development activities.

1. *Aim for cooperation.* For faculty development to become an ongoing process, it must be a cooperative effort involving the faculty members, department chairpersons, and other administrators. Lack of support at any of the three levels could result in wasted effort.

2. *Think big, but start small.* A well-planned activity for a small group of interested faculty members is more likely to be successful than a large-scale, general effort, which may suit no one. A low-profile, low-key approach keeps expectations at realistic levels and provides a better basis to begin working with faculty members. A hard-sell approach tends to alienate or intimidate many faculty members and thereby creates difficulties in working with them later. A small group of satisfied and motivated volunteers will soon set an example for their colleagues.

3. *Involve faculty members in planning development activities.* This approach will help ensure content validity for the participants and enhance their commitment to follow through. The cliché "Begin where the people are" is as pertinent when working with the faculty as with any other group of adult learners. The goals to be achieved should be set by the faculty members themselves, not by other persons in the academic hierarchy. Given adequate performance counseling, faculty members should assume the ultimate authority for determining the direction and nature of change.

4. *Be eclectic in approach.* When planning a faculty development program, the department may be tempted to concentrate on a single new technique.

TABLE 17.1 Sample of Matrix Analysis: Trends Affecting an Education Department, 1990–95

PROGRAM COMPONENTS

TRENDS	Curriculum	Faculty Members	Students	Research
More adult learners	1. Ways of crediting prior experience will be developed. 2. More evening classes will be required. 3. More in-service training will be required. 4. Practical application will be emphasized.	1. Faculty members may be required to teach on evenings or on weekends. 2. Faculty members must become knowledgeable about how adults learn. 3. Faculty members may be threatened.	1. New services may be required (e.g., babysitting). 2. There may be less collegiality among students.	1. Research money will be available to address problems of adult learners.
Energy shortage	1. Delivery systems must rely on low-cost dissemination. 2. Ways of learning through media at home or at work will be explored.	1. Faculty members may be required to go to students rather than vice versa. 2. Instruction may take place through media and correspondence.	1. Skills in independent learning may be crucial. 2. Transportation costs to schools may be prohibitive for commuter students.	1. There will be less mobility to travel to conventions. 2. There will be more emphasis on journals to keep informed. 3. Funds will be available to explore ways of disseminating information through low-cost media.
More working women	1. Ways of coping with sex bias will be included in curriculum. 2. Ways of removing stereotyping will be included in curriculum materials.	1. Faculty members may be required to adjust teaching methods to working mothers or single parents. 2. Faculty members' values regarding the career woman, dual-career families, and single-parent families may be tested.	1. More men may pursue elementary education as a career. 2. More women may pursue math and science as careers.	1. Studies in processes of stereotyping will be encouraged. 2. Studies in the educational development of children from dual-career families will be encouraged.

No single technique is suitable for everyone, however, and a variety of possible techniques would enable faculty members to choose some that suit their own style and needs.

5. *Start where the chances of success are high.* First impressions are crucial, and a few small but highly successful efforts will soon pave the way for more ambitious projects and activities.

6. *Institutionalize faculty development efforts.* A meaningful program of faculty development must address itself to the question of long-term efforts and how these efforts can be formalized to ensure longevity, adaptability, and relevance.

Strategies for Initiating a Development Program

If the chairperson has decided to begin a faculty development program and has determined his or her level of responsibility for administering it, he or she should analyze some of the conditions that would foster or inhibit the implementation of a program. Two approaches, described below, may be appropriate for initiating a faculty development program.

1. *Faculty development as a means to individual development.* This strategy begins with an activity in which a reasonable number of faculty members have agreed to participate. Determining the topic could be accomplished through the use of a questionnaire administered by a department faculty development committee. After collating the data, the committee would set priorities and consult with the chairperson for endorsement of its plans. The advantage of this strategy is that the faculty members assume the responsibility for determining areas in which they would like to improve.

2. *Faculty development as a means to department development.* Another strategy is to make faculty development a means to help the department achieve its goals. The department determines its goals by analyzing perceived trends that will affect its future. In addressing these trends and the changes required to meet them, the department should consider whether the faculty is currently qualified to meet the new demands. A faculty development program then is anchored to department goals agreed upon by the faculty. This approach addresses the matter of motivation—i.e., why faculty members should participate in an organized faculty development effort. The faculty members can then collectively monitor their progress in attaining department goals. Obviously, when faculty members perceive a faculty development effort as a means for enhancing both their indivdual goals and a department's goals, an optimum state of affairs exists.

Conditions That May Inhibit Faculty Development

Faculty development programs have met resistance for various reasons. The chairperson should be aware of common problems that impede the implementation of a program.

- The faculty members' personal goals may not be congruent with the goals of the department or the college. In this case, faculty members may fail to identify with any effort to alter the status quo.
- Faculty members often perceive development activities as unnecessary infringements on their already crowded schedules. They need to be convinced of the value of deliberate efforts toward professional growth.
- Even when faculty members become aware of the need for such involvement, they often have little idea of where to go or whom to ask for assistance.
- Some chairpersons see as a barrier the lack of funds to buy books or materials, to pay for travel, or to hire consultants. Some programs require little or no funding, however, and the chairperson should encourage development efforts even when moneys are not available.
- Physical isolation from colleagues deprives some faculty members of opportunities for stimulation and learning.
- In some departments a spirit of apathy exists, and faculty members are indifferent to the idea of continuing their professional growth. Other departments may have faculty members who feel that they have already achieved perfection and therefore see no need for organized development activities.

Many of the conditions that inhibit development efforts may be overcome by proper leadership on the part of the chairperson.

Assessing Readiness for Involvement

Before embarking on a faculty development effort, a chairperson may wish to obtain an indication from the faculty members regarding their interests. Identifying interest areas could be accomplished through a questionnaire listing areas of development and relevant activities. The following list includes some possible activities that department chairpersons can adapt for use with their faculty members:[3]

AREAS OF DEVELOPMENT AND POSSIBLE ACTIVITIES FOR FACULTY MEMBERS

A. Professional development
  1. Acquiring visiting professorships
  2. Locating and applying for sabbaticals
  3. Getting published
  4. Preparing grant proposals
  5. Establishing your own research program

3. This list is part of the Professional Seminars and Workshops Questionnaire, prepared by the Institute for Academic Leadership, Florida State University, with the cooperation of the Instuctional Systems Institute.

      6. Exploring professional exchanges with business, industry, and government
      7. Setting up joint appointment possibilities
      8. Conducting an effective committee meeting
      9. Exploring techniques for department curriculum planning

B. Instructional development
      1. Developing course objectives
      2. Preparing and using media in the classroom
      3. Preparing and delivering a lecture
      4. Stimulating class discussions
      5. Preparing classroom tests
      6. Using computers for testing students
      7. Using atypical classroom procedures
         a. Keller Plan (using student tutors to teach subsections of large lecture courses)
         b. Personalized systems of instruction
         c. Competency-based education
         d. Self-instructional systems
      8. Evaluating students' writing skills

C. Personal development
      1. Managing time efficiently
      2. Improving relationships with colleagues
      3. Improving relationships with department chairpersons
      4. Learning about faculty career patterns
      5. Using assertiveness techniques with students and peers
      6. Training in stress management
      7. Dealing with job frustrations
      8. Overcoming boredom
      9. Developing effective communication skills
     10. Exploring local recreational opportunities
     11. Improving your physical health
     12. Managing the dual-career family
     13. Countering sexism in higher education
     14. Exploring tax-deductible professional activities

D. Service
      1. Becoming a consultant for government, private industry, or other consumers
      2. Exploring consultation techniques
      3. Getting appointed to state, regional, and national professional committees
      4. Teaching special interest courses
      5. Evaluating your service contribution to the university
      6. Finding opportunities for public speaking
      7. Learning to speak effectively
      8. Planning and conducting workshops and conferences
      9. Advising students about courses and careers
     10. Recognizing, coping with, and referring troubled or disruptive students
     11. Exploring career possibilities for students in your discipline
     12. Participating on department committees
     13. Securing public support for your program

Staff, or professional, development activities existed long before the term *faculty development* was coined. Nevertheless, before a chairperson expends a great deal of energy in organizing a deliberate faculty development effort, he or she should determine whether faculty members perceive a need for it. Not surprisingly, most faculty members consider themselves "above average" teachers, and some openly claim to be among the best. With such perceptions of perfection, it is no wonder that faculty members are sometimes unresponsive to efforts to induce them to improve their teaching skills. Faculty members must perceive a need to change before they will commit themselves to participating in a faculty development effort, whether in teaching or some other professional area. Without a cogent rationale, however, such efforts will probably not elicit much faculty response.

This chapter has highlighted three critical factors that chairpersons should consider before embarking on a deliberate faculty development effort: (1) the significant local, regional, and national trends that may require of the faculty members new skills for serving their students; (2) the chairperson's own perceptions of his or her role in the area of faculty development; and (3) the extent to which individual faculty members' goals can be met by meeting the department's goals. Unless faculty members themselves can be convinced of the need to be involved in some form of faculty development and are willing to participate in a program, however, the probability of success for these types of activities is not great.

Questions

1. In view of the changes that may well affect higher education in general, select three trends or changes that are likely to have the most effect on your department during the next five years.

2. For each trend you cited above, how would your department's curriculum, faculty, students, and research programs be affected? Construct a matrix similar to the one shown in this chapter.

3. a. From the list of faculty development activities suggested in this chapter and from your own experience, list three activities that would be appropriate for helping faculty members in your department acquire knowledge and skills to cope more effectively with each of the three trends you listed in question 1.

   b. Having read the three scenarios in the chapter describing ways in which a chairperson could approach faculty development, formulate an approach that would have the best chance of success in your department.

4. To what extent is faculty development an individual responsibility of each faculty member versus a departmental responsibility?

   a. What if any should be the role of chairpersons who believe it to be an individual responsiblity of each faculty member?

    b. What should be the role of chairpersons who believe it to be a departmental responsibility?

5. To what extent should faculty members be required to submit a yearly plan for their professional development?

6. To what extent should a faculty member's involvement in professional development activities be included in the criteria used for annual performance evaluation?

7. To what extent should faculty members be expected to engage in individual professional development activities at their own expense?

8. To what extent should departmental funds be used to support an individual's professional development activities:

    a. when it is an integral part of a current plan for implementing departmental goals. Give examples of faculty development activities that might fall into this category.

    b. when it has potential for contributing to possible future plans for implementing departmental goals. Give examples of faculty development activities that might fall into this category.

    c. when it is primarily for the benefit of the individual without benefiting the department. Give examples of faculty development activities that might fall into this category.

References

BELL, DANIEL. *The Coming of Post-Industrial Society: A Venture in Social Forcasting.* New York: Basic Books, 1973.

BENNIS, WARREN G. *Organizational Development: Its Nature, Origins, and Prospects,* edited by Edgar Schein et al. Reading, MA: Addison–Wesley, 1969.

BERGQUIST, WILLIAM H.; PHILIPS, STEVEN R.; and QUEHL, GARY H. *A Handbook for Faculty Development.* Washington, DC: Council for the Advancement of Small Colleges, 1975.

BERGQUIST, WILLIAM H., and PHILIPS, STEVEN R. "Components of an Effective Faculty Development Program." *Journal of Higher Education,* March 1975, pp. 177–211.

BIRNBAUM, ROBERT. "Using the Calendar for Faculty Development." *Educational Record,* Fall 1975, pp. 226–230.

BOGENSCHUTZ, MARGARET M., and SAGARIA, MARY ANN. *Aspirations and Career Growth of Mid-Level Administrators in Higher Education.* Paper presented at the Annual Meeting of the American Educational Research Association, New Orleans, 1988. (ERIC Document Reproduction Service No. ED 296 652)

BOICE, ROBERT. "Differences in Arranging Faculty Development Through Deans and Chairs, 1985." *Research in Higher Education,* 23, 1985, pp. 245–255.

————. "Faculty Development via Field Programs for Middle-aged, Disillusioned Faculty." *Research in Higher Education,* 25, 1986, pp. 115–135.

BOYER, RONALD K., and CROCKETT, CAMPBELL (Eds.) "Organizational Development in Higher Education." *Journal of Higher Education,* May 1973 (special issue), pp. 339–351.

BRENEMAN, DAVID W., and YOUN, TED I. K. (Eds.) *Academic Labor Markets and Careers.* Philadelphia: The Falmer Press, Taylor and Francis, Inc., 1988.

BROWN, DAVID G., and HANGER, WILLIAM S. "Pragmatics of Faculty Self-Development." *Educational Record,* Summer 1975, pp. 201–206.

BUHL, LANCE C., and GREENFIELD, ADELE. "Contracting for Professional Development in Academe." *Educational Record,* Spring 1975, pp. 111–121.

CHICKERING, ARTHUR W. *Education and Identity.* San Francisco: Jossey–Bass, 1969.

COHEN, ARTHUR M., and BRAWER, FLORENCE B. *The American Community College.* 2nd ed. San Francisco: Jossey–Bass, 1988.

DOUGLAS, JOEL M. (Ed.) *Salary and Compensation Methodology in Academic Collective Bargaining.* New York: National Center for the Study of Collective Bargaining in Higher Education and the Professions, 1983. (ERIC Document Reproduction Service No. ED 230 140)

Faculty in Higher Education Institutions, 1988: 1988 National Survey of Postsecondary Faculty. Washington, DC: U.S. Department of Education, 1990.

FREEDMAN, MERVIN. *Facilitating Faculty Development.* San Francisco: Jossey–Bass, 1973.

GAFF, JERRY G. *Toward Faculty Renewal: Advances in Faculty, Instructional and Organizational Development.* San Francisco: Jossey–Bass, 1975.

GMELCH, WALTER H. "Dimensions of Stress Among University Faculty: Factor-analytic Results From a National Study." *Research in Higher Education,* 24, 1986, pp. 266–286.

GROUP FOR HUMAN DEVELOPMENT IN HIGHER EDUCATION. *Faculty Development in a Time of Retrenchment.* New Rochelle, NY: Change Magazine Press, 1974.

HAMMONS, JAMES O., and WALLACE, TERRY H. SMITH. "Sixteen Ways to Kill a College Faculty Development Program." *Educational Technology,* December 1976, pp. 16–20.

HETTICH, PAUL, and LEMA-STERN, SANDRA. "Professional Development Opportunities in Small Colleges." *Teaching of Psychology,* 16, 1989, pp. 12–15.

JACKSON, WILLIAM K. (Ed.) *National Conference on Professional and Personal Renewal for Faculty, Atlanta.* 1986. Conference proceedings available from ERIC Document Reproduction Service No. ED 276 393.

KAHN, HERMAN, and BRUCE-BIGGS, B. *Things to Come: Thinking About the Seventies and Eighties.* New York: Macmillan, 1972.

KAIKAI, SEPTIMUS M., and KAIKAI, REGINA E. *Chairpersons as Promoters of Community Service.* Catonsville, MD: Catonsville Community College, 1990. (ERIC Document Reproduction Service No. ED 321 801)

LAWRENCE, JANET H., and BLACKBURN, ROBERT T. *Aging and Faculty Distribution of Their Work Effort.* ASHE Annual Meeting Paper, San Antonio, 1986. (ERIC Document Reproduction Service No. ED 268 903)

MANN, MARY PAT. *An Analysis of Faculty Goals: Personal, Disciplinary, and Career Development Decisions.* Paper presented at the Annual Meeting of the AERA, San Francisco, March 1989. (ERIC Document Reproduction Service No. ED 305 874)

MCGEE, GAIL W., and FORD, ROBERT C. "Faculty Research Productivity and Intention to Change Positions." *Review of Higher Education,* 11, 1987, pp. 1–16.

MCINTOSH, THOMAS H., and KOEVERING, THOMAS E. "Six-year Case Study of Faculty Peer Reviews, Merit Ratings, and Pay Awards in a Multidisciplinary Department." *Journal of the College and University Personnel Association,* 37, 1986, pp. 5–14.

MIDDLEHURST, ROBIN. "Evaluation and Development of a Leadership Course for Heads of Academic Departments in the United Kingdom." *Higher Education Management,* 1(2), 1989, pp. 170–182.

NAISBITT, JOHN. *Megatrends.* New York: Warner Books, 1984.

NELSON, T. M. "Rating of Scholarly Journals by Chairpersons in the Social Sciences." *Research in Higher Education,* 19, 1983, pp. 469–497.

NELSON, WILLIAM C., and SIGEL, MICHAEL C. (Eds.) *Effective Approaches to Faculty Development.* Washington, DC: Association of American Colleges, 1980.

RASCH, CARLA. "Sources of Stress Among Administrators at Research Universities." *Review of Higher Education,* 9, 1986, pp. 419–434.

RICHARDSON, RICHARD C., JR. "Staff Development: A Conceptual Framework." *Journal of Higher Education,* May 1975, pp. 303–311.

SCHAFFER, ROBIN. "Role Conflict in Academic Chairpersons." *Occupational Therapy Journal of Research,* 7, 1987, pp. 301–313.

SCHULTZ, JERELYN B., and CHUNG, YONSUK L. "Research Productivity and Job Satisfaction of University Faculty." *Journal of Vocational Education Research,* 13, 1988, pp. 33–48.

SCHUSTER, JACK H. "The Personal Dimension: Faculty Development." *Thought and Action,* 5, 1989, pp. 61–72.

SEAGREN, ALAN T., and CRESWELL, JOHN W. *A Comparison of Perceptions of Administrative Tasks and Professional Development Needs of Chairpersons/Heads of Departments in Australia and the U.S.* 1985. Document available from ERIC Document Reproduction Service No. ED 257 328.

SEAGREN, ALAN T. *Perception of Chairpersons and Faculty Concerning Roles, Descriptors, and Activities Considered Important for Faculty Development and Departmental Vitality.* 1986. (ERIC Document Reproduction Service No. ED 276 387)

SIMEONE, ANGELA. *Academic Women Working Toward Equality.* South Hadley, MA: Bergen & Garvey, 1987.

SPICER, CHRISTOPHER H., and STATON-SPICER, ANN Q. "Communication in the Socialization of the Academic Department Chairperson." *Bulletin of the Association for Business Communication,* 65, 1988, pp. 46–54.

THOMAS, TRUDELLE. "Demystifying the Job Search: A Guide for Candidates." *College Composition and Communication,* 40, 1989, pp. 312–327.

TOFFLER, ALVIN. *Future Shock.* New York: Random House, 1970.

TWOMBLY, SUSAN B. *Boundaries of the Top-level Two-year College Administrative Market: Implications for Leadership and Cooperation.* ASHE Annual Meeting Paper, San Antonio, 1986. (ERIC Document Reproduction Service No. ED 268 865)

VAUGHN, GEORGE. *Scholarship and the Community College Professional: Mandate for the Future.* Paper presented at the Annual Convention of the American Association of Community and Junior Colleges, 1989. (ERIC Document Reproduction Service No. ED 305 965)

WEAVER, FREDERICK STIRTON. "Scholarship for the Teaching Faculty." *College Teaching,* 34, 1986, pp. 51–58.

WERGIN, JON F.; MASON, ELIZABETH J.; and MUNSON, PAUL J. "Practices of Faculty Development: An Experience-Derived Model: Virginia Commonwealth University." *Journal of Higher Education,* May 1976, pp. 289–308.

Chapter 18

Improving the Quality of College Teaching

One of the main areas of concern which appears on the agendas of many national conferences in higher education is how to improve the quality of college teaching. An increasingly strong consensus emerges at these meetings that the quality of college teaching needs improvement, and that all college (and university) teachers, regardless of how well they teach, not only need to keep up-to-date with the literature in their respective disciplines, but also should work continually towards enhancing their teaching skills. These sentiments aren't new, of course, but there is a new urgency about them, an urgency underscored by the growing pressure from governing boards and state legislatures for more assessment and accountability. These pressures are exerted on presidents, who pass them on to deans, department chairpersons, and other faculty leaders.

If indeed the quality of today's college teaching is so lacking as to attract widespread national attention, one wonders about the teaching qualifications of new faculty members when they are first hired to be college or university teachers. Are they too low? Should they be higher? What, in fact, are they? Should the department chair check the previous teaching records of candidates who are applying for vacant faculty positions?

The primary qualification for entering the professoriate at most universities is, and has been for a long time, an earned doctorate in a specific discipline. As everyone knows, the curriculum of a Ph.D. program consists of required course work and examinations on subject matter to ensure that candidates who want to be teachers or researchers have the latest knowledge in the discipline. It also includes required research methodology courses and supervised research, to ensure that those who plan to be researchers, or who want to know how to critique and evaluate someone else's research, will have the necessary skills. Most universities do not require graduate students to take either teaching methods courses or supervised teaching. Sadly, until very recently those who have sought such training independently have often been scorned for their efforts.

Graduate teaching assistantships provide some students with an opportunity to gain experience in some aspects of teaching. Indeed, the best estimates hold that approximately 30 percent of the undergraduate teaching done in American colleges and universities is done by graduate assistants. But, more often than not, teaching assistants receive little orientation or teacher training. Where orientation does exist it varies widely, and it is unusual for it to extend far beyond a general introductory briefing. A focus on research skills clearly dominates the preparation of Ph.D.s in the United States.

Is this preparation appropriate? Is it all it should be? To answer these questions, we must ask where Ph.D.s go after graduation, and what they are called upon to do in their new jobs. In 1987 (the latest year for which data are available) 50.5 percent of earned doctorates went on to find positions in academic institutions after graduation. Private industry hired 19.3 percent, government took 10.8 percent, and the remaining 20.4 percent went into other jobs or on to unknown sources of income.[1]

Within private industry, some jobs assumed by Ph.D. recipients have a research focus, but others do not. The situation is the same in government. What about the 50 percent who go back into academe? In other words, how much time do faculty spend on research activities as opposed to teaching activities?

Most faculty members teach three courses per semester, except at major research universities where the average teaching assignment is two courses. Considering preparation, contact hours, grading papers, and meeting with students, faculty report that they spend approximatley two-thirds of their time on instructional activities. That leaves one-third for everything else: research, committee meetings, and the myriad other responsibilities of being a faculty member.

Perhaps because of the preponderance of teaching in the lives of most facutly, or perhaps because of not enough commitment to research, many faculty don't do much research. In a 1984 survey on college teaching conducted by the Carnegie Foundation, 70 percent of the 5,000 faculty members in the survey reported that they were not doing any research that they expected to be published. This means that only 30 percent were involved in some type of publishable research, and that even individuals in this group were spending less than an average of one-third of their professional time on research activities.

If we are to be truthful, we must acknowledge that most universities hire new Ph.D.s to teach. Their hiring, however, is based primarily on research experience, publication record, or potential for becoming a researcher. Prior teaching experience or potential for becoming a good teacher is not a factor that is seriously considered as part of the hiring process. But new faculty members, although expected to do research, confront a job in which 60 percent to 70 percent of their work week will center on teaching and teaching-related activities, something for which they may have little formal training or experience. Some of these individuals will become effective teachers given time, but many will not.

---

1. *Summary Report 1987: Doctorate Recipients from United States Universities* (National Academy Press, Washington, DC, 1989).

Though it may be a hard reality to accept, many Ph.D. students know, even while they are carrying out the research training program for the doctorate, that they are not going to do research when they graduate. They may be planning a teaching (or some other) career and want the Ph.D. degree for status purposes, or the credentialing necessary to meet the requirements for a teaching position. Major professors often know which of their doctoral students are not planning research careers, but continue to treat them as if they were. In such instances, both parties are involved in a charade. Unfortunately, the neglect of teacher training as part of the doctoral program leaves new Ph.D.s ill-prepared for the realities they will face as teachers. It also continues to shortchange generations of undergraduates by putting before them teachers not yet awakened to, and certainly not trained for, the increasingly difficult challenge of college teaching.

The balance has not always been shifted so strongly toward research. Research really began to take the limelight in the late 1950s after the Soviet Union put its Sputnik satellite into orbit. Before that, the difference in status and reward between faculty who were primarily teachers and those who were primarily researchers was less noticeable. But after Sputnik, large amounts of government money in the form of grants to scientists changed the balance of rewards. Faculty, who are as interested in money and promotions as anyone else, naturally responded to the shift, a shift which somehow affected the humanities and social sciences as well as the hard and life sciences.

About the same time, many institutions founded as "Teachers Colleges" or "Normal Schools" began aspiring to become state universities. As they in fact achieved university status, their administrations began to insist on more research from the faculty because the real status seemed to lie in research. Good teaching thus became both less glamorous and less rewarded.

In many ways this pattern still continues: Even small regional state universities want recognition as research institutions. Ironically, however, major research universities are now increasingly interested in finding ways to encourage their faculties to put more emphasis on teaching. It is a familiar pattern in history, a pattern of trying to recover the balance lost by explosive growth in one dimension that did not give commensurate attention to another dimension—in this case the complementary rather than antagonistic dimensions of research and teaching.

It is important to be clear about this: It's not that teaching is good and research isn't, or vice versa. It is that research has stolen the rhetorical limelight. In letting that happen, we have allowed an unfortunate skewing of our image of ourselves as educators to occur. In discussions of this problem, one often hears that it's always been this way, but in fact it hasn't. In other periods we have had a more balanced understanding of these two essential components of higher education. We need to restore that balance. Within the world of higher education, if we do not understand and truly value the importance of good teaching, we have lost touch with a true understanding of the value and significance of good research. Knowing that the balance has not always been skewed should encourage us in our efforts to restore it.

But the problem of redressing the neglect that teaching has suffered in higher education in recent decades has less to to with understanding the past than it does with confronting the present and the future. In practical terms this means finding ways to enhance the instructional skills of current teaching faculty, a faculty which includes not only the tenured and tenure-track faculty members but also the graduate teaching assistants who are responsible for an estimated 30 percent of the undergraduate teaching in this country. Their needs, and the needs of the students they teach, represent the present.

The Ph.D. students we are currently guiding toward degrees are the future. What are we going to do for them and for the students they will teach that we aren't currently doing—and perhaps never have done? We know that efforts to improve teaching after the fact (the fact of graduation with the Ph.D.) achieve some success, but the greatest hope for improving college teaching over the long run lies in training new college teachers how to teach while they are still in college. Solutions for the future will undoubtedly grow out of approaches to the present, and the more sensitive and practical we are in understanding and correcting the conditions that have created the neglect of teaching, the more solid and long-lasting will be our solutions for the future.

Having set the problem within the context of historical change and removed it from the hopeless context of "That's just the way things are," we can now move on towards possible remedies for effecting the needed restoration in balance. We could present examples of what's being done at a few selected universities in the country. And these examples might be of *some* value. But every campus must, in the end, invent its own solutions to the problem, in keeping with its own identity, history, and mission. Understanding a few general principles about the dynamics of a university, and the attitudes and personalities of its faculty members—and how, perhaps, to meet a few predictable obstacles—may prove to be of *greater* value.

The problem of how to improve college teaching is not a simple one. Its solution is influenced by the extent to which many other related problems are addressed. As a starter, answers to the following questions must be obtained:

> What new or existing programs related to teaching enhancement need to be developed or modified? For whom and by whom?
>
> What obstacles need to be overcome in order to attract faculty members and graduate teaching assistants to attend and participate in the programs?
>
> What obstacles need to be overcome in order to obtain appropriate endorsements, resources, and support from the various levels of administration?
>
> How can these obstacles be overcome?

The discussion that follows will present ideas for certain types of programs, as well as a few practical observations on various approaches to overcoming obstacles. It looks at three important areas—two in the present and one for the future. Specifically, they are in-service training for current faculty, improved training for graduate teaching assistants, and an enhanced Ph.D. program which will in the not-too-distant future include some teacher training component in addition to the research training presently provided.

In-Service Programs for Faculty

One approach to enhancing faculty teaching skills involves the establishment of some sort of in-service training which would include seminars, workshops, and lectures. Designing and developing good in-service programs to help faculty enhance their teaching skills is not the problem. Getting faculty to participate in such programs, either as a member of a group or individually, is the problem. In improving teaching on campus, we are dealing with attitudes and awareness as much as with a specific group of skills. Here academe and industry differ in their understanding of in-service training. The contrast is instructive; it shows what academic leaders are up against in improving the quality of teaching on their campuses.

Corporations like IBM, AT&T, and Xerox hire people with bachelor's, master's, and Ph.D. degrees, but they aren't concerned that their new employees don't have the precise skills needed for their job assignments. Industry hires people with degrees because degrees indicate a certain level of formal education, discipline, initiative, and perseverance. Industry is willing, even eager, to teach its new employees the precise skills they need after they are hired. This is expected, common practice. And employees don't resist these in-service programs.

Some universities—realizing the need to improve instructional skills on their campuses—have attempted to follow the industry model by providing in-service programs. But faculty have often resisted these. Although they are employees of the university, faculty don't see themselves as employees in the same way as do people in industry. They insist on greater freedom. Indeed, they (rightly) insist that they were hired to exercise intelligent, intellectual independence. Faculty respond positively to power, but not so to directives. Thus, whereas industry may with confidence issue directives, academe more often must rely on persuasion.

This is where the leadership skills of department chairs and deans must come into play. With the backing of the president or provost behind them, what strategies can department chairs and deans create to get faculty to discuss what constitutes good teaching? Programs prescribed by the central administration (as contrasted with those which merely receive strong support) are generally not well supported by the faculty, because of adversarial tension between faculty and administration.

The most successful in-service programs will have two characteristics:

1. They will be sanctioned and strongly supported by the provost or president.
2. They will call upon the faculty to carry the burden of:
   a. Defining the problem in the context of their own experience as a learning community

b. Directing discussion toward formulating the best solutions for that community

c. Actively participating in whatever training program they recommend

Faculty Resistance

When faculty resist in-service training, they do so for any of several reasons. Among the most familiar are complaints that teaching is not recognized by the university's reward system in the way that research and publication are; that good teaching is impossible to define and even harder to evaluate; and that they already are good teachers, and so involvement in such a program would only cut into the already scarce amount of time available to them for research.

When faculty complain about the reward system, they have a good point. It is true, and generally accepted, that those who produce research are rewarded better than those who teach well but do not produce research. This is indeed a problem that has to be addressed by both administrators and boards of governors of universities. Provost or presidential support for enhancing instructional activities cannot be limited to exerting influence on the faculty. Top administrators must also persuade their trustees that resources—in many cases, dollars—must support such efforts if they are to be credible within the university. After all, since dollars had something to do with the elevation of research, it's only logical to suppose that dollars also can assist the restoration of a balanced emphasis on teaching and research.

This change may come about in the future, and teaching may be properly rewarded, but faculty and higher education in general cannot really afford to wait for this reform to occur to begin major efforts to improve college teaching. Legislatures and a general public already clamoring for better teaching won't wait.

Good Teaching and the Evaluation Trap

When faculty object that good teaching cannot be either defined or evaluated, they are on less-solid ground. Though the proliferation of research in teaching and learning in recent years has not come up with a single descriptive model of the good teacher, it *has* established the characteristics of good teaching, characteristics which may be realized in a wide variety of personality types and teaching styles.

Most faculty believe *they* know what good teaching is and what it does. They should be asked to share their thinking on the subject. Let them buy into the process of defining good teaching on their campus. Such participation is likely to bring out the best in their own teaching. As with other kinds of learning aimed at reforming attitudes and redirecting behaviors, much of what is known about good teaching must be discovered or rediscovered on each campus in order for it to have any effect.

Evaluation presents a more difficult problem. Many earnest efforts to improve the instructional climate on campus have become paralyzed by endless, labyrinthine debates over the problems of evaluation and the relationship between evaluation and rewards. Generally, these debates presume that if quality cannot be *quantified* it cannot be identified in any meaningful way, and so should have less importance than something which *can* be quantified, like the number of publications a faculty member has produced—whatever their quality.

In a way the emphasis on quantification and *objectivity* may also be part of the legacy of the emphasis on the sciences that began some thirty-plus years ago. Various court cases and state bureaucracies have done little to lessen the pressure of such emphasis. Once entered, it's extremely difficult to find a way out of the quantification labyrinth. The best answer to this line of thinking lies, again, in good leadership. When top scientists are asked if nonquantifiable factors have affected the formulation of their best hypotheses, they often answer yes. *Informed judgments* by well-qualified men and women make the laws of the nation, and have taken the stands for quality that have moved civilization along over many centuries. Faculty know and will say, if they are asked, what quality is—in teaching, in research, in department service. No faculty member wishes to teach badly, and all faculty members have something to contribute to an effort to enhance instruction on their campus.

Teaching Awards

Most of the resources needed to reestablish a healthy, balanced emphasis on teaching as well as on research already exist on campus—in the minds and hearts of the faculty and in the capacity for leadership in academic deans and department chairs. Often, however, valuable resources go unutilized. For example, awards for excellence in teaching. Many universities give annual awards for excellence in teaching. The number of recipients varies from university to university; sometimes it is large. This is an excellent way of recognizing good teaching. The recipients usually are selected by special faculty and student committees established for this purpose. Although in their present form such awards clearly recognize excellence in teaching, they do little to motivate other faculty to enhance their teaching skills. They aren't elective competitions after all. Researchers enter competitions to win grants, but teachers do not enter competitions to win teaching awards. Often, in fact, such awards may even reinforce the questionable notion that good teachers are born, not made.

If the awards don't really help foster better teaching in their present form, how might they be used to do so? Excellent researchers, when they receive a grant or award, often are asked to present a seminar on their work. Recipients of teaching awards, however, are seldom invited to share their knowledge or insights on good teaching with fellow faculty members. Why shouldn't they be?

Being a good teacher doesn't necessarily indicate that a faculty member would immediately know how to help his or her peers improve their teaching.

Just as reforming the community's attitude toward teaching requires some fi-nesse, so does utilizing this resource. One way to prepare award-winning faculty for the task of helping their peers is to invite them to participate in seminars in how to identify, describe, and evaluate the characteristics of good teaching. They then might also be asked to become mentors to new faculty members, and to conduct seminars on the subject of teaching excellence for the faculty at large.

At some institutions recipients of teaching awards have been encouraged to organize themselves into a committee for excellence in college teaching, under the sponsorship of the provost or president. This committee can serve as an advisory council to the president and provost, as well as sponsor various types of seminars and activities to help improve the quality of college teaching. Some support in the way of staff and a modest budget is needed to help implement these programs. Keep in mind that these recipients have been selected by faculty members and students, hence they have not been chosen and imposed from above. The point here is that awards for excellence in teaching is a fine idea that is generally not exploited as fully as it might be. As authorities on good teaching, the award winners can become the core of a faculty-owned in-service program.

The Role of the Department Chair in Improving the Quality of College Teaching

At some universities there are centrally administered programs for improv-ing teaching skills of faculty members and graduate teaching assistants. If such programs are available, it behooves the chairperson to require (or at least encourage) his or her instructors to participate. If central programs do not exist, the department should provide seminars for its own faculty and teaching assis-tants. The faculty will generally follow the lead of the department chair in this matter. If the chair feels strongly that faculty and teaching assistants need to enhance their teaching skills, and is committed to doing something about it, then it will be done. On the other hand, if chairs have a laissez-faire attitude, then chances are that very little will be done in this area.

The department chair should identify two or three of the best teachers of un-dergraduate courses in his or her department who are also reputed to be excel-lent researchers with considerable grant money. If these individuals can be per-suaded to provide leadership in improving the quality of college teaching in the department as a whole, they will make excellent role models. They would immedi-ately neutralize arguments that busy researchers don't have time to be good teachers. Some of these teacher–researchers claim that it does not take more time to be a good teacher than it does to be a bad teacher, assuming, of course, that all teachers need to spend whatever time is necessary to be current in their subject-matter discipline. Being a good teacher is a matter of attitude as much as anything else. Faculty members with teaching assignments can improve their teaching if they want to and are willing to make the effort. They must also learn how to let students know that they care about them and want to help them succeed.

With the help of two or three carefully selected faculty members, department chairs can generate a positive attitude about teaching among *all* their faculty members. This can be done effectively at a one- or two-day retreat designed specifically to discuss what constitutes good teaching in the department. Faculty need to be prepared attitudinally for such a retreat. This will take time and effort on the part of the chair and his two or three selected faculty associates. *All* of the faculty then need to be involved in planning the time, place, and agenda of the retreat. Too, an outside expert may be invited to the retreat, to serve as a catalyst and moderator. (This procedure has been followed in several major departments at Florida State University with considerable success.)

Training for Graduate Teaching Assistants

Faculty who have received teaching awards or have been otherwise honored for the excellence of their teaching should be asked to address themselves directly not only to the challenge of sharing their wisdom with their peers, but also to the problem of training the future professoriate, the graduate teaching assistants.

Should faculty be rewarded for these "extra" efforts? Of course they should. Should efforts to improve teaching wait until an adequate compensation scheme is in place? No. If a campus finds that its faculty cannot be led to participate in efforts to enhance instructional awareness without direct reward for their efforts, the need for a reform in attitudes towards higher education goes much deeper than the current imbalance between research and teaching, and it may take many years and many new hires to make any progress.

Preparing the Future Professoriate

As mentioned earlier, the best way to ensure improved teaching and a more balanced emphasis on the importance of teaching in future professors is to work some teacher training into their Ph.D. curriculum. This curriculum need not change its focus or reduce the training in research now required. The focus rather should be expanded to include at least a required unit or course in how to teach, how to design courses, and how to mount effective presentations.

If an institution has been successful in directing faculty energies toward enhancing the self-conscious profile of teaching through the kinds of seminars, colloquia, and so on mentioned earlier, it will have laid the foundation for creating and requiring such a course of its Ph.D. candidates. But there still may be political obstacles to creating a new course—especially a required one. Again, progress may require some finesse.

Normally, to add a required course to the Ph.D. curriculum would require approval of the course plan and the rationale for requiring it from several levels of curriculum committees within the institution. Members of these committees, with their usual and even traditional faculty thoroughness, would hold this and similar ideas in thoughtful hostage for many months (perhaps years), examining the context, philosophic background, and so on. If action is needed sooner, obviously other approaches need to be found.

One approach might be to provide such a course to graduate teaching assistants, required not as part of the course work for the Ph.D. but as a condition of their employment as teaching assistants. Graduate students who are not teaching assistants would also be allowed to take the course. Obviously we are talking here about steps toward changing attitudes, not a final and complete solution to this rather large and seemingly intractable problem.

Such a course, however, would translate almost immediately into better instruction for undergraduate students, and would provide for better-prepared faculty in the future. Although most graduate teaching assistants are knowledgeable in their academic discipline, at least half of them appear to lack either prior teaching experience or training in teaching (or both). Surveys conducted at some research universities indicate that "TAs" would welcome such training. Indeed, on many large campuses the teaching assistants are unionized, and almost always where they are unionized their contract requires that some sort of training in teaching be provided to them by the university. This is another good indication of a desire on the part of many graduate students for training in teaching.

At some institutions, graduate teaching assistants may be quicker than their faculty members in understanding the importance of early action to improve the quality of college teaching. In such instances it might be better to start initiating campus reform at the teaching-assistant level by selecting them to be the first recipients of teacher training programs. From there, reform might move toward a required course in college teaching for Ph.D. candidates in addition to their research training. Finally, if these activities on campus do not affect the rest of the faculty so as to move them toward a more active interest in enhancing their own instructional skills, at least participants will have the satisfaction of knowing that they are preparing more-enlightened generations of faculty to replace them.

Questions

1. Other than completed student-evaluation forms, what types of input does your chairperson get from students in your department regarding the quality of instruction they are receiving? Are negative or positive comments made about specific instructors? Give examples of the kinds of comments.

2. Have you had occasion to counsel with faculty members who have received poor evaluations for their teaching? What sorts of things are discussed? What kinds of suggestions do you give?

3. Where does teaching fit into the department's faculty culture? Is teaching a valued activity? Where does teaching rank in relation to research, service, and other activities?

4. To what extent should the improvement of teaching in the department be one of the priorities of the chairperson?

5. Are there one or more resource centers in your institution available to faculty or graduate teaching assistants who wish to enhance their teaching skills? If there are no institutional resource centers for this purpose, do you believe there should be one? If not, please explain.

6. To what extent is excellence in teaching rewarded in your department? Are there departmental or institutional awards that give special recognition to good teaching?

7. What can or should your department do to maintain a focus on the need for faculty to provide quality instruction?

8. In hiring new faculty, to what extent are efforts made to check the past teaching records of candidates by contacting their current or previous department chairs or deans?

9. To what extent are candidates who are invited to the campus for interviews given an opportunity to demonstrate their teaching ability at the undergraduate level? At the graduate level?

References

AXELROD, JOSEPH. "The Art of University Teaching." *The University Teacher as Artist.* New York: John Wiley, 1973.

COHEN, ARTHUR A., and BRAWER, FLORENCE B. *The American Community College.* 2nd ed. San Francisco: Jossey–Bass, 1988.

EBLE, KENNETH E. *Career Development of the Effective College Teacher.* Washington, DC: Association of American Colleges and the American Association of University Professors, 1971.

ERICKSON, STANFORD C., and COOK, JOHN A. *Support for Teaching at Major Universities.* Ann Arbor: Center for Research on Learning and Teaching. University of Michigan, 1980.

FARH, JIING LIH (et al.) "An Empirical Investigation of Self-Appraisal–Based Performance Evaluation." *Personnel–Psychology,* 41, 1988, pp. 141–156.

FINK, L. DEE. "The Lecture: Analyzing and Improving Its Effectiveness." In *New Directions for Teaching and Learning: The Department Chairperson's Role in Enhancing College Teaching,* 37, Spring 1989, pp. 17–30.

FREDERICK, PETER J. "Involving Students More Actively in the Classroom." In *New Directions for Teaching and Learning: The Department Chairperson's Role in Enhancing College Teaching,* 37, Spring 1989, pp. 31–40.

GAFF, GERRY J. (et al.) *The Teaching Environment: A Study of Optimum Working Conditions for Effective College Teaching.* Berkeley: Center for Research and Development in Higher Education, 1970.

GAGNE, ROBERT M., and BRIGGS, LESLIE J. *Principles of Instructional Design.* 2nd ed. New York: Holt, Rinehart & Winston, 1979.

Gordon, Thomas, and Burch, Noel. *T.E.T.—Teacher Effectiveness Training*. New York: David McKay Co., 1975.

Harlow, Linda L. "Individualized Instruction in Foreign Languages: A Survey of Programs at the College Level." *Modern Languages Journal,* 71, 1987, pp. 388–394.

Kaikai, Septimus M., and Kaikai, Regina E. *Chairpersons as Promoters of Community Service*. Catonsville, MD: Catonsville Community College. 1990. (ERIC Document Reproduction Service No. ED 321 801)

Kuh, George D., and McCarthy, Martha M. "Key Actors in the Reform of Administrative Preparation Programs." *Planning and Change,* 20, 1989, pp. 8–126.

Lee, Calvin B. T. (Ed.) *Improving College Teaching: Aids and Impediments*. Washington, DC: American Council on Education, 1966.

Mager, Robert F. *Preparing Institutional Objectives*. 2nd ed. Belmont, CA: Fearon–Pitman, 1975.

Marcus, Dora. *Lessons Learned From FIPSE Projects*. Washington, DC: Fund for the Improvement of Postsecondary Education, 1991.

Martin, Warren B. "Curriculum: Education for Character, Career and Society." *College of Character*. San Francisco: Jossey–Bass, 1982.

Near, Janet P., and Sorcinelli, Mary Deane. "Work and Life Away from Work: Predictors of Faculty Satisfaction." *Research in Higher Education,* 25, 1986, pp. 377–394.

Nelson, T. M. "Rating of Scholarly Journals by Chairpersons in the Social Sciences." *Research in Higher Education,* 19, 1983, pp. 469–497.

Noonan, John F. "Curricular Change: A Strategy for Improving Teaching." In *The Expanded Campus: Current Issues in Higher Education 1972,* edited by Dyckman W. Vermilye. San Francisco: Jossey–Bass, 1972.

O'Connell, William R., Jr., and Meeth, L. Richard. *Evaluating Teaching Improvement Programs*. New Rochelle, NY: Change Magazine Press, 1978.

Page, Jane A., and Page, Fred M. *Collegiate Instruction: Some Differences Among Faculty Members Based on Rank, Years of Experience, and School Affiliation*. Paper presented at the Annual Meeting of the Mid-South Educational Research Association, Mobile, AL, 1987. (ERIC Document Reproduction Service No. ED 289 445)

Smith, Deborah Deutsch, and Lovett, David. "The Supply and Demand of Special Education Faculty Members: Will the Supply Meet the Demand?" *Teacher Education and Special Education,* 10, 1987, pp. 88–96.

Snyder, Benson R. "The Two Curricula." *The Hidden Curriculum*. New York: Knopf, 1971.

Stone, James C. (et al.) *Toward Excellence in Teaching, Too*. Berkeley: University of California Press, 1974.

Trask, Kerry A. "The Chairperson and Teaching." In *New Directions for Teaching and Learning: The Department Chairperson's Role in Enhancing College Teaching,* 37, Spring 1989, pp. 99–107.

Weaver, Frederick. "Scholarship for the Teaching Faculty." *College Teaching,* 34(2), 1986, pp. 51–58.

Wendel, Frederick C. *Use of the Assessment Center Method in Administrator Preparation Programs,* 1988. (ERIC Document Reproduction Service No. ED 310 549)

Wilson, Robert C. (et al.) *College Professors and Their Impact on Students*. New York: John Wiley & Sons, 1975.

Part VII

Writing Goals and Developing Plans

Chapter 19. Writing Departmental Missions, Goals, and Objectives

Chapter 20. Departmental Planning

Writing Departmental Missions, Goals, and Objectives

Yogi Berra of New York Yankee baseball fame is said to have stated: "You've got to be careful if you don't know where you're going, because you might not get there!" Whether he really ever made that statement is probably a subject for debate, but it does carry a valuable message. Universities seldom have clearly defined purposes or goals which are known and understood within the institution. Instead, statements of purpose or of institutional goals are often very broad in scope, designed to satisfy every constituency, and usually impossible to measure except in the most subjective terms. In fact, they are typically developed by large committees which, through compromise, seem inclined to produce a document which keeps all options open rather than choosing specific and limited directions for future development.

Departmental faculty and the chairperson face similar difficulties at the departmental level. Statements of departmental missions, purposes, goals, objectives—whatever they may be called—seem best described as ranging from vague to nonexistent. But this is really not a criticism. The task of clearly stating departmental goals and objectives *is* formidable. It implies the existence of clearly defined and understood general goals of the college and university in which the department is a contributing unit. It requires input, discussion, understanding, and support by the faculty, the dean, and higher-level administrators. Last, but not least, it requires written statements specific enough that internal and/or external reviewers can determine whether the stated goals are being attained. Without the latter requirement, goal statements offer no basis for the kind of positive feedback that can reinforce existing activities or provide direction to improve programs.

Those who control the purse strings, especially university administrators and granting agencies, look for and expect to find mission and goal statements in the proposals and requests they read and review. The department's success in receiving funds and grants from the granting agencies may well depend on how clearly its mission and goal statements are written, and the extent to which the department's actions and practices are consistent with the contents of those statements. Accrediting agencies also look for clearly written mission and goal statements in proposals submitted by institutions or professional programs seeking accreditation or reaccreditation. The granting of accreditation is based not only on the degree to which institutions or programs meet minimum standards of quality, but also on the extent to which educational goals are being met.

Why should a department have goals? At a time when accountability is repeatedly used as a warning or a threat, department members not only should have a statement of their purpose, but also should be able to point to a set of goals they expect to achieve. They should be able to express the professional aspirations of the department in ways that will allow those aspirations to be compared with actual accomplishments. The chairperson of a department that has stated its goals clearly and realistically, and has indeed achieved its goals within a certain period of time, can make a good case for a fair slice of the economic pie that the dean keeps in the cupboard. Aside from the practical advantage of being able to say "We said we would accomplish these things, and we have done so," goal setting serves another, more theoretical, purpose: It helps academicians not only to know their purposes but also to clarify their ideas about how those purposes can be fulfilled.

Involving faculty in the process of formulating mission and goal statements helps department members articulate their feelings about their proper roles and functions in the framework of the college or the university. A hallmark of any intelligent activity, and especially intellectual activity, is that the participants know what they are about. It is not unreasonable to expect a department to have a sense of what it is doing and where it is going. The mission statement serves as the foundation on which the department builds its programs and justifies the grounds for its existence within the university. It provides guidance for departmental change and serves as a basis for comparing achievements with earlier aspirations.

Mission Statements

A mission statement should clearly identify the ongoing purposes, functions, and aspirations of a department, college, or university. A department mission statement will usually parallel the mission statement of the university, if such a statement already exists. It describes the scope and character of the teaching, research, and service activities of the department. It identifies the persons or groups that the department serves, tells how it serves them, and describes the results of the service. In addition, the statement should describe any resources or activities that distinguish the department from others, and should emphasize any unique qualities the department may have. The statement does *not* include a time sequence or a time limit for the mission to be accomplished, since the activities will be ongoing unless or until the mission is changed.

Mission statements concerned with teaching will indicate which fields of study are covered by the department, which instructional programs are being provided, at which levels (undergraduate or graduate), for which type or types of students, and which needs are being met. Following are examples of excerpts of statements dealing with the instructional part of departmental missions, but none of the excerpts is a complete mission statement in itself. Each statement comes from the mission statement of the department whose name appears at the end of the statement.

- To provide courses for students majoring in psychology leading to the bachelor's degree or master's degree [A Psychology Department]
- To provide specialized chemistry courses for students majoring in other departments [A Chemistry Department]
- To provide courses in the biological sciences to satisfy the general education needs for certain students [A Biology Department]
- To develop skills in students such as communication and analytical skills that will be useful to them in whatever careers they pursue [An English Department]
- To make graduate degree programs in educational administration available to residents of the state through off-campus credit offerings [An Educational Administration Department]
- To provide undergraduate instruction in physics for physics majors and to prepare elementary and secondary pre-service teachers to meet state certification requirements [A Physics Department]
- To teach administrators and workers to understand how to take advantage of modern computers in the workplace [A Computer Science Department]
- To train professionals who are capable of doing research in the methodology of biostatistics and to apply their statistical and quantitative knowledge to the solution of problems encountered in the community health field [A Biostatistics Department]

If research is one of the primary purposes of the department, the mission statement should indicate the specific areas of research in which the department specializes, and who are the beneficiaries of the research efforts. Examples of statements dealing with the research portion of a department's mission are:

- To conduct research on the history of mathematics [A Mathematics Department]

- Research is focused primarily on the pulmonary and cardiovascular systems and the effect of environmental agents on human and animal hearts [A Physiology Department]

If service is one of the purposes of the department, the mission statement should indicate which service or services are being provided, and for whom. An example of this would be:

- Meets the needs of commercial fisherman in the Southeast by providing extension services [A Fisheries Department]

And, as mentioned previously, any unique resources or activities of the department should be mentioned in the mission statement. An example of this would be:

- Offers programs in bilingual–bicultural education, with special emphasis in Greek and Hispanic studies [A Foreign Languages Department]

These statements are important because they set the tone, as well as some parameters, according to which the department will operate. A mission statement is not a statement of what the department *wants* to be, but of its current role and how it contributes to the university as a whole. For example, an undergraduate department may aspire to offer a graduate degree, and this may be a worthy *goal* of the department. But a graduate program is not a part of the mission statement of the department until the goal of the establishment of a graduate degree program has been reached. A mission statement should indicate the *general direction* in which the department is moving and should furnish a frame of reference from which department goals may be derived.

Chairpersons should beware of mission statements that are too broad and thus fail to show how the department differs from other departments. Mission statements that are too narrow describe activities in too much detail. Following are two examples of complete mission statements based on actual statements found in university catalogs. The first is from a behavioral science department in a school of public health:

The Department of Behavioral Sciences is concerned with the application of social science theory, methodology, and empirical findings to the study of health and illness. The department serves as a resource to the School by providing the basis for systematic consideration and study of the social and cultural aspects of health problems and theories from the disciplines of sociology, anthropology, social psychology, and political science. Departmental students are prepared primarily for careers in research and teaching. The central focus of the department is in major areas of medical sociology and anthropology, including: individual motivation in health behavior; sociocultural factors in disease; health organizations and professions; comparative healing systems; and comparative sociopolitical contexts of public health.

The next mission statement is from an English department in an urban university:

> The Department of English primarily serves the individual undergraduate student,
> the academic community, and society in general. The department seeks to de-
> velop the students' reading comprehension and writing skills in order to help
> insure maximum realization of their potential. The faculty hopes to develop
> understanding of the humanistic heritage and at the same time to stimulate the
> students' imagination and sense of joy in life by familiarizing them with British
> and American literature and with other literatures which have contributed to the
> culture. Courses are designed to foster creativity, and the department offers spe-
> cific courses for students with identified creative gifts. The department attempts to
> teach the fundamentals of research; to stimulate the use of scholarly methods and
> attitudes throughout its programs; and to encourage the individual scholarship of
> its members. Through the discharge of the responsibilities described above, the
> Department of English strives to prepare students for such professions as teach-
> ing, law, and medicine, and for an individually enriched and socially productive
> life.

These examples are not perfect. A mission statement that meets the criteria already discussed is indeed difficult to write. Nevertheless, each statement attempts to describe the particular department in a way that shows its special characteristics. The first of the two statements is more precise and specific than the other, perhaps because of the nature of the discipline. As can be seen from the preceding two examples, mission statements sometimes contain both abstract and concrete elements, which may range from the grandiose to the specific. They often contain ideological components representing widely held beliefs about the value of a college education, and they include societal as well as professional aspirations. The idealistic components of the mission statement have strong roots in American culture and continue to be affirmed, despite the odds against their being achieved. The mission statement is often based on two assumptions: that progress is an incremental movement towards some high aim, and that the aim will not actually be achieved.

Many departments write their own mission statements, but not all do. Mission statements can be prepared by planning officials, external consultants, legislative committees, administrators, and of course faculty committees. Many mission statements have a formal aura about them; they often appear in master-plan documents, budget-request documents, long-range plans, and development grant applications. Mission statements often contain information and data that serve as guides for making appropriate decisions about a department's commitments. Often the statement about the department that appears in the university catalog stands as a mission statement. The chairperson, in conjunction with a faculty committee, should conduct an annual review of the mission statement and bring it up-to-date, if necessary. Systematic redefinition of the department's mission is appropriate at certain times—for example, after the departure of senior faculty members; when curricular changes are called for; and when resources become so scarce that the department's historic mission cannot be achieved.

What some departments call mission statements, others call goal statements. Many departments that have such statements prefer to call them *goals* rather than *missions*. What they are called is relatively unimportant compared with the substance of the statements. This chapter suggests a progression of specificity of aims, using the terms *mission, goal,* and *objective* to delineate increasing specificity. Nevertheless, there are numerous nomenclatures for the different levels of specificity and the ways in which they may be elaborated. One purpose of this chapter is to discuss and clarify this conceptualization. However, the vocabulary used here should not necessarily be considered superior to others; it is simply one that is widely used.

Statements of Goals and Objectives

Having discussed mission, we can now move on to the second and third levels of specificity—*goals* and *objectives.* A *goal* is a statement of a desired accomplishment which will contribute to the realization of the educational mission of the department. It has a specified or implied end, whereas missions are continuous. The accomplishment of a goal usually requires a time period on the order of five years. This is not to say that all goal statements must indicate the period of time within which they must be achieved; goals may be long-term or short-term. Too, since predicting when a certain goal will be reached is sometimes difficult, intermediate goals may have to be set and further plans developed. But each and every goal must be realizable sooner or later. And the department most assuredly ought to be able to tell when a goal finally has been accomplished.

In addition to specifying a certain end, goal statements have other characteristics: They represent a logical extension of the mission statement; they are oriented toward specific results; they are explicit; and they are supported by a series of objectives. A *goal,* therefore, is a statement of intention to achieve a specified result that is compatible with and will contribute towards the accomplishment of the mission or purpose of the department and institution. It is the end toward which one or more activities are aimed. An *objective* is a statement of intention to achieve a specified result which, when realized, will contribute to the realization of the goal.

Both goal and objective statements indicate projected outcomes and stipulate the activities leading to them. To speak of *objectives* is to speak of the concrete, the observable, the knowable. Although missions and some goals may be ambiguous and imprecise, objectives generally specify some observable product or result. Objectives are, of course, closely related to the goals from which they are derived. For this reason, an objective taken out of context may be indistinguishable from a goal statement. Though some objectives in other contexts might constitute goals, objectives generally are more concerned with short-term effects than are goals, and usually specify a time by which the result is expected to be accomplished. Well-stated goals and objectives have these characteristics:

- They are consistent with the missions or goals from which they are derived.
- They are oriented towards specific outcomes.
- They identify activities by which the outcome or result is to be achieved.
- They are measurable in some way.
- They suggest an expected qualitative or quantitative change or accomplishment.
- They stipulate a time by which the result will be achieved.

An example of a goal in an English department is: "To identify entering freshmen with deficiencies in reading and writing skills and to improve those basic skills."

According to our criteria, the objectives derived from this goal should specify steps that must be taken to identify the freshmen, and the measure of achievement or improvement that would be considered satisfactory by a certain time. Two objectives for this goal might be:

1. To administer and score Test ABC for all freshmen by October 30
2. To raise the average score of deficient freshmen on Test ABC to the national norm of 540 by May 30

Outcome and Activity Statements

Objectives that focus exclusively on results are often called outcome statements. Statments that typically describe what students, faculty, staff members, and others do are called activity statements. The second objective in the preceding example, "To raise the average score of deficient freshmen on Test ABC to the national norm of 540 by May 30," is an activity statement. It could be converted to an outcome statement by rewording it in the following manner: "By May 30, 87 percent of all freshmen will score at least 540 on Test ABC."

Some faculty members resist stating objectives in quantitative terms because the numbers and percentages that are so often a part of those statements appear to be arbitrary. In some cases such objections are justified. Why specify 87 percent instead of 83 or 90 percent, or any other percent for that matter? There may well be no reason for designating 87 percent except that on the basis of past experience it seems to be an attainable percentage. Good judgment and common sense are needed when stating measurable outcomes.

Activity statements not linked to outcomes do not translate into good statements of objectives. Nevertheless, activity statements frequently are used *as* objectives because the activities of educational processes are more readily observable than the outcomes. To observe a faculty member teaching and to specify what, where, and for how long he or she teaches is easy; to measure the long-term effects of that teaching is not so easy. When educational objectives are stated primarily as activities, too little emphasis is placed on educational outcomes. Although clearly specifying educational outcomes is an extremely difficult task, and in some disciplines may be well-nigh impossible, faculty discussion of desired outcomes might be beneficial for all. The faculty should be able to distinguish between activities and outcomes, and wherever possible should link outcomes with activities when formulating department objectives.

A Conceptual Framework for Identifying Valid Missions, Goals, and Objectives

Universities, and departments within universities, really do not differ significantly from business and industry in terms of the existence of an operating management system. They are alike in that they all require *resources,* conduct certain *activities* utilizing the resources, and produce various *outputs.* In educational institutions *resources* include, faculty, staff, students, money, physical facilities, books, and time. *Activities* include teaching, conducting research, providing service, planning, managing, keeping records, gathering information, and procuring funds. *Outputs* include graduates, new knowledge, publications improved procedures, courses, and innovations. The lists that follow depict symbolically the operational elements of a university or department viewed from the perspective of a management system.

RESOURCES	+	ACTIVITIES	=	OUTPUTS
Faculty		Teaching		Graduates
Staff		Conducting Research		New Knowledge
Students		Providing Service		Publications
Money		Planning		Improved Procedures
Physical Facilities		Managing		Courses
Books		Keeping Records		Innovations
Time		Gathering Information		
		Procuring Funds		

The essential point of this discussion is that mission statements may include activities from the *Activities* list and/or outcomes from the *Outputs* list, and may provide information about special resources or facilities available to a department that make it unique among departments of similar disciplines and missions. What we have defined as goals and objectives are outcomes from the *Outputs* list. If academic goals are to be realized, the department must also acquire or maintain resources, and plan to use them effectively. In many cases, departments do set goals that deal with the acquisition and management of resources. A distinction may therefore be made between what are sometimes called *primary goals* and *support goals*. Primary goals are directly related to educational mission—i.e., outcomes from the familiar triad of teaching, conducting research, and providing service. Support goals are advocated not for themselves but for establishing conditions or situations whereby the primary goals can be achieved. Support goals within the department are concerned with acquiring or maintaining resources such as those in the *Resources* list.

Those activities in the *Activities* list that are related directly to the realization of the educational outcomes may be included in the primary goal statement. Activities directly related to the management or acquisition of any of the resources contained in the *Resource* list may be included in the support goal statement.

Such goals as "To increase the number of students with departmental majors," or "To obtain more funding and more faculty" are called support goals since students, faculty, and money are *resources* needed to accomplish a desired outcome. A support goal for one department may be a primary goal for another. For example, a goal to acquire a new laboratory facility is a support goal as far as an academic department is concerned, since the laboratory is a resource needed for faculty research output. For the physical plant department responsible for building the laboratory, however, the laboratory is not a resource but an output, and for that department completion of the laboratory would be a primary goal.

Following are examples of primary and support goals:

To produce graduates who will be eligible for admission to medical school [Primary teaching goal, biology department]

To maintain the department's level of publications in scholarly jounals held during the past three-year period [Primary research goal, any department]

To provide advice and assistance to teacher education centers throughout the state [Primary service goal, education department]

To establish an internship program for seniors in law enforcement [Primary goal, criminology department]

To involve faculty in a faculty development program [Support goal, any department]

To establish a system of department record keeping consistent with university policy [Support goal, any department]

To obtain additional laboratory equipment [Support goal, any science department]

As mentioned earlier, goals must be realistic and attainable. The chairperson should try to avoid ill-conceived or badly stated goals. Following is a list of reasons that many goals cannot be realized or are flawed in other ways:

- Goals may be too specific, allowing for too little flexibility to take advantage of unforeseen opportunities or to deviate from a narrow path that may become blocked.

- Goals may be too broad or abstract, to the extent that the faculty cannot agree on what constitutes achievement.
- Goals may be too simple and trivial, to the point that even when attained they have little professional or political significance.
- Goals may be too grandiose to be attained given the existing faculty, student body, or resources.
- Goals may be too optimistic given the time or administrative support available.
- Goals may be overambitious in relation to the attitudes of the administration, the public, or the legislature.
- Goals may be too pessimistic or underambitious and may not reflect adequately the abilities and aspirations of the faculty.
- Goals may be contradictory and conflicting. When goals contributed by individual faculty members are not reviewed for consistency or realism by the chairperson or a faculty committee, the resulting set of goals may be contradictory.
- Goals may lack sufficient support from the faculty. If a chairperson develops a set of goals without faculty input and consensus, the goals may not be taken seriously or may be resisted or opposed.

Involving Faculty in Setting Goals

The process whereby a department arrives at its goals is intimately related to the quality of the goals produced. An academic department is made up of persons who are likely to vary considerably in age, personality, style, and ability. Despite the stereotype of "the professor," anyone with academic experience knows that department members are rarely peas in a pod. Whereas it might be easier to get consistent and coherent department goals from a group of like-minded persons, the diversity of the faculty is probably a healthy thing, for a diverse faculty will have complementary skills. The problem the chairperson faces is how to derive a set of compatible expectations from persons whose styles and abilities differ. An unsatisfactory solution to the problem is to construct a department mold or procrustean bed that all members must fit. Such an approach is bound to stifle talent, creativity, and individuality.

How can the chairperson encourage the department to develop its goals? No matter how appropriate the goals may be for a given department, they cannot be easily implemented without the support of the majority of the faculty. The chairperson, of course, should have some ideas concerning the direction the department might take, and he or she should present those ideas tactfully to avoid having them rejected out of hand. The chairperson's leadership style will influence the way the department arrives at its goals. Some alternative approaches to goal setting are listed below.

- The chairperson can prepare statements of department goals and objectives and circulate them to the faculty to stimulate discussion and input.
- The department chairperson can ask a faculty committee to discuss and recommend appropriate goals and objectives for formal review by the entire department faculty.
- The department can form a composite of the individual goals of the department faculty and make this composite the basic department statement of goals and objectives.
- The department can survey similar departments that have already established legitimate goals and objectives.
- The department can employ a consultant or a representative from an accrediting agency to review the department's strengths and support appropriate goals and objectives.

Whichever approach to goal setting is followed, the goals that the faculty ultimately adopts must be ranked. Thus, the faculty assigns priorities to its goals. This step is critical because it provides a guide for others who might attempt to evaluate the department. A priority list is also important when the faculty wants to reward members who make significant contributions toward achieving high-priority department goals. The department priority rankings of goals could be weighted and included in the annual faculty evaluation.

One further refinement of the planning sequence—mission, goals, and objectives—should be mentioned. In implementing an objective, discrete tasks that must be accomplished should be listed. Developing a timetable for the completion of each task is sometimes useful. The term *milestone* is used to designate a task and the time by which it will be finished. Most granting agencies require that proposals for the funding of projects include a timetable with the designated milestones. A task that includes an activity, an outcome, and a timetable is a sort of mini-objective that is completed on the way to implementing the larger objective. In the same way, the completion of an objective contributes to the attainment of a goal. Objectives, then, can sometimes be seen as intermediate goals. Whether a statement of department aims or intentions is called a task, an objective, or a goal does not matter as much as whether those statements can be expressed in a logical, orderly, and precise manner.

In summary: Definitions of missions, goals, and objectives are best understood as stipulations. *Mission* and *goal* can be interchanged without doing violence to the language, and indeed some persons do so; others interchange the terms *goals* and *objectives*. So, goals as well as mission represent the department's aspirations. Goals are simply more specific and action-oriented expressions of the results that the department hopes to achieve. Some departments feel that goals must be expressed in behavioral terms—that is to say, the goal should contain a specific time frame and indicators of achievement, so that at the end of the specified time the department can easily assess whether the goal has been achieved. Other departments do not insist on such a high degree of quantification as goal statements. Certainly some areas of endeavor are more amenable to behaviorally stated goals than others.

Questions

1. Does your department have a written mission statement? If so, what is it?
2. To what extent does the department mission statement follow the guidelines contained in this chapter for developing mission statements?
3. If your mission statement does not follow the guidelines, develop a new mission statement or modify the existing mission statement so that the guidelines are followed.
4. From your mission statement, write some goal and objective statements for your department that might serve as a basis for the development of action plans.

References

ANDERSON, G. LESTER. "Organizational Diversity." In *New Directions for Institutional Research: Examining Departmental Management,* no. 10, edited by John C. Smart and James R. Montgomery. San Francisco: Jossey–Bass, 1976.

ARGYRIS, CHRIS. (et al.) *Leadership in the 1980's.* Cambridge, MA: Institute for Educational Management, Harvard University, 1980.

ARGYRIS, CHRIS. "Interpersonal Barriers to Decision-making." *Harvard Business Review,* February 1966, pp. 84–97.

ARGYRIS, CHRIS, and SCHON, DONALD A. *Theory in Practice: Increasing Professional Effectiveness.* San Francisco: Jossey–Bass, 1974.

ASTIN, ALEXANDER W., and SCHERRI, RITA A. *Maximizing Leadership Effectiveness: Impact of Administrative Style on Faculty and Students.* San Francisco: Jossey–Bass, 1980.

ATWELL, ROBERT H., and GREEN MADELINE F. *Academic Leaders as Managers.* San Francisco: Jossey–Bass, 1981.

BALDRIDGE, J. VICTOR (et al.) *Policy Making and Effective Leadership: A National Study of Academic Management.* San Francisco: Jossey–Bass, 1978.

BIRNBAUM, ROBERT. *Individual Preferences and Organizational Goals: Consistency and Diversity in the Futures Desired by Campus Leaders.* ASHE Annual Meeting Paper, Baltimore, 1987. (ERIC Document Reproduction Service No. ED 292 384)

BLAKE, ROBERT R., and MOUTON, JANE S. *The Management Grid.* Houston: Gulf, 1964.

BOK, DEREK. *Higher Learning.* Cambridge: Harvard University Press, 1986.

BOWEN, HOWARD R. "Goals: The Intended Outcomes of Higher Education." *Investment in Learning.* San Francisco: Jossey–Bass, 1977.

BOWKER, LEE H., and LYNCH, DAVID M. *Chairing a Small Department.* Paper presented at the National Conference for Department Chairs, Orlando, 1985. (ERIC Document Reproduction Service No. ED 256 222)

Brown, David G. *Leadership Vitality: A Workup for Academic Administrators.* Washington, DC: American Council on Education, 1980.

Burns, Tom, and Stalker, G. M. *Management of Innovation.* New York: Methuen, 1961.

Carnegie Commission On Higher Education. *Governance of Higher Education: Six Priority Problems.* New York: McGraw–Hill, 1973.

Carter, Charles M. "Are Small Liberal Arts Colleges Selling Out Their Liberal Arts?" *College and University,* 62(1), 1986, pp. 55–65.

Cartwright, Dorwin, and Zander, Alvin (Eds.) *Group Dynamics: Research and Theory.* 3rd ed. New York: Harper & Row, 1968.

Clark, Burton R. *The Academic Life. Small Worlds. Different Worlds.* A Carnegie Foundation Special Report. Princeton: The Carnegie Foundation, 1987.

Cohen, Arthur M., and Brawer, Florence B. *The American Community College.* 2nd ed. San Francisco: Jossey–Bass, 1988.

Cohen, Michael D., and March, James G. (Eds.) *Leadership and Ambiguity: The American College President.* Carnegie Commission on Higher Education, New York: McGraw–Hill, 1974.

Corson, John J. *The Governance of Colleges and Universities.* New York: McGraw–Hill, 1960.

Fuller, Bruce. "A Framework for Academic Planning." *Journal of Higher Education,* January–February 1976, pp. 65–77.

Gies, Joseph. *The Liberal Arts College: The Next Twenty-five Years.* 1984. (ERIC Document Reproduction Service No. ED 261 604)

Gross, Edward. "University Organizations: A Study of Goals." In *Academic Governance,* edited by J. Victor Baldridge. Berkeley: McCutchan, 1976.

Gross, Edward, and Grambsch, Paul V. *University Goals and Academic Power: A Study in Conflict and Cooperation.* Washington, DC: American Council on Education, 1968.

Guest, Robert H.; Hersey, Paul; and Blanchard, Kenneth H. *Organizational Change Through Effective Leadership.* Englewood Cliffs: Prentice–Hall, 1977.

Herr, Kay U. *Chairperson's Handbook.* 1989. (ERIC Document Reproduction Service No. ED 311 838)

Hersey, Paul, and Blanchard, Kenneth H. *Management of Organizational Behavior: Utilizing Human Resources.* 3rd ed. Englewood Cliffs: Prentice–Hall, 1977.

Kaikai, Septimus M., and Kaikai, Regina E. *Chairpersons as Promoters of Community Service.* Catonsville, MD: Catonsville Community College, 1990. (ERIC Document Reproduction Service No. ED 321 801)

Kerssen, Jeff. *Accuracy in Academia? "Professor" as a Problematic Cultural Term.* Paper presented at the Annual Meeting of the Western Speech Communication Association, Salt Lake City, 1987. (ERIC Document Reproduction Service No. ED 281 257)

Konrad, Abram G., and McNeal, Joanne. "Goals in Canadian Universities." *Canadian Journal of Higher Education,* 14, 1984, pp. 31–40.

Larson, Jon (et al.) "Higher Education Planning Perspectives: An Historical Overview, the Administrators' Perspectives, and the View from Two-year Colleges." *CUPA Journal,* 39(2), 1988, pp. 1–14.

Mager, Robert F. *Goal Analysis.* Belmont, CA: Fearon–Pitman, 1972.

MARCH, JAMES G. *How We Talk and How We Act: Administrative Theory and Administrative Life.* Urbana: University of Illinois Press, 1980.

MIDDLEHURST, ROBIN. "Evaluation and Development of a Leadership Course for Heads of Academic Departments in the United Kingdom." *Higher Education Management,* 1(2), 1989, pp. 170–182.

MITCHELL, MARY B., and WHEELER, DANIEL W. *A Grounded Theory of Chairperson Management Strategy.* ASHE 1987 Annual Meeting Paper, San Diego, 1987. (ERIC Document Reproduction Service No. ED 281 465)

PERROW, CHARLES. "The Analysis of Goals in Complex Organizations." In *Readings on Modern Organizations,* edited by Amitai Etzioni. Englewood Cliffs: Prentice–Hall, 1969.

PETERSON, RICHARD E. *College Goals and the Challenge of Effectiveness.* Institutional Research Program for Higher Education, Princeton: Educational Testing Service, 1971.

RICHMAN, BARRY M., and FARMER, RICHARD N. *Leadership, Goals, and Power in Higher Education: A Contingency and Open-Systems Approach to Effective Management,* San Francisco: Jossey–Bass, 1974.

SCHUSTER, JACK H. *Governing Tomorrow's Campus, Perspectives and Agendas.* Washington, DC: American Council on Education, 1989.

SCHUTTENBERG, ERNEST M.; MCAEDALE, RICHARD J.; and THOMAS, WARREN S. "Goal Setting in Educational Organizations: A Systems Perspective." *Peabody Journal of Education,* July 1979, pp. 272–278.

SEMLACK, WILLIAM D. *Corporate Culture in a University Setting: An Analysis of Theory "X," Theory "Y," and Theory "Z" Cultures Within University Academic Departments.* Paper presented at the Annual Meeting of the Central States Speech Association, Cincinnati, 1986. (ERIC Document Reproduction Service No. ED 269 822)

SERGIOVANNI, THOMAS J., and CORBALLY, JOHN E. *Leadership and Organizational Culture.* Chicago: University of Illinois Press, 1988.

SPRUNGER, BENJAMIN E., and BERGQUIST, WILLIAM H. *Handbook for College Administration.* Washington, DC: Council for the Advancement of Small Colleges, 1980.

TANNENBAUM, ROBERT, and SCHMIDT, WARREN H. "How to Choose a Leadership Pattern." *Harvard Educational Review,* March–April 1957, pp. 95–101.

Toward Institutional Goal-Consciousness. Princeton: Educational Testing Service, 1971.

TRIVETT, DAVID A. *Goals for Higher Education: Definitions and Directions.* ERIC/Higher Education Research Report no. 6. Washington, DC: American Association for Higher Education, 1973.

Chapter 20

Departmental Planning

Planning is something that all organizations are encouraged to do. Governments do it. Private business does it. So do educational institutions. Because planning is an important part of management, the planning process has been defined, dissected, and analyzed by many writers of "management" textbooks. Different authors perceive planning differently, and definitions vary from the vague to the very precise. Some authors subdivide the planning process into five or six substeps, whereas others divide it into twenty or more. For our purposes, planning will be defined as "the process of making decisions in the present concerning which strategies and actions are to be be taken in the future in order that certain goals or outcomes may be realized by a specified date." Decision making consists of choosing one or more courses of action from among a group of alternative courses of action. The end result of the planning process is a document containing statements of goals and objectives and when they are to be achieved, and a description of present and future strategies and actions that need to be taken in order for the goals and objectives to be achieved. If they are to be achieved in four years or less, the plan may be considered short-term. If, on the other hand, the time designated for the goals to be achieved is five years or more, the plan is considered long-term. Both short- and long-term plans should be reviewed annually to determine if the goals and courses of action are still relevant, or need to be modified in response to changing situations.

The chairperson is the department's chief planner, whether we choose to recognize this fact or not. Some departments have planning committees which, under the leadership (and with the help) of the chairperson, develop departmental mission/goal statements and plans that are submitted to the department faculty for approval. Although most chairs agree that goal setting and planning are important to a department and can provide it with stability and direction, not all departments have well-articulated planning documents. The extent to which such documents exist usually depends on the priority given to planning activities by the chairperson. In the largest sense of the term "planning," the department as a whole may in fact effect some changes. For example, departments can consciously decide to deemphasize analytical chemistry and build up organic chemistry, junk the international program in political science and concentrate on public administration, or starve the power-grid group in electrical engineering and fatten up the photovoltaic group. None of these planning decisions, however, can come to fruition if the day-to-day decisions of the chairperson and his or her committees run counter to such plans.

Some additional examples may illustrate how difficult it is for plans to be realized unless the chairperson is conscious of his or her role as planner. The chemistry department knows that all the agency funding will be concentrated in organic chemistry, yet the enrollment in analytical chemistry, particularly the graduate enrollment, keeps going up. In addition, the best candidate for the assistant professor position in the department, who was interviewed at the November national meetings, is an analytical chemist. Why did the department even interview an analytical chemist? The senior professor in the department—who also is an analytical chemist, a member of the promotion and tenure committee, and a member of the appointments committee—asked the chairperson to interview the young chemist as a courtesy because "Some of the fellows in the Society thought we ought to have a look at him."

Another example: The political science department, during the October national meeting, couldn't find just the right person for its public administration position. Lo and behold, the appointments committee chairperson, a black, puts on the chairperson's desk the stunning résumé of a young black political scientist who states that she would like to begin her professional career in that department, but whose specialty is international relations. The chairperson shifts uneasily in his seat as he reads the résumé, remembering last month's tongue-lashing from the dean *and* the provost about the department's lack of minorities and women.

And yet another example: Several members of the state's society of professional engineers, on their way home from lobbying the governor for a new building for the engineering college, stop off to talk to the chairperson of the electrical engineering department. They remind him that little work is being done on increasing the efficient transmission of electricity in power lines, and that all this nonsense about photovoltaics is simply a way of avoiding thinking about real-life power-grid problems. The chairperson, unable to enlighten this group and depressed about the recent editorial in the local newspaper concerning the eroded influence of the department's once-favored power-grid group, stares out the window, wondering "Just where is photovoltaics going?"

The chair must make many commitments on behalf of the department—and some commitments will have inevitable consequences. With every decision the chair is in effect mapping out a de facto plan for the department's future. Circumstances and opportunities present the chair with a blank canvas on which to sketch a course (or courses) of action. The accumulation of what may seem like small, discrete decisions will, at some point in the future, show patterns and trends that constitute a plan.

The chair needs to be conscious of how these decisions, and patterns of decisions, may affect the ability of the department to achieve important goals over the short and long terms. Every faculty appointment (or tenure decision), for example, has potentially long-term consequences. Searching for new faculty with cutting-edge research skills, and "stockpiling" them against predicted shortages, may result in a department with a strong position among competitors ten years down the road. Or it may just as well result in a department focused on the wrong subject! Ten years from now, new research directions in the field may require an entirely different set of skills. Similarly, a department that searches today for faculty with certain kinds of skills may find in a few years that it has negotiated away its capability to provide an acceptable level and quality of undergraduate education. Faculty may be hired with the understanding that their research assignment is primary, and that their productivity in this arena is the most important criterion for success. In years ahead, however, as the institution faces shifts in student interest, tighter funding for research and graduate education, and a strong state interest in enhancing the quality and effectiveness of undergraduate education, the department may wish it had not been so single-minded in pursuit of research "stars."

In effect there are two kinds of planning, both necessary. One is the planning that establishes goals and priorities. The other is the kind that is not perceived as planning at all. It operates on a "plan as you go" principle. Decisions and commitments are made almost daily—and every commitment made now will have consequences later, and the department will ultimately become the sum of those commitments and their consequences. Commitments made in response to unanticipated pressures or opportunities *may* have a strong positive effect on the future of the department *if* the commitments contribute to the realization of the department's mission and goals. On the other hand, commitments made without consideration of mission or goals can cause confusion, conflict, and turmoil among the department's faculty members. Departments perceived as having no direction are generally not given favored status in matters related to funding, faculty lines, and support staff positions.

Some leaders and managers plan intuitively. They seem to follow planning procedures without consciously identifying each step in the process. Others methodically follow a checklist of planning procedures developed by their faculty committees or found in textbooks written by professional planners. Regardless of how it is done, planning needs to be carried out on a continuous, regularly scheduled basis if it is to be effective. Departmental mission statements, goals, and action plans should be reviewed annually to determine if they are still relevant. They need to be updated to accommodate changes that might have occurred since the previous planning document was prepared—changes such as institutional missions and priorities, regional needs, student numbers and interests, competencies represented by current faculty, facilities, equipment, budget, and so on.

Conscientious departmental planning on a continual basis is time-consuming for those involved. Faculty members who have so many other responsibilities and deadline dates are generally not self-motivated to take time from activities that they believe require more immediate attention. Department chairpersons who place a high priority on planning as a continuous process must constantly remind their faculty of its importance, and encourage their planning committees to stay on task—all the while giving them guidance, and deadline dates for completion of specific steps in the process.

Developing Action Plans

The hierarchy of missions, goals, objectives, and tasks has been covered in some detail, but we have not discussed the process by which a department selects appropriate means for reaching goals. The careful consideration of how goals and objectives may best be reached is called *action planning.*

The following scenario has been developed as an example of how departments go about the business of developing action plans. For the purpose of this scenario, let us select the English department in an urban university mentioned in the preceding chapter. For the convenience of the reader, the mission statement of that department is repeated below.

> The Department of English primarily serves the individual undergraduate student, the academic community, and society in general. The department seeks to develop the students' reading comprehension and writing skills in order to help insure maximum realization of their potential. The faculty hopes to develop understanding of the humanistic heritage and at the same time to stimulate the students' imagination and sense of joy in life by familiarizing them with British and American literature and with other literatures which have contributed to the culture. Courses are designed to foster creativity, and the department offers specific courses for students with identified creative gifts. The department attempts to teach the fundamentals of research; to stimulate the use of scholarly methods and attitudes throughout its programs; and to encourage the individual scholarship of its members. Through the discharge of the responsibilities described above, the Department of English strives to prepare students for such professions as teaching, law, and medicine, and for an individually enriched and socially productive life.

One department goal related to the department's mission statement is "To identify entering freshmen with deficiencies in reading and writing skills and to improve those basic skills." In our scenario this goal was one of many recommended by a faculty committee appointed by the chairperson, and was formulated in response to the faculty's general feeling that many incoming students were failing because they could not handle the material assigned. Some essay examinations did not contain a single sentence that was grammatically correct.

Since there was general agreement that freshman reading and writing skills needed improvement, a committee was appointed to develop an action plan for implementing the goal. The committee first prepared a clear statement of the department's status as it related to the goal. The department had a well-qualified, hard-working faculty that had no special training in remedial work. Some older faculty members were shocked at the idea that a university should concern itself with ill-prepared students and felt that the problem could be solved by raising admissions standards. Other faculty members were actively interested in working closely with students whose skills needed improvement.

The committee then prepared a list of alternative strategies and tried to specify for each strategy objectives and tasks that might help attain the goal. In this instance, three possible means to the same end were discussed. The first alternative was a set of objectives and tasks that focused on establishing a reading laboratory, with equipment acquired through external funding. The second alternative involved using prepackaged, pretested materials from the university's resource center. The third strategy suggested using undergraduates in a program of intensive tutoring. The committee leaned toward the idea of a reading laboratory but abandoned that notion when the department failed in its initial attempts to get a laboratory funded. The second strategy, using prepackaged materials, was chosen because it seemed a better way of doing things given the available data. A minority of the faculty members preferred the tutoring plan, but they could not convince their colleagues that it was feasible.

The next step in preparing the action plan was to describe in detail the objectives and tasks that, using prepackaged materials, would help reach the goal and to specify a means of evaluating whether the action plan had been successful. The project would be considered successful if one-third of the participants brought their skills up to the average level of entering freshmen based on national norms. The goal suggested two objectives: (1) to administer and score a test for all freshmen; and (2) to take them through a program that would improve their performance.

With the help of colleagues in the education department, the faculty of the English department selected a standardized test, specified a plan for administering and scoring it, and drafted letters explaining the program to the incoming freshmen. The second objective was also broken down into discrete activities and thoroughly described. The department decided to hire two graduate students to supervise the distribution and use of the prepackaged remedial materials. The students also were to monitor the progress of the freshmen students in the program and keep records. At the end of two quarters, the students would be retested. Those whose reading skills had improved would transfer to freshman English. Those who did not improve to the specified point would continue in the program. Thirty percent of the students who participated in the program made significant gains and entered the freshman course. In this case, the program proved moderately successful.

This case has been presented to give an idea of what action planning is like. The steps of action planning can be briefly summarized as follows:

1. Start with a clear statement of a desired goal.

2. Describe the department's status as it relates to the goal—i.e., show in a quantifiable way the relationship between where the department is now and where it wants to be.

3. List alternative courses of action that might be a means to achieving the goal or objective.
4. Analyze each alternative course of action, listing the tasks required and attempting to anticipate the consequences. Specify a means of evaluating the success of the action plans.
5. Rank the courses of action in preferred order of implementation.
6. Begin to implement the top-ranked course of action. Be prepared to shift to the next-highest-ranked course of action if serious problems arise.

Some administrators use a simple technique to evaluate suggested courses of action for achieving a desired goal. Each course of action is rated in terms of (1) potential for achieving the goal, (2) cost, and (3) feasibility. The rating scale can be a simple one, such as "high," "medium," or "low."

Table 20.1 shows a table that a chairperson developed to help him choose among alternative courses of action.

Another hypothetical case may be helpful in pointing out the relationships among the statement of mission or purpose, the annual report, goals, objectives, tasks, and action plans. The department, a small physics department, provides the following statement for the college catalogue:

> The mission of the department is to provide undergraduate instruction in physics for physics majors and for elementary and secondary preservice teachers, and to fulfill some of the general education needs of the university in the physical sciences. In addition, the department shall contribute to new knowledge in physics and physics education and shall serve local and regional needs in this area through programs for in-service teachers.

The department's annual report shows that it has six faculty members, adequate office space, good facilities for instruction, and an annual budget of around $200,000. The department's assets include well-equipped teaching laboratories, two young faculty members who are especially enthusiastic and recognized as excellent teachers, and other faculty members who have good theoreti-

TABLE *20.1* **Evaluation and Selection of Alternative Courses of Action**

PROPOSED ACTIVITY OR ACTION	Potential for Achieving Goal	Cost	Feasibility
#1	High	Low	Medium
#2	High	High	Medium
#3	Low	Low	High

cal capabilities in the field of physics. The report recognizes that the department members generally lack expertise and proven performance in experimental physics.

Let us assume that state law requires that faculty members teach a minimum of twelve hours per week or the equivalent, and that the state college system has set minimum class size at twelve students. The need for general education will remain constant. The number of physics majors is expected to remain the same—i.e., about forty students. The need for elementary and secondary science teachers is expected to rise. In addition, there is a continuing need to upgrade the training of general science and physics teachers in the large regional school system.

Although this statement of the department's status is minimal, it will serve the purposes of this example. A greatly expanded information base would be essential for effective department planning and goal setting; for example, data about enrollment levels, number of majors, number of course offerings, faculty assignment patterns, and patterns of financial expenditures should be recorded over a period of several years. The resulting department "fact book" would be useful for planning and goal setting, preparing annual reports, writing grant proposals, justifying budget requests, and simplifying many of the department chairperson's other tasks.

At the urging of the chairperson, the physics department developed the following goals: (1) to increase the current level of faculty research and publications; (2) to train elementary education majors in physical science topics that are part of the public school curriculum; (3) to plan and implement a summer workshop for high school teachers; and (4) to improve the writing skills of undergraduate physics majors. Following are the goals with their objectives and tasks:

Goal 1: To increase the current level of faculty research and publications

> *Objective 1:* Increase the amount of faculty time assigned to research.
>> *Task:* Increase each faculty member's research assignment by 5 percent per year, to a level of at least 35 percent per faculty member.
>> *Task:* To compensate for increased research assignments, increase class size to reduce the number of classes to be taught.
> *Objective 2:* Seek and acquire funding for research projects from external sources.
>> *Task:* Conduct a proposal writing seminar in fall quarter.
>> *Task:* Supply clerical and technical assistance for proposal writing.
>> *Task:* Write grant proposals to potential donors.
> *Objective 3:* Publish six articles in refereed journals over the next two years.

Task: Establish a biweekly research seminar for faculty members to discuss ideas and projects.

Task: Discuss and, if feasible, implement a reward structure for publications.

Task: Provide clerical and technical assistance for research projects

Goal 2: To train elementary education majors in physical science topics that are part of the public school curriculum

Objective 1: Revise curriculum of general physics course to suit needs of education majors.

Task: Meet with science supervisors in public school system to outline topics emphasized in curriculum—October 1.

Task: Alter course curriculum to encompass desired change—December 1.

Objective 2: Teach and evaluate revised course.

Task: Teach revised course—February 1–June 15.

Task: Administer and score department evaluation forms—June 15–20.

Goal 3: To plan and implement a summer workshop for high school teachers

Objective 1: Prepare list of desired subjects for high school teachers.

Task: Appoint committee to study National Science Foundation recommendations—September 15.

Task: Meet with school board and curriculum supervisor to establish needs—October 15.

Objective 2: Plan and publicize new program.

Task: Develop curriculum and select faculty—November 15.

Task: Advertise workshop in educational journals and newspapers—December onward.

Objective 3: Conduct and evaluate summer workshop.

Task: Teach workshop as planned—July 1–July 26.

Task: Prepare and administer questionnaire to evaluate program—July 25.

Task: Prepare and administer follow-up questionnaire—December 1.

Goal 4: To improve the writing skills of undergraduate physics majors

Objective 1: Plan writing seminar for fall quarter.

Task: Contact English department and establish interdepartment committee—January 1.

Task: Develop course in technical writing—March 15.

Objective 2: Teach and evaluate writing seminar.
  Task: Announce course offering for majors, and encourage students to register—September of next year.
  Task: Read and evaluate students' efforts.

Although the goals, objectives, and tasks are presented here in outline form, the outlines themselves are the result of action planning. After the physics department established its four goals, the faculty met to plan how these goals could best be implemented. Each goal became the focus of an action plan that encompassed the steps described earlier. The objectives and tasks were formulated after the department members considered a variety of possible ways of achieving the goals.

Abandoning an Objective

When discussing the revision of the curriculum of the general physics course for elementary education majors, which is Objective 1 under Goal 2, the faculty members spent a great deal of time and effort considering an additional objective: converting the course to self-paced instruction using the computer. This objective called for the following series of tasks.

Objective: Convert the course to self-paced instruction using the computer.
  Task: Review experience of other institutions using a computerized system—September 1–October 1. Estimated cost—$600 (faculty time and travel)
  Task: Develop baseline data of test scores of students taking the course by the conventional method—September 1–June 1. Estimated cost—$500 (faculty time, student assistant time, data analysis)
  Task: Write programs needed to implement the system—September 1–January 1. Estimated cost—$6,500 (faculty time, programmer time, computer charges)
  Task: Test programs—January 1–March 1. Estimated cost—$2,500 (faculty time, computer time)
  Task: Evaluate achievement of students in computer-assisted programs—March 1–September 1. Estimated cost—$500 (faculty time, data analysis)

According to the calculations presented in the series of tasks list, the cost of implementing the program would have been more than $10,000. The results of the first task, however, revealed that computer-assisted instruction worked better with students who were already highly motivated than with students who had limited mathematical and scientific interests and skills. The goal of a computer-assisted course was abandoned before much money was spent. The experience of other institutions was sufficient to convince the chairperson and the faculty that the contemplated innovation was not likely to succeed. Instead, the department decided to identify what subjects the schools wanted their prospective teachers to know. Then the chairperson assigned the department's most dynamic teacher to the course. The course requirements were tailored to the needs and abilities of nonmajors, and the evaluation showed its popularity. Some faculty members, however, thought that the new course was not quite rigorous enough, and the debate about its merits continues.

The idea to computerize the course, which was subsequently abandoned, actually came from the action planning that was undertaken while the first goal—to increase the level of research and number of publications—was being considered. Here the department was reacting to the fact that a member's application for promotion was rejected on the grounds of insufficient publications. The goal of increased publications was a result of the department's unease over the college's increasingly rigorous promotion and tenure policy. While the faculty was trying to conceive of ways to get more time to do research, the switch to computer-assisted instruction was suggested. Teaching through the computer would save faculty teaching time, which could be spent in research. Translating the idea of computerized teaching to a goal and an action plan, which included a description of how the objective was to be accomplished, led to the rejection of the idea. Implementing the idea would have required a significant amount of computer programming, storage of large amounts of information and test items, purchase of additional terminals for student use, and payment of staff to monitor the terminals for many hours every day. Evidence of the increased costs did not lead to the immediate abandonment of the tentative objective, though it did dampen some of the early enthusiasm. Proceeding with the action plan described above, however, the chairperson and department got enough information to warrant abandoning the plan.

To be able to distinguish between ideas and goals is useful. Computer-assisted instruction seemed to be—indeed, was—a good idea. When translated into a goal, with objectives and an action plan, the idea's flaws became more and more apparent. The university has been the repository of innumerable ideas that have devoured time and money for years. Usually no one has bothered to identify the goals, the objectives, or results associated with the idea. No one has identified the measurable and desired results that the idea is supposed to produce, and no time scale for accomplishing results has been established. That the idea itself endures is not surprising, for there is no way to assess progress or lack of progress of an idea. If programs are to be effective, however, they need to develop measurable goals and objectives that are oriented toward results.

Not every goal or objective can always be attained, but when a legitimate goal is not met, an active and strong department needs to review its activities and procedures seriously. The weak department is one that does not learn from mistakes and repeats useless routines year after year.

Examples of Different Formats for Planning

From time to time, the term "planning" is embellished with attractive and attention-getting modifiers. Examples are strategic planning; planning, programming, and budgeting systems (PPBS); and integrated planning. At first glance it may appear that these new terms represent new planning procedures. In fact, however, they do not. What they do is either present different formats for the standard procedures with which we are familiar, or place increased emphasis on one or more of the steps in the process. Following are brief descriptions of standard planning procedures; strategic planning; planning, programming, and budgeting systems (PPBS); and integrated planning.

STANDARD PLANNING PROCEDURES

Most planners start out by identifying a problem or a goal that needs to be solved or achieved. They then list possible alternative courses of action that might be taken to realize the desired outcomes. The possible consequences of each of the alternative courses is considered in terms of cost, feasibility, and probability of solving the problem or achieving the goal. After eliminating those courses of action that are unrealistic, they select the course or courses of action that will be accepted, and project dates for their implementation.

STRATEGIC PLANNING

Strategic planning basically follows the same procedures. However, in setting goals or developing various courses of action, the organization or unit which does the planning "positions" itself to take the best advantage of its environment. This requires a careful study of all possible environmental conditions that may affect the planning for, or maintaining of, a new or existing program. Historically, most colleges and universities have evolved by doing just this, sometimes consciously but often as the sum of many perceptive acts of adaptation. Only recently have we begun to put a formal label on this process of intelligent adaptation, and it is now usually called strategic planning. In a commercial setting, a corporation may strategize by figuring out what products are marketable and which kinds of products it should emphasize, and why. Its goals may include maximizing profits, but it may have other goals, too. For example, a desire to be socially responsible may result in a strategic decision not to do business in certain countries. Or a company whose products may be damaging to health could decide it wants to get out of one line of business and into another.

Although universities do not always put the label "strategic planning" on their efforts to adapt to a changing environment, they may nevertheless learn to think strategically about various aspects of their "business." Environments which universities serve often undergo change. Demand for certain kinds of graduates changes (witness the decline of engineering in the '70s and its reemergence in the '80s); the availability of faculty with certain areas of expertise may change; a state or regional economy may undergo dramatic shifts; and/or student interest in certain curricula may change (such as the dramatic decline in the study of Greek and Latin). Any or all of these may have profound effects on the fortunes of individual departments.

Strategic planning, whatever the method used, is nothing more than an attempt to look ahead and study the environmental forces that may operate on the department. It is not an effort to predict the future, but rather one to anticipate and include in their planning considerations those events and trends that show a reasonable probability of occurring. A department plans strategically, for example, when it sets up a hypothetical new program and consults broadly to see if there will be any demand for graduates thereof, or prospects for external funding. It also plans strategically when it identifies potential trends that may affect existing courses and programs. For example, many institutions are implementing multicultural components in their liberal arts curricula. Too, anthropology departments might see this as an opportunity to provide a broader service course or two, and enhance cross-enrollment by students in other major fields.

PLANNING, PROGRAMMING, AND BUDGETING SYSTEMS (PPBS)

This system involves the articulation of program goals, the identification of specific activities and time lines designed to accomplish those goals, and the identification of the funding that would be required during each of one or more years to carry out all of the activities related to the accomplishment of the goals. A program is a group of related activities, functions, and objectives that contribute to the achievement of specified goals. For example, objectives and functions having to do with teaching or instruction are placed in the program of "Instruction." If a stated goal is to provide instruction to all students in an institution, the program of instruction might consist of all courses offered at the institution. If the goal is to provide undergraduate instruction to all students in an institution, the program would include all undergraduate courses offered at the institution. The program of "Research" would include related activities and objectives that contribute to the research effort, and the program of "Service" would consist of a group of related activities and objectives that have to do with service.

The difficulty in defining "Program" is so great that the definition of what constitutes a program varies from one institution to another. In addition to different types of programs of instruction, some institutions using PPBS have designated "academic support" and "student services" as separate institutional programs. Each program includes all the related activities and services that together contribute to the achievement of its respective goal. "Academic advising," including all activities related to this function, is sometimes designated as an institutional program in its own right, and sometimes as a separate component of a larger program—such as "instruction," "academic support," or "student services." Occasionally, academic advising activities are decentralized (that is, an adviser may be placed in each department), in which case they become an integral part of a program of instruction.

In PPBS, requested funding is based on the cost of achieving predetermined goals within defined programs, rather than on the cost of maintaining and/or expanding organizational units such as an English department, a biology department, or a history department. Budget categories such as salaries, expenses, and equipment are assigned to the goals and programs defined by the institution, rather than to academic departments and administrative units.

Basically, PPBS not only incorporates the idea that an organization's goals and objectives should determine its budget, but also includes a long-range planning component. PPBS is strongly influenced by the rationale and techniques of systems analysis and represents an attempt to bridge the gap between planning and budgeting. PPBS also involves attaching cost estimates to the multiyear planning goals and objectives after the most efficient and effective means for achieving the programs' objectives have been identified. The selection and number of component activities contained in a program depend on the scope of the stated goal and the preferences of the person developing the system.

A budget plan that assigns moneys to organizational units usually focuses on resources as input to the instruction process rather than on output and goals, whereas a program budget plan that assigns moneys to defined outputs provides the means to fund activities leading to the outputs and goals. In order to arrive at an institutional budget request, using PPBS program definitions, each academic department will determine a budget for each of the programs at the departmental level. For example: Of the four goals of the Physics department mentioned in the preceding section on Developing Action Plans, Goal 1 ("To increase the current level of faculty research and publications") would be included in the Program of Research; and Goals 2, 3, and 4, ("To train elementary education majors in physical science topics that are part of the public school curriculum," "To plan and implement a summer workshop for high school teachers," and "To improve the writing skills of undergraduate physics majors) would be placed in the Program of Instruction. Budget categories such as salaries, expense, and equipment are prorated among the departmental programs. Departments will submit their budget requests to the dean, who will aggregate them into college budget requests, also utilizing the same program definitions. The president's office will aggregate budget requests submitted by the deans, and develop an institutional budget request.

The statements of goals and objectives for several years, and the resources required to achieve them, become extremely tenuous during periods of rising costs. Utilizing institutional program activities as a basis for budget planning and management therefore becomes much more difficult than using organizational structures such as departments. The need to revise five-year projections during each annual budget preparation, for example, may lead to incremental adjustments. In colleges and universities, long-range projections are subject to extensive revisions, partly because the turnover rate for chairpersons is high, and program priorities within departments change as frequently. Whenever new administrators, regardless of level, search for ways to implement fresh ideas within the department, school, or college, the probability is great that older goals and objectives will be changed. Rather than trying to follow a fully developed comprehensive plan to bring about change, most administrators adopt a strategy of shifting budgeted funds gradually from one set of programs to another.

For the above reasons, most institutions no longer use PPBS in preparing and presenting budget requests. Some of the analytical techniques developed within the PPBS approach, however, still have value in department planning. For example, the planning for a new program will be much improved if objectives, alternatives, workload measures, and resource requirements are estimated before the program is implemented.

Individual departments should not attempt to implement a PPB system solely for the purpose of facilitating data compilation for the budget request, especially if the dean or administrator is not familiar with or sympathetic to the system. PPBS, properly implemented, provides a great deal of detail and clarity, but the hard work of developing a system may be wasted if the department's priorities clash with the institution's priorities. In some institutions, experience has shown that when departments attempted five-year plans, much effort was devoted to projecting needs for adding new specialty courses in the face of declining enrollments. This kind of expanded need may be inserted in any budget request, regardless of the budgeting system in use. A department has a much greater chance of being successful in its requests, however, if it fully, accurately, and realistically justifies its needs, regardless of the budgetary system used.

INTEGRATED PLANNING

Integrated planning can best be explained with an illustration. Suppose a department decides that two years hence it will offer an additional specialty or major within its degree program. To reach that goal, planning has to be conducted in several areas. One area is curriculum planning. Another is planning for enrollment of new students. Still another is planning for additional faculty assistance. Planning may also be needed for more classroom, laboratory, or office space. If new equipment is required, plans must be made for acquiring the equipment. A budget plan is also needed to ensure appropriate coordination between the availability of funds and payment schedules.

Each of these plans contains courses of action and time schedules for their completion. Moreover, these actions and time schedules need to be in phase with each other so that actions to implement related objectives will take place smoothly and in the right order. For example, it would not be wise to have new equipment delivered for installation in the new laboratory before that is a reality unless there is other space in which to store it temporarily. Likewise, students should not be enrolled until necessary classroom space becomes available, and it may not be prudent to bring new faculty to the campus until there is office space for them. And similarly, the planning for laboratory rooms needs to be coordinated with curriculum planning, and the time for purchasing equipment should be in sync with the availability of funds.

Of course many other types of coordination need to take place. Integrated planning, therefore, is the coordination and merging of several plans, each in different areas, each with different objectives, but all related to each other in that all are working towards the implementation of a single, overall, common goal. Proper integration and coordination will assure that actions from different plans will not conflict with each other, and that unnecessary lapses of time will not occur between the completion of an action in one plan and the beginning of the next required action in a different but related plan.

The Need for Sound Judgment in Planning

In this chapter we have discussed ways in which the department can report its activities and pursue a rational course in attempting to chart its future. The need for a sense of purpose, the relationship of goals to the overall purpose, and the formulation of objectives that have measurable or observable outcomes have been detailed. Planning has been discussed here mainly in the language of behavioral objectives.

Although many academicians are put off by the language of behavioral objectives and its industrial counterpart (management by objectives), others are quite taken with these concepts. Some education planners seem to think that simply stating objectives in behavioral terms with clear specification of outcomes is all that is needed to clear up confusion in the university. Even if a department can state its objectives with clarity and precision, it still must be able to assess the quality of those objectives. Whether a department's objectives are good depends on much more than the form in which those aims are stated. This chapter has suggested ways in which some clarity in the statement of purposes and goals may be attained, but their qualitative assessment depends on the good judgment and insight of the chairperson and the department. A chairperson can help unify the faculty members by involving them in developing department missions and goals.

Department members who have been successful in obtaining grants from external sources know that to specify their plans using the terminology *mission, goals,* and *objectives* is useful and convincing. Stating the department's planned activities in ways similar to those described in this chapter can be a valuable tool for obtaining resources at a time of increasing competition for available resources. The chairperson must decide how much precision and quantification can sensibly be used in reporting and planning the department's activities. Effective leadership includes the ability to forsee the consequences of one's actions. Planning a department's activities intelligently implies that the chairperson should have a good idea of what will happen to the department if the plans are carried out.

Questions

1. List, according to the following categories, some of your department's more important accomplishments during the past year:
   - Teaching—including curriculum development, new programs, and innovative methods
   - Research and publications of individual faculty members
   - Service to the university, region, and nation
   - Important decisions related to department policies concerning faculty, students, and staff; curriculum; committee structures; governance; expenditure of travel funds; and so forth
2. List, according to the categories given above, your aspirations for your department for the coming year. Formulate goal statements based on these aspirations.
3. Select a specific, genuine goal that your department wishes to implement in the near future. Develop as comprehensive an action plan as you can, including objectives and a time frame. Try to use the nomenclature suggested in the chapter.

References

ANDERSON, G. LESTER. "Organizational Diversity." In *New Directions for Institutional Research: Examining Departmental Management,* no. 10, edited by John C. Smart and James R. Montgomery. San Francisco: Jossey–Bass, 1976.

ARGYRIS, CHRIS. "Interpersonal Barriers to Decision-making." *Harvard Business Review,* February 1966, pp. 84–97.

ARGYRIS, CHRIS, and SCHON, DONALD A. *Theory in Practice: Increasing Professional Effectiveness.* San Francisco: Jossey–Bass, 1974.

ARGYRIS, CHRIS (et al.). *Leadership in the 1980's.* Cambridge, MA: Institute for Educational Management, Harvard University, 1980.

ASTIN, ALEXANDER W., and SCHERRI, RITA A. *Maximizing Leadership Effectiveness: Impact of Administrative Style on Faculty and Students.* San Francisco: Jossey–Bass, 1980.

ATWELL, ROBERT H., and GREEN MADELINE F. *Academic Leaders as Managers.* San Francisco: Jossey–Bass, 1981.

BALDRIDGE, J. VICTOR (et al.) *Policy Making and Effective Leadership: A National Study of Academic Management.* San Francisco: Jossey–Bass, 1978.

BARAK, ROBERT (et al.) *The Arizona Board of Regents Task Force on Excellence, Efficiency and Competitiveness.* Final Report and Working Papers. 4 vols. 1988. (ERIC Document Reproduction Service No. ED 306 803)

BARZUN, JACQUES. *The American University: How It Runs, Where It Is Going.* New York: Harper & Row, 1968.

BOBBITT, H. RANDOLPH, and BEHLING, ORLANDO C. "Organizational Behavior: A Review of the Literature." *Journal of Higher Education,* January–February 1981, pp. 29–44.

BOK, DEREK. *Higher Learning.* Cambridge: Harvard University Press, 1986.

BROWN, DAVID G. *Leadership Vitality: A Workup for Academic Administrators.* Washington, DC: American Council on Education, 1980.

BRUBACHER, JOHN S., and RUDY, WILLIS. *Higher Education in Transition.* 3rd ed. New York: Harper & Row, 1976.

BURNS, TOM, and STALKER, G. M. *Management of Innovation.* New York: Methuen, 1961.

CARTER, CHARLES M. "Are Small Liberal Arts Colleges Selling Out Their Liberal Arts?" *College and University,* 62 (1), 1986, pp. 55–65.

CLARK, BURTON R. *The Academic Life. Small Worlds. Different Worlds.* A Carnegie Foundation Special Report. Princeton: The Carnegie Foundation, 1987.

COHEN, ARTHUR M., and BRAWER, FLORENCE B. *The American Community College.* 2nd ed. San Francisco: Jossey–Bass, 1988.

COHEN, MICHAEL D., and MARCH, JAMES G. (Eds.) *Leadership and Ambiguity: The American College President.* Carnegie Commission on Higher Education. New York: McGraw–Hill, 1974.

CORSON, JOHN J. *The Governance of Colleges and Universities.* New York: McGraw–Hill, 1960.

CUMMINGS, L. L., and DUNHAM, RANDALL B. *Introduction to Organizational Behavior: Text and Readings.* Homewood, IL: Richard D. Irwin, 1980.

GIES, JOSEPH. *The Liberal Arts College: The Next Twenty-five Years.* 1984. (ERIC Document Reproduction Service No. ED 261 604)

GUEST, ROBERT H.; HERSEY, PAUL; and BLANCHARD, KENNETH H. *Organizational Change Through Effective Leadership.* Englewood Cliffs: Prentice–Hall, 1977.

HALSTED, D. KENT. *Statewide Planning in Higher Education.* Washington, DC: Government Printing Office, 1974.

HERR, KAY U. *Chairperson's Handbook.* 1989. (ERIC Document Reproduction Service No. ED 311 838)

HERSEY, PAUL, and BLANCHARD, KENNETH H. *Management of Organizational Behavior: Utilizing Human Resources.* 3rd ed. Englewood Cliffs: Prentice–Hall, 1977.

KERR, CLARK. "Administration in an Era of Change and Conflict." *Educational Record,* Winter 1973, pp. 38–46.

KERSSEN, JEFF. *Accurary in Academia? "Professor" as a Problematic Cultural Term.* Paper presented at the Annual Meeting of the Western Speech Communication Association, Salt Lake City, 1987. (ERIC Document Reproduction Service No. ED 281 257)

KONRAD, ABRAM G., and MCNEAL, JOANNE. "Goals in Canadian Universities." *Canadian Journal of Higher Education,* 14, 1984, pp. 31–40.

LARSON, JON (et al.) "Higher Education Planning Perspectives: An Historical Overview, the Administrators' Perspectives, and the View from Two-year Colleges." *CUPA Journal,* 39, 1988, pp. 1–14.

LYNCH, DAVID, and BOWKER, LEE. *The Status of Adult and Continuing Education Within American Institutions of Higher Learning.* Indiana University of Pennsylvania Institute for Advanced Research, 1989. (ERIC Document Reproduction Service No. ED 311 816)

MARCH, JAMES G. *How We Talk and How We Act: Administrative Theory and Administrative Life.* Urbana: University of Illinois Press, 1980.

MCGANNON, BARRY, and JAMES, S. J. "Guide to Academic Planning—St. Louis University." In *The Academic Department or Division Chairman: A Complex Role,* edited by James Brann and Thomas A. Emmet, pp. 269–296. Detroit: Balamp, 1972.

MIDDLEHURST, ROBIN. "Evaluation and Development of a Leadership Course for Heads of Academic Departments in the United Kingdom." *Higher Education Management,* 1 (2), 1989, pp. 170–182.

MILLETT, JOHN D. *New Structures of Campus Power: Success and Failures of Emerging Forms of Institutional Governance.* San Francisco: Jossey–Bass, 1978.

———. *Management, Governance and Leadership: A Guide for College and University Administrators.* New York: American Management Association, 1980.

MITCHELL, MARY B., and WHEELER, DANIEL W. *A Grounded Theory of Chairperson Management Strategy.* ASHE 1987 Annual Meeting Paper, San Diego, 1987. (ERIC Document Reproduction Service No. ED 281 465)

MURPHY, PATRICK E. "The Promises and Pitfalls of Marketing Research in Higher Education." *Liberal Education,* Spring 1980, pp. 102–115.

MURRAY, ROBERT K. "On Departmental Development: A Theory." *The Journal of General Education,* October 1964, pp. 227–236.

NEWMAN, FRANK. "Taking the Helm." In *The Third Century: Twenty-six Prominent Americans Speculate on the Educational Future.* New Rochelle, NY: Change Magazine Press, 1976.

PESEAU, BRUCE A. *Quantitatively Based Peer Program Identification.* Paper presented at the Annual Conference of the Mid-South Educational Research Association. Louisville, KY, 1988. (ERIC Document Reproduction Service No. ED 301 553)

RICHMAN, BARRY M., and FARMER, RICHARD N. *Leadership, Goals, and Power in Higher Education: A Contingency and Open-Systems Approach to Effective Management.* San Francisco: Jossey–Bass, 1974.

SCHUSTER, JACK H. *Governing Tomorrow's Campus, Perspectives and Agendas.* Washington, DC: American Council on Education, 1989.

SEMLACK, WILLIAM D. *Corporate Culture in a University Setting: An Analysis of Theory "X," Theory "Y," and Theory "Z" Cultures Within University Academic Departments.* Paper presented at the Annual Meeting of the Central States Speech Association, Cincinnati, 1986. (ERIC Document Reproduction Service No. ED 269 822)

SERGIOVANNI, THOMAS J., and CORBALLY, JOHN E. *Leadership and Organizational Culture.* Chicago: University of Illinois Press, 1988.

SPRUNGER, BENJAMIN E., and BERGQUIST, WILLIAM H. *Handbook for College Administration.* Washington, DC: Council for the Advancement of Small Colleges, 1980.

STEWART, W. G. "Selected Management Functions in the Role of Division Chairpersons in Multi-Campus Community Colleges." Doctoral Dissertation, North Texas State University, 1981. *Dissertation Abstracts International,* 42, 3034-A [University Microfilm No. 812898], 1982.

TANNENBAUM, ROBERT, and SCHMIDT, WARREN H. "How To Choose a Leadership Pattern." *Harvard Educational Review,* March–April 1957, pp. 95–101.

WHITMORE, JON. *Handbook for Theatre Department Chairs.* Association for Communication Administration. Annondale, VA: Council of Theatre Chairs and Deans, 1988. (ERIC Document Reproduction Service No. ED 305 855)

Part **VIII**

RESOURCES

Chapter 21.   Generating University and College Budgets

Chapter 22.   Funding the Department

Generating University and College Budgets

Chairpersons who are responsible for preparing or supervising the preparation of budget requests should have a general understanding of the budget process at all levels, and of the sequence of events preceding appropriation for the institution as a whole. This global view should include an appreciation of the budget review process both within and outside the university, and of budget cycles, alternative budgeting systems, and the language of budgeting. Such awareness will not necessarily lead to an increase in department allocation. It will, however, provide an understanding of those political and economic realities that affect the budgetary process; and it will also facilitate communication with a concerned faculty.

Many institutions begin preparing a budget request for the coming year's operation as much as a year in advance, and the chairperson must be able to communicate anticipated needs. The individual budgets are reviewed at each level of the hierarchy, with each department chairperson meeting with the dean, and each dean with the academic vice-president, and then all the top administrators meeting with the president. The institution's board of trustees approves the final budget request, and, in the case of a public institution, the request is submitted to the appropriate state agencies for analysis and final approval.

Private Institutions

In the case of private colleges and universities, budget requests are reviewed and analyzed within the institution, and approval by boards of trustees is the final action necessary before internal distribution of funds. In formulating budget requests, chairpersons in private colleges and universities should be mindful of the institution's general financial health. They should be aware of the status of the endowment fund and the recent pattern of gifts and bequests. Since tuition payments constitute a sizeable portion of the income of many private schools, chairpersons should be able to anticipate the effects of increased tuition on department enrollments. At many private institutions, faculty members are expected to participate actively in a variety of fund-raising activities, in addition to generating contracts and grants.

Public Institutions

Budget requests from public institutions, even if approved by boards of trustees, are subject to external review and analysis before being acted on by the state legislature and the governor. It may be useful to review the legislative budget process in a typical state. Following are the steps involved:

1. When the board of trustees of a university or a university system has reviewed, analyzed, and approved an annual budget request, it is submitted to the office of the governor.

2. The governor, with the assistance of his or her budget staff, has the responsibility of analyzing budget requests from each state agency, including universities, and incorporating all of them into what is considered the official state budget proposal. Copies are transmitted to the house of representatives and to the state senate.

3. The Higher Education and Appropriations committees of the house, and their counterpart committees in the senate, separately review the governor's higher-education budget proposal. These committees have the opportunity to recommend modifications to the governor's budget and add or subtract projects.

4. Copies of the budget request(s) that are transmitted by the universities to the governor's office are sent at the same time to the staffs of the appropriate house and senate committees. By providing the staffs with an opportunity to become familiar with the original budget requests before the governor has acted on them, they are better prepared to analyze the governor's proposal as soon as it is received by the house and senate, and to incorporate whatever priorities the legislature may have.

5. The governor's proposal, as modified by the respective legislative committees, goes to the floors of both the house and the senate, where further amendments may be made by each. Lobbyists have an opportunity to try to persuade individual legislators to support projects. The house and senate vote on their own version of the budget.

6. The final budget from each of the legislative bodies goes to a conference committee, to reconcile differences. The conference committee is made up of representatives from both house and senate.

7. The reconciled budget that comes out of the conference committee is voted on separately by the entire house and senate. The vote must be "Yes" or "No." If "No," then the budget is returned to the conference committee for further revision, and comes back again to the house and senate for the final vote.

8. Once approved by the house and senate, the budget is returned to the governor, who can approve it as received or veto parts of it on a line-item basis.

9. The budget now goes to the universities or the university system, as the case may be, for allocation within the institutions.

The depth and complexity of the external analyses depend on whether the university operates independently or is part of a university system. The University of Michigan, for example, is not a member of a university system. It will transmit its budget request directly to the governor's state budget agency and to offices of appropriate legislative staffs. On the other hand, Florida State University, because it is one of several members of a state university system under a single governing board, will transmit its institutional budget request to the central staff of the Florida university system for review and analysis. The central staff will examine budget requests from each institution in the system and submit a system recommendation to the governor's office and to the appropriate legislative staffs. In the Florida system, the budget request of each institution is identified in the system recommendation.

In other state systems, individual institutional requests are submitted to the system's office for aggregation into a system request. The aggregate request then is submitted to the governor's office and legislative staffs without identifying individual institutions. In this type of system the institution's top officials meet together with the system staff and participate in the budget development process. The system staff interprets the state budget guidelines and prepares the combined budget request, which is submitted to the system's coordinating or governing board for approval. It is then transmitted to the governor's state budget agency and the legislative budget staffs, which often meet with institutional representatives and the system staff during the preparation stages to ensure that the budget request meets the needs of both the executive and the legislative branches of government.

Thus, the institutions in the system may be listed separately in the system request and appropriations act, or they may be aggregated by program or some other classification system without institutional identification. Because many state legislatures have developed their own priorities for higher education, copies of the institutional or system budget requests may be submitted to the legislative staff at the same time that the request is sent to a governor's budget agency. In almost all states, however, the governor's state budget request to the legislature is still treated as the official budget proposal.

At the state level, the possibility for increased appropriations depends on the level of economic activity and the taxes collected. Through the process of estimating tax revenues, state officials estimate the amount of "new" money that will become available. Legislatures almost always test budget requests against these estimates and against legislative priorities. Department chairpersons can obtain a ballpark estimate of "new" money for higher education by noting the priority given to education and relating it to the estimated percent increase in state tax revenues or moneys available for appropriation, an increase that is usually well publicized.

Within a bicameral state legislature, each chamber reviews budget requests and emphasizes its own individually determined state priorities. For this reason, the "super bowl" of the legislative appropriations process is the conference committee, created jointly by the two chambers to work out their differences. Because of the complexity and magnitude of the state programs, many important funding details are listed only in work papers or exist in "understandings" among state officials, legislators, and their staffs. Usually only a few items are of sufficient priority to be listed separately in the appropriations documents. Because the house of representatives, the senate, and the state budget agency each has only one or two persons functioning as higher education budget analysts, more unwritten rules and understandings about higher education budgets and appropriations may exist than are ever listed in the published appropriations act; there often is not sufficient time to spell out all details. Sometimes, as is the case in Florida, a "letter of intent" follows the appropriations act and gives supplemental instructions regarding the use of appropriated funds.

In recent years a few states have returned to biennial budgets in the hope that reducing the number of budget cycles will stimulate better planning and program analysis preceding preparation of the budget request. Inflation and rising energy costs, however, can also require supplemental appropriations in the second year. Furthermore, when legislators meet annually, they are tempted to "redo" portions of the budget in the second year. Nevertheless, the published two-year appropriation can provide some sense of continuity and confidence for department chairpersons, since actions in the second year of the biennium tend to involve supplemental funding.

In formulating department budgets, chairpersons in public institutions that are part of state systems should be aware of the process whereby a system budget request is formulated. They should know what the main issues at their institution are and what the system's priorities are. They should stay as informed as possible about the status of the request from start to appropriation. Knowledge of the schedule of activities at the legislative and system levels may help chairpersons plan functions at the department level. This type of information, as general as it may be, helps chairpersons put their department's priorities in a wider perspective and set their expectations at realistic levels. Department chairpersons in public institutions that are not part of university or college systems should be especially sensitive to legislative schedules and actions, which are transmitted directly to the institutions rather than through the central staff of a system.

The chairperson, then, should take a more global view of the budget process and learn as much as possible about financial conditions and priorities at all levels. If the legislature uses a formula to appropriate funds, the chairperson should know what the components of the formula are. In the case of an institution that is a part of a system, the chairperson should be aware of the system's technique for distributing funds among the institutions; he or she should be especially familiar with the procedures used to derive the resources that concern academic areas.

The Budget Cycle of an Institution

An institution begins its budget cycle with the preparation of a budget request which is submitted to the board of trustees and, in the case of public institutions, to the governor and legislature of the state. When an institution finally receives an approved budget, a series of decisions are made at various levels within the institution, taking into account the funds available and the budget requested for each of the budget categories. These decisions lead to the development of an *operating budget,* which is an expenditure plan covering the period (usually a single year) for which funds are made available. At the end of each year a *financial statement* is prepared, showing the financial status at the start of the year, the activities during the year, and the financial condition at the end of the year. Finally, an *audit* is performed to verify that established rules and regulations have been followed. Budget cycles may overlap at some institutions—for example, a university could be preparing a budget request for a coming year at the same time it is preparing an operating budget for the current year. Chairpersons should be aware of budget cycles, since these cycles affect institutional decision-making processes.

PREPARATION OF A BUDGET REQUEST

This activity is usually begun well in advance of the time period for which resources are being requested—for example, an institutional budget request for a given fiscal year may have to be submitted in the early part of the preceding fiscal year. Institutions usually begin preparing their budget request about six months prior to the submission date. In the case of public institutions, the date for submitting a budget request depends on the dates of the legislative sessions.

Universities take different approaches to the preparation of budget requests. For example, in the case of some private and public institutions, the department request may be the first step in a continuous planning process that eventually results in the allocation of an operating budget. At West Virginia University, submitted department budget requests are aggregated and prioritized at the college level, and college requests are then arranged in priorities at the institutional level. During the allocation process these institutional priorities serve as the basis for distributing resources. At many public institutions, especially those funded through an enrollment formula, department requests rather than institutional priorities may serve as the basis for distributing resources among departments within a college.

Thus, in the first approach, department requests are used in a continuous process to describe the institution's needs. In the second case, department needs are not aggregated and the distribution of resources to the institution and sometimes even to the school or college may depend on some other variable, such as enrollment. A third approach, which combines the two methods and which is becoming more widespread, is to distribute resources by expenditure categories to implement defined institutional priorities.

Regardless of the approach to generating an institutional budget request, chairpersons should involve themselves in the process as much as possible. The process provides one of the few opportunities for the department to describe its past successes and future objectives. Generally, the more that is known and understood about the complex activities of an academic department, the greater the possibility that positive decisions will be made. At the same time, however, chairpersons should be careful to keep their expectations at a reasonable level. Departments often request an amount that would be sufficient to accommodate all their needs. The funds to meet such requests are rarely available, however, and the chairperson should be prepared to receive fewer resources than were sought.

ALLOCATION AND CONTROL OF THE OPERATING BUDGET

Allocation and control of a current year's budget occur after the state legislature has appropriated the funds, the college or university has received its allocation, and department operating budgets have been authorized. Chairpersons and deans exercise budget control by signing approval for proposed expenditures. They may find that, although their annual budget has been approved, the funds are not made available all at one time. This situation occurs in states that operate on a funds release schedule other than an annual one—for example, the state of Florida releases funds on a quarterly basis. If the state is on an accrual accounting basis, the accounting at the end of the fiscal year includes all obligations made during the year, and funds are "certified forward" to the next fiscal year to cover these obligations. This type of year-end activity normally occurs in states where unspent or unobligated funds "revert" to the state. Not all states operate this way, however.

BUDGET CLOSE-OUT

The budget for the academic year is closed out in the last month of that fiscal year, at which time there is usually an end-of-the-year rush to complete authorized transactions and to prepare final annual reports. In states where state funds revert, chairpersons must be aware that any allocated funds not spent or encumbered during the allocation year will be lost to the department.

EXPENDITURE AUDIT

The record of expenditures is generally audited by internal auditors during the current year or thereafter. Expenditures may also be audited by external auditors, who conduct audits of the institution for its board of trustees or for the state. Colleges or universities with large federal grants and contracts may have auditors present from different federal departments much of the year. Some foundations conduct audits simultaneously with reviews of programs they fund.

In any current budget year, all or most of these activities may be occurring at the same time, although they may be grouped variously and performed by special offices or service departments. For example, at the beginning of a new fiscal year, an institutional budget office may be allocating funds to departments, authorizing the payroll office to increase the salaries and benefits of persons receiving pay raises, compiling cost data for the budget request for the subsequent year, estimating the current and future revenues from student tuition and fees, helping close out last year's budget, and beginning planning for the future. Budget responsibilities may be centralized or decentralized within the institution. In the decentralized model, the activities may be distributed so that the planning office is concerned with the budget request, the controller's office with the implementation of current-year decisions, and the academic vice-president's budget office with all budget-related activities pertaining to academic areas.

The chairperson, aware of the complicated activities of the budget cycle, should maintain accurate records of expenditures, even though such records may also be kept in administrative offices. He or she should plan department expenditures wisely and systematically to avoid last-minute scurrying about to purchase supplies and services before the budget close-out.

Since the budget requested for a given year is usually prepared one or two years in advance, the department needs to know what activities it intends to pursue in the next year or two in order to request appropriate funds. Plans for the department's general future are linked to budget planning. The timetable and deadline dates established for completing the various stages in budget preparations are often used by chairpersons as a basis for scheduling academic planning sessions. Some chairpersons feel that planning is a wasted effort unless additional funds are expected to be made available. Such persons are not sensitive to the possibility that a department may be required to change or modify some of its academic activities to accommodate new societal needs or that at times such changes will have to be made without additional funding.

Academic planning is necessary whether anticipated funds for the coming years are more than, less than, or the same as the amounts allocated in the previous year. Departments can plan alternative courses of action to meet whatever situations occur, such as implementing new, unfunded projects in the event that unanticipated money should become available. Just as budget preparation is continuous, so should academic planning be continuous. Regular assessment of current positions and identification of key activities to be pursued will keep the department from straying too far from its missions and goals. Ideally, the planning process should take alternate possibilities into account. In reality, the tendency is to get the resources first and make the plans afterwards, especially in the case of annual appropriations.

Budgeting Systems

Institutions of higher learning use a variety of budgeting systems. When preparing budget requests, departments should follow the instructions distributed by the appropriate office of the institution. Specifically, the chairperson should be familiar with the budgeting approach used by his or her dean. Administrators who review budget requests may not attach sufficient importance to items that are not presented in a familiar format. The following summary of commonly used budget systems is presented here to expand the chairperson's language of budgeting.

INCREMENTAL BUDGETING

The system of incremental budgeting usually uses last year's expenditures as a base; it estimates and justifies an increase, or increment, above the base. This system does not require an extensive analysis or review of goals. It is widely used in colleges and universities, mainly, no doubt, because it is easily comprehensible.

Usually, each category within a budget—such as faculty salaries, expenses, travel, and so on—is increased by some percentage or flat amount of dollars. The guidelines for preparing the budget request may identify the maximum percentage increases that will be considered. When the economy becomes unpredictable and tax revenues uncertain, the budget guidelines for public colleges and universities may direct each institution to prepare and submit several different budget requests, one with perhaps a 5 percent decrease, another with no increase, and still another with a 5 percent increase. The guidelines from a state budget agency may include such specific instructions, even when an institution uses a different budgeting system. The budget request selected for approval will depend on the actual amount of state funds that will become available for higher education.

One major advantage of the incremental system is that the base is already agreed upon; further agreement is needed only on the amount of the increment. Moreover, the incremental system does not preclude the review of programs during the decision process, nor does it preclude subsequent resource adjustments to the base. Not inherent in this system, however, is a complete examination of program objectives and outcomes during each cycle.

ZERO-BASE BUDGETING SYSTEM (ZBBS)

This system assumes that a department's objectives should determine its budget and that an assessment should be made of how well objectives are reached. Zero-base budgeting starts from the premise that each time a new budget is prepared, it must demonstrate that it includes the best combination of costs and benefits for achieving each goal or the effective operation of each program. Sometimes, even the alternatives that were considered and rejected have to be specified. The base of the incremental system discussed earlier is not taken for granted in the zero-base system. In the ZBBS only demonstrable needs are to be funded. The ZBBS involves the use of "decision packages" (programs described at various funding levels) and the ranking of these "packages."

When the zero-base system is attempted annually, administrators often take the documents prepared for the previous year, reread them, and add the information provided and the funds requested. Such practice leads the system away from its emphasis on objectives, nullifies the rationale for zero-base budgeting, and leads toward a reintroduction of an incremental system. An academic department's objectives do not vary significantly from year to year, however; consequently, the complete review suggested by the ZBBS may itself be questioned on the grounds of cost efficiency. The exercise of evaluating achievement of objectives at different funding levels becomes too uncertain, and generally organizations using ZBBS arrive at set percentages to be used.

The major problem with using zero-base budgeting in academic departments is the nature of faculty costs. Faculty salaries, which are a major portion of department budgets, remain constant or increase with the longevity of faculty members, regardless of changes in department, college, or university objectives.

LINE-ITEM BUDGETING

Most institutions use organizational units and expenditure categories, rather than defined programs and activities, as the basis for budget planning. An organizational unit is an academic department, center, institute, school, or college. Expenditures include such categories as salaries, expenses, equipment, and so forth. Salaries and expenses to be budgeted for an academic department, for example, would include the cost of programs in the department, such as instruction, academic support, and advising. This itemizing is called *line-item budgeting*. By adding the budgets of all organizational units in the institution, the total institutional budget can be determined.

PLANNING, PROGRAMMING, BUDGETING SYSTEMS (PPBS)

This system has been discussed in chapter 20, "Departmental Planning." It incorporates the concept of zero-base budgeting in that budget is based on the cost of achieving institutional goals or outcomes during a given fiscal year rather than by the cost of maintaining organizational units such as academic departments. Whereas zero-base budgeting is primarily an annual process, PPBS contains a long-range planning component (perhaps five years) for which goals and outcomes are stated for each of the years (say five) and the cost is attributed to the achievement of those goals and outcomes. All the goals and outcomes related

FIGURE *21.1* Budgeting Based on Programs

BUDGET CATEGORIES	PROGRAM OF INSTRUCTION GOALS AND OUTCOMES	PROGRAMS OF RESEARCH GOALS AND OUTCOMES	PROGRAM OF SERVICE GOALS AND OUTCOMES
Salary			
Equipment			
Expense			
Other			

to instruction are grouped under the Program of Instruction, all related to research are grouped under the Program of Research, and all related to service are grouped under the Program of Service.

As we saw in chapter 20, universities have difficulty in agreeing on what should constitute a program. One university may establish "advising" as a goal or outcome that would be included in the Program of Instruction, whereas another may consider it a program in its own right. There are many definitions of programs, and each institution will decide for itself which to use.

The National Center for Higher Education Management Systems (NCHEMS) in Colorado has developed a sophisticated budgeting model that defines a program of instruction as "a discipline major or any collection of courses designed to satisfy curricular requirements for a degree or certificate."[1] This concept recognizes that students take courses in more than one department and that each department, therefore, makes only a partial contribution to the education of a degree-seeking student. With the aid of modern computer technology the cost for each student at each level of enrollment can be divided among all the departments in an institution. The total cost for producing a degree in a given major can then be estimated by summing all the costs of the educational services provided to a student in that major by all contributing departments, over a four-year period.

The matrices shown in Figures 21.1 and 21.2 will help differentiate between budgeting based on programs and budgeting based on organizational units, such as academic departments.

FIGURE *21.2* Budgeting Based on Organizational Units

BUDGET CATEGORIES	CHEMISTRY DEPARTMENT	PHYSICS DEPARTMENT	HISTORY DEPARTMENT	SOCIOLOGY DEPARTMENT
Salary				
Equipment				
Expense				
Other				

---

1. *Procedures for Determining Historical Full Costs: The Costing Component of NCHEMS Information Exchange Procedures,* Technical Report No. 65, 2nd ed. (Boulder, CO: 1977), p. 16.

A carefully prepared PPBS scenario will give the department a clear management plan and an overview of the timing and budgetary resources required to accomplish important goals. However, in fact few institutions now employ a formal PPBS process in their planning and budgeting process. In actual experience, PPBS seems to require more information, and a higher degree of rational choice, than is possible in practice.

Formula Budgeting

Formula budgeting uses formulas as a basis for preparing budget requests and for determining allocations. One purpose of formula budgeting is to provide equitable funding for all competing units, such as institutions in a state system or academic departments within an institution. The uniform application of formulas to colleges and universities in a state system tends to reduce conflict among presidents and, when applied uniformly within an institution, helps reduce conflict among deans—provided, of course, that the formulas have been agreed on and accepted by all concerned. Various formulas can be used for education budgets. Zero-base formulas, for example, derive resources based on estimated full-time equivalent (FTE) enrollment and the agreed-on cost per student. Some formulas, on the other hand, may address only increases or decreases to the existing base.

One formula, for example, involves multiplying the projected number of FTE students by the cost per FTE student. When applied to an institution across the board, regardless of discipline or student level, the formula can provide an estimate of the total cost for operating all academic programs in the university. The formula can also be applied separately to departments and programs, as well as to graduate and undergraduate students within programs. For example, estimates of operational costs can be calculated for lower-division students in biology, upper-division students in psychology, graduate students in chemistry, and so forth. The sum of the separate costs for each category will be the total operational cost for all academic programs in the institution. Before the formula can be used, however, a determination must be made of what constitutes a FTE student in each of the above categories, how many FTE students are expected to enroll in each category, and the cost per FTE student. (A more detailed definition of *full-time equivalent* appears later in this chapter.)

Another formula for developing budget requests involves multiplying the estimated number of needed faculty positions by the average faculty salary. This formula, when applied to an institution as a whole, will provide an estimate of the total faculty salary cost for the university. Before the number of needed faculty positions can be estimated, however, a determination must be made, for budgetary purposes, of what constitutes a faculty workload.

Several state university systems have, for a number of years, used workload formulas to determine the number of positions needed. "Normative" workload factors were estimated originally from turn-of-the-century teaching load data. At many institutions, as late as 1945, the average faculty workload was four courses per semester. For budgetary purposes, the average faculty workload per semester was described not in terms of total number of courses taught but in terms of total number of student credit hours generated that semester. For example, a faculty member who taught one 3-credit-hour course with 25 students in the class would generate 75 student credit hours (3 × 25). If the instructor taught four such courses during a term, the total number of student credit hours generated over that term would be 300 (4 × 75). The workload factor for this instructor, therefore, would be 300.

The number of student credit hours generated by a course may vary, depending on its assigned number of credits and the number of students enrolled in it. Originally, workload factors were calculated only for the different levels of enrollment, without consideration of discipline. Because many lower-division classes still are taught by lecture, and generally have larger enrollments than do advanced classes, the average number of student credit hours generated by an instructor teaching the lower-division courses was expected to be larger. Table 21.1 illustrates this type of approach.

Before being able to determine the number of faculty positions needed at a given level or for a given discipline, the institution must calculate the total number of student credit hours generated at each level (lower, upper, graduate), in each department or program, in each school, and in each college, taking into account all courses taught, all teaching faculty, and all students in each of the above mentioned categories.

The number of faculty positions needed at each level is estimated by dividing the faculty workload factor assigned to a level into the total anticipated number of student credit hours to be generated by the institution at that level. The total number of faculty positions needed by the institution can be estimated by totaling the faculty positions needed at all levels. Multiplying that total by an average faculty salary, regardless of rank or discipline, results in an estimate of the institution's total cost for faculty salaries.

Additional positions for research, administration, and support in each discipline are generated in fixed ratios to instructional and faculty positions. For example, one research position may be generated for every five instructional positions, one administrative position may be generated for every ten

TABLE *21.1* "Normative" Workload Factors, by Educational Status of Students

EDUCATIONAL STATUS	"NORMATIVE" WORKLOAD FACTOR (Number of student credit hours required to generate one faculty position)
Freshman or Sophomore	400 student credit hours
Junior or Senior	300 student credit hours
Beginning Graduate	200 student credit hours
Advanced Graduate	100 student credit hours

faculty positions, and one support position may be generated for every four positions.

Using the preceding ratios, a department which generates 21 instructional positions would generate 21/5 or 4.2 research positions. The instructional and research faculty together (21 + 4.2) would total 25.2 faculty positions. These 25.2 faculty positions would generate 25.2/10 or 2.5 administrative positions making (25.2 + 2.5) a total of 27.7 faculty and administrative positions. These positions, in turn, would generate 27.7/4 or 6.4 support positions. It should be understood, however, that a department will not necessarily be given all the positions it generates. Some will receive more and some less, depending on other variables as determined by the dean and the central administration. Funds for student services and library functions may be generated as percentages of the institution's total instructional and research funding, or in fixed ratios to enrollment or positions. Thus, a budget request can be built for all authorized and needed positions covering all functions within an institution.

The workload factors described in Table 21.1 present averages that do not differentiate disciplines. In reality, workload factors vary in size from one discipline to another because of the nature of the discipline. The number of students in music and art classes is much smaller than that in social science classes, thus making the workload factors in music and art smaller than that in the social sciences. The availability of the large computer makes possible the calculation, using documented or anticipated student enrollment, of workload factors for each discipline or department and for each enrollment level within each department. When data about disciplines from several previous years are averaged, more realistic workload measures can be derived. Table 21.2 contains a standard list of specific and broad discipline areas often used by institutions in reporting data to the federal government. Illustrated in the table are the workload factors in a hypothetical university, adjusted according to those disciplines and the enrollment levels within each.

The size of faculty workloads at an institution is related to an institution's tradition and history. In addition, workload factors may also be based on the most recent expenditure analysis and the amount of money available for higher education, along with a substantial dose of intuition and even arbitrariness.

At this hypothetical university, workload or productivity factors can be converted to student–faculty ratios at the undergraduate level by dividing the undergraduate workload factors by 15, and at the graduate level by dividing the graduate workload factor by 12 (15 undergraduate student credit hours and 12 graduate student credit hours equal one FTE student.)

Thus far, we have discussed ways in which formulas can be used in the preparation of budget requests. Rarely is the same formula used both to prepare a budget request for an institution and to allocate resources within the institution. Most formulas in use are zero-based and have no variable that accounts for college or institutional priorities. Therefore, more faculty positions may be assigned to some programs than would be generated according to formula. On the other hand, this excess must be balanced by assigning fewer positions than are

TABLE *21.2* Productivity (Workload) Factors in a Hypothetical University*

DISCIPLINES	LEVELS			
	Lower	*Upper*	*Graduate*	Dissertation/ Thesis (Combined)
Agriculture and Natural Resources	420.00	240.00	108.00	60.00
Architecture and Environmental Design	300.00	240.00	120.00	45.00
Area Studies	240.00	240.00	84.00	60.00
Biological Sciences	360.00	240.00	132.00	45.00
Business and Management	480.00	360.00	192.00	60.00
Communications	360.00	240.00	168.00	60.00
Computer and Information Sciences	420.00	360.00	216.00	45.00
Education	360.00	380.00	228.00	75.00
Engineering	360.00	240.00	120.00	45.00
Fine and Applied Arts	180.00	120.00	84.00	75.00
Foreign Languages	240.00	180.00	84.00	75.00
Health Professions	360.00	180.00	108.00	45.00
Home Economics	300.00	300.00	180.00	60.00
Law	0.0	0.0	480.00	60.00
Letters	240.00	300.00	168.00	75.00
Library Science	540.00	300.00	228.00	60.00
Mathematics	420.00	360.00	96.00	45.00
Military Science	0.0	0.0	0.0	60.00
Physical Sciences	420.00	240.00	168.00	45.00
Psychology	540.00	360.00	204.00	45.00
Public Affairs and Services	540.00	300.00	168.00	60.00
Social Sciences	540.00	360.00	192.00	60.00
Technology	300.00	180.00	0.0	60.00
Interdisciplinary Studies	300.00	240.00	144.00	60.00
Continuing Education	0.0	0.0	0.0	0.0

*Number of student credit hours that will generate one FTE faculty position per term at the different levels in each of the listed disciplines.

earned to certain programs with high student credit hour productivity. Thus, even though the formula for a budget request may be based on the number of FTE students generated by each department, each administrative level in a university may follow a completely different system for allocating funds to units at the next lower level. Chairpersons would do well to familiarize themselves with the formulas, priorities, and procedures used in both the requesting process and the allocation process.

Despite their usefulness, student-weighted funding formulas are creating problems for many colleges and universities today. The formulas are disliked because they usually rely on averages, and reward high enrollments in the absence of other considerations. Moreover, when student demand for a given program decreases dramatically, the amount of funds generated by the formula may not be sufficient to continue that program. Such insufficiency results because most formulas are linear and do not consider that departments have fixed costs—i.e., a class of nineteen students may cost as much as a class of twenty-one students. In addition, formulas do not take into account the difference in costs due to faculty seniority, rank, and labor market rates. Thus, some formulas fail to provide the equity that was the very rationale for their initial application.

Most funding formulas are based on a cost analysis of some kind in which data are stated in terms of cost per FTE student. The availability of computers makes it possible to process the large volume of data needed to conduct cost studies. In *A Study of Cost Analysis in Higher Education,* the American Council on Education reports that none of the existing costing systems was useful to institutional administrators in improving or managing higher education. Nevertheless, many state-required formulas continue to rely on these cost data.

Formulas that use averaged data derived from several institutions in a system generally tend to reward the teaching institutions at the expense of the research universities. Some states, like North Carolina, have different funding systems for different kinds of institutions. State budgeting systems that vary according to the mission, role, and scope of each institution in a system are now gaining much attention. Should such a system emerge formally, it would quite likely be applied to the departments within a college or university. The congruence of a department's goals and objectives with those of its parent institution would then become much more important for internal funding purposes.

The Language of Budgeting

The budgeting process is often perceived as mysterious and esoteric. Some persons find it dry and boring, and those who find it fascinating frequently choose some facet of it as a vocation. To the layperson, the jargon used by finance experts seems to be incomprehensible except to a chosen few, and those who understand it are thought to be "important." In actuality, the budget process is part of planning and is frequently less precise than it may appear. Although we may not demystify the entire process by explaining some of its intricacies, this discussion will help chairpersons become familiar with the more common terms related to budgeting. Some of these terms will be reviewed in the following sections.

FULL-TIME EQUIVALENT

FTE is a commonly used abbreviation that stands for "full-time equivalent" and refers variously to students, faculty, and staff. This concept is often used in formula-base budgeting.

    a. *FTE student.* Let us assume that a full course load for a typical undergraduate has been designated as 15 credits per term. For budgeting purposes, therefore, one undergraduate student enrolled for 15 credits of course work is considered to be one FTE student. Similarly, three students enrolled for 5 credits each, or a total of 15 credits, are considered to be one FTE. The number of credit hours designated as equaling one FTE may change according to the level of the courses or the level of the student. At many institutions, one full-time equivalent graduate student is 12 credit hours.

b. *FTE faculty and staff.* A faculty or staff member may be appointed on a full- or part-time basis for an academic or calendar year, depending on the institution's policy. Faculty members on full-time appointments are generally expected to devote 100 percent of their professional time and effort to the job to which they are appointed. What constitutes 100 percent of time and effort of a faculty member's professional life has not been clearly defined, however. Those institutions and departments who need a definition must stipulate their own.

For salary purposes, a faculty member who receives 100 percent of a salary for a designated period of time is considered one FTE faculty member for that time period. Some faculty members are appointed to two or more departments or offices simultaneously, and their salaries come from different budgets. For example, a person may receive 75 percent of his or her salary from a department and 25 percent from the dean's office. The fraction of the total salary that comes from each budget also indicates that fraction of FTE faculty assigned to each department or office. Similarly, a person who receives 25 percent of his or her salary from a contract or grant is considered to be 25 percent FTE "on the grant" and 75 percent FTE "in the department."

A faculty member whose full salary comes from a department budget and who is considered one FTE faculty member, as far as that department is concerned, is usually assigned a variety of activities, each of which is expressed as a percentage of full-time effort. For example, a faculty member's teaching effort may be assigned 50 percent of a FTE; research, 30 percent; and service, 20 percent. An institution may determine the total number of FTE faculty involved in research by adding all the individual percentage FTEs assigned to research and thereby estimate the total salary costs of the institution's research effort. Similarly, the total number of FTE faculty involved in the teaching of undergraduate lower-division courses can be estimated by adding all the individual percentage FTEs assigned to teaching lower-division courses.

A faculty member whose formal appointment is 25 percent FTE in the dean's office and 75 percent FTE in a department may devote 50 percent of his or her department effort to teaching and 50 percent to research. In this case the total teaching assignment of FTE is 37.5 percent (50 percent × 75 percent). Similarly, the total research assignment of FTE is 37.5 percent. Many urban colleges and universities employ a considerable number of part-time faculty members, each of whom is appointed to a fraction of one FTE position and is paid accordingly. If an institution hires three part-time faculty members, appointing one to a 0.5 FTE position, another to a 0.6 FTE position, and the third to a 0.3 FTE position, the three will constitute 1.4 FTE positions (0.5 + 0.6 + 0.3). Despite the many ways of calculating FTEs and their percentages, however, one faculty member can never be counted as more than one FTE, regardless of how hard or how many hours he or she works.

The FTE concept is also applied to nonacademic staff. In the case of staff, however, the percentage of FTE is based on the relationship between the number of assigned hours of work during a given period and the number of hours that constitutes a full workload for that period.

STUDENT CREDIT HOURS

SCH, another common abbreviation, usually refers to "student credit hours." One student taking a 4-credit-hour course per term generates 4 student credit hours. Fifteen students enrolled in a 3-credit-hour course per term generate 45 student credit hours (3 × 15). SCH may also refer to "student *contact* hours," the number of clock hours spent in contact with faculty members. One contact hour in a lecture class per week per term is usually equivalent to 1 credit hour. In the case of laboratory classes, however, 3 contact hours per week per term will often equal only 1 credit hour.

EXPENDITURE CATEGORIES

Resources may be allocated to institutions and departments in expenditure categories. The purpose of allocating funds in categories is to exercise control over how the money is spent. In many states and institutions, transfer of moneys from one category to another is not permitted or is permitted under restricted circumstances, such as a 5 percent limitation on transfers. Categories may vary from state to state, but the most common ones are listed and defined below.

a. *Salaries*—Includes the funds required to pay salaries of persons in permanent or regular positions

b. *Benefits*—Includes funds for additional commitments made to employees, such as retirement, social security matching funds, health insurance, and so forth

c. *Temporary personnel*—Includes funds for temporary help, such as student assistants and peak load supplemental employees

d. *Graduate assistantships and fellowships*—Includes funds for teaching and research assistantships and fellowships

e. *Expenses*—Includes funds for supplies, travel, telephones, postage, equipment lease, rent, and so forth

f. *Equipment*—Includes funds for equipment, such as typewriters, duplicating machines, laboratory equipment, furniture, and so forth, which become the property of the institution (Sometimes equipment that costs less than a designated amount may be purchased with funds from the expense category.)

g. *Capital funds*—Includes funds for construction of new buildings (In some states, funds from this category may be used to pay for building renovations.)

h. *Lump sum*—Institutional funds are sometimes allocated in "lump sums"—i.e., the funding agency does not constrain institutional expenditures by category. In such cases, the institution makes its own decisions on the percentage of funds to be spent on salaries, supplies, equipment, and so forth. Institutions with this flexibility may provide the same flexibility to individual departments.

SOURCES OF INSTITUTIONAL SUPPORT

Institutions usually get their funds from a variety of sources. Some of these funds are for general institutional support, while others may be directed toward specific purposes. The most common sources are listed below.

a. *State funds* are obtained from the general revenue of the state and usually make up the major source of a public institution's operational funds.

b. *Incidental funds* come from student tuition payments, library fines, application fees, and so forth. Sometimes contract and grant overhead funds are included in this category as well.

c. *Contract and grant funds* are obtained from foundations and government agencies for the purpose of financing specific projects and research activities.

d. *Auxiliary funds* come from revenue generated by institutional auxiliary activities, such as bookstores, housing, health center, duplicating services, and so forth. These operations are designed or mandated to be self-sufficient. Generally, normal operating funds from the university may not be used to support them. Profits generated by an auxiliary activity may be used for institutional purposes such as scholarships.

e. *Agency funds* are funds that the institution holds and disburses on behalf of an agency. A university service fraternity, for example, is in this category.

f. *Activity fee funds* are collected as supplements to tuition and are used to support such activities as student clubs, intercollegiate athletics, and other student-related activities. Although often included within agency funds, they may be handled separately. How these funds are controlled and regulated varies from institution to institution, but there seems to be a trend towards student involvement in activity fee control.

g. *Investment earnings* are generated by investing funds from the above categories if their immediate expenditure is not required. The investment earnings are generally used as discretionary funds by the institution. Sometimes state statutes prohibit public institutions from investing state funds.

h. *Other discretionary funds* may be obtained from the profits of concessions and vending machines and are generally retained by the institution for discretionary purposes.

i. *Scholarship and loan funds* may come from government or private sources. Included, usually, are funds to support the federal College Work–Study program.

j. *Foundation funds* include gifts and donations; generally these are not administered by the university but by a university or college foundation that is incorporated as a separate entity. *Restricted funds* are those given for a special purpose, such as for a particular school, college, or activity; *unrestricted funds* are those that have not been specifically designated. Usually, the foundation board decides how to use them.

k. *Athletic funds* are the revenues from the intercollegiate sports program. Usually, these funds are also external to the institution and are controlled by an athletic board.

This chapter has dealt with various aspects of how budgets are generated for colleges and universities. Those who work with and are knowledgeable about the ins and outs of budgeteering may find this chapter to be too elementary. On the other hand, those who have had little or no experience with the budget process may feel that this chapter is too general and does not go into enough detail. It was, however, written primarily for the novice. It is our firm belief that if a department chair is to be really effective, he or she needs to have a good knowledge and appreciation of the technical and political aspects of the entire budget process—from its beginning in the department, through all the internal and external hierarchies, and back to the department. Department chairs who need more information than is provided in this chapter are encouraged, therefore, to read additional literature on the subject, or consult with experienced colleagues.

Questions

1. How can or does the chairperson of your department obtain information about what increases or decreases in the institutional budget can be anticipated in the coming year?

2. If yours is a state-supported institution, does the budget request from your institution retain its identity as it is reviewed by higher levels, or does it lose its identity as it becomes a part of the budget request from a university or college system?

3. To what extent is the amount of funds allocated to your department driven by the formula used in generating institutional budget requests?

4. Are department chairs at your institution provided with seminars or workshops designed to explain how the institution generates its budget request?

5. To what extent are department chairs at your institution required to submit plans for each of the next several years (three to five) and to attach cost estimates for future activities or outcomes?

References

ADAMS, CARL R.; HANKINS, RUSSELL L., and SCHROEDER, ROGER G. *Literature of Cost and Cost Analysis in Higher Education.* A Study of Cost Analysis in Higher Education, Vol. 1. Washington, DC: American Council on Education, 1978.

BAILEY, STEPHEN, K. "People Planning in Postsecondary Education: Human Resource Development in a World of Decremental Budgets." In *More for Less: Academic Planning with Faculty Without New Dollars,* edited by James N. Nesmith, pp. 3–11. New York: Society for College and University Planning and Educational Testing Service, College and University Programs, 1975.

BARAK, ROBERT (et al.) *The Arizona Board of Regents Task Force on Excellence, Efficiency and Competitiveness.* Final Report and Working Papers. 4 vols. 1988. (ERIC Document Reproduction Service No. ED 306 803)

BRENEMAN, DAVID W., and YOUN, TED I. K. (Eds.) *Academic Labor Markets and Careers.* Philadelphia: The Falmer Press, Taylor and Francis, Inc., 1988.

BROWN, STEPHANIE. "Approaching Faculty Productivity as a Mechanism for Retrenchment." *New Directions for Institutional Research,* Winter 1979, pp. 45–54.

BUDIG, GENE A. (Ed.) *Dollars and Sense: Budgeting for Today's Campus.* Chicago: College and University Business Press, McGraw–Hill, 1972.

CARUTHERS, J. KENT, and ORWIG, MELVIN. *Budgeting in Higher Education.* AAHE/ERIC Higher Education Research Report No. 3. Washington, DC: American Association for Higher Education, 1979.

CORSON, JOHN J. *The Governance of Colleges and Universities.* New York: McGraw–Hill, 1960.

DOUGLAS, JOEL M. (Ed.) *Salary and Compensation Methodology in Academic Collective Bargaining.* New York: National Center for the Study of Collective Bargaining in Higher Education and the Professions, 1983. (ERIC Document Reproduction Service No. ED 230 140)

FLOYD, CAROL EVERLY. "State Institutional Relations" and "Planning." *State Planning, Budgeting, and Accountability, Approaches for Higher Education.* Washington, DC: AAHE/ERIC Higher Education Research Reports, 6, 1982.

GREEN, JOHN L. *Budgeting in Higher Education.* Athens, GA: The University of Georgia Press, 1972.

HALSTED, KENT. *Higher Education Price Indexes: 1990 Update.* Washington, DC: Research Associates of Washington, 1991.

HOWE, RICHARD D., and URQUHART, MARYON. *Salary Trend Study of Faculty in Social Sciences for the Years 1984–85 and 1987–88.* Boone, NC: Appalachian State University, 1988. (ERIC Document Reproduction Service No. ED 302 165)

JELLEMA, WILLIAM W. (Ed.) *Efficient College Management.* San Francisco: Jossey–Bass, 1972.

KALUDIS, GEORGE (Ed.) "Strategies for Budgeting." *New Directions for Higher Education, 2.* San Francisco: Jossey–Bass, 1973.

LESLIE, LARRY L., and ANDERSON, RICHARD E. (Eds.) *ASHE Reader on Finance in Higher Education.* Lexington, MA: Ginn Press, 1986.

MALM, LINDA. *Leadership Practice: How I Raised $100,000 This Year With No Fund Raising Experience.* 1990. (ERIC Document Reproduction Service No. ED 319 423)

MARCH, HERBERT W., and DILLON, KRISTINE E. "Academic Productivity and Supplemental Income." *Journal of Higher Education,* 51, 1980, pp. 546–555.

MARCH, JAMES G. *How We Talk and How We Act: Administrative Theory and Administrative Life.* Urbana: University of Illinois Press, 1980.

McFERRON, J. RICHARD (et al.) "Assessing and Supporting Quality in the Liberal Arts: The Role of the Chief Liberal Arts Academic Officer." *Journal of Education Administration,* 26 (2), 1988, pp. 393–407.

McINTOSH, THOMAS H., and KOEVERING, THOMAS E. "Six-year Case Study of Faculty Peer Reviews, Merit Ratings, and Pay Awards in a Multidisciplinary Department." *Journal of the College and University Personnel Association,* 37, 1986, pp. 5–14.

MICEK, SIDNEY S. (Ed.) *Integrating Academic Planning and Budgeting in a Rapidly Changing Environment: Process and Technical Issues.* Boulder: National Center for Higher Education Management Systems, 1980.

NATIONAL ASSOCIATION OF COLLEGE AND UNIVERSITY BUSINESS OFFICERS. *College and University Business Administration.* Washington, DC: NACUBO, 1975.

NATIONAL SCIENCE FOUNDATION. *Systems for Measuring and Reporting the Resources and Activities of Colleges and Universities.* NSF 67-15. Washington, DC: National Science Foundation, June 1967.

NEWMAN, FRANK. "Taking the Helm." In *The Third Century: Twenty-Six Prominent Americans Speculate on the Educational Future.* New Rochelle, NY: Change Magazine Press, 1976.

PESEAU, BRUCE A. *Quantitatively Based Peer Program Identification.* Paper presented at the Annual Conference of the Mid-South Educational Research Association, Louisville, KY, 1988. (ERIC Document Reproduction Service No. ED 301 553)

PORTER, JOHN D. *Classroom Utilization: Pacing Departments on a Scheduling Diet.* AIR 1986. (ERIC Document Reproduction Service No. ED 280 390)

Procedures for Determining Historical Full Costs: The Costing Component of NCHEMS Information Exchange Procedures. Technical Report No. 65, 2nd ed. Boulder: National Center for Higher Education Management Systems, 1977.

ROOD, HAROLD J. "Legal Issues in Faculty Termination." *Journal of Higher Education,* 63, 1977, pp. 123–152.

Salaries, Tenure, and Fringe Benefits of Full-time Instructional Faculty. Washington, DC: Center for Education Statistics, HEGIS Data available from Office of Educational Research and Improvement, Washington, DC 20208, 1986.

SOMMERS, ALEXIS N. "University Productivity." *Educational Record,* Winter 1977, pp. 251–256.

SPRUNGER, BENJAMIN E., and BERGQUIST, WILLIAM H. *Handbook for College Administration.* Washington, DC: Council for the Advancement of Small Colleges, 1980.

WATTENBARGER, JAMES L., and MERCER, SHERRY L. *Financing Community Colleges, 1988.* Washington, DC: American Association of Community and Junior Colleges, 1988. (ERIC Document Reproduction Service No. ED 292 533)

WINANS, GLEN T. *Determinants of Budget Allocations to Academic Departments: A Case Study.* ASHE 1987 Annual Meeting Paper, San Diego, 1987. (ERIC Document Reproduction Service No. ED 281 464)

WRIGHT, TED. *Who Uses Institutional Research and Why?* Research Report No. 85-22. Miami: Miami–Dade Community College, 1985.

Chapter 22

Funding the Department

Obtaining appropriate university resources for the department is one of the chairperson's more sensitive responsibilities. Since the majority of the faculty tend to believe that departments are underfunded, ability to compete successfully for institutional funds is often seen as an important indicator of a chairperson's leadership quality. This perception appears to prevail in departments that receive extensive external support from grants and contracts.

The budgetary procedures used by different institutions vary considerably. Many chairpersons, especially those who have been appointed only recently, may not be well-informed about the budget process within their universities. Further, some tend to assume, often incorrectly, that the dean possesses extensive knowledge about their departments. Frequently, what may be an obvious problem to a chairperson is not so obvious to a dean whose academic home is in another department. Unless they have been briefed, deans are often unaware of department developments. For this reason, budget requests should include complete, updated information. Generally, the dean operates within a value system; consequently, the request should indicate how the requested resources will help meet college and institution priorities.

The purpose of this chapter, therefore, is to help chairpersons formulate department budget requests and prepare effective presentations about the department during review sessions with the dean. Formal budget requests may not be required of all departments. Nevertheless, the chairperson must be able to communicate department needs effectively when the opportunity presents itself.

Continuing University Commitments and Expenses

When an institution is informed of its level of resources for a given budget period, it begins the process of internal distribution. Before moneys are disbursed to departments, however, the institution sets aside the dollars needed to pay for continuing commitments and expenses. These cuts are generally determined by an office in the central administration, such as the budget office or controller's office.

The total cost of the faculty and staff is one of the first determinations that must be made. The related question of how to deal with unfilled positions is answered in various ways by different institutions. In some cases, unfilled positions are treated as if they belong to the departments where the vacancies occurred, while in other cases all positions are reclaimed by the central administration, which reallocates them to the same or different departments on the basis of demonstrated need.

Regardless of the differences among position control policies, the computation of total institutional personnel costs is the first step in the allocation process. Next, the central adminstration must decide how much to take "off the top" to fund mandated expenditures. Money must be reserved for liability insurance, workmen's compensation, and continually increasing utility payments. Third, some funds are reserved in order to cover revenue shortfalls or unanticipated expenses. Fluctuating enrollments do not allow dependable projections of income from tuition, and in times of unstable enrollments the funds to be reserved may have to be increased.

After the necessary funds for the purposes described above have been reserved, the remainder of the budget, usually called "operating funds," is distributed to the vice-presidents, often on the advice of a university budget committee. Each vice-president, in turn, must distribute the funds to the units in his or her division. The vice-president for academic affairs allocates money to the academic deans, who subsequently make disbursements to the departments.

Managing Without Exact Budget Information

Appropriation schedules for state legislatures are often out of phase with institutional deadline dates for making and implementing planned distribution decisions. Some state universities never know for sure what their fiscal-year budgets will be until after the fiscal year has already started. Because of the number of administrative levels involved in making budgetary decisions, departments are usually the last to be informed about what resources they will have for the new budget year. For a part of the year, therefore, most chairpersons will be uncertain about resources and must make tentative decisions without exact budget information.

Even under biennial budget conditions, when the legislature appropriates funds for two years at a time, there is still bound to be a period of uncertainty while departments wait for distribution decisions to be made within the institution. This uncertainty increases the difficulty of administering a department under any sort of plan or set of priorities. For example, a chairperson cannot wait until late August to learn whether a new faculty position has been allocated; March is about the latest time to begin recruiting a new faculty member for the fall term. Similarly, the chairperson of a department with a graduate program, to avoid losing prospective graduate students because of uncertainty about available support, needs to know by February what to expect for the next year in terms of allocations for assistantships and fellowships. The chairperson should be informed as early as possible whether requests for new positions will be approved, whether he or she will be authorized to recruit for positions that will be vacated because of resignations or retirement, and what the level of support for graduate students will be. A strategy used by many chairpersons is to prepare and submit an interim request to their deans and academic vice-presidents asking them to make certain commitments in advance of the normal allocation cycle. Chairpersons may also seek early commitments for summer school operation.

The *interim request* is a procedure whereby the academic vice-president or dean, prompted by sound arguments from the chairperson, makes commitments in advance of the actual receipt of funds. Important results of early commitment may include a rise in faculty morale, improved planning for summer courses, and recruitment of good faculty members. The major effect, however, is the well-being of the department chairperson, whose uncertainty level is reduced because planning for the summer and fall quarters can proceed in a timely and appropriate manner. Everyone concerned should understand the potential for problems and the risks involved in making decisions based on early commitments, for it is possible that the anticipated funds may not become available. The chairperson must then be ready for the consequences and be prepared with contingency plans.

Although early commitments could be made quite easily in the early 1970s, when continuous enrollment increases generally assured the dean of additional resources, times have changed. Relatively stable enrollments, allocations increasingly earmarked for special purposes, and special constraints for the use of resources have caused uncertainties for the deans and vice-presidents nearly equal to those that chairpersons face.

The chairperson's ability to recognize the new uncertainties, communicate that understanding to the dean, and demonstrate willingness to share the risk with the dean can result in optimal resource planning and allocations if the dean and academic vice-president are able and willing to make early commitments. As in all high-risk situations, the chairperson must plan for and be able to deal with unanticipated consequences. In any event, when critical situations arise, the dean should be informed of the negative effect of any delay in decisions. A successful chairperson is likely to be one who is aggressive and tenacious in pursuit of a decision from a dean.

Strategies for Preparing a Department Budget Request

In times of changing enrollments and diminishing resources, the system of distributing funds to departments and programs according to enrollment may no longer serve the institution's best interests. This distribution process may have worked well in the late sixties and early seventies, when enrollments were continually expanding and institutions were generously supported by legislatures and patrons. When scarce resources are divided among departments according to their relative enrollments, however, some programs with high priority within the institution or the college may not receive sufficient funds to maintain or achieve quality. Although enrollment cannot be ignored when allocating funds, many institutions are beginning to place more emphasis on demonstrated relative need within the context of structured priorities. Consequently, clear and effective documentation justifying programs and purposes for which funds are being requested must accompany each budget request.

Academic departments compete for funds not only with each other, but also with other administrative units within the university. In the central administration the vice-president for academic affairs represents academic departments, just as the vice-presidents for administration and student affairs represent departments and units in their respective divisions. In making the budget case for academic programs, the academic vice-president uses the aggregation of documentation prepared by department chairpersons and deans. Unless the academic vice-president has sufficient and useful information at hand, he or she may be placed in an inferior negotiating position when participating with the other vice-presidents in the initial process of resource distribution. Chairpersons required to prepare comprehensive department budget requests, therefore, must give serious attention to the task of providing strong supporting documentation.

Before and during the process of preparing a budget request, the chairperson should reflect on how best to present the department's needs and what information would be most pertinent and persuasive. He or she should also make a realistic appraisal of the funds expected to be allocated to the institution for the coming year. During budget preparation time, and perhaps at other times as well, the chairperson should keep informed of legislative actions and of amounts previously allocated to higher education in general and, specifically, to his or her university for each of the last several years. If the university's allocation or expected allocation compares favorably with the previous year's allocation, there is a reasonable chance that a department's request for funds to cover basic needs, program changes, and improvements will be granted.

If the university's allocation does not compare favorably with the previous year's allocation, the chances for success in obtaining major increases are slim. Such circumstances are discouraging to the entire academic community, especially to chairpersons of departments whose programs command high enrollment and high visibility. These chairpersons feel that, without adequate funding, their departments will be unable to maintain their academic status and reputation for quality. In such instances, some chairpersons may propose that funds within the college or university be reallocated and that their departments be given additional funds, even at the expense of other departments. In theory, reallocation of resources to accommodate shifts in enrollment and changes in program priorities should be possible; in practice, major reallocations seldom occur.

The allocation patterns within universities reveal that few moneys are available for immediate reassignment. Usually, approximately 70 percent of university funds are expended for salaries; the filled positions supported by those salaries are really not susceptible to reallocation because they are held by specialized and often tenured professionals. Approximately another 10 percent of university funds is reserved for items that the university cannot control, such as utilities, leaving 20 percent to be used for operating needs. Realistically, however, only a small portion of the 20 percent is available for redistribution. Even departments whose programs have low enrollment and low priority require a minimum level of support. Any reduction in their budget could result in their demise.

One indicator of a university's ability to fund new or expanded department activities can be derived by comparing the overall increase in the university budget from one year to the next with the increase in average salaries over the same period. If the overall institutional increase is at least 2 percent greater than the salary increase, the university is in a relatively good position to meet department requests for additional operating funds. This type of situation exists, for example, when the institutional allocation has been increased by 10 percent over last year and the increase in average salaries is only 8 percent. On the other hand, if the overall institutional increase is less than the average salary increase, the university is hardly in a position to consider even minor requests for additional funds. Such would be the case with an institution whose overall allocation is 5 percent above last year's but whose increase in average salary is 8 percent. Obtaining information regarding the university's current allocation and how it relates to the previous year's allocation may take some effort. Occasionally, local newspapers will carry the information; or a call to the dean or to the budget office may produce results. Knowledge of the university's situation will help the chairperson maintain realistic expectations and see the final allocations in proper perspective.

DEVELOPING A SCHEDULE OF CRITICAL EVENTS

In preparing a comprehensive budget for a department, the chairperson should construct a schedule of critical events for which plans must be developed and budget needs identified. The following list of questions may serve as a guide for making such a schedule.

- What is the probable retirement date of each faculty and staff member?
- When will any faculty members be eligible for tenure evaluation? For an "up-or-out" review?
- Which faculty members will become eligible for sabbaticals in the next five years? Which are likely to apply for them?
- Which faculty members are likely to obtain external support and seek release time from teaching and other regular assignments in the next several years?

- Which faculty members will develop sufficient visibility to be recruited by another institution during the next five years?
- Which faculty members are likely to leave voluntarily within the next few years?
- Which faculty members are changing their career emphases from professorial to administrative roles?
- Which college or university administrators whose academic home is in this department are likely to return in the next several years?
- Given current enrollment trends and reasonably reliable forecasts of jobs for graduates and so forth, what is the probability for change in the number of student credit hours generated over the next several years?
- Is it possible, given the available data, that the department will have a surplus of faculty members in the next five years? A shortage?
- If program changes are planned for the next few years, are these likely to cause increases or decreases in enrollments?
- When is the next department self-study due? When is the next professional reaccreditation scheduled?
- Is the number of students who graduate likely to change? Will the department initiate new degree programs at existing levels? At different levels?
- Will competition with other educational institutions prove detrimental? If so, when?

UTILIZING THE TRANSFERABILITY OF FUNDS FROM ONE EXPENDITURE CATEGORY TO ANOTHER

Chairpersons should be familiar with the degree of flexibility permitted the department in transferring funds from one expenditure category to another. Such flexibility—or lack thereof—will influence the presentation of a budget request. For example, the chairperson of a department that has a justifiable need for additional instructional personnel wishes to ask for funds to meet this need. He or she can ask for salary funds, which can be used to fill permanent positions, or for temporary employment funds, which can be used to hire part-time instructors. The chairperson would prefer to add permanent positions, because once allocated they tend to remain in the department. The request for funds, however, may not be approved in time for the department to recruit adequately for new faculty positions by the fall term. If the salary line dollars can be easily converted to temporary employment funds, the funds for the new positions can be used to hire adjunct instructors. If this flexibility is not permitted, the positions will have to remain unfilled during the long recruitment period and there will be a delay in meeting instructional needs. The chairperson, if he or she knows the degree of flexibility allowed, can then decide whether to request funds for permanent positions or for temporary positions. In the latter instance, the dean should be informed of the need for additional faculty lines in the subsequent year.

Similarly, if the department is permitted to transfer money from the expense category to the equipment category, the chairperson is sometimes able to make more efficient use of moneys available. For example, a department that is paying annual leasing fees from its expense category for a duplicating machine may find buying the machine cheaper in the long run, thereby precluding the yearly outlay of expense moneys. Purchases of equipment, however, must be paid for out of the equipment expenditure category. If the department's equipment expense fund is low, the only way the purchase can be made is by transferring funds from the expense category, provided that such a transfer is permitted. By knowing in advance how much flexibility for transfer exists, the chairperson will know the best strategy for obtaining the equipment in question.

TAKING ADVANTAGE OF UNANTICIPATED AVAILABILITY OF RESERVE FUNDS

As mentioned previously, universities often keep reserves to offset possible shortfalls in incidental income. When and if a university establishes that the funds kept in reserve are not needed, these funds may be distributed to departments. Most often these reserves are held for the equipment category; thus, additional equipment needs can be accommodated late in the year. The chairperson should be aware of the department's unmet needs so that he or she may respond quickly to inquiries by the dean when unused reserve funds become available. Since the turnaround time for expending the reserves may be short, the chairperson with available information stands to gain the most.

FUNDING OF DEPARTMENTS ACCORDING TO THEIR ROLES IN MEETING INSTITUTIONAL COMMITMENTS

All departments should have a firm idea of the institutional purposes and goals they are expected to meet. Further, the chairperson should be aware that the type and condition of the department determine the nature of the budget request to be submitted to the dean. The department chairperson should be able to associate his or her budget request with department, college, and institutional goals and identify those strengths that specifically fit in with the institution's priorities. Different departments meet different institutional needs and commitments. Following are examples of five types of departments whose activities include performing specific functions needed to meet the institution's commitments.

1. *Departments that exist solely because of the university's commitment to an academic discipline.* Examples are classics and humanities departments, which generally do not attract large numbers of students or generate large amounts of contract and grant moneys. These departments often have stable enrollments and do not rank high in the institution's priorities for resource allocations. Nevertheless, they have traditionally been identified as indispensable components of the liberal arts, and their contribution to the university is felt to be important. In documenting their budget requests, such departments should

stress the quality of their programs, since their enrollment figures may not be impressive.

2. *Departments that offer large numbers of service courses.* Many English and mathematics departments belong in this category. The budget requests of these departments should use official enrollment figures as a basis for demonstrating the need for personnel and instructional support funds. Even though these departments might also have good graduate programs, their requests should emphasize service to other departments and relate needs to anticipated enrollment increases.

3. *Departments that are heavily involved in community needs.* Examples are education departments with a large number of in-service teacher training activities. (Note that these types of activities are not associated with enrollments.) Budget requests from such departments should emphasize past achievements and ask for funds to expand or improve their programs.

4. *Departments that are able to obtain outside contracts and grants to support expanding research programs.* Departments of natural and physical sciences frequently belong in this category. Budget requests should show how the outside funding augments internal allocations, as well as the extent to which the benefits derived outweigh any overhead or matching funds that the institution must provide as a condition for obtaining the contract or grant.

5. *Departments that are closely tied to professions.* Schools of law, nursing, and social work are examples. Budget requests of these departments or schools should clearly state societal and professional demands and pressures to maintain quality programs. The requests should also emphasize the added instructional costs necessary to accommodate changing certification requirements, professional regulations, and so forth.

The preceding list has been compiled to show that not all department budget requests should be developed according to the same strategy.

A further consideration is the department's perception of itself. A department that already has or is striving for a national reputation will want to emphasize its gains or losses during the current year and note the effect its national exposure has had on the university. Federal and state grant awards, prestigious publications, and improvement in student quality are developments that should be included as background in the budget request. If the department perceives itself as regionally oriented and has no serious intention of competing in the national arena, it should present information that shows its local influence. If the department is basically a service department, the budget request should include information about current faculty loads, as well as a statement of the positive effect that additional resources would have on generating credit hours.

We have discussed alternative strategies that a chairperson might use when preparing a budget. Deans, however, have their own personal styles and react in different ways to various requests. Moreover, some have their own ideas about the nature of department goals. Because the priorities that the dean has in mind are not always apparent, the chairperson should not try to outguess him or her but rather present department needs in a straightforward manner. The chairperson must maintain credibility with the dean. Overstatements and inaccuracies in budget requests may rapidly erode the chairperson's credibility. Annual budget requests that contain well-developed, accurate documentation and that reinforce department objectives and priorities will have a cumulative beneficial effect over the years in shaping the dean's perception of the department.

DRAFTING THE BUDGET REQUEST DOCUMENT

The comprehensive budget request should include relevant background information to update the dean's knowledge about the department. The information used should be "official" information, so that precious discussion time is not wasted in disagreements over facts and figures. University fact books, published financial reports, and information that has been widely distributed should serve, as much as possible, as the sources of the data presented. Each institution has an office of institutional research, which is responsible for providing accurate information to external agencies. Therefore, if published information is unavailable, that office should be consulted for data or for verification of the accuracy of unpublished data.

Several indicators of the department's workload and its relative standing within the university should be compiled and kept current. These indicators include department trends and comparative data. A recommended way of showing *department trends* is to compile the following types of data for each of the last three years and to project figures for the next year:

1. Number of credit hours produced by the department
2. Number of students majoring in the department's discipline
3. Number of service courses offered
4. Average class size of service courses
5. Number of faculty members and percent distribution of faculty effort in instruction, research, public service, and other areas
6. Number of teaching and research graduate assistants
7. Number of nonacademic staff persons, such as secretaries and technicians
8. Effect of federal and state funds

The presentation of *comparative data* should show rates of change, ratios, or statistical averages:

1. Percent change in credit hours for the department compared with percent change for the university
2. Faculty–student ratios compared with those of similar departments

3. Average faculty instruction loads compared with those of similar departments

4. Faculty–support staff ratios compared with those of similar departments

The budget request should review, as concisely as possible, the various programs within the department, stressing the program's age, its relative academic and professional standing, and its strengths and weaknesses. The presentation should be clear, logical, and brief.

The request should include a summary of how the department is organized. Faculty members' names should be associated with department functions wherever possible. Faculty members who have served on recognized university-wide committees should also be mentioned, as well as those who are active in state and national professional groups.

After providing the background information, the chairperson should present the department's precise needs for the coming year. This section of the budget request should incorporate appropriate strategies, such as those discussed earlier. Once the background information has ben clearly presented, then programs and indications of desired activities may subsequently be referred to by title.

The favorable effect of funding the proposed budget request should be described, along with the negative effect of not funding the requested improvements. If partial funding can provide some reasonable progress toward the stated goal, this information should also be stated, accompanied by a phased schedule for obtaining the remainder of the resources needed in future budget years.

A department chair's credibility is *enhanced* if his or her budget requests demonstrate how internal reallocations can be used to accomplish in whole or in part some desired objective; or how some programs and activities may be discontinued in order to undertake new programs or activities; or how departments are prepared through their own initiative to "leverage" additional resources provided by the dean or the provost in order to achieve more than the additional resources alone would support.

Credibility is dramatically *reduced* by maintaining that everything the department is currently doing is absolutely essential and already minimally and inadequately funded so that any reallocation or reduction in any program, activity, or expenditure would absolutely cripple the department, or ensure that the reputation of the department would be devastated, or defeat the department's efforts to improve itself, and (most assuredly) destroy the morale of its faculty. Any dean or provost can see this argument for what it is, and knows that any department *can* survive reasonably intact with *some* degree of budget reallocation or reduction.

A table should be provided to serve as a summary that communicates the essence of the budget request. It will further serve as a visual aid in budget discussions with the dean. The dean will become more familiar with the department and its requests if the chairperson frequently refers to the data table during budget discussions.

Budget-Related Discussions with the Dean

Much is to be gained and nothing lost by frequent discussions with the dean concerning the resources needed and the problems faced by the department. Chairpersons tend to review developments only at annual budget meetings, but they should take the initiative to call the dean's attention to problems as they occur. Conferences with the dean should be requested during the year, and matters to be discussed at these conferences should be well documented and should clearly indicate a continuous pursuit of department goals. The chairperson should provide the dean—in advance of any meeting, if possible—with facts and figures, estimates of the budget's effect, and the statement of needs. Oral presentations and face-to-face discussions should amplify, further explain, or emphasize the points set forth in the written documentation. This procedure allows for improved communication and better understanding of the request; it also helps bring about optimal results at allocation time. Consistency is necessary in describing department needs. In essence, the chairperson may help shape a dean's behavior by fostering a more rational approach and increasing the quantity and quality of the dean's response.

If the chairperson has some question about the results of a meeting with a dean, he or she should prepare a memorandum that sets down the details of the discussion, including points of agreement, action to be taken, and dates for future decisions. When shared with the dean and the department faculty, the memorandum may serve as a basis for department planning during the upcoming fiscal year.

Well-documented budget requests presented in a logically organized format will provide deans with information that may be helpful in the rational allocation of funds. The approaches described here may not always result in an improved resource allocation. They should, however, build credibility for the department. Further, they may help clarify the dean's perceptions of the department and his or her expectations about its future achievements.

Setting explicit goals—no matter how desirable for an institution, school, or department—is a difficult process, for goals are not usually formulated until the amount of available resources has been established. This process is a reversal of the rational planning model and results from increasing economic contraints placed on education. A chairperson should understand the major commitments that, in effect, are the implied goals of the school, college, and institution. Then he or she can better target the available funds for appropriate areas, programs, and components. The budget request presentation described above can elicit responses from the dean that should help the chairperson better understand the dean's philosophy. Furthermore, this presentation should improve the dean's understanding of the department.

Questions

1. a. Is your department expected to prepare and submit a budget request, formal or informal, describing resource needs?
   b. If not, how are the resource needs of your department made known to the administration? Who makes the request for you?
   c. If yes, how detailed a budget request are you expected to prepare?
2. a. Within the administrative hierarchy of your institution, how many levels must review the budget request submitted by or for your department?
   b. What external reviews, outside of your institution, are conducted? Who conducts them?
3. Speculate on the special political, social, and economic factors that might, in the next two to five years, have an effect on the funding for your department.
4. At your institution, who decides the institutional priorities? Who decides the department priorities? Who decides how many resources your department will receive?
5. How successful were you in obtaining resources for the department last year?
6. a. What calendar must your department and institution follow in preparing a budget request? What is the rationale for using this calendar?
   b. What specific deadline dates must be met by your department in preparing a budget request? How do these deadlines fit in with the other activities that must be conducted in the department?
7. What is the primary role of your department in helping the institution meet its commitments? Is the primary role to conduct research, train graduate students, train undergraduate majors, teach courses, provide community service, or provide professional training? Does it have some other role not listed?
8. a. List, in decreasing order of priority, your department's five to ten most important resource needs—such as personnel, equipment, space, supplies, services, and so forth—during the next three years.
   b. In requesting funds for each of the needs listed, what strategies would be most effective in persuading your dean or academic vice-president to provide the necessary funds?
9. Estimate the likelihood that all the needs listed will be funded.

10. Which needs have the greatest likelihood of being funded? Which have the least? List the needs in decreasing order of likelihood of being funded.

11. Would your chances for obtaining funds be increased if you included in your budget request some mention of how the department's role helps the institution meet its commitments?

12. Review the five types of departments described in this chapter under the heading "Funding of Departments According to Their Roles in Meeting Institutional Commitments."
    a. What type or types does your department represent?
    b. Are there any defining characteristics which should be added to the department taxonomy to adequately accommodate your department? If so, what are they?
    c. Do you disagree with the taxonomy? Suggest a better interpretation.

13. One of the most difficult tasks in developing the budget is to ensure that the data and the words are related and consistent. Another difficulty is preparation and presentation of tight arguments which are logical, complete, and supported by data or information. Such arguments are crucial if enrollment increases are not anticipated. Consider the following statements and determine if the justification each one presents is adequate. If you were the dean, which of the following justifications would you consider seriously? Why? Which would you not consider seriously? Why?
    a. Our faculty-to-student ratio is too high at 22. Indiana State's ratio is 15.
    b. Unless one additional position is provided we shall not be able to meet the demand for accounting courses. The demand is such that we need two more basic classes and one more intermediate class. The resulting credit hours, at current productivities, will generate two positions for the university.
    c. We absolutely must have more secretarial positions. The School of Education has 12 positions more than we do.
    d. We must have more expense money for travel and telephones.
    e. We recognize that the appropriation to the university is not sufficient to fund inflation, but if additional travel funds were available we would be able to enhance our prospects for additional grant support. Currently, I have two faculty members in Washington, and they report that we have been awarded continuation of our big training grant.
    f. We need more laboratory equipment!
    g. We would like $7,200 to purchase a Xerox duplicating machine. This will release $3,600 of expense funds which are currently being used for the lease payment.
    h. Extraordinary salary increases are requested for: Dr. Smith, who

was elected president of the national association for next year and should help enhance our national reputation; Dr. Jones, who received the university's teaching award; and Dr. Doe, who chaired the undergraduate policy council, had a full teaching schedule, and brought in a $150,000 grant which is supporting ten graduate students.

i. The salaries in the school of business are too low. We may lose some faculty next year.

j. Additional resources requested for next year include three new faculty, two secretaries, and one computer programmer.

References

BARAK, ROBERT (et al.) *The Arizona Board of Regents Task Force on Excellence, Efficiency and Competitiveness.* Final Report and Working Papers. 4 vols. 1988. (ERIC Document Reproduction Service No. ED 306 803)

CURTIS, DAN B. *Marketing the Training Course On- and Off-Campus.* 1984. (ERIC Document Reproduction Service No. ED 251–873)

DRESSEL, PAUL L., and SIMON, L. A. "Allocating Resources Among Departments." *New Directions for Institutional Research,* no. 11, San Francisco: Jossey–Bass, 1976.

HALSTEAD, KENT. *Higher Education Price Indexes: 1990 Update.* Washington, DC: Research Associates of Washington, 1991.

———. *State Profiles: Financing Public Higher Education, 1978 to 1990.* Washington, DC: Research Associates of Washington, 1991.

LESLIE, LARRY L., and ANDERSON, RICHARD E. (Eds.) *ASHE Reader on Finance in Higher Education.* Lexington, MA: Ginn Press, 1986.

MALM, LINDA. *Leadership Practice: How I Raised $100,000 This Year with No Fund Raising Experience.* 1990. (ERIC Document Reproduction Service No. ED 319 423)

MILLETT, JOHN. *Resources Reallocation in Research Universities.* Washington, DC: Academy for Educational Development, 1973.

MCFERRON, J. RICHARD (et al.) "Assessing and Supporting Quality in the Liberal Arts: The Role of the Chief Liberal Arts Academic Officer." *Journal of Education Administration,* v 26 (2), 1988, pp. 393–407.

MESINGER, RICHARD J., and DUBEK, LEROY W. *College and University Budgeting.* Washington, DC: NACUBO, 1984.

MOHANTY, DANELL Q. "Faculty Salary Analyses by Region, Rank, and Discipline from 1977–78 to 1983–84." *Research in Higher Education,* 24, 1985, pp. 304–317.

NEWMAN, FRANK. "Progress Report: The University Role in Research and Technology" and "Research Funding: A New Balance for Effectiveness." *Higher Education and the American Resurgence.* Princeton: The Carnegie Foundation, 1985.

NOVAK, RICHARD. *State Issues in Higher Education: A Bibliography.* Washington, DC: American Association of State Colleges and Universities, Center for State Higher Education Policy and Finance, 1991.

Peseau, Bruce A. *Quantitatively Based Peer Program Identification.* Paper presented at the Annual Conference of the Mid-South Educational Research Association. Louisville, KY, 1988. (ERIC Document Reproduction Service No. ED 301 553)

Vandament, William E. *Managing Money in Higher Education.* San Francisco: Jossey–Bass, 1989.

Winans, Glen T. *Determinants of Budget Allocations to Academic Departments: A Case Study.* ASHE 1987 Annual Meeting Paper, San Diego, 1987. (ERIC Document Reproduction Service No. ED 281 464)

Part *IX*

CURRICULUM MANAGEMENT, TEACHING ASSIGNMENTS, AND EFFECTIVE USE OF FACULTY TIME

Chapter 23. Curriculum Management

Chapter 24. Teaching Assignments and Effective Use of Faculty Time

Curriculum Management

Newly appointed chairpersons will find that curricula and degree programs in their departments are generally in place. Most chairpersons will seldom have the opportunity to plan and implement a brand-new curriculum unless their departments are newly established. If however such is the case and a new curriculum is called for, there are institutional guidelines and procedures regarding what information must be submitted to justify a proposal for a new curriculum, and through which faculty and administrative levels of review the proposal must be submitted in order to be approved. Chairs who plan new curricula should obtain copies of these guidelines and procedures and see to it that they are followed as conscientiously as possible.

In most cases, the chair's principal role in relation to the curriculum is one of properly utilizing feedback from all sources to assure that the existing curriculum is maintained, updated, and efficiently and effectively mangaged. The chair does not normally initiate or design curriculum changes. More likely, effective control over the curriculum is in the hands of faculty committees. In many departments, curriculum changes occur only infrequently, and reflect only major new developments in the discipline or profession. In other departments, where the curriculum may be practice-driven (as in professions like education, social work, library and information science, or applied arts), changes may be more frequent. But most such changes take place only after considerable periods of reflection and discussion among the faculty.

The chair is in a position to ask important questions about the curriculum, and to gather information that may have an impact on *how the faculty think about* needed changes. The chair's responsibility is to test for the curriculum's relevance, and this is done in a variety of ways. From many different sources, the chair gathers and uses new information to provide checks on whether curricular change is needed.

In the pure disciplines, commonly those comprising a college of arts and sciences, new ideas and modes of thought are most likely to come from developments within the field itself. National learned societies and professional journals, as well as informal correspondence among scholars, will reflect emerging ideas and perspectives. Chairs need to be in touch with the people and the media that carry these developments, and they need to hear what others may be saying— because sometimes fields are split, and different views come into contention. Often such clashes produce new syntheses that impact a department's own internal debates. Chairs who are keeping current can *anticipate* what some of the next moves may be on the part of faculty who take a special interest in an intellectual movement.

Chairs of departments responsible for teaching the applied disciplines should be alert to new theories and knowledge being developed in pure discipline departments of the university, especially the new theories and knowledge that form the intellectual foundations of their professional fields. The question to be asked is whether the professional curricula are keeping pace with these new theoretical developments. For example, are the latest advances in learning theory taught in the psychology department included in the teacher education curriculum offered in the College of Education? Students in professional programs who take classes in pure discipline departments are usually quick to perceive when they are being exposed to important new knowledge and theories not yet reflected in the curriculum of their professional field. Students, too, are a good source of information about these things, and department chairs certainly should solicit their input.

The curriculum should also be tested against information from external sources. For example, professional accrediting bodies may be especially good monitors of developments in the field. Periodic contacts (between accreditation visits) and careful reading of the literature from such bodies would be well advised. Similarly, for professions in which certification is important, the department chair should stay in touch with policy developments. In some cases, such as education, certification is handled by a state agency. In others a private national organization may be responsible. One needs to be in close touch with the trends and directions in professional certification and licensure by tracking the proposed and future directions of policy. Whether a national board or a state committee drives such change, their work will likely force change in the department's curriculum. Often the first signs of impending change appear in important states; California and Florida have been leaders in change in certain areas in recent years. While one's own state may lag behind, the pressure to change can come from significant developments elsewhere.

Relevance of the curriculum might also be measured by the demands of employers. Fields which lead to employment must remain competitive and should make serious efforts to assess the needs of the most important employers of graduates. By meeting with key employers, or polling them, or even establishing an advisory panel, the chair can gather useful perspectives and views on what future employers expect from new employees.

Students themselves may provide good information on the relevance of the curriculum. Often they know more than anyone else about what is being taught in courses, and whether it is current. They will be quick to sense that something is out-of-date, or that new developments need to be considered in the curriculum. They have contacts with employers, with certification and licensing agencies, and with courses in other departments of the university. Although they may be reluctant to speak out, their views, when carefully and patiently solicited, can lead to important ideas for change.

Curricular decisions are almost always in the hands of the faculty. The chair will usually *influence* curricular decisions, but is seldom in a position to *make* them unilaterally. There are two principal tools available to a chair whose goal is curricular change: (1) information can be developed and provided to the standing (or other) bodies charged with making curricular decisions; and (2) the chair can delegate responsibilities to consider change to the appropriate committees. Since it is sometimes difficult to achieve consensus about the need for change, the chair may have to plan an orchestrated campaign—but to do so in such a way that it is not overly obvious.

The campaign for change would involve information as the first step. Although national trends and other general information may be the best way to start focusing attention on needed change, the campaign might gradually bring the need closer to the interests of the department itself by involving employers and students in an effort to provide views on how the broader trends might effect this department. If the faculty committees have not begun to operate on their own initiative after the chair's best efforts have been expended in trying to provide information and impetus for change, then the chair may have to delegate a task to the relevant department body. With delegation comes the implication that someone will be held accountable, and the chair should establish some reasonable expectations for the committee's work. These expectations might be used as guidelines for the committee in their deliberations.

Curriculum change is almost always incremental. Chairs who expect revolutionary change are therefore almost always disillusioned. Patience is essential, and a long-term strategy for change is the only safe way to get results. By seeking current information, keeping the faculty abreast of new developments, and delegating particular questions to the appropriate committees, the chair can create a climate in which needed change can be achieved. Since most chairs cannot make unilateral decisions about curriculum, but must work through an elaborate committee structure, creating a climate for change is perhaps the most important and effective strategy they can use.

Management of Curriculum and Time

By efficiently managing its curriculum, a department can often effect savings in faculty time and instructional materials without compromising the quality of instruction or causing undue inconvenience to students. Conversely, if little or no planning time is devoted to the curriculum, the department may overextend its faculty, compromise its goals, and create morale problems that may be difficult to resolve. In other words, without planning, the teaching program may become inefficient, costly, or even obsolete.

Departments must take the time to look at their offerings objectively. For example, the information about the department contained in the university catalog may be incorrect or out of date; some courses listed may no longer be offered, and the content of others may have been altered. The chairperson should ensure that the department's course offerings are appropriately and accurately described. Courses also must be related to the task of providing a coherent and sequential program of studies within the discipline and should not be offered only to satisfy the desires of individual faculty members.

Scheduling classes and assigning rooms are important activities that are sometimes carried out without consideration either of department goals or of data derived from a systematic analysis of needs. Sometimes scheduling duties are carried out by a staff assistant without adequate faculty guidance. Clearly, curriculum management is an important task that should be supervised by the chairperson, who should analyze past experience, examine complaints, and review suggestions for improvement. In effect, he or she should develop and implement reliable and relevant procedures for dealing with the curriculum. The task of curriculum management consists of making such decisions as which new courses will be offered, who should teach particular courses, and which courses might be canceled. All these responsibilities are part of the task of managing instructional resources.

One method of monitoring the curriculum is through a department curriculum committee. In many departments, such a committee may already exist, though it usually has only the responsibility for evaluating proposals for new courses. The committee's task, however, could be expanded to include many other aspects of curriculum management. Following are some suggested responsibilities for an active curriculum committee in the areas of approval of new courses, elimination of existing ones, course schedule and sequence, and curriculum review and analysis.

APPROVAL OF NEW COURSES

Before approving any new course, the committee must take into account certain consequences. First, the committee should ask whether the new course will add to the content or perspective of the subject matter of the current offerings or whether it will substantially duplicate another course offered by this department or another.

A second consideration is the possible effect of the new course on other courses in the department. Will it draw enrollment away from department courses currently offered, or will it generate additional enrollment? If it generates new enrollment, will the enrollment in other university departments be affected? Is the course to be a core, elective, or service course? Will it primarily serve majors, nonmajors, undergraduates, or graduate students?

A third consideration is the effect of the new course on faculty members' teaching assignments. Will some department members have to assume an additional workload, or will a course currently offered be canceled so that its instructor can be assigned to teach the new course?

Finally, the committee should consider the effect of the new course on current physical or financial resources. Will the new course require materials and physical facilities that are not available to the department? Will the new course require an internal reallocation of funds or the acquisition of new funds?

When considering a new course proposal, then, the committee should analyze it in terms of, first, its educational contribution, e.g., course content, methodology, and prerequisites; second, its effect on enrollment, e.g., shifting enrollment and additional enrollment; third, its effect on workload, e.g., effect on current faculty and courses; fourth, budgetary limitations, e.g., faculty positions and the cost of new materials; and fifth, availability of space, e.g., laboratories, classrooms, and special requirements including library acquisitions and services. The committee should also examine the place of the new course within the current sequence of courses and its probable effect on the student. For students, the proliferation of courses may not only allow but even encourge early specialization. In some disciplines, specialization may narrow the opportunity to obtain a well-rounded higher education, but in other disciplines specialization may be desirable.

The department, when considering a course proposal, may need to revise its curricular goals. Such goals and objectives often include specifying the kinds of knowledge a student should obtain while majoring in the department's discipline, the competencies that the student should be able to demonstrate successfully, and perhaps even the kinds of problems the student should be able to solve. Such information may be necessary for courses currently offered as well as for proposed courses to show how the courses relate to the department's curricular goals.

The decision to approve a new course should be based on careful consideration of the information obtained during the review of the proposal. Often, a committee will not consider the effect of a new course on department enrollment. Frequently, adding a new course only disperses students majoring in the field among a greater number of courses offered by the same department. In such a case, the average class size would be reduced and the faculty workload would be increased, but the total department enrollment would remain unchanged. The effect of a new course on department enrollment, while not the major factor in deciding whether to approve the course, remains an important consideration.

ELIMINATION OF COURSES

Eliminating obsolete courses allows more efficient use of available resources and reduces the amount of misleading information appearing in catalogs and counseling manuals. Some researchers have even suggested that a course be dropped when a new course is added. Such a mechanical approach, however, may be indicative of unimaginative planning or desperation caused by declining resources.

A periodic review of enrollment in all courses is a systematic way for the curriculum committee to begin the task of designating courses to be eliminated. The ability to conduct an enrollment review depends in large part on the records kept by the department staff or on the availability of these types of data from the college or university institutional research office.

Such a review opens up at least three alternatives for the committee. First, a course that generates a minimum number of students might be retained if it were determined to be beneficial to the students enrolled in it. Enrollment could be enhanced, perhaps, by changing the meeting time or by offering the course less frequently. Second, the review could result in a course being eliminated because the committee determined that the content was no longer of interest or that another course was meeting student needs and drawing enrollment away. Third, the reviewing committee could recommend that course content, methodology, or emphasis be changed to revitalize the course. These decisions, when made well in advance of registration, enable the chairperson to allocate instructional resources wisely. Courses that continue to be offered but that are ignored by students should undergo stringent scrutiny.

The course offerings should be revised as little as possible during the registration process. Some departments allow university policies about minimum class size to determine which courses are to be dropped. The obvious drawback of this approach is that the reassignment of faculty members whose courses have been dropped is not determined by careful review of curricular or other department needs. Such inadequate curriculum planning and management usually results in ad hoc assignments, last-minute switching of instruction obligations, and "default" research or public service assignments. In addition, the department loses the opportunity to support student needs.

Some departments announce more courses than will eventually be taught and wait to see which courses actually attract the most students and which attract the fewest. Courses with few students are then dropped. The difference between this approach and the "no planning" approach is that in this case an alternative assignment has already been worked out should enrollment be insufficient to justify the course.

COURSE SCHEDULE AND SEQUENCE

When developing a schedule of classes, the department must consider the needs of students, the availability of appropriate classroom space, and the time preferred by students and faculty members. A review of past experiences and careful scheduling of core and elective or service courses may lead to an improvement in class schedules and faculty workloads. The schedule also must take into account special characteristics of the department's students; for example, if a large number of the students are working full time, scheduling morning classes makes little sense.

The department would be wise to review its courses annually. Information such as the number of approved courses, the number and frequency of courses actually offered, the enrollment gathered, and the number of students who dropped each course affords the department an opportunity to exercise control over its course offerings. Perhaps examining records of students majoring in the field as to courses taken, sequence, and so forth may help determine whether the recommended sequence is being followed.

Following are four examples of hypothetical situations that would require in-depth analysis. In each case, the academic year is based on the semester calendar with courses offered during each of three terms—fall, spring, and summer.

1. Course A was offered all three terms and had the following enrollment: fifteen students during fall; eighteen during winter; and seventeen during summer. A review of student course sequences may indicate that no disruption would occur if the courses were offered only in the winter and summer terms. (The assumption here is that faculty resources would be available in the summer.) Furthermore, because the course is required for students majoring in the field, the total annual enrollment may not be substantially reduced. Thus, by offering the course only twice a year, the department has decreased its instruction workload without substantially decreasing enrollment.

2. Course B has been taught during two terms, and each term its enrollment has been low. Examination of the situation reveals that the course has always been offered in the late afternoon. If increased enrollment is desired, the course might be moved to "prime time," e.g., late mornings at residential universities, or evenings at universities with a large number of part-time students.

3. A department has 127 approved courses, but only eighty-seven of them were offered last year and eighty-three were offered the year before. Twenty-five of the approved courses had not been offered in either of the last two years, while two of the offered courses (four sections each) accounted for 75 percent of the department's total enrollment. This situation suggests that a curriculum review, including a close examination of the department's curricular goals, is in order.

4. During the past few years the enrollment in an upper-level undergraduate course has consisted mostly of graduate students. Perhaps this course should be offered as a graduate course.

CURRICULUM REVIEW AND ANALYSIS

The importance of periodically reviewing courses before adding, eliminating, expanding, or revising them cannot be overstated. The periodic review should encompass enrollment data, revised course syllabi, statements of course objectives and student objectives, and any other special or relevant information about the courses.

Another form of curriculum analysis can be conducted using data showing department interrelationships. A given department may list all its courses and indicate the number of students majoring in other fields who are enrolled in each course. Knowing the extent to which other departments provide students for each course may be the basis for adjusting course content or method of presentation. Table 23.1 shows how such information can be arranged in a matrix. By collecting this type of data from other departments, a given department may also discover what courses are serving its own majors. Therefore, the effect of referring students to courses outside the department can be estimated. A department that offers service courses to students majoring in other fields can estimate the effect of curricular decisions by these other departments.

Almost all universities that have computerized student data files have the capability to construct such a matrix, which is usually called "the induced course load matrix." Chairpersons should contact their institutional research offices for help in obtaining the data.

DATA AND INFORMATION REQUIREMENTS

Institutional research offices amass a large body of data, often for purposes of program evaluation. If the chairperson feels that such information would be useful, even if no formal review is sheduled, he or she should contact the office of institutional research and request the information. The chairperson should understand that the data received are only as good as the data submitted to the centralized information sources. If there is a discrepancy between the data provided by the office and the chairperson's own knowledge, the chairperson should determine the reasons for the discrepancy and attempt to correct the data.

An improved curriculum, then, helps the students and the department alike. A system of curriculum management may be a departure from the common practice of allowing individual faculty members to determine the courses they want to teach. But a planned approach may be preferable to a situation where courses are frequently canceled at the last minute, contracts must be revised, and students are unable to progress systematically through their programs of study. Planning is not synonymous with inflexibility, nor need it cause a decline in academic quality. By the same token, proliferation of courses is not synonymous with improvement in academic quality. By assigning time to a faculty member to revise a course or two, the chairperson may be making a short-term investment leading to increased student satisfaction and reduced faculty workload.

TABLE 23.1 Sample of an induced course load matrix: student credit hours generated Fall Term 1987, by program major and by department, San Luis State College, Domingo, Florida

	PROGRAM MAJORS, LOWER LEVEL										Total Student Credit Hours by Department
Departments	Undeclared	Arts; Humanities	Biological Science	Science; Math	Social Sciences	Agriculture	Business	Health Sciences	Ornamental Horticulture	Food Science Technology	
Business	803	185		44	527	33	2,514	38	35		4,179
English and Foreign Language Literature	261	1,287	139	405	1,206	314	784	442	146		4,984
Fine Arts	276	1,153	14	84	230	8	149	63	20		1,997
Life Sciences	184	472	227	93	1,174	1,067	273	1,492	53		5,035
Physical Sciences	249	786	198	1,608	805	505	923	847	161		6,082
Social Behavioral Sciences	228	841	118	189	2,116	99	595	331	104		4,621
Vocational Tech.	203	12	7	31	8	22	3	756	1,927	870	3,839
Total Student Credit Hours by Major	2,204	4,736	703	2,454	6,066	2,048	5,241	3,969	2,446	870	30,737

Note: Fifteen student credit hours generate one FTE student.

Questions

1. How frequently does your department review its entire curriculum for current relevancy?
2. What procedures must be followed at your institution to delete an existing course or add a new one?
3. To what extent does your faculty review the curriculum in terms of what will be the curricular needs in five years? What procedures are followed to facilitate this type of review?
4. How much time does it take from when a decision has been made to offer a new course until the new course can be offered?
5. How many and what levels of review does a proposed new course undergo to receive final approval for its implementation?
6. In your department, what are the chances that the new course will be taught by one of the current faculty? a new faculty member? an adjunct part-time instructor employed specifically to teach the course?

References

AKST, GEOFFERY, and RYZEWIC, SUSAN REMMER. *Methods of Evaluating College Remedial Mathematics Programs: Results of a National Survey.* ERIC Research Monograph Series No. 10. 1985. (ERIC Document Reproduction Service No. ED 262 993)

ASTIN, ALEXANDER W. *Assessment for Excellence: The Philosophy and Practices of Assessment and Evaluation in Higher Education.* New York: ACE/Macmillan, 1991.

BARBER, ELINOR G., and MORGAN, ROBERT P. *Boon or Bane: Foreign Graduate Students in U.S. Engineering Programs.* New York: Institute for International Education, 1988.

BESS, JAMES L. "Classroom and Management Decisions Using Student Data: Designing an Information System." *Journal of Higher Education,* May–June 1979, pp. 256–279.

BLACKBURN, ROBERT (et al.) *Changing Practices in Undergraduate Education.* Berkeley: Carnegie Council on Policy Studies in Higher Education, 1976.

BOWEN, HOWARD R., and DOUGLAS, G. K. *Efficiency in Liberal Education: A Study of Comparative Instructional Costs and Different Ways of Organizing Teacher Learning in a Liberal Arts College.* New York: McGraw–Hill, 1971.

BOWEN, HOWARD R., and SCHUSTER, JACK H. *The American Professoriate: A National Resource Imperiled.* New York: Carnegie Corporation, 1986.

CARDENAS, KAREN HARDY. *Foreign Language Programs and Foreign Language Program Administrators: Results of a Survey.* 1988. (ERIC Document Reproduction Service No. ED 299 815)

CARNEGIE FOUNDATION FOR THE ADVANCEMENT OF TEACHING. *Missions of the College Curriculum: A Contemporary Review with Suggestions.* San Francisco: Jossey–Bass, 1977.

CURTIS, DAN B. *Marketing the Training Course On- and Off-campus.* 1984. (ERIC Document Reproduction Service NO. ED 251 873)

CHAMBERLAIN, PHILLIP C. "Resistance to Change in Curriculum Planning." In *The Academic Department or Division Chairman: A Complex Role,* edited by James Brann and Thomas A. Emmet, pp. 250–262. Detroit: Balamp, 1972.

COHEN, ARTHUR M., and BRAWER, FLORENCE B. *The American Community College.* 2nd ed. San Francisco: Jossey–Bass, 1988.

DRESSEL, PAUL L. *College and University Curriculum.* Berkeley: McCutchan, 1971.

FELDMAN, KENNETH A., and NEWCOMB, THEODORE M. *The Impact of College on Students.* 2 vols. San Francisco: Jossey–Bass, 1969.

FINK, L. DEE. *The Lecture: Analyzing and Improving Its Effectiveness. In New Directions for Teaching and Learning: The Department Chairperson's Role in Enhancing College Teaching,* 37, Spring 1989, pp. 17–30.

FREDERICK, PETER J. "Involving Students More Actively in the Classroom." In *New Directions for Teaching and Learning: The Department Chairperson's Role in Enhancing College Teaching,* 37, Spring 1989, pp. 31–40.

GORDON, THOMAS, and BURCH, NOEL. *T.E.T.—Teacher Effectiveness Training.* New York: David McKay Co., 1975.

GRANT, FRANCES L., and MAIN, ROBERT G. "Curriculum 1984: Meeting the Needs of the Information Age." *Journal of the American Society for Information Science,* 37, 1986, pp. 12–19.

GUEST, RORBERT H.; HERSEY, PAUL; and BLANCHARD, KENNETH H. *Organizational Change Through Effective Leadership.* Englewood Cliffs: Prentice–Hall, 1977.

HARLOW, LINDA L. "Individualized Instruction in Foreign Languages: A Survey of Programs at the College Level." *Modern Languages Journal,* 71, 1987, pp. 388–394.

HOUSE, J. DANIEL. *Longitudinal Curriculum Changes Instructional Design and Educational Psychology Doctoral Programs.* Paper presented at the Annual Convention of the Association for Educational Communications and Technology, Las Vegas, 1986. (ERIC Document Reproduction Service No. Ed 267 777)

JOHNSON, F. CRAIG. "Data Requirements for Academic Departments." In *New Directions for Institutional Research: Examining Departmental Leadership,* 10, edited by John C. Smart and James R. Montgomery. San Francisco: Jossey–Bass, 1976.

KINGSTON, NEAL M. *The Graduate Record Examinations Validity Study Service: Yesterday and Tomorrow.* Princeton: Educational Testing Service, 1986. (ERIC Document Reproduction Service No. ED 300 452)

LOUIS, KAREN S. (et al.) *University Policies and Ethical Issues in Graduate Research and Education.* Results of a Survey of Graduate School Deans. ASHE 1988 Annual Meeting Paper, 1988. (ERIC Document Reproduction Service No. ED 303 100)

LYNCH, DAVID, and BOWKER, LEE. *The Status of Adult and Continuing Education Within American Institutions of Higher Learning.* Indiana University of Pennsylvania Institute for Advanced Research, 1989. (ERIC Document Reproduction Service No. ED 311 816)

MALANEY GARY D. "Differentiation in Graduate Education." *Research in Higher Education,* 25, 1986, pp. 82–96.

MARCUS, DORA. *Lessons Learned from FIPSE Projects.* Washington, DC: Fund For the Improvement of Postsecondary Education, 1991.

MAYHEW, LOUIS B. "Curricular Reform and Faculty Well-Being." *Educational Record,* January 1963, pp. 53–61.

MCGEE, GAIL W., and FORD, ROBERT C. "Faculty Research Productivity and Intention to Change Positions." *Review of Higher Education,* 11, 1987, pp. 1–16.

NOONAN, JOHN F. "Curricular Change: A Strategy for Improving Teaching." In *The Expanded Campus: Current Issues in Higher Education* 1972, edited by Dyckman W. Vermilye. San Francisco: Jossey–Bass, 1972.

PAGE, JANE A., and PAGE, FRED M. *Collegiate Instruction: Some Differences Among Faculty Members Based on Rank, Years of Experience, and School Affiliation.* Paper presented at the Annual Meeting of the Mid-South Educational Research Association, Mobile, AL, 1987. (ERIC Document Reproduction Service No. ED 289 445)

RODDY, MARY ELLEN. *Qualifications and Productivity of Nontenure-track Faculty.* Paper presented at the Annual Meeting of the American Educational Research Association, Washington, DC, 1987. (ERIC Document Reproduction Service No. ED 284 488)

SAGEN, H. BRADLEY. "Organizational Reform Is Not Enough." In *Elements Involved in Academic Change,* edited by Charles U. Walker, pp. 20–29. Washington, DC: Association of American Colleges, 1972.

SEDLACEK, WILLIAM E. "Black Students on White Campuses: Twenty Years of Research." In *ASHE Reader on College Students,* Needham Heights, MA: Ginn Press, 1989.

STANLEY, BARBARA. *Teaching Research Ethics: Methods and Practice.* Paper presented at the Annual Meeting of the APA, Toronto, 1984. (ERIC Document Reproduction Service No. ED 251 019)

SCHLOSSBERG, NANCY K.; LYNCH, ANN Q.; and CHICKERING, ARTHUR W. *Improving Higher Education Environments for Adults: Responsive Programs and Services from Entry to Departure.* San Francisco: Jossey–Bass, 1989.

STIER, WILLIAM F., JR. *Physical Education Workload Policies, Practices and Procedures on the Junior/Community College Level—A National Inquiry.* Paper presented at the National Convention of the American Alliance for Health, Physical Education, Recreation and Dance, Cincinnati, 1986. (ERIC Document Reproduction Service No. ED 273 586)

TRANK, DOUGLAS M., and SHEPARD, GREGORY A. *Textbook Selection Criteria for a Multisection Basic Course Taught Exclusively by Graduate Teaching Assistants,* 1987. (ERIC Document Reproduction Service No. ED 287 183)

TRASK, KERRY A. "The Chairperson and Teaching." In *New Directions for Teaching and Learning: The Department Chairperson's Role in Enhancing College Teaching,* 37, Spring 1989, pp. 99–107.

TRINKHAUS, JOHN W., and BOOKE, ALVIN L. "The Curriculum Change Process: Participants, Strategies, and Tactics." *Research in Higher Education,* 13, 1980, pp. 307–319.

VON HADEN, HERBERT I., and KING, JEAN MARIE. *Educational Innovator's Guide.* Worthington, OH: Charles A. Jones, 1974.

WIGINGTON, HENRY. "Students' Ratings of Instructors Revisited: Interactions Among Class Instructor Variables." *Research in Higher Education,* 30, 1989, pp. 331–344.

Chapter *24*

Teaching Assignments and Effective Use of Faculty Time

As enrollments stabilize or increase and budgets remain the same or do not increase proportionately, the number of constraints on the institution will increase at all levels. Effective use of faculty time will become essential but can be accomplished only if the chairperson is fully aware of the department's workload and can project assignments over the whole academic year. In general, he or she needs to know the department's workload, understand the faculty members' professional and personal concerns, and then be able to interpret and communicate department needs while negotiating assignments with the faculty and staff. Clearly stated department goals and reliable historical data about all department resources will allow the chairperson to justify assignments in terms of the department's objectives. The ability to estimate requirements for an entire year, rather than treating each term as a unique entity, will help stimulate acceptance of heavier workloads during some terms.

Very few departments have enough faculty members to do everything that needs to be done for the university, the community, and other constituents. A department chairperson may need to juggle academic assignments to ensure that sufficient effort is expended on instructional activities to cover student demands while at the same time providing appropriate research and service time for the faculty. Careful planning of teaching assignments is required to allow time for research and service, particularly for younger faculty members, who must make reasonable progress toward promotion and tenure. Typical complications arise when established faculty members accept outside contractual obligations and have to find substitute teachers for the classroom. In addition, faculty members going on sabbatical may leave gaps in the teaching program and require replacement. As suggested in the preceding chapter, curriculum planning and management can provide a degree of flexibility. In any event, the chairperson must be able to show the faculty that each department member is treated fairly.

An equitable distribution of the department workload may be achieved by several methods. Some chairpersons make all assignments, while others depend on a committee process. A recommended technique is participatory planning. This method is not always the most efficient planning tool, since it requires extensive communication among faculty members.

Several arguments can be made in favor of the participatory planning model, however. An open discussion among faculty members who are familiar with the courses they teach can facilitate decisions about the sequence of courses, the frequency with which they are offered, the level of performance that can be expected of students following the sequence, and so on. The faculty can devise equitable procedures for assigning introductory courses as well as those courses with unusual workload requirements. Workload policy governing the balancing of large and small courses with new and old preparations can be most readily developed through participatory planning. Moreover, peer pressure tends to reinforce policies developed in an open manner.

The chairperson sometimes has the difficult task of determining whether particular faculty members are competent to teach certain courses. In a period of expanding resources and enrollment, a department may have added specialists and specialized courses. When these specialists leave, their specialized courses, having become a part of a subcurriculum, remain.

The chairperson must then choose among several possibilities: convincing another faculty member to step in temporarily; reassigning the course to another faculty member and allowing course development time; recruiting a part-time teacher; replacing the course with one that is already being offered either within or outside the department; or, with the approval of the faculty or students, dropping the course. Other considerations may include the graduate faculty status of the proposed substitute instructor or even a strong expression of preference by the dean or academic vice-president for one of the alternatives. In any event, the chairperson needs to know about the faculty members' specialty training, their current specialty interests, their reputations for teaching effectiveness, and other characteristics that are relevant to the assignment process.

If the chairperson decides to retain the course offering, he or she will usually have to persuade the most able candidate from among the faculty to accept this new responsibility. The chairperson must proceed cautiously, however, so as not to give a "proprietary deed" for the course to the substitute teacher until and unless the other faculty members concur. "Ownership" can be a prime motivating force for the teacher to develop and enhance a course. On the other hand, a faculty member who regularly teaches the same courses, year after year, may become bored with them and ineffective in the classroom.

The middle ground between ownership and boredom can be attained through a system of rotation. Even the specialized courses in many departments can be taught by more than one professor. Every faculty member might be required to be prepared at least to take responsibility for additional required or specialized courses. These arrangements can be worked out cooperatively, with the approval of the chairperson, after vitae and teaching records of each faculty member have been reviewed. The chairperson's genuine concern for faculty development will be tested in such cases. Finding the right opportunities for growth and improvement for each faculty member is a challenging task.

The problem of reassigning and revitalizing courses also occurs when enrollment in two related courses declines so markedly that they have to be combined to meet minimum enrollment standards. Prior "ownership," expertise in the subject matter, and rank and seniority in the department may complicate efforts at reassignment. The new activities required of faculty members who will have smaller teaching loads is a topic that ought to be discussed before or during the time that courses are being combined, not afterwards. A clear statement of department goals, as well as an inventory of research and service activities for each faculty member, would be helpful to those involved in reassigning courses.

Declining budgets and an increase in faculty grievances may well lead to a squeeze on **faculty time** which will, in turn, retard a department's progress toward achieving its teaching and research goals. In such situations the department's mood and productivity may depend more heavily on the manner with which faculty workload assignments are handled than on the assignments themselves. Perhaps greater involvement by the department faculty would be helpful. In essence, by using open planning to make teaching assignments, the chairperson can help change the faculty's perception of administrative capriciousness and promote unity of purpose within the department. This method, even though the results may not be ideal, may be perceived as more fair and, therefore, more palatable.

Understandably, the participatory process can create numerous problems for the chairperson. Moreover, there may be insufficient time to implement the process. Sometimes a chairperson will not know until July what the department's allocation will be for the upcoming academic year, which begins in August or September. Yet faculty assignments for a given calendar year must be made much earlier than July. One solution to this dilemma is to implement the planning process in the preceding February or March. At the least, information from the faculty can be obtained and feelings aired. An estimate of instructional resources with alternative assignments can be made, and the result can be fine-tuned in the fall.

Essentially, planning with 90 percent of the information available is superior to no planning at all. Also, decisions that are generally understood and that are accepted by the majority of the faculty are more easily implemented. An open planning process that relates operational necessities to department goals is one technique for achieving important objectives. Furthermore, a process by which all faculty members can identify their contributions and feel productive will tend to minimize friction within the department.

Most descriptions of the planning process give the impression that it is a smooth, well-oiled operation, when in actuality it is usually a fitful and uneven affair. Planning consists of the working out of tensions among various opinions and ideas, and often occurs as a result of pulling and pushing by various factions within the department. Integrating differing opinions into a working and realistic plan requires a great deal of effort.

Some Typical Problem-Solving Situations in Managing Faculty Time

Following are four examples of problems that chairpersons have encountered when trying to decide how best to allocate **faculty time**. Most discussions or problem-solving techniques contain essentially the same elements: alternative solutions to the difficulty and some method of evaluating or ranking the alternatives.

EXAMPLE #1

The chairperson of a geology department is faced with increasing demand for more frequent offerings of some of the more specialized petrology courses. He draws up a list of alternative solutions to the problem and evaluates each alternative using three criteria: (1) its potential for solving the problem; (2) its cost; and (3) its feasibility. These criteria are admittedly a bit fuzzy, but they have a certain logic. They allow the chairperson to determine what the chances are that the proposed solution, if implemented, will actually solve the problem; how much the proposed solution will cost; and what the chance is that it can be implemented. The chairperson considers five alternatives.

1. One possibility is to hire additional faculty members to meet the increased demand. More instructors would certainly solve the problem, but the cost would be high and the chances of getting new lines approved by the dean are not good.

2. A second alternative is to reduce the number of courses offered by the department and shift faculty members to the petrology courses. This approach would solve the immediate problem at practically no cost, but the faculty members whose courses would be dropped would surely object and the sequence of course requirements in other specialties would be disturbed. Therefore, the likelihood that this alternative could be implemented is only fair.

3. A third suggestion is to hire additional graduate teaching assistants to help teach the petrology courses. Unfortunately, the courses are too specialized to be taught by graduate assistants. Graduate students, however, might be used to teach other courses, especially basic courses, thereby freeing faculty members to teach petrology. In this case, the potential for solving the problem is somewhat higher. Although the cost of employing additional graduate students would not

be as prohibitive as hiring additional faculty members, obtaining funds for this purpose would not be easy.

4. A fourth alternative is to increase the use of instructional technology. Although programmed instruction is a viable technique, the faculty feels uncomfortable with it. It has the potential for partially solving the problem, but the effort involved in gearing up to use it would be fairly expensive, and the probability that the faculty could be motivated to develop such a system is not high.

5. A final alternative is to reduce the number of sections by increasing the number of students per section. With fewer sections to teach, the instructors would have time to devote to teaching petrology courses. The costs here would be negligible, and the proposed plan would be relatively easy to implement.

The chairperson draws up a list of these five alternatives. He then evaluates each alternative on the basis of the previously mentioned criteria: Potential for solving problems, cost and feasibility. Each criterion is rated on a three-point scale: "high," "medium," and "low" (see Table 24.1). Examination of the list reveals that the fifth alternative combines high potential and high feasibility with low cost. The chairperson, therefore, does select this alternative.

In many instances, however, the choice is not so easy. Two or more alternatives may be equally attractive. Approaching a problem in the manner suggested above can help eliminate some suggested solutions quickly and allow the department to concentrate its energies on deciding among the most feasible alternatives. Some chairpersons do not feel compelled to put all the alternatives in writing, preferring to debate the issue mentally. Whether the chairperson writes down the alternatives or not, the decision process is basically the same. The chairperson could also organize a group of faculty members to handle the task of listing alternatives and making rational choices.

EXAMPLE #2

Our second example of a resource allocation problem is much like the first, although more complicated. A department of interior design experiences a steady enrollment increase in a department subspecialty, nonresidential (industrial and institutional) space analysis and design. The courses in the subspecialty are taught by Faculty Member S and Faculty Member J and their graduate assistants. The two

TABLE 24.1 Ranking of Alternatives to Accommodate Course Demand

	POTENTIAL for SOLUTIONS	COST	FEASIBILITY
1. Additional faculty positions	High	High	Low
2. Reduction in course offerings	High	Low	Medium
3. Increase in graduate assistants	Low	Medium	Medium
4. Increased use of instruction technology	Medium	Medium	Medium
5. Reduction in sections per course	High	Low	High

professors are nationally recognized as experts in the field. Conscientious and productive, they are trying to implement a design internship program that requires much travel and supervision. While capable of doing research, they have published nothing in the last two years because their teaching duties have been so time-consuming.

To allow themselves more time for research, Faculty Member S and Faculty Member J request that additional faculty members be assigned to help teach the nonresidential design courses. The chairperson, recognizing that productive research is indispensable to the faculty members' careers and the department's reputation, wants to do everything possible to provide the faculty members with research time.

A review of the course enrollments in the subspecialty shows that the two faculty members are, indeed, carrying heavy instruction loads (see Table 24.2). All the courses, with the exception of IDE 4220L, are 5-credit-hour lecture courses. The exception is a 3-credit-hour laboratory class that requires supervision. The institution is on a semester calendar, and every course is taught every term. The faculty members' failure to carry out their research interests is understandable, for each course was offered three times a year.

The chairperson, when considering possible solutions, realizes that other department members will be unwilling to teach the nonresidential courses because they are not primarily interested in that aspect of interior design. Hiring new faculty members, on the other hand, is not at all feasible given the budgetary constraints at that time.

The chairperson then asks himself whether the classes could be offered less frequently without a decline in enrollment and whether the classes could be increased in size without a decline in quality. Discussions with faculty members and students indicate that the lecture courses could be taught just as effectively even if they were much larger and that they could be offered alternative terms without depriving students of the opportunity to complete their required courses within a normal time frame. The laboratory course would have to be taught each term because the number of student work stations is limited; no more than twenty students per term can be accommodated.

TABLE *24.2* Instructional Load, Courses in Nonresidential Design Subspecialty, Department of Interior Design

	FALL		WINTER		SUMMER	
Course	Enrollment	Faculty Member	Enrollment	Faculty Member	Enrollment	Faculty Member
IDE 4200	15	S	16	S	14	S
IDE 4220L	19	S	19	S	16	S
IDE 4240	23	S	25	S	20	S
IDE 4300	30	S	35	S	25	S
IDE 5943	28	J	26	J	22	J
IDE 5943r	12	J	14	J	16	J

EXAMPLE #3

The first two examples present allocation problems that involve creating additional time for faculty members to conduct research or to teach new courses. The third example deals with the opposite type of situation. Because of circumstances beyond the department's control, certain of its activities have been reduced, leaving the faculty members with considerable time that is not fully occupied. The challenge is to create activities to replace those that have been curtailed.

The department of modern languages in a large urban university suffers a drastic decrease in enrollment when the undergraduate curriculum committee of the college of arts and sciences votes to abolish the foreign-language requirement for the baccalaureate degree. Although the university is not absolutely devoted to funding departments on the basis of student credit hours taught, the situation in the modern-languages department is very serious. The department is demoralized, the funding for graduate students is reduced dramatically, and even scholarly senior professors who do little undergraduate teaching seem to be affected.

The chairperson reviews the situation in her mind. From the outset, she realizes that the least desirable solution to the problem would be to dismiss nontenured faculty members and to abolish certain programs, but she also realizes that this possibility might become a reality in the absence of other viable solutions. Aware that the university will not reinstate the language requirement, she nevertheless decides to make contact with several other departments to emphasize the value of foreign languages at the undergraduate level. She considers several ideas, but before deciding on a course of action, she needs answers to the following questions:

- How many areas and programs would continue to encourage their undergraduates to take language courses as electives for cultural or practical reasons?
- Would it be profitable for the department to reschedule and restructure its undergraduate teaching to accommodate the university's urban environment?
- Might rescheduling some courses to the late afternoon or evening attract a new student clientele? If offered to the adult community as part of a continuing education program, would such courses find acceptance?
- How many secondary school foreign-language teachers might be interested in attending in-service courses designed especially for them?
- Would the department faculty cooperate with other departments to develop interdisciplinary programs of a cultural nature?
- Could special foreign-language courses be designed to serve business needs? Foreign manufacturers need instruction manuals translated into colloquial English. Similarly, American manufacturing companies with a

large export market need staff to translate instruction, repair, and service manuals from English into foreign languages.

- Could special training be provided for persons who want to develop competencies in translating such manuals?

Some of these ideas are good ones; some are not. The chairperson must try to assess the potential benefit and the feasibility of each alternative. Perhaps all the alternatives taken together may not be able to reestablish lost enrollment. The department's survival at its present size may well depend on its importance to the university's overall mission. If that is the case, a written report justifying the retention of the current faculty members may become necessary. The chairperson should anticipate the possible need for such a document and involve the faculty in preparing it even before a request is received from the dean or vice-president.

EXAMPLE #4

In our fourth example, the chairperson of the department of urban and regional studies in a medium-sized university receives a memo from his dean, who has just returned from a conference in Washington. The dean has learned that a certain federal agency is about to initiate a new program for funding university projects in community development. In the memo, he suggests that the department consider submitting a proposal for a grant to fund a three-year project at $100,000 per year. In a subsequent telephone call, the dean again raises the subject of the desirability of the department's pursuing a federal grant in community development as described in his memo.

Before making any commitment, however, the chairperson wants to satisfy himself that a project funded by this particular federal agency would benefit the department; the faculty endorsement and support could be obtained; that certain department members have the competency to write a persuasive proposal; that sufficient department resources could be made available to those writing the proposal; and that the department would be able to carry out the proposed project successfully should it be approved.

Let us review the questions that go through the chairperson's mind: Can a project be developed that meets the goals of both the agency and the department? How will the project benefit the department and its faculty members? If the project does not contribute to the department's goals or the faculty's benefit, it should not be pursued.

Let us assume that in this case the chairperson has positive feelings about the dean's suggestion and believes that the project would be a good one for the department. His feelings are buttressed by several sound reasons: some faculty members have the necessary competencies; the project would give visibility to the department and the university; the project would provide hard data for valuable publications by faculty members; and, last but not least, funds would be available for graduate assistantships and salaries for summer faculty members.

The next step is to determine the best way to get faculty support. The chairperson remembers full well the circumstances when he tried to obtain support for an idea by presenting it for the first time to the whole faculty during one of its meetings. To overcome the department's initial negative reaction took several months of difficult lobbying. He later learned from a friend who was a seasoned administrator that a group will usually have a negative reaction to any idea that is presented for the first time to the group as a whole. Therefore, he decides to discuss the idea individually with some department members, especially those who are faculty leaders. If they cannot see the advantages to the department and their support is not forthcoming, the idea should be dropped, at least for the time being.

Once the support of key faculty members is obtained, the chairperson must think about the best time for placing the matter on the agendum of a full department meeting. At the meeting, all faculty members will have an opportunity to express themselves, and those colleagues with whom he has spoken earlier can be counted on to support the idea and emphasize its potential advantages to the department.

After satisfying himself and his faculty that the department should prepare a proposal, the chairperson must make decisions about who should write the proposal and what resources can be made available for the effort. He reviews in his mind all the department members and their respective workloads. The faculty consists of three full professors (including the chairperson), four assoicate professors, and three assistant professors. Among the faculty members are experts in the areas of transportation planning, housing and community development, health planning, and environmental planning.

Two faculty members, Smith and Jones, are recognized experts in community development and are especially suited to the task. The chairperson wonders whether the task of writing the proposal could be added to the existing assignment of either or both professors, whether a workload must be reduced in order to make time available, and who will assume the excused duties in the event a person's workload is reduced.

The chairperson now examines the existing workloads of Smith and Jones in terms of the number of courses each teaches, the number of students in each course, the time required for preparation of lectures, research involvement, committee assignments, and so forth. He finds that the workloads of both professors are approximately equal.

Smith indicates that he is willing to be the principal writer if he is given a reduced workload. When he is asked what part of his assignment he would prefer to relinquish, however, Smith produces a list of his reasons for not giving anything up. He volunteers some personal time for the assignment. Jones is also willing to write the proposal, but he is not very enthusiastic about it because much of his personal time is taken up with outside consulting activities and he depends on the income the consulting produces. In order for Jones to write the proposal, he would have to curtail his consultations.

The chairperson assigns Smith to be the writer and suggests that for the coming term Smith either cancel one undergraduate course or turn it over to a well-qualified graduate student to teach under Smith's supervision. In either case, the time saved would not be enough to carry out the entire task, so Smith will have to devote some of his personal time to the activity. Smith agrees to accept the responsibility for writing the proposal and selects one of his best graduate students to teach the undergraduate course.

The chairperson also considers the costs of writing the proposal in terms of staff time and department money. The secretarial staff consists of two full-time secretaries and a half-time typist. The chairperson must decide whether the staff can provide the necessary help to the proposal writer. If not, can expense dollars be used to hire a temporary typist for the final draft? What would have to be cut from the expense budget in order to hire the typist? Expense dollars usually pay for items such as travel, duplicating, telephone, and office supplies. A reduction in any of these categories could involve some changes in department operation. For example, what would be the effects of cuts in travel money? How would the faculty react if travel money that had already been committed could not be delivered? Might the dean be willing to provide either money or secretarial time for so worthy a project?

Finally, the chairperson ponders the personal costs of pursuing and administering the grant. How much time will he have to spend supervising the preparation of the proposal? How much time will be spent supervising the activities of faculty members who will be involved in implementing the project? The chairperson must consider the effects of any ambitious undertaking on himself as well as the department as a whole.

When resources are shifted to accommodate an added activity, the department equilibrium becomes upset. Some faculty members may feel that they are being asked to sacrifice too much for an undertaking that does not seem to benefit them personally, and the chairperson must be prepared to soothe them.

Whenever a department considers taking on some significant, previously unanticipated activity, all the variables of department operation must be carefully examined. Important decisions should be made on the basis of available data. Some of the data is to be found in department records, and some may be obtained from the office of institutional research. Chairpersons should learn about the kinds of data that are available in a college or university office of institutional research, how to obtain such data, and how to use it to the department's advantage.

Questions

1. Is there a minimum number of students that must be enrolled in a course for it to be offered? Is the minimum number part of any official regulation or is it an understanding, or rule of thumb?

2. How many courses are offered by your department and are listed in the institution's bulletin? How many are repeatedly offered every term? How many only once a year? How many once every two years?

3. How many of your courses are required for majors in your department? How many are required by majors in other departments? How many are available as electives?

4. To what extent do you believe that the teaching loads of the faculty are too light because there are too many faculty in your department to teach the optimum number of courses each term?

5. To what extent do you believe that the teaching loads of the faculty are too heavy because there are too few faculty in your department to teach the optimum number of courses each term?

6. How many of your courses that are offered each term could be offered once a year without jeopardizing the anticipated graduation dates of students? How many could be offered once every second year?

7. If faculty workloads are too heavy, how many of your courses could be assigned to part-time adjuncts without doing an injustice to the course or to the students?

References

BURKE, DELORES L. "The Academic Marketplace in the 1980s: Appointment and Termination of Assistant Professors." *Review of Higher Education,* 10, 1987, pp. 199–214.

CRESWELL, JOHN W. "Faculty Acceptance of a Workload Survey in One Major University." *Research in Higher Education,* May 1978, pp. 205–226.

CUMMINGS, L. L., and DUNHAM, RANDALL B. *Introduction to Organizational Behavior: Text and Reading.* Homewood, IL: Richard D. Irwin, 1980.

DYER, JAMES S., and MULVEY, JOHN M. "Computerized Scheduling and Planning." *New Directions for Institutional Research,* Spring 1977, pp. 67–86.

———*Faculty Activity Analysis: Overview and Major Issues.* TR 24. Boulder: NCHEMS, 1974.

———*Faculty Activity Analysis: Procedures Manual.* TR 44. Boulder: NCHEMS, 1973.

———*Faculty in Higher Education Institutions,* 1988: 1988 National Survey of Postsecondary Faculty. Washington, DC: U.S. Department of Education, 1990.

GUEST, ROBERT H.; HERSEY, PAUL; and BLANCHARD, KENNETH H. *Organizational Change Through Effective Leadership.* Englewood Cliffs: Prentice–Hall, 1977.

HARPER, RONALD L. "Faculty Activity Analysis." *New Directions for Institutional Research,* Spring 1978, pp. 73–81.

MCLAUGHLIN, GERALD W. (et al.) "Factors in Teacher Assignments: Measuring Workload by Effort." *Research in Higher Education,* 14 (1), 1981, pp. 3–17.

SCHULTZ, EVELYN B., and CHUNG, YONSUK L. "Research Productivity and Job Satisfaction of University Faculty." *Journal of Vocational Education Research,* 13, 1988, pp. 33–48.

Seagren, Alan T. *Perception of Chairpersons and Faculty Concerning Roles, Descriptors, and Activities Considered Important for Faculty Development and Departmental Vitality.* 1986. (ERIC Document Reproduction Service No. ED 276 387)

Sorcinelli, Mary Deane, and Near, Janet P. "Relations Between Work and Life Away from Work Among University Faculty." *Journal of Higher Education,* 60, 1989, pp. 59–81.

Wright, Ted. *Who Uses Institutional Research and Why?* Research Report No. 85–22. Miami: Miami–Dade Community College, 1985.

Part X

CONFLICT

Chapter 25. Managing Conflict

Chapter 26. Grievances and Faculty Unions

Chapter 27. Legal Implications of Being a Chair

Chapter *25*

Managing Conflict

Conflict, according to many department chairpersons, is something that happens in someone else's department. Academicians with preconceptions about harmonious campus life are often reluctant to speak or even think about discord and dissension in their immediate environment. Those who think of conflict as abnormal or aberrant tend to shun the subject. Some chairpersons view conflict in their department uneasily and feel that it is somehow their fault. Some chairpersons are unaware that conflict exists because they are so awe-inspiring that their faculty members conceal it from them. Even though conflict is a subject academicians do not like to talk about, they need to accept the idea that it can occur.

There seems to be an inverse relationship between the degree of conflict in a department and the level of morale: the more conflict, the lower the morale; the less conflict, the higher the morale. Although this discussion focuses primarily on types of conflict that may occur in an academic department, it also touches on promoting and maintaining good morale. Reducing conflict will not automatically raise faculty morale, but a good level of morale cannot exist in a department where energies are consumed by serious conflict.

The chairperson ought to be concerned about conflict within the department, because once it occurs, it tends to fester and grow. Conflict is divisive; it pits individual faculty members against each other and wastes time and effort that are best used in more creative endeavors. It often develops a dynamic and logic of its own. A conflict can polarize a department, forcing members into competing groups. In extreme cases, destructive and hostile behavior can destroy a department's effectiveness. Chairpersons who learn to identify and diagnose conflict at an early stage and who help their departments deal with it effectively fulfill one of the most difficult requirements of their role.

The term *conflict* is used here in a variety of ways. In psychology the term refers to the inner struggle between desires requiring immediate gratification and desires that can only be met by deferring the immediate in order to gain long-term benefits. For the purposes of this discussion, the term *inner conflict* will be used to describe tension, anxiety, turmoil, and frustration that can impair a person's activities but that do not emerge as interpersonal conflict. Webster's definition—"competitive or opposing action of incompatibles"—reflects a more common understanding of the term. Generally a disagreement becomes a conflict when it goes beyond the normal intellectual differences that characterize academic life. Serious conflict is often accompanied by feelings of fear, anxiety, or anger, and is often evidenced by intemperate or abusive language and overtly hostile actions.

Conflict may be defined either as an incident or as a process. As an incident, it occurs as a disagreement between two persons or parties in which the first acts in a way that the second perceives to be detrimental to the latter's interests and designed to force some undesired action. As a process, conflict is manifested in a series of actions by two persons or groups in which each person or group tries to thwart the other's purposes or prevent satisfaction of the other's interests. In essence, conflict is a struggle for control of another person's behavior.

Types of Conflict

Departments are made up of intelligent persons who are often ambitious, strong-willed, and competitive. Even though academicians are usually committed to the use of reason in problem solving and to the model of collegiality in interpersonal relations, conflict often arises either through personality clashes or as a result of institutional demands on faculty members. Conflict within departments can usually be categorized as one of four distinct types: (1) inner conflict; (2) conflict between employer and employee; (3) conflict among faculty members; and (4) conflict between faculty members and students.

Inner conflict concerns a person's feelings. It does not consist of a set of observable behaviors but has to do with frustrations and anxieties that a person feels and that can affect his or her normal functioning. For example, a faculty member who has long been a successful teacher but whose research skills are undeveloped fails to get promotions or merit increases as the department becomes more research oriented. He feels that the rules have been changed in the middle of his game and is angry and bitter. He withdraws from social contacts with other faculty members.

Disputes arising over matters such as promotion, tenure, merit pay, perquisites, work assignments, annual evaluations, and working conditions can usually be classified as employer–employee conflicts. These may involve faculty members and administrators, staff persons and administrators, or other types of employees and supervisors. Chairpersons who try to increase productivity by asking their faculty members to teach more or larger classes without discussing the matter with them beforehand can find themselves embroiled in employer–employee conflicts.

Conflict among faculty members can be the result of minor personality clashes or perceived inequities. Frequently such conflict arises when the egalitarian workload model is violated either by allocating varying awards for similar workloads or by allocating similar rewards for varying workloads. In the academic context, sorting out conflicting claims is extremely difficult, especially when the privileges of rank are considered. Many institutions have an uncodified, unwritten tradition that allows the senior faculty lighter course loads and more graduate courses. A more serious kind of conflict among faculty members is related to academic matters—e.g., what activities are worthwhile and what methodologies and techniques are best. Conflicts concerning the practice of the discipline are very difficult to resolve and sometimes lead to a kind of academic warfare in which entire factions are banished from the department.

Conflict between faculty members and students commonly begins either with student complaints about a faculty member's teaching performance or grading practices or with a faculty member's charge of cheating or plagiarism. Student complaints about faculty members sometimes grow into wholesale protests or demonstrations, especially when students feel that their right to due process has been violated.

In all types of conflict the disagreement can concern territory, clientele, and intergroup relations. Debates over humankind's territorial nature aside, conflict often does involve territory or "turf." Administrators, faculty members, and students at times all identify certain subjects, courses, or areas as exclusively their own and attempt to defend them against encroachment by others. Territorial disputes can break out over such seemingly trivial matters as the decision to assign some persons to windowless offices. Disagreements can arise when a new clientele is identified—as, for example, when a department adopts an off-campus program and faculty members argue with each other about who must teach in the program. Faculty members might also quarrel over a particularly able student, with whom they all may want to work, or a particularly poor student, with whom no one may want to work. Students may protest being assigned to particular faculty members.

Conflict in intergroup relations is often ideological. It may develop when various factions argue about what constitutes the proper methodology of a discipline. Intergroup conflict can occur when students organize and press demands. Student activism usually involves more than a department, however, and thus will not be discussed here. Other frequent sources of intergroup conflict in the academic environment involve relations between one department and another or relations between the university and the department. Neither of these sources of conflict is especially relevant to this discussion, but they are mentioned because the chairperson may be involved in such disputes. When departments are reviewed by policy councils or as part of accountability procedures, the chairperson may be thrust into the role of leading the struggle for the department's survival.

Attitudes Toward Conflict

The way a person acts in a conflict situation may well be related to his or her attitude towards conflict. These attitudes vary considerably from person to person. Institutions in general and colleges and universities in particular also have "attitudes" toward conflict that are represented in institutional policy and procedure. Social theorists have, since antiquity, developed different views on the matter that are still with us.

Let us examine two extreme views and see how they are reflected in present-day approaches. The first, the "Rousseauian" perspective, assumes that men and women are innately good, but that this goodness is perverted by society. Hence, conflict is unnatural. If society's unjust conditions and institutions were removed and humanity's natural goodness allowed to emerge, conflict would disappear. The opposite view—which might be called an "original sin" view or, in a more secular context, a Hobbesian view—assumes that each person attempts to maximize his or her goods and opportunities until he or she is stopped by someone else who is doing the same thing. In this view, conflict is natural as well as normal. Improving social conditions will not reduce conflict and might even increase it. Conflict is regulated by strict rules and procedures and accompanying sanctions.

These two views are, of course, mutually exclusive. While neither is intended as an empirically verifiable description of reality, these and similar attitudes toward conflict are prevalent. From these examples we can say that a person's behavior in conflict situations is related to his or her attitudes and beliefs about the nature of conflict and its role in human affairs.

J. Victor Baldridge, in *Power and Conflict in the University,* identifies three models of university governance based on attitudes toward conflict. The first governance model, the *collegial model,* views conflict as abnormal. This view holds that a true community of scholars would eliminate conflict altogether. When disagreements arise, they are solved by deliberation and reason, not by negotiation and arbitration. Moreover, professors are civilized men and women, not brawlers, who prefer to live in an atmosphere of harmonious consensus.

The second model, the *bureaucratic model,* also views conflict as abnormal. This model of governance, however, assumes that conflicts will occur but that they will be controlled by bureaucratic sanctions. Although the bureaucratic model does not adequately describe traditional faculty behavior in most colleges and universities, it seems to be increasingly appropriate in large systems where collective bargaining is practiced and where guides to organizational behavior are increasingly codified.

The third model, the *political model,* accepts conflict as a normal part of organizational life. This model assumes that contention among competing interests precedes almost any policy change. In the language of the model, the social structure of the university is not a homogeneous community of scholars. Instead, the professional community is said to be pluralistic, fractured into subcultures and divergent interest groups, and composed of fairly autonomous professional practitioners. The general style of decision making and policy development involves negotiation, political influence, and bargaining (i.e., making trade-offs).

Political influence is attained by persuading and mobilizing persons of like opinion into an interest group or faction. It assumes neither a community of professional interests nor agreement about the ends of higher education beyond the need to preserve academic freedom.

To view the collegial, bureaucratic, and political governance models as ideal types, abstracted from reality, is helpful. Most institutions have elements of all three models within them, and members of the institutions often behave in ways that are consistent with the model to which they personally subscribe. Comparing the governance models to the attitudes toward conflict, the collegial model seems compatible with the Rousseauian "natural goodness" attitude; the bureaucratic model, which assumes that people must be constantly watched and supervised, is compatible with the Hobbesian model, which sees people as inherently selfish.

The three models also emphasize communication and its role. The collegial model stresses the importance and value of communication in consensual decision making. The bureaucratic model emphasizes the need for clear channels of communication to avoid mistakes and get the messages through. The political model rejects the view that conflict is due to misunderstandings and communications breakdowns and labels such belief "the communications fallacy." Indeed, the political model, while admitting the desirability of authentic communication, denies that communication is in itself sufficient to reduce conflict. Even though two disputants may clearly understand each other, such understanding well may lead to increased rather than reduced hostility, as may a clear communication that one side is losing and the other winning. In fact, the perception of "them" winning and "us" losing almost always precedes conflict. The political model sees conflict resolution essentially as a trading off of advantages and favors in a process called "rational selfishness."

A continuum reflecting the various stages of conflict within a department—from an anarchic state of total conflict at one end to a bland and blissful state of total cooperation at the other—can easily be constructed (see Fig. 25.1).

One interesting aspect of this continuum is the central position of competition. Friendly competition lies to the right of center; unfriendly competition lies to the left of center. On the continuum, the balance point is the competitive state, and the implication is that life in an academic department goes on in a state of nonconflictual competition. Conflict can be constructive when it enables antagonists to make their beliefs and dissatisfactions explicit, thus clearing the air. In such a case, a step toward problem solving has been taken, and, it is generally agreed, conflict ought to be reduced to problem solving.

FIGURE *25.1* Department Conflict Continuum

Total Conflict	Controlled Conflict	Competition	Collaboration	Total Cooperation

Stages of Conflict

Another way of understanding conflict is to view it as a series of stages that make up a conflict episode. This theory permits taking a developmental view of conflict and treating the separate stages individually. The four steps are *latent, perceived, manifest,* and *aftermath.* Each stage, it should be noted, contains the elements of the preceding stages as well as elements of its own.

LATENT CONFLICT

The first stage is called *latent conflict.* In this stage the conditions are being set for future conflict. Common sources of conflict include competition for scarce resources, drives for autonomy, divergence of individual goals, incompatible role expectations, and the frustrations of a person or group resulting from events beyond its control.

Latent conflict, deriving from the causes mentioned above, exists in almost every department in every college and university in the country. We need hardly discuss competition for scarce resources, which has characterized academic affairs for the last decade. Drives for autonomy or independence can be interpreted in several ways: faculty members can become frustrated when they feel that they have no role in the department's decision-making process; a department chairperson may desire more authority than the administration is willing to delegate; a faculty member may claim the right to teach anything she sees fit, even while teaching a section of a colleague's course. Faculty members who pursue their own goals without regard for others in the department are common figures, often creating dissension and frustration by their tactics. Faculty members serve as teachers, researchers, providers of service, and, sometimes, as administrators, and the demands of these many roles can often lead to frustration and conflict. So too can the role expectations of the faculty of professional schools when it clashes with the liberal arts faculty at promotion committee meetings. Finally, of course, many academicians feel they are losing control of their professional lives.

This stage of conflict is called "latent" because the conditions that lead to conflict are present but, for a variety of reasons, are suppressed. Some persons avoid conflict, perhaps because it can be painful and threatening, and ignore or withdraw from a situation that promises to erupt. Clearly, within any department there are many examples of latent conflict.

PERCEIVED CONFLICT

The next stage of conflict is called *perceived conflict.* In this stage, one element from the latency stage emerges as problematic. The persons involved are aware of a disagreement but do not yet feel tense or anxious. This stage is sometimes called the "semantic" conflict stage, because the perception of conflict comes from information that may be erroneous or incomplete. At this stage, if the perception really comes from misinformation, improved communications may nip a crisis in the bud. If the information, once clarified, proves the perception correct, however, the conflict can rapidly move on to the next stage, *felt conflict*. Felt conflict moves beyond intellectual awareness to a personalized feeling of anxiety and tension. Some persons at this stage withdraw and become uncommunicative. Nevertheless, once tension, unease, and anxiety emerge, the progression to open conflict is simple.

MANIFEST CONFLICT

The stage of open conflict, often called the *manifest conflict* stage, is marked by open aggression, generally verbal but occasionally physical. Instances of faculty members engaging in physically aggressive behaviors are few but not unheard of. Occasionally, a frustrated student will attack a faculty member he sees as having prevented him from achieving his goals.

CONFLICT AFTERMATH

The final stage is *conflict aftermath*. Every conflict ultimately comes to an end. The conflict may not have been satisfactorily resolved, but hostilities have simply ceased. Sometimes one side is clearly victorious. Sometimes an external party may intervene and impose a settlement. Sometimes a genuine solution satisfactory to every party is achieved. Unfortunately, many a conflict aftermath merely sets the stage for a new conflict.

Understanding conflict as a process that encompasses several stages can help the chairperson recognize the importance of maintaining department morale. The subject of maintaining morale will be discussed in some detail here because low morale is often an indication that conflict is moving from the latency stage to a higher stage. Moreover, much conflict, especially inner conflict, comes from the perception that the interests of human beings are pitted against the interests of the system. The feeling that the system, whatever *system* means, is becoming larger, more powerful, and more oppressive, and that the person is powerless to do much to oppose it contributes to the anxiety and frustration that leads to conflict.

Diagnosing and Dealing with Conflict

A number of factors that affect department morale have been identified. The chairperson has little control over many of these, but he or she can nevertheless try to minimize the feelings of dissatisfaction that lead to inner conflict. Two of these factors are the salary and working conditions of the department members. Faculty members can easily become depressed about the fact that their income declines in inflationary times. They also resent the imposition of heavier teaching loads or larger classes. Although the chairperson cannot magically produce salary increases for the entire department, he or she can reduce resentment by showing that, compared with departments elsewhere, the department is not doing as badly as its members think. If the department actually is in a poor position compared with similar departments in other institutions or other departments in the university, the chairperson can boost morale by showing that he or she is actively lobbying for a fair share of the funds available. Similarly, faculty members often feel that they are being discriminated against with respect to the allocation of travel funds. Again, the chairperson should be able to show them that they are no worse off than anyone else in the college or the institution.

Another factor that contributes to low department morale is the sense of ever-increasing bureaucratization—the proliferation of meaningless rules and regulations and increasing outside pressure on the department. The chairperson can raise department morale by showing that he or she opposes the proliferation of administrative trivia. When the chairperson is seen as the defender of the department's welfare, he or she helps create a climate of solidarity within the department. Faculty members will come to feel that by sticking together in the face of adversity they can overcome some of the difficulties that appear insurmountable.

A common source of frustration and inner conflict for faculty members is the feeling that they are losing control over crucial department decisions affecting their future. One way to reduce feelings of alienation and powerlessness is to establish a set of policies within a department that permit the faculty to participate in the decision-making process. There should be formal means for allowing debate over department policy and procedures, such as faculty meetings that allow open discussion and debate. Written reports on policy decisions should contain evidence that a variety of points of view have been reviewed. In this way, the chairperson can show that minority opinions have been considered and respected.

Conflict can be reduced when the lines of authority and responsibility in the department are clarified. For example, a chairperson assigned a faculty member the task of making up teaching schedules for the entire department but failed to inform the department members that he had given this responsibility to one of their colleagues. When the schedule was distributed, the faculty members were confused and resentful. Had the chairperson informed the faculty that he had delegated this task and had he instructed the schedule maker to consult with each member of the department, this conflict would have been avoided. Whenever a chairperson delegates administrative responsibility to faculty or staff members, the lines of authority must be clarified.

Department meetings should allow open confrontation over controversial issues. Confrontation need not lead to destructive conflict. Free debate and free expression can ensure a fair hearing for diverse viewpoints about significant issues. Debate can also bring out conflicts at an early stage of development, allowing them to be dealt with before they become critical. The chairperson can help develop an atmosphere of commitment to orderly change within the department. Autocratic methods should not be advocated, and both majority opinions and minority rights should be respected and upheld.

This discussion of minimizing latent and inner conflict has emphasized what a chairperson can do to identify conflict before it becomes destructive. Chairpersons are advised to establish an atmosphere that prevents conflict from escalating, since conflict is difficult to resolve once the department is polarized. A chairperson who does not hear of conflicts—particularly a chairperson of a large department, where the probability of their existence is high—should ask whether there is something about his or her administrative style that causes the faculty, staff, and students to avoid discussing difficult situations. Perhaps the chairperson is perceived as too authoritarian or unyielding. If so, the chairperson might begin to visit briefly but regularly with every member of the faculty and staff. These visits, which may be held once a month, should be on a one-to-one basis and should not be held in the chairperson's office. Meetings on neutral ground, such as a faculty club or restaurant, or on the faculty member's turf, such as his or her office or home, are much less threatening. The purpose of the meetings is not to solve problems but to listen and look for the emergence of latent or inner conflict.

One skill the chairperson can learn is the technique of "active listening," developed by Thomas Gordon, which is useful for discovering latent conflict. Active listening is an extremely effective communications technique that is used by many thousands of parents. Academicians have some difficulty with the technique because the listener does not lecture, teach, give logical arguments, judge, criticize, question, interpret, analyze, or diagnose. In other words, all the logical and conceptual skills that are indispensable to a university career are temporarily put aside. Active listening consists of the listener (or receiver) "feeding back only what he feels the sender's message meant—nothing more, nothing less."[1]

By listening patiently and "feeding back" the feelings of the speaker, chairpersons may promote a good relationship between themselves and their faculty, facilitate problem solving, and, in general, foster a cooperative spirit in the department. To be an effective listener, the chairperson must want to be helpful, believe in the speaker's sincerity, and be willing to accept the speaker as a fellow human being. A chairperson who gets good results by listening quietly, with an occasional empathetic grunt and a few gestures showing he understands the speaker's feelings, would be well advised to read Gordon's book in order to perfect the listening technique.

Occasionally, conflict in a department may be related to a faculty member's mental state. Recent research has examined and brought to the public consciousness the existence of "life crises" that most people undergo. The chairperson should be sensitive to each faculty member's state of mind. Reading some of the literature on life stages, such as Levinson's *The Seasons of a Man's Life* or Sheehy's *Passages,* can help the chairperson understand some of the personal

---

1. Thomas Gordon, *Parent Effectiveness Training* (New York; London; and Scarborough, Ontario: New American Library, 1970 and 1975), p. 53.

crises that can lead to unhappiness and consequent strife within a department. Many personal crises, such as divorce or a death in the family, can temporarily impair or disrupt a faculty member's normal functioning. The chairperson can arrange for substitutes in the classroom and on committees. But how long can a chairperson cover for a faculty member? There are no hard and fast rules. Some persons take longer to recover from crises than do others. The chairperson who is thoroughly aware of university rules and policies on leaves of absence and sick leaves can support faculty members in times of personal adversity.

Academicians, like all other professionals, may suffer from serious personality disorders or develop patterns of behavior that are disruptive or dangerous. The chairperson must be able to distinguish between a person who is frustrated or temporarily disabled and one who is chronically disabled. When a faculty member is in constant conflict with colleagues or students, the chairperson must exercise judgment. Sometimes the chairperson may wait patiently in the belief that the crisis will be temporary. At other times the chairperson may decide to suspend the person from work. A decision such as this is a painful one; it may ease or erase conflict in a department, but only at the expense of that faculty member's professional life.

The matter of faculty members who behave erratically is complicated by the legal and the psychological aspects of the issue. To suggest to a colleague that he or she is sick and needs help may result in a charge of character assassination and a lawsuit. Chairpersons must remember that they have no legal or professional authority to counsel a department member. When someone with no training attempts to counsel an emotionally unstable person who is incapacitated by inner conflict or actively engaged in a dispute, serious and unpleasant consequences may result. If a faculty member needs to be referred to a counselor or psychiatrist, the chairperson should discretely discuss the matter with the dean and the legal staff before proceeding.

Thus far, we have discussed situations in which the chairperson has been dealing with inner conflict, latent conflict, and feelings of powerlessness against the system. We have not discussed in detail manifest or overt conflict. But conflicts, despite strenuous efforts to control them, do emerge and, in most cases, are destructive and costly. There is, of course, no clear blueprint of what to do when conflict occurs. The chairperson who is aware of the stages of a conflict episode and who has a finger on the department's pulse will not be surprised if conflict does emerge, because he or she will have been watching it develop. Yet there is more to dealing with conflict than simply not being surprised by it, since some persons who are not surprised by events are still unable to handle them.

Much department conflict can be managed effectively by an astute chairperson. What does *conflict management* mean? For our purposes, it means the shaping of conflict in such a way that it is reduced to a process of problem solving. In many cases, this transformation can be accomplished if the chairperson is able to develop a clear idea about the basic attitudes of the disputing parties toward, first, the conflict they are engaged in and, second, the stakes involved. This understanding is important because attitudes toward conflict influence persons' behavior and because conflict over low stakes is much easier to resolve than conflict over high stakes.

Analyzing the participating parties' attitudes towards the conflict need not be complicated. The chairperson should know whether they feel that the conflict was avoidable and whether they feel that some agreement or compromise is possible. If disputants feel agreement is possible, they can generally be persuaded to convert their dispute into an opportunity for problem solving. If, on the other hand, they feel that an agreement is impossible, they may engage in a fierce struggle to the bitter end, especially if the stakes are high. Generally, if the stakes are high, the conflict will be much more vigorous, and the possibility exists that the conflict will not be settled amicably.

Chairpersons can settle a dispute if they can make the opposing parties believe that an agreement is possible or if they can get the parties to lower the stakes in their dispute. For example, an anthropology department was engaged in a bitter dispute between its structuralists and its functionalists. Each side was accusing the other of not being "real" anthropologists and was preventing the promotion and tenure of young faculty members in the enemy camp. The stakes were the survival of each faction in the department. The chairperson, even though a member of one of the factions, was able to persuade the groups that they could live with each other and that their ideological differences need not lead to the expulsion of half the department. In this case, the stakes were not lowered, but the attitudes were changed.

The question of what "high" stakes are, compared with "moderate" or "low" stakes, is somewhat subjective but certainly includes such matters as promotion, tenure, and status in the department. Low stakes might include a large office, allocation of a typewriter, and travel funds. Nevertheless, serious conflicts have erupted over the last three examples. Someone once said that the reason academic politics is so sordid is that the stakes are so small. Low stakes for one person may be high stakes for another.

The question of whether parties to a conflict think the conflict was avoidable is of little concern here. Some persons believe that conflict is avoidable but that, if it should occur, an agreement is impossible. Research indicates that such persons often tend to withdraw from the conflict when it occurs. Generally, however, if persons see conflict as inevitable, agreement as impossible, and stakes as high, they are likely to engage in the most bitter of conflicts. Sometimes attempts to lower stakes and change attitudes do not succeed, and the results can be serious indeed.

When diagnosing a conflict, a chairperson must exercise analytical ability. He or she must use good judgment in deciding whether to intervene and strive to reduce conflict or channel it creatively. If the chairperson can identify an emerging conflict, uncover the faculty's attitudes and beliefs about the nature of conflict, and assess the stakes involved in the conflict, he or she will be better equipped to decide what to do in a particular situation. Often, the best decision is not to act. When intervention obviously will not improve the situation or even make it worse, the chairperson's best strategy is to remain aloof from the conflict while staying alert to the situation and sensitive to the conditions that produced it. For example, two senior faculty members have been bickering for years. Their differences do not impede the operation of the department, and the chairperson does not attempt a peacemaking role. On the other hand, if the quarreling department members attempt to pressure the rest of the faculty to choose sides and build up factions within the department, some intervention is called for.

As stated earlier in this discussion, the chairperson should try to transform conflicts into opportunities for problem solving. It may be useful here to make a conceptual distinction between *conflicts* and *problems*. A problem exists when a set of expectations is not being fulfilled; a conflict exists when one or more persons is intentionally or unintentionally thwarting the needs or wants of another person or persons. For example, several faculty members taught an introductory graduate seminar on a rotating basis. Students who took the course from a particular faculty member had great difficulty passing the department qualifying examination. This difficulty caused conflict between the students and the faculty members, as well as among the faculty members themselves. The chairperson arranged a meeting of all the teachers of the course. Instead of permitting them to dwell on their differences, he limited the agendum to a discussion of what the students were expected to know at the completion of the course and what the examination should cover. By concentrating on the problem rather than on the dispute and by reaching a mutually satisfactory solution, the chairperson defused the conflict.

The chairperson can resolve some conflicts by acting as clarifier. An emerging conflict may be reduced if the chairperson can show the parties that their expectations are based on incorrect information. For example, conflict in a department over inequitable teaching loads may be reduced if the chairperson supplies precise information about who teaches what. On the other hand, such information, if it gives evidence of real inequities, may widen the conflict.

When the chairperson receives reports of a conflict, he or she would be wise to begin a discreet inquiry into the situation before taking any overt action. For example, two faculty members were engaged in a bitter feud because one believed the other had misrepresented her ability and record to a Washington funding agency and thus was responsible for its rejection of her grant proposal. By conducting a few interviews, the chairperson was able to clarify the situation. Discreet inquiry was also effective in a case involving rumors of sexual misconduct by a faculty member. When the chairperson met with some graduate students, he discovered evidence of a pattern of sexual exploitation in which the faculty member threatened the careers of students unless they granted him favors. In some instances when rumors of misbehavior were ignored, the university was later subjected to adverse publicity and legal action.

The department as a whole or committees within the department can be used to settle or reduce conflict. For example, a bitter quarrel over who was to teach a certain course threatened to disrupt the activities of a statistics department. The department referred the problem to a committee and asked its members to develop a set of criteria and procedures for determining who would teach specific courses in the department. The decision of who was to teach each course, including the one in question, would henceforth be made on the basis of established policy.

Some conflicts are caused primarily by problems that the chairperson may be able to identify but not be authorized or suited to address. In such cases, the use of an outside authority may be required. For example, a faculty member's alcoholism was ignored and even concealed by his colleagues and chairperson until a committee of graduate students spoke with an attorney about the man's chronic absenteeism and erratic behavior. The chairperson then discussed the matter with the dean, and they contacted a staff member who was an effective alcoholism counselor. Together they worked out a program of action that they offered to the faculty member.

Occasionally a chairperson will encourage an emerging conflict in the belief that getting things out in the open will help correct misunderstandings and ultimately result in a more positive relationship. Some chairpersons may even induce conflict in order to discover the intensity of feelings about a particular issue. Only a skilled conflict manager should attempt to introduce a dispute into the department. The potential for damage is high and probable outcome too unpredictable.

When thinking about the kind of strategy to use to reduce a conflict, the chairperson should examine the values held by the opposing parties. He or she should be aware that intervention might unwittingly lend support to one party's values. Examining values is especially important when the department has no clear priorities or goals. In such instances, the chairperson, by supporting a value or goal, is causing a conflicting value to be downplayed or rejected. The chairperson then becomes a party to the conflict rather than a mediator, part of the problem rather than part of the solution. In departments that have no clear-cut goals, the value supported by the chairperson establishes priorities and creates a latent conflict situation. For example, in a department that had established no priorities concerning the value of research or teaching, the faculty members began to argue about the relative merits of generating large numbers of student credit hours rather than publishing research. The chairperson sided with the advocates of teaching large classes. By so doing, he established a priority that would later cause conflict between the disaffected researchers and the rest of the department.

Although it is wise to adopt a neutral stance toward conflict in the department, the chairperson must sometimes become embroiled in a conflict because the role demands it. On such occasions, one of the parties in conflict may perceive the chairperson's action as partisan or punitive. Thus far we have emphasized the chairperson's role as a problem solver, but there are times when the attempted solution to a conflict requires that the chairperson make a decision that arouses someone's anger and hostility. Indeed, on occasion traditional ways of reducing conflict are not successful and a party to conflict must be warned, disciplined, or reprimanded. Chairpersons should know what authority they have to order persons to desist from certain behaviors. They should be aware of institutional rules and regulations and know the extent of their legal powers as chairpersons.

In some cases of conflict the best action is to intervene immediately. If equipment, students, or faculty or staff members are threatened with danger, the chairperson must act quickly and effectively. In the rare case of hostile or threatening behavior, the chairperson and the staff should know how to contact police or security officers. The chairperson should also know what to do in the case of fire, storms, and accidents. Thefts should be reported promptly, since they may be part of an organized and systematic activity that the police might be able to identify and stop.

Some disputes can be settled only by consultation with a dean or other official. Such disputes include quarrels between departments, quarrels between a department and the administration, and quarrels between a department and a university committee. With chairpersons vigorously advocating the claims of their own departments, quarrels can escalate into conflict. In such an event, the dean or the academic vice-president must try to settle the fight. For example, a school of education offered statistics courses to its own students, while a statistics department offered courses to the university in general. When many arts and sciences students began to take courses in the school of education, the statistics department pressed for a regulation that would prohibit crossing college lines for statistics courses. Each department began accusing the other of proselytizing, so the chairpersons decided to cool things down by taking the problem to the academic vice-president. Another example: When the graduate policy committee suspended a department's authorization to grant graduate degrees, the department claimed it was treated unfairly. The chairperson took the problem to the dean. In both instances, the chairpersons were part of the conflict, but they used their knowledge of the dynamics of conflict to arrive at a solution.

The chairperson is sometimes called on to appear as an expert witness or as an independent observer in proceedings that arise as a result of conflict. During grievance procedures and in the course of official hearings, the chairperson may be required to present evidence or give testimony about the conduct of department members. The chairperson should keep journals or records that recount in detail the actions of the parties in a dispute, especially if he or she intervenes in the conflict. The chairperson should take into account the legal aspects of building a case history or record and should comply with requirements of due process and with laws respecting privacy. Ordinarily, if a file is being kept, the person or persons who are the subject of the documentation should be informed of its existence. The file should not simply document the errors or misdeeds of persons or parties; it should also record the steps taken to resolve the dispute or transform it into an opportunity for problem solving.

A conflict poses a more difficult dilemma for chairpersons when none of the possible interventions seems likely to resolve the whole problem. On occasion a chairperson may hesitate to intervene in a conflict for fear of losing his or her effectiveness as chairperson, alienating powerful members of the department, or possibly losing his or her position. Suppose that two very influential faculty members who generally disagree about each other's principles and practices and who both are extremely vindictive have joined forces to deny junior faculty members the opportunity to teach certain courses and the opportunity for released time to do research. The two faculty members are politically strong enough to threaten the chairperson's position. The junior faculty members have approached the chairperson and asked for assistance in the conflict. What should the chairperson do?

Another hypothetical dilemma: The short-tempered dean of the college is a tenured faculty member in a certain department. He thinks of himself as a superb teacher and insists on teaching a required undergraduate course. In fact, he has the deserved reputation of being one of the worst teachers in the university. The students are outraged at the poor quality of instruction and the lack of organization in the course and are vigorously protesting. In addition, one of the younger faculty members in the department is upset because he feels he is more qualified than the dean to teach this particular course. What can the chairperson do about his own dean?

The chairperson's role in dealing with conflict and maintaining morale is crucial to the smooth operation of the department. He or she must be aware of the conditions in the department that might give rise to conflict and be prepared to use analytic ability, good judgment, and creativity in order to handle conflict effectively. He or she must be able to recognize and analyze a conflict when it occurs and to exercise good judgment when deciding whether or not to intervene. The kind of intervention depends on the facts and dynamics of the situation. The chairperson must be creative and deal with each situation individually. In the case of recurring conflict, the irrational and emotional elements of the situation can be defused if the chairperson can find or get the department to develop a regulation or policy covering that type of conflict. As a general rule, conflict that can be reduced to an opportunity for problem solving has the greatest chance of being settled. This transformation requires that the chairperson explore the limits of his or her own creativity.

GUIDELINES FOR DEALING WITH CONFLICT

Although no formula exists that can be applied to all conflict situations, the following guidelines can be of help to the chairperson.

- Keep in touch with the feelings and attitudes of faculty members. Through frequent meetings, the chairperson can discover latent conflict situations before they emerge.
- Be aware of the four stages of conflict episodes in order to be able to deal with them at the earliest opportunity.
- Use techniques of active listening to raise morale and to understand the perceptions of faculty members who may be engaged in conflict.
- Structure the department in such a manner that conflicts can be discussed, aired, and dealt with through normal governance procedures.

- Be sensitive to faculty members with personal problems but do not necessarily get involved. Intervene only if the operation of the department is impaired.
- In cases of conflict, determine what conflicting values are held by the parties.
- Do not take sides in a conflict that does not concern the welfare of the department.
- Do not intervene in conflicts unless you have reason to believe that intervention can help the situation.
- Find out whether disputants perceive the stakes as high or low. If they are perceived as high, try to reduce them.
- Find out whether parties believe the conflict is amenable to solution. Try to persuade them that solutions are possible.
- Try to change any conflict to an opportunity for problem solving.
- Be prepared to make discreet inquiries about reported potential and actual conflict.
- When appropriate, use department committees to establish policies and procedures that govern situations in which conflicts have occurred and may occur in the future.
- As soon as possible, clarify misconceptions that may cause conflict.
- Communicate clearly with the faculty about any unprecedented action that might cause conflict.
- Be prepared to be called as a witness to, or observer of, a conflict. Keep records of action and involvement in conflicts.
- Do not violate laws or institutional regulations when dealing with conflict.

We have briefly discussed, from both a theoretical and a practical point of view, conflict as it occurs in academic departments. Chairpersons of academic disciplines other than the social sciences may be unaware of the great amount of research conducted by sociologists and psychologists on the problems of identifying, analyzing, and resolving conflict. Knowing how to deal with conflict can be useful in managing families, schools, churches, businesses, legislatures, and international affairs. Chairpersons, in order to be effective, must continually be alert to the possibility of conflict in their departments. They must be sufficiently wise to determine whether they should get involved. If they decide to become involved, they must select the strategy that has the best chance of solving or defusing the conflict.

Questions

1. What factors or influences outside the university have caused latent conflict among the faculty members in your department?

2. What factors or influences *within* the university but outside the department have caused latent conflict among your faculty members?

3. What kinds of issues, situations, or relationships that exist within your department have contributed to latent or emergent conflict?

4. a. Review one or more conflicts in your department or in another department that have been constructive. How were they resolved?

   b. Review one or more conflicts in your department or in another department that have been destructive. How were they resolved?

5. Do any serious conflicts exist in your department at the present time? What are they?

6. In this chapter we have discussed morale in general terms. Identify factors that at one time or another have lowered morale in your department. How did you react to those factors? Do you think your reaction was appropriate?

7. Identify factors that have raised morale in your department. Did you have any influence over these factors?

8. What elements in the governance structure of your department serve to minimize conflict?

9. This chapter contains a list of guidelines for helping resolve conflicts. For each guideline on the list, think of two or three examples of conflict situations and stages of conflict for which the particular guideline might be helpful. Try to find a colleague or two who are willing to join you in this exercise.

10. Described below are five skeleton sketches of conflict situations in a department. Assume that you are the chairperson who must resolve each of the conflicts. Use your experience and imagination to expand each sketch into a more comprehensive case study by adding more details. Try to interest one or two of your colleagues in joining you in this exercise.

    1. Half the faculty of a department have signed a letter to the dean, asking for the chairperson's resignation.

    2. A faculty member has a personal problem that is affecting his performance and relations with others in the department.

    3. Students complain, with some justification, that an instructor's grading practices are discriminatory.

    4. Faculty in a department have polarized into two camps and are feuding. Students are suffering because of the conflict.

    5. Two faculty members are fighting with each other. Their areas of specialization overlap and they are competing for resources. In developing the hypothetical case study try to include the following:
       • Background information describing the history and development of the conflict.

- A description of the personality and character of the individuals involved. Be specific about their roles and status.
- Give details of various incidents in the conflict.
- Using information from this chapter, analyze the conflict in terms of the stakes involved and the attitudes of the actors.
- Describe your reasoning about whether or not to intervene.
- Describe the strategies you will use to try to reduce or settle the conflict, if you decide to intervene. Which strategies from those described in the text can be applied?
- Describe how you anticipate the conflict will be resolved.

References

ABRELL, RONALD L. "Educational Leadership Without Carrot and Club." *The Clearing House,* February 1979, pp. 280–285.

ADAMS, HAZARD. *The Academic Tribes.* 2nd ed. Champaign, IL: University of Illinois Press, 1988. (ERIC Document Reproduction Service ED 297 632)

BALDRIDGE, J. VICTOR. *Power and Conflict in the University: Research in the Sociology of Complex Organizations.* New York: John Wiley & Sons, 1971.

BASKIN, OTIS W., and ARONOFF, CRAIG E. *Interpersonal Communication in Organization.* Santa Monica: Goodyear, 1980.

BLAKE, ROBERT R.; SHEPARD, HERBERT; and MOUTON, JANE. *Managing Intergroup Conflict in Industry.* Houston: Gulf, 1964.

BOLTON, ROBERT H. *People Skills: How to Assert Yourself, Listen to Others, and Resolve Conflicts.* Englewood Cliffs: Prentice–Hall, 1979.

BRAMMER, LAWRENCE M. *The Helping Relationship.* 2nd ed. Englewood Cliffs: Prentice–Hall, 1979.

BUCKLEY, WILLIAM F. *God and Man at Yale: The Superstitions of "Academic Freedom."* Chicago: Regnery Books, 1986.

BURNS, TOM, and STALKER, G. M. *Management of Innovation.* New York: Methuen, 1961.

CARTWRIGHT, DORWIN. "Achieving Change in People: Some Applications of Group Dynamics Theory." *Human Relations,* November 1951, pp. 381–392.

CONRAD, CLIFTON F. "A Grounded Theory of Academic Change." *Sociology of Education,* April 1978, pp. 101–112.

CUMMINGS, L. L., and DUNHAM, RANDALL B. *Introduction to Organizational Behavior: Text and Reading.* Homewood, IL: Richard D. Irwin, 1980.

ETZIONI, AMITAI. "Human Beings Are Not Very Easy to Change After All." *Saturday Review,* 3 June 1972, pp. 45–47.

GORDON, THOMAS. *Parent Effectiveness Training.* New York; London; and Scarborough, Ontario: New American Library, 1975.

GOULDNER, ALVIN W. "Cosmopolitans an Locals: Towards an Analysis of Latent Social Roles." *Administrative Science Quarterly,* December 1957, pp. 281–306; and March 1958, pp. 444–480.

GREENLAW, PAUL S., and BIGGS, WILLIAM D. *Modern Personnel Management.* New York: Holt, 1980.

GROSS, EDWARD, and GRAMBSCH, PAUL. *University Goals and Academic Power: A Study in Conflict and Cooperation.* Washington, DC: American Council on Education, 1968.

GUEST, ROBERT H.; HERSEY, PAUL; and BLANCHARD, KENNETH H. *Organizational Change Through Effective Leadership.* Englewood Cliffs: Prentice–Hall, 1977.

HEFFERLIN, J. B. LON. *Dynamics of Academic Reform.* San Francisco: Jossey–Bass, 1969.

————. "Hauling Academic Trunks." In *Elements Involved in Academic Change,* edited by Charles U. Walker, pp. 1–10. Washington, DC: Association of American Colleges, 1972.

HERSEY, PAUL, and BLANCHARD, KENNETH H. *Management of Organizational Behavior: Utilizing Human Resources.* 3rd ed. Englewood Cliffs: Prentice–Hall, 1977.

JENKS, CHRISTOPHER, and RIESMAN, DAVID. *The Academic Revolution.* Garden City, NJ: Anchor Books, 1969.

LAWRENCE, PAUL R. "How to Deal with Resistance to Change." *Harvard Business Review,* May–June 1954, pp. 49–57.

LESLIE, DAVID W. "The Status of the Department Chairmanship in University Organization." *AAUP Bulletin,* 59, 1973, pp. 419–426.

LEVINSON, DANIEL J. *The Seasons of a Man's Life.* New York: Alfred A. Knopf, 1978.

LOEWENBERG, PETER. "Love and Hate in the Academy." *The Center Magazine,* September–October 1972, pp. 4–11.

LUTHANS, FRED (Ed.) *Contemporary Readings in Organizational Behavior.* 2nd ed. New York: McGraw–Hill, 1976.

————. *Organizational Behavior.* 2nd ed. New York: McGraw–Hill, 1976.

MILGRAM, STANLEY. "Group Pressure and Action Against a Person." *Journal of Abnormal and Social Psychology,* August 1964, pp. 137–143.

NEUMANN, YORAM. "The Perception of Power in University Departments: A Comparison Between Chairpersons and Faculty Members." *Research in Higher Education,* 11(4), 1979, pp. 283–293.

PETERSON, MARVIN W. "Faculty and Academic Responsiveness in a Period of Decline: An Organizational Perspective." *The Journal of the College and University Personnel Association,* Spring 1980, pp. 95–104.

PONDY, LOUIS R. "Organizational Conflict: Concepts and Models." In *Contemporary Readings in Organizational Behavior,* edited by Fred Luthans. 2nd ed. New York: McGraw–Hill, 1976.

RICHMAN, BARRY M., and FARMER, RICHARD N. *Leadership, Goals, and Power in Higher Education: A Contingency and Open-Systems Approach to Effective Management.* San Francisco: Jossey–Bass, 1974.

SCHUSTER, JACK H. "The Faculty Dilemma: A Short Course." *Phi Delta Kappan,* 68, 1986, pp. 275–282.

SERGIOVANNI, THOMAS J., and CORBALLY, JOHN E. *Leadership and Organizational Culture.* Chicago: University of Illinois Press, 1988.

SHEEHY, GAIL. *Passages.* New York: Dutton, 1976.

SHERTZER, BRUCE E., and STONE, SHELLEY C. *Fundamentals of Counseling.* 3rd ed. Boston: Houghton–Mifflin, 1980.

STEINMETZ, LAWRENCE L. *Managing the Marginal and Unsatisfactory Performer.* Reading, MA: Addison–Wesley, 1969.

TANTER, RAYMOND (Ed.) "Why Fight? Conflict Models for Strategists and Managers." *American Behavioral Scientist,* July–August 1972 (special issue).

TEGER, ALLAN I. *Too Much Invested to Quit.* Elmsford, New York: Pergamon Press, 1980.

Chapter 26

Grievances and
Faculty Unions

In the days of rapid expansion of colleges and universities, little attention was given to resolving problems relating to the conditions and procedures of employment of faculty members. Because the academic market was strong, faculty members who were dissatisfied with their jobs could escape their problems by changing institutions. Moreover, many faculty members were of patrician background, and their upbringing taught them to disdain strident, overt conflict. Colleagues "were done in quietly"; they simply disappeared in June, to emerge at another school the following September.

By the end of the 1960s, much had changed. Students had frightened university administrators into making various reforms, and issues of war and peace had become campus concerns. Faculty members from the working class, ethnic backgrounds, and, to a lesser degree, minority cultures had joined the profession. Legislators voted to punish university communities for real or imagined transgressions, and most traditional disciplines faced declining markets. For many faculty members the idea of organizing themselves and their professions no longer seemed outlandish.

At one time, faculty members who were denied tenure or whose contracts were not renewed might have respectably transferred to other institutions. With few employment opportunities available, they now were increasingly willing to challenge negative evaluations by administrators and colleagues. They tried to retain their jobs through existing, though sometimes impotent, procedures, and their cases frequently reached federal or state appellate courts.

Some institutions changed their procedures, although most did not. A few institutions, especially those supported primarily by private sources, developed formal procedures that were included in their constitutions and faculty handbooks. Others, particularly those state universities supervised or coordinated by state boards of higher education, developed procedures that became part of state law. At some institutions where procedures were actually included in the law, faculty members still felt that they had no strong advocates to ensure that the procedures were applied impartially. When they were not satisfied with the implementation of the procedures and mechanisms designed for appealing individual nonrenewals, de facto tenure quotas, or layoffs, faculty members often designated unions to represent them in negotiating with the administration and in filing grievances. This cooperation frequently resulted in the development of official faculty union contracts that contained conditions and procedures of employment. Contracts at some state universities—for example, the state universities in Florida—contain the same conditions and procedures as those stipulated in the state law concerning university personnel policies.

In several states the difference between the legislation and the contracts is that the contracts are monitored by union officials who act as faculty advocates. In states with legislation but no negotiated contract, the conditions are monitored by the administration, a situation that many faculty members perceive as the fox guarding the henhouse. The spirit of the legislation appears to be remarkably similar to the spirit of the negotiated contracts. Perhaps if a mechanism were developed that carried out the legislative intent fairly, faculty members might not feel such a strong need to unionize.

Faculty personnel problems occur whether a union exists or not. In fact, although the power and influence of faculty unions are increasing dramatically in some areas of the country, the personnel problems facing faculty members have remained the same. These problems have led to formal grievances or informal complaints, depending on the procedures at any given institution.

Regardless of whether a faculty union exists, a department chairperson may confront many kinds of grievances. The following list contains examples of typical problems that have led to grievances:

- Conflict with colleagues, administrators, students, or community over teaching methods, course content, research design, or subject matter
- Complaints about rank or pay; claims that inequities were due to discrimination against race, sex, religion, or handicap
- Dissatisfaction with status or classification; claims that existing status or classification did not reflect training, experience, or responsibilities
- Disagreement over assignment; claims that assignment was made late, represented an undesired overload, constituted disciplinary action, or was made arbitrarily and capriciously
- Problems concerning evaluation; claims that evaluations were biased, that supervisors failed to notify employees of the results of their observations, that the evaluation procedures and instruments used were in violation of the contract, that the evaluation file was stacked with negative information, or that evaluation was based on materials not contained in the evaluation file
- Problems concerning nonrenewal of contract; claims that employees were not notified of nonrenewal within contractual time limits, that

reasons for nonrenewal were not provided on request, or that reasons provided were in violation of the contract, the law, or university rules or constitution

- Problems concerning layoff; claims of failure to follow contractual guidelines for layoff or failure to pursue actively recall and placement procedures

- Problems with peer review; claims of failure to conduct peer reviews so that administrative decisions would be based on consistent criteria and procedures established by the contract, the law, or university rules

- Problems concerning promotion and tenure; claims that decisions were not based on established criteria, were arbitrary and capricious, or contradicted supportive materials in the evaluation folder; claims of unwillingness to overturn an erroneous review on its merits; claims of total disregard for a favorable peer review

- Problems concerning reprimand or censure; objections to negative letters placed in personnel file; objections to suspension or termination

- Problems concerning access to records, documents, or information; disagreements over administrative use of "relevance" or "privilege" arguments to refuse access

- Problems concerning efforts to solve problems; claims that administrators failed to observe time lines, to conduct impartial meetings, or to make good faith efforts to reach a settlement or to issue decisions based on the merits of the grievance

The issues of greatest conflict between faculty members represented by a faculty union and the board of regents in one state university system have been identified in a recent dissertation.[1] The study found that during the period from 1976 to 1988, 298 conflicts reached the second step of the formal grievance procedure—i.e., review by the chancellor of the board of regents or his or her representatives. These conflicts were filed by faculty members in tenured or tenure-earning positions only, and the 298 grievances filed represented 0.61 percent of the faculty, or an average of six faculty members per 1,000. The top ten conflict issues arose from complaints about Promotion Procedures (14.08 percent or 42 cases); Assignment of Responsibilities (13.38 percent or 40 cases); Tenure Procedures (12.91 percent or 38 cases); Discrimination (10.56 percent or 31 cases); Performance Evaluation (8.23 percent or 25 cases); Salaries (8.22 percent or 25 cases); Appointment (7.28 percent or 22 cases); Personnel Evaluation File (5.63 percent or 17 cases); Termination and Other Actions (5.40 percent or 16 cases); and Reappointment (2.11 percent or 6 cases). The top ten conflict issues represented 88 percent of all the cases filed.

In this study, those who filed grievances most often came from the follow-

---

1. Cheryl D. Lovell, "Faculty Grievances: A Longitudinal Study of Conflict Issues in the State University System of Florida," Ph.D. Dissertation, Florida State University, 1989.

ing groups of faculty: female, minority (nonwhite), assistant professors, and nontenured.

Most of the inequity grievances grew out of a sex discrimination clause of the contract. Once the initial inequities were rectified, this cause of grievances became of secondary importance in subsequent years. Tenure, promotion, assignments, nonrenewals, and evaluations still remained major grievance areas. Since these 298 cases reached an advanced step in the grievance process, certain matters of faculty relations clearly deserve close scrutiny. With these conflicts in mind, the chairperson may be able to anticipate personnel problems. In many cases, when the reason for a problem is understood, the potential difficulty can be resolved to everyone's benefit before it becomes critical.

Sometimes personnel problems result in formal grievances. A *grievance,* as the term will be used here, is a claim that a contract negotiated under collective bargaining has been violated or that university or college rules, state statute, federal law, or constitutional rights have been violated. When a faculty union perceives that its members have a problem, it may "find" an article of the contract that it will claim is being violated. Such a claim does not necessarily mean that a violation has occurred but that the union can be expected to interpret the contract liberally when the interests of its clientele are involved. If a faculty member's unhappiness stems from something other than a violation of the contract or of any of the above laws, rules, or rights, he or she may simply choose to write a letter of complaint to some upper-level administrator in the college or university.

An unusually large number of complaints or grievances within a department, whether based on alleged violations of a faculty contract or not, is often symptomatic of deep-seated conflict. A wise chairperson will try to create a department environment that minimizes grievances and maximizes openness and trust. In discussing how to minimize grievances, we have assumed that a better understanding of grievance procedures will lead department chairpersons to adhere to the spirit and letter of the faculty contract (if one exists) or of current university rules and regulations governing faculty personnel. Unfortunately, some department chairpersons are not cognizant of these rules and regulations or choose to ignore them. As faculty members expend greater efforts defending their rights, it is increasingly important for chairpersons to understand the faculty contract or other operative personnel rules and regulations, as well as alternatives for dealing with personnel problems.

A chairperson can minimize grievances, contractual or other, by assigning responsibilities in a clear and forthright manner; providing a process for faculty members to dispute and change an arbitrary or capricious assignment; regularly evaluating employees on the basis of their assignments, rather than on personality or social considerations; instructing committees engaged in peer evaluation also to evaluate a faculty member on the basis of that person's assigned responsibilities; and counseling faculty members who have performed poorly. A good personnel policy is one that is fair, provides means of improvement, and minimizes complaints and grievances.

When a faculty member files a grievance, considers doing so, or simply has a complaint or problem, the chairperson should be willing to discuss the problem with the potential grievant and his or her representative. A chairperson should not be offended if a department member feels the need for a representative when dealing with a serious career matter. Unions usually advise faculty members to have a colleague witness such discussions with supervisors. Moreover, to the chairperson, the faculty member may be a colleague, but to the faculty member with a problem, the chairperson may simply be the "boss." Even a professional may need the moral support of a colleague or grievance specialist.

Faculty members with grievances are under enormous pressure. They do not want to offend friends or administrators, but they do want a just resolution of their problem. A simple description of the grievance process does not begin to reveal the strain that a grievance creates, even among innocent bystanders in a department or college.

Resolving personnel problems is easier when the complaints are still informal. Clearly, doing whatever possible to eliminate potential causes of grievances and attempting to solve them informally is in the best interests of all persons in the university community. Possibilities of settlement may arise at informal meetings early in the grievance process and should be seriously pursued. An experienced party might be recruited to suggest solutions. Early resolution keeps the complaint within the chairperson's control; avoids time-consuming hearings, depositions, or court appearances; spares upper-level administrators the need to deal with the department's headache; and prevents the intradepartment bloodletting that often results when factions form behind protagonists.

The Grievance Procedure

If the problem is not resolved, it may become a formal grievance. When a contract exists, only matters covered by the contract may constitute the subject of a grievance. The contract encourages administrators and employees to communicate openly and to make every attempt to resolve problems before a grievance is filed. Once a grievance is filed, however, the contract stipulates three steps to be followed in the attempt to settle the grievance. The grievance procedure for the State University System of Florida will serve as our model for the three-step grievance procedure.

The first step consists of the grievant and his or her representative presenting evidence supporting the grievance to the university president or his or her representative. At this time, the "acts or omissions" leading to the grievance and the university officials involved are identified, and a solution is proposed. The president or his or her representative must give a written decision within a defined time. If the grievance is not satisfactorily resolved within the institution, the process moves to the second step, which consists of a prompt review by the chancellor of the university system or his or her representatives, who must give a decision with supporting reasons within a defined time. If no satisfactory resolution results, the third step is taken at the discretion of the union. This step consists of a process of arbitration conducted by a neutral arbitrator chosen from a preselected panel. The arbitrator's decision is binding on the board of regents, the union, and the grievant, though the arbitrator's decision may be appealed to a court of law if he or she appears to have acted outside his or her jurisdiction.

The three-step approach gives the impression that grievances are primarily resolved at one of the three official levels. Many grievances, however, never reach the first step but are worked out informally between the local union steward or chapter grievance specialist and the department chairperson or, occasionally, a dean. In addition, many grievances are worked out along the way as "settlements" that are satisfactory to both sides. Still others end in ad hoc committees, acceptable to both the administration and the faculty union, which successfully resolve the problems. The distasteful prospect of arbitration encourages both sides to strive for an acceptable settlement. The grievance procedure with the possibility of a review by a neutral party introduces an element of accountability into contract administration.

The situation is considerably different when a union contract does not exist. At universities that provide due process, usually one or several peer committees exist to deal with complaints. The committees may be appointed by administrators, chosen by senates, or elected at large. Such committees hear charges, examine evidence, and keep records. The committee members are colleagues of the grievant and rarely, if ever, have authority to change personnel decisions on their own. Their charge is to make a recommendation to a high-level management representative, who may or may not choose to follow the recommendation.

Several states have legislation modeled on the federal Administrative Procedures Act, and a considerable number of academic rules and procedures for state universities are usually included in these state statutes. Florida law, for example, provides for standard university governing policies, such as criteria for tenure and promotion, acceptable reasons for nonrenewal, and even the relationship of teaching to research and publication in the promotion criteria. The state's Administrative Procedures Act provides a mechanism for faculty members to deal with violations of those procedures.

The shortcomings of the Administrative Procedures Act in Florida, however, are typical of those throughout the country. Under this act, a party has the right to have a grievance placed before a neutral hearing officer, who is chosen on the basis of his or her expertise in the matter in question. In the absence of a collective bargaining contract, the hearing officer's ruling on whether a faculty member's rights have been violated is only a recommendation to the university. If the university does not choose to implement the recommendation, the aggrieved faculty member can litigate, but in so doing faces considerable financial costs. Moreover, in Florida the courts have rarely upheld the hearing examiner when he or she ruled against management. The unions, of course, point out that the standard grievance procedures in collective bargaining contracts culminate in neutral arbitration, which the courts almost universally support. For this reason neither management nor labor enters into litigation over arbitration decisions, except in the rare instance in which the arbitrator exceeds his or her authority.

The chances of a grievant winning his or her argument seem to be much greater on those campuses where faculty members have union contracts. Nevertheless, the chairperson may face even greater involvement in a noncontractual case because so many separate hearings may need to be conducted for a single case. The strain on the department, the loss of faculty members' time, and diversion of department administrative effort can be significant. For example, one standard noncontractual tenure grievance case was in intrauniversity system hearings for two years and in litigation for another three years. Faculty members and especially chairpersons are frequently required to take part in hearings and litigation. Although the department will not have to incur legal costs for such cases, the university will. In addition, upper-level administrators will have to take part in this unpleasant diversion. University administrators may view chairpersons who are involved in a great many grievances as problems in themselves. Chairpersons should not acquiesce to unreasonable claims made by some department members but should understand the rules under which they function and minimize grievances through sound personnel practices.

A grievant or the union will occasionally blame the chairperson for the problem leading to the grievance. The grievant will sometimes demand that the chairperson be disciplined or receive psychiatric counseling. Grievants often vent their hostility in this way, and the chairperson should not succumb to emotional reactions. Such reactions not only make resolution more difficult and final adjustment to the situation unlikely, but they also may weaken the argument for the chairperson's position. The goal of both sides is to reach an equitable settlement, but the chairperson will have to live with whatever settlement is attained. Department members may have difficulty accepting an uncomfortable situation, but the chairperson must acquiesce gracefully for the sake of the department and its development. In such instances, it helps for the chairperson to have a thick skin.

A Case Study of a Grievance Filed Under a Union Contract

The following case study is based on a grievance that took place in the State University System of Florida. The procedures that were followed are outlined in a contract negotiated between the United Faculty of Florida and the Florida Board of Regents. The Florida contract is not presented as a model for other states to follow, nor is this study to be viewed as advocating or opposing the cause of faculty unions. It is presented in order to inform department chairpersons of the dynamics of a grievance process. Other states with similar contracts usually have similar, though not necessarily identical, processes. This case study should also be of interest to chairpersons in institutions that do not have union contracts, because it deals with a grievance about tenure and closely resembles cases that have occurred in the absence of a contract.

The facts of the case presented here have been slightly modified in order to protect the privacy of the persons involved. The actual case involved several steps, but it has been restructured as only a one-step case. The names of the persons have been changed, minor facts altered, and some events deleted, but the case is based on an actual incident.

A BRIEF BACKGROUND OF THE CASE

John O'Hara, a member of the department of educational foundations for six years, filed a grievance after being denied tenure. During his fifth year he had been promoted to associate professor, and the promotion was unanimously approved by his department's tenure and promotion committee. When he applied for tenure the next year, the same committee rejected him unanimously. When O'Hara formally asked why he had failed to receive tenure, the university president's representative responded that the department would state only that it had rejected O'Hara because a majority of the committee had voted against him.

O'Hara filed a grievance citing several documents: a letter from the department chairperson. C. B. Rhodes, a collective bargaining unit member [at certain institutions in the State University System of Florida, some chairpersons are designated as members of the collective bargaining unit and some are designated as part of management]; a letter from Jason Smith, the chairperson of the tenure and promotion committee; and a letter from James Deles, the leading scholar among the full professors serving on the committee. The initial series of letters supported O'Hara's promotion; a subsequent series supported his tenure approval. These letters were uniformly positive, praising O'Hara's qualities as both a teacher and a scholar. Deles, for example, described him as "the strongest scholar in the department." O'Hara also included letters from the same persons that were written following the department's rejection of his request for tenure. These three letters, all written in a remarkably similar style, considerably modified the earlier praise and indicated unspecified doubts about the candidate.

The file contained several other letters. Among them were two unsolicited communications to O'Hara from nationally known scholars praising his latest book and a related article of his that had appeared in the leading journal in the field. The file also included a copy of the chairperson's annual evaluation of faculty members, which rated as "excellent" O'Hara's teaching and research for each year that he had served at the university. Student evaluations of O'Hara's teaching were also quite positive. His publications list was formidable.

In the area of service, however, O'Hara had received only a "satisfactory" rating for his first three years with the department; for the last three years, he was not evaluated for service. Included in the grievance file was a statement by O'Hara pointing out that he did not understand why he had received only a "satisfactory" rating for meeting his service obligations. O'Hara noted that he had served on as many committees as anyone else in the department, had several doctoral students working under him, and had obtained more money in grants in the last four years than the three most successful grant recipients in the department had obtained in their combined academic careers. O'Hara also coached a peewee-league softball team, an activity he felt constituted community service of a sort. He stated, however, that he was not sure what "community service" meant for someone in the field of philosophy of education. O'Hara noted that when he asked Rhodes what he should do to improve his service rating, Rhodes assured him—verbally—that O'Hara need not worry about the matter. Subsequently, he was not assigned a service obligation for the last three years.

AN INFORMAL ATTEMPT TO DEAL WITH THE PROBLEM

A union grievance representative brought the O'Hara matter to the attention of the dean of the college of education, Carmine Calabrezi. The dean chose not to have the assistant to the president for labor relations present, indicating that on principle he would not overturn a unanimous vote of a department. In addition, Dean Calabrezi emphasized that he had utmost confidence in the department chairperson, Rhodes. Dean Calabrezi would not speak of the substance of the grievance. If Rhodes indicated to him that a serious error had taken place, Calabrezi assured the representative that he would be happy to reconsider the tenure recommendation.

The union representative then met informally with Rhodes, who also refused to discuss the substance of the case. Rhodes began by noting that the union had filed this grievance only after the dean had rejected O'Hara's tenure. Rhodes emphasized, "I'm in the collective bargaining unit, not an administrator who has to justify his decisions." After his meeting with Rhodes, the union grievance representative gave a report of "no progress" to O'Hara.

GRIEVANCE MEETING

A meeting was scheduled to discuss O'Hara's grievance. Greivance meetings at this stage in the process take on different forms at different institutions. At some universities, the president's representative meets first with the representatives of one party and then with the representatives of the other. At O'Hara's grievance meeting, the union's representative and the president's representative remained for the entire meeting.

At the meeting, O'Hara and his union representative discussed the grievance matter with the president's representative. O'Hara based his argument on documents from his personnel file and on relevant sections of the collective bargaining contract, board of regents rules, and state law. The president called on O'Hara's department chairperson, Rhodes, to testify against O'Hara's charges. The union representative asked Rhodes many questions, but Rhodes refused to cite any specific reasons for the denial of O'Hara's request for tenure other than the fact that a peer committee had unanimously made that recommendation. He also refused to answer any substantive questions regarding the case, citing the secrecy of the tenure process. In addition, he claimed that, as a collective bargaining unit member, he had no official responsibility in the matter.

The representatives of the union and the president both countered that merely citing the unanimous vote against O'Hara's tenure application was an inadequate response by the chairperson. The president's representative added that although Rhodes was a unit member, a chairperson serves in a management role when deciding about promotion and tenure matters and should be responsible enough to aid the grievant in his right to due process. The representative added that any chairperson who does not accept supervisory responsibilities should meet with the dean to redefine the chairperson's role or else resign the position. He also pointed out that if the chairperson were not able to provide the evidence on which the rejection of O'Hara's request was based, the department would have to grant O'Hara tenure. "If, Mr. Rhodes, you persist in hiding behind the argument that you are in the unit, you will be stuck with a man you claim you do not want in your department," the president's representative said.

Other members of the tenure and promotion committee appeared at the meeting or were contacted directly by the president's representative. All but one member of the committee presented the same arguments as Rhodes and refused to give any substantive reason for opposing O'Hara's request for tenure.

The one exception, Jason Smith, chairperson of the department's tenure committee, stated that he did not feel strongly about O'Hara's request for tenure one way or the other. He considered O'Hara an "overly aggressive man who cared only about research and his own career" and stated that O'Hara had little loyalty to the department. The union representative asked Smith if any criteria such as "department loyalty" or "lack of aggressiveness" were included in the qualifications for tenure drawn up by the university or the board of regents. Smith said that he was not familiar with the specifics of tenure criteria found in official documents. His vote had been based on his intuition, on information he had received from students and colleagues, on his personal impression of the grievant, and on a careful examination of O'Hara's promotion file. He also noted that because of O'Hara's overconcern with research, he had a weak service record. Smith stated, however, that he intended to vote for O'Hara's tenure next year. [In this institution, candidates could be considered for tenure during the seventh year even though they have been formally notified of nonrenewal.] Smith felt that another year of seasoning would provide O'Hara with some much-needed humility.

Before examining the president's decision about O'Hara's grievance, let us review certain relevant excerpts from the contract that was in effect at that time between the Florida Board of Regents and the faculty union, as well as excerpts from the Florida Administrative Code, the Board of Regents Manual.[2] Chairpersons should have some familiarity with the language of contracts, statutes, and rules that define the rights and responsibilities of faculty members and administrators. Note that the language of each is similar.

EXCERPTS FROM THE FLORIDA ADMINISTRATIVE CODE, FLORIDA BOARD OF REGENTS MANUAL

Each faculty member, tenured and non-tenured, shall be evaluated at least once annually on the basis of his or her individual total performance in fulfilling responsibilities to the university. The basic purpose of the evaluation is faculty improvement in the functions of teaching, research, service, and any other duties that may be assigned, with the resulting enhancement of learning, cultural advancement, and the production of new knowledge. This evaluation shall precede and be considered in recommendations and final decisions on tenure, promotions, and salary for tenured and non-tenured faculty members and on retention or non-renewal for non-tenured faculty members. [6C-5.05(1)(a)]

When first employed, each faculty member shall be appraised of what is expected of him or her, generally, in terms of teaching, research and other creative activities, and service, and specifically if there are specific requirements and/or other duties involved. If and when these expectations change during the period of service of a faculty member, that faculty member shall be apprised of the change. [6C-5.05(1)(b)]

Tenure is that condition attained by the faculty member through highly competent teaching and research, or other scholarly activities, service, and contributions to the university and to society. . . . [6C-5.06(1)(a)]

Each nomination for tenure shall be acted upon with careful consideration being given to the qualifications of the faculty member, including evaluations by colleagues and the immediate superior. . . . [6C-5.06(2)]

Tenure recommendations shall be based on the institution's evaluation procedures. . . . [6C-5.06(4)(a)]

[The areas of performance to be evaluated are:]
(a) Teaching. . . .
(b) Research and Other Creative Activities—Contribution to the discovery of new knowledge, development of new educational techniques, and other forms of

---

2. The BOR has contended that such BOR rules, state law, and state and federal constitutions do not, as such, constitute the subjects of a grievance. The union has continually cited BOR rules and state law in grievances. The issue has not yet been decided either in arbitration or litigation. Whether the BOR or the union eventually prevails in this issue, the chairperson should understand the material involved. Also, non-unit grievants will likely utilize these citations.

creative activity shall be considered and evaluated. Evidence of research and other creative activity shall include, but not be limited to: published books; articles and papers in professional journals; . . . and current research and creative activity that has not yet resulted in publication, display, or performance. The evaluation shall include consideration of:

1. Productivity, including quality and quantity of what has been done during the year, and of the faculty member's long-term research and other creative programs and contributions, and

2. Recognition by the academic or professional community of what is done.

(c) Service—Service shall include, but not be limited to, service on departmental, college, and university committees, councils, and senates; service in appropriate professional organizations; involvements in the organization and expedition of meetings, symposia, conferences, workshops; participation in radio and television; and on local, state, and national governmental boards, agencies and commissions. Only those activities which are related to a person's field of expertise or to the mission of the university shall be evaluated. [6C-5.05]

In evaluating the competency of a faculty member, primary assessment shall be in terms of his performance of the assigned duties and responsibilities, and such evaluation shall be given adequate consideration for the purpose of salary adjustments, promotions, re-employment, and tenure. . . . Flexible criteria for rewarding faculty members, consistent with the institution's educational goals and objectives, shall be established, which criteria shall include quality teaching as a major factor in determining salary adjustments, promotions, re-employment or tenure. [Florida Statute 241.731, a portion of what is known as the Omnibus Education Act of 1973]

[Although not a part of the statute proper, the Title of the bill conveys the legislative intent] that no denial of promotions, salary adjustments, re-employment or tenure be solely for failure to do research, publish, or perform other scholarly activities. . . . [Laws of Florida, Chapter 73–338]

ARTICLES FROM THE FLORIDA BOARD OF REGENTS–UNITED FACULTY OF FLORIDA AGREEMENT

Article 8
APPOINTMENT

8.4 When first employed, each employee shall be apprised of what is expected, generally, in terms of teaching, research and other creative activities, and service, and specifically if there are specific requirements and/or other duties involved. If and when these expectations change during the period of service of the employee, that employee shall be apprised of the change.

Article 9
ASSIGNMENT OF RESPONSIBILITIES

9.1 The professional obligation is comprised of both scheduled and non-scheduled activities. The parties recognize that it is a part of the professional responsibility of employees to carry out their duties in an appropriate manner and place. For example, while instructional activities, office hours, and other duties and responsibilities may be required to be performed at a specific time and place, other non-scheduled activities are more appropriately performed in a manner and place determined by the employee.

9.2 Employees shall be apprised in writing, at the beginning of their employment and at the beginning of each year of employment thereafter, of the duties and responsibilities in teaching, research and other creative activities, service, and of any other specific duties and responsibilities assigned for that year.

9.3 Except for an assignment made at the beginning of an employee's employment, the person responsible for making an assignment shall contact the employee prior to making the final written assignment. Such contact shall also take place prior to changes which become necessary in an assignment, and such changes shall be specified in writing. The employee shall be granted, upon request, a conference with the person responsible for making the assignment to express concerns regarding:

(a) the employee's qualifications and preferences; and

(b) the character of the assignment, including the number of hours of instruction, the preparation required, whether the employee has taught the course in the past, the number of students and time required by course, whether travel to another location is required, the number of preparations required, the employee's assignments in other semesters, and the availability and adequacy of materials and equipment, secretarial services, student assistants, and other supportive services needed to perform the assignments.

An employee may request which two of three terms the employee wishes to work and this request shall be honored where appropriate. Available assignments to a summer term shall be offered equitably and as appropriate to qualified employees in sufficient time to allow voluntary acceptance or rejection.

9.4 ... No employee's assignment should be arbitrarily and capriciously imposed. If an employee believes that the assignment has been so imposed, the employee should, prior to the effective date of the assignment, take the matter up with the individual who has the responsibility for making the assignment. If that discussion does not resolve the dispute, the employee may discuss the matter with the dean or other appropriate administrator. If no satisfactory resolution is accomplished after consultation with the dean or appropriate administrator, UFF may, prior to the effective dates of the assignment, refer the matter to a neutral umpire acceptable to both parties or, failing agreement, to a member of the Arbitration Panel in accordance with the procedures in Article 20.11. The umpire shall determine whether or not the employee's assignment has been arbitrarily and capriciously imposed. Upon a finding that the assignment has been so imposed, the President or designee shall take appropriate corrective action. ...

Article 10
ANNUAL EMPLOYEE PERFORMANCE EVALUATION

10.1 Employee's performance shall be evaluated at least once annually and they shall be advised of the term during which such annual evaluation will be made. Personnel decisions shall take such annual evaluations into account, provided that personnel decisions need not be based solely on written employee performance evaluations.

10.2 The employee, if assigned teaching duties, shall be notified at least two weeks in advance of the date, time, and place of any direct classroom observation or visitation made in connection with the employee's annual evaluation.

10.3 The evaluation shall be in writing and shall be discussed with the employee prior to being placed in the employee's evaluation file. The evaluation shall be signed by the person performing the evaluation, and by the person being evaluated, who may attach a concise comment to the evaluation. A copy of the evaluation shall be made available to the employee.

10.4 Those persons responsible for supervising and evaluating an employee shall endeavor to assist the employee in correcting any performance deficiencies reflected in the employee's annual evaluation.

10.5 The annual performance evaluation shall be based upon assigned duties, and shall take into account the nature of the assignments, in terms, where applicable, of:

(a) Teaching effectiveness, including effectiveness in presenting knowledge, information, and ideas by means or methods such as lecture, discussion, assignment and recitation, demonstration, laboratory exercise, practical experience, and direct consultation with students. The evaluation shall include consideration of effectiveness in imparting knowledge and skills, and effectiveness in stimulating students' critical thinking and/or creative abilities, and adherence to accepted standards of professional behavior in meeting responsibilities to students.

(b) Contribution to the discovery of new knowledge, development of new educational techniques, and other forms of creative activity. Evidence of research and other creative activity shall include, but not be limited to: published books; articles and papers in professional journals; musical compositions, paintings, sculpture; works of performing art; papers presented at meetings of professional societies; and current research and creative activity that has not yet resulted in publication, display, or performance. The evaluation shall include consideration of the employee's productivity, including the quality and quantity of what has been done during the year, and of the employee's long-term research and other creative programs and contributions; and recognition by the academic or professional community of what is done.

(c) Service on departmental, college, and university committees, councils, and senates; service in appropriate professional organizations; participation in meetings, symposia, conferences, workshops; participation in radio and television; and service on local, state and national governmental boards, agencies and commissions. Evaluation of service shall include consideration of contribution to:

(1) the orderly and effective functioning of the employee's academic unit (program, department, school, college) and/or the total university;

(2) the university community; and

(3) the local, state, regional and national communities, and scholarly and professional associations.

(d) Other assigned university duties, such as advising, counseling, and supervision of interns, or as described in a Position Description, if any, of the position held by the employee.

(e) Such other responsibilities as may be appropriate to the assignment.

Article 11
PERSONNEL EVALUATION FILE

11.1 There shall be one file in which all written materials used in the evaluation process are maintained. When evaluations and personnel decisions are made, the only documents which may be used are those contained in that file. Employees shall be notified upon request of the location of the personnel evaluation file and the identity of the custodian.

11.2 An employee may examine the evaluation file upon reasonable advance notice, during the regular business hours of the office in which the file is kept, and under such conditions as are necessary to insure its integrity and safekeeping. Upon request and the payment of a reasonable fee for photocopying, an employee may obtain copies of any materials in the evaluation file and may attach a concise statement in response to any item therein. A person designated by the employee may examine that employee's evaluation file with the written authorization of the employee concerned and subject to the same limitations on access that are applicable to the employee.

11.4 In the event a grievance proceeds to arbitration, the Board, UFF, the arbitrator, and the grievant shall have the right to use copies of materials from the grievant's evaluation file relevant thereto in the arbitration proceedings.

11.5 No anonymous material shall be placed in an evaluation file, except for student evaluations which are part of a regular evaluation procedure of classroom instruction.

11.6 Evaluative materials or summaries thereof prepared by peer committees as part of a regular evaluation system may be placed in an evaluation file when signed by a representative of the committee.

11.7 Materials shown to be contrary to fact shall be removed from the file. This section shall not authorize the removal of materials from the evaluation file when there is a dispute concerning a matter of judgment or opinion rather than fact. Materials may also be removed pursuant to the resolution of a grievance.

11.8 Except as noted above, only university and Board officials responsible for the supervision or evaluation of employees shall have access to such files except under order of a court of competent jurisdiction.

Article 15
TENURE PROCEDURE

15.1 A tenured employee may be terminated only for cause in accordance with the provisions of Article 16, Termination and Other Actions, or laid off only in accordance with the provisions of Article 13, Layoff and Recall.

15.3 Except for employees who, by virtue of prior service credited at time of appointment, are eligible for consideration earlier, an employee shall normally be considered for tenure during the fifth year of continuous service in a tenure-earning position or, at the option of the employee and with the concurrence of the appropriate administrative officials, during the sixth such year in a tenure-earning position. Part-time service of an employee employed at least two academic semesters in any 12 month period shall be accumulated. For example, one year (at least two semesters) of half-time service shall be considered one-half year of service for purposes of tenure eligibility. By the end of six full years of service within the State University System, an employee eligible for tenure shall either be awarded tenure or given notice that further employment will not be offered. The notice shall be accompanied by a statement of reasons by the President or representative why tenure was not granted.

15.4 The decision of the Board to award or deny tenure shall be made by September 15 and the employee shall be notified in writing by the President within five days of the decision of the Board. An employee being considered for tenure prior to the sixth year may withdraw from consideration on or before April 15 without prejudice.

15.5 The performance of an employee during the entire term of employment at the institution shall be considered in determining whether to grant tenure.

GRIEVANCE FINDING

A grievance report was drawn up by a member of the president's committee, which acted in lieu of a single representative. After reading the report, the president sent a letter to O'Hara indicating that he would recommend to the Board of Regents that O'Hara be granted tenure. The president cited the following reasons for his decision:

1. The documentary evidence indicated that without any doubt John O'Hara had fulfilled two of the three standard criteria for tenure, those of teaching and research, in an exceptional manner. These criteria, it should be noted, had been cited to all chairpersons by the dean of faculties in a memorandum. [The established criteria for promotion and tenure are cited in Florida Statutes 241.731, the Florida Administrative Code Section 6C-5.06, and the BOR/UFF Collective Bargaining Agreement, Articles 10 and 15.]

2. Neither the members of the tenure and promotions committee nor the department chairperson could or would adequately explain their negative votes. They could not explain how O'Hara failed to meet the existing criteria for tenure. Only one member of the tenure committee even discussed the substance of the grievance, and that member's only relevant argument was that O'Hara's service record had been weak. O'Hara had been rated "satisfactory" in the area of service for three years and had not been given a service assignment during the next three years. If he had not performed the service responsibilities well, this weakness should have been noted on the evaluation forms. In addition, the chairperson should have counseled O'Hara about the matter and given him an opportunity to improve in that area.

3. Senior faculty members in the department had repeatedly rated O'Hara's performance in both research and teaching as "excellent," ratings that were recorded on the evaluation forms used for considering his requests for promotion and tenure. O'Hara had letters in his file from program leaders indicating strong support for his candidacy. In addition, he had received two "high merit" raises. [Criteria for such salary adjustments are the same as for promotion and tenure under Florida Statute 241.731.] The tenure committee could not adequately explain the inconsistency of O'Hara's continued high ratings and the negative tenure vote. If the committee had not changed the criteria on which its earlier judgments had been based, then this judgment was clearly inconsistent, arbitrary, and capricious. If the criteria had in fact changed, O'Hara had not been informed of the changes. Failure to inform him of such changes is in violation of Florida Administrative Code 6C-5.05 (1)(6) and Article 8.4 of the BOR/UFF agreement.

4. Before the vote on the tenure application, the department chairperson

had at no time informed O'Hara of any inadequacies in his performance of his teaching, research, or service responsibilities. Following the tenure vote, the tenure committee and the department chairperson evaded O'Hara's request to cite specific inadequacies on his part so that he could work to overcome these immediately. By not informing O'Hara of his inadequacies, if in fact they existed at all, the department and the chairperson clearly violated both Florida Administrative Code/BOR Rule 6C-5.05 (1)(a), which states that those being considered for tenure shall be evaluated in order to improve "the functions of teaching, research, service," and Article 10.4 of the BOR/UFF Collective Bargaining Agreement, which states that "persons responsible for supervising and evaluating an employee shall endeavor to assist the employee in correcting any performance deficiencies. . . ." To refuse to reveal the inadequacies of the candidate clearly contradicts the purpose of the evaluation, namely faculty improvement.

Rhodes, the department chairperson, had the specific responsibility of ensuring that the department tenure committee not act in an arbitrary and capricious manner. Clearly, Smith, who chaired the tenure committee, had little knowledge of the official criteria. In addition, Rhodes, who had the responsibility of ensuring that O'Hara knew of his performance inadequacies in time to correct them before the tenure vote, had been totally unresponsive and continued to insist that a peer committee vote should not be overruled on any grounds. This argument was rejected since it would deny O'Hara his due process in any grievance or appeal process following a peer committee vote. In addition, Rhodes argued that the BOR/UFF Agreement provisions were new and that therefore it was unnecessary to follow them this year. When it was pointed out to him that these provisions had recapitulated long-standing Board of Regents rules, university rules, and state law, he claimed that these rules had not been traditionally followed. In all, Rhodes' approach to the tenure process and the appeal procedure seemed to be at best cavalier. O'Hara should not be penalized because of his chairperson's poor judgment and inadequate leadership.

5. Rhodes' position that as a chairperson in the bargaining unit he had no responsibility in the matter was rejected. This argument is not unique. Some members of the state university system collective bargaining unit who supervise and evaluate other members have filed grievances stating that they should no longer have the obligation to evaluate members of their own bargaining unit. The viewpoint is invalid since the collective bargaining contract was never intended to change the assignment of any unit members. The collective bargaining agreement also gives the administration the right to make assignments and to determine the types of duties and responsibilities. Faculty members in the unit have, of course, traditionally taken on management roles such as the evaluation of peers for tenure and promotion purposes. Chairpersons should continue in a similar manner.

The president concluded that the administration of the department of educational foundations violated both the letter and the spirit of the BOR/UFF Collective Bargaining Agreement, Florida Statute (241.731), Board of Regents rules, and reasonable standards of academic administrative judgment. He would add O'Hara's name to the recommended tenure list and officially forward it to the Board of Regents.

After the case was completed and the decision rendered, other facts that revealed the source of O'Hara's actual problems with his colleagues came to light. O'Hara's tenure was opposed primarily because his peers resented his large grants and because he made little effort to include any of his peers in his bounty. In fact, he did invite several members from another department within the university to join him in his work. Although O'Hara had rejected collaboration with his department colleagues, he had nevertheless fulfilled all the requirements for tenure. Incidentally, O'Hara had never been specifically told of the department's resentment, and neither the union's representative nor the president's representative had even surmised the crux of the problem.

Other Case Studies

Following are brief descriptions of other grievances filed under a variety of conditions. Some of them have been resolved; others have not. These abbreviated case studies are examples of the kinds of grievances chairpersons might face, regardless of whether a union contract exists.

GRIEVANCE HEARD BEFORE A FACULTY SENATE COMMITTEE

The following grievance was processed through university procedures at an institution that had no collective bargaining contract.

Three associate professors in the classics department argued that the dean had rejected their promotion requests even though each of them had fulfilled all the department's requirements for promotion. In a subsequent memo, the dean noted that the classics department promotion committee did not recommend any of the three applicants for promotion and that the chairperson supported the committee's recommendation. In response to the grievants' request for the reasons for not being promoted, the dean replied that the information he had received from the department chairperson indicated that none had adequate publishing records.

In the formal grievance the candidates for promotion pointed out, with substantial supporting evidence, that the publishing records of previously promoted candidates were rarely stronger than their own records and often appeared somewhat weaker. In addition, they noted that the only senior woman in the department was promoted, even though she had a publishing record considerably weaker than any of theirs. They claimed that she was promoted because of affirmative action pressure. The grievants also pointed out that the classics department consisted mostly of full professors; that the department's promotion and tenure committee was made up entirely of full professors; that full professors in the department taught half as many hours as associate professors; and that many in the department believed that if the associate professors were promoted, the full professors would have to increase their teaching loads in order to maintain department productivity.

The faculty senate was asked to establish an intrauniversity committee to hear the grievances and to make a recommendation to the university president. The committee established by the senate consisted of four full professors and one assistant professor. In addition to the points already discussed, it considered the following counterarguments: the associate professors were hired as part of a quality improvement program that was designed to upgrade the department; they were involved in developing the changes in promotion and tenure criteria; and the allegations that the full professors were motivated by selfish, personal considerations were untrue.

The committee rejected the grievance. The grievants then threatened a lawsuit, alleging that the senate committee was stacked against them. To avoid an acrimonious public airing of the controversy, the university president agreed to promote two of the associate professors and to consider the third application the following year.

GRIEVANCE HEARD BEFORE A STATE HEARING OFFICER

The following dispute occurred at a state university that had no collective bargaining contract. The case was heard before a state hearing officer.

The university hired Howard Gibson to serve as director of the university art gallery and as assistant professor of fine arts. At the time the department chairperson, Roger Smythe, assured Gibson that an assistant gallery director would be employed within six months. The assistant director, however, was never employed. In addition to administering the gallery and teaching, Gibson was expected to create and display his own works on the same basis as other members of the art department. Some of his associates asserted that Gibson had the heaviest workload in the department.

Four years after Gibson's appointment, the art department evaluated its untenured faculty members. Gibson was not formally informed that this evaluation was going to take place; therefore he did not submit any of his material. He later indicated that he thought the session was being held only to review the files of those faculty members being considered for tenure. The committee voted 7 to 2 in favor of abolishing Gibson's position. The chairperson's report to the dean stated: "The position is simply too big for any one person to handle. Since the administration cannot provide the funds for the department to employ an assistant galley director, we must do away with this aspect of our program entirely." Gibson's contract was then not renewed.

After the nonrenewal, several students circulated a petition that endorsed Gibson's retention and that received considerable student support. Four members of the department's evaluation committee, each of whom had voted to abolish Gibson's position, stated that they had never intended to recommend nonrenewal of his contract and would have voted against the measure if they had understood that it would result in his termination. Nevertheless, the university administration acted in accordance with Smythe's recommendation, and Gibson was sent a notice of nonrenewal. He filed a grievance that resulted in a formal hearing, with a state-appointed hearing officer serving as an umpire. The officer's decision was not binding but merely served as a recommendation to the president.

Smythe, the chairperson, was the administration's chief witness and the defender of his department's recommendation. The university administration depended on Smythe's verbal and documentary evidence in putting together its case. The chairperson was rigorously cross-examined by the grievant's attorney. Members of Smythe's department, some students, and some upper-level administrators attended the meeting. Charles Jones, university attorney, represented the administration in the hearing. Jones requested and received from the department chairperson evidence in support of Gibson's termination.

Gibson's attorney was extremely successful in buttressing the argument that his client had not been properly informed of the nature of the evaluation. He also had several committee members testify that their vote to abolish the position of gallery director was not a vote to abolish Gibson, whose abilities they respected and admired. The hearing officer's decision was in Gibson's favor. He asserted that the grievant's rights to due process were violated in several ways and that even though the university had the right to abolish the position of gallery director, it did not have the right to terminate Gibson's employment in a manner inconsistent with established university practice. The university accepted the recommendation of the hearing officer and renewed Gibson's contract.

POTENTIAL GRIEVANCE AT A PRIVATE UNIVERSITY WITH NO COLLECTIVE BARGAINING CONTRACT

Mary Ellis, a member of the social work department, complained to her chairperson that she had been discriminated against. First, she had received no merit pay during the previous four years. Although she admitted that she had not published a great deal, Ellis pointed out that the department's thrust had been toward teaching and service and that she excelled in both areas. In addition, Ellis's publishing record was no weaker than those of other department members who had received higher salary increases. She therefore felt she was entitled to merit pay.

Ellis also protested that she had not been treated fairly in her teaching assignments. Although her course load was not heavier than that assigned to other department members, she was denied her request to teach late afternoon courses. Late classes in her department constituted an overload and provided extra pay. The late afternoon courses were applied courses taken by students already employed in the field, and Ellis did not have expertise in the applied area.

Ellis basically supported her department's democratic tradition of forwarding to the dean, directly and unchanged, the salary recommendations of an elected committee. An elected committee also determined the annual assignment. Ellis claimed, however, that faculty members with Master of Social Work degrees dominated all key department committees and received "high merit" raises at the expense of faculty members with Ph.D.s in fields other than social work. Ellis holds a Ph.D. in sociology.

Discussing the matter with the dean, the chairperson asserted that since Ellis's degree was in sociology and her background was strong in research methodology, he expected her to have a stronger publication record than her colleagues. The dean suggested that the chairperson review Ellis's case carefully, since there seemed to be some merit to her argument. The dean further stressed the need for documenting the facts of the case in the event of a formal grievance, which could conceivably end up in court if the problem were not satisfactorily resolved. He urged the chairperson to advise Ellis about what she might do to upgrade her expertise so that she could teach some applied courses. He also suggested that the chairperson assign a research role as part of Ellis's workload.

The chairperson followed the dean's advice and met with Ellis several times to discuss her concerns. Ellis made an earnest attempt to heed the chairperson's suggestions and qualified for a merit raise the next year.

POTENTIAL GRIEVANCE UNDER A UNION CONTRACT

Bosley Cowpens had been an assistant professor of history for five years. The department tenure committee voted 7 to 2 against his being granted tenure in the department, and he contemplated filing a grievance. Although the department placed a high priority on research, Cowpens had only a mediocre publishing record. His record showed improvement, but the improvement did not satisfy the department committee. He claimed that his publication record for the last two years was equal to the record of two senior tenured professors. The department had thirty members, sixteen of whom were tenured. On the basis of student evaluations, Cowpen's teaching record was below the department average. Moreover, on numerous occasions he had failed to meet his classes, and a letter of reprimand concerning his unexcused absences was on file. He did, however, have a small but loyal following among the students. His service record showed an enormous amount of time and effort spent on the United Fund campaign but very little service to the profession or department.

Cowpens claimed that the real reason for his failure to gain promotion was his iconoclastic behavior on committees. The promotion and tenure committee called his behavior abrasive and reported that he had withdrawn from committee work whenever he had quarreled with other members. The chairperson had discussed his previous unsatisfactory annual evaluations with him, but Cowpens had refused to accept the substance of the evaluation. He was kept on, according to the chairperson, in the hope that his performance would improve, but the degree of improvement had not been deemed satisfactory. The chairperson kept records of his discussions and his attempts to counsel Cowpens and informed him of his record keeping.

Cowpens insisted that he was being denied tenure because he was not a team player and because of personality differences with other faculty members. He also insisted that his community service deserved to be recognized and that his teaching was as good as that of many other department members.

The department union representative, a close friend of Cowpens, expressed his willingness to support the assistant professor if he wanted to file a grievance. The chairperson feared that Cowpens, if he were not granted tenure, would file a formal grievance and would receive union support. Nevertheless, the chairperson was determined to support the findings of the tenure committee. He felt confident that the department committee was properly constituted, had followed established procedures, and was justified in its decision.

The chairperson then met with the university (not the department) union representative to discuss the issue. Despite the fact that Cowpens was counting on union backing, the union, in this instance, decided not to support a faculty member whose case was so weak and informed Cowpens accordingly. Cowpens received notice of nonrenewal of his contract. A grievance was never filed.

By anticipating the kinds of personnel problems that are occurring in postsecondary education, by understanding the nature of grievance mechanisms and the chairperson's role in them, and by becoming familiar with the way rulings, recommendations, and settlements occur, chairpersons can prevent many potential grievances. Personnel problems, however, will be with us as long as there are bosses and workers, managers and employees, and administrators and faculty members. Thus there will always be grievances, whether a collective bargaining contract exists or not. Formal bargaining may result in a greater number of officially filed grievances, but unofficial grievances have always existed.

Chairpersons will no doubt see some changes in their roles as a result either of collective bargaining or of conscientious support of state law and institutional personnel rules. (The latter often emerges when a collective bargaining contract seems probable.) Chairpersons will give greater attention to formal evaluations and personnel decisions and will thus be faced with more paperwork. They will have to provide evidence and appear at various kinds of hearings, while administrators will be transmitting more rules and directives to the department level. Chairpersons will assume the task, often avoided in the past, of counseling less productive department members and suggesting ways to improve their work. If chairpersons avoid such tasks or attempt to reject them because they see themselves as faculty members and not administrators, the administration will shift the position of chairperson upward into the management bureaucracy.

Such trends have not occurred solely because of collective bargaining. For example, institutions of higher education, with or without collective bargaining, have become increasingly centralized. In addition, chairpersons have always had both academic and administrative responsibilities; they were sometimes colleagues and sometimes bosses. Thus some chairpersons have always perceived themselves as centaur-like creatures—half man and half beast. Whether the beast is the management half or the employee half depends on the chairperson's philosophy.

Questions

1. Give examples of unfair treatment of faculty members at the hands of the chairperson in the areas of workload, evaluation, and financial matters, in which the chairperson *may not be aware* that he or she is treating a faculty member unfairly.

2. Give examples of unfair treatment of faculty members at the hands of the chairperson in the areas of workload, evaluation, and financial matters, in which the chairperson *may be aware* that he or she is treating a faculty member unfairly.

3. Give examples of treatment perceived by faculty members to be unfair in the areas of workload, evaluation, and financial matters, in which upon investigation it was found that the treatment *was really not unfair.*

4. In some departments, committees are designated to make decisions in the areas of workload, evaluation, and financial matters. What might a chairperson do in the event that he or she believes that the committee decision is unfair to a faculty member?

5. The following questions are based on the O'Hara case:
   a. Distinguish between a grievance and a complaint according to the definitions given in the chapter.
   b. How was the union contract violated in O'Hara's case?
   c. What instructions should the department chairperson have given the tenure and promotion committee about its charge as well as about the contract?
   d. What might the chairperson have done in order to avoid the situa-

tion? What should have been his reaction to the 9–0 vote against O'Hara?

    e. What effect will the retention of O'Hara now have on the department?

6. The following questions are based on the Gibson case:

    a. How might Chairperson Smythe have countered the argument that the department committee members did not understand what they were voting on?

    b. If the university had no clear policy or rules regarding evaluation and review of faculty members, on what grounds could Gibson have filed a grievance?

7. The following questions are based on the Ellis case:

    a. As department chairperson, how would you have attempted to resolve this problem?

    b. What specific measures might a chairperson institute within a department in order to keep this type of problem from occurring?

8. The following questions are based on the Cowpens case:

    a. If Cowpens had filed a grievance, he probably would have lost. If you were the chairperson, what arguments would you use to persuade Cowpens to resign?

    b. Under what altered circumstances might Cowpens have won a grievance?

9. If a college or university has no faculty union and its board of trustees prefers not to have one, what can the administration do to bolster the faculty members' feeling of security so that they might not feel the need for union representation?

10. If a college or university has a faculty union and wants to keep grievances to a minimum, how should administrators and department chairpersons deal with faculty problems on a continuing basis so that faculty members will not feel the need or the urge to file grievances?

Case Studies of Faculty Personnel Problems and Possible Grievance Situations

The following are examples of faculty personnel problems which have arisen in the university setting.[3] Select the problems which may be of interest to you and contemplate how you might deal with them. These types of situations are generally addressed in such documents as faculty handbooks, college or university constitutions, institutional contracts with faculty members and other employees, collective bargaining agreements (if faculty are unionized), and state

---

3. Developed for use in seminar discussions for department chairpersons and other university administrators by Catherine Archibald Longstreth, associate vice-president for Academic Affairs, University of Florida, with James Perry, associate vice-chancellor, and other staff members, from the Office of Human Resources, Florida Board of Regents.

statutes. It will be helpful to obtain copies of documents that are applicable to your institution and to refer to appropriate chapters, articles, or sections in them as you consider the problems described below.

1. A faculty member has demanded a copy of the following materials:

Current résumés of all of the members of your department; all evaluations that you, as department chair, have made regarding these faculty members' performance; any grant applications these faculty members may have submitted, and any correspondence regarding the approval of such applications; and all documents relating to your department's budget for the past five years.

You have conservatively estimated that a response would consume fifty hours of staff time and involve copying over 2,000 pages. What are your options?

2. A delegation of senior faculty members in your department comes to you to complain about what they term "the inflated salaries" offered to new appointees. The faculty say that, at times, newly hired assistant professors begin their employment making more money than senior faculty members who have given years of dedicated service to the university. They demand that this matter of salary equity be resolved, beginning with the next academic year's salary increases. Further, they inform you that if satisfactory resolution does not occur, they will file an age discrimination suit against the university, the college, and *you*. What response can you offer to this group of faculty members?

3. A tenured faculty member in your department has not been in the office during most of the week. You have tried to contact this person for several days, and discover that you have hit on a pattern which has occurred for the last two weeks because of a consulting position the faculty member has taken for two days each week for this month. This faculty member does not miss scheduled classes, but is not available for student advisement. You had no formal knowledge of the faculty member's consulting work. When you confront this individual, the response you receive is that you are harassing this person and that as long as the scheduled activities are performed, it is none of your business where the faculty member is. What should you do?

4. One of your faculty members is arrested by city police for the possession and distribution of child pornography (photos, motion pictures, etc., of teen-agers). The individual is released on bail; a trial date is set for a date six months after the arrest. What would you do prior to the trial? The faculty member then pleads "No contest" to the charges. Adjudication of guilt is withheld, and all the records relating to the arrest and charges are sealed by the court. What is your response now?

5. A faculty member was hired five years ago as an assistant professor. Neither the letter of offer nor the initial employment contract mentioned any special conditions of employment. The faculty member claims that the previous chair gave assurance that qualification for tenure would be possible if performance in the teaching and service areas was good; research productivity was not a necessity. The chair, who retired three years ago, tends to support the faculty member's recollection of the statement. Upon your assuming the position as chair two years ago, you revised the tenure criteria to place more emphasis on research. The faculty member, who claims unfamiliarity with the revised tenure criteria, has been turned down by the college tenure committee after receiving a mixed, but favorable, vote at the departmental level. This individual now asks you to meet with the dean to assist in the faculty member's request for a redress of the wrong and to recommend that the dean support the application for tenure. What is your decision?

6. One of your unmarried faculty members, while attending a professional meeting along with one of your married faculty members, is discreetly propositioned by the married faculty member during an evening social after the professional meeting is completed. The unmarried faculty member ignores the proposition. However, it occurs a second time, a day later, under similar circumstances. The unmarried faculty member approaches you with this information. How should you respond? Would your response be different if the person propositioned were a graduate assistant studying with the married faculty member?

7. A faculty member has been absent from assigned duties for two days during each of the past four weeks. A sick-leave request was submitted for one of the two days on each occasion; however, the faculty member claimed that it was not necessary to take sick leave for the other day because no classes were assigned. You ask that medical verification of the illness be submitted, but the faculty member refuses. What should you do?

8. A faculty member has been reassigned to a branch campus. The faculty member complains that this assignment is a violation of the individual's academic freedom because he or she will be isolated from colleagues, the university library, and technical equipment available only on the main campus and necessary for current research projects. How would you handle this situation?

9. A tenured faculty member in your department with twenty years of service will reach the age of sixty-one within a year. You want him to retire so you can replace him with a faculty member who can contribute more to the research role of the department. You arrange a meeting with him to inform him of your decision, including the fact you want to replace him with a junior faculty member. How would you handle the discussion so you could accomplish your goal?

10. A faculty member (12-month) asks to use her accrued annual leave, but the period for which she has requested to take the leave conflicts with a conference that all members of the department should be attending. On this basis, you do not approve the leave. You advise the faculty member of your decision, suggesting that she change her request for annual leave to another time. The faculty member claims you have violated her rights since she has earned the leave and can use it when she desires, and informs you she will fight your denial all the way to the vice-president's office. What would you do?

11. A faculty member has been observed by his colleagues to have had an alcohol problem for several years. They have covered for him when he has occasionally been unable to teach or perform other scheduled assignments. His

condition has recently been deteriorating—he recently collapsed in class, and attended several departmental functions in a clearly inebriated state. The department members have met and are asking that his tenured appointment be terminated immediately. How would you respond to the faculty?

12. A faculty member is nominated for tenure, but does not receive a positive vote from his colleagues in the department, and you (the chair) do not support the nomination. The faculty member requests a conference to discuss the tenure vote with you and to seek information on the appeal process. During the discussion you explain that the denial was based on a lack of distinction in two of three categories: teaching, research, and service. The faculty member claims, and you must acknowledge that his claim is valid after reviewing his personnel file, that he has continually demonstrated outstanding performance in teaching. He further claims that the members of the department, and particularly you, have misled him and treated him unfairly by allowing him to reach a point in his career where he is to be denied tenure and not reappointed, without appropriate assistance and equitable assignment(s). Each year he has received a 5 percent service and 5 percent research assignment, along with positive annual evaluations and commensurate merit pay. How would you respond to his claims?

13. You have appointed a faculty member to a three-year, grant-funded, soft-money position. You would like to make it quite clear that the appointment is subject to renewal each year and requires no further notice of cessation of employment, so that the university is protected in case the grant is not renewed, or in case the faculty member's performance is unsatisfactory. How would you make this point clear to the faculty member?

14. In accordance with college procedures, you have conducted the annual evaluation review in May, and at that time also provided faculty members with their written assignments for the coming year. In July you find that there is a need to increase the teaching load of half of your faculty for the Fall term, but are not able to advise three of your faculty members about the change in assignment because they were out of town for the entire summer term. When they return to campus on the first day of classes they are informed of the change in their assignment. They meet with you to discuss the assignment. One faculty member informs you that he refuses to teach additional courses assigned. How would you deal with this situation?

15. A faculty member from a department wherein all regular appointments are for nine months complains that she has not received a supplemental summer appointment for three years, even though she has met the departmental criteria for such appointments. She teaches courses that attract only modest student enrollment during the academic year, but at least one course in her specialty is offered each summer. A departmental colleague, who has been named Teacher of the Year in the department, has been offered a supplemental appointment to teach this course for the past four years. The course is scheduled to be taught next summer by a newly hired faculty member who was offered summer employment during his first year of employment as a recruitment incentive. How would you respond to the complaint?

16. As a new chair, you decide to improve the evaluation of teaching in your department. Accordingly, halfway through the spring semester you begin weekly unannounced classroom observations of each of your eight department members. During these observations you discover that a newly hired faculty member from China is extremely difficult to understand—students are frustrated and confused by his lectures. You are now prepared to use the information you have gathered in the annual evaluation. Any problems?

References

ANGELL, GEORGE W. (Ed.) *Faculty and Teacher Bargaining: The Impact of Unions on Education.* Lexington, MA: D. C. Heath, 1981.

BERGMANN, THOMAS J., and O'MALLEY, JOHN T. "The Department Chairperson in Campus Governance." *College and University Personnel Association,* Fall 1979, pp. 7–17.

BETTEN, NEIL, and OLDSON, WILLIAM. *Contract Administration: From Grievance to Arbitration.* Tallahassee: UFF/Florida AFL–CIO Publications, 1978.

BOK, DEREK. *Beyond the Ivory Tower: Social Responsibility of the Modern University.* Cambridge: Harvard University Press, 1982.

BUCKLEY, WILLIAM F. *God and Man at Yale: The Superstitions of "Academic Freedom."* Chicago: Regnery Books, 1986.

CARNEGIE COUNCIL ON POLICY STUDIES IN HIGHER EDUCATION. *Making Affirmative Action Work in Higher Education: An Analysis of Institutional and Federal Policies with Recommendations.* San Francisco: Jossey–Bass, 1975.

CORSON, JOHN J. *The Governance of Colleges and Universities.* New York: McGraw–Hill, 1960.

CSORBA, LES (Ed.) *Academic License: The War on Academic Freedom.* Evanston, IL: UCA Books, 1988.

DOUGLAS, JOEL M. (Ed.) *Salary and Compensation Methodology in Academic Collective Bargaining.* New York: National Center for the Study of Collective Bargaining in Higher Education and the Professions, 1983. (ERIC Document Reproduction Service NO. ED 230 140)

EDMONSON, WILLIAM F. *Grievance Arbitration and Its Role in the Settlement of Professional Negotiation Disputes in Higher Education.* Ed.D. Dissertation, University of Mississippi, 1973.

ELLIS, JOHN M. "Grievance Procedures: Real and Ideal." *New Directions for Higher Education,* Autumn 1974, pp. 63–76.

FENCHEL, ALLAN H. *The Academic Corporation: Justice, Freedom, and the University.* New York: Black Rose Books, 1987.

FERGUSON, TRACY H., and BERGAN, WILLIAM L. "Grievance Arbitration Procedures and Contract Administration." *Journal of College and University Law,* Summer 1974, pp. 371–391.

FLEMING, JOHN E.; GILL, GERALD R.; and SWINTON, DAVID H. *The Case for Affirmative Action.* Washington, DC: Howard University Press, 1978.

HAY, ELLEN. "The Variable of Teaching Effectiveness in Tenure and Promotion Decisions." *ACA Bulletin,* vol. 68, 1989, pp. 52–59.

KELLEY, EDWARD P., JR., and RODRIGUEZ, ROBERT L. "Observations on Collective Bargaining: Implications for Academic Management." *Liberal Education,* March 1977, pp. 102–117.

KEYNES, MILTON. "Academic Freedom and Responsibility." *Society for Research into Higher Education.* Philadelphia: Open University Press, 1988.

KLUGER, ELIZABETH. "Sex Discrimination in the Tenure System at American Colleges and Universities: The Judicial Response." *Journal of Law and Education,* 15, 1986, pp. 319–339.

LESLIE, DAVID W. *Impact of Collective Bargaining on Conflict Resolution Practices.* Research Summary, no. 2, Washington, DC: Academic Collective Bargaining Information Service, 1975.

LESLIE, DAVID W. "NLRB Rulings on the Department Chairmanship." *Educational Record,* 53, 1972, pp. 313–320.

———. "The Status of the Department Chairmanship in University Organization." *AAUP Bulletin,* 59, 1973, pp. 419–426.

LOVELL, CHERYL D. *Faculty Grievances: A Longitudinal Study of Conflict Issues in the State University System of Florida.* Ph.D. Dissertation, Florida State University, 1989.

MANNIX, THOMAS M. "Community College Grievance Procedures: A Review of Contract Content in Ninety-Four Colleges." *Journal of the College and University Personnel Association,* April 1974, pp. 23–40.

MOORE, KATHRYN M., and JOHNSON, MICHAEL P. "The Status of Women and Minorities in the Professoriate: The Role of Affirmative Action and Equity." In *New Directions for Institutional Research,* no. 63 (Managing Faculty Resources), 16, 1989, pp. 45–63.

NASH, NANCY S. *Private College Faculty as Managers: An Empirical Test Under "Yeshiva."* ASHE Annual Meeting Paper, San Antonio, 1986. (ERIC Document Reproduction Service No. ED 268 898)

REYES, PEDRO, and SMITH, GREGORY. *Faculty and Academic Staff Participation in Academic Governance: The Social Contract Model.* ASHE 1987 Annual Meeting Paper, San Diego, 1987. (ERIC Document Reproduction Service No. ED 281 446)

REYES, PEDRO, and TWOMBLY, SUSAN B. "Perceptions of Contemporary Governance in Community Colleges: An Empirical Study." *Community College Review,* 14, 1987, pp. 4–12.

RUFF, RAYMOND T., JR. *A Description and Analysis of Faculty Grievances and Faculty Grievance Procedures in New York State Community Colleges.* Ph.D. Dissertation, State University of New York at Buffalo, 1972.

SATRYB, RONALD P. *The Art of Settling Grievances: A Study in Campus Conflict Resolution.* Special Report, no. 27. Washington, DC: Academic Collective Bargaining Information Service, 1976.

SCHRECKER, ELLEN. *No Ivory Tower: McCarthyism and the Universities.* New York: Oxford University Press, 1986.

TIGHT, MALCOLM (Ed.) *Academic Freedom and Responsibility.* Philadelphia: Open University Press, 1988.

ZIRKEL, PERRY A. *Faculty Bargaining and Campus Governance: Rhetoric vs. Research.* 1986. (ERIC Document Reproduction Service No. ED 267 727)

Chapter 27

Legal Implications of Being a Chair

We often cast the department chairperson in the role of mediator, concilia-tor, advocate, and judge, so it should come as no surprise that the role of the chairperson involves legal obligations and risks of legal liability. As an employee of the institution, the chairperson nominally acts as agent for the principal; his or her acts, when committed within the scope of employment, are attributable to the college or university. Although the incidence of individual liability is remote, the acts of the chairperson may result in costly and unnecessary litigation for the institution, consuming time and diverting efforts that could otherwise be di-rected to essential educational objectives.

"Lawyers," Supreme Court Justice Oliver Wendell Holmes is said to have remarked, "spend a great deal of their time shoveling smoke." It might also be suggested that when the smoke clears, little of substance is left to guide conduct and protect against liability. Courts have decided relatively few cases that directly affect the role of the department chairperson, and of the cases resolved, subtle distinctions make unerring generalization difficult.

While it is undoubtedly true that the law has recognized few principles that would serve to guide the administrator, some generalized legal notions relating to the department chairperson's role can be identified. From the limited case law available, one can draw conclusions that may not always apply in a given circumstance but that so closely parallel standards of appropriate administrative practice that they deserve elaboration.

Learning by example may be a desirable method for conveying the mean-ing of legal principles applicable to the department chairperson. The opinions of judges, based as they are upon the facts of a particular controversy, offer a case study approach to the analysis of legal issues and permit the extrapolation of guidelines for the department chairperson. However, these legal generalizations require a few initial qualifications. First, the department chairperson must look to state statute, regulatory standards, institutional policy, and, where appropriate, collective bargaining agreements in order to clarify the legal obligations unique to each state jurisdiction. Second, applicable legal standards vary depending on the institutional type involved, particularly where an institution is exclusively private or pervasively religious in character in contrast to state-supported public institutions and land grant colleges.

Judicial Restraint

Judges are reluctant to intervene in matters outside their area of expertise or susceptible to resolution through expeditious administrative process. Since the responsibilities of the department chairperson relate both to academic decision making and administrative procedure, judicial restraint is particularly appropriate as a basis for limiting judicial review of the chairperson's decisions. As a corollary to this principle, the department chairperson should welcome the development of administrative procedures which permit review of his or her decisions and advise those who are adversely affected by these decisions to initiate the review process in the event they are dissatisfied. Furthermore, it is a wise chairperson who emphasizes the central role of academic policy implementation in his or her actions and who takes care to harmonize decision making with the educational objectives of the department and the institution. The chairperson who always assumes the correctness of his or her decision making forgets that "Assumption is the mother of all foulups."

Rational Relationship and the Rule of Reasonableness

In general, courts indulge a presumption in favor of the chairperson's exercise of authority on behalf of an institution. The presumption assumes that the chair has acted reasonably, in good faith, for motives consistent with the bona fide purposes of the institution. Such a presumption, however, is not irrebuttable and may be subject to judicial review when facts are presented from which a judge may infer the lack of a rational relationship between the actions of the chairperson and the bona fide purposes of the institution.

If the court is initially persuaded that such actions leave some doubt about the reasonableness or the rational relationship between actions and institutional policy, the burden of proof may shift from the person or persons who allege the impropriety to the department chairperson. Under this circumstance the chair's obligation is to go forward with a showing that his or her action was both reasonable and warranted.

Once the burden of proof has shifted to the chairperson, both argument and evidence are required in order to establish substantial proof in support of the propriety of the chair's action. It is extremely helpful for the chairperson to provide an evidentiary record corroborating the "reasonableness" of his or her action. A personal notebook detailing the basis for a particular administrative decision, anecdotal records substantiating observations and evaluations, written memoranda establishing that proper notice has been provided are among the sources of evidentiary material on which the chairperson may need to rely at some later date. Such a record, which may be accessible to both the person bringing the suit and the institution, should reflect the chair's concern for fair dealing and adherence to the academic and professional standards of the institution.

Legal Liability

Legal liability can be established only where a complaint properly alleges and a plaintiff proves the elements of a legal claim. "Plaintiff" is the title given to the individual who brings suit. Plaintiffs, whether students or employees, must demonstrate that a duty was owed to them, that the duty was breached, and that the breach of duty is the principal cause of an injury for which the court should grant relief. Depending on the nature of the injury, the court may grant relief in the form of an award of damages or an order enjoining or compelling some institutional practice.

It is a popular maxim among lawyers that what really matters is the name a litigant succeeds in imposing on the facts—not the facts themselves. It is possible to categorize the differing allegations that might be argued as a basis for the chairperson's and the institution's legal liability. Among the various types of liability that may be associated with the role of the department chairperson, five types are of particular importance because of the frequency with which they appear in litigation. The types of liability most likely to involve the performance of a department chairperson would include allegations of arbitrary and capricious action, breach of contract, denial of constitutional rights, discriminatory practice, and unintentional or intentional breach of a common-law duty which resulted in injury to the individual.

ARBITRARY AND CAPRICIOUS ACTION

Courts have long recognized that behaviors which appear arbitrary or capricious may be actionable by law. Evidence that a student or a faculty member has been treated radically different from others tends to establish arbitrary and capricious action, particularly when the department chairperson fails to follow recognized institutional procedures, when irregularities in the application of standards are discovered, or when there is a lack of uniformity in the administration of standards.

Typically, where a court does discover evidence of arbitrary or capricious action, the court will turn to the institution for a justification of its policy. Courts generally follow a "rule of reasonableness" under such circumstances, inquiring whether the chairperson's action can be shown to have employed some understandable, unified standard. Obviously, the failure to establish and maintain such standards leaves the chairperson open to a charge of impermissible abuse of discretion and breach of a duty of good faith or fair dealing.

This is not to suggest that every deviation from accepted policy constitutes arbitrary or capricious conduct by the chairperson. Exceptions to the uniform application of a standard are widely recognized in law, but it is an unwritten presumption that a justification accompany the exception to policy. The most often encountered situation is one in which exceptions to a policy have been permitted, then the policy is suddenly enforced by the chairperson with adverse and injurious consequences for the person affected.

Clare Booth Luce's observation that "No good deed goes unpunished" seems apt for such a circumstance. The benevolent chairperson who has granted exceptions to a rule or policy suddenly finds that the enforcement of the policy can conceivably be legally enjoined as arbitrary. Courts will insist upon a rationale for the disparity in treatment, and it behooves the chair to clarify every exception to a rule of policy, adopting the exception whenever later cases present the same or conspicuously similar circumstances.

Nowhere is the allegation of arbitrary or capricious treatment more likely to appear than in cases involving students. Usually, the denial of the degree or dismissal for academic deficiencies engenders the litigation. In an illustrative case, a law student whose cumulative grade point fell below required standards for graduation was informed that he could continue for a fourth year, but that regardless of whether he improved his overall average, he would not be given the degree. He refused to accept the conditions, but was permitted to enroll and managed to bring his cumulative average up to the requisite graduation standard in his fourth year. Despite his improvement, he was denied the degree.

While the court recognized that the law school had absolute discretion to deny the request for readmission to a fourth year, it took cognizance of the institution's previous practice of allowing other probationary students to enroll and correct deficiencies during a fourth year. In some cases these students had met requirements and been awarded the law degree. The imposition of a condition that the student could not be granted a degree even if he satisfied degree requirements was deemed by the court as arbitrary and a manifest abuse of discretion.[1]

In another case, a student successfully alleged a cause of action for arbitrary treatment when singled out from other students and compelled to meet special requirements not originally outlined in order to complete a degree.[2] Similarly, a student dropped from medical school for failing to pass a second-year final examination successfully challenged the dismissal by establishing that the examination had been incorrectly administered and that other affected students had been granted the opportunity for reexaminations.[3]

---

1. Paulsen v. Golden State University, 156 Cal. Rptr. 190 (Cal. Ct. App. 1979).
2. Shuffer v. Trustees of California State Univ., 136 Cal. Rptr. 527 (Cal. Ct. App. 1977).
3. Maitland v. Wayne State Univ., 256 N.W. 2d 195 (Mich. Ct. App. 1977).

Allegations of arbitrary and capricious treatment have seldom been sustained where the department has applied clear, unambiguous academic policies relative to retention and graduation. In a case that proves the rule, a student sought to invest the department's minimum grade point policies with an alternative meaning which the court described as "frivolous" and inconsistent with the institution's uniform application of academic policy.[4] In another, the student was unable to establish that a faculty adviser's interpretation of the procedure for awarding grade changes should prevail over the express written policy of the school. In the latter instance, the court was particularly impressed by the extent to which the institution had accorded the student procedural due process in the administrative appeal of the dismissal decision.[5]

BREACH OF CONTRACT

A contract is an agreement between parties involving mutual understandings relative to specific considerations and obligations. The law in every jurisdiction prefers to enforce the express, written agreements of the parties, but oral understandings and actions of the parties during the performance of the contract have frequently influenced the court's interpretation of a contractual obligation. The departmental chairperson is seldom considered to be a principal party to a contract involving faculty, staff, or students and does not normally act as an agent for the institution in the negotiation of a contract agreement. However, the chair is often responsible for the administration of a contract and must faithfully execute the obligations the institution has agreed to assume. The acts of the chairperson may also influence the determination of whether a contract can be implied between the institution and another party.

When it comes to the obligations of a contract, brevity and ambiguity are often concomitants. Since ambiguity is often the source of contract disputes, it is not surprising to see considerable detail in express agreements, whether they be college catalogues, graduate bulletins, or collectively negotiated agreements. For the department chairperson, the administration of any contract often involves rigorous attention to detail as well as a fine eye for resolving ambiguities in a fashion consistent with institutional policy and the intent of the parties.

CONTRACTS WITH STUDENTS. Courts consider college bulletins, program guides, and brochures as contracts that create mutual obligations between institution and student. Fundamental fairness to the parties involved in a lawsuit requires that the court consider the extent to which a contractual relationship did exist between parties and the potential harm when one party has breached a duty under terms of the contract. As a consequence, the oral representations of faculty advisers, deans, and chairpersons have been relied upon as a basis for initiating a suit for breach of contract. However, courts do not appear to apply

4. Watson v. Univ. of South Alabama College of Medicine, 463 F. Supp. 720 (S. D. Ala. 1979).
5. Hines v. Rinker, 667 F.2d 699 (8th Cir. 1981).

contract standards rigorously, choosing to resolve many ambiguities in favor of the institution and often abstaining from resolving substantive matters of academic policy.

Two contractual situations that are particularly relevant to the relationship between student and department chairperson have received significant consideration by courts. Where department or college programs constitute a contractual inducement to enroll and students can be said to have reasonably relied upon these contractual terms in undertaking a field of study, students may sue to enforce specific compliance with the proposed program or seek an award of monetary damages for their reliance on the contract. In a second situation, oral and written representations related to degree and program requirements, often the result of inaccurate or improper advisement, have been the basis for suits in which students seek award of the degree or program modifications consistent with the alleged contractual obligation.

An illustration of the first instance involved students enrolled in the school of architecture at Ohio University. The school had lost accreditation, but its faculty and college administrators repeatedly assured students they would obtain an accredited degree. Provisional accreditation was secured when institutional representatives gave assurances to accrediting officials that the institution would work toward meeting all requirements for accreditation. Subsequently, this provisional accreditation was withdrawn when the university elected to phase out the architecture program in response to institution-wide financial problems. The students enrolled in the architecture program sued, alleging that an implied contract based on the oral representations of university faculty and administrators was breached when the university failed to maintain accredited status.

The reviewing court recognized a contractual obligation because the faculty and staff of the school continually conveyed the promise that the institution would work toward full accreditation. Since students acted upon this promise and continued to enroll, pay fees and tuition, and attend classes, the court concluded that the students had acted reasonably in reliance upon these promises and that the institution breached the implied contract when it withdrew funding and support for the program. In recognizing that college governing boards have the authority to discontinue programs, the court qualified this authority by emphasizing that contractual commitments that have been undertaken must be honored or, alternatively, damages for breach of contract awarded unless the institution can show financially exigent conditions so overwhelming as to permit a defense of impossibility of performance.[6]

A student's reliance on the oral representations of faculty advisers or written academic policies has often been the basis for contract suits. Often, the court will regard oral representations as too speculative to constitute an enforceable contract as in the case in which the student sought to enforce an advisor's

---

6. Behrend v. State, 379 N.E. 2d 617 (Ohio Ct. App. 1977).

statement that she would graduate "soon."[7] In cases involving a contract based on a college bulletin, judges will sometimes defer to a written disclaimer which stipulates that information is subject to change.[8]

In another case, a student sought award of a master's degree when he relied upon a professor's erroneous advice relative to the scoring of a final comprehensive examination. When the college applied a higher standard than the professor had indicated, the student was denied the degree and sued to force the institution to make the award of the master's. Although the student asserted that he would have passed the examination using the criteria articulated by the professor, the court showed a characteristic judicial reluctance to intervene in academic policy and refused to require the award of the degree. An important consideration in the court's judgment for the institution was the department chair's willingness to grant the student an opportunity to retake the examination.[9]

Any contract between a student and the institution implicitly requires the student to demonstrate academic competence and the institution to act fairly and in good faith. Even though courts are extremely reluctant to compel the award of a degree, it is important for the institution to meet its obligations and avoid irreparable injury to the student. Statements guaranteeing special service such as remedial or tutorial programs for the disadvantaged or specifying academic procedures which the student must follow are frequently recognized as actionable contract claims by courts.[10] Although the judicial branch is reluctant to interfere by requiring award of an academic degree, the courts will not defer to the professional educator when it comes to the contractual obligation to provide student services expressed or implied by the institution or its representatives.

CONTRACTS WITH FACULTY AND STAFF.   In employment contracts, whether collectively or individually negotiated specified obligations are generally interpreted with greater emphasis on strict construction by courts. The department chair would be well advised to avoid commitments to faculty and staff that are beyond the chair's authority and to seek consultation with other administrators before resolving ambiguities in employment contracts. As chairpersons, doing nothing may seldom be appropriate, but saying nothing, particularly when it relates to interpreting the institution's obligation under a contract, is often the wisest course until clarification can be obtained.

A department chairperson who failed to take appropriate action under tenure denial of a contract was held to have violated the contractual obligation of a private college in Tennessee. The contract of employment specified that once a faculty member was given a contract to teach for the fourth consecutive year the institution must give notice within ten days after the beginning of the second semester of the fourth year if a decision has been made not to grant tenure. The

---

7. Cuddihy v. Wayne State, 413 N.W. 2d 692 (Mich. Ct. App. 1988).

8. Easley v. University of Michigan, 627 F. Supp. 580 (E.D. Mich. 1986).

9. Olsson v. Bd. of Higher Education, 426 N.Y.S. 2d 248 (N.Y. 1980).

10. *See* Craft v. Board of Trustees of the Univ. of Illinois, 516 F. Supp. 1317 (E.D. Ill. 1981).

court noted that the institution had an affirmative duty under the contract provision to provide timely notice if the faculty member was not to be continued. Since the department chair did not provide notice of tenure denial until three months after the start of the second semester, contractual notice had not been provided and the faculty member could be considered to have acquired tenure.[11]

Alternatively, a department chairperson's letters and off-hand statements can often be incorporated as part of a contract provision. In a case from New Hampshire, a professor was considered to have violated his contract when he failed to give adequate notice of his sabbatical leave plans. When the professor signed his employment contract, a letter attached to the agreement stipulated that he would be expected to take a year's sabbatical at half-pay rather than a one-semester sabbatical at full pay unless he notified his administrative representative prior to a date set in the letter. Several times after the date for notification passed, the professor was requested to inform the college of his sabbatical plans. Finally, the professor was advised by letter that he would be on a one-year sabbatical at half-pay and that if he objected, he should notify the college president.

The basic issue in this case was whether the professor failed to perform a condition of his employment contract when he postponed notice to the department of his plans for sabbatical leave until after the deadline stipulated in the chairperson's letter. The court held that the letter attached to the contract was binding and incorporated material elements of the contract of employment. Further, the request for notice of sabbatical plans within a specified time was a reasonable request of the department. The professor's failure to give timely notice, particularly after repeated requests to do so, constituted a breach of the terms of the sabbatical leave provisions, and the college could compel the full-year leave at half-pay.[12]

Despite the protection of employment rights guaranteed by a contractual obligation, an institution may act to dismiss an employee prior to the end of a contract term if good cause to do so can be established. In public institutions, good cause most often includes dismissal for insubordination, incompetence, or immorality. Other grounds are sometimes inferred, including neglect of duty, persistent misconduct, and conditions that compel layoffs such as financial exigency or declining enrollment.

In most cases, the role of the department chairperson in instances of faculty dismissal, reprimand, or layoff will be that of investigator and information gatherer. In such a role, the chair will find it hard to avoid the position advocated by the man who sought reelection to a judgeship on the basis that he had always endeavored to "seek a balance between impartiality on the one hand and partiality on the other."

The formal administrative processes established for dismissal or layoff of employees will normally specify the standards to be applied in these adverse employment decisions. The chairperson should endeavor to conduct a confiden-

---

11. Sawyer v. Mercer, 594 S.W. 2d 696 (Tenn. 1980).
12. Daum v. New England College, 422 A.2d 1035 (N.H. 1980).

tial inquiry, providing reasonable disclosure to the employee under scrutiny and emphasizing that the inquiry is limited to an investigation of conduct that may be reasonably expected to have an adverse effect on the employee's performance on the job or on relations with students and colleagues. Immoral behavior should be shown to have some nexus with job-related activity, such as a negative impact on classroom performance or students. Insubordination should relate to a repeated refusal to obey reasonable institutional rules or administrative directives and should be tied to the chairperson's previous notification and warning to the employee that the behavior must be corrected. Incompetence, always a most difficult ground to establish, usually involves a burden of proof in which periodic evaluations, anecdotal records, and complaints by students and colleagues create a cumulative record of job-related deficiencies that the employee is unable or unwilling to remediate.

DENIAL OF CONSTITUTIONAL RIGHTS

Public colleges and universities are obligated to respect the federal constitutional rights of students and employees. In recent years, the doctrine of state action has extended this obligation to ostensibly private institutions who receive substantial federal or state funds for programs. (A program at a private institution may receive so much federal or state financial support as to be "infected" with a public purpose and liable for the denial of constitutional rights.) The protections of federal constitutional law most often involve the guarantees of due process under the fourteenth amendment and the right to free speech and association secured by the first amendment.

DUE PROCESS, PROPERTY RIGHTS, AND LIBERTY INTERESTS. Under the fourteenth amendment, an individual's interest in property or liberty may be protected from arbitrary governmental action. In the public higher education setting, property interests would include the student's entitlement to continued enrollment and participation in the academic program after the payment of fees or notice of admission. An employee's property rights would be defined by his or her contractual status at the institution during the period of a contract or indefinitely for those who hold tenure status. Liberty is related to the individual's interest in protecting his or her reputation, particularly from any stigmatizing information that might foreclose other employment or educational opportunities. Typically, the student or employee must establish that a protected property or liberty interest has been denied in order to compel procedural or substantive constitutional protection.

Particularly as applied to public institutions of higher education, the denial of a liberty or property interest may require that the institution provide basic elements of due process. These elements may vary with the nature of the interest that is threatened, but fundamental due process will include a showing that procedural and substantive guarantees of due process have been extended. Procedural due process often includes notice of changes and timely opportunity for a hearing. Substantive due process relates to more subjective elements of fundamental fairness and reasonableness, usually tied to uniformity and lack of bias in the application of due process protections.

DUE PROCESS RIGHTS OF STUDENTS.   Although courts have regularly expressed reluctance to intervene on behalf of students in the academic decision-making process, adherence to procedural safeguards of due process has been a basis for judicial scrutiny of administrative action. As guardians of process, courts first consider the nature of the property right or liberty interest, then assess the requisite amount of procedural due process required. While disciplinary standards of due process have long been codified as part of the public institution's honor code or student judicial review board, academic standards involving students remain largely within the province of the faculty and department chairperson in the academic department.

Disciplinary due process involves issues related to misconduct rather than to identified deficiencies in academic performance. Courts have insisted on fundamental elements of due process in cases involving disciplinary due process, and usually insist that student disciplinary codes be followed when allegations of cheating, plagiarism, or falsification of information are involved. However, courts do not compel rigid standards of due process like those involved in criminal prosecutions, relying instead primarily on adequate notice of charges and an opportunity for a fair and impartial hearing of essential elements. In an actual case, the court upheld the decision of an institution to revoke the doctoral degree of a former graduate student who was charged with fabricating data used in the dissertation. The court concluded that the department chair had acted appropriately in granting the former student notice of charges, an opportunity to review the evidence on which the charges were based, and the right to appear and respond to the charges. The fact that the graduate insisted on additional due process protections, and refused to attend the hearing when these were not granted, did not convince the reviewing court that the institution could be barred from rescinding the degree.

Courts have applied even fewer restrictions on the discretion of academic decision makers relative to due process in academic affairs. The principal case on the amount of due process required in such circumstances is *Board of Curators of the University of Missouri v. Horowitz,*[13] a case in which the United States Supreme Court ruled that no hearing need be afforded to a medical student who was fully informed of academic deficiencies in her clinical performance and given adequate opportunity to correct those deficiencies prior to dismissal. For purposes of this case, the Court assumed that the student could demonstrate the existence of a protected liberty or property interest but held that the school had met its obligation by informing the student of her unsatisfactory performance, warning of the consequences of a failure to improve, and giving her sufficient time to improve.

Academic decisions are recognized by courts as generally more subjective

---

13. 98 S. Ct. 948 (1978).

and evaluative, requiring subject matter expertise and an assessment of cumulative information not easily reviewable by judges. In contrast to disciplinary actions, which are adversarial, associated with the resolution of factual questions and determination of standards of proof, academic judgments are typically nonadversarial, subjective judgments involving specialized knowledge. What seems required under such circumstances is adequate notice of deficient performance, specifying the inadequacies that must be remedied and giving reasonable opportunity to correct deficiencies. Such a notice could be challenged where reasons given were arbitrary and capricious, but otherwise no right to an adversarial hearing is automatically conveyed by constitutional standards of academic due process.

In *Horowitz,* the stigma of dismissal was the principal basis for the medical student's contention that she had been denied a liberty interest without due process of law. While the Court recognized that a stigma foreclosing any opportunity to transfer and matriculate at another medical school might result, it refused to grant the student a hearing. However, if the decision to dismiss for academic deficiencies is a subterfuge for a dismissal decision unrelated to academic performance, the student may be able to compel a due process hearing to clear his or her good name. A student engaged in a required course for teacher certification was administratively dropped when he refused to withdraw after being advised of his academic deficiencies. In a note outlining the student's academic deficiencies, the supervising faculty member expressed the opinion that the student was in need of psychological help. The note was not disclosed to anyone besides the student and the associate dean, who advised the student of his academic deficiencies and instituted the administrative drop. Was the note a stigma which necessitated a due process hearing?

A federal district court reasoned that the administrative and supervisory record of the student's academic deficiencies was sufficient to justify removing the student from the course and, ultimately, denying teacher certification. Among the deficiencies noted were charges of failure to develop and follow lesson plans, failure to detect and correct grammatical errors, inability to accept criticism, and difficulty in focusing on day-to-day matters relative to student learning styles and teaching details. No evidence tended to show that the dean's decision was predicated on that part of the note which referred to the student's alleged psychological problems. Furthermore, there was no publication or dissemination of the note's contents beyond the student, supervising teacher, and the dean. The district court concluded that no stigma was created, and found that the decision to drop the student was substantiated by identified academic deficiencies of which the student had periodic notice during the course; thus no hearing was required.[14]

The observance of procedural safeguards could be influenced by the nature of the property interest claimed. While the contract between student and institution will usually meet the requirement for some legitimate claim of entitle-

---

14. Aubuchon v. Olsen, 467 F. Supp. 568 (E.D. Mo. 1979).

ment to due process, this property right would appear to grant nothing more than periodic notice of academic progress. However, the denial of some property rights extended to students would require even more due process, including a right to a hearing. At least one court has extended a right to a limited hearing, creating an exception to the *Horowitz* standard. Recognizing a graduate student's property right to remain in good standing in order to receive an assistantship, and taking cognizance of the university's policy requiring consideration of the student's motivation and attitude toward academic work in any dismissal decision, a United States district court granted a student an opportunity to explain the reason for his poor scholarship in order that the university could take into account circumstances that might have influenced the student's motivation and attitude. The court's view of the hearing required was limited to granting the student an opportunity to explain mitigating factors relative to his performance; it would not appear to extend to a right to an adversary proceeding at which he could contest evaluations.[15] Interestingly, this case conflicts with another federal court decision in which a student who lost a scholarship due to academic deficiencies was properly denied a right to a hearing.[16]

The situation in which minimum grade point average is the sole determining factor in academic decisions would not admit to any right to a hearing, unless institutional policy extended due process protection going beyond that provided by the fourteenth amendment. In one such instance, a student dismissed from a private institution was granted due process rights to notice and a hearing on the dismissal because the institution's policy required these elements of due process.[17] Although fourteenth amendment standards do not normally apply to private colleges, how much due process is granted to the student will depend not only on constitutional guarantees but also on those property entitlements a student is granted by contract with the institution and by reference to institutional rules.

A former student's right to due process, including written notice and the specification of reasons, was recognized by a state court when the student sought readmission to a program in medicine after more than a year's leave of absence. The student had completed two years of the program with a B-plus average but was forced to reapply after his one-year medical leave of absence had lapsed by two months. He reapplied, submitting statements of fitness from physicians and psychiatrists, but was denied admission without explanation. The court ruled that the student was entitled to complete his education unless the institution could show specific circumstances preventing his continuation. Two years of matriculation in good standing created a property right to due process which was not forfeited by a one-year and two-month hiatus from matriculation.[18]

Although courts consider the nature of the property right protected by due

---

15. Ross v. Pennsylvania State University, 445 F. Supp. 147 (M.D. Pa. 1978).

16. Hankins v. Temple University, 829 F.2d 437 (34d Cir. 1987).

17. Tedeschi v. Wagner College, 427 N.Y.S. 2d 760 (N.Y. 1980).

18. Evans v. West Virginia Bd. of Regents, 271 S.E. 2d 778 (W. Va. 1980).

process, they do not challenge the institution's right to apply reasonable academic standards nor do they require successful completion of preconditions for receipt of a degree. A graduate student pursuing his doctorate repeatedly failed his written examinations, but was granted review after alleging personal bias on the part of a faculty member. After a long and elaborate review and evaluation, including readers selected from outside the university, the graduate school determined that the student passed the written examinations and directed the department to administer the student's orals. Two years had elapsed in the appeal process, and the student sought to waive the orals and receive the degree. The court rejected any entitlement to a degree and refused to intervene in the circumstances. The court's holding emphasized that the student's refusal to sit for the orals constituted a deficiency in establishing a property right worthy of due process.[19]

DUE PROCESS RIGHTS OF FACULTY AND STAFF. Under the fourteenth amendment, an employee's interest in public employment may be constitutionally protected. Procedural fairness must be observed whenever the public university threatens an employee's property rights or liberty interest.

To compel due process protections, a faculty or staff member might show that a certain property interest is sufficient to justify court intervention. Typically, whether a legitimate claim of entitlement to continued employment exists will be defined in reference to employee contracts, negotiated agreements, institutional regulations, and state laws. Faculty in public institutions who are dismissed or otherwise denied property rights during the contractual term of employment are entitled to due process of law. This view is consistent with the decision in *Perry v. Sindermann,*[20] in which the Supreme Court ruled that a teacher who had held his faculty position for four years in reliance upon a de facto tenure arrangement could establish a legitimate claim of entitlement worthy of due process protection. The Court cautioned, though, that "If it is the law (of the state) that a teacher . . . has no contractual or other claim to job tenure, the . . . claim would be defeated."[21]

The faculty member involved in the *Perry* case was able to establish de facto tenure by coupling the institution's lack of a formal tenure system with oral and written representations by various deans and department chairpersons that satisfactory performance would be rewarded with continuing employment. The faculty member submitted the statements of his administrative superiors as proof that a contract existed which granted him a long-term property right tantamount to tenure. Numerous appellate decisions have distinguished the *Perry* case by emphasizing that an established system with published standards and procedures for granting tenure would not allow for a de facto grant of tenure.

---

19. Goldberg v. Bd. of Regents of the Univ. of Colorado, 603 P.2d 974 (Colo. Ct. App. 1979).
20. 408 U.S. 593 (1972).
21. *Id.* at 599.

Assurances of tenure given a faculty member by a department head would not appear to create a sufficient expectation of continued employment to guarantee due process protection provided the assurances are clearly contradicted by published tenure policies. A promise by a department chair that a new professor would receive tenure "as a matter of course" or assurances by tenured colleagues that a professor is progressing satisfactorily and would eventually receive tenure would not create an implied right to tenure when the nontenured faculty member is given notice of a formal tenure process.[22] Since formal tenure standards preclude reliance on the assurances that a new employee may receive, it is wise for the department chairman to lobby for the adoption of such a formal, written policy to put new faculty on notice of the existence of such a policy and to avoid statements that might reasonably be construed to create a genuine expectation of continued employment. With regard to the creation of a property right to continuing contract, the chair might well rely on the evidentiary proposition that "If you don't say it, he or she (the faculty member) can't repeat it."

A liberty interest may be infringed when the results of administrative action impose a stigma or other disability on the employee that forecloses the individual's freedom to take advantage of other employment opportunities or otherwise injures good name, reputation, or standing in the community. In *Board of Regents v. Roth,*[23] the conditions that would impose such a stigma were expressed as "a charge that (the employee) had been guilty of dishonesty or immorality."[24] Roth, hired to teach for one year at the university, was informed without explanation that he would not be rehired. He alleged that the true reason for nonretention was his criticism of the university and insisted that a due process hearing was required in which the university must justify its nonrenewal decision. The United States Supreme Court held that Roth failed to establish a violation of first amendment free-speech rights, and no fourteenth amendment liberty interest was denied because the university had made no charges against Roth that would bar him from employment at another institution.

There is no legal obligation on the part of the department chairperson to give reasons for nonrenewal of contract unless there is a stipulation in state law, institutional regulations, or negotiated contract requiring that reasons be given. Although it is a general rule that timely notice be given if the employment contract is not to be renewed, the employee does not have a federal constitutional right to reasons for nonrenewal. However, the department chairperson would be well advised periodically to evaluate and confidentially to inform the faculty or staff member of his or her performance in order to avoid any possible allegation of arbitrary treatment. Giving reasons for a nonrenewal decision is permissible and appropriate provided the reasons are communicated to the employee in confidence and have to do with job-related concerns, such as

---

22. Davis v. Oregon State Univ., 591 F.2d 493 (9th Cir. 1978) and Haimowitz v. Univ. of Nevada, 579 F.2d 526 (9th Cir. 1978).

23. 408 U.S. 564 (1972).

24. *Id.* at 573.

inability to cooperate with colleagues, poor evaluations of teaching, declining enrollments, and budget constraints.

In *Roth* no reasons were given for the professor's nonrenewal, but in *Beitzell v. Jeffrey*[25] a faculty member who was denied tenure was made aware of several factors which influenced the denial of tenure. The faculty member's chairperson had submitted a memorandum to a grievance committee which described the professor's professional behavior as "irresponsible" and indicated that other faculty had expressed concern about the faculty member's drinking. The departmental committee had voted against a recommendation for tenure after a discussion that included references to the professor's lack of adequacy as a teacher and adviser and to his drinking. In all communications relative to the decision not to grant tenure, the department chairperson maintained a high level of confidentiality, disclosing the basis for the committee's decision to the professor, and forwarding his memorandum to the grievance committee only when the professor's attorney insisted that the memo become a public record in the grievance proceedings. The appellate court observed that the professor failed to show that the personal aspects of these discussions, including references to drinking habits, became public as a result of the actions of the department chairperson. Since the chairperson did not make the charges public, the university could not be said to have stigmatized the former employee in such a way as to interfere with his ability to take advantage of other employment opportunities.

The requirement that a stigma seriously damage the faculty member's ability to take advantage of other employment opportunities, coupled with the requirement of public disclosure of the reasons for the employment decision, has limited the number of cases in which faculty have successfully claimed a right to due process based on a denial of a liberty interest. A charge of inadequate teaching performance would appear to be insufficient to establish a stigma denying a liberty interest; rather, a showing that the institution made public charges that the employee had been guilty of dishonesty or immorality would seem required.[26]

The extent of process which is due a faculty or staff member depends on a balancing of the public institution's interest in efficient operation of the system against the weight of the property of liberty interest of the individual. The seriousness and permanence of an adverse employment decision will influence the requirements for notice and/or hearing and the extent to which administrative appeal and review are necessary. Where the faculty member has established a property or liberty interest worthy of due process, minimal elements afforded to the employee would include the following:

1. The employee must be advised of the cause or causes for the adverse employment decision in sufficient detail to fairly enable the employee to show any error that may exist.

25. 643 F.2d 870 (1st Cir. 1981).
26. Swain v. Bd. of Trustees, 466 F. Supp. 120 (N.D. Ohio 1979).

2. At a reasonable time after notice of cause, the employee must be accorded a meaningful opportunity to be heard in his or her own defense.
3. A hearing should be granted before a tribunal that both possesses academic expertise and has an apparent impartiality toward the charges.

Generally, the institution's formal grievance procedures established for administrative review of employment decisions accord the minimal elements of due process. The department chairperson is often charged with the responsibility of providing notice to the employee, informing the employee of the charges, procedures, and consequences of any action which might be taken and outlining the route of appeal. Failure to provide timely notice to the employee has resulted in a court-ordered continuation of employment, specifically when the college or university has promulgated rules on notice of nonrenewal and the chairperson, as agent of the institution, fails to notify within the period established for notice of nonretention.[27] Similarly, a department chairperson's failure to discuss his renewal recommendations with a nontenured faculty member, when college procedural rules specifically required such notice to the individual faculty member under consideration for renewal, has resulted in continuation of employment for the affected employee.[28] Both these results indicate the importance of adhering to procedural safeguards in employment situations, whether those procedures are developed by the institution, required by negotiated agreement, or extrapolated from state or federal law.

DENIAL OF FREE SPEECH AND ASSOCIATION

In the public sector, the first amendment provides some protection to individuals in the exercise of speech and association. In colleges and universities, these protections are often linked to notions of "academic freedom," but it is probably more accurate to characterize these rights as constitutional protections. Largely because United States courts have been reluctant to recognize an entitlement beyond the grant of free speech and association available to every citizen, few courts have recognized a right to "academic freedom" which transcends the protections already granted by the first amendment.

Public colleges and universities have a special obligation to avoid actions which punish or retaliate for the exercise of free speech and association rights. Particularly when the exercise of these rights by a student or employee involves a matter of public concern related to religious, political or philosophic speech, federal courts have been quick to enjoin actions which would subject the individual to reprimand or other discipline. However, courts have placed some limits on the speech and associational rights of individuals, limiting the range of speech which enjoys constitutional protection and granting institutions the authority to place reasonable restrictions on exercise of these rights.

---

27. Jacobs v. College of William and Mary, 495 F. Supp. 183 (E.D. Va. 1980).
28. Nzomo v. Vermont State Colleges, 385 A. 2d 1099 (Vt. 1978).

FREE SPEECH AND ASSOCIATION FOR STUDENTS.   Students enjoy a constitutionally protected right to the reasonable exercise of free speech and association in the public higher education setting. The leading case on the subject is *Healy v. James,*[29] a decision in which the United States Supreme Court recognized that students may organize and demand recognition as a valid student group unless the institution's agents can show a compelling state interest that would overcome the constitutional right to freedom of association. The case arose when a local student group was denied recognition by a state college president because of the group's avowed political activism. While the president sought to deny recognition on the basis that similar student groups had interrupted classes and fermented disruption on other campuses, the court took notice that the students had promised to abide by reasonable campus restrictions on advocacy and action and disassociated themselves from the national organization (Students for a Democratic Society). Adopting the view that the students' right to speech and association was of paramount constitutional importance, the Court required that the student group be recognized in the absence of strong evidentiary proof that the students acting in concert could reasonably be predicted to substantially disrupt or materially interfere with the operation of the institution.

The department chairperson is more likely to be a student's advocate than a detractor when it comes to the rights of free speech and association. Universities and colleges have long been recognized by courts as institutions in which the free exchange of ideas is vital, and any actions that "chill" the right to expression are given close scrutiny by courts. It should be noted that a faculty committee had recommended college recognition for the student group in *Healy,* a recommendation that influenced the Court's decision to reverse the president's action denying recognition. The chairperson's principal obligation in such circumstances would be to insure that academic or disciplinary action taken by the department against a student or students is free of any hint that the institution sought to penalize the individual for the exercise of free speech or associational rights.

FREE SPEECH AND ASSOCIATION FOR FACULTY AND STAFF.   To protect the right of the employee to constitutionally guaranteed first amendment freedoms, courts have elaborated a series of tests which balance the rights of the individual against the state's interest as employer. Typically, a faculty member would be required to show that his or her conduct was constitutionally protected, and that it was the exercise of this constitutionally protected right that was the primary or motivating factor in the department chairperson's decision to deny some employment benefit or invoke some penalty. In the specific case of a faculty member, even when a faculty member could have been discharged for no reason whatever, with no constitutional right to a hearing on the administrative decision, he or she may establish a claim for reinstatement if the decision not to rehire was made on the basis of that faculty member's exercise of first amendment freedoms.

---

29. 408 U.S. 169 (1972).

The application of free-speech constitutional protections is illustrated in a case involving a nontenured teacher whose contract was not renewed following her sixth year of teaching in a junior college. The official reason for nonrenewal, "declining enrollment and poor evaluation of her work," was appropriate enough, but the faculty member introduced evidence that the real reason for nonrenewal was retaliation for her vigorous support of her husband's candidacy for the college board of regents and her efforts to promote a faculty association. The court noted that the department chairperson admitted advising the teacher to have her husband withdraw from the election, voiced objection to her activity on behalf of the teachers' association, and recommended nonrenewal to discipline the teacher for trying to create ill will and lack of cooperation with the administration. This evidence supported a jury verdict awarding damages after a finding that the teacher had not been rehired because of her exercise of constitutionally protected rights.[30]

In similar cases involving allegations that a faculty member was discharged for a constitutionally impermissible reason, courts have insisted that the plaintiff first establish that the conduct is constitutionally protected. A questionnaire soliciting the views of faculty on a broad range of subjects, some of which were related to evaluating administrative efficiency and effectiveness, has been held to be protected under the first amendment. When the university refused to review a nontenured teacher's contract solely because he helped construct and circulate the questionnaire, the court held that this refusal denied free speech and ordered reinstatement.[31] An avowed Marxist, openly critical of textbooks and politically active on behalf of the Progressive Labor Party, was reinstated by a federal court when it was determined that the administration's ostensible reason for nonrenewal, alleged student complaints, had never been discussed with the professor nor verified by the department chair. After finding that the teacher had never used his classroom to proselytize nor deviated from required curriculum, the court concluded that the teacher's nonrenewal was attributable to his exercise of free speech and held that the administration had acted in a constitutionally impermissible fashion.[32] In another case, an untenured faculty member's circulation of memoranda critical of university practices, characterized by a department chair as evidence of frustration and hostility, was sufficient to raise an inference that the teacher may have been denied renewal for his criticism of his employer. If the faculty member's criticism was the primary or motivating factor in the nonrenewal, then a claim of a denial of free speech would be substantiated.[33]

The department chairperson can withstand a charge of denying free speech and association if it can be shown that the employee could have been disciplined notwithstanding the exercise of constitutionally protected rights. It is

30. Goss v. San Jacinto Junior College, 588 F.2d 96 (5th Cir. 1979).
31. Lindsey v. Board of Regents, 607 F.2d 672 (5th Cir. 1979).
32. Cooper v. Ross, 472 F. Supp. 802 (E.D. 1979).
33. Eichman v. Indiana State Univ. 597 F.2d 1104 (7th Cir. 1979).

permissible for a teacher to be denied salary increases when the actual basis for denial is unsatisfactory scholarship rather than public criticism of university projects.[34] Similarly, it would be considered reasonable for a chairperson to deny summer teaching and offer a relatively small salary increase to a professor in order that the lowest paid faculty members might be provided additional compensation as an inducement to keep highly competent but underpaid young faculty, despite allegations that the denial of salary increases and summer teaching was in retaliation for the professor's opposition to departmental policy.[35] In one instance, a faculty member who was not renewed after protesting a reassignment challenged the department chair's recommendation not to renew on the basis that his criticism of the chair's directives and the faculty member's reassignment was protected free speech. However, the record supported the testimony of the department chairperson that the decision not to renew had been reached some months before the teacher's protests and criticisms of the chairperson. The reviewing court concluded that the decision not to renew could not have been predicated on the faculty member's exercise of free speech, and upheld the nonrenewal.[36]

Evidence of a potential denial of a free speech or associational right may often be manifest in communications from the department chairperson. Following is an example. The chair's memorandum to the state college faculty member began by chastising the professor for failure to complete and submit required reports on scholarly publication and service activity, but continued: "Your contentious attitude toward university policies reflected in public protests of institutional investment in countries that do not observe principles of human rights, and your attacks on the administration, particularly your circulation of a flier urging faculty to censure the dean for alleged misappropriation of funds, will be the focus of this year's annual evaluation unless I see evidence of a cooperative attitude and heightened professionalism for the remainder of the year." The memorandum opens the door to a charge that the chair sought to limit the faculty member's right to free speech by threatening punishment for its exercise. A court might regard the memorandum as establishing a "chilling effect" on the exercise of free speech, characterizing the communication as one intended to threaten an unsatisfactory evaluation if any further speech should occur. Vague demands for "cooperation" and "professionalism" may only heighten judicial sensitivity to the possibility that the chair intends to punish the faculty member for any exercise of free speech.

Given extraordinary circumstances, even the constitutional exercise of free speech will be balanced against the interests of protecting the campus from substantially disruptive or materially interfering conduct. While the difference between advocacy, which enjoys constitutional protection, and action, which may not be so protected, is difficult to assess, there are times when courts recognize

---

34. Berry v. Battey, 666 F.2nd 1183 (8th Cir. 1981)
35. *See* Stone v. Board of Regents, 620 F.2d 526 (5th Cir. 1980).
36. Hillis v. Stephan F. Austin State Univ., 665 F.2d 547 (5th Cir. 1982).

the authority of the chairperson and the institution to act despite the potentially "chilling" effect on the exercise of free speech. Another case involved a tenured assistant professor, dismissed for playing a prominent role in unauthorized protest activities. The professor contended that his dismissal was in retaliation for his exercise of free speech and assembly rights granted by the constitution. The facts were that the professor tried to stop a motorcade bringing officials to a campus ceremony, led student demonstrators in raucous catcalls to disrupt the ceremonies, and encouraged demonstrators to leave their seats and enter the stadium field, thus creating a danger of violent confrontation. The court upheld a finding that the professor's actions went beyond advocacy of ideas and that he engaged in a course of conduct which interfered and disrupted the regular operation of the school in a manner which left him outside the protection of the first amendment.[37]

DISCRIMINATION

Congress has enacted several federal statutes designed to extend and elaborate the prohibitions against invidious discrimination contained in the equal-protection clause of the fourteenth amendment. This plethora of federal statutory entitlements prohibits discrimination on the basis of race, sex, religion, age, national origin, and handicap in programs receiving federal financial assistance.[38] The laws protect employees and "participants in, or beneficiaries of" programs that receive federal financial assistance. Methods available for enforcement of these laws include federal agency reporting and regulatory standards, compliance reviews, affirmative action agreements, institutional self-regulation, and suits by private parties.

It may be small comfort to the department chairperson, but the legal standards applied to a proof of discriminatory practice remain consistent across most of these statutes. In the principal cases, the burden is on the party alleging discrimination to establish the existence of an intent to discriminate prohibited by law. The crucial issue for resolution of most allegations of discrimination remains a showing that the defendant was motivated by a discriminatory animus.

Generally, this discriminatory animus must be shown to have been overt. Evidence of an expressed intent to exclude a handicapped student or give preferential treatment to a male employee in relation to a female of equivalent skills and ability would be compelling for a court. While statistical proof of disparities between men and women and between blacks and whites relative to salaries, hiring practices, or admissions would contribute to a case for discrimination, the department chair can be most effective in negating a charge of discriminatory practice by scrupulously avoiding any overt action that might be characterized as

---

37. Adamian v. Lombardi, 608 F.2d 1224 (9th Cir. 1979).

38. See, for example, 42 U.S.C. § 2000e (Title VII), 29 U.S.C. § 794 (Rehabilitation Act of 1973), 29 U.S.C. § 623 (Age Discrimination in Employment), 29 U.S.C. § 206(d) (Equal Pay Act).

exhibiting a discriminatory intent and by showing a willingness to investigate and intervene in situations where discrimination within the department is alleged.

This is not to suggest that federal law prohibits any form of discrimination. Courts recognize that it is the nature of the academic process to evaluate and discriminate on the basis of factors that relate reasonably to an institution's valid educational mission. It is for the department chair, in concert with colleagues and institutional representatives, to justify the standards that will be applied to that process of discrimination. Particularly where the discriminatory processes of the institution appear to have a substantial deleterious effect on members of an identifiable sex or race, however, the justification offered by the institution may be judicially required to go beyond a simple showing of a reasonable relationship, extending to a proof that the practice is necessary, essential, or compelled to realize valid institutional objectives.

DISCRIMINATION AGAINST STUDENTS. Most cases alleging discrimination against students have involved the admission policies of the institution. Since admission policies may often include departmental criteria, the chairperson has a responsibility to insure that reasonable standards are applied. The department's authority to establish admission criteria is seldom challenged by the courts, but the established criteria or the way in which criteria are applied should avoid discrimination on the basis of race, sex, or national origin, nor should the criteria exclude "otherwise qualified handicapped individuals."

While courts have struck down admissions quotas based upon race, they have been quick to point out that race may be used as one of several factors which may be considered in insuring an institution's legitimate interest in a diverse student body. The celebrated decision of the United States Supreme Court in *Bakke vs. Regents of the University of California*[39] struck down a medical school admissions program which allocated a number of admission slots to minority and disadvantaged students through application to a separate minority admissions council. In declaring the university's policy discriminatory, the Court did sanction an alternative strategy for the admission of minority and disadvantaged students by adopting the view that race could be given additional weight as one of a number of factors to be considered in an admissions policy applied uniformly to all applicants. The key element in any such admissions system would be a set of admissions criteria reasonably related to the institution's educational goals and uniformly applied to all students. The Court suggested that insuring a diverse student body would be an appropriate justification for a "weighted" admissions program.

In a more recent decision by the Court, *Southeastern Community College v. Davis,*[40] the justices refused to require that a hearing-impaired student be admitted to a clinically oriented educational program in nursing. The Court's rationale emphasized that provisions of the Rehabilitation Act of 1973 did not

---

39. 438 U.S. 265 (1978).
40. 442 U.S. 397 (1979).

require the admission of a handicapped applicant where it could be demonstrated that the handicapping condition would require substantial modification of the college and that the likelihood of placing the handicapped graduate in a job related to the training offered was remote. In a similar decision by a federal court of appeals, an applicant to medical school who was denied admission due to a history of psychological disorders was unable to obtain court-ordered relief. Recognizing the *Davis* case as controlling, the court noted that the applicant's disability had not responded to treatment and would seriously impair her ability to practice medicine; consequently, she could not be considered an "otherwise qualified handicapped person" under the law.[41]

In another example, an applicant to the psychiatric residency program at the university was denied admission on the basis that he was confined to a wheelchair and disabled in his ability to write and walk. The department's admissions committee, chaired by the department head, emphasized that the rejection of the application, which followed an interview with the candidate (at which time the handicap was discovered), was based on the view that the applicant's physical limitations would inhibit his full participation in the clinical aspect of the program, which involved hospital rounds and contact with patients who might endanger the applicant.

Whereas a department may consider handicap when substantial revision of the educational curriculum to accommodate the person would be necessary, or when it is unlikely that the training could effectively be utilized by the handicapped individual in seeking later employment, handicap may not be used as the sole basis for excluding an otherwise qualified applicant. In the case of the applicant confined to a wheelchair, the decision of the department's admissions committee will be subject to judicial scrutiny should the student elect to challenge the denial of his application. Absent further evidence that would support the committee's justification for denying admission, this applicant may successfully argue that reasonable accommodation could have been made in order to permit his participation in the clinical component. Arguing that physical barriers such as lack of wheelchair access would prohibit participation are not convincing, and opinions as to the risk factor related to clinical rounds may not persuade a court that reasonable accommodation cannot be realized so that the student can participate fully without any significant modification in the clinical program.

DISCRIMINATION AGAINST FACULTY.   For the department chair in an institution receiving some form of federal financial support, the primary constitutional and statutory provisions governing issues of employment discrimination focus on the equal protection clause of the fourteenth amendment, Title VII of the Civil Rights Act of 1964,[42] and Title IX of the Educational Amendments of 1972.[43] In recent years, faculty alleging a discriminatory animus on the part of colleges and univer-

---

41. Doe v. New York Univ., 666 F.2d 761 (2nd Cir. 1981).

42. 42 U.S.C. § 2000e.

43. 42 U.S.C. § 1681.

sities have relied on the provisions of Title VII rather than on the rigorous proof of official intent to discriminate required under the fourteenth amendment or on the as yet unresolved standards to be used in Title IX proceedings.

Title VII of the Civil Rights Act of 1964 prohibits employment discrimination against individuals on the basis of race, color, religion, sex, or national origin. Employment practices resulting in disparate treatment of a person or class protected by the act constitute one form of discrimination; however, the employer can justify the discriminatory practice by articulating a legitimate, nondiscriminatory reason for the employment decision such as an occupational qualification bearing a reasonable relationship to the job in question. Legal controversy in most of these cases has alternated between the employee's burden to establish a prima facie case and the defendant employer's burden to articulate some legitimate nondiscriminatory reason for the allegedly discriminatory practice.

The principal case involving disparate treatment in higher education is *Board of Trustees of Keene State College v. Sweeney,*[44] a case which involved allegations of sex discrimination in the denial of promotion to a female associate professor. Dr. Sweeney was successful in establishing a prima facie case of sex discrimination by a statistical showing that the promotion of women at Keene was substantially confined to the lower ranks. The college sought to demonstrate that its decision not to promote Sweeney to full professor was based upon legitimate factors, citing insufficient service to the college, primarily in committee work, and personality considerations which allegedly interfered with her teaching and relationships with colleagues. The United States Supreme Court ruled that once the college articulated a legitimate nondiscriminatory basis for its adverse employment decision, the burden of proof shifted once again to Dr. Sweeney, who must establish that the articulated reason offered by the college was a subterfuge or pretext for a discriminatory practice.[45] Sweeney carried this burden. She demonstrated that her complaints concerning discrimination had largely been ignored by her department head and the administration and that the "personality variables" which were a basis for denial of promotion had not been introduced when she was granted tenure at the college two years previous to the initial denial of promotion. Sweeney had been promoted to full professor two years after the initial denial of promotion. Reasons cited for promotion by the department chair emphasized her committee service, excellence in teaching and community service, factors cited as negative performance indicators during the initial promotion decision, yet Dr. Sweeney's qualifications had not changed in any significant way in the interim between promotion decisions.

Disparate treatment in the *Sweeney* case was manifest in administrative indifference to the concerns of women faculty, statistically significant differences in hiring and promotion practices, inconsistent application of promotion and tenure criteria, and a preoccupation with trivial criticisms as a justification for the

---

44. 604 F.2d 106 (1st Cir. 1979), *cert. denied,* 444 U.S. 1045 (1980).
45. Bd. of Trustees of Keene State College v. Sweeney, 439 U.S. 24 (1978).

promotion decisions. In another case, disparate treatment was established by a showing that a female faculty member was evaluated for tenure using criteria different from those applied to male candidates and that personnel advisement practices of the department discriminated on the basis of sex.[46] Similarly, a department chairman's imposition of degree requirements not initially required nor reasonably related to a position as athletic administrator and coach were held to be evidence of a discriminatory animus.[47]

Sex-role stereotyping has become a frequently cited basis for a proof of discriminatory animus in employment decisions. An example is the case of a female faculty member who repeatedly sought consideration for additional teaching assignments that would have meant supplemental salary. Although male faculty received such assignments at periodic intervals, female faculty did not. In response to her request for an explanation, the department chair candidly explained that the assignments were reserved for male faculty who were married and needed extra income to support a wife and family. Additional compensation, in the eyes of the department chair, should be made available to those who needed it the most. The department chair's rationale for awarding supplemental compensation to male faculty members reflects the sexual bias that only males should be awarded the additional compensation because only males have the responsibility to support a family. This presumption will not withstand judicial scrutiny and does not meet the test for a legitimate, nondiscriminatory reason which would justify disparities in the treatment of male and female faculty.

The college or university must demonstrate that its employment decision (whether related to hiring, promotion, award of tenure or benefits, demotion, or termination) is based upon legitimate factors and not on explicit or implicit considerations prohibited by Title VII. Such a proposition does not rule out peer review, nor does it hold that consideration of teaching, research, and service (essentially subjective criteria) are inappropriate to the employment decision. What is important is that there be no differential treatment in the employment decision-making process. Uniformity of procedures and criteria for evaluation are essential. The articulation of a rationale for employment decisions that bears a reasonable relationship to departmental, college, and institutional objectives is extremely important. The articulated basis for adverse employment decisions should relate to legitimate, performance-related reasons, which might include negative student evaluations, unwillingness to assume responsibility for teaching or service assignments, refusal to accept student advisees, and the like.

While statistical evidence of a disparity in hiring and promotion may be sufficient to establish a prima facie case of discrimination, it must often be coupled with overt discriminatory treatment in order to require a legal remedy. Evidence that a chairperson engaged in or condoned differential treatment of employees or made compliance with unwanted sexual overtures a condition of employment or advancement in employment would substantially strengthen a

46. Kunda v. Muhlenberg College, 621 F. 2d 532 (3rd Cir. 1980)
47. Hill v. Nettleton, 455 F. Supp. 514 (D. Colo. 1978).

case of employment discrimination. Coupled with evidence of a statistical disparity, even the slightest manifestation of an overt discriminatory intent may be actionable. In these latter situations, evidence that the chairperson had difficulty cooperating with racially or sexually identifiable employee groups, ignored the employee's expressed concern for alleged discrimination, or demeaned an employee because of the employee's race or sex could be influential in proving discriminatory animus.

SEXUAL HARASSMENT. One aspect of federal civil-rights law which has special significance for the department chair is the prohibition, contained in Title VII and Title IX, on sexual harassment. These titles have been accompanied by regulatory provisions prohibiting two forms of harassment: bargain transactions and hostile environment. Bargain transactions (also known as quid pro quo sexual harassment) involve unwelcome sexual advances, requests for sexual favors, or other verbal or physical conduct of a sexual nature, whereby submission to the request or advance is either an explicit or implicit condition of employment or is used as a basis for decisions affecting the student or employee's status. Hostile-environment sexual harassment involves conduct which has the purpose or effect of unreasonably interfering with a person's work performance, or of creating an intimidating, hostile, or offensive sexually-charged environment. Unpermitted touching, sexual advances, demands for sexual favors, sexually stereotyped insults, and demeaning propositions are among the forms of behavior which, particularly if shown to be continuous or repeated would establish sexual harassment.

The following hypothetical example contained in a legal commentary on sexual harassment is utilized by the authors of the commentary to illustrate hostile-environment sexual harassment as it might occur in a college classroom.[48] In this example, a professor regularly illustrates his lecture on human anatomy by projecting a photo of a nude female from the centerfold of a men's magazine. Although this faculty member is highly respected and considered an outstanding teacher by students and faculty, several female students have brought complaints to the department chair concerning this practice. These students express concern that the centerfold projection is offensive to women and creates a classroom environment in which sexist remarks and improper jokes are initiated by male students. While the harassment involves students, the issue is also an employment concern. Under the circumstances presented in the hypothetical, the department chairperson would be compelled to investigate the complaints registered by the female students and, if those complaints were substantiated, to direct the professor to discontinue the practice. Failure to act expeditiously to investigate and address an instance of sexual harassment might lead to liability for both the department chair and the institution. In such cases

---

48. Steven Olswang, and Barbara Lee, "Faculty Freedoms and Institutional Accountability: Interactions and Conflicts," ASHE–ERIC Higher Education Research Report No. 5 (Washington, DC: Association for the Study of Higher Education, 1984), pp. 38–39.

the administrator must know the institution's policy, disseminate that policy, and act affirmatively to address complaints.

Common-Law Liability: Law of Torts

Once described as a "brooding omnipresence," the common law consists of duties and obligations as defined by court cases. While previous discussion has centered upon those duties of the department chair that relate to constitutional, statutory, or contractual provisions, there exists a judicially imposed set of standards which in some cases predate constitutional laws. These duties may loosely be categorized as falling under the law of torts, a category of civil wrongs not actionable under general principles of contract or constitutional law, but recognized as meriting relief under judge-made standards.

Two classes of tort law liability are particularly relevant to the department chair despite a paucity of actual case law involving the liability of the chairperson. First, there are those tort law cases involving the negligent breach of a duty of care. Typically, these cases involve a determination that the chairperson could have reasonably foreseen a danger to another person to whom the chair owed a duty of reasonable prudence. Second, there are those cases which involve an intentional or willful act, the injurious consequence of which could only have been intended by the person who so acted. The two forms of intentional tort of particular relevance to the department chairperson are defamation and fraudulent misrepresentation.

NEGLIGENT TORTS: DUTY OF REASONABLE PRUDENCE

A department chairperson provides services to several constituencies (students, staff, faculty) which imply obligations beyond those recognized under contract or constitutional mandate. The provision of service implies a duty to act with reasonably prudent care in foreseeing possible dangers to the individual and in mitigating any potential risk of injury. The meaning to be attached to "reasonably prudent care" is subject to the evaluation of a lay jury or judge using the hindsight available only after an injury has occurred; hence a definitive statement of meaning is difficult. However, it is possible to extrapolate at least the following three common law duties that may apply to the department chairperson under certain circumstances: (1) Assignment of appropriate supervisory staff, (2) Promulgation of reasonable safety rules, and (3) Notification about possible dangers.

Consistent with the chair's responsibility for scheduling and employee assignment, a duty to act with reasonably prudent care to *assign appropriate faculty or staff* can be inferred. A risk of injury might not be anticipated in a history class, but it could reasonably be foreseen if a chemistry lab program were overenrolled and inadequately staffed. Under such circumstances, the failure to assign employees with the requisite training to provide proper instruction and adequate supervision might ultimately be construed as a breach of reasonably prudent care by the chairperson. The chair's duty to act with reasonable care in assigning faculty or staff would generally require consideration of the foreseeable dangers attendant to an activity and provision of a level of supervisory expertise consistent with reducing that risk to within acceptable limits.

As the administrator most often charged with implementing faculty and administrative policies, the role of chairperson may carry a *duty to promulgate reasonable rules for the safety of others.* If a danger can reasonably be foreseen, then action to mitigate the risk often takes the form of a rule or regulation to guide the conduct of others. The chair might be charged with a duty to promulgate and inform staff, faculty, and students of an office or building security policy designed to protect against intruders. Where previous acts of vandalism or assaults have occurred on the campus, the chair's negligence in failing to develop and disseminate a security policy might be construed as the proximate cause of any injury in which an assailant gained entrance and attacked a building occupant or invited guest.

In most circumstances the chairperson's obligation extends no further than insuring that proper notice of a safety hazard has been provided to others. The *duty to notify of dangerous conditions* may involve dissemination of the institution's policy on building security, arranging for posting of radiation warnings, or informing other administrative personnel of a building hazard which needs to be corrected in order to insure the safety of those who can reasonably be anticipated to use the facilities. Notice to others through memoranda or posting of conspicuous signs is generally considered to relieve the chair of responsibility in the event of a later injury and offers concrete evidence that the chairperson took positive steps to alleviate any foreseeable danger to persons or property. It is worth pointing out that a policy of *immediate* notification is a convenient method for transferring liability to another party, who, once aware of a dangerous condition, may be said to have assumed an obligation to act reasonably in relationship to the danger.

Following is an example of a situation that sometimes occurs in science laboratories at colleges facing long-term financial difficulties. Lack of sufficient financial resources forced a certain college to make repeated cutbacks in plant and building maintenance. The chairperson of the chemistry department is particularly sensitive to these cutbacks, because reductions have meant that laboratory renovations have been repeatedly postponed. Within the last month, a facilities inspection led to the discovery that shower units located in the labs were clogged by rust and inoperative. The inspection was undertaken after a student, working on a chemistry laboratory assignment without instructor supervisions, spilled a beaker of acid on his lab partner and the partner sustained painful burns when he was unable to irrigate his face and hands using the showers.

The chair in this case faces a number of concerns which relate to foreseeable risk and the duty to effectively manage risks in the institutional setting. An incident has occurred which makes it imperative that the shower units be repaired or certain laboratory activities be curtailed. The instance establishes a foreseeable risk of potential injury, and the duty on the department chair, after discovering that the shower units are no longer operational, is to reduce the likelihood of injury to students and staff. It is impossible to eliminate all risks in an educational setting, but it is imperative that once an injury can be foreseen, the department chair take affirmative steps to reduce the known or anticipated risk.

INTENTIONAL TORTS: DEFAMATION

A former faculty member sued for libel and slander based on a letter read at a faculty tenure committee meeting which accused the former professor, a married man, of having attempted to seduce a young woman who was a student in one of his classes. The author of the letter was unnamed, the accusations were unverified, and the professor was not afforded an opportunity to see or respond to the letter. Charging defamation, the professor alleged that his professional reputation and standing in the community had been injured, that the letter referred to a rumor that had been discredited months earlier, and that he was denied tenure as a result of the reading of the letter. These allegations constitute the basic elements of a defamation.[49]

A defamatory statement is one which injures reputation or standing in the community. The communication may be written (libel) or oral (slander). It has been considered defamatory to report that a faculty member drinks liquor excessively,[50] is a racist,[51] or has falsified credentials. An accusation that a professor has attempted to seduce a student, when coupled with a correspond-ing denial of an employment opportunity (promotion or tenure), has been recognized as a defamation.[52]

Department chairpersons are regularly compelled to appraise faculty and students. To protect against the risk of legal liability for defamation, two defenses are available. First, the chairperson may establish the truth of the allegation, coupling this proof with evidence that the alleged defamatory communication was made in good faith without malice or intent to injure. Since the burden of establishing that the defamation is true may prove too demanding, an alternative is to establish that the communication was qualifiedly privileged. This latter defense is conditioned upon the absence of malice in circumstances where the law recognizes that the communication was uttered in a reasonable manner, limited in scope, for a proper purpose.

Qualified privilege was the appropriate defense to a charge of racism when black medical students sought to grieve the allegedly discriminatory practices of a professor in the university's medical school. The professor contended that the students had libeled him when they filed a written grievance charging him with

---

49. *See* Stukuls v. State, 366 N. E. 2d 289 (N.Y. 1977).
50. Dauterman v. State-Record Co., 154 S.E. 2d 919 (S.C. 1967).
51. Scarpelli v. Jones, 626 P. 2d 785 (Kan. 1981).
52. Stukuls v. State, 366 N.E. 2d 829 (N.Y. 1977).

willful acts of discrimination. The court found that a qualified privilege existed since the students had acted in good faith to redress a grievance and had limited their communication to university officials who had an interest or duty to respond to such a concern.[53]

In another example the department chair, in response to a directive from the president, prepared a letter expressing an opinion that the candidate for tenure and promotion from the department "exhibited limited and superficial scholarship coupled with a contentious and belligerent attitude that had other faculty intimidated into voting to support the award of tenure and promotion." After discovering a copy of the letter in the promotion file, the faculty member threatens suit.

In this situation which called for the opinion of the department chair, the faculty member is unlikely to prevail on a claim of defamation provided the communication by the department chair was limited in dissemination and communicated for a proper motive. The statement related to the professor's scholarship is within the range of fair comment in the context of a tenure and promotion decision and was compelled as part of the responsibilities of the department chair. The comment that other faculty were intimidated by the professor's belligerent attitude is suspect in that it suggests malice in the department chair's viewpoint, but the degree of insulation from liability which qualified privilege conveys would generally extend to this comment as well.

A defense of conditional privilege may be overcome by evidence that there was excessive publication of the defamation, or that the communicator acted out of malice. In the case of the faculty member accused of seducing a student, the court recognized that a prima facie case of defamation had been established by the faculty member. Nevertheless, the case was remanded for a determination of whether malice had prompted the reading of the letter. The court was unwilling to find an inference of malice in a showing that the letter was false, adopting the position that it may have been appropriate to provide information of a mere suspicion or a rumor when the communication is made to faculty who have a legitimate interest in the matter.[54]

INTENTIONAL TORTS: FRAUDULENT MISREPRESENTATION

While a student's or employee's reliance on statements made by university administrators may be a basis for a contractual obligation, there are few cases in which the agent's representations have been construed as attempts to fraudulently induce the individual to pay fees or perform services. Cases of fraudulent misrepresentation are rare, confined primarily to proprietary institutions in which inducements were considered gross and the defrauded person was unable or unlikely to be sufficiently informed to know better.[55]

---

53. Scarpelli v. Jones, 626 P. 2d 785 (Kan. 1981).
54. Stukuls v. State, 366 N.E. 2d 829 (N.Y. 1977).
55. *See* Joyner v. Albert Merrill School, 411 N.Y.S. 2d 988 (N.Y. Civ. Ct. 1978).

Nevertheless, as recruiting practices and marketing strategies signaling increased competition for students and faculty proliferate, it is advisable to exercise caution in representing the program of an institution. Courts seem particularly protective of students who have been induced to enroll in programs that provide placement assistance bordering on a guarantee of employment or mislead students into believing they have special aptitude through the use of inappropriate testing and bogus courses. A public community college lost a jury verdict to a student who complained that he was induced to enroll in a one-year welding technology program through representations of faculty and administrators. These representations induced him to believe that certain classes would be taught, specific equipment would be available, and program completion would prepare the student for employment in the trade. The representations were false in that several courses were not offered, machines and materials were not available at the college, and the year-long course of study was not sufficient to prepare him adequately for employment as a welder. A jury verdict awarded $125,000 to the student, but it was overturned by the trial judge and appellate court on the grounds that Oregon statute law grants governmental immunity for state college officials in the exercise of their role as counselors.[56] (No such defense would be available to a private college official.)

Conclusion

It may be argued that this chapter raises more questions than it answers. For the conscientious department chairperson, the answer to what constitutes a "reasonably prudent person" or "good faith" behavior may appear ambiguous, vague, and uncertain. As in any situation involving the use of case study, the ability to generalize from individual cases is limited and the applicability of a particular standard may be subject to variables which remain undetermined. If the chair's quest is for certainty and unerring guidance, then an inquiry into the law of the case is nothing more than a modern quest for a yet to be discovered holy grail.

What the case law does convey is a sense of the issues that occupy courts in the administration of justice. Some sensitivity to how liability may be determined provides a conceptual framework for the department chairperson in assessing the risk of liability. The outcome of particular cases may provide an intuitive guide to factually related circumstances. There are no absolutes, but a sufficient number of qualified answers gives rise to a few guiding generalizations.

When risk of legal liability exists, consultation with legal counsel is often an appropriate preventive measure. Particularly when the institution employs in-house counsel or has a competent attorney on retainer for consultation, the chairperson is advised to seek advice before undertaking any action that would deny identifiable rights or result in injury. Often, the effort to obtain advice of

---

56. Dizick v. Umpqua Community College, 577 P.2d 534 (Or. Ct. App. 1978).

counsel coupled with the chair's conscientious effort to act on that advice will serve as evidence of good faith and further limit the risk of individual liability.

The corollary to consultation with legal counsel is consultation with appropriate and knowledgeable colleagues. Appropriate colleagues are those whose formal status in the administrative hierarchy of the institution creates a measure of responsibility for supervision and articulation of the department chairperson's role. Knowledgeable colleagues are those with the experience and training to inform the chairperson on institutional objectives and traditional past practices or procedures. Observing existing standards, remaining consistent with past policies, and informing a superior of this intention prior to action is no guarantee against a lawsuit, but it is one of the best ways of making your problem the institution's problem and thus avoiding individual liability.

In addition to observing the traditional policy and procedures of the institution, the chairperson should strive to identify and implement those often illusive "best professional practice standards" related to the chairperson's role. The appropriate standard of conduct for a chairperson is a factual question which neither an attorney nor a judge can resolve without the aid of expert testimony or the opinion of other administratively competent academicians. In this sense the guidance upon which a chairperson might wish to rely in order to avoid legal liability is contained in those chapters of this text which suggest a best practice standard. While it might appear self-serving for the chairperson to explain his or her conduct on the basis of practices proposed by a treatise on the department chairperson, courts have shown extraordinarily deferential attitudes when a chair's action is consistent with recognized professional practice.

The law is replete with references to words of art such as "good faith," "reasonable prudence," and "fundamental fairness." These terms suggest a host of behavioral maxims with varying degrees of relevance to the chairperson. Principally, it behooves the chairperson to avoid acting precipitously in decision making. Whenever possible, allow time for the necessary information gathering before acting on a problem. Rather than rely upon a single account or hearsay, seek confirmation and corroboration of facts and circumstances surrounding an event. Consider the possible consequences of any course of action and always evaluate possible alternatives which may accomplish the same or similar results with less risk of harm. Document your efforts to resolve problems, always articulating the basis for your authority to act and relating your action to the valid objectives or statement of purposes adopted by the institution.

Another homily that rings true is the admonition to act with honesty and candor. Nothing is more damaging to a chair's defense in a legal action than evidence of duplicitous behavior, deceit, or misrepresentation in the role of chairperson. Such a proof will frequently give rise to a presumption that the chair acted with a malicious intent to injure, creating potential for individual liability and the award of punitive damages against the chairperson. The chairperson who adopts a Machiavellian mode of operation may find that chicanery, coupled with political scheming and half-truths, will result in retribution that reaches deep into the individual's pocketbook.

Although it is important to avoid the allegation of malice, a level of candor which admits that an institutional duty has been breached is not appropriate. Just as a physician would never say "Oops!" in the operating room, never admit liability in your effort to be fair to all concerned. Liability can be decided by the court as an ultimate question relating facts to law. Being sorry an injurious situation occurs is perfectly permissible, but admitting responsibility for the injury is unwise. Send a card of condolence, but do not confess guilt.

A chairperson should always keep in mind that courts are first and foremost the guardians of process. A number of substantive legal questions have been addressed in this chapter, but it is the procedural defect in an institution's policy that most often creates the basis for litigation. In this regard, the role of chairperson is particularly critical. Courts will often abstain from hearing a case if the aggrieved party has failed to utilize the institution's procedures for redressing an alleged wrong. Courts will intervene when the chairperson has failed to follow appropriate procedural standards or has created a potential injury for which there is no institutional appeal.

In most institutions, the department chairperson is uniquely situated to resolve procedural problems and reduce the likelihood of litigation. By encouraging the adoption of procedures that provide notice, impartial hearing, and timely administrative appeal, the chair can facilitate institutional arrangements that provide for self-regulation and mitigate the potential effects of arbitrary action. In a conscientious and earnest effort to inform others of and comply with the institution's procedural standards, the chair demonstrates good faith and fair dealing.

Neither Solomon nor Moses, the chair is recognized by courts of law as the institutional agent who must ensure compliance with administrative procedures, defend the academic standards of the department, and act in a multitude of ways to realize the valid educational objectives of the institution. Few judicial decisions have ever held the chairperson individually accountable for errors committed in a genuine effort to realize any of these purposes. In most cases, courts have granted a presumption of reasonableness and substantial discretion to the chair in order to ensure a measure of autonomy and authority consistent with effective and efficient management. The chair who recognizes those limited constraints imposed by courts is most likely to continue to exercise the authority so essential to his or her role.

Questions

1. List all the documents that have been published by your institution which contain commitments to students and faculty and which could be considered contractual in nature and perhaps legally binding. Examples: catalogs, bulletins, faculty handbooks, schedules, program and recruitment brochures.

2. Obtain copies of the documents you have listed and try to identify portions that imply legal obligations on your part as a department chairperson at your institution.

3. As chairperson of your department, what situations might arise where you could be charged with behaving in an arbitrary and capricious manner? If you have witnessed actions of chairpersons that might be deemed arbitrary and capricious, please describe these actions.

4. In your own academic department, what special areas of possible liability exist for which you need to take special precautions? (For example, hazardous experiments in laboratories, and field trips.)

5. Each institution has its own policies for providing or not providing legal assistance in instances of litigation. What are the policies of your institution with regard to providing legal counsel or economic assistance to chairpersons? In what areas will your institution come to your aid or defense in a lawsuit, and in what areas may it refuse to assist you? If you do not know the answers to these questions, you should consult appropriate officials at your institution.

References

ALEXANDER, S. KERN, and SOLOMON, ERWIN. *College and University Law.* 2nd ed. Charlottesville, VA: The Michie Company, 1979.

CUNNINGHAM, PATRICK J. "Disciplinary Counseling: The First Step Toward Due Process." *The Journal of the College and University Personnel Association,* Summer 1980, pp. 1–6.

DOUGLAS, JOEL M. (Ed.) *Salary and Compensation Methodology in Academic Collective Bargaining.* New York: National Center for the Study of Collective Bargaining in Higher Education and the Professions, 1983. (ERIC Document Reproduction Service No. ED 230 140)

EDWARDS, HARRY T. and NORDIN, VIRGINIA DAVIS. *Higher Education and the Law (with Cumulative Supplement).* Cambridge: Harvard Institute for Educational Management, 1979.

HOLLANDER, PATRICIA A. *Legal Handbook for Educators.* Boulder: Westview Press, 1978.

LESLIE, DAVID W. "NLRB Rulings on the Department Chairmanship." *Educational Record,* 53, 1972, pp. 313–320.

———. "The Status of the Department Chairmanship in University Organization." *AAUP Bulletin,* 59, 1973, pp. 419–426.

KAPLAN, W. A. *The Law of Higher Education.* 2nd ed. San Francisco: Jossey–Bass, 1986.

MARCH, JAMES G. *How We Talk and How We Act: Administrative Theory and Administrative Life.* Urbana: University of Illinois Press, 1980.

McCARTY, DONALD J., and REYES, PEDRO. "Organizational Models of Governance: Academic Deans' Decision-making Styles." *Journal of Teacher Education,* 38, 1987, pp. 2–8.

McConnell, T. R., and Mortimer, Kenneth P. *The Faculty in University Governance.* Berkeley: Center for Research and Development in Higher Education, University of California, 1971.

Nash, Nancy S. *Private College Faculty as Managers: An Empirical Test Under "Yeshiva."* ASHE Annual Meeting Paper, San Antonio, 1986. (ERIC Document Reproduction Service No. ED 268 898)

Olswang, Steven, and Lee, Barbara. *Faculty Freedoms and Institutional Accountability: Interactions and Conflicts.* ASHE–ERIC Higher Education Research Report No. 5. Washington, DC: Association for the Study of Higher Education, 1984: 38–39.

Schrecker, Ellen. *No Ivory Tower: McCarthyism and the Universities.* New York: Oxford University Press, 1986.

Young, D. Parker (Ed.) *The Yearbook of Higher Education Law.* Topeka: National Organization on Legal Problems of Education, 1980–1981 editions.

Part XI

DEALING WITH DEANS, UNIVERSITY ADMINISTRATIVE OFFICES, AND EXTERNAL AGENCIES

Chapter 28.   Dealing with Deans and University Administrative Offices

Chapter 29.   Dealing with External Agencies

Dealing with Deans and University Administrative Offices

The chair's role is partly a first-among-equals faculty position, but it is also partly an administrative role. The chair is expected to implement university policies, to enforce rules, and to respond to directives from the dean and other administrators. The chair's appointment is usually at the dean's pleasure, and the dean usually conducts the chair's annual evaluation. The university bureaucracy, although it may seem alien and impenetrable, is also potentially a tool the chair can use to get things done. Chairs will be effective in direct proportion to their mastery of relations with deans and the bureaucracy.

Deans and Their Motives

Deans once were faculty, and usually will return to the faculty when they finish their terms as deans. Some have broader ambitions in administration, but only a few go on to vice-presidencies or presidencies. While serving as deans, they are expected to assume a corporate management perspective—their most pressing and urgent duties have to do with budgeting and resource allocation, public relations, and the management of people. Deans are considered successful (in the eyes of presidents and trustees) when they can show increases in external funding, improvements in the national reputation of their departments or programs, increasing enrollments, and demonstrable gains in the efficiency of college operations. If they can be innovative in improving the quality of teaching and learning, especially if this pays off in publicity, so much the better.

Deans are expected to play a very public role, one which shows the university off to best advantage. They play corporate promoter with the press, with potential donors, with important political supporters of the university, and with the corporate and civic leaders of the community, state, and nation. They help presidents translate needs into funding opportunities, and they help articulate the university's ambitions to the professional and lay public. Successful deans work hard to recruit the best faculty and students, raise whatever money they can, blend people and money into excellent programs, and promote the results in a continuing entrepreneurial quest. They are judged by how much they contribute to the university's bottom line—measured in money, image, and prestige.

Deans are expected to have goals and strategies. They have to deal with a variety of higher-level bureaucracies, each of which expects them to be able to say they have rational plans in place to do what the bureaucrats expect. Budget planners like to think ahead, and they particularly like to think about numbers that increase. Program planners like to think about quality and excellence, and they especially like to have numbers that demonstrate quality and excellence. Facilities planners like to think about new facilities. Deans seem to be constantly trying to satisfy various planners' deadlines, and, in the process, to be setting goals for time horizons that are quite beyond most chairs' ambitions for their own terms of office.

Although ambitious deans may drive chairs to distraction, deans who do not fit the entrepreneurial, promotional pattern are probably going to hurt their colleges in the long run. Those who merely preserve the status quo, who serve as brokers and mediators rather than as promoters, who follow rather than lead, who "satisfice" rather than challenge, will be viewed from the top levels of the university as "losers," as deans without ambition, and as place holders more concerned with their own security and salary than with the greater glory of the university. Successful deans learn quickly to play on the fast track, and they need very much to be supported by chairs and by faculty who can keep up to top-competition speed.

Deans' Styles

Deans are as varied in their styles as chairs are in theirs. But a few characteristic patterns *can* be outlined—with of course the caveat that none exists in its pure form. Chairs may well reflect on the dean's style in order to anticipate how the dean might behave in predictable situations.

The "tyro" dean is young, enthusiastic, energetic, and slightly smitten with the heady responsibilities and status that go with the job. The tyro often enters the deanship with high ideals and ambitions, and is particularly quick to adopt the trappings and symbols of corporate management. The tyro will be under considerable pressure to "look good" to presidents and provosts, and will be quick to respond with tough decisions, grand plans, and projections. The young, fresh dean is likely to be politically naive, and may be particularly obtuse about how the faculty view him or her. This dean will be quick to give inspirational speeches, and to lay out for the faculty a planned route to greatness.

Tyro deans are unknown quantities. Some will quickly become disillusioned, and resign after short terms. Others will learn and persist, growing in office and ultimately doing the college a great deal of good. Chairs can adapt to younger deans by helping them form realistic goals and plans, by assisting them with contacts, by supporting and shaping their image with faculty, and by offering whatever counsel and advice their experience may equip them to offer. Tyro deans often are viewed as investments in the future by the university hierarchy, and they may receive a great deal of higher-level support in the early going. When a university hires a young, energetic, visionary dean, it is often sending a signal to the college that it expects a good deal more in the future. Chairs should be able to perceive that message, and orient themselves to helping the tyro dean realize the ambitions he or she was sent to pursue. Young deans who are successful frequently have enough time left in their careers to advance in higher-level administration.

At the other end of the continuum are deans who achieve their positions as senior statesmen. Not only do these deans bring considerable personal stature to their positions, but they probably have relatively distinguished records in their own academic fields. Unencumbered by personal needs for achievement and recognition, statesmen deans sometimes outrank vice-presidents in prestige and power.

Statesmen deans see their enterprise in baldly objective terms. They know where the strengths are, where the weaknesses are, and who has political connections and power. They waste little motion or energy on bureaucratic games, and they cut through fantasies with a terrible swift sword. On the other hand, statesman deans are capable of both realistically planning and achieving their objectives with admirable effectiveness. They know how to put initiatives together, and they know how to achieve results. Although they may be very happy to share the public credit for their achievements, they also have no illusions about the roles that the various actors may have played.

Chairs almost always wind up playing subordinate roles to statesman deans. There is no dishonor in this; a chair may, in fact, benefit enormously from a statesman's achievements. Statesmen welcome solid, sensible, goal-directed chairs. They are not threatened by independence and initiative, but they have little patience or regard for chairs who signal that they are simply going along for the ride—without making any real contribution to the advancement of the department or college. Chairs working under statesman deans are well advised to act as team players and to keep their departments up to speed during this kind of regime. Statesmen do not have to spend much time ingratiating themselves to faculty, and are quite able to walk away from the weaker units without fearing political reprisals.

Many deans are best characterized as managers. They move into deanships from middle-of-the-road careers, often having moved in orderly fashion from positions in faculty governance through department chairs to associate deanships. They are tested, safe, conventional, and well-known and regarded within the institution. Although they will respond to, and function in, the promotional culture of top management, they do so with relatively limited vision and with considerable attention to the consultative processes they have undoubtedly learned well over the years. Managers' regimes are usually marked by no dramatic departures from the status quo (unless by accident of unusually good luck). Their terms in office are also marked by stability, and so are often forgettable because there are no achievements of any momentous dimensions. Managers survive during periods of relative prosperity, but may be less well suited to periods of stress and change.

Chairs can almost always work comfortably with manager deans. Managers are insiders, familiar with the status quo, and not anxious to make upsetting changes. They readily horse-trade and compromise, and they respect the sacred processes of collegial governance. On the other hand, they can hurt the college by failing to push, promote, or provoke change and development. Chairs may have to assume a greater responsibility for leadership under these regimes, particularly if the manager seems to be avoiding opportunities, neglecting public relations, or operating too conservatively. Manager deanships often require of chairs a delicate balance between being loyal team players and being entrepreneurial.

Some deans, whether out of insecurity or because they have never learned how to lead, operate very much as tyrants and bullies. Chairs can almost never be effective under such regimes. Dictator deans usually focus on achieving power and personal status—and usually do so at others' expense. They may promote new ideas and progressive programs, but they do so with an almost pathological sense of ownership. They expect obedience and loyalty in all matters, and, particularly, they expect subordination of others to their will. In some cases, dictators do make great strides in improving a college's visibility and image—largely because doing so is associated with their own self-promotional needs. However, they also leave a trail of bitter feelings, low morale, and disorganization. They are often impulsive, secretive, opportunistic, and vindictive. They are successful in coercing people to do their bidding, but they almost always alienate these same people.

Chairs can take small comfort in knowing that tyrants universally sow the seeds of their own downfall. Their only hope is to hunker down and outlast the regime. However, knowing that they may very well succeed in outlasting what may be a brief reign, chairs can be quietly active and effective during such periods. Most importantly, it is a time to build alliances—with faculty, with the central administration, and with important people outside the institution. None of this alliance-building can be visible, because it will threaten the tyrant, but it must go on, and it should be seen as an investment in the department's long-term stature.

Obviously these caricatures do not do justice to the wide array of styles. They merely represent some common "types" to the extent that typing is at all fruitful. Mainly, chairs should be aware that each dean is different from every other dean, and that he or she should plan to adjust and calibrate his or her behavior to play to a dean's strong points and compensate for the weaknesses.

Developing Trust

Deans and chairs have to trust each other if they are to work together effectively. Because the chair will ultimately be judged by the dean, it is important to build a relationship in which the dean is able to communicate expectations and in which the chair is able to seek advice and feedback in an open and honest fashion. The chair must also be able to get the dean's support when it is needed. The dean must therefore have confidence in the chair's judgment and in his or her political legitimacy with the faculty.

Building and nurturing a good relationship with a dean may take a substantial effort. If a college is large, a dean may have a dozen or more chairs to deal with, as well as a cast of center directors, assistant and associate deans for various things, and the university bureaucracy. The dean may be virtually uninformed about important departmental matters because he or she is almost always overloaded with information from the many channels that feed into the office. On the other hand, the chair may be substantially uninformed about the dean's perspectives, plans, and problems. Deans are often off-campus, closeted in meetings, bedeviled by problems and crises, and preoccupying themselves with promotional activities which are just as often command performances for central administrators as self-initiated.

Certainly, deans have every opportunity to be superficially informed. Annual and more frequent reports reach the dean's office through formal channels. Memos, records of grant and contract activity, publicity from all quarters, and voluminous records of committee and council proceedings all are funneled through the dean's office. Most deans make a responsible effort to screen their own mail, and to pick up information that is useful. Some use the telephone or computer mail networks to stay in touch. But deans are busy people, and they cannot possibly find out everything it would be useful for them to know. They depend on their department chairs to play an active role in communicating. Chairs should learn what the dean considers an effective way to communicate, and master it.

There is one extremely ineffective style of communicating with deans: keeping secrets and waiting until problems become crises. Chairs who go to a dean with a plea for a budget bailout, or who undertake to discipline a faculty member, or whose faculty votes to reject a new program proposal initiated by the dean without having taken the trouble to pass along useful information and perspective prior to the fact, will find—at best—a cool reception in the dean's suite. Chairs may feel that the dean is paid to deal with crises, and that problems can simply be dumped at the door. Chairs who adopt this attitude will have short terms in office; short and unhappy. Deans are human, and they mightily resent having to solve others' problems. They especially resent being blindsided by situations already out of control.

Chairs, on the other hand, may fear the open and candid sharing of their own problems. Deans, they assume, will not want to hear bad news, nor hear that the chair needs advice and support. To the contrary, a dean is experienced enough to know that no department is free of problems. The dean, understandably, does not want to be in the position of solving every such problem. Chairs are expected to take as much responsibility as possible. But deans need to *know about* potential problems, and their support for the chair is more likely to follow if they have had a hand in counseling the chair through early efforts to achieve resolution.

Since deans seldom have the time to seek out chairs for regular consultation, chairs should assume that the burden is on them to schedule reasonably frequent face-to-face meetings. Usually, important issues need to be discussed, options explored, and solutions worked out jointly. Communication by memo or electronic mail seldom permits the kind of understanding that can be achieved in a personal conversation.

Depending on the dean's calendar and routine, such face-to-face meetings may be as regular as a standing weekly lunch date, or as infrequent as a half-hour talk every two months. The chair should be highly sensitive to the way in which this schedule affects the dean's impression, and he may even want to keep an informal diary as a reminder of things that have been discussed, agreements that have been reached, follow-up activities to be conducted, and sources of potential disagreement or conflict. If meetings are infrequent such a record becomes critical, because the chair's memory may be selective, and he or she may approach subsequent meetings with agenda that do not bear any relationship to the dean's expectations.

Chairs should prepare carefully for each meeting with the dean. Although the relationship may be a personal one, and although the dean may be relaxed and informal, his or her time is valuable, and there is an expectation that the chair will have an agenda, information worth sharing, and questions that only the dean can answer. Deans like to hear good news, so it is almost always a good idea to let them be the first to hear about accomplishments that bring credit to the university. Deans are not afraid to deal with problems, but rather like to be involved in preventing them or in helping the chair solve them while they are still manageable. Part of the agenda should be in dealing with anticipated events and issues—items on which the chair seeks perspective and advice prior to any action. Obviously, if a problem is developing and the chair is in less than complete control of events, this should be shared.

In some cases the chair must communicate immediately, not waiting for a routine standing appointment. But deans should never be surprised with unwelcome news. They especially should not have to deal with faculty, staff, or students referred to them without notice. Sending an angry person to one's superior is guaranteed to create the impression that one is incompetent or out of control, or both. The dean will undoubtedly lose some confidence in the chair after two or three such episodes.

Obviously, trust is best developed when both sides in a relationship learn how to anticipate what another is likely to do. It is also built through open communication and a mutual effort to keep each other fully informed. Chairs often must take more of the burden in this relationship; they put themselves at considerable risk if they fail to find the best way to communicate with the dean and if they do not use available channels effectively.

Dealing with the Bureaucracy

As large corporate entities, universities accumulate bureaucracy. These offices are needed to maintain facilities, to keep money flowing, to hire and supervise literally thousands of employees, to process grants and contracts, to admit students, to house and feed them, to assure compliance with dozens of state and federal laws, to publicize the institution, and to secure gifts and contributions. To new chairs the scope and power of the bureaucracy may be intimidating, or at least discouraging. Certainly its complexity is daunting.

Although the bureaucracy may appear neither helpful nor useful to the chair, its reason for being is to be both. The chair will find getting things done is easier in direct proportion to the extent that he or she has the cooperation and assistance of specialists in the various departments, nooks, and crannies of the bureaucracy. Several offices are likely to be particularly worth cultivating.

Departments depend heavily on having competent, efficient staff. These people are usually recruited, screened, classified, and evaluated by a university-wide personnel department. Personnel specialists also negotiate contracts with unions for various civil service units, and are thoroughly knowledgeable about the rules for all nonfaculty employees. The personnel department is particularly helpful in two respects: They can assist a department in analyzing its staff needs and locating employees of the right class to fill jobs. They can also provide guidance and support when disputes or problems arise in the performance of a staff person. Getting to know the institution's personnel officer (or staff) may smooth the way when help is required.

Budgeting sets the stage for many decisions about the department's future. The department chair may have to deal with several key people in the process of putting the budget request together. Formally, the dean and his or her staff will ordinarily transmit information about the calendar for budgeting, guidelines as to what should be included, and how the department's case should be presented. The dean may set general policy guidelines in response to directives from the provost and/or president. The dean also will have particular guidelines in mind for the college's budget. Since all of these guidelines are well established before the department chair ever sees a call for his or her own budget request, any special issues that may be important to the department should be raised and discussed with the dean well before the formal process gets under way. This means that the chair must be thinking about the actual budget year two years ahead of time.

There is usually a person in the dean's office whose responsibility is to handle the technical routine of budgeting, and to implement all the procedures and guidelines according to deadlines and time frames. These individuals, although they typically play a very limited role in making judgments about budget policy, are also very likely to be the best-informed people about how to get what one needs from the budget process. They may also be powerful if they have been in place very long, and if they have information with which to be influential. It is wise to use these people for counsel and guidance, and to be prompt and responsive when information is requested by them.

There are also people in the dean's office who are in a position to help the department chair. They process vouchers and faculty or staff contracts, approve purchases, distribute paychecks, and handle all the routine business functions that keep the college and department going on a day-by-day basis. Almost always invisible to the chair, the business office is the hub of the college's operational work, and is often the key unit from which departmental staff take their cues. Because they can make a very large difference in the department's ability to do its business, the staff of this office are people who should be cultivated. Not only are they in a position to process paperwork and approve or disapprove important transactions, but they are often avenues to other university business operations wherein it may be helpful to have good contacts.

Many departments have grants and contracts with various agencies. The university almost always delegates responsibility for processing grants through a separate office—sometimes housed in a vice-presidential unit, and sometimes in the graduate dean's office. This office may have final authority to obligate the university in any grant or contract relationship. Faculty, department chairs, or deans may not have any authority in these matters at all. Grants and contracts people can decline to approve a grant application, and they can insist that faculty principal investigators live up to grant or contract terms during the project. They also may have the power to audit projects to assure fiscal responsibility, protection of human subjects, and compliance with various laws and regulations. Grants and contracts administrators are sometimes in a position to take the side of the funding agency in any dispute. They are potentially important people to any department that processes a significant amount of external funding.

Chairs will find that there are other university administrative offices on campus whose work, while comparatively anonymous, may nevertheless affect substantially the ability of the department to do its work. Although almost always nonfaculty, these people are relatively senior in standing, know a great deal about the rules and operations of the university, and sometimes have substantial power. A chair may be unaccustomed to working with or socializing with nonfaculty, and may even be uncomfortable in doing so. But an effective department chair will personally take the time to learn from and cultivate the key actors in the university bureaucracy. He or she will also encourage department support staff to get to know the support staff in these administrative offices. They can help plan, assist with the inevitable flow of paperwork, and serve as resource people when problems arise. They sincerely want to be helpful and to do their jobs in a constructive way. To be treated with respect and to feel that they are authorities about their specialties is flattering—especially when they seldom experience deferential treatment from academics. A chair who takes the time to get to know and respect the nonacademic bureaucracy may have unusual success in cultivating allies and supporters who will be tremendously useful when the chair finds he or she most needs help.

Among the units the chair may wish to cultivate are the travel office, through which faculty travel requests and expense reimbursements pass (more or less smoothly); the payroll office, which processes paychecks; and the purchasing office, which processes orders, vouchers, and other evidence of dealings with vendors. Building maintenance and campus security can be particularly important units for departments that have laboratories, storerooms, and other substantial facilities to maintain and protect. If people in these units feel comfortable approaching the chair, they may be quick to point out hazards and potential security problems, and serve to prevent losses.

In this chapter the chairs' relations with various important administrative offices has been explored. For most chairs, learning the administrative side is a considerable challenge. That challenge can be reduced to the extent that the chair is willing to make friends and allies of people in the administrative chain of command. These individuals are in a position to help keep the machinery of the department running smoothly so that the faculty under the leadership of the chair can perform their teaching, research, and service functions with a minimum number of unnecessary delays and interruptions.

Questions

1. How would you describe the leadership and management style of your dean? In what ways does this dean differ from other deans you know or have known?

2. List several ways that your dean's decisions affected your department within the last two years. To what extent were the outcomes beneficial to you or to your faculty?

3. To what extent do you have regular meetings with the dean on a one-to-one basis? Are these meetings frequent enough to ensure a strong communication link between yourself and the dean?

4. To what extent is the dean aware of the achievements of your department? Of honors or awards received by your faculty members or students? Of the problems in your department?

5. To what extent are you aware of the goals or aspirations that the dean has for the college as a whole, or for your department in particular?

6. To what extent do you as chairperson, or the support staff of the department, have positive working relationships with individuals in the institution who have administrative responsibility for processing budget expenditures, contracts and grants, travel, personnel, and so on?

7. Think of an area in your department which needs improvements that can only occur with the dean's help. Develop a plan to enlist the dean's

assistance in making the necessary changes. Can you name support staff in your department and in the dean's office who can help you implement this plan?

References

ANDERSON, G. LESTER. "Organizational Diversity." In *New Directions for Institutional Research: Examining Departmental Management,* no. 10, edited by John C. Smart and James R. Montgomery. San Francisco: Jossey–Bass, 1976.

BLUMBERG, ARTHUR. "Beyond Something Called the Deanship: A Story About a Memorable Academic Leader." *Teachers College Record,* 1988, pp. 85–98.

BOGGS, GEORGE R. *Pathways to the Presidency.* Paper presented at the Annual Convention of the American Association of Community and Junior Colleges, 1988. (ERIC Document Reproduction Service No. ED 306 973)

BOK, DEREK. *Higher Learning.* Cambridge: Harvard University Press, 1986.

CARTWRIGHT, DORWIN, and ZANDER, ALVIN (Eds.) *Group Dynamics: Research and Theory.* 3rd ed. New York: Harper & Row, 1968.

CHACKO, HARSHA E. *Administrators' Method of Upward Influence and Perceptions of Their Supervisors' Leadership Styles.* Paper presented at the Annual Meeting of the AERA, New Orleans, 1988. (ERIC Document Reproduction Service No. ED 296 476)

CLARK, BURTON R. *The Academic Life. Small Worlds. Different Worlds.* A Carnegie Foundation Special Report. Princeton: The Carnegie Foundation, 1987.

COHEN, ARTHUR M., and BRAWER, FLORENCE B. *The American Community College.* 2nd ed. San Francisco: Jossey–Bass, 1988.

COHEN, MICHAEL D., and MARCH, JAMES G. (Eds.) *Leadership and Ambiguity: The American College President.* Carnegie Commission on Higher Education. New York: McGraw–Hill, 1974.

CORSON, JOHN J. *The Governance of Colleges and Universities.* New York: McGraw–Hill, 1960.

GAINES, FRANCIS P. *Presidents and Deans: A Changing Academic Scene.* Tucson: University Associates, 1987.

HERR, KAY U. *Chairperson's Handbook.* 1989. (ERIC Document Reproduction Service No. ED 311 838)

KINGSTON, NEAL M. *The Graduate Record Examinations Validity Study Service: Yesterday and Tomorrow.* Princeton: Educational Testing Service, 1986. (ERIC Document Reproduction Service No. ED 300 452)

LOUIS, KAREN S. (et al.) *University Policies and Ethical Issues in Graduate Research and Education.* Results of a Survey of Graduate School Deans. ASHE 1988 Annual Meeting Paper, 1988. (ERIC Document Reproduction Service No. ED 303 100)

LYNCH, DAVID M. (et al.) "Chief Liberal Arts Academic Officers: The Limits of Power and Authority." *Studies in Higher Education,* 12 (1), 1987, pp. 39–50.

MACCOBY, MICHAEL. *The Gamesman.* New York: Simon & Shuster, 1977.

MARCH, JAMES G. *How We Talk and How We Act: Administrative Theory and Administrative Life.* Urbana: University of Illinois Press, 1980.

MARTIN, JOSEF. *To Rise Above Principle: The Memoirs of an Unreconstructed Dean.* Champaign: University of Illinois Press, 1988. (ERIC Document Reproduction Service No. ED 295 548)

McCarty, Donald J., and Reyes, Pedro. *Models of Institutional Governance: Academic Deans' Decision-making Patterns as Evidenced by Chairpersons.* ASHE 1985 Annual Meeting Paper, Chicago, 1985. (ERIC Reproduction Service No. ED 259 641)

―――. "Organizational Models of Governance: Academic Deans' Decision-making Styles." *Journal of Teacher Education,* 38, 1987, pp. 2–8.

McFerron, J. Richard (et al.) "Assessing and Supporting Quality in the Liberal Arts: The Role of the Chief Liberal Arts Academic Officer." *Journal of Education Administration,* 26 (2), 1988, p. 393–407.

Millett, John D. *New Structures of Campus Power: Success and Failures of Emerging Forms of Institutional Governance.* San Francisco: Jossey–Bass, 1978.

Rasch, Carla. "Sources of Stress Among Administrators at Research Universities." *Review of Higher Education,* 9, 1986, pp. 419–434.

Richman, Barry M., and Farmer, Richard N. *Leadership, Goals, and Power in Higher Education: A Contingency and Open-Systems Approach to Effective Management.* San Francisco: Jossey–Bass, 1974.

Reyes, Pedro, and Smith, Gregory. *Faculty and Academic Staff Participation in Academic Governance: The Social Contract Model.* ASHE 1987 Annual Meeting Paper, San Diego, 1987. (ERIC Document Reproduction Service No. ED 281 446)

Reyes, Pedro, and Twombly, Susan B. "Perceptions of Contemporary Governance in Community Colleges: An Empirical Study." *Community College Review,* 14, 1987, pp. 4–12.

Sagaria, Mary Ann D., and Johnsrud, Linda K. *Administrative Intrainstitutional Mobility: The Structuring of Opportunity.* ASHE Annual Meeting Paper, San Francisco, February 1987. (ERIC Document Reproduction Service No. ED 281 445)

Sagaria, Mary Ann D., and Krotseng, Marsha V. "Deans' Managerial Skills: What They Need and What They Bring to a Job." *Journal of the College and University Personnel Association,* 37, 1986, pp. 1–7.

Semlack, William D. *Corporate Culture in a University Setting: An Analysis of Theory "X," Theory "Y," and Theory "Z" Cultures Within University Academic Departments.* Paper presented at the Annual Meeting of the Central States Speech Association, Cincinnati, 1986. (ERIC Document Reproduction Service No. ED 269 822)

Sprunger, Benjamin E., and Bergquist, William H. *Handbook for College Administration.* Washington, DC: Council for the Advancement of Small Colleges, 1980.

Tight, Malcolm (Ed.) *Academic Freedom and Responsibility.* Philadelphia: Open University Press, 1988.

Tote, Lawrence S. *The Successful Presidency as a Shared Responsibility.* Abstract of remarks and survey data for distribution to Pennsylvania Community College Presidents and Trustees. Harrisburg: Pennsylvania Association of Colleges and Universities, 1986.

Tucker, Allan, and Bryan, Robert. *The Academic Dean: Dove, Dragon, and Diplomat.* 2nd ed. New York: American Council on Education/Macmillan, 1991.

Twombly, Susan B. *Career Lines of Top-level Two-year College Administrators: Implications for Leadership in a New Era.* ASHE Annual Meeting Paper, San Antonio, 1986. (ERIC Document Reproduction Service No. ED 268 884)

Whitmore, Jon. *Handbook for Theatre Department Chairs.* Association for Communication Administration. Annondale, VA: Council of Theatre Chairs and Deans, 1988. (ERIC Reproduction Service No. ED 305 855)

Chapter *29*

Dealing with External Agencies

Departments do not exist in isolation. They depend on other offices or agencies for resources, for program approval, for policies that support or regulate professional practice, and for accreditation. Sometimes public attention comes to the department whether it seeks such or not. Chairs may find themselves dealing with many different people and agencies external to the university, and frequently these people and agencies have the power to affect public perceptions of the department, as well as its long-term success and health.

Alumni and Friends

The most significant external group is the alumni and friends who feel at least a nominal loyalty to the department. They have either completed a degree or received a valuable service from the department. They are in a position to know some of the faculty and students, and often are in a position to help the department in a variety of ways. Occasionally a department is fortunate enough to have an alumnus in a position to help in some very major way—perhaps donating an endowed chair, or helping to recruit others who could do so.

Although a new chair may not have personal connections or other contacts with alumni and friends, it is very important that they be cultivated at appropriate opportunities. The chair may feel at first that this is a task best handled by the alumni association or fund-raising office. After all, these offices are equipped with mailing lists, staff, information, and marketing expertise. But communications from the alumni office (or any other office, including the president's) frequently suffer from being very broad in theme, and seldom cover developments of real interest within individual departments. If the chair is interested in keeping its alumni informed and their attention focused on the department, then some kind of specialized media may be needed.

Alumni like to feel that their degrees have at least as much value as ever before. This means they would like to know how well-known the department and its faculty are. They take pride in knowing about new grants, projects, and publications, and about attention the department may have achieved in the news media; and that new students are (a) more numerous and (b) more able than ever. They also like to feel that the department remembers them and takes pride in their achievements. They relish news of both their own accomplishments and those of their classmates, mentors, and friends.

Although informing alumni is a way of maintaining their loyalties and interests, an even better way to engage them is to ask their help with occasional projects. They may find it mildly alienating to be remembered only when the university mounts a fund-raising campaign, but will feel flattered to be asked to serve on a committee or task force. The assignment may be as benign as serving with a group that will recruit new students in a given city or state, or that will help students find jobs in a certain industry or professional field. Alumni whose professional achievements represent real leadership and substance can be of particular help. Not only can they serve as role models for students (and perhaps even for faculty) in the department, but they also can represent the department to great advantage in public or professional forums. In some cases they can serve as particularly good advisers on curriculum, research, and other academic matters.

Communication with alumni may not yield any immediate measurable results. But keeping the lines of communication open will help sustain the loyalties of the department's supporters. It can also help by occasionally prompting someone to lend a hand when he or she might otherwise not have been aware of a need. On rare occasions, staying in touch with alumni will produce a major coup—the endowed chair, a research fund for graduate students, scholarship aid funds, or something of the sort.

One word of caution is in order: Not all alumni are benign. Some nurse grudges or hostilities, perhaps the result of a long-forgotten incident, and perhaps even of something that had nothing to do with the department itself. Whatever the causes, real or imagined, an occasional alumnus is sure to be motivated to vent dissatisfaction. There is no formula for dealing with this kind of person, except to put as much distance as possible between him or her and the department. There is usually no way to satisfy the complainant, nor any point in trying to do so unless there is actually something the chair can and should do to provide a remedy. Under most conditions the vengeful or vindictive alumnus is to be studiously avoided, if not totally ignored.

Occasionally an alumnus will become overinvolved to the point of harassing the chair with "good" ideas. While one welcomes support from almost every quarter, this sort of helpfulness can be distracting. The chair may best attempt to be cordial and receptive in an indirect way without ever passing judgment on the merits of the ideas proffered, and without ever acting on them. Of course, after several attempts the alumnus may express hurt that his or her ideas are never put into effect. The chair may then have to explain to this person why his or her support is important and welcomed, but also that perhaps another and better channel for this enthusiasm can be found.

Parents

Although not a formal "agency," parents form a powerful external constituency. At many institutions parents are organized into formal groups, and provide both feedback and support. They represent important consumer interests, and their overall satisfaction can be both politically and financially important. Many parents are loyal supporters of their children's institutions, and become long-term donors.

Parental involvement is to be welcomed, particularly when it is informed involvement. Some parents will simply take a defensive posture, becoming contentious whenever their son or daughter encounters a problem of an academic or personal nature. Most parents, however, expect the institution to educate in the broadest possible terms. Their expectations are high, and they know their children will be challenged and stretched during their college years.

The most difficult aspect of parents' roles during their children's college years is coming to terms with independence. In the traditional middle-class family, parents have assumed tremendous responsibility for eighteen years, and have often involved themselves on a daily basis in their children's lives. Suddenly they are no longer involved, and they miss the daily feedback on activities and progress. Chairs must realize that privacy laws prevent them from communicating to a substantial degree with *any* third party, including parents, regarding a student's progress and achievement. College or university guidelines about such communication should be carefully reviewed, but chairs may have to tell a concerned parent that he or she will have to discuss the matter directly with the student. The chair may, of course, represent to the student that it would be wise to keep parents informed, and that talking with parents does not compromise newly found autonomy. But students relish their freedom and their perceived adult independence. In short, chairs may have to find a way to mediate when students want to flee the nest and parents want to maintain control and involvement.

As much as they have invested in the institution, parents who are paying tuition and other expenses will want to have the value of their investment preserved and enhanced. They will be interested in how well the institution compares to others, and to any particular news about their own sons and daughters. New grants and programs, faculty accomplishments, and honors and awards achieved by students all are newsworthy. Periodic college or university-wide reports to parents can be a good way to reassure them that they have invested in an active and thriving institution, and that their children are benefiting in some concrete way.

Boards of Trustees

Almost every institution in the U.S.—and the university as an institution is no exception—is controlled by a board of trustees. They are empowered to act on behalf of the corporate university, and usually have full power to approve programs, employment contracts, and policies governing all aspects of institutional life. Although boards of public institutions may be politically appointed, and although those of private institutions are self-perpetuating, most board members are lay people of considerable ability and stature. They may be prominent corporate or civic figures, or they may be present or former government officials. Individually, they have no authority. The board acts only as a board. But board members often work hard at their duties, and know a great deal about the university.

The principal contact with board members is the president, who is essentially hired directly by the board and serves as its agent in managing the university. Their official agenda is usually developed through consultation between the board chairman and the university president within guidelines established under bylaws and other legal requirements. The president also is responsible for information provided to board members, and often is an ex officio member of the board.

Chairs seldom have opportunities for direct communication with the board. They may occasionally prepare items of information for the board's benefit. They may now and again be invited to a dinner or social occasion at which board members may be present. They may even get to know one or two individual board members fairly well, especially if there has been a special interest shown by the same in the department's subject matter, or the alumni are represented thereby. But the chair seldom is invited to attend a board meeting, and may even less often be asked to speak to the group in its official capacity. The board prefers to work directly with the president, and to be able to hold the president accountable for all aspects of institutional management. The chair may best serve his own interests and those of the department by communicating through regular administrative channels on matters of potential concern to the board.

Instructional and Professional Accrediting Bodies

Regional accrediting agencies accredit the university or college. Professional accrediting bodies accredit individual degree programs or departments. In law, medicine, business, education, and other professional fields, professional accrediting agencies may accredit the entire school (or certain groups of programs). In addition to external accreditation, many institutions have internal program reviews, and some states conduct their own program reviews at public institutions. The chair may have to contend with as many as two or three different program reviews during a normal term in office.

The ultimate goal of all program reviews is an objective, factual assessment of conditions under which students are educated. Essentially, such program reviews look at whether the conditions are those normally associated with acceptable quality. If not, the review normally concludes with recommendations for change and improvement. Seldom does an external agency make direct qualitative judgments about an individual program. It usually assesses a set of indicators, and those indicators are customarily *associated with* quality.

The key to dealing with program reviews and external accrediting bodies is preparation. Procedures vary from one agency to another, and each defines and describes the standards by which it will review the program. Considerable advance notice of such reviews is almost always available. Generally, a department or program will know at least a year in advance when a review team will be visiting. In the case of a regional accreditation, the lead time is virtually always longer than that.

Once notice of a review is confirmed, the protocol for preparing a self-study report is almost always put in the chair's hands, along with suggested time frames for completing the essential tasks. With a long period of time available before any formal report is due, the chair may be tempted to procrastinate. It is important to point out, though, that the chair will serve the department and institution far better by taking the review seriously, and proceeding to conduct the self-study according to the timetable.

The most important factor is that a valid program review requires good data. Often this means conducting surveys of alumni, students, and others. It also may mean extensive data-gathering in departmental files which may be organized different from the way that accrediting bodies' information needs demand. It is important that the data gathered be as complete and valid as possible, because the department will have to live with the results of the program review for some years. Waiting until the last minute before organizing or collecting the required data will, in itself, leave an impression of a poorly administered department, and may even result in having less than complete or accurate data on which to rely.

The second reason to begin work on the self-study promptly is that this is an opportunity to involve faculty and others in a serious and objective review of the status of departmental programs. If the chair involves as many of the key actors as possible, a self-study can heighten awareness and prepare the faculty for eventual changes. Furthermore, involving people in the self-study and providing them with the time and resources to do a thorough job will result in an informed and consistent set of interviews when the accrediting team visits and conducts its review. (Even if there is no clear consensus on recommended changes, at least everyone will have the same information from which to begin the conversation.)

Sometimes, departments will use the accrediting process as leverage against the dean or the central administration. They will purposely represent their situation as requiring more new resources and a higher level of priority on the dean's or president's agenda. Professional accrediting bodies may be susceptible to such an appeal. But the chair should be aware that deans and presidents receive reports from all accrediting bodies that visit the institution, and that many of these bodies reach the same conclusion. The resulting impression is that *all* accredited fields seem to need more resources and more attention.

It may be good strategy to put one's case in the strongest terms when an accrediting body is available to support the argument. But there are risks, too. If the field looks too weak, it might provoke the central administration to wonder if it can be fixed at any price—and, therefore, if it would be better to discontinue the program. Chairs are well advised to use the accreditation process to conduct nothing more or less than a strictly objective review. They should foster openness and candor in the process, and should work toward getting the best data available. A cooperative attitude and good faith preparation of the self-study will serve the whole process well.

Government Agencies and Legislators

Some departments have extensive relations with state agencies. They may consult or advise, as a biology or forestry department may advise a state department of natural resources. They may have research and development grants, as a college of education may support a department of education's test-development section. They may be regulated by a department with responsibility for licensure of a certain profession. Or they may have relations with several agencies across a wide spectrum of issues.

Public institutions have special concerns insofar as they may have to satisfy several agencies with considerable authority over colleges and universities: The governor's office, the legislature, state coordinating boards for higher education (or governing boards), the department of education, state controllers and auditors, and agencies that regulate labor relations and public health and safety may all request information or action that will require the chair's attention. Although these contacts are usually mediated by someone in the university's central administration, they are not always handled this way; and, in any event, there are special concerns whenever a state agency is involved. Almost any contact with a government agency may have legal and/or political implications for the corporate university. Whatever may prompt a chair to pursue such contact should be carefully and thoroughly considered. Except in the case of consulting or research agreements, both of which will likely have to be approved by the grants and contracts offices of the university and the government agency, other contacts with state government are best managed through the central university administration.

From time to time, chairs may develop acquaintances with legislators. They may share information, and serve an occasional legislator in helpful ways. It may be tempting to try and turn such a relationship to the department's advantage by engineering a special appropriation or program in return for the good will one has engendered. Occasionally this kind of arrangement works and works spectacularly well. But there may be hidden costs, and the chair should be fully aware of the risks. Most public university appropriations are the product of as much as two years' preparation. Many different claims to new resources are filtered through the university's budget request process, and delicate balances are struck with many different units on campus about the queuing of priorities.

The chair should obtain approval from the dean and the provost prior to negotiating over a separate issue, and this should be part of the university's overall budget plan. If the dean and provost do not know about a special appropriation that has been engineered outside the normal process, they may perceive the resulting allocation as a challenge to their authority. The chair can anticipate that a dean or a provost may be upset that someone has "gone off the reservation," and may very well decide to take compensating action against the chair. Among other possibilities, the chair could find the department's original budget reduced by the same amount as the special appropriation, thereby neutralizing whatever effort has gone into achieving new funding. Certainly the chair will find that his or her future actions get much tighter scrutiny from other offices, and that precious credibility with key administrators may suffer.

There may be times when the chair (and faculty) will be tempted to involve themselves in issues that have political ramifications. As citizens, and as professional people, they have the right and duty to speak and to advocate. However, they are also employees of the university. Those at state-supported universities often are considered employees of the state. Sometimes, faculty members are not sensitive to the line between these two roles. For example, a faculty member might write a strong letter to a legislator on official stationery, opposing that legislator's position on an issue of concern to the university. The legislator could properly question whether university funds were used to produce the letter, and could embarrass the university by pointing out that lobbying with state funds is not only wrong, but illegal.

Faculty may also attend legislative hearings, testify on their own initiative, and visit with legislators in their offices. As citizens, they are certainly free to do so. But they are not free to do so if they are using university time and resources, or if they appear in their official capacity to oppose positions taken by university administrators. The chair should be sensitive to the fine line that must be drawn between the role of citizen and that of university employee. That distinction applies to faculty, and particularly to chairs, who are essentially members of the administrative team.

It is probably wise to separate contacts with government (state or federal) into two categories, one involving expertise and the other the corporate interests of the institution. Chairs and faculty alike may field calls from government agencies with requests for consulting and other kinds of assistance. Usually there is good reason to facilitate this kind of assistance. Chairs would want to have the best-qualified faculty supporting the research, development, and policy-making activities of government. On the other hand, the corporate university has numerous contacts with government, too—contacts that may cover a range of issues (many with long and tangled histories) and affect virtually all departments in the university. Furthermore, "government" is not a single entity pursuing a single agenda. It is a highly pluralistic set of agencies and interests.

Frequently the agendas being pursued by the various actors have more to do with power than with substance. Corporate university relations with government take account of both the jumbled political scene and the traditional interests of the university. Occasionally the university will want to engage a chair or a faculty member in preparing testimony for the president or a vice-president, but more often these corporate relations are handled as a matter of policy established by the board of trustees upon advice and counsel from the president. Unless called upon to assist in these matters, chairs are well advised to leave contacts with government to the central administration. Certainly if one feels strongly about an issue involving state or federal policy, the best avenue to express that concern would be through university administrative channels.

Foundations

Sometimes departments will seek support from private foundations for specific projects or occasionally for support of longer-term thematic work. (Preparation of minority and female scientists, for example, might attract long-term support of a particular foundation.) Foundations are generally cautious and conservative about supporting projects. They are besieged with "good ideas," and often have to deal with several informal approaches from people connected with one university.

There are a few ground rules that chairs might remember when dealing with foundations. The most important is that foundations have limited resources and establish very strict priorities for grants. Although a particular foundation may have established a set of priorities at one time, there is no guarantee that the same priorities will be in place when a department wishes to make application for funding. The first step, therefore, must be to establish that a foundation's priorities permit them to consider a project such as the one being proposed.

The second major principle is that foundations do not and cannot provide substantive program support for an indefinite period of time. They can provide startup or seed funding to get a good idea into operation, but they will expect a commitment from the university or college to take over funding and keep the project alive in the future.

Third, foundations must deal with the corporate institution. They may support individual projects, and even individual investigators, but they usually act as one corporate entity relating to another. This usually means they will require letters of endorsement from the university president, and it also means that they will not support more than a limited number of projects from any given institution at any one time. If they are already funding several projects at the chair's institution, they probably will entertain a new proposal, no matter how deserving, with considerable reservations.

Finally, foundations seldom fund projects at first sight. They almost always want some kind of introduction to the prospective principal investigator and some kind of discussion about the nature of the project. Essentially, this boils down to having an opportunity to get to know who will be spending the foundation's money, for what it will really be spent, and whether the program officer can promise the foundation board that the project will reflect well on the foundation. If the chair does not know someone well at the foundation, it may be very important to find an intermediary at the institution who can handle introductions and smooth the way. Often a letter from the university president accompanying a preliminary inquiry to a foundation is helpful and persuasive.

The Press

Media attention, particularly for accomplishments by faculty or students, is to be welcomed. Chairs may wish to attract such attention by developing a public relations strategy, but they will also have to deal with press contacts that are unexpected and sometimes unwelcome. How the chair manages these contacts and inquiries will have an effect on how the department (and the chair) is represented to the public.

Virtually every university maintains a helpful and effective media relations office. Often staffed by professional journalists, such offices can help in a variety of useful ways. They can, for example, help the chair plot a public relations strategy. If they are aware that certain people in the department, or certain projects, might be of considerable (and positive) public interest, they can help pull information together that will be useful in developing a public relations effort. They will also have some feeling for the media that will be most appropriately interested in the theme or story. The media relations office knows what goes into making a good newspaper story or television news item, and they know how best to present that information to the reporters or editors working on the story. They may also have a good feeling for the timing factors involved in placing news or special-interest stories. (Is it of interest today? Or is it something that a newspaper is more likely to use in a Sunday edition?) Some information will be useful to have on file in the media relations office for use when the volume of press inquiries becomes particularly heavy.

The media relations office can be particularly helpful when dealing with press-initiated inquiries. Chairs may be contacted about a variety of subjects. Sometimes they are contacted because the press may think of them as experts on some particularly newsworthy subject. Other times it may be regarding a dispute with a faculty member or student. Or it may be about some other university issue on which the reporter is seeking comment from many different people, such as the impact of a newly passed appropriation on how the university does its work.

There is no law that requires the chair to respond to any press inquiry, and there is no law that requires the chair to respond immediately, either. If the chair is being contacted for his or her own academic expertise, and feels able to respond in an effective way, then a response is probably appropriate. On the other hand, if the chair is being contacted as a university official, or is doubtful that his or her own point of view is sufficiently informed to be useful, then it may be better to ask the reporter to call back at another time. The chair should report this sort of media contact to the media relations office, and would be wise to seek counsel about responding.

The chair should treat all unsolicited media contacts with caution. The chances are good that the reporter already has a substantial amount of information (or opinion) to work with, and that the chair's answers or point of view will be tested for consistency with those of others. It is usually not a good idea to offer opinionated responses, or judgmental statements, as these will almost surely appear in a divisive light. It is always a good idea, on the other hand, to respond as factually as possible. This is only possible, though, if one has valid and current factual information on hand. For this reason, chairs should feel free to put reporters on hold until the chairs are comfortable that they have needed factual material available with which to frame responses to questions.

Chairs should also assess whether they are the best respondents to media inquiries. Sometimes reporters are unfamiliar with university organization, and may not know whom to contact. Chairs who get calls from media persons might reflect on the questions being asked, to see if they can help locate a better-informed or more appropriate person whom the reporter might best contact. It may be, for example, that the call is about a faculty member's project, public mention of which would do the department some good. The chair might take the time to locate and help prepare the faculty member for an interview, perhaps by alerting the media relations office and requesting their help in preparing.

Most reporters are trying to write fair and objective stories—stories that will have legitimate interest among a wide range of readers or viewers. They appreciate cooperative and helpful story subjects. Chairs who find themselves being interviewed can help by sympathizing with reporters' needs. Short, concise, factual responses are useful. Reporters need concrete examples and specific, operational details. They cannot use abstract or theoretical material, and will be less likely to publish or air a story that cannot be told effectively to the average consumer. They are also not impressed by academics! So the chair is well advised to help the reporter by working with him or her to prepare a story that the editor will like and use, perhaps even in a prominent spot. The reporter will be a far better judge than the chair of how this can be achieved.

Questions

1. List the types of external agencies that deal directly with your department. Create suggestions for strengthening the relationship with each type of agency listed.

2. Does your department publish a newsletter for alumni, friends, and associates? If not, would it be a good idea to start one? To what extent could your support staff and graduate or undergraduate students be involved in such a project?

3. When was the last time your department was mentioned in the institutional alumni publication? Think of several faculty accomplishments

worthy of recognition in any institutional publication and/or the local media. Were these accomplishments described in any news releases?

4. To what extent does your department keep an updated media file containing a record of faculty and student accomplishments?

5. Cite all the accrediting bodies associated with your department and with the school or college. When did the last review take place? Have you seen your department's ratings?

6. To what extent were there additional incentives available to faculty who seek untapped sources of funding? Do you provide adequate support and collaborative opportunities for faculty and students?

7. To what extent do members of the support staff or your faculty members possess particularly strong grant-writing abilities? To what extent are there individuals who might work well with members of your department on joint projects?

8. To what extent does your department have clear-cut written guidelines for handling grants and contracts?

References

BARAK, ROBERT (et al.) *The Arizona Board of Regents Task Force on Excellence, Efficiency and Competitiveness*. Final Report and Working Papers (4 volumes total). 1988. (ERIC Document Reproduction Service No. ED 306 803)

BIRNBAUM, ROBERT. *Individual Preferences and Organizational Goals: Consistency and Diversity in the Futures Desired by Campus Leaders*. ASHE Annual Meeting Paper, Baltimore, 1987. (ERIC Document Reproduction Service No. ED 292 384)

CLARKE, MARIANNE (et al.) *The Role of Science and Technology in Economic Competitiveness*. Final Report. National Governors' Association Center for Policy Research and Analysis. Washington. DC 1987. (ERIC Document Reproduction Service No. ED 293 696)

CORSON, JOHN J. *The Governance of Colleges and Universities*. New York: McGraw–Hill, 1960.

CURTIS, DAN B. *Marketing the Training Course On- and Off-campus*. 1984. (ERIC Document Reproduction Service No. ED 251 873)

HALSTEAD, KENT. *State Profiles: Financing Public Higher Education, 1978 to 1990*. Washington, DC: Research Associates of Washington, 1991.

HINES, EDWARD R. "State Leadership in Higher Education." *Higher Education and State Governments, Renewed Partnership, Cooperation, or Competition*. Washington, DC: ASHE/ERIC Higher Education Research Reports, 6, 1982.

KAIKAI, SEPTIMUS M., and KAIKAI, REGINA E. *Chairpersons as Promoters of Community Service*. Catonsville, MD: Catonsville Community College, 1990. (ERIC Document Reproduction Service No. ED 321 801)

LYNCH, DAVID, and BOWKER, LEE. *The Status of Adult and Continuing Education Within American Institutions of Higher Learning*. Indiana University of Pennsylvania Institute for Advanced Research, 1989. (ERIC Document Reproduction Service No. ED 311 816)

MALM, LINDA. *Leadership Practice: How I Raised $100,000 This Year with No Fund Raising Experience.* 1990. (ERIC Document Reproduction Service No. ED 319 423)

MILGRAM, STANLEY. "Group Pressure and Action Against a Person." *Journal of Abnormal and Social Psychology,* August 1964, pp. 137–143.

NEWMAN, FRANK. "Taking the Helm." In *The Third Century: Twenty-six Prominent Americans Speculate on the Educational Future.* New Rochelle, NY: Change Magazine Press, 1976.

NOVAK, RICHARD. *State Issues in Higher Education: A Bibliography.* Washington, DC: American Association of State Colleges and Universities, Center for State Higher Education Policy and Finance, 1991.

RAINES, MAX (et al.) *Thinking Together About the New Century in Michigan Higher Education.* Project 90: A Priority Assessment from Professors of the College of Education, Michigan State University, 1987–1989. (ERIC Document Reproduction Service ED 311 943)

WATTENBARGER, JAMES L., and MERCER, SHERRY L. *Financing Community Colleges, 1988.* Washington, DC: American Association of Community and Junior Colleges, 1988. (ERIC Document Reproduction Service No. ED 292 533)

WOLANIN, THOMAS R. "Federal Policy Making in Higher Education." *AAUP Bulletin,* 61(4), December/Winter 1975.

Part XII

ASSESSMENT

Chapter 30. **Evaluating the Department**

Chapter 31. **Evaluating the Chair**

Evaluating the Department

Depending on its discipline and mission, a department may be evaluated in a variety of ways, and by as many as five or six different agencies. It is evaluated annually by the dean of its college. Graduate programs are periodically evaluated by university graduate councils. Undergraduate programs are occasionally evaluated by institutional or college councils or committees. Statewide governing and coordinating boards may conduct evaluations of programs and departments every five to ten years. State agencies responsible for issuing licenses to professional practitioners will evaluate programs and colleges that provide training to those professions. Regional institutional accrediting agencies regularly evaluate departmental programs as part of institutional accreditation. Accrediting bodies of national professional associations routinely evaluate departments and colleges that offer professional training. Federal agencies are sure to evaluate departments and programs applying for federal contracts and grants. Newspapers, magazines, and private organizations and associations conduct national surveys, or analyze data published by various federal and other agencies, and will assign national rankings to institutions and departments.

A department chair, during a typical term of office, may experience several evaluations, and in some instances more than one at the same time. In most cases the chair is required to assist the evaluators by providing them with information about the department. The chair is also expected to respond to evaluations, and when appropriate to present plans for change and/or improvement. A general perspective on what kinds of evaluations take place and how they are conducted can help the chair deal with these responsibilities. This chapter will therefore discuss some of the different types of evaluations that academic departments undergo.

Evaluation by the Dean of the College

The most important evaluation of a department or program is made by the dean of the college. It is the dean, after all, who determines how scarce resources will be allocated, and the grounds on which such decisions are made. Deans have to put each department in the broader context of the college's mission and their own plans for the college's future development. In evaluating the program, at least three criteria are considered—namely, the program's *worth, quality,* and *cost effectiveness.*

WORTH OF A DEPARTMENT

A dean's judgment of a department's or program's worth is based on at least three considerations. The first has to do with how essential the program is to the college's and university's mission. Does it have historic value for the college or university? How many other departments in the university depend on this department to offer service and elective courses to their majors?

The second consideration is concerned with the degree to which there are regional or national social needs for the program. The idea of social need often is judged in the marketplace or in the political arena—e.g., a program meets a social need if its graduates receive many job offers and command impressive salaries when they enter the job market. Many colleges and universities have special interpretations of social need. These interpretations are based on perceptions that students need to be educationally prepared to function as knowledgeable and intelligent citizens in public policy areas of society, to function effectively in a technological world, to be able to work effectively in foreign countries, and to be able to adapt to the possibility of multicareers.

The third consideration is concerned with the size of the student demand for courses offered by the program. How many students are majoring in the program, and how many majors from other programs are taking courses in this program? Changes in student demand do not by themselves tell a complete story. A high-quality program may lose students simply because of changes in social demand. During the decade of the mid-'70s to the mid-'80s, for example, enrollment in teacher education programs fell nearly by half nationally. There were significant demographic reasons for this, just as there will be significant demographic reasons for future increases in teacher education enrollments. High- and low-quality programs alike were affected by these trends.

On the other hand, enrollment trends can indicate whether programs are improving or failing to improve. In the case of departments with decreasing enrollments, the dean will want to know whether faculty members have become too narrow and specialized or whether the programs have lost their relevancy. Departments that have significant enrollment increases will also attract the attention of the dean. He or she will want to know whether students are enrolling to take advantage of low standards, or whether the departments are addressing positive social needs in ways that attract more conscientious students.

QUALITY OF A DEPARTMENT

In evaluating the quality of their departments and programs, deans consider many things. How well has a department articulated its goals and objectives; and, compared to other departments in the college, how much progress during the past year has this department made in achieving its goals with the resources available to it? How does the quality of a department compare with the quality of others in the same college? Departments in some colleges such as Arts and Sciences are of different disciplines (for example chemistry, sociology, English, literature) and may have different goals. Even though comparisons of departmental quality in such colleges are difficult to make, deans nevertheless must make them. They also must have an interest in knowing how their departments compare in quality to similar-discipline departments in other universities of similar size and reputation. For example, how does *this* biology department compare with biology departments in other institutions; and what kind of reputation does a given program have among peers regionally and nationally, and among those who employ significant numbers of the program's graduates?

Before discussing measures that are used to identify quality, let us review briefly the activities in which colleges and universities are engaged. Such activities include teaching, learning, research, and service. At some institutions, teaching is the priority activity and research is given much less importance. In some departments at larger and older universities, however, research may have a higher priority than teaching. These activities, translated into managerial terms, are called "process." What goes into the process is called "input," which at academic institutions consists of students, faculty, and resources. What comes out of the process are products or "outcomes," which include educated graduates, professional people, scholarly papers, and (in the case of research institutions) new thinking and new knowledge.

The term "quality" is difficult to define and, like "beauty," may in fact be in the eyes of the beholder. There is continuous debate among academics as to what constitutes quality in educational outcomes, and how to measure it. It is less difficult to assign quality factors to some of the ingredients in the input. The assumption is that if the ingredients are considered to be of both high quality and sufficient quantity, and the process is carried out well, it can be assumed that the outcomes will also be of high quality, even if the quality cannot always be measured exactly or quantitatively.

INPUT AND PROCESS.   The quality of a program, therefore, often is judged on the basis of input and process. For example, the quality of students in the program is measured by their SAT scores, where they placed in their high school graduating classes, and the academic reputations of the high schools from which they graduated. The quality of faculty is gauged by the prestige of the department or university from which they received their graduate training, and how they measure up against standard indexes of performance: Are they effective teachers? Are they current with respect to emerging trends and specialties? How well do they relate to practitioners and academics in the field? How frequently do their publications show up in the "good" journals? How well are they known among leaders in the field? Another input measurement sometimes used as an indicator of quality is how much external funding the department has received in the past several years.

Each of the "input" and "process" measures described above says something about whether the conditions for excellence are present in the department. None taken by itself would guarantee that the department is effective in either educating students or creating new knowledge. Nor would a "higher" standing on any of these measures guarantee that a department is "better" than another. Although it is certainly appropriate to compare departments for purposes of evaluation, it is not logically possible to infer that having more of some particular quality necessarily means that a department has achieved an outcome that is better.

OUTCOMES. Deans are also interested in learning about the "outcomes" of a program. What do the graduates of the program gain? What special values does the program add to its students, and how does it fit with overall university expectations? How does it fit with demand for graduates in the marketplace? How well do graduates in professional programs perform on state certification examinations such as the nursing examination, a basic-skills examination for beginning teachers, or the state bar examination for law school graduates? Have the faculty of the program made an effort to work cohesively toward some kind of intended outcome for program graduates? What kind of publication record do faculty members have? How much regional or national visibility have faculty members brought to the university through publications in nationally recognized journals and through leadership roles in national professional associations and learned societies?

COST EFFECTIVENESS OF A DEPARTMENT

Most institutions have at least comparative data on the cost effectiveness of their various programs. Each program is expected to generate a specified number of student credit hours in order to be cost-effective in terms of the number of faculty members it currently employs. Departments that generate fewer student credit hours than the specified number may face increasing pressure to justify their budgets and staffing. Departments that produce surplus credit hours may also cause concern to a dean who is worried about how the surplus enrollments will impact upon the quality of students' experiences in and out of the classroom. A dean, of course, will usually consider with favor programs that return new and/ or additional resources to the university for dollars invested. External funding in the form of grants for training or research projects may help departments with low enrollments receive an acceptable grade for cost effectiveness.

BALANCING WORTH, QUALITY, AND COST EFFECTIVENESS

Deans inevitably have to make *comparative judgments* among departments. Comparisons are complex, involving balancing the three criteria—worth, quality, and cost effectiveness. A department that is relatively inexpensive to operate may not be contributing at all to the institution's overall mission. Or it may even be detracting from the institution's drive to enhance its stature. In this situation, the department or program would not be considered cost-effective, since any cost that does not help the institution achieve its overall goals is arguably too high.

On the other hand, a department that may have demonstrable evidence of its effectiveness (e.g., it sends 90 percent of its majors to high-prestige graduate schools) may nevertheless be operating outside the boundaries of acceptable cost. This department may have relatively few students, a relatively high number of tenured full professors earning comparatively high salaries, and an annual travel budget that requires subsidies every year from the dean's contingency fund. Such a department may be living at an unsustainable level when other institutional demands are considered. Merely being effective does not prevent a conclusion that the department is too costly. Likewise, merely being inexpensive does not mean that the department will be judged effective.

In the end, the dean bases funding decisions on an overall evaluation of each department in the college. What should be done, for example, about a department that is high on worth but low on quality and cost effectiveness? Or conversely, what should be done about a department that is low on worth but high on quality? In some cases, the dean may decide to fund an almost excellent department to make it excellent rather than a less-than-adequate department to make it adequate. Sometimes the decision will be to provide funds for improving a less-than-adequate department, if its accreditation is in jeopardy.

Deans seek to "optimize," or balance, the distribution of resources to all departments in ways that support the university's mission. However, they will not tolerate for long a pattern of funding that drains resources for unaccountable purposes.

Evaluation by the Institution

Increasingly, colleges and universities are finding it useful to conduct their own internal evaluations of programs—whether for purposes of appearing accountable or, more substantively, for strategic planning. Internal evluations usually are conducted by teams of faculty peers and sometimes by students. Although the evaluators may have had some training, orientation, and/or experience in the conduct of evaluations, they may also vary widely in the interests, skills, and sensitivity they bring to the task. Often the department or program can do a great deal to assist and support the team.

The team's report may be important in setting the tone for negotiations with the dean or provost, regarding the department's or program's needs in future years. It is thus in the interest of the chair to think through carefully what the report ought to say, and to assist the evaluation team in gaining a full and candid picture of the program's current status and needs. Three major types of evaluation have emerged: assessment of institution-wide programs, in-depth assessment of selected departments, and assessment of graduate programs. These are discussed in the following sections.

ASSESSMENT OF INSTITUTION-WIDE PROGRAMS

Assessment of institution-wide programs provides data on the outcomes of undergraduate education across all fields and majors. Students are assessed to confirm that they can perform with the desired skills at the desired levels. In some cases these assessments may be very broad, including attention to the formation of esthetic and ethical judgments (in addition to the more common and traditional outcomes of undergraduate education). Departments can be compared to see if their majors are developing the outcomes desired by an overall college or university plan for the education of undergraduates.

IN-DEPTH ASSESSMENT OF SELECTED DEPARTMENTS

A second kind of assessment looks in depth at selected departments. Reviews of these selected departments are usually requested by the dean, the provost, or the department itself for a variety of reasons—a major change in program emphasis is being considered; a decision needs to be made about the continuation of the program; conflict among faculty is so great that activities in the program have almost slowed to a standstill. These reviews may be scheduled on an ad hoc basis and at such times as deemed necessary by the dean or the department chair. The review methods may vary from institution to institution, but often are similar to those followed by accrediting bodies. A review team may visit the department, examine a self-study report, interview faculty and students, consult with external experts in the field from other universities, and make a report to a provost or dean about important issues facing the department and its programs at all levels.

ASSESSMENT OF GRADUATE PROGRAMS

The third kind of internal review is limited to those aspects of a department that are related to its graduate and research programs. This kind of review may be under the jurisdiction of a special faculty committee, such as a university graduate council, rather than a campus provost or president. Its focus is usually on academic quality, with a particularly heavy emphasis on strengthening those programs that do not measure up to the faculty's standards for high-performing graduate education. The reviews may be very fine-grained, including substantive review of faculty publications and dissertations completed by the program's recent graduates.

Evaluation by State Coordinating and Governing Boards

Public institutions in a state may be subject to several layers of program review and evaluation above the level of the institutions themselves. Most states have a coordinating or oversight board watching over their colleges and universities. These boards generally have strong advisory powers in making recommendations to legislatures, state governors, and governing boards of individual institutions. In some states, public universities do not have individual governing boards. All are under the governance of a single governing board, and the universities together are referred to as the state university system. Sometimes the responsibilities for both the coordination and governance of institutions in a state university system may be assigned to the same board. For example, universities in the State University System of Florida are governed and coordinated by the Florida Board of Regents.

States that have too many colleges and universities to be governed and coordinated by a single board have divided their institutions into several university systems. Each system consists of two or more institutions, and the institutions in each system are governed and coordinated by a university system board. In such states the activities of the system boards are coordinated by the statewide coordinating board. Each statewide or system board has a professional staff headed by a director (who is sometimes considered head of the system). Illinois is an example of a state that has many university systems. Each institution is a member of a system. Institutional requests must be reviewed and approved by the system board, and again by the statewide coordinating board (the Illinois Board of Higher Education).

As complex as statewide governing and coordinating boards may be, their goals and procedures for academic program review and evaluation are not difficult to understand. Their agenda is to assure that:

- The state's needs for a trained work force and for research and development are being met.
- The state's resources are being spent prudently without unnecessary program duplication among institutions.
- The existing programs meet conventional expectations for academic quality.

Statewide boards (whether coordinating, governing, or both) conduct two kinds of program review and evaluation. All new programs must undergo some kind of "approval" process. Approval represents permission to create the program using public resources, and to grant degrees as authorized by the appropriate governing body. Program approval is commonly preceded by a lengthy period of planning and preparation. Extensive market surveys to establish the demand may be necessary, and the institution's ability to articulate an acceptable program design (acceptable to professional accrediting bodies, for example), recruit faculty, and dedicate resources to the program may need to be demonstrated.

In addition to program approval, statewide governing and coordinating boards conduct systemwide reviews of existing programs, either in response to special concerns or as a matter of routine policy. Coordinating boards may respond to legislative direction to review certain kinds of programs for particular reasons. Health programs, for example, are fairly often the target of such special reviews because costs for such programs are relatively high. Likewise, maldistribution of health professionals occurs in some locations, prompting the concern of politicians. Economic development is another concern prompting such special program evaluations. Business interests may, for example, express an interest in expanded programs for management training, engineering, or certain other technical specialties.

Although quality of existing programs may be a central interest, cost and distribution of programs may assume an equal role in the evaluation. In system or statewide reviews that are conducted as a matter of routine policy, program quality may be the central issue, but other issues may also become important. Access, success rates of minorities, statewide distribution of specialities, and other factors may be important issues to policy makers. System or statewide program reviews usually are conducted using a standard cycle, such as every five years. In system or statewide reviews, biology departments in all state universities, for example, are reviewed at the same time, or all engineering programs in the university system are reviewed at the same time. A team of "experts" from outside the state is employed to conduct the review, and site visits are usually made to all state institutions.

Reports from state or systemwide evaluations are most commonly made to the head of the university system, and to the appropriate boards, via the board staff. There may or may not be an opportunity for program chairs or faculty to see draft reports and/or to comment in response. Sometimes the specific recommendations may only reach the department head via the official chain of command—university system head to president of the institution to provost to dean to department head. Depending on how each university system is organized, and the purpose for which such reviews are conducted, the impact may be great. For example, the statewide resource allocation may be restructured. An underrepresentation of minorities in a field like engineering, or in certain specialties in education, may prompt a state system to reallocate funding for such fields to institutions with historically strong records of minority enrollment. This illustration is not meant to advocate such use of program evaluation reports, but only to suggest the importance that their results may have in the shaping of systemwide policies.

Evaluation for Membership in Associations

Institutions may elect to seek a membership in prestigious associations that screen candidates. Two examples are the Association of American Universities (AAU) and Phi Beta Kappa. Departments may be called upon to provide data to support their institution's application for membership.

Such applications may require considerably more than routine descriptive information about programs and activities. If the organization is dedicated to ideals of excellence, or some other demonstrable standard of high performance, it may seek assurance that candidates for membership are worthy representatives. Whether by measured amount of external research funding, or by demonstration that faculty are collectively committed to rigorous standards of excellence in the classroom, the burden of proof is on the candidate institution to show that it should be granted the privileges of membership. Achieving such stature can be both symbolically and practically important for an institution and its departments, but it may require a long-term strategy of development and achievement, coupled with a solid evidentiary record, to accomplish the goal of membership.

Evaluation by Government Agencies

Departments may be subject to evaluation by many different governmental agencies. Federal agencies preparing to award a major grant or contract, for example, often conduct site visits to assess firsthand the strength of a faculty, the adequacy of the physical infrastructure, and the commitment of the administration to an important project.

At the state level, evaluation usually is conducted by agencies concerned with professional licensure or certification. One criterion for certification may be "graduation from an approved program." Program approval is granted by a certain agency after evaluation according to specified criteria or guidelines. In many cases, state approval of a program requires regional and/or professional accreditation as a precondition.

Criteria for program approval vary from state to state, and from field to field. In some cases approval may rest partly on past performance by program graduates on a licensing examination, such as a minimum-competency exam for teachers, or the bar exam for attorneys. Too high a failure rate could result in removal from the approved program list, a catastrophe in certain fields.

Evaluation by Accrediting Bodies

Virtually all institutions, and most professional programs, seek accreditation by the appropriate accrediting body. Such accreditation is required in order to be eligible for federal funding. It is also viewed as an essential part of the institution's or program's public credibility. Accrediting agencies look at all aspects of an institution's operations, including academic programs and departments, educational support services, and administrative processes. Reviews are conducted to ensure that:

1. The institution or program has well-articulated and clearly defined mission and goal statements, and maintains conditions that facilitate achievement of the goals.

2. The efforts of the faculty are consistent with the mission and goal statements of the institution or program, and are directed towards achieving the stated goals.

3. The institutions or programs meet established standards.

INSTITUTIONAL ACCREDITATION

For accreditation purposes, the United States is divided into six geographical regions. Each region has been assigned to an accrediting association (Southern Association of Colleges and Schools, North Central Association of Colleges and Schools, etc.) that has authority to accredit all postsecondary institutions in that region. These associations are essentially organizations of educational institutions whose purpose is self-regulation through voluntary accreditation. In effect, institutions of higher education accredit each other, without interference from governmental agencies. For the most part, such accreditation follows a similar method in all six regions.

An institution's accreditation is reviewed every ten years. It conducts a year-long self-study according to the regional association's specified format. All aspects of the institution's operation are subject to a detailed and searching review. The lengthy period of self-scrutiny is designed to encourage the college or university to propose ways to better focus its resources and programs in pursuit of the overall goals it sets for itself.

At the conclusion of the self-study, a team of faculty and administrators, usually from similar institutions, conducts a site visit to assess the institution's own report and to formulate a recommendation for approval, probation, or nonapproval that can be presented to the assembly of member institutions at the next annual meeting of the association. Although the site visit is usually only a few days in length, it is normally a focused and energetic review, terminating with an exit interview with the president. Institutions that are candid about areas in which they propose to make improvements usually find the visiting team to be supportive.

Accrediting bodies may well change their standards between one review and the next. There are currently two trends among regional accrediting bodies that may impose dramatic changes on what is expected. Most now require that institutions demonstrate an adequate effort to attract, enroll, and graduate minorities. This affirmative-action requirement may also be used to scrutinize employment practices.

The other major trend is to require that institutions assess outcomes of their programs. The concept of "value-added" has been widely discussed in this connection. "Value-added" refers to demonstrable gains in student knowledge, or other indicators of growth and development. Institutions are expected to be able to show that students' experiences while on campus have resulted in some kind of intended outcome, such as a positive change in what they know, how they think, and/or how they perform. Although institutions have been accustomed to reporting the accomplishments of their graduates, the publications of their faculty, and the qualifications of newly admitted students, comparatively few have given serious thought to how a systematic assessment of learning *outcomes* can be accomplished. There is an emerging body of theory and practice to which one might turn for guidance, but equally important is that departments examine their own goals and methods for assessing student learning, in anticipation that they will soon be required to justify and implement a formal program to demonstrate value-added.

PROFESSIONAL PROGRAM ACCREDITATION

Accrediting of professional programs is conducted by commissions of national professional associations, of which there are about forty in the United States. They accredit programs in individual disciplines and professional fields such as business, law, and health professions, and follow procedures similar to those of regional accrediting associations. It is not unusual for a department to find that it is undergoing reviews by both the regional *and* professional accreditation bodies during the same academic year. It can also happen (but not often) that a department such as a Department of Health Administration located in a School of Public Health may undergo *three* accreditations during the same year. The Southern Association may be accrediting the institution, the Council on Education for Public Health may be accrediting the School of Public Health, and the Commission on Education for Health Services Administration may be accrediting the Department of Health Administration.

There is a lot of work involved for a department that must provide data to three separate accrediting bodies in one year, but to have three site visits occur during the same week is almost overwhelming. (Attempts have been made by accrediting bodies to coordinate their efforts when they are reviewing the same department at the same time, but these have not always been successful.) Procedures used in professional accreditation are parallel in many respects to those of institutional accrediting agencies; however, professional accreditation may require that more explicit standards be met. The process of self-study, followed by a site visit and formal recommendations to a national assembly, is characteristic.

National Rankings

Departments may be subject to national comparisons conducted by official and unofficial arbiters of quality, quantity, or performance. Some data gathered and published routinely by government agencies are used as a basis for ranking institutions and programs. They reveal, for example, which universities rank highest in terms of the dollar amounts obtained for research and development via grants and contracts, or in terms of funds raised from private sources. Too, they indicate how peer institutions compare in terms of numbers of faculty members, faculty salaries, numbers of students, admission standards, funding per student, etc. And, they show which institutions rank highest in the numbers of graduates who go on to leading graduate and professional schools, or are employed by prestigious firms.

One frequently cited standard of comparison is the student–faculty ratio, the assumption being that the smaller the ratio, the more contact a student will have with faculty members, resulting in education of higher quality. Another way of comparing accomplishments with those of other departments of the same discipline at other institutions is to count the number of times a particular author is cited in the professional literature. Departments having the most frequently cited scholars are ranked highest in the areas of research scholarship and publication.

News media frequently publish "rankings" of colleges or programs. They like to compare institutions in terms of "value for money," or "overall excellence." Regardless of how such rankings are determined, they enjoy wide and popular circulation, and may be reinforced when others use them in unrelated settings. One should be aware, however, that they are (at best) no more than the product of a poll, or a collection of opinions by informed observers. Individual disciplines or professions sometimes undertake a national ranking of departments or programs within a given field. Department heads or prominent people in that field are surveyed and asked to grade departments on indexes of performance—faculty strength, teaching excellence, research performance, and so on. Often a composite index is constructed, and individual departments assigned a "score." Once a number is assigned, departments can be put in rank order, and decisions made about where to draw lines between those that are "excellent," "prominent," "strong," or "adequate." Although the methods for obtaining such rankings are questionable, the rankings nevertheless persist. Sometimes the person doing the study declines to make the method public, or refuses to publish raw data from which the rankings are compiled. Such studies should be treated with appropriate skepticism.

Reputational studies in general suffer from the phenomenon of "lag." If one is asked to rate all the prominent departments in his or her field, he or she inevitably has to rely on less-than-perfect knowledge of each of the departments. Characteristically, one's knowledge lags behind developments, and so that party's rankings are based on "data" that may be twice-removed from reality. Without firsthand experience of teaching performance in a given department, one evaluates it—under the best of conditions—by using hearsay evidence. And that evidence usually is several years out-of-date. It is therefore common for national rankings to seem (to the cognoscenti) hopelessly dated and out of phase with current developments. Departments that dominated the field in years past enjoy a halo (and commensurately strong rankings) on the basis of their former accomplishments and reputation. That they may no longer even have viable programs after some key retirements or departures is often ignored. Just as likely, reputational rankings will miss departments or programs with a strong upward trajectory—and do those departments a disservice by leaving an impression on campus that they are perhaps not as upwardly mobile as they really are.

Preparing for External Reviews

In this chapter we have so far discussed the many and various types of evaluations to which departments are subjected by agencies other than the department itself. As part of these evaluations, departments are required to conduct self-evaluation studies and to submit evaluation reports indicating, among other things, their self-perceived weaknesses and strengths. Departments are also expected to provide whatever other kinds of data that may be requested by whoever is doing the evaluating. In each case, program evaluators will have specific expectations about what data should be available and when they might make a site visit to interview faculty and students. Chairs will find themselves faced with potentially substantial demands on faculty and staff time to meet these varied and overlapping requests. With this in mind, it is important to anticipate repeated and inevitable evaluations by organizing data that will be both required by and useful to more than one external agency.

Departments will almost invariably be asked for the following information, albeit in varying formats, in advance of every evaluation that is conducted:

- Current, orderly, standardized student records
- Annual records of faculty activity, including grant applications and awards, publications, awards and prizes, and other indicators of quality
- Records of applications, admissions, enrollments, and scores on competitive entry exams
- Records of alumni achievements, employment, and addresses
- An archive of the chair's annual reports, including graphic displays of trends on important measures of quality

A department that maintains a useful core of data on its programs and on the outcomes will provide evaluators with a good starting point, help establish good will between the chair and the evaluating team, and save time and energy in creating reports every time another evaluation is due.

Department chairs may develop cynical or distrusting attitudes towards external evaluation. Sometimes such an attitude can lead a chair to misrepresent the department, or to be recalcitrant about sharing important data. A department that does this may lose in several ways. Most immediately, it loses a bona fide opportunity to gain support for improvements it may wish to make. It also may sacrifice its own credibility, because deans and others will immediately suspect an inaccurate or dishonest report. A chair may have to answer for such a transgression of the process.

Responding to External Reviews

Departments often can anticipate how they will fare in an external evaluation or program review. Knowing in advance where the strong and weak spots are can help the chair work with the review team to locate the areas in which further support and development may result in improvement. In the end this is the most useful outcome of a program assessment, and it is the basic purpose behind most such exercises.

For most departments or programs it is not so much the outcome of external evaluations that produces uncertainty as it is how to implement the recommendations. A chair would do well to follow up the evaluation with a sequence of actions that will help set changes in motion:

- Assess the evaluators' report thoroughly and objectively, focusing on the most important recommendations and on the facts or conditions that underlie these recommendations.
- Communicate these facts to administrators and faculty in simple, clear, repeated messages.
- Seek allies and partners who can help rethink, reshape, and rebuild (if necessary).
- Develop strategies and plans for change.
- Test new ideas and directions with constituencies who can validate them.
- Inform others of the department's commitment to implement changes.
- Translate new solutions into budget or program requests.
- Solicit faculty involvement in implementing changes.
- Prepare to begin the program review cycle again.

Sooner or later, a chair will be faced with conflicting recommendations from several evaluators. In this case, the chair should seek broadly based advice from those best positioned to help validate whatever course of action the department may choose to take. Key faculty members, deans, and perhaps leaders of the profession or discipline may have useful perspectives on the consequences of choosing among alternatives.

Self-Evaluations

Self-studies are generally conducted as one of the requirements of an evaluation by an agency other than the department being evaluated. In many instances, departments do the minimum necessary to satisfy that requirement. Some departments, however, will use the occasion to do an in-depth self-evaluation study, since they have already collected considerable data for annual reports and external reviews. For example, faculty have compiled records of their accomplishments for the purpose of annual merit reviews. Publications, grants, and teaching performance may be recorded in considerable detail in these reports. End-of-course student evaluations may also be compiled for study. Similarly, performance of students on end-of-course examinations or on standardized tests may provide some perspective on trends in achievement. Institution-wide assessments of learning outcomes may allow comparison with other departments. Quality of student applications and enrollees may show trends and help the department assess its own reputation and visibility.

A department may wish to obtain information about its program that is not usually collected on a routine basis, such as the aforementioned value-added. A number of institutions are experimenting with this concept as an appropriate measure of quality. Determining how much value has been added requires a measure of outcomes. Obviously, using a value-added criterion in evaluating a department's programs requires a considerable amount of information about *both* inputs and outcomes. It requires, in fact, a demonstrable improvement in student performance that can be tied to experiences the student has had as a result of enrolling in the department or program.

A number of institutions are also experimenting with the assessments of outcomes related to *basic skills* in reading, writing, and mathematics. Outcome assessment may also be related to the development of certain *professional or technical competencies.* Such competencies may be defined by a state agency responsible for professional certification, or they might be defined by an industry or a labor union. Outcomes may also be defined in broader terms as "The desirable qualities of a liberally educated person." Some assessment programs, for example, attempt to measure the level of a student's esthetic judgment or ethical reasoning.

Some of the experiments with outcome assessment now going on are quite creative. Although some rely on traditional paper-and-pencil tests, standardized in the classical way, others have tried much more inventive means. Two promising techniques are those of "portfolio" assessment, and the "assessment center" idea. A portfolio is a record of the student's work over time, an accumulation of creative effort that can be judged by a panel of experts. A portfolio should include copies of papers and critiques prepared by students as well as other pieces of work submitted for evaluation. It should show how the student has grown and developed along those dimensions considered important by the department. An assessment center is also a juried performance, except that the student appears personally and reacts or responds to a series of exercises. The jury scrutinizes and evaluates the student's performance, again using dimensions related to the desired outcomes. Increasingly, regional accrediting bodies are recommending or requiring such outcome-oriented assessment measures. As pressure to account for results increases, and as such accountability becomes the basis for either public funding or accreditation, most institutions will feel compelled to implement some kind of process that demonstrates value-added.

It is not the purpose of this chapter to offer specific kinds of measures or methods for conducting such an assessment. Many other sources are available that deal with this topic in depth. Regardless of the specific method used, all such assessment focuses on demonstration that some kind of learning has taken place, and that students can do something (or know something) that they could not do (or did not know) when they entered the program.

All of these data, and others, that chairs might elect to gather can help the faculty to sense the course that the department is taking, and provide important feedback. Most importantly, self-evaluation can help establish consensus about directions for change and improvement. A faculty that is voluntarily aware of its own strengths and weaknesses is far more likely to accept the need for change than a faculty not challenged to reflect on its own performance. The department, through carefully orchestrated information-gathering and sharing, can establish an ethic of self-evaluation. Departments that consciously examine their own performance are usually in a far stronger position than otherwise to shape and influence the conclusions of external evaluators.

Developing a Data Base for Review and Evaluation Purposes

Because the demand for data is so continuous, departments should set up a routine data-gathering operation to build a data base from which self-studies can be conducted. Departments should not only anticipate the needs of external evaluators, but should also consider relevant questions about their own operations and programs. For example, they need to collect data that will help demonstrate the department's worth, quality, and cost effectiveness. A department that maintains adequate records about students, faculty, activities, and so on, and files these in an orderly manner can conduct evaluations and compile reports much more efficiently than a department that must send its members scurrying one or more times a year to find information that might have been amassed just as routinely and easily.

Answers to the following questions are useful in evaluating a department, developing a good annual report, and creating a data base for planning future activities.

INFORMATION ABOUT STUDENTS

- How many students are majoring in the department's field?
- How many students are enrolled in each course?
- How many degrees in the department's field have been conferred?
- How many students have received scholarships, fellowships, assistantships, grants, and gifts?
- How many students have won honors?
- How many new majors have been accepted for the coming year?
- How many minority students have been recruited, trained, and graduated?
- How are the students performing in terms of grade point average and national tests? How does student performance compare with that of past years?
- What theses, dissertations, or research reports have been completed?
- What percentage of the total number of lower-division, upper-division, and graduate students in the university is majoring in this field? Is the

percentage increasing, decreasing, or remaining relatively stable? What accounts for the change or stability?

- What evidence indicates that students are receiving the courses and information necessary for the next stage of their academic or employment careers? How many and what percentage of graduating seniors in the department were admitted to graduate school? To what graduate schools were they admitted? How many and what percentage of graduates were employed in jobs for which they have been trained?
- What other schools and colleges within the university are sending students to this department? Are other departments asking for service courses? Has a systematic needs survey been conducted? What are the past, present, and anticipated student demands for courses in this department? What are the past, present, and anticipated job market needs for graduates of department programs?

INFORMATION ABOUT DEGREE PROGRAMS, COURSE OFFERINGS, AND CURRICULUM

- What courses were offered at each level during each term of the year and how many students were enrolled in each course?
- How many full-time equivalent students were generated by the department at each level?
- Have course syllabi been updated?
- Have courses been changed by using other media or more individual modes of instruction?
- Have new courses been added? How do these courses contribute to the program?
- Do the courses in the program meet the present and anticipated needs of the students and the job market?
- Has the program been reviewed? If so, by whom? A university committee? A state agency? Has the program been reviewed for accreditation?

INFORMATION ABOUT FACULTY MEMBERS AND THEIR ACHIEVEMENTS

- How many full-time faculty members are in the department?
- Have new faculty members been added to the department?
- How many faculty members are on leave or sabbatical?
- Have any faculty members resigned?
- Have any faculty members been dismissed? Have any contracts not been renewed?
- Do any faculty members have reduced workloads?

- How many faculty members are temporary or part-time? Is the number of part-time or temporary faculty members increasing?
- Which faculty members have received professional honors or teaching awards?
- Have any faculty members received grants and contracts for research, development, or training?
- What is the record of publications by faculty members?
- Have any faculty members received awards for research or publication?
- What service activities have faculty members performed? For the school or institution? For professional associations? For the community?

INFORMATION ABOUT EQUIPMENT, FACILITIES, AND SUPPLIES

- Are resources adequate to meet demands?
- Do any programs not have adequate resources? Are additional resources needed?
- Has new or special equipment been acquired for the department?

INFORMATION ABOUT DEPARTMENT GOVERNANCE AND ADMINISTRATION

- How is the department structured? What are the roles of department committees? To what extent do students participate in department affairs?
- Have any new policies been implemented for the department's operation?
- How is travel money allocated within the department?
- Is the level of faculty morale satisfactory?
- What other important activities or actions should be mentioned?

Aside from the official information that is required by the central administration and the dean, each department must determine for itself what data it wishes to collect and maintain on a regular basis. Answers to the questions above illustrate the kinds of statements that appear in annual reports, though requirements for these statements differ from one institution to another. Departments can obtain much information from the university's institutional research office, which collects and stores much of this data.

Questions

1. How would you evaluate the quality of record keeping in your department? To what extent are sufficient data available to respond quickly to a dean's request for information?

2. To what extent can an institutional research office or an alumni affairs unit at your institution provide information you can use to assist in departmental evaluation efforts?

3. List several of your department's strengths and weaknesses. For each item, define an essential element for maintaining the strengths and reducing the weaknesses.

4. What is the critical factor in determining the department's success or failure?

5. To what extent does the state legislature or other government agency impose assessment criteria on your institution? What is the regulatory impact on your department?

6. In anticipation of the national trend toward statewide assessment policies, in what ways does your department measure student learning outcomes?

7. To what extent does your department use a committee structure for internal evaluation and assessment activities? Might the committee benefit from student representation?

References

ARGYRIS, CHRIS. "Interpersonal Barriers to Decision-making." *Harvard Business Review,* February 1966, pp. 84–97.

ARGYRIS, CHRIS, and SCHON, DONALD A. *Theory in Practice: Increasing Professional Effectiveness.* San Francisco: Jossey–Bass, 1974.

ASTIN, ALEXANDER W. *Assessment for Excellence: The Philosophy and Practices of Assessment and Evaluation in Higher Education.* New York: ACE/Macmillan, 1991.

ASTIN, ALEXANDER W., and SCHERRI, RITA A. *Maximizing Leadership Effectiveness: Impact of Administrative Style on Faculty and Students.* San Francisco: Jossey–Bass, 1980.

ASTIN, ALEXANDER W., and LES, CALVIN B. T. "Current Practices in the Evaluation and Training of College Teachers." *Educational Record,* Summer 1976, pp. 361–375.

BALDRIDGE, J. VICTOR (et al.) *Policy Making and Effective Leadership: A National Study of Academic Management.* San Francisco: Jossey–Bass, 1978.

BARAK, ROBERT, (et al.) *The Arizona Board of Regents Task Force on Excellence, Efficiency and Competitiveness.* Final Report and Working Papers. 4 vols. 1988. (ERIC Document Reproduction Service No. ED 306 803)

BARE, ALAN C. "The Study of Academic Department Performance." *Research in Higher Education,* 12(1), 1980, pp. 3–22.

BIRNBAUM, ROBERT. *Individual Preferences and Organizational Goals: Consistency and Diversity in the Futures Desired by Campus Leaders.* ASHE Annual Meeting Paper, Baltimore, 1987. (ERIC Document Reproduction Service No. ED 292 384)

BOWEN, HOWARD R., and SCHUSTER, JACK H. *The American Professoriate: A National Resource Imperiled.* New York: Carnegie Corporation, 1986.

BOWKER, LEE H., and LYNCH, DAVID M. *Chairing a Small Department.* Paper presented at the National Conference for Department Chairs, Orlando, 1985. (ERIC Document Reproduction Service No. ED 256 222)

BRASKAMP, LARRY A.; ORY, JOHN C.; and PIEPER, DAVID M. "Student Written Comments." *Journal of Educational Psychology,* 73(1), 1981, pp. 65–70.

BRENEMAN, DAVID W., and YOUN, TED I. K. (Eds.) *Academic Labor Markets and Careers.* Philadelphia: The Falmer Press, Taylor and Francis, Inc., 1988.

COOK, MARVIN J., and NEVILLE, RICHARD F. "The Faculty as Teachers: A Perspective on Evaluation." ERIC Clearinghouse on Higher Education, Report no. 13, Washington, DC: George Washington University, 1971.

DAVIS, BARBARA GROSS. "Demystifying Assessment: Learning from the Field of Evaluation." In P. J. Gray, ed., "Achieving Assessment Goals Using Evaluation Techniques". In *New Directions for Higher Education,* 67, Fall 1989.

DAVIS, C. GRIER, JR., and STROTZ, ROBERT H. "The Politics of Accreditation and the Role of COPA in Self-Regulation." In John B. Bennett and J. W. Peltason, eds., *Contemporary Issues in Higher Education: Self Regulation and the Educational Roles of the Academy.* New York: Macmillan, 1985.

DENT, PRESTON L., and NICHOLAS, THOMAS. "A Study of Faculty and Student Opinions on Teaching Effectiveness Ratings." *Peabody Journal of Education,* January 1980, pp. 135–143.

EBLE, KENNETH E. *Professors as Teachers.* San Francisco: Jossey–Bass, 1972.

FARH, JIING LIH (et al.) "An Empirical Investigation of Self-Appraisal–based Performance Evaluation." *Personnel–Psychology,* 41, 1988, pp. 141–156.

FREDERICK, PETER J. "Involving Students More Actively in the Classroom." In *New Directions for Teaching and Learning: The Department Chairperson's Role in Enhancing College Teaching,* 37, Spring 1989, pp. 31–40.

GUEST, ROBERT H.; HERSEY, PAUL; and BLANCHARD, KENNETH H. *Organizational Change Through Effective Leadership.* Englewood Cliffs: Prentice–Hall, 1977.

HIND, ROBERT R.; DORNBUSH, SANFORD M.; and SCOTT, W. RICHARD. "A Theory of Evaluation Applied to a University Faculty." *Sociology of Education,* Winter 1974, pp. 114–128.

JOHNSON, F. CRAIG. "Data Requirements for Academic Departments." In *New Directions for Institutional Research: Examining Departmental Leadership,* no. 10, edited by John C. Smart and James R. Montgomery. San Francisco: Jossey–Bass, 1976.

LADD, DWIGHT R. *Change in Educational Policy: Self-Studies in Selected Colleges and Universities,* with commentary by Katherine McBride. New York: McGraw–Hill, 1970.

MARCUS, DORA. *Lessons Learned from FIPSE Projects.* Washington, DC: Fund For the Improvement of Postsecondary Education, 1991.

MARSH, HERBERT W.; OVERALL, J. U.; and KASLER, STEVEN P. "Validity of Student Evaluations of Instructional Effectiveness: A Comparison of Faculty Self-Evaluations and Evaluations by their Students." *Journal of Educational Psychology,* April 1979, pp. 149–160.

MCKEACHIE, WILBER J. "Student Ratings of Faculty: A Reprise." *Academe: Bulletin of the AAUP,* October 1979, pp. 384–397.

MCINTOSH, THOMAS H., and KOEVERING, THOMAS E. "Six-year Case Study of Faculty Peer Reviews, Merit Ratings, and Pay Awards in a Multidisciplinary Department." *Journal of the College and University Personnel Association,* 37, 1986, pp. 5–14.

MIDDLEHURST, ROBIN. "Evaluation and Development of a Leadership Course for Heads of Academic Departments in the United Kingdom." *Higher Education Management,* 1(2), 1989, pp. 170–182.

NATIONAL SCIENCE FOUNDATION. *Systems for Measuring and Reporting the Resources and Activities of Colleges and Universities.* NSF 67-15. Washington, DC: National Science Foundation, June 1967.

NEUMANN, YORAM. "The Perception of Power in University Departments: A Comparison Between Chairpersons and Faculty Members." *Research in Higher Education,* 11(4), 1979, pp. 283–293.

Salaries, Tenure, and Fringe Benefits of Full-time Instructional Faculty. Washington, DC: Center for Education Statistics. HEGIS Data available from Office of Educational Research and Improvement, Washington, DC 20208, 1986.

SCOTT, W. RICHARD (et al.). "Organizational Evaluation and Authority." *Administrative Science Quarterly,* June 1967, pp. 93–117.

SELDIN, PETER. *Successful Faculty Evaluation Programs; A Practical Guide to Improve Faculty Performance and Promotion/Tenure Decisions.* New York: Coventry Press, 1980.

SERGIOVANNI, THOMAS J., and CORBALLY, JOHN E. *Leadership and Organizational Culture.* Chicago: University of Illinois Press, 1988.

TRASK, KERRY A. "The Chairperson and Teaching." In *New Directions for Teaching and Learning: The Department Chairperson's Role in Enhancing College Teaching,* 37, Spring 1989, pp. 99–107.

Chapter *31*

Evaluating the Chair

The chair's job has been described in great detail earlier in this book as complex and important. The chair's most fundamental responsibility is to do what it takes to keep the department solvent, functioning, and changing with the field For the chair, evaluation is the total of accumulated impressions of others about whether he or she is doing the job that is expected.

Who Evaluates the Chair

Chairs are evaluated by faculty and deans, both of which depend heavily on them to administer the department. Each has very specific ideas about what an effective chair should be doing, and how he or she should be handling the job. These evaluations may or may not be handled in a formal way, but either way the chair should be aware of the significance of the impressions formed, and of the potential impact of individual acts, on the evaluation. Sometimes the chair will find that expectations of deans and faculty are not entirely consistent with one another, and that it is inviting stress to try to satisfy more than one set of criteria for effective job performance.

Expectations may develop in a variety of ways. Chairs may enter their jobs without a clear description thereof, and even without otherwise knowing very much about what they are expected to do. They may also enter with marching orders from the dean and/or the faculty—only to discover that this kind of imperative is too narrow with respect to other things the chair will be expected to do on the department's behalf. It is up to the chair to discover the totality (for the time being) of what is expected, and how to apportion effort so that at least a good percentage of these expectations have a reasonable chance of being met.

Although the specific expectations of faculty and deans may vary from situation to situation and time to time, there are certain bedrock things that chairs *must* do in order to serve the department well. They must see that routine work is done. They must handle the flow of management tasks required by not only the dean but also the university. They must communicate well with both faculty and administration. They must exercise supervisory authority over the faculty while respecting the faculty's professionalism. They must acquire and control fiscal resources to accomplish the department's work. They must plan.

Even when there is agreement about what the chair is supposed to do, there may be differences among faculty, and between faculty and deans, about how the chair is performing. A dean, for example, may place heavy emphasis on prompt and thorough reports. Faculty, on the other hand, may come to see the reporting process as burdensome and bureaucratic. While a chair puts forth great effort to meet the dean's expectations, he or she may also find that faculty do not value (and indeed may criticize) these efforts. On the other hand, the faculty may wish to see schedules changed to accommodate their expectations for a new curriculum sequence. So, the chair may work hard over several months to accommodate individual teaching-schedule preferences, and to move large classes from one time period to another. But then the dean may not be aware of, or appreciate, the amount of attention the chair gives to making these changes. In fact, the dean may only hear from his or her staff about the *problems* that these changes are causing—for example with the registrar, and with departments whose schedules also must be shifted to accommodate change. Thus the criteria used by deans for judging the chair's performance may differ from those used by faculty. Both may have limited information on which to base their evaluations. The chair must be aware of these potentially conflicting and sometimes incomplete perspectives, and would be well advised to leave a well-marked trail of performance, so that all sides are able to make reasonably valid judgments.

Faculty Expectations

Faculty view the chair through many lenses. They are independent and judgmental by training and experience, and they may be very free in providing critical feedback to the chair. Nevertheless, they do form one of the chair's most important constituencies, and their views can ultimately determine how successful a chair will be. Faculty perspectives on the chair's performance come from their own contact with the chair, and with the kind of impact the chair has on their ability to do their jobs. Faculty usually evaluate the performance of department chairs in at least three areas: managerial, academic, and political.

MANAGERIAL PERFORMANCE

Although chairs at most institutions consider themselves principally to be faculty members, their acceptance of the position of department chair places them in a managerial relationship to faculty. Faculty do not like to perceive themselves as being managed, but some management is necessary nevertheless. The chair is expected to assign teaching and other duties, to establish equity among the loads carried by individual faculty, to communicate expectations on behalf of the university, and to hold faculty accountable for performing their duties. If the chair handles these duties with fairness, objectivity, candor, and a reasonable amount of flexibility, faculty will (for the most part) appreciate the chair's management efforts.

ACADEMIC PERFORMANCE

Chairs are also expected to have a clear sense of the academic and professional norms and issues that drive what faculty do. Faculty are participants in a discipline or profession that requires them to pay attention to developments far beyond the boundaries of their employing institution. Their teaching, their research support, and their success at publication all derive from their ability to master the key intellectual issues of the field. This, rather than slavish observation of the conventions and daily routines of one's own college or university, constitutes the meat of a faculty member's self-defined "work." A chair who does not appreciate the intensity of faculty members' involvement in this external world of professional colleagues and pure intellectual pursuit, or who is not "up to speed" on the latest developments, may well be perceived in a negative light.

Some chairs, of course, may be far more engaged intellectually than are members of the faculty in general. For these chairs, the hazard is of a different kind: They may be perceived as *too* disengaged from the routine matters of departmental management, and not sufficiently effective at getting the normal work done. They may also be active enough on the national scene to be perceived with some envy by those faculty who have lost touch, or who have lost interest in, and commitment to, the genuinely intellectual life.

Obviously, chairs need to balance and calibrate their own involvement in the field. Perhaps they need to work hard at keeping up to speed in departments that are alive and leading the field—but they also need to provide leadership in focusing people's attention and energy on the day-to-day business of the department. On the other hand, they may need to push for more attention to important intellectual and professional issues in a department that has grown too comfortable with its own way of doing business. In either case, it pays for the chair to be perceived as at least *adequately* interested in the major trends and developments in the field.

Occasionally, chairs will be asked to administer departments that are actually more like holding companies for programs that do not share genuinely similar intellectual traditions or foundations. A Foundations of Education department, for example, may house not only quantitatively oriented professors of educational psychology but also historians and philosophers who apply tools of humanistic inquiry to issues in education. For chairs in departments such as this, satisfying the demands for intellectual currency and engagement can be a serious challenge.

POLITICAL PERFORMANCE

The third area in which faculty expectations provide a basis for evaluating the chair is the exercise of political skills. All departments experience more-or-less visible struggles over power and resources in which faculty may compete to control others and to get at least their own share of scarce commodities (merit increases, "essential" equipment, the best students, and so on). Chairs usually are in a strong position of influence over the distribution of advantages considered valuable by faculty. And faculty are quick to perceive the fairness and justice with which chairs handle the distribution of valuable resources. They also are quick to perceive whether a chair is effective or ineffective in managing the peculiar political conflicts in the department.

Chairs may expect that faculty will *differ* among themselves in how they evaluate the managerial, academic, and political dimensions of the chair's performance. Inevitably some faculty will find themselves feeling deprived, ignored, and unappreciated. However, although the chair will try to be as fair and humane as possible, there is no way to satisfy everyone. Negative feedback is inevitable, and the chair will just have to put such feedback in an appropriate context.

The Dean's Expectations

Chairs are perceived by deans to be members of a management team. Deans therefore evaluate chairs according to criteria that differ greatly from those used by faculty. Although deans may associate a chair's performance with the overall performance of his or her department, they also evaluate chairs in terms of how well they seem to behave as managers.

Deans expect chairs to be advocates for their departments, but they also expect them to condition their advocacy upon an awareness of the larger picture. There are limits to what deans can do for individual departments without damaging others, and they depend on chairs to be intelligent and mature enough to see this reality. Although it may create inner problems for the chair in terms of divided loyalties, the dean expects members of the college's administrative team ultimately to act in the interest of the greater number—namely, the college as a whole.

Deans will value chairs who are open and communicative, and honest with the dean and themselves alike. Chairs who hide information from the dean, who are secretive, who avoid talking with the dean, are not perceived as being helpful. They often become objects of suspicion to the extent that they themselves are suspicious, and perhaps afraid, of open contact with the dean. Deans themselves must have timely and reliable information in order to be effective managers, and so must rely in turn on chairs to provide them with precisely that. Being open about problems helps everyone to cope with situations that may, in fact, be larger than just a single department. Open lines of communication foster problem-solving behavior and help avoid the kind of festering conditions that invite open conflict and publicity. Thus, a dean's major interest is in having chairs communicate clearly and accurately concerning their departments.

Deans appreciate chairs who are decisive, and willing to act. Although they want to know what is going on in departments, deans do not want to be expected to solve everyone's problems. They may be willing to consult and support chairs in making decisions, but they hire chairs to manage the departments. They will not appreciate having every decision "kicked upstairs" by chairs who do not have the courage to act. A chair's passing of the buck in this manner puts the dean in the position of being the "bad guy" and is a transparent ploy by the chair to salvage his or her own position *at the dean's expense.*

Deans value chairs who are able to look at a situation objectively and to plan appropriately for a course of action that meets the demands of the situation. It often is tempting for the chair to "play to the audience"—in this case, the departmental faculty. A chair who sees his or her role as principally that of an advocate for the department may act in a partisan manner that ignores the realities facing the dean. Just as government at all levels is faced with strident "single issue" lobbies that refuse to compromise their interests, so a department chair who cannot look at objective reality will be perceived as nettlesome and unhelpful to a dean who must stretch resources over ever-expanding needs.

On the other hand, chairs who are adaptable and try to work within the limits of the situation are likely to be seen by deans as valuable members of the management team. Chairs who work to construct advantage for their departments within the rules and the available resources benefit from the dean's respect and usually earn themselves more latitude for initiative. Yet chairs are not expected to be bootlickers or uncritical handmaidens of the dean's whim; weak chairs are not usually seen in a positive light by deans. Articulate advocates for departmental needs and interests who can work constructively within limits are the ones invariably viewed with high regard.

Being a member of a team puts a premium on showing certain other qualities as well. Deans will expect chairs to be both loyal and discreet. They will have conferences with chairs in which both sides speak candidly and openly about their views and objectives. Sometimes deans will share information with all chairs at a meeting, sometimes individually. In either event, the dean is depending on the chair to behave professionally and to preserve confidences in appropriate ways. They will expect chairs to use information, but to do so in the best interests of the college. Chairs who use their contacts with the dean to bolster their own stature with leaks and rumors based on information the dean has provided in confidence will be perceived as disloyal and indiscreet. Deans will quickly learn who can be trusted and who cannot.

Loyalty is not limited to maintaining confidences. Deans and chairs typically maintain a working relationship over a period of years. Neither can do an effective job without the other's support and confidence. They must have a tacit understanding that they are going to work as a team, and the dean must have confidence in the chair's trustworthiness. Chairs who engage in manipulation, intrigue, power plays, and end-runs that thwart a dean's ability to manage will not long enjoy the dean's confidence.

Deans will evaluate chairs on the basis of the latters' ability to act selflessly or altruistically. Administrators are supposed to promote the greater good. They should be secure enough in their own careers and personal lives to be able to serve others' interests and needs in ways that advance educational objectives of the institution. Chairs who take the job to stroke their own egos or to advance themselves for personal reasons, chairs who assert powerful motives for self-gratification, may find that deans have little patience or sympathy for behavior that is fundamentally egocentric. Chairs' time and energy should be directed towards supporting others and providing a productive educational environment in which faculty and students alike can thrive. Deans do not long support chairs who insist on perks, special attention, public notice, or funding for pet projects. On the other hand, chairs who unstintingly help others achieve their own ends will always be seen in a very favorable light.

Deans expect chairs to show a reasonable amount of courage, but also the good judgment to balance decisiveness with prudence. Chairs must make decisions that are not always popular with faculty or students. Sometimes chairs will try to maneuver themselves into positions that allow them to evade the taking of such responsibility. Typically, a chair who fears making an unpopular decision will try to make it appear as if the dean is making him or her do it. Deans are no more anxious to play the role of tough decision-maker than are chairs. They are particularly unhappy when a chair repeatedly shies away from taking a strong stand.

On the other hand, deans are not so unrealistic that they expect chairs to be trigger-happy, or so full of bravado that they relish making controversial decisions. Prudent chairs, those who can make decisions that are carefully considered and proportional to the circumstances, will earn deans' respect. Such chairs do what the circumstances require, but do not needlessly entangle the dean (or others) in controversy or imbroglio.

Deans value energetic and productive chairs. A chair who is distracted by or committed to other activities, or who simply cannot sustain a level of effort needed to do the job, will eventually begin to cause distractions for the dean. Being unavailable for telephone calls, missing (or skipping) meetings, failing to follow up on correspondence, being late with reports, and otherwise appearing uncommitted or disinterested are behaviors that signal to the dean that the chair is not able to handle the requirements of the job. Deans need chairs who will work hard to help things run smoothly, who will complete assignments, and who will not complain about onerous but essential chores. As in any setting where teamwork is essential, chairs will have to calibrate their contributions and their productivity to the expectations and norms of the leader. Deans will be very sensitive to who is able to keep up with the pace they demand and who is lagging behind and letting others carry the burden.

HANDLING FEEDBACK

Chairs will receive both formal and informal feedback on their performance in a variety of forms. The chair needs to sort out what kind of feedback is useful and valid, and what kind is not. Sometimes chairs will be subject to public or private comments about their leadership (or lack of leadership) from faculty or others who may be upset and are lashing out at convenient targets. Or a faculty union may publish an annual "rating" of administrators' effectiveness that is less than flattering. Although the chair must take all evaluative comments and feedback seriously, he or she should also be cautious about lending too much weight to random individual comments. It would be far wiser and more productive to be watchful for, and attentive to, any patterns that may develop in the kind of feedback that comes from many faculty over a significant period of time. If a chair finds him- or herself reacting in a highly sensitive way to each incident in which another offers evaluative comments (either favorable or unfavorable), perhaps the chair has psychic needs that require more or less feedback than the job has to offer.

While successful chairs do not grow elephant hides that protect them from all compliments or criticisms, they do develop a healthy perspective on feedback. They view feedback as just that—information they can use to help adjust their own behavior or to remedy conditions that need to be altered. Evaluation is viewed as diagnostic or "formative" in the sense that it provides a starting point for change and for the further development of one's skills and performance.

Negative feedback is inevitable in any administrative position. All chairs receive criticism; none escapes it unless serving a very short term. Following the rule of thumb that the source should be considered in interpreting what negative feedback means, the chair should not ignore the criticism but rather try to understand the message. As often as not, negative feedback means that a chair has in fact gotten his or her point across—say perhaps that some sort of change is desired. Chairs who make a difference will inevitably meet with resistance and be forced to endure some criticism as a result. But they need not view that criticism as evidence that they are doing a poor job. Quite the contrary, they may view negative feedback as evidence that they are accomplishing exactly what they want to accomplish. Movement may be occuring in the desired direction, albeit movement with some resistance or friction along the way.

"Consider the source" does not mean that all negative feedback is benign. A chair may well find that negative evaluation is sufficiently widespread among key constituents, and sufficiently consistent in its content, to warrant careful attention. It may be a message to institute changes in one's own style or agenda. Is the chair pushing too hard on a certain issue on which change is unlikely? Are faculty upset about not being consulted? Is the dean unhappy about lax supervision of staff? Are these things that a chair can do something about? If not, the chair may be in a situation in which he or she cannot hope to be effective. But it is always constructive to look at negative feedback as information one can put to use for the purposes of making needed change. Sometimes that change is in one's own behavior; sometimes it is in other factors.

Just as negative feedback may have two sides, so may positive feedback have connotations that are not unconditionally good. Chairs who spend most of their time and energy "stroking" others and meeting others' needs may be very popular. But they are not always addressing the tough problems a department may need to confront. If a department faces clear and objective problems, a chair is obliged to deal with these in a realistic way, and to accept a certain amount of criticism and discomfort in the process. A chair who pursues the path of least resistance in order to achieve personal popularity can do great damage to an impaired department that desperately needs leadership.

Again, the chair is well advised to consider the source of unconditional positive feedback or evaluation. If it comes from people who have good reason to criticize the chair, and if it acknowledges specific accomplishments, positive feedback can be extraordinarily gratifying. If, on the other hand, it is unconditional and more personal, of the "hail fellow" variety, the chair might question whether there is real substance behind it. Just being a good-natured and vaguely popular person is hardly an indicator of effective performance by the chair.

Chairs may get a good deal of random feedback on their performance, but neither systematic nor valid feedback. New chairs should have an agreement with the dean about what kind of evaluation will be conducted, and about how the information from such evaluation will be communicated and used. It is important for the chair to secure regular and dependable feedback above and beyond a ritual, year-end conference with the dean. Although such a conference is important (usually it is required), the occasion may become ritualistic and perfunctory. A year is too long a time to wait for feedback. The chair will be performing in a vacuum, and may be unable to make timely adjustments in either style or substance as required.

The chair who fails to get timely feedback will, often unconsciously, seek out cues. Sometimes a chair fishes for compliments from colleagues, or in the heat of immediate events becomes overly sensitive to both positive and negative comments. Without a more systematic and reliable source of information, the chair may be at the mercy of his or her own sensitivities as well as that of the idiosyncrasies of a few faculty who express themselves freely on any and all occasions.

Open lines of communication with the dean, including regular monthly conferences, would be helpful if they can be arranged. Likewise, departments often have a faculty advisory or executive committee that could serve as a useful sounding board for chairs to rely upon. Such a standing body of faculty might be a particularly good source of feedback. Occasionally a chair may be fortunate to have a trusted confidant(e) among the most senior and experienced faculty. Such a person may be able to serve as an informal mentor. He or she may be familiar with the department's history, and with the way in which chairs have typically succeeded or failed in dealing with important and persistent problems. A chair would be fortunate indeed if this kind of relationship could be cultivated to the point where the faculty person would feel free to provide candid feedback. Such a relationship should, of course, be discreet, and the chair would want to take care that the mentor not be perceived as such—and certainly that he or she would not be seen as having unusual access to, or influence upon, decisions and resource allocation.

Chairs obviously walk a very fine line between satisfying the dean and satisfying the faculty.In the end, chairs must decide to do what they consider best for their departments. It is the department's interest, and not the faculty's or the dean's, that they are supposed to represent.

In summary then, a chair's career will be marked by both positive and negative evaluation. The challenge to the chair is to treat all such information as useful feedback with which to work in charting the course of future decisions and actions. Chairs who are sensitive to what is going on around them will be able to adjust and carry on. Chairs who do not listen carefully to what significant others have to say will ultimately serve the department poorly. Evaluation is nothing more than the process by which others communicate with the chair about how well important messages are being received and acted upon. Chairs should welcome good and frequent feedback as a source of information about how they can do their jobs better.

Questions

1. Are department chairpersons at your institution formally evaluated by their faculty members on a regular basis? Do you think they should be? Give reasons for your response.
2. What do you perceive to be your strengths and weaknesses as a chairperson?
3. In what areas do you think your faculty members would agree or disagree with your perceptions of yourself?
4. When you became chairperson, what did your dean tell you about the problems of the department, and what he or she would expect of you as the chairperson?
5. To what extent was the dean's explanation accurate?
6. To what extent does the dean formally evaluate your performance as a chairperson?
7. To what extent does the dean discuss with you your strengths and weaknesses as a chairperson, and to what extent does he or she give suggestions and advice as to how you might solve some of the department's problems?
8. Are there colleagues in or out of your department that you can turn to for feedback and support?

References

ALLEN, PAUL M.; (et al.). *Teacher Self-Appraisal: A Way of Looking Over Your Own Shoulder.* Worthington, OH: Charles A. Jones, 1970.

ARGYRIS, CHRIS; CYERT, RICHARD M.; RAILEY, STEPHEN K.; and MAEROFF, GENE I. *Leadership in the 1980's.* Cambridge, MA: Institute for Educational Management, Harvard University, 1980.

ARGYRIS, CHRIS. "Interpersonal Barriers to Decision-making." *Harvard Business Review,* February 1966, pp. 84–97.

ARGYRIS, CHRIS, and SCHON, DONALD A. *Theory in Practice: Increasing Professional Effectiveness.* San Francisco: Jossey–Bass, 1974.

ASTIN, ALEXANDER W., and SCHERRI, RITA A. *Maximizing Leadership Effectiveness: Impact of Administrative Style on Faculty and Students.* San Francisco: Jossey–Bass, 1980.

AVI-ITZAK, TAMAR E. "On "First-timers" Vis-à-Vis "Experienced" Department Chairpersons' Perceptions of Role Fulfillment: The Case of Fluid Participation in Organization." *Higher Education in Europe,* 10, 1985, pp. 31–36.

BALDRIDGE, J. VICTOR (et al.) *Policy Making and Effective Leadership: A National Study of Academic Management.* San Francisco: Jossey–Bass, 1978.

BARE, ALAN C. "Managerial Behavior of College Chairpersons and Administrators." *Research in Higher Education,* 24, 1986, pp. 128–138.

BENNETT, JOHN B., and FIGULI, DAVID J. (Eds.) *Enhancing Departmental Leadership: The Roles of the Chairperson.* New York: Macmillan, 1990.

BROWN, DAVID G. *Leadership Vitality: A Workup for Academic Administrators.* Washington, DC: American Council on Education, 1980.

COHEN, MICHAEL D., and MARCH, JAMES G. (Eds.) *Leadership and Ambiguity: The American College President.* Carnegie Commission on Higher Education. New York: McGraw–Hill, 1974.

EHRLE, ELWOOD B. "Selection and Evaluation of Department Chairmen." *Educational Record,* 56(1), 1975, pp. 29–38.

GUEST, ROBERT H.; HERSEY, PAUL; and BLANCHARD, KENNETH H. *Organizational Change Through Effective Leadership.* Englewood Cliffs: Prentice–Hall, 1977.

HAY, ELLEN. "The Variable of Teaching Effectiveness in Tenure and Promotion Decisions." *ACA Bulletin,* 68, 1989, pp. 52–59.

KNIGHT, W. HAL, and HOLEN, MICHAEL C. "Leadership and the Perceived Effectiveness of Department Chairpersons." *Journal of Higher Education,* 56, 1985, pp. 677–690.

MCINTOSH, THOMAS H., and KOEVERING, THOMAS E. "Six-year Case Study of Faculty Peer Reviews, Merit Ratings, and Pay Awards in a Multidisciplinary Department." *Journal of the College and University Personnel Association,* 37, 1986, pp. 5–14.

MIDDLEHURST, ROBIN. "Evaluation and Development of a Leadership Course for Heads of Academic Departments in the United Kingdom." *Higher Education Management,* 1(2), 1989, pp. 170–182.

MILLER, RICHARD I. *Evaluating Faculty Performance.* San Francisco: Jossey–Bass, 1972.

MITCHELL, MARY B., and WHEELER, DANIEL W. *A Grounded Theory of Chairperson Management Strategy.* ASHE 1987 Annual Meeting Paper, San Diego, 1987. (ERIC Document Reproduction Service No. ED 281 465)

MITCHELL, MARY B. "The Process of Department Leadership." *Review of Higher Education,* 11, 1987, pp. 161–176.

SAMUELS, KEITH T. *A Study of Community College Division Chairpersons with Comparisons to University Department Chairpersons in Florida's System of Higher Education.* Unpublished Doctoral Dissertation, Florida State University, 1983.

SELDIN, PETER. *Evaluating and Developing Administrative Performance: A Practical Guide for Academic Leaders.* San Francisco: Jossey–Bass, 1988.

Seagren, Alan T. *Perception of Chairpersons and Faculty Concerning Roles, Descriptors, and Activities Considered Important for Faculty Development and Departmental Vitality.* 1986. (ERIC Document Reproduction Service No. ED 276 387)

Sergiovanni, Thomas J., and Corbally, John E. *Leadership and Organizational Culture.* Chicago: University of Illinois Press, 1988.

Singleton, Brenda S. "Sources and Consequences of Role Conflict and Role Ambiguity Among Department Chairs." *Capstone Journal of Education,* 7, 1987, pp. 39–50.

Smart, John C., and Elton, Charles F. "Administrative Roles of Department Chairmen." In *New Directions for Institutional Research: Examining Departmental Management,* no. 10, edited by John C. Smart and James R. Montgomery. San Francisco: Jossey–Bass, 1976.

Tannenbaum, Robert, and Schmidt, Warren H. "How to Choose a Leadership Pattern." *Harvard Educational Review,* March–April 1957, pp. 95–101.

Wattenbarger, James L. "Evaluation of College Administrators." *New Directions for Community Colleges,* 11, pp. 45–55.

Wigington, Henry. "Students' Ratings of Instructors Revisited: Interactions Among Class Instructor Variables." *Research in Higher Education,* 30, 1989, pp. 331–344.

Winner, Cornelia W. *The Role of the Department Chairperson at Delaware Technical and Community College.* Dover, DE: University of Delaware, 1989. (ERIC Document Reproduction Service No. ED 308 898)

Part XIII

PERSONAL AND PROFESSIONAL WELFARE OF THE CHAIR

Chapter 32. Getting the Position, Finding Satisfactions, Coping with Stress, and Moving to the Next Job

Getting the Position, Finding Satisfactions, Coping with Stress, and Moving to the Next Job

Why Faculty Members Become Chairpersons

There are many reasons why faculty members become chairpersons. Following are a few.

Faculty members who have had good and successful experiences chairing important committees wonder if perhaps they should try their hand as an academic administrator. As a department chair they can test their ability as an administrator without completely leaving the faculty role. For them, this may be a first step towards a deanship or even a presidency. Other faculty members find themselves frustrated and dissatisfied with the performance of the current department chair. They feel they can do a much better job, and decide to seek the position for one term, not for their own sake but for that of the department. (At least initially it may be for the sake of the department.)

Some faculty members may not even be thinking about the possibility of being a department chair. Their colleagues, for whatever reason, identify them as a potential chair, tell them that they are the only ones in the department who can handle the job, and persuade them to accept the position.

There are a few faculty members who persuade themselves that no one else will take the job, and so they must accept it to save the department. A few others feel that their research and publication skills are not as strong as their leadership and organizational skills, and that they would be more successful if they were administrators—so they seek an administrative post.

How the Chairperson Is Selected

The person selected to be a chair of a department is most often a faculty member of that department, but sometimes is from another university. Procedures for selecting an inside person for the position vary. In some departments, usually small ones, the position rotates. That is, every faculty member gets a turn at being chair. In other departments (larger ones) the chair is elected by fellow faculty members for a specific term (say three years) and may be eligible for reelection for an additional term or two. In departments with this procedure, not every faculty member gets to be a chair. In still other types of departments, the dean will ask a faculty committee to select three candidates from among the faculty of the department and submit their names. The dean will then appoint one of them to the position. Here again, the term of office is generally three years and is renewable if all concerned parties are satisfied. Some chairs come to the department from another university after a national search. They usually are appointed for terms of three years after having been recruited and screened by an officially appointed search committee.

Before Accepting the Job

HUMAN AND FISCAL RESOURCES CONSIDERATIONS

A candidate for chairperson should try to obtain as much information as possible about the department before agreeing to take the job. First of all, what does the faculty expect from the chair? Secondly, what does the dean expect? Are these expectations consistent with each other, or do they conflict? Is the condition of the department such that the expectations are realistic in terms of available human and fiscal resources? What is the maturity level of the department in terms of faculty members being able to work together cooperatively? Candidates for chairperson should ask themselves whether they have the temperament and personality to provide the type of leadership needed for this particular department.

Examples of other questions that need to be asked are: Is the department viable? Does it have a sufficient enrollment and fiscal base to survive and achieve a desired level of excellence? (In a research university, does the department have outside funding for its projects, and are the prospects good for the continuation of such funding?) What kind of reputation does the department have with regard to undergraduate teaching? What is the culture of the department like? What are its values, and how do people work together to achieve its goals? Do faculty pull together, or are there schisms and factions? Is there a premium placed on colleagueship, or on being contentious and obstreperous? Is the morale of the faculty high or low? What are the problems currently facing the department? What issues are likely to arise? Why did the previous chair leave? Does the department have the support of the dean? Is there a clean slate with accrediting bodies, or are there recommendations from recent reports that need to be addressed? Is there a departmental strategic plan?

Who does the candidate ask to get answers to the above kinds of questions? The candidate must ask anyone who might have information, such as faculty members of the department, the current or former chairperson, the dean, chairs of other departments under the same dean, representative students, a budget officer, or executive officers of appropriate professional associations. A candidate must analyze the answers to these questions and determine whether he or she is the right person for the job, whether the conditions are satisfactory, and whether or not to accept the position.

RANK AND TENURE CONSIDERATIONS

Ideally, one should not accept the position of department chair unless he or she already is a full professor and has tenure. Being a full professor with tenure will assure the necessary academic stature and job security one may need to feel confident and independent enough to handle all of the decisions a chair has to make.

If the opportunity to become a chair arises under different conditions, it would be wise to seek some firm agreement about the future. For example, taking on the chair position in a large department with many administrative demands may mean giving up one's own research agenda. If the candidate has not yet attained the rank of professor, and ultimately wishes to do so, remaining current in one's field of research will be important. Some kind of understanding must be reached with the dean about how much time one can expect to invest in scholarly pursuits while serving as chair. If it seems unlikely that the chairmanship will permit significant scholarly work, and if one is still willing to take the job, then it will be important to negotiate an understanding about leave time *following* service as chair, to provide a jump start to the resumption of scholarly work.

Sometimes a chair will assume the position without tenure. Either tenure has not yet been achieved, or the chair moves to a new institution and must serve at least a nominal "probationary" period without tenure, rank and length of service notwithstanding. Needless to say, there are hazards and pitfalls in agreeing to such an arrangement. A chair must sometimes make decisions or take actions that are unpopular with precisely the people who may ultimately vote on the chair's tenure. It is not in anyone's interest to work under conditions that may compromise either personal integrity or the integrity of the department, and for this reason one who accepts a chairmanship without tenure must have some kind of understanding with the dean about how tenure can be achieved.

In some cases it may be possible to get a firm agreement that the dean will recommend tenure at the earliest permissible date. It may also be possible to get a waiver of the normal rules regarding waiting periods for the award of tenure. If the chair will be expected to do any significant amount of research in order to achieve tenure, it ought to be made clear at the time of the appointment. The prospective chair would want a clear commitment from the dean—at minimum—that service as chair will not hurt the chance to achieve tenure.

If one accepts the chairmanship without tenure and without any understanding about how or when tenure is to be achieved, he or she must be prepared to accept the risks that go along with the situation. The obvious hazards include acting too tentatively to satisfy the dean, and acting too boldly to satisfy the faculty. The dean may later decide that the chair has not carried out the agreed-upon mandate, and decide not to renew the chair's contract. Or the faculty may decide that the chair is too demanding, and vote against awarding tenure. Since no chair can ever permanently satisfy both sets of demands, the chair without tenure is particularly at risk. It is simply good sense to begin one's term in office with tenure, or with at least a firm agreement about when tenure will be granted.

The Chairperson's Reaction to the Concept of Middle Management

Some writers classify academic department chairpersons as middle management in educational institutions. Although this classification may be correct from the standpoint of an organizational chart, the reaction of chairpersons to this classification ranges from amusement to irritation. After all, chairpersons are faculty members who have been chosen to assume the additional responsibility of providing leadership for their colleagues. How dare anyone call them middle managers! Nevertheless, that is what they are, and they are prone to the conflicts and pressures well documented in such roles. Essentially, middle managers have to serve as buffers between the individual aspirations of those who do the organization's production work (teaching, research, and service), and the press for efficiency, quality, and accountability that come from the organization's management hierarchy. Middle managers have to deal with these conflicting pressures by finding ways to satisfy *both* parties. Usually, the best that can be expected is that the middle manager will succeed over a finite period of time in satisfying some of the people some of the time, but not all of the people all of the time. In so doing, he or she will experience some successes and failures, some satisfactions and frustrations.

Satisfactions

Despite their claims to the contrary, most chairpersons receive enough satisfaction from the job to want to continue in the position for as long as possible. One young chairperson of a sociology department stated, only somewhat facetiously, that the only thing worse than being chairperson of the sociology department is not being chairperson of the sociology department. Despite complaints about paperwork and other so-called unpleasant duties, 90 percent of chairpersons serving three-year terms said that they would seriously consider serving an additional term if invited to do so.[1]

For some reason, faculty members expect the chairperson to suffer while carrying out his or her duties, and they tend to get suspicious or anxious when the chairperson appears to be enjoying the job. Chairpersons, who were once faculty members themselves, are aware of those feelings, and play along by complaining of the rigors of the role. When chairpersons meet together socially, outside the hearing of their faculty members, they sometimes admit to each other that there are indeed joys in being a chairperson. Becoming a department chairperson often brings with it an initial sense of pride and accomplishment.

Colleagues will treat the chair with deference and respect. The chair will find his or her social agenda expanded with invitations to many university and community events. New networks are formed, and the chair has a great deal more access to information and decisions. His or her advice is sought, and there are many opportunities to make decisions that affect the department and its academic programs.

What are the areas that are most satisfying to chairs? They enjoy the status and prestige that goes with the position, even though it is sometimes greater in the community at large than it is within the institution. Even when the chairperson receives no additional material benefits for undertaking the responsibilities of office, there may be considerable psychic rewards. For example, there is the personal satisfaction derived from helping others with their professional development, and from helping to guide and build an effective academic program. There is the challenge of leadership, which many people find invigorating. They find rewards in guiding the guiders of students, shaping curricula, defending the interests of the department, and interacting with other academic leaders, including deans and vice-presidents. Many have come to feel that their ability to motivate others to greatness perhaps exceeds their ability to motivate themselves. Some of these chairpersons want to enhance their administrative effectiveness by developing whatever additional skills are necessary to implement the management processes. Some see the acquisition of such skills as a prerequisite for further advancement in academic administration.

Sources of Stress

Of course, stress comes with the job. Not all chairs tolerate stress equally well. For some, stress is an elixir. They find it exhilarating to deal with difficult people or difficult decisions, and they welcome the challenge, no matter how stressful. For others, a minimum amount of stress can be overwhelming, and may even affect their health.

---

1. Survey conducted in 1987 by Allan Tucker, unpublished.

Typical causes of stress for the chair are numerous. One source is trying to obtain faculty consensus on important issues. Often the chair will feel that agreement must be reached on a matter of great importance to the department's future. But the faculty may not share the chair's sense of urgency, or may not agree with the chair's position on the issue. Sometimes the chair will invest months in the process of seeking a working consensus, and risk his or her own credibility and legitimacy in the process. Compromises made along the way may also lead the chair to feel that some unacceptable sacrifices have been made.

Some departments experience chronic conflict. Faculty are contentious and fractious; they habitually argue over matters large and small. Sometimes the divisions are deep and extend to serious policy issues that affect the department's future. If faculty cannot get along, and if the chair cannot find a way to make the department effective in spite of such conflict, the job will be perpetually unpleasant and stressful.

Faculty evaluation—the chair's inescapable duty—often is a source of serious stress. Although some chairs may have a department in which all faculty perform at a high level and are cooperative colleagues, most will be faced with the task of giving unwelcomed feedback to at least some faculty who do not live up to even minimum expectations. One source of stress comes from the direct personal confrontation that accompanies an unsatisfactory-performance evaluation. A second source of stress related to performance evaluation arises when the chair is asked to explain the *comparative* rankings he or she has made. A faculty member may want to know why another has been ranked higher, and what was perceived to be less adequate in his or her own performance. A third source of stress has to do with the nature of the evaluation decisions a chair has to make. Some faculty will be performing in just barely adequate or just barely superior ways. The judgment is a close call, and the chair will have to deal with the consequences no matter which way he or she decides to go.

Another source of stress may arise from the need to make a very important decision. The chair may feel that there is not enough good information available, or that there are no good precedents to follow. Few people can offer advice, and the decision will have to be made without knowing whether the result will benefit or harm the department. If it is particularly difficult to foresee the consequences of a decision, and if the consequences are likely to be major, the chair may feel under a great deal of stress both during and after the decision process.

Stress may also build up over the chair's relationship with the dean. Some deans have conflicting expectations, vacillate over decisions, send unclear or mixed signals, or simply avoid making hard choices. Deans who are ambivalent or indecisive make it hard for chairs to figure out what they themselves should do. Deans who are uncommunicative make it particularly difficult for chairs to take signals about how to act. Working under deans who show these patterns may put chairs in particularly stressful situations: They do not know with any confidence when the dean will be supportive, or when they may make a decision that the dean will fail to support. And adopting the same indecisive or uncommunicative style displayed by the dean may only make the chair's situation worse, because faculty will then begin to apply pressure on the chair for more clarity and more decisive actions.

Many times the chair is faced with an unreasonable workload. Deadlines pile up in close proximity to one another. Staff may be out on vacation, or on sick leave. Equipment may not be operating at full efficiency. The chair will occasionally have to take on a number of routine chores to keep the department functioning. The greater the time demands, and the more important the deadlines, the greater the stress.

For many chairs, stress may arise from conflicts over how much effort to devote to their research and teaching interests. Being a dedicated and competent chair requires much time and energy, plus attention to purely administrative tasks. Finding the time to do scholarly work—particularly the large blocks of time required to do serious research—and at the same time trying to be a full-time chairperson is very difficult, and for some people almost, if not fully, impossible.

Chairs who do not have tenure may be particularly subject to stress. They will find that they do not have enough time to meet all the requirements for achieving tenure. Even if they are able to continue some of their research, it will not be at the level that many promotion and tenure committees would require. Chairs without tenure may also have to face a vote by faculty whose interests have been affected by some of his or her decisions. Knowing that a tenure decision will be made at a certain time, and feeling that one may not be able to satisfy all the conditions required for a favorable decision, may keep the chair in a constant state of stress, particularly if one begins to overwork in the interest of trying to satisfy everyone.

Ambivalent chairs not only have to accommodate all the other pressures of the job, but must use extra energy thinking about whether they are interested in pursuing an administrative career or returning to the faculty as a full-time faculty member. The ambivalent chair also may weigh the feedback cues of others more heavily—he or she expends energy trying to figure out how others view each action, and therefore how these actions might reflect on the chair's future as an administrator or faculty member.

Chairs may well find it stressful to suppress their own achievements in order to let others take credit. Although everyone has certain ego needs (the need to be recognized, to be given rewards, to achieve the respect of others), the chair's job requires *giving* credit, rather than receiving it. If the chair needs more public recognition than he or she is getting, and also finds it difficult to let others take credit for the department's accomplishments, he or she will probably begin to resent others, and simultaneously begin to feel stress.

A final source of stress may affect a chair who has very strong needs for affection and approval. Once a person has assumed administrative duties, old friendships and support groups may be less approving and less accessible. Often a chair does not realize how much he or she may have depended on these groups for psychic support. They perhaps provided a zone of safety and comfort that satisfied many unconscious or unacknowledged needs. The sudden change to a chairmanship may leave one feeling suddenly unloved. Depending on the individual's own needs, this perceived rejection by former friends may be deeply stressful.

Coping with Stress

The preceding sections describe some aspects of the chair's role that may be sources of stress. This stress is actually caused by excessive concern that one of the chair's tasks is not being done as well as it should be—or that the chair hasn't sufficient resources or control to see the task done well. Some level of stress is good, however, and may stimulate the chair to put great effort into performing the task at hand. Usually the task will attract the chair's attention and energy in proportion to the level of stress he or she attaches to it. A moderate level often will increase performance and result in both better-quality work and better-quality decisions.

On the other hand, there are chairs for whom stress significantly reduces the ability to perform on the job. In excess, it may cause the chair to divert attention from the task at hand to trivial pursuits. Attending stress-reduction or time-management seminars may be helpful to some individuals in reducing the discomfort associated with stress. In any event, chairs must accept the fact that there will *always* be some stress associated with the job, and the best way to cope is to identify the causes and engage in the problem-solving thereof.

If a chair feels stressed, it is important to acknowledge these feelings and to make a list of all the tasks that may be at cause. Once the causes have been identified, they can be grouped into categories: those about which the chair can do something; those that need the help or advice of others in order to afford progress; those perhaps requiring a change in the chair's own attitude (from negative to positive) about the importance or difficulty of the task; and those that might call for acceptance of the situation as it is. Some situations will neither go away nor be controlled, and the chair cannot waste time and energy on such. Perhaps others can deal with these issues more constructively than the chair, and it may be possible to delegate to them these onerous tasks.

Common sources of stress mentioned earlier can be dealt with constructively for the most part. Others have dealt with them in the past, because they are perennial problems. For example, if stress is caused by trying to get the faculty to reach consensus and cooperate with each other, the chair should read the literature on conflict management. He or she may find suggestions in the literature about what motivates faculty and how their conflicts might be brought to more satisfactory conclusions. Discussing the problem with other department chairs may provide new perspectives on the causes of the conflict, as well as ways to resolve it. Networking with other chairs and finding others with whom to talk over concerns and problems does much to help put issues and actions in the larger context, too.

If making a decision is causing stress because the chair hasn't enough good information, or because the consequences of the decision are not clear, the chair should discuss the problem with other chairs who may be facing, or have faced, similar decisions. Chairs who have had experience in dealing with the same situation can offer valuable guidance. Alternatively, it would be a good idea to share responsibility for such decisions with a departmental committee. If the department has an executive committee, they should be involved—partly to help *make* the decision, and therefore share responsibility, and partly to educate the faculty on the likely consequences of the decision.

Stress associated with evaluating faculty performance can be minimized (but certainly not eliminated) to the extent that the process is perceived as fair and rational. It is usually a good idea to have carefully prepared criteria and standards by which to evaluate job performance. If faculty have had a hand in developing the criteria and the procedures for rating performance, they are more apt to accept the results of the evaluation. Although it is difficult to reduce faculty performance to strictly quantitative ratings, some quantification may serve to eliminate the perception of bias. Confronting faculty members with poor evaluations will be less stressful if the chair can show the faculty member numerical ratings for each category of performance and, with appropriate protections for confidentiality, how others were rated, as well. For example, if Professor X believes that he performs as well as Professor Y and wants to know why Professor Y received a higher evaluation, the chair can show him that Professor Y received a higher overall numerical rating. Professor X may not be happy with this information, but he might be less argumentative. It would be helpful if such ratings were also carried out by a faculty panel, or were at least validated by some other rater than the chair alone.

If stress is caused by ambiguous signals from the dean, leaving the chair wondering what is expected, the chair should initiate a candid discussion with the dean as soon as possible. The chair should make it plain that he or she needs a better understanding of the dean's expectations and signals. Often the dean will not realize that people are having trouble getting a message, and will find the discussion helpful. The chair should also be prepared to find that the dean may be deliberately obfuscating, allowing the chairs to make their own decisions (and suffer the consequences). It is not common, but some deans are poor communicators and no amount of patient prodding will reveal their intentions.

If the work and the deadlines accumulate to the point where the chair's stress level becomes dysfunctional, tasks must be prioritized, and the chair must evaluate his or her own capabilities to complete them. The chair should delegate as much as can be delegated, and decide which tasks will be done as a last priority, if at all. Under some conditions the chair simply cannot find a way to do everything, and so everything will not get done. This is a reality with which the chair must learn to live.

If chairs worry to the point where they are stressed about how little research and writing they are able to accomplish, they need to *make* time available to do scholarly work. Keeping the office door closed and the telephone turned off for half a day a week is one solution. Finding another place to work for a set period every week is another. Perhaps the chair could arrange to take a month off in the summer to devote to research. Chairs who really want to conduct research *can* make time. If they are unable or unwilling to make time for this purpose, they probably do not have serious commitments to conducting research. They may conclude that research can be resumed upon completion of their terms in office as chairs, or perhaps reflection will show that they are really more interested in administrative work, and ought to think about pursuing administrative careers.

Chairs who feel stressed because they can't decide whether they want to continue as administrators or return to the faculty need to make a decision sometime between the first and second year in office about what their next move is likely to be. A chair whose ambivalence persists beyond this point is not very committed to an administrative career, and should plan to return to the faculty. Since an administrative career will only add to the kinds of stress one experiences in the chair, one should not be ambivalent about wanting to move in this direction.

Finally, if stress results from not getting enough credit, a chair must make a conscious effort to learn how to obtain (vicarious) satisfaction from the accomplishments of others, and from the personal knowledge of what one did to help that individual achieve recognition. For example, a chair must learn how to experience satisfaction and success from knowing that a young faculty member has achieved tenure, or that another faculty member has finally obtained a prestigious grant, or that a third had received student ratings showing that his teaching had improved dramatically.

Reasons for Leaving the Chairmanship

Chairs whose stress level is so high that it affects their health and ability to do their work effectively should leave the job. Chairs who feel that they have made whatever contribution they are capable of, and cease to find satisfaction and reward in doing their job, should leave, especially if their work begins to seem repetitive and routine. When people's complaints and quirks become less objects of challenge and interest and more tiresome, and when the job begins to seem more like a burden than an opportunity, the chair ought to leave.

Faculty members who have served as chairs for several years may decide that they have no particular love for administration and may want to return to their academic careers. They may feel that their scholarly work has suffered long enough, and decide to return to their first priority. On the other hand, chairs with interests in administration will probably encourage others to nominate them for administrative jobs, either at their own institution or elsewhere. A chair who is able and whose record is strong as both scholar and adminstrator will sometimes be actively recruited for deanships and other administrative positions. Some chairs, of course, will be attractive to other institutions as faculty members. They will leave the chairmanship to accept the new position.

Sometimes the chair has made (or not made) tough decisions, and the department develops factions supporting or opposing the chair's continued tenure. This is, fortunately, a relatively rare circumstance, but some chairs do face considerable hostility among the department's faculty. They may be tempted to give up being chair as a way of escaping an uncomfortable situation. Before doing so, however, the chair should assess the situation and decide whether the issues being confronted are really relevant to his or her performance in office. Many issues are simply written into the script and so will confront anyone occupying the chair. Intellectual splits in the field, a controversial tenure decision, falling enrollments, and many other imaginable problems may arise at uncontrollable times and have nothing at all to do with the current chair. If the chair can honestly say that the issues causing tension are unrelated to his or her own decisions and behavior, then a more dispassionate self-analysis of his or her performance should be substituted for the natural distress one feels when things are not going smoothly. The dean, senior faculty, the department executive committee, and perhaps other chairs may be able to provide an objective assessment.

Some chairs do bring controversy to their terms in office, and some eventually lose credibility and legitimacy because of acts they commit or fail to commit. Faculty who have lost confidence in the chair will find a way to express their feelings—often indirectly, but sometimes with brutal directness. A chair is faced with a difficult decision when it becomes clear that the faculty no longer has confidence. If he or she is an elected chair, then parliamentary procedure (via a vote of confidence on some convenient issue) can resolve the matter if the chair wishes to put it to a test. On the other hand, a chair who has been appointed by the dean may wish to test the dean's own confidence by submitting a letter of resignation. It would be easier for all concerned if the chair could talk openly with the dean prior to any irreversible move, thereby getting some sense of how the dean felt. In some cases the dean will express full confidence in the chair, praise the current direction being taken, and ask the chair to stay on. In other cases the dean may waver and suggest further inquiry and consideration of faculty views. This may be a vote of marginal confidence in the chair, or it may be the dean's way of telling the chair it is time to go. Without the dean's full confidence, the chair should start thinking seriously about leaving.

The most difficult situation of all comes when a dean or a chair's faculty decides the chair must go. These conditions will result in a voluntary or involuntary departure, and every chair should be alert to signals that his or her time has come. The key is to anticipate; waiting to be fired, sometimes in a very public way, puts everyone in an awkward position. There are no winners when a chair must be fired.

When to Leave

Inevitably all chairs will leave their positions. The question is, "When?" Will they leave when they want to or when someone else wants them to? Will they have a choice? The answer to the second question is "Yes," if they have personal career goals in mind, if they assess their situations on a continuing basis to determine whether their performance is satisfactory to their faculty and dean, and if they have been able to acquire appropriate new skills, experiences, and contacts that will make it possible for them to qualify for another position if and when a change is needed. If they don't do any of these things they may not have a choice, or at least not as good a choice, with regard to departure time or the type of job they would like to move into.

A chair should not resign and leave in a sudden fit of anger or emotional stress. Sometimes a run of bad luck or the press of business over an extended time may leave him or her feeling fatigued and depressed. No one should make an irreversible decision under such circumstances. If in the past there have been considerable satisfactions in serving as chair, then temporary setbacks, fatigue, or similar conditions can be readily discounted. If, however, the setbacks continue indefinitely, it probably is time to leave.

As a general rule, chairs should stay in their positions through the end of their contracts. Leaving earlier, for whatever reason, gives the impression (perhaps erroneously) that the chair is quitting under pressure, and may create as many problems as it solves—except when the chair cannot physically or emotionally handle the work. Deans and faculty will be expecting the chair to serve for a given period of time, and, in fact, depend on the chair to be in place for that period.

Quitting the chair for another administrative job after only a short time in office, the attractiveness of the new position notwithstanding, can be hazardous. It leaves a bad feeling at the institution, and in the department as well. It also means that a fair and searching test of one's administrative staying power has not been conducted. A period of two or three years in office is barely sufficient to see how well one plans, implements, and builds on new programs and ideas. It is also barely sufficient to test one's mettle in handling serious conflicts or resource deficiencies. Most seriously, it does not give the person a clear sense of how well he or she will perform in higher-pressure positions. A short term as chair may provide too many satisfying experiences and not enough really tough tests, or vice versa. It is equally possible that one will have too many negative experiences in a short term and reject an administrative career unrealistically.

A departing chair should leave at a propitious time. The department should not be in great difficulty, and the chair should feel that he or she is "ahead." It is always best to leave a position with one's dignity and record intact. Staying on too long may result in an involuntary departure, or a departure overdue because problems have been allowed to develop and fester. Leaving too soon after assuming the role may reflect badly on the chair with respect to his or her reliability and commitment or, as mentioned above, may give the impression that the chair is leaving under pressure. It is best if one can serve at least the obligatory and expected time in office, leaving while things are going well.

What Comes After Chairing, and How to Prepare For It

Most chairs return to their academic careers and pick up their teaching and research interests. For some this proves difficult. If a chair served for five or eight or ten years in a large department where it was difficult to isolate time for research or writing, he or she may find that the field has moved ahead rapidly. Catching up will take a great deal of time and energy, perhaps more than is reasonable to devote at a late stage in one's career. The chair who clearly expects to return to academic work would be wise to abide by two rules: First, limit the time spent in the chair position, especially if the administrative demands are heavy. Second, find a way to stay current in at least one important aspect of the field so that work on some ongoing problem can be under way when the term as chair is complete. Chairs who return to the faculty on a full-time basis are almost like new faculty members. They have to recarve a niche for themselves and become valuable for their expertise, their national visibility, their teaching skills, and all of the academic qualities that may have been important in their selection for the chair in the first place. Ironically, service in the chair has probably led to some decline in all of these skills. Although the first few months out of office will be marked by deference and the kind of regard in which the chair was held while in office, this will soon evaporate, and the chair will have to quickly readjust to being but one among many colleagues—colleagues who expect him or her to resume standard academic behavior.

Some chairs decide that they don't like the academic life after all, and move out of academe and into a government or business career. Those who plan to do this should make early contacts with people in appropriate government agencies or business organizations, to let it be known that they are interested in that sort of work.

Some chairs move into deanships or other administrative positions. If one anticipates an administrative career, then one's term as chair should be focused on learning new skills and behaviors. Developing progressively more sophisticated ways of dealing with administrative problems and becoming familiar with how the purely administrative side of the university runs should both be high on the chair's agenda. Since it helps to have a mentor, sponsor, and promoter of one's administrative career, an ambitious chair might cultivate a dean or vice-president and seek their advice and support for opportunities to advance.

There have been exceptions, of course, but most academic deans have started their administrative careers as department chairpersons. Most academic vice-presidents and provosts once were deans, and most college and university presidents have gone through the ranks, from chair to dean to vice-president to president. Department chairs, however, remain the bulwark of academic administration in American higher education—in spite of their problems and frustrations.

Questions

1. Under what circumstances did you become chairperson of the department? Did you apply for the position? Did others persuade you to accept it? Did you have an interest in the possibility of becoming an academic administrator?

2. To what extent did the job turn out to be what you expected? What surprises, if any, did you get after having been in the position for a while?

3. From your experience as a chair, what parts of the job frustrated you the most? What parts of the job caused the greatest stress? How did you deal with the frustrations?

4. What parts of the job brought you the greatest satisfactions? To what extent are you able to get satisfaction from the accomplishments of others? To what extent are you frustrated when others are given credit for what you know wouldn't have happened without your involvement?

5. How long would you like to stay in the position of department chairperson? What is the basis for your answer?

6. Thinking beyond your present role, where do you see yourself five years from now: Returning to full-time faculty? Continuing as a department chairperson? Moving into academic administration, such as a deanship? What plans do you have to get there?

References

ADAMS, HAZARD. *The Academic Tribes.* 2nd ed. Champaign, IL: University of Illinois Press, 1988. (ERIC Document Reproduction Service No. ED 297 632)

ANTHONY, JOHN H. *Moving Up the Administrative Ladder.* Paper presented at the Conference of the National Council on Community Service and Continuing Education, Toronto, Canada, 1986.

BENNETT, JOHN B., and FIGULI, DAVID J. (Eds.) *Enhancing Departmental Leadership: The Roles of the Chairperson.* New York: Macmillan, 1990.

BOGENSCHUTZ, MARGARET. M., and SAGARIA, MARY ANN. *Aspirations and Career Growth of Mid-Level Administrators in Higher Education.* Paper presented at the Annual Meeting of the American Educational Research Association, New Orleans, 1988. (ERIC Document Reproduction Service No. ED 296 652)

BOGGS, GEORGE, R. *Pathways to the Presidency.* Paper presented at the Annual Convention of the American Association of Community and Junior Colleges, 1988. (ERIC Document Reproduction Service No. ED 306 973)

BOICE, ROBERT. "Differences in Arranging Faculty Development Through Deans and Chairs, 1985." *Research in Higher Education,* 23, 1985, pp. 245–255.

——. "Faculty Development via Field Programs for Middle-aged, Disillusioned Faculty." *Research in Higher Education,* 25, 1986, pp. 115–135.

CLEARY, ROBERT. "University Decision Making." *Educational Forum,* November 1978, pp. 89–98.

EHRLE, ELWOOD B. "Selection and Evaluation of Department Chairmen." *Educational Record,* 56(1), 1975, pp. 29–38.

FENCHEL, ALLAN H. *The Academic Corporation: Justice, Freedom, and the University.* New York: Black Rose Books, 1987.

GAINES, FRANCIS. *Presidents and Deans: A Changing Academic Scene.* 1987. (ERIC Document Reproduction Service No. ED 285 474)

GMELCH, WALTER H. "Dimensions of Stress Among University Faculty: Factor-analytic Results from a National Study." *Research in Higher Education,* 24, 1986, pp. 266–286.

GREEN, MADELEINE (Ed.) *Leaders for a New Era: Strategies for Higher Education.* New York: ACE/Macmillan, 1988.

JACKSON, WILLIAM K. (Ed.) *National Conference on Professional and Personal Renewal for Faculty, Atlanta, 1986.* (Conference Proceedings Available from ERIC Document Reproduction Service Ed 276 393)

KOWITZ, ALBERT C., and KNUTSON, THOMAS J. *Decision Making in Small Groups: The Search for Alternatives.* Boston: Allyn & Bacon, 1960.

LAWRENCE, JANET H., and BLACKBURN, ROBERT T. *Aging and Faculty Distribution of Their Work Effort.* ASHE Annual Meeting Paper, San Antonio, 1986. (ERIC Document Reproduction Service No. ED 268 903)

LESLIE, DAVID W. "The Status of the Department Chairmanship in University Organization." *AAUP Bulletin,* December 1973, pp. 419–426.

LEVINSON, DANIEL J. *The Seasons of a Man's Life.* New York: Alfred A. Knopf, 1978.

LYNCH, DAVID M. (et al.) "Chief Liberal Arts Academic Officers: The Limits of Power and Authority." *Studies in Higher Education,* 12(1), 1987, pp. 39–50.

MARCH, JAMES G. *How We Talk and How We Act: Administrative Theory and Administrative Life.* Urbana: University of Illinois Press, 1980.

MARCUS, DORA. *Lessons Learned from FIPSE Projects.* Washington, DC: Fund for the Improvement of Postsecondary Education, 1991.

MCGEE, GAIL W., and FORD, ROBERT C. "Faculty Research Productivity and Intention to Change Positions." *Review of Higher Education,* 11, 1987, pp. 1–16.

MCKEACHIE, WILBERT J. "Memo to New Department Chairmen." *Educational Record,* Spring 1968, pp. 221–227.

MIDDLEHURST, ROBIN. "Evaluation and Development of a Leadership Course for Heads of Academic Departments in the United Kingdom." *Higher Education Management,* 1(2), 1989, pp. 170–182.

MITCHELL, MARY B. "The Process of Department Leadership." *Review of Higher Education,* 11, 1987, pp. 161–176.

RASCH, CARLA. "Sources of Stress among Administrators at Research Universities." *Review of Higher Education,* 9, 1986, pp. 419–434.

REDMAN, GEORGINE M., and ANDREW, LOYD D. *Deans of Nursing: Pathways to the Deanship.* Paper presented at the AERA Annual Meeting, New Orleans, 1988. (ERIC Document Reproduction Service No. ED 299 864)

ROACH, JAMES H. L. "The Academic Department Chairperson: Functions and Responsibilities." *Educational Record,* Winter 1976, pp. 13–23.

RODMAN, JOHN A., and DINGERSON, MICHAEL R. "University Hiring Practices for Academic Administrators." *Journal of the College and University Personnel Association,* 37(2), 1986, pp. 24–30.

SAGARIA, MARY ANN D. and KROTSENG, MARSHA V. "Deans' Managerial Skills: What They Need and What They Bring to a Job." *Journal of the College and University Personnel Association,* 37, 1986, pp. 1–7.

SCHAFFER, ROBIN. "Role Conflict in Academic Chairpersons." *Occupational Therapy Journal of Research,* 7, 1987, pp. 301–313.

SCHULTZ, MAX F. "Management of the Multi-Department." *ADE Bulletin,* May 1978, pp. 34–39.

SCHUSTER, JACK H. "The Personal Dimension: Faculty Development." *Thought and Action,* 5, 1989, pp. 61–72.

SEAGREN, ALAN T., and CRESWELL, JOHN W. *A Comparison of Perceptions of Administrative Tasks and Professional Development Needs of Chairpersons/Heads of Departments in Australia and the U.S.* 1985. (ERIC Document Reproduction Service No. ED 257 328)

SELDIN, PETER. *Evaluating and Developing Administrative Performance: A Practical Guide for Academic Leaders.* San Francisco: Jossey–Bass, 1988.

SHEEHY, GAIL. *Passages.* New York: Dutton, 1976.

SHREEVE, WILLIAM. *University Department Chairs: Who Are We?* Washington, D.C.: 1987. (ERIC Document Reproduction Service No. ED 285 464)

SIMEONE, ANGELA. *Academic Women Working Toward Equality.* South Hadley, MA: Bergen & Garvey, 1987.

SINGLETON, BRENDA S. "Sources and Consequences of Role Conflict and Role Ambiguity Among Department Chairs." *Capstone Journal of Education,* 7, 1987, pp. 39–50.

SNYDER, ROBERT A.; HOWARD, ANN; and HAMMAR, T. "Mid-Career Change in Academia: The Decision to Become an Administrator." *Journal of Vocational Behavior,* October 1978, pp. 229–241.

SPRUNGER, BENJAMIN E., and BERGQUIST, WILLIAM H. *Handbook for College Administration.* Washington, DC: Council for the Advancement of Small Colleges, 1980.

STATON-SPICER, ANN Q., and SPICER, CHRISTOPHER H. "Socialization of the Academic Chairperson: A Typology of Communication Dimensions." *Educational Administration Quarterly,* 23, 1987, pp. 41–64.

THOMAS, TRUDELLE. "Demystifying the Job Search: A Guide for Candidates." *College Composition and Communication,* 40, 1989, pp. 312–327.

TWOMBLY, SUSAN B., and MOORE, KATHRYN M. "Job Search: Career Changes Among Community College Administrators." *Review of Higher Education,* 11, 1987, pp. 17–37.

TWOMBLY, SUSAN B. *Boundaries of the Top-level Two-year College Administrative Market: Implications for Leadership and Cooperation.* ASHE Annual Meeting Paper, San Antonio, 1986. (ERIC Document Reproduction Service No. ED 268 865)

————. *Career Lines of Top-level Two-year College Administrators: Implications for Leadership in a New Era.* ASHE Annual Meeting Paper, San Antonio, 1986. (ERIC Document Reproduction Service No. ED 268 884)

VAUGHN, GEORGE. *Scholarship and the Community College Professional: Mandate for the Future.* Paper presented at the Annual Convention of the American Association of

Community and Junior Colleges, 1989. (ERIC Document Reproduction Service No. ED 305 965)

WATTENBARGER, JAMES L. "Evaluation of College Administrators." *New Directions for Community Colleges,* 11, pp. 45–55.

ZORN, JENO C. "The Chairman's Return." *Educational Record,* Spring 1978, pp. 121–133.

Index

Academic dean
administrative staff of, 490
in budgeting process, 363–364
chair's role compared with, 33
departmental evaluation by, 509–513
in recruiting, 175
stress in relations with, 548–549, 551
Academic freedom, 11, 103–104, 107–108. *See also*
Freedom of speech and association
Academic Freedom and Tenure, 103, 108
Academic vice-president, budget and, 356
Accrediting agencies, 34, 497–499
review by, 517–519
Action plan
developing, 314–319
evaluating, 316–317, 316*t*
for faculty research activity, 205–206
Active listening, 405
Activities, vs. outcomes, 221
Activity statements, 303–304
Adamian v. Lombardi, 465
Administration. *See also* Central administration; Governance
department committees and, 92–93, 94–95
in healthy department, 6–7
procedures of, and litigation, 477
Administrative officers in American colleges, 14. *See also* Academic dean
Administrative Procedures Act, 422–433
Administrative staff
budget process and, 489–490
chair's relations with, 489–491
Admissions policies, 466–467
Adult students. *See* Students; adult
Advertising of position vacancies, 162–166, 169
Affirmative action, 160–161, 165, 184
Altruism, 534
Alumni
chair's need to cultivate, 494–495
demands of, 34
American Association of University Professors, 103, 107–108, 196
American Council on Education, 103, 267
Applications for positions, requirements, 163–164
Applied sciences departments, chairs of, 90–91
Arbitrary and capricious action, 448–450
Arbitration, for faculty grievances, 422–423
Aubuchon v. Olsen, 456
Audit. *See* Expenditure audit
Authority
clarifying within department, 404
formal, 44–45
Autocratic-democratic leadership model, 59–60
Awards, for teaching, 289–290

Bakke v. Board of Regents of Univ. of California, 466
Baldridge, J. Victor, 400
Behavioral objectives, in department planning, 325
Behavioral science department, mission statement for, 300
Behrend v. State, 451
Beitzell v. Jeffrey, 460

Bell, Daniel, 265–266
Berry v. Battey, 464
Blanchard, Kenneth H., 16
Board of Curators of the Univ. of Missouri v. Horowitz, 455, 456
Board of Regents v. Roth, 459, 460
Board of Trustees of Keene State College v. Sweeney, 468
Breach of contract, 450–454
Brown, David G., 268
Bruce-Briggs, 266
Budget. *See also* Planning, programming, and budgeting systems (PPBS); Resources
chances of increasing, 357
inflation and, 323–324
institutional: allocation patterns, 356–357, 359–360; continuing financial commitments, 353–354; cycle of, 335–338
mission and goals statement and, 298
negotiating, 36–37
strategies, 355–363, 359–360, 362
Budget, department, expenditure categories, 347
Budget process
administrative staff and, 489–490
"guesstimating," 354–355
interim request, 355
language of, 345–349
in private institutions, 331–332
in public institutions, 332–335
request document, 361–363
reserve fund availability, 359
schedule of critical events, 357–358
special appropriations, 499–500
stages in, 335–338
transferability of funds, 358–359
Budget systems, 338–341
formula, 341–345
incremental, 338
line-item, 339
planning, programming, and budgeting (PPBS), 339–341
zero-base (ZBBS), 338–339
Bureaucracy. *See* Administrative staff

Career paths, of faculty members, 111–114
Carnegie Foundation, 284
Catalog, revising, 374
Central administration
chair as advocate of policies of, 37–38
contacts with state government and, 499–501
demands of, 34
departmental evaluation by, 513–514
foundations and, 501
recruiting new faculty and, 159–160
Chair. *See also* Responsibilities of chair
characteristics of effective, 40
as chief department planner, 311–313
dean's expectations of, 533–538
faculty expectations of, 531–533
performance counseling and, 246–247
reasons for leaving, 552–553
reasons for taking position, 543
selection of, 27–28, 544

sources of power, 46–47
support staff relations with, 134–135
when to resign, 552–554
Change in academic organizations, 74–75
administrative impediments to, 78
faculty opposition to, 77–79
implementing, 76–77, 80–81
Chemistry departments, fragmentation in, 19
Civil Rights Act of 1964, Title VII, 467–471
Closing dates, in advertising faculty positions, 164
Collective bargaining. *See also* Employment contract;
union
changes in chair's role and, 438–439
Committees, department. *See also* Curriculum committee; Salary committee; Tenure and promotion committee
ad hoc, 93–94
appointment of, 48–49
conflict resolution and, 408–409
elected, 95
guidance and direction for, 94–95, 97–98
listing of, 96–97
standing, 93–94, 109
structure of, 92–98, 109
students as members, 151
tasks, 95–96
women and minority faculty on, 187–188
Committees, institutional, grievance procedures, 422
Common-law liability, of chair, 471–473
Communication, external
between dean and chair, 487–488, 533, 537
as source of chair's power, 47–48
Communication, internal
change and, 78
faculty evaluation and, 216, 250–253
in healthy department, 9–10
models of governance and, 401
over faculty assignments, 212
with part-time faculty, 126–127
as source of chair's power, 46–47
Community colleges
chair's responsibilities, 30–31
divisional structure, 16
evaluating faculty, 218, 220
faculty in, 35
transfer students from, 143
Community service
in healthy department, 8
ideal of, 105
mission statement for, 300
performance criteria for, 206–207, 220–221
point allocation system for, 235
Competition
in academic governance, 401
within mature large departments, 19
Conflict
among faculty members, 398–399
attitudes toward, 399–401
between chair's faculty and administrative roles, 34
between faculty and chair, 250–252
between faculty and students, 146–147, 399
between faculty and support staff, 136–137
between graduate students and faculty, 144–145
chair's resignation and, 553
definitions, 397–398
diagnosing, 403–404
efforts to resolve, 404–412: guidelines, 410–411
employer-employee type, 398
grievances as symptom of, 420
in healthy departments, 3–4, 6

ideological, 399
over curriculum, case study, 82–83
stages of, 402–403
stress and, 548
unresolvable, 410–411
vs. problems, 408
Conflict management, 406–411, 550–552
Conservatism
in American higher education system, 73
of faculty senates and committees, 109, 110
Constitutional rights. *See also* Due process; Freedom
of speech and association
denial of, 454–461
Contact hours, 210
Contract. *See* Breach of Contract; Employment contract
Cooper v. Ross, 463
Cost studies
annual, 208
of department's effectiveness, 512–513
Counseling of students, 148–149. *See also* Performance counseling; Psychological counseling
Courses. *See* Curriculum
Craft v. Board of Trustees of the Univ. of Illinois, 452
Credit hours, 210, 347, 351
as workload measure, 202
Criticism of chair, 535
Cuddiby v. Wayne State, 452
Culture
of faculty, 106–107
of healthy department, 10–11
Curriculum
adding new courses, 371, 374–375
assessing, 371–373
changing, 75, 373
data and information requirements, 378, 525
eliminating courses, 375–376, 384
innovations in undergraduate teaching, 149
review and analysis, 377–378
Curriculum committee, 48–49, 374–378

Daum v. New England College, 453
Dauterman v. State-Record Co, 473
Davis v. Oregon State University, 459
Deans. *See also* Academic dean
characteristics and responsibilities, 483–486
demands of, 34
evaluation of chair by, 530–531
expectations of chair, 533–538
resolving interdepartmental conflicts, 410
Decision making
collective nature of, 107
faculty involvement in, 68–70: case study, 82
stress and, 548, 550–551
styles of in academic department, 66–68
Defamation, 473–474
Department, academic. *See also* Goals, department
administrative staff responsibilities, 132–133
appraisal by candidate for chair, 544–545
faculty development and, 276
healthy mix of faculty types in, 113–114
historical development of, 15, 103
immature large, 18–19
immature small, 17
mature large, 19–20
mature small, 17–18
national ranking of, 519–520
pure vs. mixed, 15–16
self-evaluation by, 498, 522–524
theory of development of, 20–21

Directive-supportive leadership model, 56–59, 58f
Disabled, discrimination in admissions policies, 466–467
Discipline of students, due process rights, 455
Discrimination. *See also* Employment discrimination; Gender discrimination; Racial discrimination
federal laws prohibiting, 465
legal standards applied to proof of, 465–466
Dismissal of faculty member, grounds for, 453–454
Dizick v. Umqua Community College, 475
Documentation
for budget requests, 356, 361–362
of chair's exercise of authority, 447–448
for department review and evaluation, 521, 524–526
of faculty activities, 207–210: categories for, 207–208
faculty hiring procedures, 161, 166–167, 168, 176–177
of performance counseling, 254
for performance evaluation, 237–238: sample contract clause, 430–431
for program reviews, 498
Doe v. New York Univ., 467
"Donated time" concept, 210
Due process, 454–455
minimum protections under, 460–461
students' rights, 455–458

Easley v. Univ. of Michigan, 452
Eble, Kenneth E., 267
Educational Amendments of 1972, Title IX, 467–471
Education, higher
changing social environment for, 73–74, 265–267
"property rights" in context of, 454
Eichman v. Indiana State Univ., 463
Elementary schools, partnerships with, 185–186
Elton, Charles F., 90
Employment contract, 176, 198–199, 418
breach of, 452–454
chair's legal obligations, 459–460
union, 422, 423: example of, 428–432; grievance case study, 423–434; grievance procedure under, 437–438
Employment criteria, case study, 81–82
Employment discrimination, faculty hiring practices and, 184–185
Employment, memorandum of, with part-time faculty, 124
English department
action plan for, 314–315
mission statement for, 301
Enrollment
budget request and, 355–356
diminishing, 121
Enrollment, in department programs, 510
Entrepreneurs, faculty as, 113
Etzioni, Amitai, 74
Evaluation form, in interviewing faculty candidates, 174–175
Evans v. West Virginia Bd. of Regents, 457
Expenditure audit, 337–338

Faculty, academic. *See also* Faculty members
decreasing demand for, 158
historical development of, 103–104
statistics for women and minorities, 183–184
Faculty assignments
based on outcomes, 222

chair's role in, 195
equitability of, 199–204, 203t
evaluation based on, 221–222
explicit, 196–197
faculty involvement in, 222–223, 224
nonperformance of, 199
performance criteria for, 204–207
performance evaluation and, 218–219
procedures, 197–199
rotating courses, 384–385
sample contract clause, 428–429
strategy for, 211–212
Faculty development
chair's role in, 263–264, 271–273
defined, 267–268
enhancing teaching skills, 287–288
inhibiting conditions, 276–277
initiating program, 274, 276
planning a program, 273–274
Faculty member, ideal, 104–105
Faculty members. *See also* Community service; Faculty development; Full-time equivalents; Performance evaluation; Unsatisfactory performance
change and, 77–79
characteristics of full-time, 105–106
curriculum change and, 373
delegation of administrative responsibility to, 92
department decision making and, 68–70
department goal setting and, 306–308
discrimination against, 467–470
due process rights, 458–461
encouraging good performance, 253
evaluation, 511–512: list of activities for, 235–237
evaluation of chair by, 530–531
expectations of chair, 531–533
freedom of speech and association, 462–464
gathering information about, 525–526
institutional commitment to, 112–113
loss of confidence in chair, 553
mix of, in healthy department, 8–9
morale, 404
new, orientation for, 36, 178–179
psychological and personal difficulties, 405–406
retention of, 177–180
self-development activities, 268–271
self-evaluation by, 224
support staff and, 133, 136–137
types of leadership by, 109–112
workload distribution and, 384–385
Faculty, part-time
benefits and costs of using, 119–120
categories of, 120–121
growth of, 118–119
institutional policies for, 121–122, 124–126
management of, 125–127
Faculty positions, restructuring, 160
Failure, of student, 147–148
Fair employment practices, interview requirements, 173–174
Feedback, handling, 535–537
Florida, community college system, part-time faculty in, 118
Florida Board of Regents, Office of Human Resources, 440
Florida State University
Board of Regents Manual, administrative code, 427–428
faculty assignment in, 195
faculty grievances: case study, 423–434; procedures, 421–423; statistics, 419–420

faculty union contract, 428–432
Force field analysis theory (Lewin), 79
Foreign language division, case study of leadership styles, 65–66
Formula budgeting, 341–345
Foundations, dealing with, 501–502
Freedman, Mervin, 267
Freedom. *See* Academic freedom
Freedom of speech and association, denial of, 461–465
Fringe benefits, for part-time faculty, 123–124
FTE. *See* Full-time equivalents
Full-time equivalents
    budgeting formulas and, 341
    faculty and staff, 346–347
    faculty workload reporting and, 208–210
    students, 345–346
Funding, external, 104, 207
Future shock, higher education and, 265–267

Gamesman leadership model, 60–62
Gender discrimination, 420
    legal precedents, 468–469
Goals, department, 3–4
    abandoning, 319–320
    assessing faculty member's contribution to, 39
    changing, 75
    conceptual framework for, 304–306
    involving faculty in setting, 306–308
    primary and support, 305–307
    problems with, 305–306
    recruitment and, 158–159
    statement of, 302–303: example, 317–319
    strategies for accomplishing, 4
Goldberg v. Bd. of Regents of the Univ. of Colorado, 458
Gordon, Thomas, 405
Goss v. San Jacinto Junior College, 463
Governance. *See also* Administration
    faculty participation in, 108–109
    gathering information about, 526
    models of, 400–401
    student role in, 150–152
Government agencies. *See also* Funding, external
    chair's relations with, 499–501
    departmental evaluation by, 517
Grades, student complaints about, 147–148
Graduate programs, evaluation of, 514
Graduate students, 144–145
Graduate teaching assistants, 127–128, 291
Grants and contracts office, 490
Grievances
    case studies, 423–438
    chair as witness in, 410
    faculty assignment process and, 219
    faculty assignments and, 197
    performance counseling and, case study, 256–257
    procedures, 417–418, 421–423: for part-time faculty, 127
    typical causes, 418–420
Group for Human Development in Higher Education, 267
Guidelines
    for dealing with conflict, 411–412
    for department evaluation committees, 97–98

Haimowitz v. Univ. of Nevada, 459
Hanger, William S, 268
Hankins v. Temple University, 457
Harassment. *See* Sexual harassment

Health insurance. *See* Fringe benefits
Healy v. James, 462
Hefferlin, J. B. Lon, 74, 76
Hersey, Paul, 16
Hillis v. Stephen F. Austin State Univ., 464
Hill v. Nettleton, 469
Hines v. Rinker, 450
Holmes, Oliver Wendell, 446
Human resource inventory, 158

Illegal conduct, 247
Independence, of faculty. *See* Academic freedom
Induced course load matrix, 378, 379t
Institution, academic. *See also* Budget: institutional; Governance; Private institutions; Public universities
    evaluation by accrediting agencies, 518–519
    funding sources, 348–349
    operational elements of, 304
Integrated planning, 324–325
Interventions, 81–85
Interview techniques, 172–175

Jacobs v. College of William and Mary, 461
Job descriptions
    circulating to faculty, 160
    for part-time faculty, 122
Job registries, 164–165
Joyner v. Albert Merrill School, 474
Judicial restraint, 447

Kahn, Herman, 265, 266
Kerr, Clark, 77
Kunda v. Muhlenberg College, 469

Ladd, Dwight, 75
Leadership
    in academic environment, 46–47
    determining style of, 62–65, 64f: case study, 65–66
    by faculty members, 109–112
    models of, 56–62
Learning styles, students', changes in, 149–150
Lee, Barbara, 470
Lee, Calvin, 267
Legal action. *See also* Liability, legal
    over employment discrimination, 184–185
    over grievances, 423
    psychological counseling and, 406
    by students, 147–148, 409
Legal counsel, consultation with, 475–476
Legal principles, relating to chair's role, 446–447
Legislation, governing faculty employment, 417–418
Legislators, chair's relations with, 499–500
Legislature, in university budget process, 332–334
Letters of reference, 163, 170–171
Lewin, Kurt, 79
Liability, legal. *See also* Common-law liability
    of chair, 448–477
    chair's protections against, 473, 476–477
Libel. *See* Defamation
Lindsey v. Board of Regents, 463
"Loans and borrows" concept, 210
Lovell, Cheryl D., 419
Lowell, (president of Harvard, 1938), 76

Maccoby, Michael, 60–62
McLaughlin, Gerald W., 90
Maitland v. Wayne State Univ., 449
Malpass, L. F., 90
Management by objectives. *See* Behavioral objectives

Market conditions, for academic organizations, 74–75

Marketing concepts, applied to academic department, 5

Matrix analysis, as development planning technique, 274, 275*t*

Maturity of academic department
defined, 16
determining, 21–22, 22*t*
leadership models appropriate to, 58–62

Media, dealing with, 502–503

Media relations office, 502

Meetings
between dean and chair, 488–489
in mature large department, 20
minimizing conflict, 404–405
with students, 152

Merit raises, 218
rating point averages and, 238–240, 238*t*, 239*t*

Middle management, chair's position in, 546

Minority faculty
increasing pool of, 185–186
recruiting, 186–189
sensitivity to concerns of, 189
special difficulties of, 187–188
statistics for, 183–184

Misrepresentation of department program, 474–475

Mission, department. *See also* Goals, department
conceptual framework for, 304–306
statement of, 298–302: action plan for, 314–315

Montgomery, James R., 90

Multiculturalism, of student populations, 143–144

Murray, Robert K., 20

National Center for Higher Education Management Systems, 207, 340

Negligence, chair's liability, 471–473

Nepotism rules, 167

Niche, seeking, 5–6

Nzomo v. Vermont State Colleges, 461

Objectives, department. *See* Goals, department

Office hours, failure to hold, 248

Ohio University, School of Architecture, 451

Olsson v. Bd. of Higher Education, 452

Olswang, Steven, 470

Organizational unit budgeting, 340*t*

Outcomes
assessing, 518–519, 523
in departmental evaluation, 512
statements of, 303–304
vs. activities, 221

Outside employment, of faculty members, 248

Parents of students, chair's interaction with, 496

Part-time faculty. *See* Faculty, part-time

Paulsen v. Golden State University, 449

Performance counseling. *See also* Unsatisfactory performance
purpose of, 246–247
record keeping for, 254
for support staff, 135–136

Performance criteria, 224–226
for faculty assignments, 204–207
in healthy department, 9
for students, 147

Performance evaluation. *See also* Performance criteria
chair's role in, 38–39, 52, 223
of department: by academic dean, 509–513; by

central administration, 513–514; by state review boards, 515–516

due process rights of students, 455–458

external: by government agencies, 517; preparing for, 521; responding to, 521–522

guidelines for faculty committee, 97–98

necessity for, 217–218

of part-time faculty, 126

by professional associations, 516–517

record-keeping, 237–238

research vs. teaching in, 288–289

sample contract clauses, 429–431

stress and, 548, 551

of support staff, 135–136

types of, 226–237: component evaluation, 228–229, 228*t;* subjective, 226–228; weighted, 229–232; weighted, by department mission, 232–234, 233*t*, 234*t*

Perry v. Sindermann, 458

Personnel department, 489

Personnel problems
chair and, 438
grievances and, 420: case studies, 440–444

Ph.D. programs, teaching skills and, 283–285, 291–292

Physics department, goal statement for, 317–319

Planning, department. *See also* Action plan
budget process and, 337–338
chair's role in, 35, 311–313
curriculum, 373–378, 379*t*
formats for, 321–325
kinds of, 313–314

Planning, programming, and budgeting systems (PPBS), 322–324, 339–341, 340*t*

Point system. *See* Rating scales

Policy making, department committees and, 93

Political activities of faculty, 500

Power, sources of chair's, 44–46

PPBS. *See* Planning, programming, and budgeting systems (PPBS)

President, college, 76, 497

Press. *See* Media

Privacy laws, communication with parents and, 496

Private institutions
budget requests in, 331–332
constitutional rights at, 454, 457
grievances, case study, 436–437

Problems
of students, 145–149
vs. conflicts, 408

Professional associations. *See also* Accrediting agencies
evaluation by, 516–517
faculty service in, 206–207
as source of faculty candidates, 165

Professional development for support staff, 138–139. *See also* Faculty development

Professional programs, evaluation by accrediting agencies, 519

Program, academic
establishing new, 50–51
in healthy department, 7–8
reviews of, 497–498

Program budgeting, 340*t*

Promotion, chair's power over, 52

Property rights, in academic context, 454–455

Psychological counseling, avoiding, 253, 406

Publications, point allocation system for, 235

Public universities
budget process in, 332–335